Ex Líbrís

On Many a
Bloody Field

On Many a Bloody Field

FOUR YEARS IN THE IRON BRIGADE

ALAN D. GAFF

INDIANA UNIVERSITY PRESS
Bloomington & Indianapolis

The paper used in this publication meets the minimum
requirements of American National Standard for Information
Sciences—Permanence of Paper for Printed Library
Materials, ANSI Z39.48-1984.

Manufactured in the United States of America

Library of Congress Cataloging-in-Publication Data

Gaff, Alan D.
  On many a bloody field : four years in the Iron Brigade / Alan D.
Gaff.
    p. cm.
  Includes bibliographical references (p.   ) and index.
  ISBN 0-253-33063-7 (alk. paper)
  1. United States. Army. Indiana Infantry Regiment, 19th
(1861–1864). Company B. 2. United States—History—Civil War,
1861–1865—Regimental histories. 3. Indiana—History—Civil War,
1861–1865—Regimental histories. I. Title.
E506.5 19th.G34 1996
940.54'12772—dc20   96-1728

1 2 3 4 5 01 00 99 98 97 96

This book is dedicated to H. B.,
the other half of my soul.

This book is dedicated to H. B.,
the other half of my soul.

I knew him! By all that is noble, I knew
This commonplace hero I name!
I've camped with him, marched with him, fought with him, too,
In the swirl of the fierce battle-flame!
Laughed with him, cried with him, taken a part
Of his canteen and blanket, and known
That the throb of this chivalrous prairie boy's heart
Was an answering stroke of my own.

—H. S. Taylor, "The Man with the Musket"

CONTENTS

ILLUSTRATIONS

MAPS

ACKNOWLEDGMENTS

Researching this book has brought me in touch with a number of wonderful people who willingly shared their talents and materials. I regret being unable to list them all.

No Iron Brigade book can be complete without the approval of Alan T. Nolan, whose name has become synonymous with that unit's history. Alan's support and encouragement for over twenty years have been matched only by his patience as he waited for the appearance of this manuscript. He is a true gentleman and I am proud to call him my friend. Thank you, Alan.

Other Iron Brigade friends provided assistance over the years, including a sharpshooting trio of Badgers—Lance Herdegen, Bill Beaudot, and Howie Madaus. Lance and Bill are the authors of that popular book, *In the Bloody Railroad Cut at Gettysburg*, to which Howie added a detailed appendix on the Iron Brigade uniform. Being devoted to the "Babies" of the 6th Wisconsin, they will be surprised to learn that there was indeed an *Indiana* regiment in the famous Wisconsin brigade.

Marc and Beth Storch speak for the 2nd Wisconsin and they have generously shared material that their searches have uncovered. No one is more familiar with researching in the various government agencies than this talented duo and I am anxiously waiting for their history of the "Ragged Ass Second."

Many people generously arranged for the loan of photographs and manuscripts and their contributions are greatly appreciated. I regret that space allows me to list only a few of them: James Biltz, John W. Green, Craig Johnson, Mick Kissick, Thomas R. Pratt, Rick Saunders, Frances M. Vander Weide, Bob Willey, and Jerry Wise.

I am most indebted to Jeff Krull, director of the Allen County (Indiana) Public Library, and his staff. The library's general collection contains a solid Civil War section, but its genealogy department, under the direction of Curt Witcher, is a world-class jewel. This genealogy collection is the second largest in the entire country and is a wonderland for anyone researching American military history. This department's material is complemented by another section of the library where an extensive set of government documents is readily available. Many ACPL staff members assisted me during my research, but perhaps none more so than the cotillion-trained

Katherine Smith, who was always ready to answer any question, no matter how obscure, even if it was for a Yankee.

The late Ruth Harrod, librarian at Helmke Library, Indiana University–Purdue University at Fort Wayne, was instrumental in securing copies from the Orr Collection in the Lilly Library, Bloomington, Indiana.

John Selch of the Newspaper Section, Indiana State Library, was particularly helpful. His knowledge of nineteenth-century Indiana newspapers is amazing and he allowed me to check many sources that I otherwise would not have known existed.

Two very close friends, Cathleen Arnoldy and Cheryl Hackworth, provided emotional support and technical assistance during critical stages of the writing process.

Words cannot express how much my wife, Maureen, has contributed to this book. When we married back in 1969 Maureen did not realize that she would be spending over twenty-five years of her life with 115 of my closest friends. She has been supportive throughout the whole period, acting unofficially as researcher, editor, proofreader, and indexer. My love for her grows stronger every day. I have dedicated this book to her.

INTRODUCTION

When the Civil War began, many of the firemen in Richmond, Indiana, left that city to join the Union Army. On February 20, 1863, the editor of the *Richmond Palladium* wrote, "We venture the assertion that there is not another Fire Company in the State of Indiana that has had more volunteers in the service of their country, than the 'Quaker City No. 2's,' since the war broke out." Members of the company were praised for their pluck and patriotism, the former best illustrated by "their promptness at fires" and the latter proven by a list of forty-one members who had already enlisted.[1]

Included on that list of firemen who were serving their country was the name of Charles H. Petty, a sergeant in Company B, 19th Indiana Infantry. Shortly after the *Palladium* article appeared, Sergeant Petty was seriously wounded in the leg, on April 29th, during a preliminary movement of the Chancellorsville campaign. He languished in a hospital near Fredericksburg, Virginia, until his death on June 9, 1863. Petty's comrades made arrangements to have the corpse embalmed and then had his coffin shipped home for burial.[2]

Charley Petty's remains were met at the railroad depot on June 15th by the Quaker City Fire Company No. 2 and the Richmond Guards, a local militia organization. Their precious burden was taken to the No. 2's engine house where it remained overnight. Family members, friends, firemen, and other citizens came by to view the body, which was "in an excellent state of preservation." At 9 A.M. on June 16th, the funeral procession left the engine house for Earlham Cemetery, located on the western outskirts of Richmond. The hearse was followed by all of the city's fire companies, the Richmond Guards and a vast number of carriages and wagons. The editor of the *Quaker City Telegram* observed, " As the funeral cortege passed through our streets to the step of the mournful Dead March, many eyes unused to weeping, were suffused with tears."[3]

Charley Petty's friends in the fire company had hurriedly taken up a collection in order to buy two lots in Earlham Cemetery "for the purpose of burying those of their own members, who may be stricken down by death, and who desire to be buried therein; and, also, as a place to deposit the remains of those of our brave boys who have gone out from our midst to fight for their country." The fire company lot was atop a small slope overlooking the cemetery entrance, just a stone's throw from the National Road. After Elder A. J. Hobbs made a few appropriate remarks, the Richmond Guards interred Charley's body with suitable military honors. The *Telegram* called the ceremony "a fitting consecration of the ground for the purposes intended," while the *Palladium* referred to the new grave as "his last resting place in the beautiful cemetery of Earlham."[4]

There was much praise for the departed soldier. A member of the No. 2's said simply, "he was a brave soldier, as he was a fireman." General Solomon Meredith, home on leave, referred to Petty at a public meeting as "an excellent soldier," who "was never known to complain—he was always at his post, and did his duty faithfully and willingly." The editor of the *Telegram* commented, "All who were acquainted with the deceased speak of him as being an excellent young man, a dutiful son, and an agreeable companion."[5]

A stone marker was soon erected at the head of Petty's grave, but the fire company thought a more impressive monument was needed for their cemetery lot. In September 1863, the No. 2's began a fund drive to raise a suitable memorial, "ornamenting and embellishing this receptacle of the brave and honored dead." A monument was ordered, at the cost of $400, but although other members of the No. 2's died in the service, none of them were ever interred in the firemen's plot.[6]

Charles H. Petty remained the only burial in the fire company lot. He rested there for over seventy years, beyond all earthly care and worry. Summer's scorching heat and winter's harshest storms came and went with regularity. The grass sprouted every spring and brown leaves piled up against his headstone every autumn. Other Indiana soldiers went off to fight other wars, this time in faraway places like Cuba and the Philippines and France. But the dead hero slept calmly through it all, safely tucked away in the embrace of Mother Earth.

This, however, was not to be Charley Petty's final resting place. In 1935, right in the midst of the Great Depression, the Nicholson family, which was prominent in Richmond society and best remembered for its successful printing and publishing business, approached the manager of Earlham Cemetery. The Nicholsons wanted to acquire the engine company property in order to increase the size of their family plot. Earlham Cemetery was agreeable. Since the volunteer fire company had been disbanded for many years, the ground apparently belonged to the City of Richmond. Lawyers representing Earlham Cemetery, the Nicholsons, and the city met to work out legalities of transferring the property. Apparently no one represented Sergeant Charles Petty.

On September 3, 1935, the Common Council of the City of Richmond passed a resolution approving transfer of the following real estate to Earlham Cemetery:

A strip of ground in uniform width of Eight (8) feet, measured north and south from the south end of Lots No. 228 and 229, Section No. 1, of Earlham Cemetery, as recorded in Plat Book 3, page 16, in the Recorder's Office of Wayne County, Indiana, and on the Plat in the Secretary's Office of the Earlham Cemetery.

Justification for the transfer was addressed by the statement that "said lots are of no use or value to said City and require upkeep and maintenance." On the following day, after receiving $100 from the cemetery, Mayor Joseph M. Waterman signed a Quit-Claim Deed and gave to Earlham the land described above.

Earlham Cemetery quickly sold lot 229 to Edith B. Nicholson for twenty dollars on September 12th. Lot 228 could not be immediately transferred to the Nicholson family because Charley Petty was buried there. Petty's coffin would have to be dug up and his remains moved before the Nicholsons could take possession. Clem Zwissler, a cemetery caretaker, participated in the removal and would always remember the experience. Charley had been buried in a hermetically sealed, zinc-lined shipping coffin. Petty's uniform was "very well kept" and his hair and bones were "in good shape," although some of his ribs were out of position. The mortal remains of Charley Petty were placed in a new coffin and reburied in the Soldiers Section, near the graves of other veterans from the Civil War, Spanish American War, and World War I. The now-empty grave was filled in and lot 228 was sold to Edith B. Nicholson for twenty dollars on September 21st.[7]

When he died of his wounds after having served his country for two years, Charley's fellow soldiers, at great expense, had sent his body home for burial. Comrades from the No. 2's had purchased a special plot for his burial. Family members and friends and acquaintances had shed many tears while attending the funeral for this young fireman turned soldier.

But how different the second burial! People who knew Charley Petty before his death had now themselves been dead for many decades. Memories of the Civil War had faded and the sacrifices made during those terrible years had been forgotten. This time Charley would be interred by strangers, in a plot of ground with no special significance, because his old burial site was "of no use or value" to the city he defended, first as a fireman and then as a soldier.

There is one great irony to this whole story. The Nicholsons never buried anyone on lot 228 and to this day Charley Petty's original grave site still lies empty.

The Civil War has now been over for 130 years and, despite continuing efforts by historians, its real military experience has never been told. Like poor Charley Petty's resting place, the history of our Civil War has been shifted from its original focus. Veterans tried to write their own histories of the Civil War, but they were unable to maintain any objectivity. The old soldiers did realize, however, that historians were not getting the story right. It was simply a matter of perspective—veterans had lost their innocence on the battlefield, but could not write about it, and historians had been trained to write well, but did not really understand what had happened. Unfortunately, only historians remain to tell the story.

An objective examination of the military experience during our Civil War is long overdue. The only effective way to accomplish this goal is to examine a small group of men over the course of the entire war. The most logical choice for such an examination would be an infantry company, the basic unit of the Civil War military, both tactically and socially. This book is a history of one such unit—Company B, 19th Indiana Infantry—and the 115 men who served in its ranks.

Slavery, politics, economics, religion, and law, all popular and sanitized topics for current historians, are mentioned only in passing. General officers move in and out of the narrative as the war progresses, but this is not a view from headquarters. Instead it offers a glimpse of the war as seen by those men who experienced the mud and blood and horror of combat, but who never became famous. This book gives soldiers of the 19th Indiana a long-delayed opportunity to tell their story, in their own words.

Charley Petty was one soldier who saw the Civil War in its most horrible form, but a steadfast devotion to duty kept him at the post of danger until a rebel shot him down. Many had fallen before him and many more would follow him to the grave, but his surviving comrades, by now hardened to tales of unbearable sorrow, continued the struggle until their final victory. Amid the euphoria that came with peace, few would remember the final poetic tribute to Sergeant Charles H. Petty:

> Hark, 'tis the funeral knell,
>   The muffled drum;
> The solemn tread,
>   The measured beat
> Comes down the street,
>   The soldier's going home.[8]

A NOTE ON
QUOTED MATERIAL

Every effort has been made to be scrupulously accurate with the numerous quotations used herein, misspellings and all. However, in letters home where the soldier omitted periods at the end of his sentences (not uncommon in the 1860s) these have been supplied, and all underlinings have been rendered as italics.

1

Richmond City Greys

At the age of nineteen, John M. Snider had left the comfort of his parents' home in Centreville, Indiana, to begin life on his own. He would later write, "I have learned to stay away from home and form my own acquaintances," but John thought often of Jacob and Sabilla Snider because he worried constantly about their welfare. Some ten years previously, Jacob had been stricken with erysipelas, a streptococcus infection commonly known as St. Anthony's fire. The disease slowly spread through his left arm and left leg so that by 1856 John's father had become a "confirmed invalid" and incapable of supporting the family. Determined to assist his parents, John went to work for J. T. Bohrer at a saddlery and harness-making shop in Hagerstown.

Bohrer remembered that John kept only enough money to pay for his board and clothing. For about four years, the remainder of John's wages, usually ten to fifteen dollars a month, was sent to his parents in Centreville. According to his employer, John Snider "was the main support of his mother's family, and that by his kind and filial conduct to her, he endeared himself to the whole community."

John spent the morning of Sunday, April 14, 1861, at church where he listened attentively to a new preacher whose sermon was from the Gospel of Saint Matthew, chapter 28, verses 19–20:

> Go ye therefore, and teach all nations, baptizing them in the name of the Father, and of the Son, and of the Holy Ghost.
> Teaching them to observe all things whatsoever I have commanded you: and, lo, I am with you always, even unto the end of the world.

After church concluded, John talked with friends for a few minutes and then walked home for dinner.

At noon John began to write a letter to his sister, Anna, who was then visiting relatives at Greenfield in Hancock County. It was obvious that he missed his family and the old home in Centreville, as he wrote:

> I will go to Centreville on Satturday the 27th Sunshine or raining, would like to come out to see you all. will not have the money after giving to Mother for I want to give to her all I can spare and have been saving for that purpose.

He advised Anna that the visit home would be a short one since "I am alone in the shop and have plenty of work." John then shared the biggest news in Hagerstown—the appointment of Walkin Williams as postmaster. John closed his letter by wishing "regards to all."[1]

Although John Snider did not yet know it, the country had already plunged into civil war. Secessionist military forces in South Carolina had opened fire on Fort Sumter in Charleston Harbor. After sustaining a prolonged bombardment, Major Robert Anderson and his detachment of the First United States Artillery surrendered the post on the morning of April 14th. At noon, South Carolina time, Anderson's artillerymen fired a salute to the national flag and abandoned the post.

A telegraphic dispatch announcing the bombardment of Sumter arrived in Centreville, the seat of Wayne County's government, at 1 P.M. on April 15th. One hour later, a train pulled into the Centreville depot on the tracks of the Indiana Central Railroad amid a snowstorm. A tall man, "who looked still taller by reason of the high hat he wore," stepped from a passenger car and made a beeline for the court house. Solomon Meredith, clerk of Wayne County, had heard the remarkable news at his home near Cambridge City and caught the first train to the county seat. He quickly located the janitor and sent the man scampering to ring the court house bell.

Court was not in session and no cries of "Fire!" accompanied the clanging bell, so a large crowd pushed into the court room to learn the cause of this alarm. After a few minutes, Meredith stepped onto the judge's desk and began to talk to the assembled citizens. The speaker announced that the American flag had been fired upon at Charleston, South Carolina, and that the people of Indiana must respond to the secessionist challenge. One member of the audience remembered:

> He said prompt action should at once be taken by the people who lived in the home town of Governor Morton, their distinguished fellow citizen. He soon had the crowd aroused to the highest pitch of enthusiasm, and when he closed his address by suggesting that the meeting take form by the election of a president and secretary, the speaker . . . was promptly chosen president and Frank Beitzell, a young attorney at Centreville, was named as secretary.

A motion was unanimously adopted to raise a company of volunteers and horsemen carried the news throughout the county.[2]

A similar public meeting was held at Richmond on April 15th where John A. Bridgland had been chosen president of that assembly. Speeches were made, but no action was taken in Richmond until the following day, when Governor Oliver P. Morton's call for six regiments reached the city. Judge William P. Benton announced his intention to raise a company of three-months troops and opened a recruiting office near the intersection of Pearl and Main Streets. Volunteers flocked to enlist and the company's ranks were filled in a single day. Benton's company marched to the Indiana Central depot on the morning of April 18th and boarded cars for their trip to Indianapolis. After picking up additional detachments from Centreville and Cambridge City, Benton's company became the first to reach Indianapolis in response to Governor Morton's call and formed a part of the 8th Indiana Regiment.

Volunteers continued to come forward during this exciting time. The country was in peril and able-bodied men were needed at once. Military companies sprang into existence almost overnight in every village of Wayne County. Men said goodbye to their wives and children and rushed to enlist. Mothers and fathers fought back tears as their young, strong sons strode off to sign the enlistment rolls.

Another volunteer company was organized in Wayne County by April 23rd, but Indiana's quota of six regiments had already been filled. Instead of turning away eager volunteers, Governor Morton authorized the organization of six additional regiments for a one-year term. These new regiments would be sworn into state service, the Indiana Legion, where they would be held in readiness in case the Federal government needed additional manpower. One of these regiments, the 16th, was to be organized at Richmond and would contain a large number of boys from Wayne County. The county fairgrounds were converted to military use and designated as "Camp Wayne," so soldiers in uniform became a common sight on the streets of Richmond.[3]

The "Richmond City Greys" was another volunteer company raised during this initial burst of recruiting activity. Formation of the company was communicated to the citizens of Wayne County by an announcement in the *Broad Axe of Freedom* on April 27th:

> RICHMOND CITY GREYS. — A new Military Company has been recently organized in this city, bearing the above title, designed as an independent home guard. The Company will be made up of our most respectable young men, and we learn already numbers forty members. This is a good move, and we hope to see it carried out, and encouraged by our citizens. This evening the Company meets for drill, and on Tuesday the Committee on Uniform reports. The Greys will probably appear on parade in a few weeks.

1. William W. Dudley.
From the Collection of the Library of
Congress. Used by permission.

On Saturday night, May 4th, the City Greys assembled and voted for their officers. The following men were selected: William W. Dudley, captain; Davis E. Castle, first lieutenant; Edward W. Gorgas, second lieutenant; Henry E. Robinson, first sergeant; and Frederick O. Strickland, ensign.[4]

Captain Dudley had been born into a distinguished New England family at Weathersfield Bow, Windsor County, Vermont, on August 27, 1842. His father, Reverend John Dudley, was a descendant of the earliest settlers of Connecticut, a graduate of Yale Seminary and a Congregational minister. Dudley's mother was Abigail Wade, a granddaughter of Colonel Nathaniel Wade, one of General George Washington's staff officers during the Revolutionary War. Young William obtained a basic classical education at Phillips Academy in Danville, Vermont, then continued his studies at Russell's Collegiate Institute at New Haven, Connecticut. The course of instruction at this latter school included classes on military science and tactics. William had planned to enter Yale in 1862, but he was compelled to abandon that plan in order to assist in supporting his family. Dudley first worked as a bookkeeper and accountant in New Haven, Connecticut, but in 1860 he moved to Richmond, where he worked as a salesman for an uncle engaged in the milling business. The newcomer to Richmond refrained from enlisting in the first Wayne County companies because of a promise made to his mother to avoid military life. Only after receiving her full consent to come to his country's aid did he begin to recruit the City Greys.[5]

Davis Castle, first lieutenant of the City Greys, was a native of Oswego, New York, who had worked as a railroad hand while boarding with William Patterson in Richmond. A few months prior to his enlistment, Castle found employment as "an unpretending, quiet clerk" at the Cincinnati Dry Goods Store. Second Lieutenant Edward W. Gorgas had much in common with Davis Castle, since he had also worked as a clerk in the Cincinnati Dry Goods Store and on the railroad. First Sergeant Henry E. Robinson was a descendant of Sir William Robinson, who had come to America with William Penn. Henry's father was Francis W. Robinson, owner of the Robinson Machine Works, which manufactured threshing machines and grain separators. Ensign Frederick O. Strickland, who was responsible for carrying the company flag during drills, was a salesman for J. A. Bridgland, tobacco merchant.[6]

Although he was only eighteen years of age, William Dudley's election as captain was assured because he had received at least some military training and most volunteers in the City Greys were wholly ignorant of military affairs. John Leander Yaryan, or "Lee" as he was commonly known, had received a classical degree from Miami University in 1860, but later recalled his only exposure to military affairs prior to his own enlistment:

> I know that as a boy I listened with delight to the stories of an old soldier in the Mexican War, who would stump into the village blacksmith shop on his wooden leg, and with its iron-shod heel, mark, in the cinders and dust of the clay floor, the positions of troops, and how they drove the enemy from this point, and were in turn repulsed from that. These were about the only lessons I took in war until 1861.

Lee's delight at listening to these tales of the old soldier was tempered somewhat when he later learned that the man was an ex-convict who had served ten years in state prison after his conviction on a charge of murder.[7]

Captain Dudley first drilled the City Greys in public on Saturday, May 18th. Although only a portion of the volunteers were present, the editor of the *Palladium* praised their efforts, writing, "They presented a fine appearance, and Capt. Dudley is a most excellent and efficient drill officer." The editor of the *Broad Axe of Freedom* wrote that the City Greys "marched well," then concluded his observation with the statement, "This is one of the finest military companies of this part of the State." The military appearance of Dudley's men increased dramatically on May 22nd when a shipment of old muskets arrived and were incorporated into the drill.[8]

Since the company was now parading through the streets of Richmond on a regular schedule, members felt that they should present a statement of their intentions during the national crisis. On May 25th, the

Broad Axe of Freedom published a resolution, probably authored by Dudley, which had been adopted by the volunteers:

> *Resolved,* That, from the troubled condition of our native land, and the possibility of a disgrace to the Flag we have worshipped as the emblem of Peace, Liberty and Justice, we believe it to be the duty of all American citizens to defend it, and more particularly, we who are in the prime of life, with none of the ties which bind those of more advanced age. We, therefore, resolve to tender our services to the Governor of the State of Indiana, in case our services are required, in the subjugation of those who have forgotten the noble blood of our revolutionary Fathers, which was spilled in the establishment of this, the greatest and freest government since the existence of man, and whose flag has been disgraced, for the first time, by those who should have died in its defense.

Volunteers continued to come forward, including men and boys from Wayne Township who came into Richmond after spring planting.[9]

On Friday evening, May 31st, hundreds of citizens, despite the stormy weather, gathered in Starr Hall at the corner of Main and Marion Streets to witness a flag presentation. Captain Dudley commenced the ceremony by marching the City Greys to the front of the hall where John A. Bridgland, the tobacco merchant, waited with a national flag. Speaking on behalf of the committee members who had carefully crafted the banner— Misses Robinson, Strickland, Castle, Potts, McWhinney, and Fox—Bridgland first addressed his remarks to the residents of Richmond, then to the volunteers:

> *Ladies and Gentlemen*: As many of you are aware, we have come here for the purpose of presenting a flag to this band of young gentlemen, who have formed themselves into a military company to vindicate and defend the honor of their country. I have been selected, by the young ladies present, to present that flag, and I beg to offer them my sincere acknowledgments for the honor they have thus conferred upon me.

> *Young Gentlemen of the Richmond City Greys:* I have the honor tonight, in behalf of the young ladies before us, of presenting to you this flag. I see by your countenances, by the emblems of the soldier upon your persons, and by the arms you bring with you, that it is about to pass into hands fit to receive it. May God help you to honor and protect it; and when you return, may it come back to the fair hands that gave it, unstained, unless by the blood of your enemies.

> But twice, since this flag has been made the emblem of our nation's glory, has it been dishonored by an American hand, betrayed by Arnold, in 1777, and at Fort Sumter, in 1861, it was pulled down in disgrace by

a band of traitors. Let us know no rest till it again waves in the walls of Sumter, the glorious emblem of our patriotism and our valor.

While it seems almost like turning against my mother, and proving recreant to the fond memories of my childhood, to take up arms against Virginia; yet rather than see the Government succumb to rebels and traitors, I am ready and willing to march with my fellow-citizens, and expend my life, if need be, in defense of the glorious old flag of the Stars and Stripes.

The man who bears these colors is the prominent mark for the enemy's fire; his breast is the target for the deadliest shafts in battle. But the soldier knows full well the post of danger is the post of honor, and if there is a man who will make himself bearer of these colors for his company, let him *present arms!*

The City Greys instantly snapped to the position of "present arms," then Ensign Strickland stepped forward and accepted the banner. Captain Dudley followed with a response to Mr. Bridgland's address:

> *Ladies,* in behalf of the members of this Company, I would accept this emblem of our once peaceful land which you have so kindly offered, and return as the only manner now within our power of expressing deep gratitude, their sincere thanks. To say that its image inspires us with patriotism, is but the expression of every true American. But, presented as this is by hands too weak to strike a blow in its defense, every star has received additional luster and every stripe new endearments, that will make our hearts throb with emotion when its sacred folds are unfurled to our view. That constellation which has been eighty years in forming, shall not now be robbed of a single one of its luminaries, or this small band shall fall with the vast multitude which now rushes to the call of the Executive and *that* flag shall be taken to the battlefield a silent witness to our efforts. The insult, not the war, is ours, and the blood spilled in the subjugation of traitors will paint in letters too vivid for posterity to overlook, what Americans can, and will sacrifice to maintain their honor. Again accept our thanks and believe me this treasure and the motive of its donors are fully appreciated.

Following Dudley's remarks, two prominent attorneys, Herman B. Payne and John Yaryan (Lee's father), made patriotic speeches in which they praised both the ladies and the volunteers. After these speakers concluded, the remainder of the evening was devoted to music and dancing, a celebration that was termed as "merry as a marriage bell." One spectator at the event commented on the determination exhibited by Richmond's newest military company: "If called upon, we have no fear but what the 'Greys' will bring back their Flag, marred and torn though it may be by the crash of battle, yet covered with laurels, if there is but one of them left alive to carry it."[10]

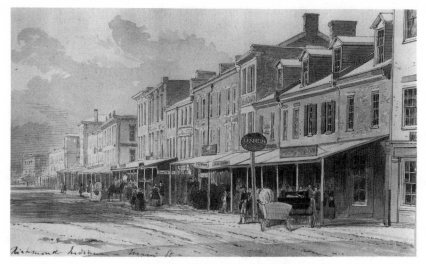

2. Main Street in Richmond, Indiana.
From the Lefevre Cranstone Collection, Lilly Library, Indiana University.
Used by permission.

One topic certainly much discussed that evening was the passage of Solomon Meredith through the city on Thursday night, bearing, it was said, important dispatches from Governor Morton to President Abraham Lincoln. Of course, he could not discuss the nature of those messages, but Sol did intimate to friends that Indiana would soon have an opportunity to furnish additional regiments for Federal service. The editor of the *Broad Axe* observed that Meredith was just the man for such a mission, then predicted that the war would continue "long enough to give all who are 'spilin' for a fight,' an opportunity to 'go in on their muscle.'"[11]

Most of the volunteers in the City Greys were sons of middle-class families who lived and worked in Richmond. Two of the young men who quickly learned their drill were Thomas H. Benton and Samuel McCown, both of whom were twenty years old. Tom worked in his father's hardware and cutlery store at 48 Main Street, next door to the dry goods store at 50 Main Street owned by Sam's father. Across the street and down the block was the dry goods store of Edward G. Potts, whose son Jesse was learning how to dispense prescription drugs. Robert Conley and Charles Petty worked for Bob's father by day at the Richmond Gardens, a nursery and greenhouse on South Pearl Street, and drilled with the City Greys at night. Asa Blanchard was the son of James M. Blanchard, the railroad agent, and, although only seventeen years old demonstrated an aptitude for military life. Luther Hall was the son of William Hall, foreman for Wiggins & Company, a large local tanning firm. Dr. Anselm Butler's son, John, lived at home but worked as a carpenter. A few members of the company, like the blacksmith, James Livengood, were independently pursuing their trades, but most were still living with their folks.[12]

Many of the available young men were enlisting in the 16th Regiment at Camp Wayne, so Dudley and his officers began recruiting residents on the outskirts of the city and in outlying towns. Concentrating on the more populous townships in northern Wayne County, the City Greys were soon augmented by men such as Thomas Jefferson Wasson, son of J. Macamy Wasson, hotel keeper and postmaster in Chester, and Timothy Hart, the orphaned son of Irish immigrants and a former bound boy. From the vicinity of Washington, in Clay Township, recruiters signed up the Sykes brothers, Joseph and William, both natives of North Carolina, and Charles Davis, grandson of the man who had laid out the village of Dublin. In Hillsboro, near the Ohio state line, Jacob and Joseph Addleman signed the roll, although their elder brother John stayed home to help with the farm. The Addlemans were joined by Noah Craig, the oldest son in a cooper's family of ten children. From Williamsburg came Benjamin B. Duke, a young farmer whose maternal ancestors came west from New Jersey and whose father's family emigrated from North Carolina, a unique blend of North and South in the current crisis.[13]

Recruiting for the City Greys was spurred by news that Solomon Meredith had been commissioned colonel and given authority to raise a new regiment. Meredith's call for troops was issued on June 14th:

> Having been authorized by the President of the United States to raise a regiment for three years' service, I desire that all captains, who wish to form a part of my regiment, report to me at the Bates House in Indianapolis within the next ten days.
>
> 　　　　　　　　　　　　　　S. Meredith

A Wayne County colonel must have Wayne County troops, so Captain Dudley telegraphed the Indiana Adjutant General that the City Greys wished to assume a place in Meredith's new regiment. By the evening of June 15th, eight companies, including the Richmond company, had been accepted. Two additional companies soon filled the roster, but other companies still tendered their services to the tall colonel from Wayne County.[14]

Acceptance of the City Greys into Meredith's regiment alienated the company from the Fifth District's most influential politician, Congressman George W. Julian. Although both men were devoted members of the Republican Party, Sol Meredith and George Julian were bitter personal enemies. In fact, the colonel would later declare, "The people of his neighborhood will remember that during the early part of the war, he never opened his mouth or raised his hand in behalf of the Government." That silence was attributed to Julian's malice toward Meredith, a deep-seated hatred that had to be gratified "even at the expense of whatever influence he could bring in favor of a vigorous prosecution of the war."[15]

Unable to appeal to their congressman for support and encouragement, the City Greys placed the following advertisement in the press:

> VOLUNTEERS
> FOR THE WAR
> WANTED!
> THE RICHMOND CITY GREYS, having been tendered a position of honor in the United States' service, for the war, want a few more able bodied men, to fill up the ranks of the Company. An election for officers will be held as soon as the Company is full, when they will go into service immediately. By order of the Company.

The ranks of the City Greys were only half-filled when all companies of Colonel Meredith's regiment, now designated as the 19th Regiment Indiana Volunteer Infantry, were instructed to gather at Camp Morton in Indianapolis. Captain Dudley's company was to report on July 6th. The Greys opened a recruiting office on July 3rd and chose Lee Yaryan to man it after their departure. Lee was to find able-bodied men, enlist them into the Greys, and forward the recruits to Captain Dudley at Indianapolis.[16]

On Saturday morning, July 6th, the Richmond City Greys were escorted to the depot by Mitchell's Cornet Band and the 16th Indiana. The editor of the *Broad Axe* witnessed their departure:

> The Greys are a fine looking company, composed for the most part of young men "native and to the manor born." As they paraded the streets they were seen and admired by most of our citizens, and many a prayer doubtless went up for their success and safe return.

After a short ceremony at the depot, eager volunteers filed into the passenger cars for a sixty-eight mile trip to Indianapolis. With family members crying and cheering on the platform, the train pulled away from the depot and their young men waved and shouted back through the windows until Richmond faded into the distance.[17]

2

Camp Morton

 After reaching Indianapolis, Captain Dudley formed the City
Greys into line at the depot, then marched them over to the State
house behind Mitchell's Cornet Band. There the company stood at attention and the men entered state service by taking the following oath of
allegiance:

> I ———, solemnly swear that I will honestly and faithfully serve the
> State of Indiana against all her enemies or opposers, and that I will do my
> utmost to support the Constitution and laws of the United States, and
> of the State of Indiana, against all violence of whatever kind or descrip-
> tion. And I further swear that I will obey the legal orders of all officers
> legally placed over me, when on duty; so help me God!

Captain Dudley's soldiers were then conveyed by wagon to Camp Morton,
where the quartermaster issued woolen army blankets and cooking equipment: coffee pots, camp kettles, frying pans, wash basins, tin plates, tin pans
deep enough to hold soup, tin cups, tin buckets, knives, forks and spoons.
The fifty-five volunteers then marched to the camp commissary where they
received their first issue of army rations: pork, bread, rice, coffee, sugar,
vinegar, pepper, salt, potatoes, molasses, and hominy. Although the boys
were not able to duplicate the home cooking they were accustomed to,
state rations were at least passed out in greater quantities than the standard
Federal issue.[1]

On the very day Dudley's men reached camp, Colonel Meredith
issued his first "General Order," which outlined the rules that would govern
his regiment at Camp Morton:

Head Quarters, Camp Morton,
Indianapolis, July 6th, 1861

The following will be the hours of service:
  1. Reveille — 5 o'clock A.M.
  2. Roll call — immediately after.
  3. Signal for breakfast — 5:30 A.M.
  4. Surgeon's call — 6:30 A.M.
  5. Fatigue call — 6:40 A.M.
  6. Reports and issues — 7:10 A.M.
  7. Officer's drill — 7:40 A.M.
  8. Guard mounting — 8:00 A.M.
  9. Company drill — 9:00 A.M.
  10. Signal for dinner — 12 M.
  11. Battalion drill — 2:30 P.M.
  12. Dress parade — 5:00 P.M.
  13. Supper call — 6:30 P.M.
  14. Retreat — Sunset
  15. Tattoo — 8:30 P.M.
  16. Taps — 10:00 P.M.

  1. Drums will not be beaten nor bugles sounded except in making regular calls, and in practice. Practice hours for musicians from 11:30 A.M. to 2:00 P.M.

  2. Orders as to persons passing the lines will be given from headquarters.

  3. Passes of soldiers will be regulated by special order from headquarters.

  4. Sergeants failing to relieve sentinels at the exact hour, will themselves be compelled to do guard duty; and all the sentinels, not relieved at the proper time, are required to report the delinquents to the officers of the guard, who will report the same to headquarters.

  5. No unmarried soldier will be permitted, under any circumstances, without special leave from headquarters, to pass the night out of his company quarters.

  6. Silence and strict order will be enforced in barracks, except from 11:30 A.M. to 2:30 P.M. and from tattoo to taps.

  7. At taps every light will be extinguished, and any soldier, not on duty, found out of his company quarters after taps, will be taken to the guardhouse, and kept there till after reports in the morning.

  8. Further orders will from time to time be issued.

S. Meredith, Col. commanding.

It may be inferred that the individual points addressed in Meredith's order were efforts to correct abuses by hundreds of young men who were still unused to army discipline.[2]

The City Greys was the eighth company to join the 19th Indiana at Camp Morton, so the Richmond boys spent Sunday getting acquainted with soldiers from other commands. Captain Valentine Jacobs's "Invincibles," an Indianapolis company, had been the first to arrive, marching through the camp gates on July 2nd. Captain Jacobs, described as "a man of the John Morrisey stamp," maintained order in a unique fashion, since he "didn't pretend to govern them according to military discipline, but would go to work and knock down three or four of them at once." Jacobs shared his taste for pugilism with Private Abram J. "Jack" Oliver, "a powerful man" who deemed it his "duty" to thrash people. However, not all of the Invincibles were brawlers itching for a fight. One of Jacobs's men had been assaulted on June 29th, near the White River, by a gang of ruffians who knocked him down and stole his watch.[3]

The Invincibles were joined on July 2nd by seventy-seven men of the "Delaware Greys," who hailed from Delaware County and were commanded by a Muncie resident, Captain Luther B. Wilson. Two of Wilson's volunteers, Frank Ethell and Abram Jay Buckles, were natives of Delaware County. Frank, the son of William J. Ethell, had been born and raised in Muncie, attending class in the county schools until his enlistment. He was also one of the smallest soldiers in the regiment. Abe Buckles was the second son of Thomas and Rebecca (Graham) Buckles. His father's family had settled in Virginia long before the Revolution, but his mother's people were more recent immigrants from Ireland. This young volunteer had received but little education in the county schools and would not celebrate his sixteenth birthday until August 2nd.[4]

Three additional companies for Colonel Meredith's regiment had arrived on July 3rd—the "Spencer Greys," "Selma Legion," and "Elkhart County Guards." Captain John H. Johnson's Spencer Greys came into camp with the ranks, including one clergyman serving as a private, at full strength, the only company to do so. One of the noncommissioned officers was Chauncey B. Patrick who, at the age of forty-one, was one of the oldest men in the regiment. Sergeant Patrick's father was a Methodist minister who had died in 1844, but by that time the son was married and working as a carpenter at Bainbridge, Indiana. Chauncey moved his family to California in 1858, but returned to Spencer, in Owen County, after the death of his wife. His eldest son, Albert, would eventually enlist in the same company.[5]

The Selma Legion, commanded by Captain Samuel J. Williams, was one of the most dapper companies in camp, each man outfitted with a frock coat of "butternut grey," with red flannel trim and brass buttons. Williams had been born in 1830 in Virginia, but the family moved to Indiana soon after his birth. Samuel's father died in 1845, leaving the youngster as the sole support of his mother. After devoting sixteen years to farming, stock dealing, and mercantile pursuits in the village of Selma, Williams became the prime mover in forming the Legion. Before leaving for Camp Morton, Captain Williams had drilled his volunteers for several weeks on the village commons, even though the area was still inconveniently filled with stumps and logs.[6]

Captain John R. Clark's Elkhart County Guards was a combination of several companies from northern Indiana. Clark's men included his Elkhart County contingent, a sizable group from the Lagrange County Guards, and a number of recruits from DeKalb County. While the boys from Lagrange and Elkhart counties carried on a running feud over possession of a flag presented by the citizens of Goshen, the DeKalb volunteers had the most interesting story to relate. When the townspeople of Waterloo gathered to bid farewell to their departing heroes, an amateur artillerist had recklessly loaded the village cannon to within a few inches of the muzzle. As the gunner, Mr. J. H. Shoemaker, fired, the cannon exploded, "bursting the gun to atoms and scattering the pieces in all directions, over houses and treetops, carrying several heavy pieces to a distance of over eighty rods." Although no one in the crowd was injured by the explosion, a fragment tore through Shoemaker's body, killing him instantly.[7]

On July 5th, the "Union Guards" and "Meredith Guards" marched in to join the 19th Indiana. Sixty members of the Union Guards arrived under command of Captain Isaac M. May, a native Virginian who had moved to Anderson, Indiana, where he worked as a cabinetmaker. One of May's lieutenants was Alonzo S. Makepeace, whose parents were among the early settlers of Madison County. In 1856 Alonzo, at the age of twenty-one, had joined a company of young men on an expedition to California via Central America. Unrest in Nicaragua resulted in the company turning back to New York, where Alonzo returned home to Indiana by way of Niagara Falls and Ontario. Makepeace was working as a carpenter in Anderson when he joined the Union Guards.[8]

Acceptance of a second Indianapolis company into Colonel Meredith's regiment was virtually assured when the men adopted the *nom de guerre,* "Meredith Guards." Captain John F. Lindley brought only thirty-four men out to Camp Morton, the smallest company to join the 19th Indiana except for Captain Jacobs's Invincibles. Apparently, the married men of these two commands were allowed to return home when not on duty, at least for the first weeks of their training. One volunteer who surely needed to attend to matters at home was John Andis. He and his wife were parents of seven

3. John M. Lindley.
Used by permission of the Indiana
State Library.

children, aged seventeen, sixteen, twelve, nine, seven, five, and one. Among
Captain Lindley's men were the Cly brothers, John and Abraham. John was
small of stature and quick of movement, while his older brother was "big,
burly, good-natured and stout as an ox." Abe was generally known as "Bull
of the Woods."[9]

Before the City Greys could make the acquaintance of all their
comrades in other companies, they had to say goodbye to some of their own
men. On July 8th, about a dozen of the Greys, claiming that they could not
serve under Colonel Meredith, "immediately volunteered to go home
again." The *Broad Axe* reported the unusual incident and pointed out that
Captain Dudley, even before the company left Richmond, had explained to
his men that they had been assigned to Colonel Meredith's regiment. The
editor had no sympathy for the dissenters, observing that "if they had
'conscientious scruples' to serving under him, it would have looked better to
'back down' before starting." Although no specific reason was given for the
return of these volunteers, the incident may have somehow been provoked
by Congressman Julian. Colonel Meredith would later write that Julian, his
archenemy, "endeavored in every possible way to clog and thwart my efforts
to complete my regiment."[10]

On the day the dissenters from Dudley's company left for Richmond, Captain Richard M. Kelly arrived with ninety-three men from the
"Edinburgh Guards," which had been raised in Johnson County. Kelly, a

Mexican War veteran, was originally from Jackson County, but had been admitted to the Johnson County bar in 1856 where he was "a close student, and tried his cases with a good deal of skill." Kelly's first lieutenant was Theodore Hudnut, a partner in Hudnut & Tilford, a hominy mill erected by Hudnut in Blue River Township in 1857.[11]

The 19th Indiana was finally filled on July 15th with the arrival of its tenth company, the "Winchester Greys." Although its captain, Dr. Robert W. Hamilton, claimed to have never lost a case of diphtheria or scarlet fever, he was not so lucky in his new position. Of the 101 men on the original muster roll, only sixty-seven stayed around long enough to be mustered into Federal service. William W. Macy was one of Captain Hamilton's steadfast volunteers. He was a descendant of Thomas Macy, one of the first settlers of Salisbury, Massachusetts, who had emigrated from England in the 1630s. William represented the ninth generation of Macys in America and spent his winters in school and his summers hauling logs by ox team to his father's steam mill near the village of Farmland.[12]

Once all ten companies were assembled, the first order of business was to assign them posts in the regimental line of battle. The following assignments were made:

Company A	Captain	Isaac M. May	Madison County
" B	"	William W. Dudley	Wayne County
" C	"	Robert W. Hamilton	Randolph County
" D	"	Valentine Jacobs	Marion County
" E	"	Luther B. Wilson	Delaware County
" F	"	John F. Lindley	Marion County
" G	"	John R. Clark	Elkhart County
" H	"	Richard M. Kelly	Johnson County
" I	"	John H. Johnson	Owen County
" K	"	Samuel J. Williams	Delaware County

The individual companies were aligned in the following order, with Company A on the right of the line:

B   G   K   E   H   C   I   D   F   A

For the purpose of maneuvering by the drill manual, Meredith's companies were numbered one to ten, from right to left. In addition, the regiment was divided into divisions of two companies each, which were numbered one to five, right to left. A sergeant with the national colors and eight corporals as color guards were posted in the middle of the regiment, between companies C and H, with the five right companies designated as the right wing and the color guard, and the five left companies as the left wing.

Counties Which Sent Companies for the 19th Indiana

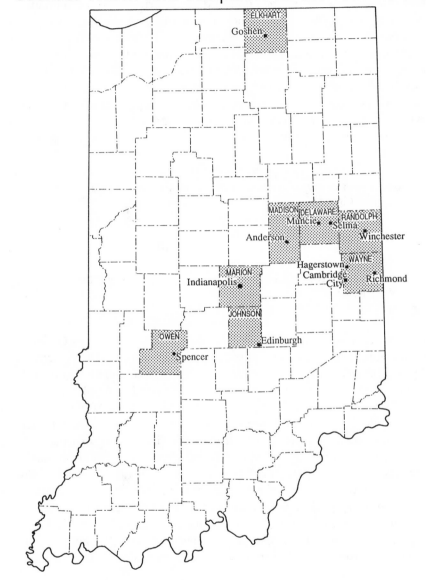

Company B, like all the other companies, was formed in two ranks with the tallest men on the right and the shortest men on the left. The company was further broken down into platoons and sections for the purpose of maneuver. Corporals were posted in the front rank where they could help direct the men and act as pivots for the various maneuvers, the tallest corporal on the right. Officers and sergeants, called file closers, marched behind the company's two ranks and directed or corrected the line as necessary. According to this arrangement, dictated by the manual, Horace Wharton, the tallest corporal in Company B, would be posted in the first rank, first section, first platoon, tenth company, fifth division, left wing of the regiment.[13]

William R. Moore, a private in the Selma Legion, remembered those first days spent in trying to master the intricacies of an infantry drill almost mathematical in its precision:

> Our life in Camp Morton was not exactly a picnic, even if on that order to some extent. It was quite warm (hot) weather, as is apt to be at that time of year. We were being drilled vigorously in military maneuvers, learning how to march in twos, fours, squads, platoons and Company in line, learning "hay-foot, straw-foot," marching, counter-marching, quick time and double quick, etc.

Lieutenant Colonel Thomas J. Wood of the 1st United States Cavalry was responsible for the Hoosiers' introduction to William J. Hardee's *Rifle and Light Infantry Tactics*. The boys did not take kindly to Wood and his complicated maneuvers and he was quickly branded "a regular martinet."[14]

Hardee's *Tactics* commenced with the "School of the Soldier," in which officers began the progressive instruction of their men. Instructors, often just one lesson ahead of their students, first read an explanation of a movement, then executed that movement themselves and finally put their charges through seemingly endless repetitions of the drill. New soldiers were first taught the position of a soldier, how to face and how to march at common time, quick time and double-quick time. When these lessons had been learned, the men were taught the manual of arms, how to load and fire their muskets, and the proper use of their bayonets. Finally, the soldiers received instructions on how to march together and how to change direction while marching.

Even before mastering these basic elements, the individual squads were united for drill in the "School of the Company," in which the soldiers applied their acquired knowledge as a cog in the larger unit. When some degree of proficiency was achieved in this stage, the companies were assembled and drilled in the "School of the Battalion." Company and battalion drill became increasingly complex, but hours upon hours of practice brought confidence and the soldiers learned to move in unison "with only a tangle-leg, now and then."[15]

When officers learned their lessons only hours before implementing a new drill, the result was a complete dependence on the manual. Colonel Meredith found himself in an embarrassing position one day while giving orders from his open copy of Hardee's *Tactics*. Isaac Julian, brother of George W. Julian and editor of the *Indiana True Republican,* gleefully reported the incident. Everything went smoothly until the colonel came to the optional command, "Right or left oblique—March!":

> Solomon followed the book to the letter, improving however upon the pronunciation thus: "Right or left oblicu—March!" The soldiers of course did not comprehend the order, and so informed him, and someone told him it was wrong, to which he replied "that could not be, for he *had taken it from the book*."

The Hoosier colonel was learning that a transition from agriculture and politics to the military field was not as easy as it first appeared.[16]

Solomon Meredith's appointment as colonel of the 19th Indiana was the latest in a long series of political successes by the Tarheel native. It was accurate to say that "Long Sol" always stood out in a crowd, since he stood a towering six feet, seven inches, but he was most notable for his limitless ambition and an uncanny ability to get what he wanted.

Born on May 29, 1810, in Guilford County, North Carolina, Solomon was the youngest child of David and Mary (Harington) Meredith. Solomon's paternal grandfather had been a soldier in the Revolution and was a veteran of the battle at Guilford Court House. In addition to this patriotic connection, Solomon was raised in a home that emphasized involvement in political affairs and devotion to the Society of Friends.[17]

At the age of eighteen, Solomon, in company with Richard Hubbard, walked from North Carolina to Wayne County, Indiana. After remaining a few months, the young man returned home and told his parents of Indiana's wonderful farmland. Sol's parents decided to make a new home in the Hoosier State and in 1829 settled on a farm seven miles north of Richmond. David Meredith was unable to support his youngest son, so Sol set out on his own with only twelve and one-half cents in his pockets. He earned his first wages of eight dollars per month by cutting timber and hewing logs.[18]

After establishing himself in the community of Cambridge City, Meredith was elected sheriff of Wayne County in 1834, just five years after his arrival, and reelected to the office in 1836. During his second term, Sol married Anna Hannah, a daughter of Samuel Hannah, a prominent politician who would later serve as treasurer of the State of Indiana. Content to breed stock on Oakland Farm and fill several local offices in Cambridge City, Meredith did not seek political office again until 1846, although he did serve as a delegate to the Whig National Convention at Columbus, Ohio, in 1840. During this period Sol became a spokesman for internal improvements in the state, supporting the development of the Whitewater Canal, whose northern terminus was at Cambridge City, and the Indiana Central Railroad, whose tracks just happened to run behind his home.[19]

Sol's political career began in earnest in 1846 with his election to the Indiana House of Representatives, to which body he was reelected in 1847 and 1848, where he successively held the chairmanships of the Committee on Roads, the Committee on the State Bank and the Committee on Ways and Means. From 1849 to 1853 Sol served as United States Marshal for the State of Indiana, much of this term overlapping a ten-year tenure as vice president, director, and agent for the Indiana Central Railroad. In 1852, while serving as marshal, Long Sol visited England on behalf of the Indiana Central and arranged for the shipment of Irish laborers to Wayne County. A strong supporter of the Whig party during this period, Marshal Meredith did everything in his power during that year to ensure the election of Winfield Scott to the presidency. On one occasion he gathered over 100 of the new Irish immigrants in their shantytown, marched them in a body to the court house, delivered a stirring speech extolling the virtues of General Scott, and issued citizenship papers to the crowd. But Sol's efforts resulted in his most embarrassing political moment when a local contractor marched these new citizens to the polls on election day and instructed them to vote for Franklin Pierce, the Democratic candidate.[20]

Meredith's career of public service continued with his election to the Indiana House of Representatives in 1854 (now a two-year term under the new state constitution) and he was again selected as chairman of the Committee on Ways and Means. The Wayne County representative explored the possibility of gaining a seat in the United States Senate, going so far as to entertain the entire Indiana legislature at Oakland Farm, but he did not make a serious attempt for the office. When the Whig party fragmented, Long Sol briefly joined the Know-Nothing party and served as a delegate to its Grand Council in Philadelphia in 1856. Switching his allegiance to the emerging Republican party, Meredith was elected Clerk of the Wayne County Court in 1859. An Indianapolis visitor called on the Wayne County leader shortly after his election to the clerkship and recorded his impression of the politico: "He has been Marshall of the State & in politics a great many years. He looks on them as vain pursuits. Promises to be honest & reasonable." Quickly rising to prominence in the Indiana Republican organization, Meredith had the honor of presenting a motion that Henry S. Lane's nomination for governor be by acclamation at the state convention in 1860.[21]

His support of the Republican ticket resulted in Sol's selection as a member of the Republican National Committee. During the party's national convention in 1860, solid support of the Indiana delegation, under the leadership of Henry Lane, assured the nomination of Abraham Lincoln. After the election of 1860, Meredith kept in touch with Lincoln by providing letters of introduction for prominent Wayne County Republicans and, on at least one occasion, by visiting the president-elect in Springfield, Illinois. In late January of 1861, the officers of the Indiana Central instructed Meredith to write Lincoln on their behalf, offering the use of a special train, one coach to be set aside for the president, and sent "free of charge" for his trip to Washington. Sol concluded his letter, "I sincerely hope we may have the pleasure of greeting you 'the people's choice' at our State Capitol, on your way to Washington City." On February 11, 1861, Lincoln stopped overnight in Indianapolis on the way to his inauguration. A large crowd assembled outside the Bates House and called for a speech. Although Lincoln did not address the assembly that evening, he stepped onto a balcony where he was introduced to the citizens of Indianapolis by his Hoosier friend, Solomon Meredith.[22]

Part of Solomon's political success was based on his uncanny ability to remember names and faces. He could begin any conversation by referring to topics discussed the last time he had met with the person. Although denied a classical education, Meredith displayed the courtesy, friendship, and manners of a true gentleman. He was a prominent member of the International Order of Odd Fellows and served as Grand Master of Indiana, as well as Grand Representative to the Grand Lodge of the United States. As a father, Sol was devoted to his wife and sons—Samuel, David, and Henry. A daughter, Mary, died in infancy.[23]

If Sol's quest for political office and prestige were considered "vain pursuits," his real loves were agriculture and stock breeding. He bought Oakland Farm in 1851 and soon became "one of the most prominent of the early Indiana breeders, and afterward acquired international reputation for his herd." One writer summed up Meredith's contributions in the field of husbandry:

> As an importer of rare and expensive stock, especially of cattle, hogs and sheep, Mr. Meredith perhaps outranks all others in the western country. For the period of ten years he was Vice President of the Agricultural Society of Wayne County; for many years he was a leading member of the State Board of Agriculture, and he has been a constant and always successful exhibitor at the State and United States Agricultural Fairs. It is quite safe to say that he has received more premiums at these exhibitions than has any gentleman in the West.

4. Solomon Meredith.
From the collection of the author.

Sol could always be counted on to have his own tent or building at these agricultural fairs, where he entertained friends and directed his array of entries. As an example of his success, Meredith, at the Wayne County Fair in 1860, won three sweepstakes awards worth $50 apiece. In addition, his entries garnered four first place and eight second place awards, for a total of $265, just over twice the yearly pay of a private in his regiment at Camp Morton in July of 1861.[24]

As Colonel Meredith tried to instruct his regiment on the drill field, his captains searched for more men to fill their ranks to the full complement of 101. Keeping the men already in camp was also a major problem. Second Lieutenant William Orr of the Selma Legion described for his parents the delicate process of keeping his company together:

> By great exertion our company was organized in the first place, by great nursing it was maintained as an organized company. By a continued and well directed effort the Company was accepted in Col Meredith's regiment. By great exertions we succeeded in bringing down 60 men on the 2nd day of July. By great exertions we succeeded in holding our company together here. Once or twice I thought the whole thing was gone up and that we would be under the necessity of returning to you with our fingers in our mouths or else join some other company as high privates.

Apparently the most critical time for the Selma company came when the men heard a rumor that they would receive no pay until the 19th Indiana was formally organized. Renouncing the oath with which they had entered state service, the volunteers announced that if they were not paid, the regiment would never be organized. Speeches by their officers and citizens visiting in camp calmed the agitated soldiers until the companies were sworn into Federal service on July 17th.[25]

On that day Colonel Meredith's regiment was marched to Camp Sullivan, where the soldiers were hastily inspected before being sworn in. They all subscribed to the standard oath of allegiance:

> I, ———, do solemnly swear that I will bear true allegiance to the United States of America, and that I will serve them honestly and faithfully against all their enemies or opposers whatsoever; and observe and obey the orders of the President of the United States, and the orders of the officers appointed over me, according to the Rules and Articles for the government of the armies of the United States.

Lieutenant Colonel Wood and his examining surgeon were able to weed out some men who were obviously too old, too young, or too drunk, but most of the men were accepted without question. Thomas P. Davis, a private in Captain Dudley's company, remembered the cursory process: "I was thoroughly examined on enlistement but not stripped." As might be expected, some men managed to conceal their ages, ailments, and infirmities in their eagerness to be accepted. Two volunteers from Captain Dudley's company were accepted despite disqualifying physical limitations. John Winder passed his physical exam although his arm had been broken and had healed so as to prevent him from ever carrying a musket for an extended period. Milton Franklin, a diminutive fifer from Hagerstown who stood only five feet, two inches, must have walked on his tiptoes to fool the inspector since he was two full inches under the minimum standard for a soldier. There were undoubtedly other cases of fraud perpetrated on Lieutenant Colonel Wood that day.[26]

The most common sort of fraud was lying about one's age. At least ten members of the Richmond company were accepted, despite being under the legal age for enlistment, including Henry Zook and Sanford Wallick, who were both only fifteen. But the examiners were able to apprehend a few youngsters. Albert B. Beneway, "a little blue-eyed, brown-haired and beardless boy," attempted to become a drummer boy, but his age, size, and "the importunity of his mother" foiled the attempt. Undeterred, young Beneway ran away from home and followed the 19th Indiana to Virginia, where he contracted typhoid fever. Upon his recovery, Beneway returned home and later enlisted in Company C of the 75th Indiana. Leroy Magee's experience was nearly identical to that of Albert Beneway. Magee went to Indianapolis with the City Greys, but was rejected because he was only fourteen. Leroy stayed on with the company by signing up as a servant for Lieutenant Davis

Castle and remained until the fall of 1861. Returning home, Leroy soon bluffed his way into Company A, 63rd Indiana, where he served about eight months. The youngster requested a transfer to the 18th United States Infantry, where he served another ten months before his discharge for disability. Leroy returned home, but died of consumption only a few days later. Probably the most astounding case was that of Jacob Mays who enlisted in Company A, but was rejected on account of his size and age, being only fifteen. On September 5, 1861, "Jakey" enlisted in Company F, 34th Indiana, and a few days later was "accepted by the same examining officer who had rejected him but a few days previous!"[27]

Captain Dudley's company was just over half-filled when it was sworn into Federal service, but recruits continued to flow into Camp Morton. The fierce competition for men of military age had forced Lee Yaryan to search new territory for volunteers to fill the City Greys. Trips to Knightstown, Millville, and Coffin's Station in neighboring Henry County brought in almost a dozen more soldiers. But Yaryan's best luck came at Hagerstown, in the northwestern corner of Wayne County, where he signed up almost two dozen volunteers. These new men included Alexander C. Walker, son of Dr. James H. Walker, and Benjamin F. Jewett, the son of Parker Jewett, who had been raised in "a home of prayer." John Snider had written his sister on June 19th that he was so busy in the harness shop that he could not possibly come home for several months. But now he, too, had enlisted and was headed for Camp Morton.[28]

By the end of July, Company B of the 19th Indiana no longer resembled the City Greys organization which had proudly marched down the streets of Richmond only three weeks before. Captain Dudley still commanded the company, with Davis Castle his able first lieutenant, but Samuel Hindman had replaced Edward Gorgas as second lieutenant with the latter now serving as a sergeant. Ensign Strickland and First Sergeant Robinson were both gone, the former post having no place in the Federal organization and the latter post now filled by Samuel B. Schlagle of Williamsburg. Henry Robinson would later enlist in the 57th Indiana, but Fred Strickland would see no additional military service.[29]

Two valuable young men left the City Greys when promotions beckoned. After closing his recruiting office, Lee Yaryan was rewarded with a commission as first lieutenant in Captain Clark's Company G, thereby terminating his connection with Captain Dudley's company. Yaryan resigned on January 24, 1862, in order to accept a commission as adjutant of the 58th Indiana. He eventually reached the rank of captain and served as a division staff officer in the Army of the Cumberland. Jesse Potts was appointed hospital steward of the 19th Indiana upon its formal organization. Jesse would be commissioned a second lieutenant in Company C during the spring of 1863 and would serve as a division staff officer during most of 1864.[30]

The ranks of Company B were now scattered with "foreigners" from outlying Wayne County villages and other nearby counties, the Richmond boys not able to muster a majority in the company. But Captain Dudley's company was still typical of the volunteer organizations that formed in 1861. The majority of the soldiers were young, the median age being twenty years. Three boys admitted to being only seventeen years of age when they enlisted with their parents' approval. But three other seventeen-year-olds in the City Greys, Asa Blanchard, Luther Hall, and Jeff Wasson, swore they were eighteen. The contingent from Hagerstown supplied three more underage recruits—Henry Gordon, seventeen; Sam Lutz, sixteen; and Henry Zook, fifteen. "Hen" Zook shared the distinction of being the company's youngest member with Sanford Wallick, a resident of Cambridge City. In the other extreme, Benjamin Thornburg was forty and James Bradbury was forty-two.

Over one-half of the men of Company B were Indiana natives and all but one of them had been born in the United States. More than one-half of Dudley's men stated they were farmers, along with seventeen mechanics, eight laborers, and a scattering of other trades. In height, the men ranged from the six-feet-four-inch Horace Wharton on down to the pint-sized Milton Franklin, all five feet two inches of him. As far as personal appearance, the majority of the soldiers were dark-complexioned, with blue eyes and brown hair. The only apparent oddities were Dick Jones from Cambridge City, whose eyes were two different colors, one hazel and one gray, and Dick Williams, who sported the only red hair in the company.[31]

Organization of the 19th Indiana slowed for a week in late July when Colonel Meredith, still the only field officer in the regiment, fell ill and was forced to leave camp for a room at the Bates House. One journalist made inquiry and learned that "the boys are not disposed to take advantage of his absence," displaying obedience not only to their colonel but also to their captains. The boys were evidently enjoying their soldier life. A visitor to Captain Clark's Elkhart County Guards described the company as "a happy set of fellows," while one of the Selma Legion advised his father, "Tell the boys up there if they want to see fun to gist come down here." Levi Yost summed up the prevalent feeling when he wrote his parents, "The soft side of a poplar board is as good to sleep on as a fether bed almost, While defending our Country." There were occasional interludes of a non-military nature, such as the afternoon in late July when the entire regiment was invited to a picnic in Walnut Grove. Camp duties were forgotten for the afternoon as soldiers spent a few joyous hours with the supportive citizens of Indianapolis, including, no doubt, a number of young, attractive women.[32]

On July 29, 1861, Lieutenant Colonel Thomas J. Wood mustered the 19th Indiana Volunteers into Federal service in a ceremony at Camp Morton. The roster of Company B, formerly the Richmond City Greys, included the following:

CAPTAIN
William W. Dudley

FIRST LIEUTENANT
Davis E. Castle

SECOND LIEUTENANT
Samuel Hindman

FIRST SERGEANT
Samuel Schlagle

SERGEANT

Thomas H. Benton	Charles Davis
Edward W. Gorgas	Samuel McCown

CORPORAL

Noah Craig	Thomas J. Crull
Benjamin F. Jewett	Abraham Luce
Allen W. Ogborn	John M. Snider
John R. Thornburg	Horace Wharton

FIFER
Milton Franklin

DRUMMER
Henry Gordon

WAGONER
James Bradbury

PRIVATE

Jacob O. Addleman	Joseph O. Addleman
Bartley Allen	Jerome Barker
Peter Baughan	George V. Beetley
William Beck	William J. Bennett
Daniel Blain	Asa Blanchard
Samuel Bradbury	Milton M. Burket
John P. Butler	Anthony P. Carr
William H. Castator	Gershom W. Conger
Robert G. Conley	Daniel Curry

Joel B. Curtis
Ira Dillon
William H. Edwards
Lot Enix
David P. Fort
James C. Fulkerson
Luther M. Hall
Charles W. Hartup
Henry H. Hiatt
Jacob Hunt
Richard Jones
George W. Kemp
Gardiner Lewis
William M. Locke
Patterson McKinney
George Marquis
John Morgan
John Motz
George W. Parsons
Daniel Pierce
George Pool
Charles C. Sater
Charles Sponsler
Joseph Sykes
Benjamin Thornburg
William Thornburg
Alexander C. Walker
Thomas J. Wasson
King S. Whitlow
Richard Williams
James Wine
Charles W. Woolverton

Thomas P. Davis
Benjamin B. Duke
Hugh L. English
William Ford
Randolph Fort
James Grunden
Timothy Hart
Thomas C. Henderson
William G. Hill
Jesse E. Jones
Edward Jordan
Jefferson Kinder
James D. Livengood
Samuel Lutz
John Markle
James H. Mills
Edward W. Morse
James M. Palmer
Charles H. Petty
Joseph H. Pike
John T. Rariden
Samuel Sparklin
Ambrose H. Swain
William Sykes
James Thornburg
Joseph W. C. Titus
Sanford Wallick
James W. Whitlow
Grear N. Williams
John M. Winder
Joseph Wisenberg
Henry Zook

The 19th Indiana was only one of a number of regiments then in Camp Morton, which was overflowing with thousands of young men, their tempers shortened by heat and overcrowding. On July 29th, Levi Yost, of Company C, described one problem that resulted: "There was a soldier killed to-day. he was stabbed beneath the eye. He died immediately after it was done. There has been five killed since we have been here."[33]

With the 19th Indiana now officially in the service of the United States, the first priority was the issue of clothing and arms. Tents were given out on July 29th with thirty wall tents going to the officers and 218 A-frame tents handed out to the enlisted men. Two days later the camp took on a more military aspect when the men finally received their state uniforms— wool cassinette suits manufactured by the firm of Menderson & Froham in Cincinnati. These uniforms (breeches and roundabouts purchased at a price of $8.75 per complete uniform) were described by a Richmond visitor as "grey doeskin cassimere, all wool, and well put together," prompting the claim that they were "the best uniforms furnished any of the regiments sent forth by this State." In addition to uniforms, the quartermaster issued to each man a hat, two gray woolen shirts, two pairs of cotton drill drawers, a pair of shoes, two pairs of stockings, a leather strap, a canteen and a haversack. Enough wool blankets were also given out to assure that nearly every man had two of them. On August 1st, tenor drums and B fifes were issued to the company musicians. The rest of the quartermaster stores were issued on August 5th: 146 axes, 146 hatchets, 120 spades, and 120 picks, along with five blank books for miscellaneous record keeping.[34]

Stores sufficient to stock a ten-bed hospital were also issued on August 5th: seven boxes of medicine, two boxes of furniture, ten cots, twenty woolen blankets and a lot of India rubber cloth. One Indianapolis visitor observed:

> We saw yesterday, in the Quartermaster General's warerooms, numerous boxes of physic, packed and marked for the Nineteenth Regiment. Dr. Kendrick goes along to help administer these drugs, more dangerous than the cannon balls of the enemy.

The hospital equipment was entrusted to Dr. Calvin J. Woods, a friend and neighbor of Governor Morton from Centreville, who was commissioned surgeon of the regiment. Born on June 2, 1819, Woods had served with General Zachary Taylor in the Seminole War and had assisted in the removal of the Cherokee Indians. His assistant was Dr. William H. Kendrick of Indianapolis, whose wife was already packing to accompany the regiment wherever it might be sent. A small library, assembled at a cost of $15.55, was prepared for the medical men and included: *United States Dispensatory, Formulary, Surgery, Methodology, Military Surgery,* and two blank books. The two doctors and their small hospital would soon prove to be woefully inadequate.[35]

At dress parade on August 3rd orders were read for the soldiers to cook and pack three days' rations in preparation for a move to the front on August 5th. A typical daily issue of commissary stores for the 101 men in Company B consisted of: 25 pounds of pork, 76 pounds of beef, 101 loaves of bread, 13 pounds of beans, 10 pounds of coffee, 15 pounds of sugar, one gallon of vinegar, one pound of pepper, one and one-half pounds of candles, 4 pounds of soap, 4 pounds of salt, 40 pounds of potatoes, one gallon of molasses, and 13 pounds of hominy. During the three-week sojourn of the 19th Indiana at Camp Morton, Colonel Meredith's boys consumed the following staples from the Commissary Department: 16,305 pounds of pork, 8,322 pounds of beef, 27,989 loaves of bread, 2,379 pounds of beans, 1,912 pounds of rice, 2,885 pounds of coffee, 4,214 pounds of sugar, 269 gallons of vinegar, 247 pounds of pepper, 438 pounds of candles, 1,133 pounds of soap, 1,125 pounds of salt, 9,738 pounds of potatoes, 105 gallons of molasses, 504 pounds of dried apples, 2,717 pounds of hominy, 200 pounds of cornmeal, and 1,535 pounds of hardtack.[36]

On August 4th Lieutenant Orr confided that "all is hustle and excitement today," but the preparations took an earnest tone on the morning of August 5th when the men were marched to the armory and received their arms. Company A, the right flank company, had been issued fifty .577 caliber Enfield rifled muskets on July 30th. Now the remainder of Company A, along with most of the regiment, received .69 caliber percussion muskets, a few of them old flintlocks converted to the new percussion system. Company B, the left flank company, and Company C, the color company, received .577 caliber Enfield rifles from a lot of weapons recently purchased in Canada by an agent of Governor Morton.[37]

The Indiana Arsenal also issued ammunition to the men—7,500 round ball cartridges for the smoothbores, 900 minie ball cartridges for the Enfields, and 10,200 percussion caps. Accouterments were also passed out, each man receiving a cartridge box, cartridge box belt, cartridge box plate, waist belt, waist belt plate, bayonet scabbard, frog, cap pouch, cone pick, and gun sling. The men shared a few screwdrivers, wipers, ball screws, and spring vices. By order of Governor Morton, Colonel Meredith, Lieutenant Colonel Robert A. Cameron, Major Alois O. Bachman, and Adjutant John P. Wood were each issued .36 caliber Colt Navy revolvers with an appropriate supply of ammunition.[38]

To offset Colonel Meredith's lack of military knowledge, Governor Morton had finally filled the other field officer posts in the 19th Indiana with two captains recently discharged from the state's three-month regiments. Lieutenant Colonel Robert A. Cameron had been born on February 22, 1828, in Brooklyn, but moved to Porter County, Indiana, in 1843, where he attended the Indiana Medical College until his graduation in 1850. Cameron augmented his flourishing medical practice in 1857 when he purchased a Valparaiso newspaper and renamed it the *Republican*. Cameron edited that journal until he took his seat in the Indiana House of Representatives, to which he had been elected in 1860. Dr. Cameron first entered military service as captain of Company H, 9th Indiana, on April 25, 1861, and led his command in the campaign against the rebels in western Virginia. Just before the regiment started its march, some of his company complained that rations had not been issued, but Captain Cameron silenced the grumblers by threatening to leave them behind if they continued their carping. Cameron became available for service in Meredith's regiment when the 9th Indiana returned for its muster out on August 2nd.[39]

Major Alois O. Bachman had been born in 1839 to Swiss settlers in Madison, Indiana, and received a college education at Hanover College and the Kentucky Military Institute. Bachman organized a militia company known as the "Madison City Greys" before the Fort Sumter crisis, then entered military service as captain of Company K, 6th Indiana, the first Hoosier regiment organized during the war. After participating in the western Virginia campaign, Bachman returned to Indianapolis for the regiment's muster on August 2nd. Governor Morton immediately tapped him for the majority in Colonel Meredith's regiment. Cameron and Bachman provided practical field experience to complement the theoretical knowledge contained in Hardee's *Tactics*.[40]

Despite the addition of a lieutenant colonel and major to the officer corps, there was still unrest in camp. A lieutenant in Company K recorded that on the evening of August 3rd "our boys tried to break and go home," although the attempt was successfully blocked by the officers. The Indianapolis press reported that on the morning of August 5th "some difficulty originated concerning the Sutler's department of the 19th regiment." For some unknown reason a mob of soldiers formed and threatened the property and person of the regimental sutler. Colonel Abel D. Streight and an armed guard arrived on the run to enforce order, but they were treated "somewhat rudely" by the unruly crowd, which went so far as to pelt the officer with stones. The soldiers refused to obey Colonel Streight, claiming that he was not their commander and they would obey only Colonel Meredith, but he stood his ground and gradually won control of the situation. The editor of the *Daily State Sentinel* summed up the shocking affair: "We lay no blame whatever upon the troops, but certainly their officers in immediate command, ought to have known of their grievances and attended to the remedy before matters had proceeded to a point threatening a general mutiny."[41]

Affairs got even worse on August 5th, the last morning in Indianapolis, when a few company commanders used bad judgment when leaving Camp Morton:

> Some of the captains, in marching from camp, did the foolish thing of putting their men through the "double quick" for nearly a mile before reaching the armory, and then forcing them hurriedly through the

building where the air was close and heated. The result was that several men were "sun struck"—going from a shady camp where they had been for weeks into dusty streets with the sun broiling hot, and made to "go it on the lope" with the thermometer at 98 was a little too heavy. There was no necessity for this severe exercise, as the regiment rested for four or five hours before starting on the cars.

The incident proved to be a classic example of the "hurry up and wait" military tradition.[42]

After receiving their arms and equipments, the soldiers were marched to the depot where they were loaded into freight cars, which were promptly remodeled by knocking out pieces of siding to improve ventilation. Eight companies, under the command of Lieutenant Colonel Cameron, were loaded onto the train that would travel on the Bellefontaine Railroad. Colonel Meredith, who took along two of his best horses, and the other two companies climbed aboard a smaller train that would leave on the tracks of the Indiana Central a few hours later. The regimental brass band, under the direction of Earl Reid, an experienced band leader from Indianapolis, stayed behind because the band uniforms had not been completed. The band, numbering twenty-six musicians, would catch up with the main body of the 19th Indiana in about two weeks at the nation's capital.[43]

3

Camp Kalorama

The train carrying Lieutenant Colonel Cameron's detachment, including Captain Dudley's Company B, pulled out of the Indianapolis depot amid the cheers of friends and well-wishers. Nothing of note occurred until the train reached Muncie, where citizens showered all of their attention on Captain Wilson's company of hometown boys, the soldiers in other companies "feasting our eyes but not our stomachs." A large crowd met the train when it stopped at Bellefontaine, Ohio, at 6 A.M. on August 6th. The patriotic residents prepared "a magnificent breakfast free of charge" for the officers and loaded down the enlisted men with cakes, pies, and other tempting morsels from Ohio kitchens. This scene was repeated at the town of Marion, where the boys were invited to pitch in, an invitation which was "cheerfully accepted." After giving three times three cheers for Marion, Ohio, the regiment proceeded on to Crestline, where another crowd offered cakes and lemonade while the cars were switched from the Bellefontaine Railroad to the Pittsburgh, Fort Wayne & Chicago Railroad.[1]

Lieutenant William Orr observed that, all along the route during the daylight hours, "every house we passed had ladies at the doors waving handkerchiefs." At Mansfield, Wooster, Canton, Alliance, and Salem, then on into Pennsylvania at Rochester, large crowds met the Indiana soldiers, one of whom remembered that the people "cheered, applauded, watered and fed us, as though we were heroes returning victorious from war instead of raw recruits going forth to war." Captain Jacobs agreed, saying, "At several places along the line of travel provisions were passed through the cars and we were invited to take hold without money and without price." John Hawk remembered the ride through Ohio as a joyous trip for the enlisted men, where the generous residents "stuffed us Hoosiers until we were as stiff as gut sausage."[2]

Arriving in Pittsburgh at 9 P.M. on August 6th, Lieutenant Colonel Cameron's detachment was joined by Colonel Meredith and the other two companies and the reunited regiment enjoyed a "bountiful repast." The boys in Meredith's detachment were quick to share their accounts of a reception by the residents of Richmond. A notice had been read in the city churches on Sunday, August 4th, announcing that Colonel Meredith's regiment would arrive in town at noon on the 5th and requesting that all friends of the Union greet their departing heroes with a special dinner. People from the city and surrounding countryside flocked to the depot bearing aromatic baskets filled with treats usually reserved for holiday entertaining. Tables were erected and the meal readied, but after an anxious wait a telegram announced that the 19th Indiana had taken the Bellefontaine route.

One of those in the crowd who hoped to send off the Wayne County boys in grand style noted, "The news fell with almost crushing weight on the hearts of many fathers and mothers who had come—some of them ten and fifteen miles—to take leave of their brave boys who had volunteered to defend the flag of their country." The dinner was eaten by the crowd, but their bitter disappointment was relieved when a later dispatch announced that Colonel Meredith and 200 men would arrive in Richmond at 9 o'clock that evening. The women went to work and had another meal ready when the gallant colonel and his men arrived amid the cheers of a reassembled crowd that numbered at least 3,000. After supper, Colonel Meredith was called on for a speech and obliged with a few remarks thanking his friends and neighbors for their show of support for himself and his regiment, then the train pulled out of the depot shortly after 11 o'clock.[3]

Taking the Pennsylvania Central Railroad from Pittsburgh to Harrisburg, the 19th Indiana, "by preference," rode in freight cars which had previously held livestock. Company B was assigned to three cars with an officer aboard each, all of the freight cars being temporarily modified with benches and air holes. Sleep was haphazard at best. By daylight on August 7th the Hoosiers were traveling through the Alleghenies, "huge, rugged steep rock mountains." At one point the boys experienced the thrill of literally going through the mountains in a tunnel that seemed to be a mile long, a new experience for the flatland Hoosiers. The receptions in Pennsylvania were somewhat cooler than in Ohio, demonstrations of patriotism being nearly non-existent and meals lacking the "goodies" handed out by the Buckeyes.[4]

As the regiment passed over into Maryland, the boys were somewhat surprised to hear cheers of "Hurrah for the Union!" but the officers still anticipated an attack by the Baltimore mob. An ominous sign was the presence of squads of the 20th Indiana posted as guards at intervals along the

North Central Railroad from Harrisburg to Baltimore. The cars were stopped a mile or two short of the latter city, ten rounds were issued to each man and the soldiers were ordered to load their muskets. Colonel Meredith's Hoosiers would be ready for trouble in the streets of Baltimore.[5]

On August 8th, the Indiana soldiers were pleasantly surprised at their reception by the citizens of Baltimore who "cheered as lustily as at any other place." Although the Hoosier officers quickly learned that the 5th Wisconsin had been stoned and insulted only a day or two previously, Lieutenant Orr boasted, "It was generally remarked that we were the greatest devils that ever went through Baltimore." Soldiers jumped from the cars and formed a line of battle in the hot sun, standing at parade rest for over an hour until the order was given to march to the Camden Depot, where the regiment would embark on the Baltimore & Ohio Railroad for the last leg of its journey. Buckets of water were provided along the line of march, followed by ice water for the canteens at the Camden Depot where the officers had a good meal, although they had to pay for it. One private remembered that after having some of the ice water, "We cooled down, inwardly and out-wardly." After an hour's wait at the depot, the Hoosiers climbed on board passenger cars for the short ride to Washington.[6]

As the cars picked up speed, some of the men committed "a dastardly act," as one of the regiment termed it. Tempted to use their loaded muskets on the property of Marylanders of questionable loyalty, a few of the boys began to discharge their weapons at ducks and chickens near the tracks. Within minutes, muskets were blazing from the windows. When a group of horses was spotted at a distance of one-half mile, the Hoosiers turned their sights on them. After a short fusillade, one horse reared up and fell to the ground, apparently dead. Colonel Meredith, outraged by this senseless slaughter of livestock, started through the cars, demanding in his peculiar accent, "Byes who shot that horse?" No one admitted shooting the horse, but a member of Company K remembered:

> Our colonel went for the boys at a lively rate for such a showing of their ingratitude towards the people who had but recently treated us so thoughtfully and kindly. And said he wouldn't be surprised now if the people of Baltimore did not follow us up and attack us.

There was a brief scare shortly afterwards when the engine stopped on a grade for a few minutes, but the boys eventually laughed off the incident. The train pulled into the Washington depot shortly after 6 P.M. on August 8th. The men were marched to the Soldiers Rest, a large building capable of sleeping the entire regiment, and the Hoosiers took much needed baths before bunking down for the night.[7]

Environs of Washington, D.C. – 1861

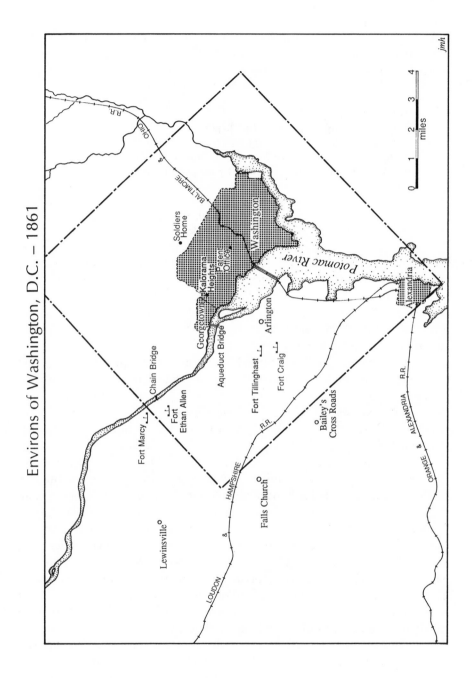

jmh

On Friday, Colonel Meredith received the following summons, indicative of a move to more permanent quarters:

U. S. Military Telegraph
August 9th, 1861

From War Dept.
To Commanding officer 19th Ind Regt
Genl McClellan directs that you report forthwith at his
headquarters—corner 19th & Penna avenue for the
purpose of securing instructions as to the position your
Regiment is to occupy
          Answer by telegraph
                              S. Williams
                              Asst Adj Genl

While Sol was off conferring with the army commander, one of his lieutenants thought he would go out into the city and trade his Indiana currency for some of the local variety. Henry Vandegrift assumed that he, holding the exalted office of first lieutenant in Company D, should be able to come and go at will, but the Hoosier officer was quickly halted by an unappreciative sentinel and sent back to the Soldiers Rest.[8]

Colonel Meredith returned in the afternoon with news that the regiment would be assigned to a provisional brigade in the suburbs until it was in a fit condition to cross the Potomac River into Virginia. The 19th Indiana would join two Wisconsin regiments, the 5th and 6th, which were already in camp on Kalorama Heights under the command of Brigadier General Rufus King. The brigadier, a West Point graduate who had abandoned army life in favor of a newspaper career, had been appointed minister to the Vatican by President Lincoln, but declined to serve overseas when his military expertise was badly needed at home. One of the Wisconsin men, himself a new arrival in the Kalorama camp, remembered the novel sight that presented itself to the Badgers on the night of August 9th: "Looking up, our boys saw, astride a black horse, what seemed to us the tallest man we had ever seen." In true military fashion, the clouds, which had been threatening showers all afternoon, let loose a rainstorm while the regimental tents were still being loaded in wagons back at Washington. The Hoosiers spent their first night in the mud "without a murmur" until the tents arrived, then pitched them haphazardly in the inky darkness.[9]

Lieutenant Orlando M. Poe of the Topographical Engineers laid out the camp of the 19th Indiana on Kalorama Heights in an old tobacco patch that had recently been plowed and turned into a quagmire by the rain. Poe thought the location to be dry and airy, although the natives knew it to be prone to heavy fogs and miasmas. The unhealthy atmosphere was made even worse by the camp's water supply which was described as "surface water, warm, flat, and unpalatable." The summer weather was unpredictable, according to one officer, "More fickle, disagreeable and trying weather I have rarely experienced. One day so cold that we wore our overcoats, and the next so hot that we are nearly melted." Jefferson Crull of Company B wrote at the end of August that "it is awful wet weather heare it rains every other day and is so slipery that one can hardly stand up."[10]

The soggy conditions naturally resulted in an explosion of the mosquito population. One soldier compared the mosquitoes to the Old Testament curse of the flies in Egypt, exaggerating only a little:

> They are of all sizes and kinds, from the diminutive torments called "gnats," to the hornet-like "gallinipper," with black body and yellow legs, and big enough, almost, to digest salt horse and hard tack. They prefer, however, to take their rations by proxy, after WE have manufactured those delicacies into good loyal blood. The only possible good these things were created for must have been to prevent sentinels from sleeping on post.

In addition to adversity presented by the elements and the insects, Indiana enlisted men were furnished with what was called the wedge tent. But with six men in each, the group forming one mess for culinary purposes, shelters were "*wedged* inside in fact, and outside in shape." Under these conditions, the sick list of the regiment, which numbered forty after the exhausting ride from Indiana to Washington, ominously lengthened.[11]

Whenever the rains abated, this new campground featured a magnificent view of Washington, Alexandria, Arlington Heights, and Fairfax Seminary. General King's camp was located about two and one-half miles from Washington and about one mile from Georgetown, overlooking the Long Bridge, where ships came and went every day on the Potomac River. A sluggish little stream called Rock Creek meandered nearby before emptying into the river. A scant eight rods from the camp of the 6th Wisconsin stood the campus of Columbia College, now a temporary hospital containing many of the wounded from the Union defeat at Bull Run. Near the camp of the 19th Indiana stood the Kalorama House, "one of the most magnificent places that imagination can picture." One visitor gave a glowing description of the estate:

> You enter the large gate guarded by a beautiful white cottage for the janitor, and by a circuitous route through a dense grove of deciduous and evergreen forest, you rise, rise, rise, by easy and gradual ascent, the great swell of ground on which stands the beautiful mansion, shut out from the view of the visitor till he is almost on the threshold,

but overlooking even its own growth of forest, and the whole country for miles around.

Despite its idyllic setting, this imposing estate quickly fell victim to military necessity and the medical department appropriated the residence, transforming the majestic old home into a pest house for contagious diseases, thereafter discouraging curious callers.[12]

From the Kalorama House soldiers could walk across a little valley filled with white tents to Meridian Hill, where stood the Porter Mansion, occupied in mid-August by General King and his headquarters staff. According to bearings inscribed upon a slab of granite at the northwest corner of the house, this mansion stood at latitude 38°55' 38" and longitude west from Greenwich 79°56' 59" 1'". The aristocratic old stone mansion, with its front supported by four massive pillars, commanded probably the finest view of Washington available anywhere. Evergreens and aspens had once abounded on the property, complemented by ornamental shrubbery, climbing roses, clematis, and honeysuckle, but now the place had a seedy appearance and exhibited merely a shadow of its former greatness. On the grounds, many trees were mutilated by names of soldiers carved in their bark and most of the shrubs were broken down by constant traffic about the headquarters building. Horses were hitched to trees in clumps of evergreens and the gazebo had been taken over by a commissary officer for the distribution of beef, pork, and beans. Inside the main building, walls were blackened and broken, floors badly soiled, and window sills, sashes and moldings all marred by soldiers' knives. While the best rooms were used for official business and officers' quarters, other rooms were filled with corn and oats for horses of staff members. Even the marble shaft marking the grave of Elizabeth Porter served as a place to play cards, write letters, and drink. The desolation was depressing to everyone who visited the site.[13]

General King's provisional brigade, established by Special Order No. 18 of the Division of the Potomac on August 9th, was originally composed of the 19th Indiana and 5th and 6th Wisconsin, but a number of other regiments were attached for varying lengths of time. The 14th Massachusetts, known as the Essex County Regiment, and 15th Massachusetts, raised primarily in Worcester County, were assigned to duty on August 11th. One officer in King's command remarked of the Massachusetts men that they were the "most neatly uniformed, the best equipped, the best provided for, and the best drilled regiments I have seen." These Eastern boys only stayed for two weeks before being ordered to other posts, the 14th to Fort Albany and the 15th to Poolesville, Maryland. The 67th New York, also called the 1st Long Island Volunteers or Brooklyn Phalanx, and the 4th New York stopped briefly with the brigade before moving on to other assignments. The 73rd New York, or 2nd Fire Zouaves, arrived without muskets but with a characteristic eagerness to fight the rebels. The 79th New York and 2nd Wisconsin were assigned to King's command when William T. Sherman was sent to Kentucky and his brigade of Bull Run veterans broken up.[14]

Of all the regiments that surrounded the Porter Mansion, the Fire Zouaves created the most stirring sight, one of their admirers being Jeff Crull of the Hoosier regiment:

> the fire Zuaves is the nicest regiment in the World. they have light blue pants with two stripes down the lags of a shade lighter with white leather boots and roundabouts of dark blue trimed with light blue cords and red collars and blue caps trimed with cord like the coats. thair band have pants like the rest with red coats.

Another regiment of Zouaves camped nearby, although not assigned to King, and were the object of curious eyes:

> They are funny looking creatures with their faces closely shaved, their hair closely cropped, and head covered with a red turban. The dress is red, white and yellow, green and grizzly, and every other color, and the pants look like a bag with a hole cut in the bottom, through which both feet are stuck. By looking at them I can imagine something about ladies' running gear, and that is about all. They are lively as crickets, fly around, swing their arms as if they were pendulums to clocks with springs broken, smoke in the ranks when drilling, and pay no attention to drill whatever; nearly all saw service in the Crimean war, and as they are Frenchmen, will, no doubt, fight better than they drill, and be a strong arm of whatever brigade they are attached to.

The 79th New York Highlanders (Scots), along with their 69th New York (Irish) comrades from Sherman's old brigade, were "ethnic" regiments, but both regiments were dismissed as "drunken rowdies" by one of King's officers.[15]

The most important addition to King's command occurred August 27th with the arrival of the 2nd Wisconsin, a combat-experienced regiment that would remain with the brigade and provide leadership both in camp and on the battlefield. The other soldiers thought their comrades in the 2nd were rather hard cases and styled them the "Rowdy Second." The Badgers still wore gray Wisconsin uniforms and their appearance was a stark contrast to the nattily dressed Massachusetts regiments that had recently departed:

> They present the appearance of having passed through the wars. Instead of the uniform hats furnished by the State, they are now supplied with hats and caps of every conceivable pattern, many of them

picked up on the battle-field at Bulls Run, and their clothes are, in
many cases, "tattered and torn."

The ragged appearance of the 2nd Wisconsin soon resulted in a new and more
permanent nickname. General King was a close personal friend of Secretary of
State William H. Seward, who often visited the camp on Kalorama Heights,
occasionally accompanied by President Lincoln. On September 2nd, the two
statesmen, accompanied by a large crowd of gentlemen and ladies, drove out
to the Heights for a review. Carriages pulled up behind the 2nd Wisconsin,
which was drawn up in line, "but very suddenly the ladies began to blush
furiously when the teams as suddenly drove to the front of the line." The
problem was the old, worn trousers, many of which were ripped in the rear,
with the result that the men's drawers were plainly visible. This was too good
a joke on the veterans, so some wag christened that command "The Ragged
Ass Second," a name that stuck like glue throughout the war.[16]

Monotony of company and battalion drill, the latter a two-hour
affair held every day, in the unpredictable August weather was broken by a
series of reviews. On August 18th, the Hoosiers were paraded in front of
Governor Morton, who was in Washington and could not leave without
visiting his "pet" regiment. After going through their maneuvers, the men
greeted their governor with hearty cheers, then politely listened to a short
address which elicited even more enthusiastic cheering. General King reviewed the brigade on August 24th, a preliminary to an August 26th review
by General McClellan of all the troops assembled in the Meridian Hill-
Kalorama area. The day after this general review, King's regiments were
formed at 9 A.M. on the parade ground of the 5th Wisconsin near Columbia
College in anticipation of seeing "general Scot gen Mclelan the president and
the war department." At 10 o'clock General McClellan and his large staff
watched as King's seven regiments marched in review, an important part of
the army commander's plan to increase confidence and *esprit de corps* in the
volunteers. The effect was not lost on Jeff Crull, who later described the
event: "it was a beatuful sight to see the seven regments fall in collum by
plattoons and march by the genarl with the bands a playing." It was no
wonder that one of the boys in Company K could write that "we will be able
to knock the dog water out of Jeff Davis and not half try."[17]

There were ten bands playing when McClellan reviewed the brigade, their military music adding to the martial spectacle. Bands were an
important part of the Civil War army and the volunteers were treated to
stirring tunes every morning at guard mounting and every evening at dress
parade, as well as impromptu concerts between supper and tattoo. The best
bands were unquestionably those belonging to the Brooklyn regiment,
whose bandsmen played silver instruments, and the 5th Wisconsin. While the

Badgers and Brooklyn boys vied with one another for the title of best band in King's brigade, there was no doubt about which band was the worst. The bandmaster of the 6th Wisconsin seemed to cherish playing "The Downfall of Paris" and his musicians were constantly practicing the old tune, always careful to do so out of stone's throw of the sentries. One captain of the 6th Wisconsin indignantly referred to the musicians as "that contemptible brass band of ours" and Charles King, the young son of General Rufus King, claimed, "I have seen men dive into their tents and burrow under their blankets—ostrich fashion—whenever they began." As soon as the band members began to thump out "The Downfall of Paris" on Kalorama Heights, cursing became so loud that it rivaled the profanity used by teamsters in moving a quartermaster train after a hard rain.[18]

A welcome change from drill came in late August with the beginning of target practice, a routine judged necessary after the poor showing of many Federal regiments at Bull Run. Every day the individual companies were marched to an improvised firing range where, after the men became familiar with their muskets and the principles of judging distance, the officers observed the men firing singly, by rank, and by company.[19]

Colonel Meredith was clearly unimpressed with the old arms furnished by the State of Indiana, so he wrote directly to General McClellan on August 29th to complain about them:

> When my Regiment left Indiana it was furnished with inferior arms— and *accepted* them with the *promise* that they *would be exchanged* on my arrival here for *improved Arms*. The "Enfield Rifle" with which the flank companies are armed are *constantly* getting out of *order* and soon 1/2 will be unfit for use. A large share of the men composing my Regiment have from childhood been accustomed to the Rifle and are accomplished Marksmen. If *armed* with the *Springfield Gun,* I would desire whenever you think us competent, an advanced position—And will cheerfully perform the outpost and Picket duty.

Robert Dale Owen concurred with Meredith's assessment of his weapons, particularly the 240 Enfield muskets:

> They had already sent 48 of them (one fifth of the whole) to be repaired, and the armorer declared a portion of them to be not worth repairing. Some of them, however, were good guns & had done good service. . . . I ought to state further, as to the Enfields, that in many the calibre was irregular & in some the ramrods were too short.

McClellan was certainly aware of the acute shortage of modern weapons, but nothing could be done about Meredith's request until Northern factories could increase production of the Springfield Rifled Musket.[20]

Shortly after Colonel Meredith's complaint to McClellan, President Lincoln visited the Hoosier regiment again. While the Indiana soldiers stood in line waiting for the review to begin, the president and his commanding general rode up behind Company D and dismounted. McClellan's intention was to demonstrate the unsuitability of these old Springfield altered muskets which many of the Hoosiers carried. He took Private Augustus D. Shaw's weapon, which was "conspicuously dirty," and handed it to Lincoln, who examined the musket and pronounced it unacceptable. Little Mac returned the musket to Shaw with a polite "Thank you." The nervous private later recalled the incident and claimed, "I do believe it was the first, and perhaps, only instance on record where an officer thanked a private for carrying a dirty gun."[21]

Colonel Meredith wrote directly to McClellan a second time on September 1st, presenting a plan for increasing the size of his regiment:

A large number of companies in Indiana desire to attach themselves to my Regiment. I would like very much to increase it to sixteen hundred two Battalions or twenty four hundred three Battalions.

The companies are picked men and would render good service. I am extremely anxious to gratify the wishes of those who desire to join my Regiment and if permitted to do so, I shall endeavor to make it worthy of the cause in which we are engaged and the State we represent.

I ask the favor if consistent with your views and the interest of the public service as my Regiment is the only one from Indiana under your command.

McClellan, undoubtedly irked by this ambitious colonel who ignored the chain of command when so many other matters needed attention, wisely ignored the suggestion.[22]

While Sol badgered McClellan with his correspondence, the 19th Indiana was kept in a constant state of readiness for action. In the words of Corporal Jeff Crull, "We expect an hourly attack on the city." Cannon fire to the southwest added to the anxiety, which was compounded by officers dashing to and fro, artillery rumbling about and new regiments arriving daily. By August 30th, Jeff was advising the folks at home:

We are under marching orders. instead of sleeping on our blankets we rool them up lay them under our heads sleep with our catrige boxes on and our guns by our side. we expect to leave every half hour.

Most of the boys were caught up in the excitement and Christopher C. Starbuck of Company C confessed, "wee have great times here now and all the fun."[23]

Quartermaster James Drum did his best to keep the Indiana boys provided with good, nourishing "grub," but, although his efforts were

5. James Drum.
Used by permission of the Indiana State Library.

appreciated, he could not duplicate the delicious fare of Camp Morton days. Captain Jacobs assured the folks at home that the rations "will support life," but the enlisted men, according to Private Moore, had to make some adjustments in their appetite:

> The most of us built up stomachs that would digest almost anything from sandwiches of raw pickled pork laid between a couple of "hard-tacks," to what some of the unregenerated boys dubbed a son-of-a-bitch. . . . This latter dish was made . . . by breaking up a skillet full of hard tack, pouring a little water over it, adding seasonings, possibly a good deal of pork fat, and then cooking it to a turn.

One Wisconsin soldier described the hardtack which was issued at Camp Kalorama:

> There is only one difference between these crackers and a kind of fish I have seen, called sheepshead. The difference is, the fish could float, and the crackers cannot. The more you boiled the fish the tougher he got, and it's ditto with the crackers.

It was no wonder that the boys sought supplements to their army diet.[24]

Fruit was cheap and abundant, so the boys bought melons, tomatoes, peaches, berries, and all sorts of delicacies from peddlers who wandered through the camps. One afternoon an enterprising businessman pulled a wagon up to the camp of the 15th Massachusetts and began to sell pickles. But a large crowd indicated more for sale than the pickles which were so prominently displayed. After orders to move on were ignored, Colonel Charles Devens had a squad remove the boxes from the wagon, when it was discovered that liquor bottles outnumbered pickle jars by five to one. Devens ordered the liquor bottles smashed, gave his name to the peddler, pointed to General King's headquarters and walked off, confident that he had at least put a dent in the liquor trade on Kalorama Heights.[25]

By the end of August the Hoosiers had become familiar with their commanding officers and had formed opinions of them. Drum Major Clint Smith tactfully referred to Long Sol's ability in a letter intended for publication, saying, "Colonel Meredith talks right, acts right and in fact does the very best he knows how. I think he means well. He also commands the respect of his officers and men."[26]

In contrast to this lukewarm portrait of Meredith, Smith heaped praise on the regiment's second-in-command, "Lt. Colonel Cameron is a splendid officer, good natured, and commands the respect of the whole Regiment; at the same time he enforces the military law, and the rules and regulations of the Regiment, to the letter." To illustrate Cameron's character, Smith described the following incident:

> I detailed a drummer to beat the first call for tattoo, and not understanding the call very well, being the first time he was detailed for the purpose, he made the roll too long, making the call something near like an alarm. At this time Lieut. Colonel Cameron was in bed, he heard the call, and in a moment he was in the centre of the camp, ready for fight, with nothing on but shirt and pants. So you may judge the kind of material Col. Cameron is made of. He was in the act of putting the drummer under guard, when I came up, explained the matter to the Col., and everything was all right again.

The boys in Captain Dudley's company were also admirers of Cameron. According to Jeff Crull, "our leutendant Col is the best man i ever seen. We all just love him. i would rather hear him talk to us than eat any time. he has bin tried. he will fight if he can get to where it can be done."[27]

Major Alois Bachman (pronounced "Backman") apparently kept a low profile in the shadows of Meredith and Cameron. Talk among the boys was that he had been a captain in western Virginia, where he had been shot in the breast at Laurel Hill, "a fighting man" sure. Bachman's chest wound was a camp rumor, but the enlisted men had little personal contact with their field officers and often repeated any stories that sounded the least bit plausible.[28]

Privates had much more contact with Adjutant John P. Wood, whose responsibilities included forming the regiment for inspections and parades, mounting the camp guards, and communicating orders from Colonel Meredith. His duties brought him into constant conflict with some soldiers who did not appreciate his methods. One man grumbled, "Adjutant Wood is a good officer, but rather tyrannical; he takes delight in 'putting a man through,' especially when he can do it before the whole Regiment, therefore he is making enemies every day, I find." Another soldier recalled how Wood "when inspecting guard mount would walk in both front and rear of the line, sometimes he'd lift up the bottom of one's trousers and if the heels of that one's shoes were not properly polished he would send him to his quarters." Adjutant Wood was not unknown to the Wisconsin soldiers in King's brigade since he had served for a time in the ranks of the Milwaukee Light Guard before the war, but his association with the Badgers was probably of a more cordial nature.[29]

While visitors to the Hoosier camp spoke of it in glowing terms, there were serious problems that were not evident to the casual observer. Disease was rapidly spreading through the ranks of all the new regiments in the Washington area, including Camp Kalorama. Medical Director Charles Tripler explained the lack of hygiene which existed in the early days of the war:

> The individual man at home finds his meals well cooked and punctually served, his bed made, his quarters policed and ventilated, his clothing washed and kept in order without any agency of his own, and without his ever having bestowed a thought upon the matter. The officer in ninety-nine cases in a hundred has given no more reflection than the private to these important subjects. When the necessity for looking after these things is forced upon his attention, he is at a loss how to proceed. Too frequently he lacks the moral courage and the energy to make his men do what neither he nor they stipulated for or understood when they entered the service. To bad cooking, bad police, bad ventilation of tents, inattention to personal cleanliness, and unnecessarily irregular habits we are to attribute the greater proportion of the diseases that actually occurred in the army.

The 19th Indiana was no exception to this general observation. At the time of Governor Morton's visit on August 18th, the health of the regiment was found to be "very good" with only a few cases of diarrhea under care of Surgeon Woods and some half-dozen more cases sent to hospitals. Ominously, Dr. Kendrick, the only professional assistant, was confined to his bed with a case of typhoid fever.[30]

On August 31st Colonel Meredith's regiment was mustered for pay. The bi-monthly muster, held on the last day of February, April, June, August, October, and December, was the army's way of keeping track of its personnel. The muster of an infantry company was preceded by a careful inspection, which concluded with the troops in open order and at the position of "Order Arms." The captain then commanded his company to "Support Arms" and the mustering officer called the company roll. Upon hearing his name called, each soldier answered "Here" and brought his musket to the position of "Order Arms." All absences were verified by the mustering officer. Results of the muster were recorded on printed muster rolls, along with notations of monies due the United States for damage to clothing or equipment. These muster rolls served as the official record of a soldier's service and his pay was based on the entries made upon them.[31]

Companies were supposed to be paid on the day of muster, but in fact very few times would payments actually be made on the specified date. The 19th Indiana was formally mustered on August 31st, although the soldiers were not actually paid until September 12th. The volunteers in Company B received their wages according to the following table:

Captain	$60 per month, 4 rations per day, 1 servant								
1st Lieutenant	$50	"	"	"	"	"	"	"	"
2nd Lieutenant	$45	"	"	"	"	"	"	"	"
1st Sergeant	$20	"	"						
Sergeant	$17	"	"						
Corporal	$13	"	"						
Private	$13	"	"						
Wagoner	$14	"	"						
Musician	$12	"	"						

Captain Dudley, as company commander, was allowed an additional $10 per month for assuming responsibility for the company's clothing, arms, and accouterments.[32]

4

Affair at Lewinsville

By September 3rd, the 19th Indiana's morning report listed 157 officers and men as sick, 103 under the care of Surgeon Woods and fifty-four distributed almost equally between the hospitals at Columbia College and Georgetown Seminary, with a couple of men in a hospital on K Street in downtown Washington. There was great concern over the large number of cases of fever and Robert Dale Owen sought to explain the situation in a report to Governor Morton dated September 16th:

> First, they were very much exposed, the very first day of their arrival here; being turned out & compelled to spend the night in an open field, during a severe storm of rain. This, of itself, though tents were speedily procured and put up, caused some sickness. Then a spot was selected for encampment, apparently dry & airy, but noted (though Col Meredith knew it not,) for miasma. There the sickness rapidly increased.

Colonel Meredith was quick to shift the blame onto Calvin Woods and implored Morton, through his agent, Owen, to remove the doctor. Owen passed along the message, saying that Sol "is very much dissatisfied with the surgeon of his regiment & considers him not only inefficient but careless." Company officers confirmed Meredith's claim that Woods often would not get up at night to attend to seriously ill soldiers. Sergeant Joel Newman of Company C wrote of Dr. Woods: "wee have a Doctor here in this regment that is not worth a dam or I think the boys would git along better. if I only would Dare I would give him a cusing for neglecting the boys." Whatever the source of the problem, it seemed that whenever one patient recovered, two others fell sick.[1]

Medical problems were forgotten on Tuesday evening, September 3rd, when the telegraph operator at General King's headquarters listened to his clicking instrument and announced the arrival of a dispatch from McClellan: "Have your Brigade ready to move at any moment." Orderlies were sent scurrying to the various regiments, where officers got essentials packed and their men under arms within thirty minutes. About 10 o'clock another message arrived from the commanding general:

> Proceed immediately with your Brigade to Chain Bridge, and report to Gen. Smith for further orders. Take knapsacks and forty rounds of ammunition. Let the wagons follow with rations in the morning.

Charles D. Robinson, General King's quartermaster, sat on his horse and watched the brigade march away from Camp Kalorama:

> It was a grand night. There was no moon, but every star was out, and though the day had been oppressively hot, the air was beginning to grow cool enough for pleasant marching. The only drawback was the dry state of the roads, and there being no wind, clouds of dust arose and at times half smothered the men. The column formed with Col. Cobb's regiment, the Wisconsin Fifth, on the right. It marched out upon the road to the music of its splendid band, and as its last company moved from the encampment Col. Cutler's regiment, the Sixth Wisconsin, filed in. Then followed Colonel O'Connor's Second Wisconsin. As we passed down the road to where the Seventy-ninth New York (Highlanders) were encamped, we found them drawn up in line, and Col. Stevens (late Gov. Stevens, of Washington Territory) was addressing them. I could not hear what was said, but it evidently was to the point, for the cheering was like the roar of a battery. They fell in on the left of the Second, and then the last regiment of the Brigade, Col. Meredith's Indianians, the Nineteenth, brought up the rear.

The long roll had beaten at half past ten in the Hoosier camp, resulting in a great "commotion and excitement" as canteens were filled, haversacks were stuffed with rations and extra ammunition issued. Tents and baggage of the Indiana regiment were left behind at Kalorama, guarded by a detail of sixty men, who also doubled as nurses for the large number of sick unable to march.[2]

No one in the brigade, not even General King, knew where the regiments were going or why they were ordered out. There had been rumors of a rebel advance, as well as frequent alarms, but only the sealed orders which awaited King at Chain Bridge held the answers. One Badger officer graphically described the night march:

> There was scarcely a word spoken; the bands were not permitted to play after the march was fairly commenced; and there was no noise but the

dull and heavy tramp of four thousand men, and the occasional clatter of the wheels of the provision wagons and ambulances upon the loose stones along the road. The route led through Georgetown; and so little noise was made, even upon the pavement, that the sleeping citizens were not even disturbed. Occasionally a window was suddenly raised, and a head or two thrust inquiringly out, but nothing more, and we left the sleeping city behind and marched out upon the road which led along the Potomac.

The marchers were closed in between the Chesapeake and Ohio Canal and Georgetown Heights, and across the river the steep Virginia bluffs loomed in the darkness. Lights were clearly visible on distant Arlington Heights, where friendly Northern forces were in camp, but there was no sign of life across the river from Georgetown, not even the light from a farmhouse window or the barking of a watchdog. One man in the marching column observed, "The black ban of secession has put all the inhabitants to flight, and desolated that shore like a pestilence." After leaving Georgetown a good share of the march was conducted, by order of General King, at a double-quick, which left many men scattered in the rear.[3]

King's brigade reached Chain Bridge at 2:00 A.M. on September 4th, when the men were halted in the road for thirty minutes while the general and his staff hunted for orders. No written orders were located, but a verbal message had been left that one regiment should cross immediately and advance two miles to the outposts, while the other four regiments were to remain at the northern end of the bridge until daylight. General King led the 5th Wisconsin over the heavily guarded Chain Bridge and up a narrow road in a wooded ravine made even darker by a cloudy sky. The Wisconsin regiment was halted from time to time by stalled wagons and lumbering artillery, as well as one occasion when a loyal Virginia guide named Tennant was carried back to the river after having been shot by nervous pickets. At the very front of the column was fifteen-year-old Charles King, son of the general, who was along with the soldiers as a mounted orderly, outfitted with buff leggings, red fez, and a "volcanic rifle" capable of firing forty rounds without reloading. Aside from their wounded guide, there were no other casualties; indeed, there was no fighting since the movement was made only to reinforce approaches to the important river crossing.[4]

General McClellan's orders to King instructed him to report directly to General William F. Smith, an awkward situation since Smith was a junior officer. Charley King remembered how his father reported that September morning, "General Smith, I have brought my entire brigade with me, and am here to support you in any way that you may designate." Charley noticed that Smith was embarrassed as he told General King to return to the north bank, retaining one regiment there and sending the balance of his brigade south of the river to carry out McClellan's orders. Rufus King graciously accepted the arrangement, although he could have asserted command over the combined brigades, and retired back over Chain Bridge until the arrangement could be straightened out.[5]

After entering the Old Dominion, Colonel Meredith marched his regiment about a mile northwest to the site of Fort Smith, where the Hoosiers halted briefly. After about ten minutes, Colonel Meredith led companies A, F, G, and B off on a scout along the Leesburg and Georgetown Turnpike toward Langley, where a rebel force, estimated at 200 cavalry, was reported to be firing on Federal pickets. The detachment started off on a double-quick, but the enemy disappeared just twenty minutes before Meredith's reinforcements arrived. Hoosiers did capture "a notorious secessionist" and three Negroes who had run away from a South Carolina regiment. The Negroes were sent back to army headquarters for interrogation, but the success was tarnished somewhat when the "secessionist" eagerly took the oath of allegiance and was set free. Meredith's men, disappointed at missing a fight, returned to camp.[6]

That afternoon the Hoosiers made their camp in an old orchard where they constructed shelters of brush in a vain attempt to keep dry. Private Jesse Jones, one of Captain Dudley's boys, remembered his stay on the slopes overlooking Chain Bridge, "We had no tents at that time and were exposed to hot days, cool nights and rain." Private Joseph Slack was more succinct when he wrote, "When We gote to chain bridge it reigned and We got sum Wet." There were few pleasant memories of "Camp Advance." The boys of the 19th Indiana, in addition to being exposed to inclement weather, were detailed on alternate days to dig ditches and cut timber as General Smith pushed his command to complete Fort Smith, now renamed Fort Marcy.[7]

This fort was built on the land of a "secesh" farmer whose son was an officer in the rebel army, although both father and son were now safely quartered in Washington. John Hawk explained how the Federals were remodeling the site:

> We have took posesion of a Secesh farm, we are clearin it up for him and digin him a selar on the south side of his house, about one hundred yards, it is a large one, there are about three acres in it.

Several regiments worked on the fort each day and the activity was compared to a beehive. Wide ditches were dug around the perimeter of the fort and dirt thrown to the inside, where it was formed into ramparts for the mounting of heavy cannon. Lieutenant Reed was particularly impressed by the industry of the Irishmen in Colonel Meredith's regiment, saying, "'tis beautiful to see them twirling the shovel as I saw them yesterday in the trenches." A New Yorker who worked in the ditches joked that "spades were trumps, and every man held a full hand." As Fort Marcy neared completion, work began on a new fort southwest of Chain Bridge, first named Fort Baker after Colonel Edward Baker of the 71st Pennsylvania, but later called Fort Ethan Allen.[8]

In addition to digging ditches, building ramparts, and mounting guns, the regiments at Camp Advance spent weeks cutting down vast stretches of timber, including valuable stands of oak, chestnut, and cedar. As many as a thousand soldiers would be felling trees at one time, leading one old Negro grandmother who lived in a nearby hut to exclaim, "De Lor' knows I never heard such a cutting of trees since I war born." The axmen, primarily experienced timber cutters from Wisconsin and Maine, would begin in a line at the bottom of a hill and chop part way through the trees, working upwards. When the crest was reached, some trees at the top were cut through, falling downward on those below "like the billow on the surface of the ocean" until the entire hillside was cleared with a thundering crash. Some of the trees were dragged up to Fort Marcy, where their branches were intertwined to impede an enemy attack, but most of the timbering operation was simply to clear fields of fire for the cannon. With rebel outposts visible in the distance, regiments were kept constantly on the alert, men working within arm's length of their muskets by day and sleeping in line of battle by night until Fort Marcy was completed.[9]

On September 7th, General Smith conducted an impressive test of his artillery, one solid shot striking within three feet of a target 2,000 yards distant. Similar success was reported with shells. One Indiana officer wrote that the missiles had "a very thrilling effect" as they sped through the air, "especially when sent over your head." Such precise firing inspired confidence, as did the rumors that fully 150,000 soldiers were assembled in Virginia from Chain Bridge to Arlington Heights and across the river in the District of Columbia. A private in Company K wrote on September 8th that "All the soldiers is in good spirits" and another Hoosier confided, "Ours is a regiment of fighting devils," then added, "Old Sol is anxious to cover us with glory."[10]

The only opportunity for glory came with the daily details for picket duty, three Hoosier companies performing that coveted role every day. A few soldiers were shot or captured on both sides of the brigade picket line, although Indiana boys managed to escape the casualty lists while protecting Camp Advance from rebel scouts. Picket duty was a refreshing change from the manual labor of working on Fort Marcy and it made the boys feel as if they were striking back at the rebellion, if only in a small manner. According to one soldier, the duty had some benefits:

> We had to stand 24 hours and wee was not allowed to go to sleep a moment the whole time under the pain and penalty of being shot. wee had all the peaches wee could eat and all the roasten ears wee could eat. wee had to go to some of the houses and boil them for wee was not allowed to have any fire on post.

Joseph Slack boasted of how "the boys goes out on picket and bring in a trator and sumtimes they bring in a niger boy or woman." Christopher Starbuck elaborated on his comrade's assessment, "We are taking Secessionists by the groups and some of the colored population known as slaves. The people are coming in for protection here in our camp. One man came in this morning with 4 horses saying the seceshers were after him." John Hawk, one of Captain Williams's impatient privates, sent a message home in anticipation of his first encounter with the enemy: "Tell old House that I am going to have them scelps for him when I come back and I want him to have me a good snort when I come back."[11]

The pickets were fired on almost nightly by rebels probing the defenses at Camp Advance. Just past midnight one morning a soldier of the 33rd New York, stationed at a post about two miles from the Hoosier camp, fired at an enemy scout. Nervous pickets continued firing into the darkness until headquarters became alarmed. A rocket went up from Fort Marcy and two signal cannon were fired, rousing nearly 15,000 troops from their blankets. But the alarm proved false—there was no attack. Soldiers in the 33rd New York were understandably nervous on guard, one of their number having been mortally wounded while at his post, "a hard looking sight" when carried past an Indiana picket post. Such false alarms were common and many a night's sleep was lost as a result.[12]

Jeff Crull and Anthony P. Carr were on a picket post near Fort Marcy one day and the former described their adventure:

> a boy by the name of Carr and myself was standing in some bushes when two of their scouts came by. thay was a talking about things. one said he did not expect to get back the other one said he did not eather. thay went a bout 1/2 mile further. thay started in to the woods on our side of the line. one of our pickets shot one in the leg he took him prisner the other got a way. in a bout 1/2 an hour a bout 50 of the enimy cavelry came. they made us get though the woods a kiten. i dident think i could run though the Bushes as fast as i could. i went Back to the reserve. some of our cavelry went out made them get as fast as thay made us. We have some mighty exciting times here.

While most of the Hoosiers were hoping for a battle, there were a few level heads among them, including Clint Smith, who confessed, "Our boys seem anxious to get in to a fight but my opinion is that they will get enough of it before they are through. I am satisfied to stay behind a fort, provided I had a chance."[13]

Attention to duty on the picket lines outside Camp Advance increased dramatically when William Scott, a private in Company K, 3rd Vermont, was arrested for sleeping at his post, court-martialed and sentenced to death for the offense. Scott, described by one Hoosier as "a short, thick-set boy, of somewhat stolid disposition, though an honest, noble youth," was confined before his scheduled execution in a small, old log house, possibly a smokehouse, only a few rods from the camp of the Hoosier regiment. The condemned man was guarded by a detachment under the command of Lieutenant Davis B. Castle. Scott's execution was set for September 9th, but soldiers of the 3rd Vermont lobbied for a pardon. The Green Mountain boys won the support of General Smith, their original colonel, and Lucius E. Chittenden, Register of the Treasury. General McClellan had already approved the death sentence, so a delegation of Vermonters visited the White House, where they advised President Lincoln of the facts in this celebrated case. Lincoln's intervention on behalf of William Scott, combined with the Vermonters' petitions and political pressure, resulted in McClellan issuing a pardon for the private on the very day he was scheduled to be shot. This was the first such case in McClellan's army and newspaper reporters gave the story a wide circulation, embellishing the tale of "The Sleeping Sentinel" to heroic proportions after Scott's death on April 16, 1862, during a small action at Lee's Mill on the Peninsula.[14]

Protected by a screen of now-vigilant pickets, the soldiers at Camp Advance amused themselves in various ways. Charley King spent several days with T. S. C. Lowe observing the rebel camps from the balloon *Union,* which made a number of ascensions near Chain Bridge during the month of September. Less well-connected soldiers contented themselves with an occasional excursion into Washington, walking back to the river where they took the ferry across the Potomac to Georgetown, at which point they climbed into a horse-drawn bus for the ride into the capital. On Sunday mornings the religiously inclined Hoosiers gathered in a pine grove where Chaplain Lewis Dale held services reminiscent of a camp meeting back home.[15]

After McClellan stated that he would not conduct military movements on Sundays, Sabbath afternoons were devoted to camp chores such as washing clothes. One writer from Company C managed to capture the novelty among the mundane:

> You ought to see us washing shirts, handkerchiefs, &c. it is really laughable. Lieut. Campbell has but one pair of pants, and they are torn

about the unmentionables. I see him now sitting under the shade of a pine, without pants or drawers, waiting for his pants to be patched with oil cloth. He looks like a scared Secesh.

Gray uniforms of the 2nd Wisconsin soldiers were replaced in September by Federal blue and the Indiana boys, knowing their turn would soon come, looked on apprehensively as the quartermaster issued new suits of clothing. Cornelius Wheeler, one of the Badgers in the 2nd, affirmed that government clothing was not meant to fit and that picking clothes at random was just as effective as sorting through an entire pile. Describing his own new trousers, Wheeler claimed, "I think cloth could be taken out of my pants to make Charley a pair of pants and a jacket and then have a *roomy* pair left for myself."[16]

The chopping, digging and picketing by regiments of General Smith's command were interrupted by several expeditions to Lewinsville, a small crossroads village four miles due west of Chain Bridge, which would be an important point to occupy before any Federal advance upon Falls Church or Vienna. The first offensive operation saw three companies from the 5th Wisconsin advance on Lewinsville with orders to capture or drive off a small cavalry force reported at the village. The enemy at Lewinsville was dispersed and rebel reinforcements were ambushed by a detachment from the 79th New York. General Smith's first probe toward Lewinsville was a success, so the commander decided to send a more substantial expedition the following day.[17]

Five roads concentrated at Lewinsville—one from Langley and the Federal outposts, a second from the north connecting with the Leesburg Turnpike, a third coming from Falls Church to the south, a fourth from Vienna to the west, and the fifth parallel to and south of the Vienna Road, known as the New Vienna Road. General Smith's plan was to send Lieutenant Orlando Poe of the Topographical Engineers, accompanied by a sizable force, to reconnoiter the village and surrounding countryside. Isaac I. Stevens, colonel of the 79th New York, was selected as commander of a combined force of cavalry, infantry, and artillery. Stevens's expedition consisted of the 79th New York Highlanders; four companies of the 65th New York (1st Regiment U.S. Chasseurs); Companies A and F, 2nd Vermont; 3rd Vermont; Companies A, D, F, H, and I, 19th Indiana; Captain Charles Griffin's Battery; fifty Regular cavalry under Lieutenant William McLean; and forty volunteer cavalry.[18]

Colonel Stevens left Camp Advance with his expeditionary force at 7:30 A.M. and reached Lewinsville at 10 o'clock. Half of the volunteer cavalry scouted along the Leesburg Turnpike. McLean's Regular cavalry picketed the two roads to Vienna, backed by two companies of the 3rd

Vermont, and the road to Falls Church, supported there by Company I, 19th Indiana, under the watchful eye of their lieutenant colonel. Company H of the Hoosier regiment was detached as a reserve at the village while Colonel Meredith led his remaining three companies, with one of Captain Griffin's guns, north on the road running to the Leesburg Pike. Long Sol detached two parties of skirmishers, one to the west and one to the north, and placed the bulk of his command under cover. Colonel Meredith's boys, still outfitted in their state-issue gray uniforms, wore strips of white muslin tied on their arms to distinguish them from the gray-clad rebels. The Chasseurs and 79th New York were halted short of Lewinsville with a heavy body of skirmishers from the latter regiment extending toward Falls Church.[19]

Lieutenant Poe's reconnaissance continued entirely uninterrupted, although individuals and small parties of rebels were often visible in the distance. Poe's work was concluded about 2:15 P.M., when Colonel Stevens ordered his skirmishers recalled and the column formed for the march back to Camp Advance.[20]

There was a considerable delay in collecting the skirmishers, particularly those from the Hoosier company protecting the Falls Church Road. When Lieutenant Colonel Cameron discovered that Lieutenant John Baird's Company I did not return promptly, he first sent a mounted sergeant after his men, then rode personally to bring off the skirmishers. Inquiry disclosed that the boys were awaiting the return of a small party that had disobeyed orders and left the skirmish line in order to fire on some rebel infantry deploying one-half mile ahead.

After a few minutes of sharp firing, Private Hiram Antibus came running back to the skirmish line, so hotly pursued that he had lost his shoes and cartridge box, although he still clutched his musket. Second Lieutenant Benjamin F. Hancock, Sergeant Samuel M. Goodwin, and Private Oliver Hubbell failed to return and were thought to be shot down, although the three men had actually been captured by rebel troops assembled by Colonel J. E. B. Stuart to defend Lewinsville. Lieutenant Hancock's party had encountered skirmishers from a battalion of the 13th Virginia under command of Major James B. Terrill, who personally captured the Federal lieutenant. Under Lieutenant Colonel Cameron's direction, Company I retired to the crossroads where it rejoined Colonel Meredith and the other Indiana companies.[21]

When the Indiana battalion was reassembled, the Owen County boys learned that their comrades picketing the road to the Leesburg Pike had also encountered the enemy. Company F had been deployed in front of Captain Griffin's guns along a line of woods. After remaining concealed for a short time, a rebel dressed in gray pants, black coat, and broad-brimmed hat jumped up in front of the battery and ran toward the Hoosier skirmishers, who immediately captured him. Scouts ventured into the woods and discovered that they had been occupied only a few minutes earlier by a small force of graycoats which had retreated so quickly their rations had been left cooking in camp kettles.[22]

Although Company B was still back at Camp Advance, Orderly Sergeant Sam Schlagle and Corporal Jeff Crull, along with two band members, shared the adventure after obtaining permission to accompany the column. As Colonel Stevens's command began to retrace its path back to the Federal lines, the boys were no longer looking for an attack, but suddenly two cannon opened fire on the column and Crull watched as "the bombs came aflying over our heads thick and fast." Southern infantrymen concealed in a wooded ravine and cornfield added long-range musketry to the shells and spherical case shot of the rebel artillery.[23]

Private W. H. H. Wood of Company D was killed by a shot in the head and Private Asbury Inlow of the same company was seriously wounded by a ball which entered his left cheek and passed out behind his ear. The Hoosiers were under this galling fire, with no real opportunity to reply, for five to ten minutes. Ordered forward along the road, Meredith's men stumbled over the body of a private from the 3rd Vermont who had been horribly mangled by a shell and lay beside his mortally-wounded filemate, who was feebly trying to drink from a canteen. Lieutenant Benjamin F. Reed watched one shell hurl fragments of a rail fence high into the air just moments after the Indiana boys had left their position there. Reed noted that the Indiana soldiers behaved well under the cannonading even though there was a display of "artful dodging" and the bowing of many a head at the performance. One shell burst directly over the heads of Reed and Lieutenant John Cottman. A chunk of iron buried itself in the ground about six feet from the pair and a cool corporal dug up the fragment as a souvenir.[24]

Captain Griffin's rifled guns were speedily put into action and responded to the rebel artillery. A section of Captain Thaddeus Mott's 3rd New York Battery soon galloped up and unlimbered, accompanied by General William F. Smith, who had ridden forward to take personal command of the expedition. Mott's 32-pounder was mentioned by several participants as instrumental in silencing the rebel guns. When the column prepared to move on, Colonel Meredith's five companies were assigned to the rear guard along with Griffin's battery and Lieutenant McLean's Regular cavalry, "dragoons" according to Long Sol. The Hoosier companies covered the retirement of General Smith's command under a fitful artillery fire, losing Private John Hamilton of Company D when a spent ball wounded him in the foot. The firing at Lewinsville was clearly heard in Washington, so the returning soldiers found the road lined with reinforce-

ments which had been hurried forward by the generals. Among the reinforcements were four companies of the 19th Indiana—Company C being
detailed as camp guards after a night on picket—whose men had moved to
assist their comrades "not on common time, not on double quick, but on the
run." The spirits of the returning Hoosiers, now "quite exhausted" by their
exertions during the warm fall afternoon, were buoyed by the cheers of the
newcomers.[25]

This cheery greeting was forgotten later that night when a hard rain
soaked everyone and everything in Camp Advance. Lieutenant Reed could
not sleep and walked through the Hoosier camp, reflecting on the way his
men accepted their fate:

> I arose after receiving a thorough drenching, and walked up and down
> our column the balance of the night, listening to the remarks of the men,
> some of which were jocular, some were angry in tone, bewailing their
> condition, some were snoring, all unconscious of the water which was
> actually rippling over the feet of some, or of the fact that they had
> miraculously escaped death but a few hours previously.

There were grumblers in Captain Dudley's company, but Corporal Crull
dismissed them with the comment, "some of the boys growl but i think thay
dont know what thay do want."[26]

After the abandonment of Lewinsville by Smith's command, Captain Thomas Rosser of the Washington Light Artillery inspected the area
where his rebel gunners had aimed their sights and reported, "The road here
was plowed by my projectiles, and thick with fragments of shell, and strewn
with canteens, haversacks, and a few muskets of the enemy." Despite the
effects of Rosser's cannonading, Colonel Meredith's loss in the skirmish at
Lewinsville was one private killed, two privates wounded and one lieutenant,
one sergeant and one private missing. Sol concluded his first battle report in
the following manner:

> My men were under fire about two hours, and during the whole of
> that time behaved with the utmost coolness and gallantry, obeying all
> orders promptly and with but little confusion, their chief anxiety
> seeming to be that the enemy's infantry might advance from their cover
> or that they might have a chance to try their hand on Stuart's cavalry.
> Though discrimination seems almost invidious when all behaved well,
> yet I cannot close my report without adverting to the conduct of
> Lieutenant Colonel Cameron, whose courage and coolness were con-
> spicuous throughout the whole of this affair. While shells were bursting
> around us he rode the lines, giving orders with an equanimity which was
> not even disturbed when one of them passed so close that his horse,
> sinking under him, with difficulty recovered the shock.

Colonel Isaac Stevens reported the successful conclusion of his expedition to Lewinsville, summing up the information gained concerning the region about the village, "It has great natural advantages, is easily defensible, will require but a small amount of ordnance, and should be permanently occupied without delay."[27]

The body of Private Wood, the first man killed in battle from the 19th Indiana, was recovered on September 12th by a detachment of the 3rd Vermont, which had returned to Lewinsville to look for the missing from that regiment. The appearance of Wood's corpse indicated that he had died instantly from a bullet wound in the head. Rebels had removed his shoes, emptied his pockets and cut the buttons from his uniform coat, the latter apparently intended for trophies. Wood's body was carried back to the Hoosier camp, cleaned up and laid out among the tents for a few hours. The coffin was then carried with military ceremony, including a dirge by the regimental band, to a grave on a hill adjoining the regimental campsite. Wood's grave was located next to the final resting place of Daniel Ward of Company G, who had drowned on September 9th after being swept over the Little Falls in the Potomac.[28]

Private Asbury Inlow, the regiment's first man wounded in battle, was the object of great curiosity in camp, but he was not much of a hero. His head wound left Inlow incapable of opening his jaws more than one-half inch and he was discharged on October 29, 1861, because of his "inability to bite a cartridge." Returning home to Indianapolis, Inlow resumed his former lifestyle, drinking heavily and cruelly abusing his wife while under the influence of liquor. He also associated with a number of lewd women, including a Miss Oliver who was described as possessing a "notoriously bad reputation and dissolute character." Private Inlow would eventually receive a government pension for his wound.[29]

Morale, already high after the skirmish at Lewinsville, received a boost on September 13th when the detachment from Kalorama arrived with the regimental tents. These boys also brought news of a case of attempted poisoning. On September 10th, soldiers mysteriously became ill after drinking water from a spring near the Kalorama camp. An investigation revealed that the water was impregnated with arsenic. Dr. Kendrick, who had recovered enough to do limited duty, examined leaves removed from the bottom of the spring and found "large portions of arsenic still adhered" to them. Kendrick treated about ten men who became very sick from ingesting the poison. Rebel spies were blamed for the cowardly act.[30]

Boys who had not gone on the expedition to Lewinsville became highly excited after listening to tales of those who had been under fire. A few veterans of the 2nd Wisconsin, always on the lookout for a good practical joke, dressed a private to resemble a secesh and marched him as a "prisoner" past the camp of the 5th Wisconsin. Just as the detail passed the Wisconsin tents, their "prisoner" was allowed to escape. The rookies fell over themselves as they scampered after the escapee, but when they discovered the trick "they looked rather cheap." There were real Southern visitors to Camp Advance—Negroes leaving the desolated region between the two armies that had been abandoned by its white inhabitants. An Indiana officer observed the arrival of one particular family:

> I noticed one old father, who had provided himself with a cart and horse, and his two daughters, with their children, some three or four, together with all their clothing, and a coop of chickens, stowed therein, two good, stalwart boys walking by the side, and their faithful dog.

After hiring the most promising Negroes for cooks and servants, officers sent the remainder on to Washington as fast as they appeared.[31]

While Colonel Meredith's boys resumed routine duties at Camp Advance, General Smith pondered all the forage he had seen in the unmolested region around Lewinsville and decided to return to that village. Smith ordered his quartermaster to gather ninety army wagons for a foraging expedition to Lewinsville, while he assembled troops for their protection. Colonel Isaac Stevens's operation had been conducted with an aggregate of 1,800 fighting men, but this new movement, scheduled for September 25th, would be protected by 5,100 infantry, 150 cavalry and 16 guns. General Smith's force consisted of the 19th Indiana, 33rd New York, 79th New York, 71st Pennsylvania, 2nd Vermont, 3rd Vermont, two companies of Berdan's United States Sharpshooters, five companies from the 6th Maine, two companies from the 72nd Pennsylvania, four companies from the 2nd Wisconsin, eight companies from the 5th Wisconsin, Griffin's battery, Mott's battery, Barr's Pennsylvania Battery and two companies of cavalry, one Regular and one volunteer. The troops were ready for action, as evidenced by the statement of Lieutenant George H. Otis of the 2nd Wisconsin: "All due preparations were made, the shooting-irons cleaned up, and with smiling countenances all hands 'fell in,' supposing we were going to have a brush with the foe."[32]

General Smith marched his command from Camp Advance at 9 o'clock on the morning of September 25th and, moving by way of Langley, arrived unmolested at Lewinsville, which was occupied by only a few enemy scouts. Wayne County soldiers were unimpressed with the village, which was found to contain a church, schoolhouse, grocery, blacksmith shop, and four houses, all deserted. Colonel Meredith's Hoosiers were positioned, along with the other regiments, to protect the quartermasters, who had their wagons stuffed with forage by 3 P.M. Having seen the countryside swept clean, Smith's command retired about an hour later under long-range artillery fire. At one point, about a mile from town, the Indiana soldiers were ordered to lie down in a clover field to avoid the shell fire and enemy projectiles struck so close that Company B was several times pelted with sand and gravel. Union artillery soon drove off the rebel cannoneers and kept the enemy cavalry and infantry, advancing on the Falls Church Road, at a respectful distance.[33]

The Federal column returned to Camp Advance by 7 o'clock that evening with its plunder: 60 tons of hay, large quantities of corn and oats, 160 head of cattle and a number of horses and sheep. General Smith reported a loss of one man and the capture of one rebel, "a most impudent sort of a fellow" and purported to be an aide to Colonel J. E. B. Stuart. As the prisoner was being escorted in handcuffs past the 2nd Wisconsin, the Badgers noticed that he wore a regulation army hat and naturally asked him where he got it. The captive cavalryman made no friends when he alluded to the recent battle at Bull Run, boasting, "When you ran I got the hat you left behind." No wonder the Wisconsin boys thought him impudent![34]

Lewinsville lost its significance when McClellan's army advanced on September 28th and General Smith's command occupied Falls Church. The Hoosiers participated in this movement to Falls Church, where marauders caused a great deal of destruction to private property, as witnessed by one Indiana boy, "I went over to a cecesh house and our men was tearing nearly every thing up. they tore up a pianno. I tried to play a tune on it but it was so shattered that it would not sound like any thing." Foragers killed all the hogs and chickens, then divided up the staples with special attention being given to molasses, which was not included in their regular rations. The house was then burnt. While soldiers had no regrets about looting rebel homes, they were, according to John Hawk, constantly bothered by one nagging concern, the marital status of the girls back home—"Tell them that the boys are all in good spirits and the only thing that makes them uneasy is that they are afraid the girls will so far forget themselves as to marry some of the cowardly dogs who are left behind."[35]

On September 27th, General Winfield Scott Hancock's brigade was ordered to reinforce General Smith's provisional division, thereby relieving King's regiments, which were ordered to concentrate on the Potomac's northern shore. On September 28th, the order was modified by permanently detaching the 5th Wisconsin to Hancock's brigade, replacing the departing Badgers with another of Governor Alexander Randall's regiments, Colonel Joseph Vandor's 7th Wisconsin, which was then en route to Washington. General King's headquarters tents were pitched at Montgomery Hall, rumored to have once been the headquarters of General George Washington, although the building was now "in a somewhat dilapidated condition." The 6th Wisconsin, the only regiment under Rufus King's command since September 4th, was camped north of the Leesburg and Georgetown Turnpike. When General Hancock rode up to King's headquarters on the stormy afternoon of September 30th, he was leading a long column of infantry, "drenched and bedraggled by the downpour." General King was absent in Washington with some of his staff, while other aides were off on business of one kind or another, leaving sixteen-year-old Charley King in charge. When Hancock asked for a mounted guide to direct his brigade to General Smith, young Charley spoke up, "I can take you, sir. I go there every day." So the youngster mounted his horse and guided the handsome general down a ramp that engineers had carved in the riverbank and across an old truss bridge to the southern shore.[36]

Somewhat reluctantly, boys in the 19th Indiana and 2nd Wisconsin left Camp Advance on October 1st to rejoin King's brigade across the river at Camp Lyon, their displeasure a combination of abandoning a foothold in the land of secession and the necessity of leaving behind many of their personal possessions. These Western soldiers, like soldiers everywhere, displayed "a remarkable faculty for accumulating property" and had finally begun to get settled at Camp Advance after the belated arrival of their tents. Most of this amassed treasure was abandoned by necessity whenever the regiments changed camp. The twenty wagons allotted to each regiment were barely enough for the tents and other camp equipment, enlisted men being forced to carry what they wanted to retain and, according to one private, "then we leave our common furniture, and a good share of our every day clothes." Leaving an old camp for a new one was rather like setting up housekeeping as pioneers, abandoning the comforts and beginning again with only the absolute essentials.[37]

The replacement regiment for the departing 5th Wisconsin also reached Camp Lyon on October 1st, General Rufus King's brigade thereafter being composed of the 19th Indiana, Colonel Solomon Meredith; 2nd Wisconsin, Colonel Edgar O'Connor; 6th Wisconsin, Colonel Lysander Cutler; and 7th Wisconsin, Colonel Joseph Vandor. The stay at Camp Lyon was brief—an order came to strike the tents at 8 A.M. on October 5th in preparation for a march to Arlington Heights at 10 A.M. This movement did not commence until about noon, when the temperature had reached ninety-four degrees and the boys began their march with the sun beating down upon them and no breeze to cool the air. It was one of the hottest days encountered since their arrival at Washington. Some claimed it was the hottest they had ever seen and Indiana boys suffered severely from the heat, dropping from the ranks to seek shade until evening when they straggled on to Arlington.[38]

    With Professor Lowe's balloon bobbing above them as they left Camp Lyon, King's brigade marched along the turnpike to Georgetown, where the soldiers crossed back into Virginia on the Aqueduct Bridge, which had been recently drained and floored. Climbing the Heights, King's Western boys marched past the imposing Arlington Mansion to camps recently occupied by General James S. Wadsworth's brigade. The Badgers and Hoosiers would not leave their new camps until the following spring.[39]

5

Indiana Hospital

When the 19th Indiana marched off for the Chain Bridge on September 3rd, Surgeon Calvin Woods, in anticipation of an imminent battle, accompanied the regiment. With Assistant Surgeon Kendrick prostrated by typhoid fever and confined to his bed, care of the 103 sick men in camp was left to the guard detachment, whose members were expected to perform hospital service in addition to guard duty. In many cases the sick men nursed each other, patients presenting "a most forlorn and helpless condition." Elizabeth Smith, wife of Secretary of the Interior Caleb Blood Smith, discovered the abandoned Hoosier boys at Kalorama during a visit to that camp on September 4th and immediately returned to the city. After hearing Elizabeth's description of the deplorable situation at Kalorama, Secretary Smith assembled all the Indiana clerks in his department, jokingly referred to in Washington as the "Department of Indiana." These clerks quickly made plans to alleviate the suffering of their fellow Hoosiers.[1]

Warren T. Lockhart, Hallet Kilbourn, Richard M. Hall, Edward Mothershead, and Samuel Alter were appointed to a committee charged with ascertaining the number of sick, arranging for their removal to comfortable quarters, and providing nurses and medical attention. R. O. Hedrick and E. C. Mayhew were selected to head a finance committee and instructed to collect funds to defray any expenses involved in the relief effort. Richard Hall described the actions taken by the concerned Indiana clerks:

> We found about *ninety* on the sick list and incapable of duty. Ambulances were at once procured, and twenty-eight taken to the Georgetown Seminary, which has been put in order to receive sick, and secured proper attention for them, and then removed *sixty-two* to a large hall of the Patent Office, for which we procured mattresses, sheets, &c., provided nurses and medical attention, as well as means by which proper food would be regularly and abundantly supplied.

In addition to those removed to Georgetown Seminary and the Patent Office, Mrs. Smith took several, including Assistant Surgeon Kendrick, into her own home.[2]

Sick soldiers were carried up flights of stairs to the top story of the Patent Office, where a hospital was created in a large unfinished wing. Secretary Smith suspended further construction on that wing and the floor was cleared of dust, shavings, nails, and carpenter scraps. Debris was shoveled into barrels, which were stacked at one end of the new ward. Pieces of scaffolding were nailed together to form rude tables, each "bed" capable of holding six patients. These beds, so high and large that the sheets and blankets could only be straightened with brooms, ran the full length of the room. Mattresses were thrown atop stacks of marble slabs, converting the future flooring into beds that were given to the most serious cases. But as the crisis continued, more space was urgently needed. A volunteer nurse recorded the response:

> As the number increased, camp beds were set up between the glass cases in the outer room, and we alternated typhoid fever, cog wheels and patent churns—typhoid fever, balloons and mouse traps (how *many* ways of catching mice there are!)—typhoid fever, locomotives, water wheels, clocks—and a general nightmare of machinery.

Upon admission to the hospital, each man was given a new shirt and a new pair of drawers. At first, food and water were carried by hand up to the top floor, but soon massive pulleys were erected in a window and, thereafter, "any time through the day, barrels of water, baskets of vegetables, and great pieces of army beef might be seen crawling slowly up the marble face of the building." Gradually, confusion gave way to system and order.[3]

R. O. Hedrick, Superintendent of the Interior Department, assumed the responsibility of collecting funds for the Hoosier relief effort, a duty he discharged admirably. Contributions from Indiana clerks in Secretary Smith's department amounted to over $200, a sum augmented by donations from other residents of Washington. The most substantial contribution was made by E. S. Alvord, an Indianapolis resident in town on business, who inquired for the treasurer of the hospital fund one day in September. When informed that Mr. Hedrick was out seeking donations, Alvord sat down and stuffed two $50 Treasury notes into an envelope, "remarking that he knew none of the men personally, but they were his fellow citizens, soldiers waging a holy war, and his mite should be freely circulated for their relief." Expenditures for bedding, clothing, medicine, food, cooking utensils, and other necessities quickly depleted the fund, despite economical management.[4]

On September 11th Robert Dale Owen, who was visiting the Hoosier regiments around Washington as an agent of Governor Morton, described the establishment of this "Indiana Hospital" and concluded:

> In view of these circumstances I earnestly recommend that five hundred dollars be sent from the State Treasury & placed in the hands of M Smith, to defray the main expenses of this supplemental hospital. About half that sum has already been disbursed; and, as I could judge, used with the strictest economy. It is proper I should state, that I suggest this, (to prevent the heavy burdens now falling exclusively on a few,) without the slightest prompting or request, direct or indirect, either from M Smith, or from any other person concerned.

Owen's recommendation prompted Governor Morton to telegraph that his agent was to "incur whatever expense may be reasonably necessary to provide for our sick." Later that year $439.23 from Morton's Military Contingent Fund was sent to W. T. Lockhart, head of the Executive Committee, with the money earmarked for "Sick soldiers at Washington City belonging to Indiana reg'ts."[5]

Although the Indiana congressional delegation did not become actively involved with this volunteer project, other prominent Hoosiers lent their time and talent. Most notable of these, of course, were Caleb and Elizabeth Smith, who recognized the need and inaugurated a plan to care for the sick of the 19th Indiana. Commissioner of Patents David P. Holloway, along with his wife, Jane, was prominently mentioned in several early accounts of the hospital and, as a former resident of Richmond and founder of the *Palladium,* probably saw to it that the Wayne County boys were well treated. Librarian of Congress John G. Stephenson, formerly a doctor in Terre Haute, received praise for his generosity. Judge David Kilgore, who as a former member of Congress had represented many of those now lying low with fever, lavished attention on the 19th Indiana, where his son James served as first lieutenant in Company A.[6]

Almira Fales, whose husband had a government position and whose sons were in the army, screened applicants for nurses at the hospital. One such applicant was Maria M. C. Hall, but she was initially rebuffed by the "kind-hearted but eccentric" Mrs. Fales, who followed Dorothea Dix's belief that "youth, grace, and talent were poor recommendations for a hospital nurse." But the young and cultivated Miss Hall was adamant. Mrs. Fales then tried to dissuade the young lady:

> She tried to discourage the warm-hearted girl by telling her that the work to be done was very plain, very practical, and sometimes repulsive; that the men were dirty, and needed washing; and their hair was all in

tangles, and must be combed out and brushed; that they were very hungry, and cared for nothing but to get something good to eat.

Such descriptions served only to stimulate Maria Hall, so the older woman gave in and escorted the young lady and her sister to the Patent Office, where she opened the door and said, "Now, girls, here they are, and everything to be done for them. You will find work in plenty."[7]

Robert Dale Owen was impressed with the newly created Indiana Hospital when he stopped by on his inspection tour:

> There I found 85 patients, tended by ladies of the city who had volunteered their services, while the actually essential (clean bedding, food, medicine, cooking apparatus, etc.) had been purchased by the Subscription. Most of the men seemed to be in a fair way of recovery; some able to sit up & walk about; a few, as far as I could judge, more hopeless cases, chiefly of fever, sometimes accompanied by delerium. They had secured the services of a physician. No one had yet died there, but five had died from this regiment, in the other hospitals.

Summing up the rescue effort orchestrated by Secretary Smith, Owen wrote, "I am satisfied, that the prompt action by himself & other Indianians in removing them at once in carriages to the present quarters, saved many lives." Despite Owen's upbeat message the crisis was far from over.[8]

On September 3rd there were 157 officers and men sick, both in camp and in hospital, but that number increased to 234 on September 8th, only eighteen of these men being with the regiment at Camp Advance. On September 15th, the total sick had dipped slightly to 229, but during the following week the sick list began to grow—255 on September 16th, 257 on the 17th, 270 on the 18th, 273 on the 19th, 282 on the 20th, and 289 on the 21st. The 289 soldiers sick on Saturday, September 21st, represented the climax of the illness that ravaged Colonel Meredith's regiment. Of those soldiers, four officers and 93 enlisted men were sick in camp while nine officers and 183 men were sick in Washington area hospitals or at Camp Kalorama. It will be remembered that those remaining at Kalorama were under the care of camp guards, but, if attention to duty was an indication of medical performance, the sick boys must have suffered. The lackadaisical attitude at Kalorama became apparent on the night of September 20th, when a lieutenant inspecting the guard posts went into one of the deserted headquarters tents and walked away unopposed with the regimental flag![9]

After Robert Dale Owen had visited the Indiana Hospital, he made a careful investigation south of the Potomac and sent Governor Morton his report on the continuation of fevers in the 19th Indiana:

After a time every able-bodied man was ordered across the river to "Camp Advance" where they now are; and no tents were sent with them. Thus ever since they crossed, they have slept on a bare hill-side, without the slightest protection except what a single blanket can afford; often in drenching rain.

A. F. Scott, an old friend from Centreville now acting as a military agent, also advised Morton that exposure at Camp Advance was primarily responsible for the fevers sweeping through the Indiana ranks. After describing the unhealthy site at Kalorama, Scott reported:

After remaining at this camp several weeks, they were moved across the Potomac, to a location equally unhealthy; compelled to work in ditches during the day, and stand on picket at night for some two weeks, and without tents, and many without blankets, and the whole regiment slept on their arms seven nights in an old field, during most of which time it was raining.

While representatives of the governor gave their opinions on the cause of these fevers, Surgeon Woods confided to Morton, "This will always be a sickly regiment. Too many young loafing vagabonds and snipes of boys in it, who have no constitution, muscle or stamina."[10]

Dr. Woods candidly expressed his discouragement with military life in a letter written to Governor Morton on September 24th. The doctor confessed:

I have been sick twice but soon got well. Surgeon of a Rgt is not the nice job I thought it would be. I thought I would only have to cut off a few legs and arms instead of which I have to mix constantly with fevers of the worst kind. I long since got tired Doctoring in common sickness such as fevers.

The surgeon then began to enumerate some of the problems he had experienced since the 19th Indiana reached Washington, beginning with the case of Dr. Kendrick, his only assistant, who was lying near death at Secretary Smith's home. Woods then pointed out that after Meredith's regiment marched to Chain Bridge the sick were scattered to various places, making it impossible for one man to attend them all. Then his hospital stewards were struck down by fever and Colonel Meredith would not approve asking for additional medical help. On top of these troubles, Woods was notified that he must appear before a board of examination and prove his ability as a medical officer. After passing his examination, the surgeon then had to discharge the regimental matron, whose presence was apparently undermining good order.[11]

By the end of September, Surgeon Woods was desperate and admitted that he was "having a hard time generally." Bypassing the official chain of command, he declared that an additional doctor for the regiment was "a Stern and absolute necessity" and claimed, "I must have someboddy or die." Governor Morton responded by sending Dr. John N. Green to Washington, but he was diverted to the Indiana Hospital upon his arrival and Woods toiled on without a professional assistant. As a stopgap measure, Governor Morton appointed Dr. John G. Stephenson, the Congressional Librarian, to his personal military staff and ordered him to duty with the 19th Indiana, where he brought much-needed relief. It was mid-October before the surgeon general detached D. Cooper Ayres from the 7th Wisconsin to assist in ministering to the Hoosiers, leading Surgeon Woods to write with relief, "The Sickness of our Rgt is gradually abating."[12]

In addition to his problems with assistants, Woods no longer had any use for his superior:

> Col. Meredith thinks or pretends to think it is all my fault. Public opinion naturally seeks for the cause of all our Sickness and Sol is So fearful that he will be *blamed* that he insidiously tried in all the influential quarters to have it charged up to me.

But the beleaguered surgeon preferred to stand on his record and, although about twenty men had died of disease, stated bluntly that no deaths had occurred under his treatment.[13]

No detailed case histories survive from the Indiana Hospital, but the symptoms of patients and treatments given them by their physicians may be surmised from existing records of two Hoosiers who were, by chance, sent to Seminary Hospital rather than the Patent Office. One such example concluded favorably:

> Private Eli Sulgrove, Co. D, 19th Ind.; age 18; had a chill about Aug. 25, 1861, and was admitted September 4. Diagnosis—typhoid fever. He had headache, pain in the bones and back, and slight diarrhoea with fever, which was aggravated daily about noon. On the morning of the 5th there was tinnitus aurium but no fever; the pulse was 78, skin cold and moist, tongue coated, pale and flabby, appetite good, bowels regular. Quinine was ordered. In the evening the pulse was 72 and strong, tongue pale, flabby, red at the edges and white at the base and centre. During the day he had one thin stool and was weak and giddy. Dover's powder was given at night. Until the 11th the patient continued without change, a slight febrile action occurring every evening, manifesting itself in flushing of the face, but the pulse in no instance rose higher than 80; there was one stool daily, with, on one occasion, pain in the left iliac fossa. He usually rested well and had a fair appetite,

although his tongue continued pale, flabby and coated. On the 11th a few rose-spots appeared, which faded next day, but were replaced by others and an eruption of sudamina; the pulse was 68, the skin cool, bowels quiet and not tender, tongue coated brownish but red at the tip. On the 13th he was sent to hospital at Baltimore, Md.

Private Sulgrove eventually made a complete recovery and served until the close of the war.[14]

The typhoid and malarial fevers that scourged the 19th Indiana were often lethal, as indicated in the case study below:

Private Henry Martindale, Co. F, 19th Ind. Vols.; age 24; was taken Aug. 28, 1861, with headache, pains in the bones, languor and chill. He took quinia and had no recurrence of the chill; but the fever which followed was generally worse in the morning. He was admitted September 4. Diagnosis—typhoid fever. On the 5th: Pulse 76; skin warm and moist; tongue heavily coated, pale and flabby; slight diarrhoea; stools, but no pain or tenderness in the bowels; appetite fair. Dover's powder at night. On the 6th and 7th the symptoms were unchanged. On the 8th the mind was somewhat dull; the patient continued to be up and to walk about occasionally. Sugar of lead and opium were given. No material change took place until the 11th, when the warm and moist skin showed sudamina and some rose-colored spots on the abdomen, the tongue at this time being pale, flabby and coated gray, the bowels but slightly relaxed and the appetite good. Whiskey-punch was prescribed. The patient was drowsy on the 12th, and on the following day the tongue became brown and cracked but remained pale at the tip, the skin hot and dry, the breathing hurried, and the bowels moved eight times but free from pain and distention. On the 14th the tongue was dry and the countenance haggard. Two grains of quinine and one of calomel were prescribed for administration three times daily. Profuse perspirations occurred on the 15th, but the diarrhoea continued and sordes appeared on the teeth. Turpentine emulsion was given. On the evening of the 16th there was some tenderness of the abdomen and the patient kept tossing his head from side to side. On the 18th the pulse was 80, weak and small, tongue heavily coated, brown in the middle and red at tip and edges, skin hot and moist, bowels not tender but quite loose, especially at night. On the 19th there was some tenderness in the right iliac region. Ten stools were passed on the 22d, and on the following day the abdomen was tympanic.

The case history closed abruptly with the announcement of Private Martindale's death on September 28, 1861. His remains were conveyed to the cemetery at the Soldiers Home, where three dozen of Colonel Meredith's men would be buried before the year was out.[15]

While the original group of patients in the Indiana Hospital were being nursed by Washington citizens, sick soldiers continued to be sent to the Patent Office from Camp Advance, where fevers continued unabated. Second Lieutenant William Orr of Company K was one of those who was stricken and he left a detailed account of his suffering. On September 9th, Orr felt "a little unwell" and reported to Dr. Woods, who gave him two pills and explained that he "was going to have a sick spell." Resolving to stay with the company as long as he could, Orr remained in camp "not feeling very well and not feeling very sick," although he did cut back on his work, leaving many of the details to his sergeants. On September 11th, the lieutenant had "a violent headache," but led Company K on the double-quick when reinforcements rushed to support Colonel Meredith's detachment at Lewinsville. While most of the regiment spent that night unprotected in the rain, Lieutenant Orr passed the night under shelter. The following night the Selma boys were sent on picket, but Lieutenant Castle of Company B took command of that portion of the picket line so that Orr could rest on the porch of a house with the reserve. On the 13th the debilitated lieutenant supervised the pitching of his company tents and on the 14th he watched while the company was paid, but then went to his bed and stayed there until the morning of September 15th. On that day, his twenty-third birthday, Lieutenant William Orr, "wearied, worn out, sick," was loaded into an ambulance and carried back across the Potomac to the Indiana Hospital.

Lieutenant Orr's recollection of his first two weeks of hospitalization was very dim, but he did remember that Edward Rodman, convalescent after recovering from his own case of fever, faithfully looked after him. The lieutenant never knew how sick he was and curiosity prompted him to inquire about his condition:

> The Dr. never told me what he thought. Kilgore said he always thought I would get well. Donahue, a lawyer of Greencastle who came 3 or 4 times to see me, told the Col he thought I never would get up. The nurses say I was very sick But with the exception of some sickness at the stomach I felt no pain at all.

Judge Kilgore's optimism for William's recovery was somewhat guarded, as indicated in a letter to James Orr written on September 22nd:

> Your son is quite sick though I think not dangerously so. he is in the hospital where I visit him together with some one hundred and fifty of the 19th Regt daily and try to give them all the aid in my power. I have just left the room of your son, he appears quite cheerful and full of hope. Should he suddenly become dangerously ill I will telegraph you at Muncie and you had better make some arrangement there to have it sent to you at once.

On the 26th Kilgore again wrote to James Orr and advised him, "I have just left the Hospital. Your son is much better and I think will be able to be up in a few days though quite weak."

On October 14th Lieutenant Orr, confiding that "both hands and head not working by a good deal as they used to when I was well," composed a long letter to his father. Describing his current condition, Orr wrote:

> I am much better. I can walk around. I am not able to go down into the street yet & when I walk about I always carry a cane. I have a good appetite, and go down to the kitchen every time now for my meals. But still I am very weak. This morning I weighed only 105 lbs. and when I was taken sick I would weigh at least 140 as I was fleshier than I ever was in my life.

Through a combination of attentive nursing, Dr. Green's prescriptions, a naturally strong body and prayer, Lieutenant William Orr made a complete recovery and returned to duty with Company K on October 29th.[16]

Although a few officers suffered along with the enlisted men at the Patent Office, most of them were cared for in private homes when they fell sick. When Lieutenant Davis Castle became ill in mid-October, Jesse Potts, the hospital steward, took him in a carriage to the boardinghouse of Mary Roche at 417 12th Street West. Castle was under the care of a Dr. Richards until Dr. John G. Stephenson returned from his stint as an assistant surgeon with the 19th Indiana and took over the case. Dr. Stephenson attended to the stricken lieutenant daily, with Mrs. Roche serving as a nurse through a long and extreme course of "nervous and muscular prostration." Jesse Potts remembered that Lieutenant Castle was "at one time very low from the disease, and not expected to live," news which was communicated to friends back home when Lieutenant Lee Yaryan returned to Richmond on furlough. After Lieutenant Castle felt well enough to travel and applied for a leave of absence, he reported to the Indiana Hospital, where Dr. Green offered his assessment of the case:

> I do hereby certify that I have carefully examined this officer and find that in consequence of a protracted attack of Typhoid Fever which has confined him to bed four weeks and which left him in a feeble condition his debility is so great that he is unable to perform any kind of duty and will not be for less than four weeks.

By November 23rd, Lieutenant Castle had received a furlough and was among friends in Richmond "for the purpose of recruiting his health." Despite attentive care and an opportunity to rest at home, Castle's health was permanently damaged and he would soon be detached from the company to a less strenuous post than that of an infantry officer.[17]

Many of the boys in Captain Dudley's company were sick with fever when the regiment marched away to Chain Bridge. After the relief effort was organized, Gershom Conger and Randolph Fort were conveyed to the Georgetown Seminary. James Fulkerson, a nineteen-year-old native of Ohio, was carried to Columbia College, where he died on September 9th, the first man from Company B to lose his life in the service. Grear Williams was diagnosed with a case of measles, so he was packed off to the Eruptive Hospital at Kalorama, but he deserted a few days later and returned to the company. The majority of patients were taken to the Patent Office. Company B's contingent included Lieutenant Samuel Hindman, Corporal Abraham Luce, and Privates William Castator, Hugh English, Thomas Henderson, George Marquis, Ambrose Swain, James Thornburg, Alexander Walker, John Winder, and Joseph Wisenberg. By November 16th these soldiers had been joined by Sergeant Edward Gorgas, Corporal John Thornburg, and Privates Ira Dillon, James Livengood, William Locke, James Mills, John Morgan, Daniel Pierce, Samuel Sparklin, William Thornburg, Joseph Titus, Grear Williams, and James Wine. The average stay for the boys from Company B lasted just over five weeks. Corporal John Thornburg died on December 6th and six other Wayne County men were eventually discharged for disability, the remainder being returned to duty.[18]

Of all the tragedies associated with the Indiana Hospital, no case was more pathetic than that of Sergeant Edward W. Gorgas. Ed had been born and raised in Philadelphia, where his father had died in the 1850s. In 1860 Edward said goodbye to his mother Sarah and set off to live with relatives in Richmond, Indiana. Gorgas was "a strong hearty vigorous man" when he joined the City Greys and Captain Dudley remembered the decline of one of his favorite soldiers:

> Edward W. Gorgas . . . bade fair to become a splendid soldier. Shortly after his service began and the drilling and hard work of the service commenced, I noticed that he became quite misanthropic and moody, and would frequently go away by himself, shunning the companions with whom he was formerly intimate. This continued to grow worse until late in the fall of 1861, at Fort Craig, when he became so palpably insane that I found it necessary to send him to the hospital.

Ed was admitted to the Indiana Hospital on October 16th and was diagnosed as suffering from camp fever and insanity.

Dr. Green wrote to Sarah Gorgas and advised that her son was a patient in his hospital and suffering from an attack of camp fever. A few days later, Green posted another letter to Sarah which stated that her son had recovered from his bout of fever, but the illness had left him hopelessly insane. Following Dr. Green's instructions, Sarah arranged for a nephew, George Pierce, to start for Washington, where he could obtain Ed's discharge. Pierce met the doctor at the Patent Office where Green told him, "This man's mind seems to be entirely gone from the terrible case of fever he has had. We have no place to care for insane people and I think you had better ask for his discharge and take him home."

Dr. Green explained the sad case in a brief note that he addressed to Secretary of War Simon Cameron. George Pierce arranged an interview with the secretary, presented Green's note and asked for a discharge for his cousin. Secretary Cameron replied, "Dr. Green says this man cannot get well; we want active soldiers, not imbeciles. I will give you his discharge at once." On October 27th, Headquarters, Army of the Potomac, issued a memorandum that read, "Private Edward Gorgas 19th Indiana Regiment has authority to proceed to his home at Philadelphia pending an application for his discharge on the ground of insanity." Ed was discharged on October 29, 1861, by Special Order No. 122, Headquarters, Army of the Potomac.

George Pierce later recalled his cousin's behavior when he first encountered Ed that fall:

> When I saw the said soldier at the Patent Office Hospital at Washington, D.C. he had the appearance of a maniac. He talked in an incoherent and rambling manner and was impressed with a mania that all around him were conspiring to poison him. I remember distinctly while on our road home, in the cars, he talked of the attendants putting pieces of broken glass in the butter, and this species of mania has stuck with him ever since.

Ed required constant care and his presence soon proved a burden to the family. After about a year, acting upon medical advice, Sarah Gorgas made arrangements for her son to live with a farmer in Bucks County. Gorgas stayed in the country about a year and the farmer watched over him. But then Ed turned violent and one day attacked his caretaker with a hatchet. After that, according to Pierce, the farmer "refused to take care of him any longer."

Following the hatchet attack, Sarah had no choice but to place Ed in an institution. She chose the Friends Asylum at Frankford, Pennsylvania. Henry Kates, a brother-in-law with whom he had lived in Richmond prior to his enlistment, was appointed Ed's guardian. Kates eventually obtained a pension based on Ed's disability, thereby relieving the family of the expenses incurred in caring for the invalid. After Kates's death, Ed Gorgas's financial affairs were handled by the Dickinson Trust Company of Richmond. Although the bout of camp fever had destroyed his mind in 1861, Ed's body survived without additional injury and remained healthy and robust. Edward Gorgas remained at the Friends Asylum without hope of a cure until his death on October 21, 1915—fifty-four years after his discharge from the Indiana Hospital.[19]

Overcrowding in Washington hospitals, including the Indiana Hospital, resulted in soldiers falling victim to contagious diseases while confined with other maladies. Nearly two dozen patients from the Indiana Hospital were sent into quarantine, often with fatal consequences. William H. Kepler of Company C fell ill with typhoid and "complained mostly of his head whenever he raised up he took light headed and could not stand without help." After a brief stay at the Patent Office, Kepler was transferred to Kalorama Hospital, or the Eruptive Hospital as it was then called, where men suffering from smallpox and measles were quarantined. He died there of measles on October 19th. George W. Ribble of Company K suffered through a series of diseases—typhoid fever, measles, rheumatism, and smallpox before his death on January 12, 1862.[20]

James W. Lloyd of Company G was one sufferer who was sent off to Kalorama after developing measles. He described the situation in a letter to his mother:

> they will not allow any contagious disease to be in the hospitals. there is a hospital where they send all those that have the measles or small pox. the hospital is crowded to excess. . . . I was pretty near starved at the measles hospital. We got nothing to eat but dry bread & tea not even any butter on the bread.

Private Lloyd was overjoyed when he was returned to the Indiana Hospital. He assured his mother, "I have plenty to eat here & that of the best kind. the city folks are very kind. they bring in grapes & lemons oranges & give to the sick."

Although Dr. Green applied for James Lloyd's discharge, his patient died before the paperwork could be completed. The surgeon felt obligated to inform Lloyd's mother of her son's death:

> It becomes my paneful duty to inform you of the decease of your son J W Lloyd. he departed this life this morning in this hospital. . . . Allow me to offer you my heart felt simpathy in this your great Affliction. I trust you will have strength and fortitude given you to bear your loss with resignation. your son was verry low with typhoid fever when I took charge of the hospital in sept but he ralied from that and was able to be about until the last ten days he had kept his bed. he had had a verry troublesome cough ever since recovered from the fever . . . your son had every posable atention and kindness shown him during his last illness. I think the immidiate cause of his death was an affusion of fluids about his hart with extensive softning and braking down of the left lung. he will be decently buried and his grave marked

The attentive physician also enclosed the forms necessary for his mother to submit a claim for James Lloyd's back pay and bounty.[21]

When patients succumbed to disease at the Patent Office, it was the painful duty of friends to relate details of their death, often a difficult task under the circumstances. Joseph Slack of Company C wrote of "the loss of 1 of our party from home":

> Eli Abernathy brethed his last at the pattent office hospital on the 5th inst. his disease was the typhoid fever. he was sick about 4 weeks and he was over there about 3 weeks. we never got to go and see him at all. wee tried to get a pass to go and see him but we could not. wee heard the night before he died that he was not expected to live through the night and next morning the boys tried to get a pass to go and see him but they could not get 1. there is 1 of our Co just come here that saw him die. he says he died very easy.

Captains diligently reported deaths in their companies and requested that hometown newspapers publish their names, along with expressions of deep sympathy to surviving family members. Grieving comrades collected money, personal effects, blankets, and clothing "that is fit to send" for shipment home. Despite the wishes of dying soldiers and their families, most remains were buried at the Soldiers Home instead of being sent home. Some bodies, like that of John L. Keller of Company G, were immediately embalmed and shipped back to Indiana. A few others, like James Franklin of Company E, were buried at the Soldiers Home "until cold weather," then were disinterred and taken home by family members.[22]

The only bright spot among the depressing letters about disease, death, and burials was a constant reassurance sent to grieving families about the care given patients at the Indiana Hospital. According to Christopher Starbuck of Company C:

> You must rest easy on this for all the boys that have gone to the hospital are all well cared for and they all praise it when they come back to Camp. Eli Abernathy W. H. Kepler and D. B. Johnson were all as well cared for as if they were at home. They hire the best women in the city for nurses to wait on the sick soldiers there.

In conclusion, Starbuck stated bluntly, "The hospital at the Patent Office is the best hospital at Washington or in any eastern city." Captain Valentine Jacobs agreed with these sentiments and wrote, "While we have had sickness we also had the best conducted hospital in the United States, set apart almost exclusively for the 19th Indiana."[23]

Dr. John N. Green, who took on not only the medical duties but the hospital administration as well, was responsible for this efficient management. Governor Morton had dispatched Dr. Green in mid-September with orders to report to the 19th Indiana and serve as an assistant to Dr. Woods. But upon Green's arrival in Washington, Secretary Smith advised him that the sick in the Patent Office were in dire need. After being made aware of the situation, Medical Director Charles Tripler agreed with Smith, overruled Governor Morton and assigned Green to the Indiana Hospital with Special Orders No. 82, Headquarters, Army of the Potomac. Despite a dispatch from Morton, dated September 27th, directing him to immediately report to the regiment and assist Surgeon Woods, Green would remain at the Patent Office.[24]

On October 16th Dr. Green reported his efforts on behalf of the Indiana boys to Governor Morton:

> I now have 110 patients in hospital, all in a fair way for recovery. I have returned to duty since I came here 97. We receive about as many as we return every week. I have had the whole care of the hospital and sick on my hands with no help except such as convalescents could give all the time. I have labored unceasingly for the good of the poor afflicted boys and trust my labors have not been in vain.

He also pointed out that he still had not received his commission, a document that was needed before he could receive his army pay.[25]

One of Dr. Green's major problems was with those soldiers detailed to act as nurses. The men were often selected while still convalescing from their own bouts of fever and many proved unable or unwilling to help their sick comrades. Acting as if he exercised an independent command, Green wrote directly to Seth Williams, General McClellan's adjutant general, on November 14th:

> I desire a change made in the detail from the 19th Ind. Vol. for service in this hospital. Two of those detailed proved so inefficient that I was compelled to return them to the regiment. One other is lying very low with general paralysis with slight hope of recovery.

Two days later Green again wrote to General Williams with yet another complaint:

> I desire private Fred Meyer Company G 19th Ind Vol, acting as nurse in Indiana Hospital to be returned to his regiment and David Dunlop Company F same regiment detailed in his place. Cause habitual intoxication on the part of Meyer.

This second letter was emphatically endorsed by Williams, "Make the detail."[26]

Another of Dr. Green's major problems was his superior officer. Colonel Meredith endured what he saw as a series of challenges to his authority by his new assistant surgeon, but finally complained to brigade headquarters:

> Dr. J. N. Green Ast Surgeon of the 19th Regt. Ind'a Vol. now in charge of the Ind'a Hospital Washington D.C. does not furnish me with a notice of deaths of the members of this Regt. and the Commandants of Companies have nothing official to report from.
>
> Many irregularities have occured in his reports. Men have been detailed by order of Genl McClellan for duty at that Hospital and afterwards granted furloughs without my Knowledge and others detailed in their places. I would most respectfully request that these irregularities be corrected.

Meredith's letter went from King to McDowell to McClellan to Tripler and finally to Green, who responded as if on trial at a court-martial:

> In response to the first specification of Col Meredith I reply that since I have understood it to be my duty to make official reports to the Commanders of Regiments and companies of deaths occurring in hospital I have invariably done so.
>
> I do not know what irregularities he refers to as he specifies none.
>
> In relation to granting furloughs to men detailed for service in the Indiana Hospital I reply that I have granted but two and they were approved by Adj't General Williams and I did not understand it to be my duty to report the fact to the Col Commanding or to ask his permission to grant the furloughs.
>
> I have never detailed or had detailed a man from any regiment to serve in place of those absent on furlough.

Colonel Meredith's attitude apparently confirmed some of Surgeon Calvin Woods's advice to Governor Morton that he send a surgeon "as *corrupt* and *treacherous* as Sol himself," telling his old friend, "If a Physician in this Regt does not pander to all the Cols treachery, he will be opposed in everything."[27]

Despite its problems, the overall success of the Indiana Hospital led to a widening of its sphere of operations. Invitations to send in their sick were sent out to Lieutenant Colonel Scott Carter of the 1st Indiana Cavalry, Colonel Pleasant Hackleman of the 16th Indiana and Colonel Silas Colgrove of the 27th Indiana. The distinct Hoosier character of the hospital continued into November, with only one threat to its existence. Richard M. Hall related how an unnamed, but influential Indianapolis physician attempted to remove the sick Hoosiers to regular hospitals under the guise of an order from the War Department. The doctor had gone so far as to take down names of patients when he was confronted by Elizabeth Smith. While Mrs. Smith argued and stalled, her husband, Caleb, hurried off and persuaded Simon Cameron to countermand the order. After listening to a brief description of the Hoosier relief effort, Secretary Cameron commended Smith's employees at the Interior Department, then entered into an agreement recognizing the Indiana Hospital as one "for the *exclusive* benefit of Indiana men."[28]

By mid-November the Indiana Hospital began to lose its distinctive status when patients from other states were admitted as beds became available. On November 16th, the *Washington Evening Star* listed a total of eighty sick at the Patent Office with sixty-one being Colonel Meredith's men and the remainder representing other Indiana regiments, the 7th Pennsylvania Reserves and both regiments of Berdan's United States Sharpshooters. On November 27th, Dr. Green reported that he "Had quite a rush yesterday from the 1st Mich Cavelry & Berdans Sharpshooters." On that same day Private Austin Conyers, a soldier from Company C detailed as a nurse, described the hospital staff:

> Thare is twenty in my ward and ninty two sick in bed and a bout eight men for nurses four woman four cooks and two Docters and three negros for waiters. That constitutes the hospital of the ninteenth

The Hoosier institution was eventually renamed the United States General Hospital at the Patent Office and was enlarged to accommodate nearly a thousand patients. Secretary Caleb Smith later reported on the effect that this temporary hospital had on operations in the Interior Department, stating, "The use of these rooms for hospital purposes has been the cause of much inconvenience to the Patent Office, and to every other bureau in the department. This inconvenience has, however, been cheerfully submitted to, in view of the benefits conferred upon the suffering soldiers."[29]

Despite their misfortune at being ill, patients at the Indiana Hospital had an enjoyable holiday season. According to one soldier:

> I must not forget to tell you that we sick and convalescent soldiers had a "happy" if not "merry Christmas." Mrs. Smith, and several of her lady friends from Indiana contributed the material, and Miss Hall, our matron, and her corps of assistants, under the direction of our good surgeon, Dr. Green, attended to the "cuisine" and distributing of the good things furnished.

Newspapers and magazines relieved the boredom of confinement, while toilet articles, jellies, preserved fruit, farina, and other delicacies were passed out among the appreciative soldiers. One demoralized newcomer carried into the Patent Office just before Christmas was astonished by the upbeat atmosphere:

> At sight of the rows of neat cots and clean linen, with the comfortable and cleanly surroundings, hope revived and, as I looked into the contented faces of my fellow invalids, I knew they must be the recipients of that "home" care and sympathy so seldom enjoyed by soldiers, and the lack of which adds so much to their life of hardships. I soon learned from my comrades, who represented several of the loyal States, that the institution was under the special patronage of Mrs. Secretary Smith, who visited them almost daily, and supplied deficiencies from the hospital store.

Many articles for distribution were consigned directly to Secretary Smith by aid societies, but when stocks occasionally ran low, Smith or Judge Kilgore or some other public-spirited citizen made up the difference.[30]

Probably the most commonly seen male faces in the hospital belonged to Judge David Kilgore and Dr. John N. Green. From the very first day, Judge Kilgore had been a regular visitor to the sick, spending his private funds every day on chickens, soups, and broths. One convalescent happily remembered his efforts, writing, "Not a day passes that his portly person and smiling countenance is not seen among the sick, cheering them and strengthening them at the same time, with his never-to-be-forgotten bucket of chicken soup." One observer declared that Kilgore's devotion deserved "infinite praise," while another man wrote hopefully, "Such a true friend to the afflicted will not, I trust, go unrewarded by the people of Indiana." Appreciation for Dr. Green's dedication to his patients took a more tangible form. On January 11, 1862, Steward John P. Butler, on behalf of current and former patients in the hospital, presented the astonished doctor with "a costly and magnificent dress sword," a token of the esteem in which he was held by all associated with the Indiana Hospital.[31]

While great praise was due Dr. Green for his work among the fever-ravaged soldiers, even more credit was due the ladies of Washington who bore the burden of caring for their fellow Hoosiers. In summing up the operations of the Indiana Hospital, one Washington resident wrote in June of 1862:

> Woman, ever forward in noble and good works, led off. Mrs. Sec'y Smith, Mrs. Hedrick, her sister, and Mrs. Holloway, were the heroines, the ever present, the ever beautiful spirits in this benevolent work. but all labored with devoted energies, doing good and visiting the sick ones.

The patronage of Elizabeth Smith, who visited the boys almost daily, was an essential ingredient in the Indiana relief effort, as one patient pointed out:

> My own experience leads me to infer that Mrs. Smith's visits not only procured for us materials, but contributed to incite better care, on the part of the attendants, by her example. For if Mrs. Smith, high in position, thought it worth her while to interest herself in the soldier's welfare, there was honor in their task. This reasoning secured us extra care from nurses who, otherwise, are more than ordinarily tidy and attentive.

Jane Holloway was also conspicuous, being singled out as "assiduous and devoted in her attentions to the sick."[32]

Recognition should also be given to Maria Hall for her determination to assist the sick, despite many obstacles placed in her path. In the words of one admirer:

> The surgeons afforded her few or no facilities for her work; and evidently expected that her whim of nursing would soon be given over. Then came the general order for the removal of volunteer nurses from the hospitals; this she evaded by enrolling herself as a nurse, and drawing army pay, which she distributed to the men. For nearly a year she remained in this position, without command, with much hard work to do, and no recognition of it from any official source; but though the situation was not in respect agreeable, there was a consciousness of usefulness, of service of the Master in it to sustain her; and while under her gentle ministrations cleanliness took the place of filth, order of disorder, and profanity was banished because "the lady did not like it," it was also her privilege occasionally to lead the wanderer from God back to the Savior he had deserted, and to point the sinner back to the "Lamb of God that taketh away the sins of the world."

In the summer of 1862 Miss Hall joined the Hospital Transport Service aboard the *Daniel Webster,* where she applied on a larger scale many of the lessons learned while nursing Hoosier boys in the Patent Office.[33]

Richard M. Hall, a member of the Executive Committee, realized exactly who should receive the credit for the success of the Indiana Hospital:

> Wherever humanity suffers women like merciful angels are found, and beside these poor emaciated, fever-scorched soldiers, they stand unweariedly through the long hours, soothing with their hands, and cheering by words and smiles these afflicted defenders of our Nation's unity.

Eliza Woolsey Howland remembered with obvious satisfaction how she was able to aid one poor man:

I remember rushing about from apothecary to apothecary, in the lower part of the city, one Sunday afternoon, to get, in a great hurry, mustard, to help bring life into a poor Irishman, who called me Betty in his delirium, and, to our surprise, got well, went home, and at once married the Betty we had saved him for.

The presence of female nurses threw "a cheerful gleam across the otherwise lonely hours of these poor sick ones," leading one patient to proclaim, "May God bless them all!" Long after the crisis had passed, Hoosiers in Colonel Meredith's regiment held dear the memory of their friends at the Indiana Hospital. When some of the volunteer nurses chanced to visit the regiment in the summer of 1862, Henry Marsh recorded the event in his diary:

The ladies were well received by the boys as many of them have been under their care. They are noble true women—women whose names ought to be remembered in History, they surely will be in the hearts of the soldiers.[34]

6

Arlington Heights

While ailing Hoosiers languished in the Patent Office and other Washington hospitals, Colonel Meredith's regiment settled into its new camp between the Arlington House and Fort Craig. The Arlington estate, named for an older family property on the Eastern Shore, had been purchased in 1776 by John Parke Custis, a stepson of George Washington. Upon John's death, the estate passed to his only son, George Washington Parke Custis, who had been adopted by George and Martha Washington. Shortly after the death of Martha Washington, work on the mansion began on the brow of a hill overlooking the District of Columbia. The house was built of stuccoed brick, painted buff and white, with an imposing portico that boasted eight massive Doric columns. Stones for the foundation and timber for framing came from the surrounding slopes, while bricks were manufactured by slaves from native red clay. The Western troops discovered that the estate was still occupied by about thirty-five slaves, one of whom was eighty years old and could distinctly remember serving Washington. Another slave, a coachman, claimed to have lived at Arlington for sixty-five years, but had never gone farther than across the river to the capital.[1]

Upon the death of George Washington Parke Custis, Arlington House and its surrounding acreage passed to his daughter, Mary Anne Randolph Custis, who had married Robert Edward Lee in 1831. Lee had recently resigned his commission as colonel of the 1st United States Cavalry and was now a rebel general in western Virginia. General Lee's wife and children were refugees and in their flight had left behind many relics relating to the Washingtons. Some of those historic artifacts had been stolen long before the mansion was appropriated by General Irvin McDowell and used as his division headquarters. Colonel Meredith's boys joined in the hunt for souvenirs and Jeff Crull sent a memento home to his mother:

this Leaf is of ov a picture frame in genarl Lees house. it was on a fancy
frame that hung in the hall. i was on guard at the house. i went in to get
a flag to put up at sun rise. i got a gun of the guard and Bayneted it of.
it has hung up in the hall fer three or four years.

The historic nature of this mansion and a constant throng of officers kept
serious vandals at bay, so that the residence escaped being torn up or burnt
down like other Virginia properties.[2]

On October 15th, General McDowell's division was composed of
three infantry brigades. General Erasmus D. Keyes commanded the 22nd,
24th, 30th, and 84th New York regiments, while General James S. Wadsworth
led another brigade of New Yorkers, the 12th, 21st, 23rd, and 35th
regiments. General Rufus King's four Western regiments formed McDowell's
third brigade. The 2nd New York Cavalry and two Regular batteries completed the division organization. The 12th New York, 2nd New York
Cavalry, and artillery were soon transferred, but the remaining New Yorkers
served alongside King's Western boys until their terms of service expired.[3]

Drills, inspections and reviews left McDowell's soldiers little free
time during the fall of 1861. A Badger volunteer remembered:

> Every day of this period was full of active duty. There were guard mount
> in the mornings, company drill in the forenoons, regimental drill in the
> afternoons, and dress parade in the evenings. There were picket duty at
> the front; brigade and division drills and frequent reviews.

Marching to the tune of fife and drum, General King's brigade marched daily
down toward the Potomac, where the four regiments practiced brigade drill
on a large, level field. The men were maneuvered from place to place by their
commanders, always accompanied by the "Chorus of Sergeants":

COLONEL — Column forward, guide right, march.
CHORUS OF SERGEANTS — Close up, boys, close up.
COLONEL — By the right flank, march.
CHORUS OF SERGEANTS — Close up, close up, boys, *close* up.
GEN. KING — On head of column, close *en masse*.
CHORUS OF SERGEANTS — Close up, boys, Damn you, close up.
GEN. KING — On first Battalion, deploy column.
CHORUS OF SERGEANTS — Close up! close up! close up!

This irritating chatter by the file-closers became most offensive when the
boys were drilled while loaded down with knapsacks, a process designed to
harden the soldiers for active campaigning.[4]

Reviews by the generals were the most taxing duty, since much individual preparation had to be done beforehand, such as brushing clothing, blacking shoes, polishing brass, and cleaning muskets, the latter especially time-consuming because they rusted badly following every rain. One of King's soldiers described the brigade review held on October 9th:

> Yesterday we had our Brigade reviewed by Gen. McDowell; we were marched to the field about 10:30 A.M., and drawn up in line of battle, the 6th Wisconsin and 19th Indiana and, behind them, the 2d and 7th Wisconsin. Gen. McDowell first reviewed us in line of battle, in rear open order; then the columns were formed and we were marched in review past the Staff, and returned to our post, where our arms were inspected by the Aids, and our clothes by the General.

Jeff Crull offered a description of another brigade review, this one held on October 18th:

> it was the pretiest sight i ever saw to see the regiments maneuvering on double quick and to see the genarls and aids galoping over the field and to see the glisning barls and bright bayenet of the men and butens and belt plates that glisen in the sun. it was a nice sight to see the Brigade as thay wheeld in to companys on double quick to pass the reviewing oficers. it looked like solid walls of steel. our company looked nice and done well. Thay done the best i ever saw them. *every* man had the step and the line could not be made any straiter.

General McClellan was under great pressure to advance against the rebels, but he refused to do so until his army was thoroughly trained, thereby avoiding another Bull Run disaster. Corporal Crull's comments indicate that McClellan's policy was building confidence within his army.[5]

A succession of generals, cabinet members (especially Secretary of State William Seward and Secretary of the Interior Caleb Smith), and foreign visitors dropped by to view the troops on Arlington Heights. Prominent among the distinguished observers were Prince de Joinville, son of King Louis Phillipe of France, and his two nephews, the Comte de Paris and the Duc de Chartres, both sons of the Duc d'Orleans. Prince Felix Salm-Salm, a Prussian officer who wore a uniform "highly adorned with decorations and gold lace," occasionally ventured over from General Louis Blenker's division. While these European noblemen rendered important service as staff officers, King's boys were unimpressed by royalty and dismissed the lot of them as "McClellan's French Ducks" and "Prince Slam Slam."[6]

Some of the American "noblemen" in Captain Dudley's company lost their status shortly after arriving at Arlington. Corporal Jeff Crull explained the circumstances:

i have been acting as Sergant for two weeks. there is one of our sergants discharged. he could not stand to march. there is three of our coperels put Back in the ranks fer geting drunk. it served them right. we dont want any Non commised oficers that get drunk and we wont have them.

Crull replaced Sergeant Ed Gorgas, who had been sent off to the Indiana Hospital and would soon be discharged for insanity. The corporals who had imbibed too heavily were probably Noah Craig, John Thornburg, and Horace Wharton. After being under arrest for several weeks, two of the corporals were reduced to private, Craig on October 17th and Wharton on November 1st. Thornburg was probably the third culprit, but he escaped punishment when he came down with a serious case of fever and was sent off to the Indiana Hospital.[7]

General King's brigade was strengthened by the arrival of Battery B, 4th United States Artillery in late October. The battery had arrived in Washington on October 13th after a long journey from its previous station in Utah. The artillery unit, although it was woefully short of its authorized strength, was quickly assigned to McDowell's division. Eager recruits had flocked to volunteer organizations raised locally, but enlistments in the Regular Army companies had virtually ceased. The first priority was to fill those depleted ranks, so McDowell authorized Captain John Gibbon to select volunteers from infantry regiments in his division. The captain picked his men after carefully observing "their bearing and appearance," asking a question or two when in doubt about an individual. Gibbon's non-commissioned officers were soon inspecting and drilling over 100 new artillerymen.[8]

At full strength, Battery B was authorized four commissioned officers, an orderly sergeant, a quartermaster sergeant, six sergeants who were designated "chiefs of piece," six corporals acting as gunners, six corporals assigned as "chiefs of caisson," five artificers (mechanics), two buglers, one guidon, and 120 cannoneers and drivers. Gibbon's battery was outfitted with six 12-pounder Napoleon guns, officially designated "light twelves," which were bronze, muzzleloading smoothbores. Each gun and its carriage, weighing a combined 3,820 pounds, were towed behind a limber pulled by a team of six horses. Six-horse teams also pulled the twelve caissons and traveling forge, while eight horses pulled the battery wagon. Officers, sergeants, artificers, buglers, and guidon were all mounted on saddle horses.[9]

In addition to instructing his new recruits from the infantry regiments, Captain John Gibbon was responsible for training volunteer batteries in McDowell's division. To familiarize new officers and enlisted men with firing loaded guns, Gibbon created a firing range twenty feet wide and one-half mile long in a nearby tract of forest. Near the end of this improvised artillery range a large pine tree was left standing as a target. Each day a couple of gun crews were ordered out to fire a smoothbore cannon at the pine tree. All went well for the gunners from Gibbon's Battery B, George A. Gerrish's New Hampshire battery and George W. Durell's Pennsylvania battery.

When it came time for Captain J. Albert Monroe's Battery D, 1st Rhode Island Light Artillery, John Gibbon, the professional artillery instructor, learned a valuable lesson. Captain Monroe furnished the story:

> At that time I had rifled Parrott guns, and one day, in compliance with Captain Gibbon's orders, I took out one of my guns, he accompanying me, and we commenced blazing away at the tree. We observed the effect of the fire, discussed its effectiveness, scientifically considering whether it were better to elevate or depress the piece a little more or not, and so on, when we heard all at once, "What the devil are you trying to do? Stop that or I will cut you to pieces; you have been firing right into my camp." Looking behind us we found a squadron of cavalry, whose commanding officer had thus summarily ordered us to cease our practice. Of course we stopped, for the idea of being cut to pieces was not a healthy one.

Captains Gibbon and Monroe discreetly waited until afternoon before riding around the timber to the cavalry camp where they discovered that "our shot had struck plump into their drill ground, which adjoined their camp, and where they were drilling at the time of our firing." Artillery practice by the long-range rifled cannon in McDowell's division was thereafter conducted with an eye to keeping peace between the cannoneers and their neighbors.[10]

Such mistakes seem humorous now, but many of the new officers were making far too many mistakes and were obviously unsuited to lead troops. Despite his impressive political pedigree, Colonel Sol Meredith had no previous military experience. Although no one doubted his devotion to the cause or his zeal as colonel, Long Sol was just not developing into a competent military officer.

Surgeon Calvin Woods offered his assessment of Meredith's ability in a private letter to Governor Morton on October 2nd:

> Our Col has no practical Sense. The officers have all found it out. I knew it before, so did You. Lieut Col is a Good man, or we would have all gone to Sticks before now. Bad Administration is seen and felt throughout all the Regt. our Col unfortunately wants to attend to all departments down to the Smallest minutiae. Of course he fails of necessity.

The physician continued his candid observations in another letter to Morton on October 20th:

> You would be Startled to hear the *officers* and *Soldiers* talk about "old Sol." It Seems that he is about being promoted to a Brigadier. If he is not

there will Soon be a petition Signed by the whole Rgt. for him to resign. Two officers tell me to night Since I began this letter that it cannot be staved off much longer. The Regt one and all have now the most contemptible opinions of the Col. Pride and fear together have detered the men from Saying or doing anything So far, but I fear it cannot long continue. If you could hear the captains laugh and talk about him, You would think a *change* was imminent.

Surgeon Woods put up with Meredith's inept leadership until March 24, 1862, when he resigned his commission, citing "Personal considerations." Governor Morton quickly appointed him an agent of the Indiana Sanitary Commission, in which capacity he performed many valuable services for Hoosier soldiers and their families. Calvin Woods published his *Reminiscences of the War* in 1880 and died in 1907.[11]

Enlisted men also exhibited "a lack of confidence in our Colonels Millitary qualifications" and the rumor about camp was that General McDowell had urged Meredith to resign. The company officers were especially disgusted with Colonel Meredith's performance. Lieutenant William Orr wrote bluntly that Colonel Meredith was "notoriously unfit to command," explaining that "every day he attempts to command the Regt on Brigade drill, he exposes him self to the contempt of the officers and becomes a laughing stock to his men." In order to rid the regiment of its colonel, his company officers devised a plan to get Sol promoted. Colonel Meredith, his staff and six captains, backed by Governor Morton, made an assault on the War Department, but the delegation was informed that Indiana already had enough generals. Sol took the news hard and "plainly manifested his disappointment by his bitterness to all parties." Then the officers flirted with a plan to resign in a body, but that scheme also failed, leaving the regiment "with prospect for disaster."[12]

In order to remove persons unsuited for command, Congress enacted legislation, approved July 22, 1861, that provided for the establishment of boards of examination to inquire into the fitness of volunteer officers. General James S. Wadsworth was president of a board that examined officers from King's brigade during mid-October. The aim was to remove incompetent and incorrigible officers, but many good men had to suffer through the "fiery ordeal" of examination before the onset of winter.[13]

Six officers from the 19th Indiana resigned before the end of the year. First Lieutenant Benjamin F. Reed, Company F, was the first to go. His letter of resignation, dated September 19th at Camp Advance, read:

My domestic matters at home are of such a nature as to require my immediate attention in order to avoid considerable suffering. I regret

the matter extremely, but it is absolutely necessary for the well being of
my family that I devote my attention unto them at once.

In addition to his official duties, Reed had acted as correspondent for the
Indianapolis Daily Journal, so his departure meant the Hoosiers lost their
best means of informing Indiana citizens of their adventures.[14]

 This "domestic matters at home" excuse was the best way out for
unqualified officers facing the formidable threat of General Wadsworth's
board of examination. Four officers—Captain John Johnson (I), and
Lieutenants Henry Vandegrift (D), Theodore Hudnut (H), and James L.
Kilgore (A)—cited "domestic" considerations when offering their resignations and all were discharged under Special Orders 98, Headquarters,
Army of the Potomac, dated October 11, 1861. Kilgore, however, was
determined to serve and he reenlisted in Company A, this time as a private,
on February 1, 1862. His second enlistment ended with a serious attack of
rheumatism and the congressman's son left the regiment for good on April
23, 1862. One other officer, Lieutenant Frederick Hale of Company D,
resigned at Fort Craig on November 28th, but he blamed "business affairs"
for his departure.[15]

 One officer who was in no danger of forcible resignation was Quartermaster James S. Drum. He was a native of Cincinnati who had moved to
Indianapolis with his family when he was just a boy. After receiving an
education in the city schools, Drum became a merchant and enrolled in the
National Guards, a capital city militia unit. His first military appointment was
Commissary at Camp Morton, but he longed for active duty and was offered
a post in the 19th Indiana. Drum was promoted to captain in the Commissary Department in 1863 and was assigned to Nicholasville, Kentucky, where
he died of disease. Indiana boys did not want for food or clothing while under
Lieutenant Drum's care. One correspondent described the regimental quartermaster department:

> I am writing now surrounded by blankets, shoes, socks (thick woolen
> ones), drawers, shirts, pants, caps, haversacks, canteens and all the
> necessaries in the clothing line except overcoats, and one thousand and
> ten of them are on the way to us. The next tent to me is full of sugar,
> coffee, salt beef, pork, beans, rice, hominy, molasses, and to which may
> be added fresh beef twice a week. The men have so much clothing that
> General McDowell talks of taking some of the blankets away from them.

Despite Drum's best efforts, the 19th Indiana wore a hodgepodge of Federal
and State uniforms for several months. At one October review, "They were
dressed, some in blue coats, some in gray; some in overcoats and some
without; some with leggins and some without." The regiment's appearance

6. Thomas Jefferson Crull.
From the Collection of Thomas R. Pratt.

led General McDowell to exclaim that "a look at the 19th Indiana would put Hogarth in ecstacies."[16]

Lieutenant Drum soon after issued the Hoosiers a "new suit of blue" that consisted of caps, coats, and pants, the latter "made of very thick heavy goods." Each man also had two shirts of white flannel, two pairs of canton flannel drawers, and two pairs of socks, actually knee-high stockings that were held up by garters. To complete the military outfit, Colonel Meredith's boys were issued "thick heavy canvass legings."[17]

Sergeant Jeff Crull listed some of the government items that Quartermaster Drum had issued to each of the boys: uniform, knapsack, gray blanket with stripes, blue blanket with stripes, rubber blanket, "blue and Big and Heavey and warm" overcoat, cartridge box, shoulder strap, two belts, musket, haversack, and canteen. He then enumerated those personal items that added to his load:

> i have two combs a looking glass a testament one prayer book three novels one mony purse three pocket hancrceif some needles and thried some butens a guard role Book a Port folio a lot of paper envelops etc.

It was little wonder that the sergeant would remark, "i have got used to carying an army Brigade Wagon on my Back fer the Knap sack."[18]

While the soldiers staggered about feeling like army wagons, their officers were overwhelmed by miles of red tape, a veritable maze of which enveloped each regiment. One officer who served with the Army of the Potomac later described the various papers that found their way to a regimental headquarters during the war:

> Here are, to begin with, orders—no end of orders; orders from the War Department, from army headquarters, from division, brigade and regimental headquarters; here are infinite reports, returns, requisitions, receipts, abstracts, vouchers, blanks in duplicate, triplicate and quadruplicate; here are applications "approved and respectfully forwarded," applications returned with disapproval and endorsements of all sorts; here are details for courts-martial, courts of inquiry and military commissions; here are endless details for guard, for picket, for police, for the pioneer corps, for the ambulance corps, for the quartermaster's, commissary and ordnance departments, details as orderlies, guards and provost-guards at the several headquarters, details for fatigue and working parties; an occasional detail for recruiting service (a rare and soft thing); leaves of absence and furloughs granted, ditto refused; here are circulars, certificates, discharges, descriptive lists of recruits, descriptive lists of deserters, inventories of the effects of deceased soldiers, abstracts of unserviceable ordnance stores, boards to assess value of officers' private horses, pay rolls, muster rolls, muster in and muster out rolls; and here are inspection reports, criticizing one regiment for unsanitary condition, another for neglect of military courtesy in saluting, a third for want of schools of tactical instruction.

Literally tons of forms generated by this military routine were transported hither and yon by thousands of staff officers, orderlies, and couriers.[19]

7

Headquarters Guard

In mid-November King's brigade, under the immediate supervision of General McDowell, was selected to prepare the grounds for McClellan's grand review near Munson's Hill. In order to judge the suitability of the grounds, McDowell marched all of his brigades out to the field, actually several contiguous farms, and held a division review on November 18th. After marching his men back and forth over this 1,000 acre tract, McDowell saw that improvements were necessary. King's men returned to the field on the following day in order to clear away "trees, fences, barns, secession tenements, etc." The hard labor was eased somewhat by canteens of beer obtained from Germans in Blenker's division who were camped along the road to Munson's Hill.[1]

A startling incident occurred after police work on the parade field had been completed. A brisk skirmish on the picket line prompted McDowell to order King's brigade to reinforce the threatened point. But there was one slight problem—*the entire brigade was without ammunition*! Because the arduous work at Munson's Hill was well within the Federal lines, the colonels had given their boys "tacit permission" to lighten the load by removing their cartridges. The colonels were forced to admit their transgression to General King, who appeared somewhat displeased. McDowell, on the other hand, stormed about "in a great rage, and ordered the brigade to quarters with a sharp rebuke." As the Western regiments marched back to camp in disgrace, a brigade of New Yorkers selected in their stead trotted past "simply swearing mad."[2]

On November 20th, General McClellan staged the grandest review ever held on the North American continent. Seventy thousand soldiers assembled for the great event, "one of which Caesar or Alexander need not to have been ashamed." A Delaware County boy wrote that "the North winds blew with terrible fury from morn to dewy eve, the skies assumed a dreary leaden hue, the sun was a masked battery." King's men had eaten breakfast before daylight and were first to arrive; they watched as the field became "one living, moving mass of bristling steel." Finally it was time to begin:

> About twelve o'clock President Lincoln and his Cabinet, Gen. McClellan and his staff, arrived upon the field, when a hundred cannon thundered forth in flame and smoke their greeting to the Chief. McClellan and the President then rode along the lines, greeted every-where with loud and enthusiastic cheers, save when they passed the troops of Indiana and Wisconsin, where profound silence evinced the respect of the Western legions.

One soldier in the 2nd Wisconsin wrote that the brigade "stood motionless and gave no shout . . . like the pines and oaks of the Northwest."[3]

After the dignitaries had ridden along the lines, they took up a position on a small knoll, watching the troops pass in review for over three hours. Soldiers marched in close order in column by division, or the width of two companies, through stiff mud that had been churned to the consistency of kneaded bread dough by the time King's brigade took its turn. One of the Hoosiers bragged, "The 19th marched with the precision of veterans, and were highly complimented by Gen. McClellan." General King sent a note to Meredith, praising the 19th for "their splendid and soldierly bearing" during the review. Everyone tried to describe the pageantry of McClellan's review, but most of the enlisted men would have agreed with the private who confessed, "It was probably a grand thing, but I could not see much of it, and my knapsack endeavored to make me think it was not so good after all." Even *Harper's Weekly* and *Frank Leslie's* could not accurately capture the spectacle, one soldier commenting on the engravings in those papers, "They resemble it as much as Stanley's Gallery of Aborigines in the Smithsonian Institute would."[4]

As mentioned previously, individual, company, and battalion drill in the 19th Indiana had been conducted according to Hardee's *Rifle and Light Infantry Tactics*. This system of instruction was supplemented by two other manuals: George B. McClellan's *Manual of Bayonet Exercise* and Henry Coppee's *The Field Manual of Evolutions of the Line*. King's brigade also simulated combat by firing blank cartridges while arrayed in line of battle. One such exercise occurred on December 7th after a review. The Western regiments were drawn up facing toward Washington, "each regiment firing in succession from right to left; after firing a few rounds by regiment, two or three were fired by right and left wing, then by company." Although the Wisconsin regiments fired well together, Colonel Meredith's boys were a bit sub-par, "their battalion firing sounded more like firing by file."[5]

A series of sham battles in December completed the instruction process for King's Western brigade. One participant described one such event:

> The cavalry charge was the most imposing, although the artillery is by no means uninteresting. The Parrott and rifled guns sputtered forth flames and smoke with a wicked spite and made one believe almost that there was a real enemy in front. The enemy moved in squares through brush and briers, trailing arms when they could not march upright. Then all reducing squares and forming in line, when we loaded and fired at will, which the boys enjoy more than any other part of their exercises.

Sergeant Jeff Crull remarked on a similar sham battle that "it was nice" but then added, "We would rather that it was in reality."[6]

Some of the boys overloaded their muskets to create more noise during these sham battles, often using as many as six cartridges at a time. One soldier in the 2nd Wisconsin burst his gun by doing so and luckily shattered only his hand and not his head. This accident was just the latest in a long series of injuries that occurred after assembling thousands of young men and giving them all firearms. Accidental wounds were common in King's brigade. A young Norwegian in the 2nd Wisconsin was leaning on his musket one day, with the muzzle placed under his armpit, when it discharged through his shoulder. In Company E of the 19th Indiana, Frank Ethell was accidentally shot in the thigh by a bullet from the revolver of Isaac W. Witemyre, his first sergeant. After three such injuries from carelessly handled revolvers in the 7th Wisconsin, all pistols and bowie knives (looking so fierce in those early photographs) were taken away from the boys so they would not hurt themselves.[7]

Company B had its own share of accidental injuries. The first instance occurred on the night of September 4th, near Chain Bridge, when James Grunden's musket accidentally discharged while he was standing on picket guard with Jacob Hunt. After the excitement had died down, it was discovered that Grunden had shot off the forefinger of his right hand, a wound that would prevent him from ever using a musket. Surgeon Woods dressed the injury and sent him to the Indiana Hospital. After his wound healed, Grunden returned to the regiment, but he was assigned to drive an ambulance because of his disability. On October 15th, Bartley Allen became the second of Dudley's company to shoot off a finger, this time the middle finger of his right hand, an injury that eventually led to his discharge. Bowie knives were also dangerous in camp. Captain Dudley remembered how George Beetley was peacefully standing at the sutler's tent when he was suddenly stabbed in the back by a fellow soldier who had mistaken him for another man. By the end of 1861, the soldiers in the 19th Indiana had inflicted more wounds on themselves than they had on the rebels.[8]

On November 17th the Ordnance Department issued weapons to Colonel Meredith's regiment. This new arm was the United States Rifle Musket, Model 1861, commonly referred to as the Springfield Rifled Musket. Effective at a range of 500 yards, this .58 caliber musket was the basic infantry weapon of the Civil War and could be fired three times per minute. A complete set of accouterments had been issued the previous week, so Colonel Meredith's regiment was now armed and equipped better than the Wisconsin regiments in King's brigade. Old muskets and accouterments that had been issued at Camp Morton were boxed up and returned to Indiana. When the material was uncrated in Indianapolis, officers found that much of the equipment was worthless. Some muskets were incomplete; leather boxes and straps were either old or worn out or unserviceable. Outdated when first issued to Meredith's regiment, these weapons and accouterments could not hold up during active service and the new Springfields were a welcome change.[9]

There would be no campaigning until spring of the following year, so the Hoosiers began to prepare for cold weather. More than 1,000 greatcoats arrived on November 10th and were issued by Quartermaster Drum. The 19th Indiana received orders on November 25th to build winter quarters at Fort Craig. The boys immediately began to clean up the area, ditch around tents and company streets, and build fireplaces. The tents were soon winterized, a process described by Robert J. Patterson:

> The boys are chopping poles and building small pens, or foundations for their tents, they are generally made about three feet high with small fire-places, (and the brick of which they are made, the boys carried or wheeled two miles,) the tent is then put upon the pen and made fast by hooks, so when daubed it is completed, and you may be sure the boys feel happy as kings in their palaces of mud and logs.

After describing this typical log and tent construction, Sergeant Crull listed some of the contents of his personal "palace":

> but the best part is We have a nice iron stove in it on which we do all our cooking. We had corn cakes fer supper and plenty of butter. thay was good two and fresh beef. we get more than we can eat. We have plenty of wood pine and cedar. We stay in the tent play checkers and read novels and newspapers all day. We have five in our tent. there is milt [Franklin] and myself and Dick Jones of cambridge Tom henderson from below richmond and John Mots from cincinnati all good boys. the stove cost us 75 cents a peace. it is sheet iron has two holes on top and is a good one.

With such quarters, Jeff could truthfully assure his mother that "We have fine times now."[10]

The Hoosiers and their Wisconsin comrades all took turns at standing guard around the Arlington House, which now served as division headquarters. Day and night, rain and shine, even during the "Potomac fogs" which were said to aggravate rheumatism and lung ailments, these guards stood diligently at their posts around the beautiful home and a nearby collection of tents that formed General King's brigade headquarters.

One cold, rainy night in December, General McDowell was pacing up and down the portico when he noticed a Hoosier sentinel shaking his hands in a vain attempt to warm them. McDowell walked over and, after returning the sentinel's salute, remarked, "My man, you are cold, and will not give place to a relief for more than an hour. I am warm. Let me take your musket and stand guard while you go into my room and get warm." Colonel Meredith's man, fearing a trick, declined the offer, but the general insisted, "It's all right, my man, I'll take your place. Go and get warm." Reassured, the astonished soldier handed his musket over to the major general, who stood guard over his own headquarters for half an hour. While walking his beat, McDowell chanced to spot General King and rendered the proper salute. Receiving no response, McDowell accosted him, "Gen. King, when a guard salutes you it is your duty, as an officer, to answer him." King responded with a hearty laugh, but, after a few minutes of conversation, McDowell said, "Look here, King, my fingers are getting cold; take this gun and stand guard awhile." The original guard took his time coming back to relieve General King, but lost no time at all in spreading the story of two generals who had walked his beat. For a long time thereafter, the appearance of either McDowell or King in the camp of the 19th Indiana prompted the outburst, "There's the headquarters guard!"[11]

To their surprise, the Hoosiers found their generals to be kind and courteous. One of Captain Dudley's noncoms explained:

> i was on duty at genarls Mcdowels on Thursday with 15 men. the genarl talked with me a good bit. he said i done well and kept good order a mong them. I also talked to mcclellan. he said we had a nice set of men that knowed how to be have them selfs.

Although the volunteers could feel comfortable with their own officers, whom they had known for many years in civilian life, there was no familiarity allowed between enlisted volunteers and officers from the Regular Army. As one soldier would later say of John Gibbon, the stern West Pointer who commanded Battery B, "you'll just feel that you hadn't better call him Johnnie."[12]

Colonel Meredith's Indiana boys often found themselves the odd men out in the otherwise Wisconsin brigade. It was with considerable amusement, however, that they watched and listened as the Badgers competed with one another, each regiment pitted against the other two in a contest of wits. This rivalry became so intense that officers from the 6th Wisconsin went out and bought copies of *Burton's Encyclopedia of Wit and Humor* and, "by a felicitous turn of words," made the boys of the 7th the butt of their jokes. The clowning reached its zenith with two incidents that occurred on the picket line. One night late in the year, a detachment from Colonel Cutler's regiment became alarmed by a loud banging noise nearby. Unable to identify the sounds and receiving no response to shouted challenges, the Badgers opened fire. The banging continued unabated, so an officer quietly slipped out into the darkness where he found a barn door swinging on its hinges. One of the 7th's boys gleefully recorded the damage inflicted by the Belgian muskets of the 6th: "40 shingles killed, ten mortally wounded, and two boards slightly injured."[13]

Although this first round went to the 7th, the boys of that regiment made the mistake of firing on a small herd of cows that was about to overrun their picket post a few nights after the barn incident. This new "tale" quickly spread through camp and the returning pickets were accosted by the cry: "Hi, you Huckleberries, where are those calves that charged you last night?" The Huckleberries, so named for the regiment's fondness for that fruit, quickly tossed back a reply: "Those calves are all right, Bloody Sixth. We shut them in the barn that charged on you fellows." The Babies, short for King's Pet Babies, of the 6th were bested and had no more to say about embarrassments on the picket line.[14]

That section of the Washington defenses assigned to General King's brigade stretched from Fort Craig on the south to beyond Fort Tillinghast on the north. The 19th Indiana protected the area around Fort Craig, with the 2nd Wisconsin, 7th Wisconsin, and 6th Wisconsin, in that order, prolonging King's line to the right. Soldiers of the Ragged Ass Second, those swaggering veterans of Bull Run, looked upon their Hoosier neighbors as "good boys who, somehow or other, can't understand the free and easy style of the bloody Second." With perhaps a touch of arrogance, one of the Badgers explained, "They are a little too far off to be practically under our instruction, or we would break them in and make soldiers of them, as we have the Sixth." In the opinion of the Indiana boys, they were already good soldiers and did not need any Badgers telling them how to behave.[15]

The ten orderly sergeants, including Sam Schlagle of Company B, were of necessity brought into close contact with one ex-Badger, Adjutant Wood. William H. Campbell related a few of the duties he performed as an orderly sergeant:

> it is five times wors than school teaching. I have to get up at day light in the morning call the roll, make out a report and take it to the adjutant,

detail the guard from our Co, black my shoes, and see that the guards have their shoes blacked, and then march them up to guard mounting and then make out a report of the sick that are in our company and take it up to the surgeon and bring him to the tents and see that they get their medicin, and then form the company for company drill and go out with them, and after noon go out on battallion drill.

Adjutant Wood was responsible for ensuring that regulations were strictly observed and his attention to minute details made life difficult for the orderly sergeants.[16]

The John Winder affair was one example of how things could get out of hand when regulations were ignored. Winder was sent to the Indiana Hospital on September 4th with remittent fever and he returned to Company B on October 29th. Discouraged by military life, the private applied for a discharge on the first day of November. In addition to his bout of fever, Winder's medical problems included an arm that had been broken and then healed so as to prevent him from carrying a musket. Winder had fraudulently concealed his disabled arm at enlistment, but he would soon discover that getting out of the army was much more difficult than getting into it.

Winder obtained certificates attesting to his disability from Dr. Green and Dr. Woods. He presented those documents, along with his application, to Lieutenant Samuel Hindman, who was commanding Company B in Captain Dudley's absence. Hindman listened scornfully to Winder's request, took his documents and, "accompanied by the use of profanity and a bravado spirit and manner," tore up the papers and threw them into a fire. The private obtained duplicate documents and sent them directly to Surgeon General Tripler, who approved Winder's request after an assistant had examined him. Private John M. Winder was ordered to be discharged on December 4th, the necessary paperwork being sent to the 19th Indiana on that day. Despite prompting from army headquarters, Winder was not discharged.

Seth Williams, McClellan's adjutant general, ordered General McDowell to investigate the matter and determine why Colonel Meredith had disobeyed four emphatic telegrams to discharge Winder. On the 10th McDowell dispatched a letter to Meredith, asking for "an immediate explanation of the cause of your delay" in the Winder matter. To emphasize the urgency, McDowell instructed his colonel, "You will please send your answer by the bearer."

According to Meredith's reply, the first telegram arrived when he was absent in Washington. When he returned, Sol deferred action until the return of Adjutant Wood, who was also in Washington on business, because he was familiar with Winder's case. Upon the adjutant's return, he entrusted the papers to Chaplain Dale, but the minister misunderstood his instructions and gave the documents to Dr. Green at the Indiana Hospital. Green, not knowing what to do with the papers, sent them back to the regiment. The approved application for discharge was finally sent to army headquarters on December 12th, but Seth Williams was absent and did not get them until two days later. Winder called at Williams's office some one-half dozen times regarding his status, but received no satisfaction. Finally, the exasperated private retained a lawyer who wrote directly to General McClellan on December 17th. This last communication had the desired effect and John Winder was discharged from Federal service with an effective date of December 6, 1861.[17]

While Winder was struggling with bureaucratic red tape, Captain Dudley's other boys were selected for a number of interesting duties. On November 12th, the Wayne County company was chosen to escort Mrs. Meredith from Washington to Long Sol's headquarters tent. Two weeks later, a squad of men under Sergeant Crull were instructed in artillery drill, manning a huge rifled cannon in Captain Abner Doubleday's battery. Individual soldiers also found themselves detailed to positions of importance. Corporal John Snider, the young harness-maker from Centreville, stood but five feet, four and one-half inches tall, but his stature increased tremendously on December 20, 1861, when he was appointed sergeant major of the 19th Indiana. Although remaining with the regiment, his service with Company B had ended and Snider's subsequent history would be as part of the regimental staff. Young Henry Zook, "Hen" to his friends, was made an orderly at regimental headquarters, carrying messages for Colonel Meredith. Asa Blanchard was appointed an acting ordnance sergeant with responsibility for the regiment's arms and ammunition. Asa discharged his duties so well that on December 10th his commanding officers would recommend that Governor Morton commission him a lieutenant whenever a vacancy should occur.[18]

8

Winter Camp

 The year 1862 began with a controversy surrounding the resignation of Lieutenant Lee Yaryan, one of the original City Greys. Governor Morton had promised Lee, the son of an old lawyer friend, a position in the 57th Indiana during a visit to the Army of the Potomac in October. In fact, John W. Shafer, a private from Elkhart, had been instructed by the governor to replace Yaryan on October 27th. Shafer received a commission, dated November 22, 1861, as first lieutenant in Company G, although Yaryan still held the office. Lee continued to draw the pay of lieutenant despite being reported as absent without leave after December 16th, a charge that made him liable to dismissal from the army. Meanwhile, "Lieutenant" Shafer was shocked to see that, according to the pay rolls for November and December, he was only due a private's pay.

Shafer obtained no satisfaction from Colonel Meredith in settling this complicated affair, so he addressed a letter directly to Governor Morton and pleaded for justice. To aid his case, Shafer enlisted the help of Surgeon Calvin Woods, who appended a short note to Morton, describing Shafer as "a good deal embarrassed and even distressed about the way Col Meredith treats him." Woods's message to Morton was clear, "Justice and right require that you attend to this matter promptly." Shafer was sent a new commission, this one dated December 10th, but that solved nothing, since Yaryan still held the post.[1]

Relations between Colonel Meredith and John Shafer deteriorated. On January 5, 1862, Shafer wrote to W. R. Holloway, Morton's personal secretary, "I give it as my honest opinion that Col Meredith will use every means in his power to keep me out of the position." He continued, "I know Gov Morton will do me justice so far as it is in his power, despite the excentricities of Col Meredith." For his part, Long Sol wrote to Morton that

7. Leander Yaryan.
From the Roger D. Hunt Collection, U.S.
Army Military Institute. Used by permission.

"Shafer has been behaving badly left Camp without my permission and stayed in Washington three days and in fact he is not a man that I can trust." After recommending that Sergeant Julius Waldschmidt be commissioned in place of Yaryan, Meredith concluded, "I cannot be bothered with Shafer any longer." The entire matter ended on January 24th when Lee Yaryan's resignation from the 19th Indiana was accepted and Shafer took his place as first lieutenant in Company G. The 57th Indiana was fully officered by this time, so Yaryan was given the post of adjutant in the 58th Indiana. Sol Meredith never forgot an enemy, whether real or perceived, and he and Shafer would never be friends after this tangled affair.[2]

Solomon Meredith had already alienated the medical staff of the regiment. By January, Sol was also criticizing Lieutenant Colonel Cameron and Major Bachman. The colonel complained to Morton about the openly ambitious Cameron, "I would be glad if you could give Lt Col Cameron a place. he is as restless as he can possibly be all the time. thinks that he must be Col or he will never die happy." As for Bachman, Sol described the major as "a man of no energy and is very little advantage to me." Meredith recommended that Cameron be given his own regiment and expressed hope that Bachman would follow him. They could then be replaced by Sol's "true friends"—Captain May as lieutenant colonel and Captain Hamilton as major.[3]

Although Robert Cameron was not one of Colonel Meredith's "true friends," the lieutenant colonel was popular with the enlisted men. One soldier described him as "a man of energy and always has a word of kindness, always on hand in any emergency, and never shrinks from the duty of his country's cause." The enlisted men demonstrated their admiration for Cameron on January 16th when they presented him with a magnificent sword, belt, and sash. The sword, which cost $175, bore the inscription: "Presented to Lieut. Col. R. A. Cameron, by the enlisted men of the 19th regiment, Jan. 16, 1862."

The regiment was formed in a hollow square with Cameron, the Stars and Stripes, and the regimental colors in the middle. Sergeant George H. Finney, of Company H, came forward with the sword and made a few remarks:

> Accept this sword from your friends, through me. Wear it, and wherever it goes, let me assure you there is not a "wild Hoosier" but will follow. May that blade ever be found fighting in defence of our glorious old banner, till not a rebel dare raise his arm to assail its sacred folds. May you be spared to see the end of this unparalleled war, and enjoy the blessings of that peace which your valor will have aided in establishing. May the "Red, White and Blue" again flaunt joyously over city, town and hamlet, from the snow-capped hills of Maine to the golden plains of California—from the peninsula of Florida to the remotest bounds of Oregon. These our heart-felt prayers accompany this emblem of esteem. And when in coming years you gaze upon this trusty weapon, perchance dimmed by rust, remember that it is a token of kindly feeling from your fellow soldiers.

Cameron graciously accepted the gift and, "filled with inexpressible emotions," made the following reply:

> I feel doubly proud of this beautiful blade, coming, as it does, from one of the noblest bands of men any cause ever enlisted together—men who left their homes and firesides, their wives and little ones, and the idols of their souls, to rally around their country's insulted flag, to render safe a time-honored Constitution and a glorious Union, who, despising all danger, all hunger, fatigue and cold, thought of nothing but how they could save their country.

After commenting on his regiment's honorable service, the officer wound up his remarks in the following manner:

> Brave, patriotic and generous men! You have gained my deepest regards and kind feelings, and all I would ask would be with such men to meet the foe. *Then* would the dark clouds now hanging over the

horizon be lighted up, and soon the monster rebellion would be crushed, and the weapons of war laid aside for the arts of peace. But I will not weary your patience. I will conclude by saying that from a full and overwhelming heart, I thank you.

Lieutenant Colonel Cameron, clutching his valuable treasure, started off amid three rousing cheers and inspiring music from the fifers and drummers.[4]

On the following day, the 19th Indiana's commissioned officers presented Colonel Solomon Meredith with his own elegant sword and belt. The sword, described as "a beautiful specimen of workmanship, heavily elaborated with pure gold," was carefully valued at $180, five dollars more than Cameron's new outfit. General King, his staff and all officers in the brigade attended the ceremony. The presentation was made by the Honorable James Orr, Lieutenant William Orr's father:

> Recognizing in yourself a perfect gentleman, frank, affable, courteous and dignified to your equals in rank; kind to your inferiors; a man of indefatigable energy who, neglecting his own comfort, has devoted his whole time, his untiring energy and personal influence to the benefit of his men. The officers of your command take pride in presenting to you this fitting testimonial of their high consideration of your character.
>
> Permit me, then sir, in the name and in behalf of the gallant commissioned officers of the brave 19th regiment of Hoosiers, to present you this beautiful and elegant blade as a token of the high esteem, love and regard they entertain to you for your untiring zeal to our glorious Union, and the energy you manifest in suppressing this wicked, sin-conceived rebellion, and for your indefatigable energy in elevating the gallant 19th to the dignified position which they now occupy. We trust, sir, that there never will be any act done by you that will cause the 19th to be ashamed, or an Indianian to blush.

Long Sol accepted his gift with a short speech that ended with the following words:

> I cannot close my remarks without referring to the officers and men of the 19th Ind. My confidence in the restoration of the Constitution and the Laws is based upon the strong arms and patriotic hearts of those who are to defend them. I know the men around me—those who are to follow my lead in the coming struggles, you are inspired with impulses of patriotic pride to deeds of noble daring in defense of constitutional liberty. To you and those who are associated in arms with you, the country looks with anxious hopes for a restoration of peace and a suppression of this wicked rebellion. They will not be disappointed when the proper time arrives to go forward. I know that you will do your duty, if necessary, at the sacrifice of your lives. Mr. Orr, will you, sir,

convey to the donors of this beautiful sword my grateful acknowledgments for the confidence and respect they have manifested for me after an association of six months together. I cannot express my feelings on this occasion; but will promise you, however, to devote myself to the service until the stars and stripes shall wave over the shattered walls of Fort Sumter.

After the speeches had concluded, Colonel Meredith held a dinner for all of the brigade officers, followed by an eloquent speech by General King. Although the enlisted men were not invited to dine, Sergeant Major John Snider managed to mingle in the crowd and get a generous helping of cider.[5]

Hosting large dinners was one way for Sol Meredith to increase his stature and pile up political capital. Just a few weeks before the sword presentation, a holiday feast given by the ambitious colonel had led a correspondent of the *Indianapolis Daily Journal* to declare, "Old Sol never does things by halves." Invitations had been sent to Secretary Caleb Smith, Commissioner Holloway, and the entire Hoosier congressional delegation. Leaving no stone unturned, Sol also invited William H. Russell, of the *London Times,* and reporters from various New York newspapers. The *Journal* writer summed up the affair by saying, "The collation was a splendid one, and was another evidence of the generous and big souled impulses of 'Sol's' heart." Festivities concluded with toasts honoring Colonel Meredith, the Army of the Potomac, and General McClellan.[6]

Boredom in winter camp led to a dependence on alcohol for amusement. One of King's soldiers wrote, "There would be a vast deal less of drinking and swearing among the men if a sufficiency of reading, such as newspapers, historical novels, and magazines, could be had." Of course, there were regulations against the use of alcohol, but they were not uniformly enforced. A Wisconsin man described some of the methods used to combat liquor smugglers:

> At the bridges and ferry the argus-eyed guards are ready to pounce upon anything that looks like whiskey, and nothing is allowed to pass without a strict and thorough examination. Every private has his pockets examined; every wagon is searched; every box must be open; every barrel is probed with a long iron, so that the old subterfuge of putting a keg into a barrel of vinegar or cider, or bottles into sugar and molasses, does no good.

The Badger candidly continued that all liquor thus discovered was immediately destroyed, "except choice morsels that are saved for the guard."[7]

Diligence by guards and the fact that their sutler was "a strictly temperance man" forced the Hoosier boys to look elsewhere for refreshments. The mecca for thirsty soldiers could be found in the nearby camps of General Blenker's division, where as many as two dozen establishments sold lager beer and whiskey. Blenker's regiments contained sizable German contingents and the open sale of alcoholic beverages was condoned, even though it resulted in widespread "dissipation," as many as 500 soldiers being unfit for duty each day because of intoxication. William Wilson, one of Blenker's officers who had many friends in the 19th Indiana, said of the Hoosiers, "I know that many of them come over to our camp and get liquor, and go home intoxicated." John Hawk confessed to patronizing the German liquor dealers, "Andy Knapp and I went over to Blenkards and got a half gallon of tangle toe and we felt as independent as a hog on ice."[8]

Contraband whiskey that reached King's brigade sold for between $1.50 and $2.50 a pint, depending upon the arrival of smugglers. Whiskey was called "corn juice" by many, but some of the names were a little more descriptive. The most potent brand was "Kill at the Counter," so called because victims would die before the seller could make change. "Slow Torture" and "Death Bed Confession" were only a little less potent. Drinkers wisely did not inquire about ingredients in these concoctions. Rumor held that dealers sold hard cider made by combining sweetened water, tartaric acid, and sulfuric acid, so the recipe for whiskey must have been truly frightful. Whatever its composition, whiskey had its intended effect. Joshua Jones, of Company E, wrote that men with needy families spent their money getting drunk instead of sending it home. Fights among drunken soldiers were common, such as one on January 13th that was described in William Murray's diary: "Whiskey aboard. A great pugilistic exhibition in Company C."[9]

Drinking, smoking, and gambling helped pass the long hours in this first winter camp, but some soldiers fought off boredom by giving themselves tattoos. Private William R. Moore, of Company K, described the popularity:

> I was picking Indian ink in my arm and Henry Williams come in. nothing would do but that I must pick some in his arm and William he come in and because Henry had som picked in his arm nothing would do but he must have some in his arm. . . .

This particular tattoo artist was put out of business after Captain Williams learned that Moore had decorated his young son, who was visiting camp. It was no wonder that Henry Marsh would write that "the army is a fearful place for a young christian," and would add later, "I feel that to be in the army is as if in a bar room and a gambling saloon."[10]

On January 23rd, McClellan's adjutant telegraphed McDowell and inquired whether any of his regiments were unfit to take the field, either due to deficiencies in equipment or discipline. McDowell reported that his New

York regiments were "equipped and well disciplined for volunteers," although his assessment of King's brigade was a little more harsh:

> The brigade is equipped, with some slight exceptions, and well disciplined for volunteers. The Nineteenth Indiana the least so. A special report will be made as to this regiment after a special inspection next Monday.

McDowell's special report has apparently been lost, but the muster roll for January and February indicates that discipline and instruction in the 19th Indiana were only "fair." Notations on the roll for April 30, 1862, suggest that problems persisted, since the muskets were "indifferently cleaned" and the accouterments were in "bad condition." Obviously, the 19th Indiana was lagging behind in its military development. This could be traced to a number of factors, such as the wave of fevers that curtailed training, the suspicion that Sol Meredith was probably not fit to command and the consequent division of subordinate officers into pro- and anti-Meredith factions.[11]

Colonel Meredith's problem with his ambitious lieutenant colonel ended on February 3rd when Robert Cameron was transferred to the 34th Indiana. Major Bachman did not follow Cameron, as Meredith had hoped, but was instead promoted to fill Cameron's vacancy. Governor Morton granted Long Sol's wish to be surrounded by true friends when he commissioned Captain May, Company A, to the post of major. The commissions for Bachman and May were dated February 6, 1862, but for some unexplained reason the new major was never officially mustered into Federal service at that rank. Though Isaac May served as major of the 19th Indiana until his death, the Pension Bureau made his widow furnish affidavits attesting to such service before it would consider her application.[12]

Medical affairs in the regiment continued on their chaotic course. Dr. Woods returned to Wayne County for a much deserved rest in January, being replaced by a Dr. Prunk, who had been sent out from Indiana at state expense. On January 14th, Meredith recommended that Morton recall the newcomer, writing candidly, "Jesse Potts the Hospital Steward and him cant get along together and I think Jesse knows much more than Dr Prunk and I would much prefer to retain Jesse than the Dr." Jesse, originally a member of the City Greys, stayed and Dr. Prunk was sent back home.[13]

There was also trouble in the regimental band. One continual annoyance was the State of Indiana's demand for reimbursement for the original band uniforms purchased from the firm of Messrs. Glaser & Bros. In reply to an inquiry from J. H. Vajen, Indiana's Quartermaster General, Bandmaster William Earl Reid complained that the clothier "did *not* fulfil their contract to have the uniforms completed as to time, by near *two days*."

This delay prevented Reid's band from accompanying the regiment to Washington. According to the bandmaster, after accepting delivery, "there was scarcely *one* coat in the *whole Band,* manufactured by Mess Glaser & Bros, that could be pronounced a *fit,* or *fit to be worn* by a musician on parade." After protesting the unfairness of paying this firm of "Princely Jews" for worthless goods, Bandmaster Reid assured Vajen that if the issue were pressed, the account would be settled.[14]

While letters were exchanged between the band and authorities in Indianapolis, Drum Major Clint Smith had grown tired of his position. Smith wrote directly to Governor Morton and asked for a commission in a new regiment, citing his political qualifications:

> If serving a party is any inducement, I have only to say, and as you know, that I have always labored for the success of the *Republican Party,* and while laboring for that Party, was broken up by the *Geo. W. Julian* Faction.

The drum major confessed that he finally was forced to ask for such a favor because he was "not receiving pay sufficient to support my family," a fairly common complaint among Hoosier soldiers.[15]

John M. Snider had been jumped from corporal in Company B to sergeant major of the 19th Indiana on December 20th. He thus bypassed the regular order of promotion from corporal to sergeant to orderly sergeant. The office of sergeant major was often used as a reward for corporals of demonstrated ability who would otherwise languish in their respective companies. An appointment to sergeant major often meant a "fast track" career and an impending officer's commission. Although obviously aware of his good fortune, Sergeant Major Snider modestly told his family, "I was corporal untill lately and went a little higher."

On January 18th, after a guard-mount where it was "raining like fourty," John wrote to his family and described his new situation:

> I am all alone in the big round tent occupied by our Adjutant, where I Sleep as well as loaf through the day; this is my headquarters where I have to be nearly all the time. to day is *Sunday.* it Seams more like *Monday,* than the Lords Day; for I have just as much to do to day as any other. I have not Seen a Sunday to have a day of rest for Six months or more; for there is no *Sunday* in the Army as you are probably aware of.

Duty left little opportunity for personal interests, although John did assure his sister that he did not indulge in the typical army diversions, "I generaly pass the spair time I have in reading the Papers or Some book; and frequently writing to those that are far away."[16]

The first winter snow occurred on January 4th, just enough "to make the ground gray." Two inches of snow fell the following day, with like amounts blanketing the camp on January 14th and February 11th. In addition to the snow, frequent rains swept over Arlington Heights. Temperatures were mild and Sergeant Tom Benton could write that "there has not been a day so cold that a person was obliged to wear an overcoat unless they were out for some time." The precipitation and relatively mild temperatures meant that the ground alternated between frozen solid and sloppy mud. By the end of January, William Murray would record in his diary, "mud beautifully deep and swimmingly sloppy apparently at its maximum." Military operations were impossible and the Arlington camps were virtually shut down by mid-February—drills, parades, reviews and even guard mount were dispensed with and the army ground to a standstill. But the boys did find ways to occupy their new-found vacation:

> Eat, drink, sleep, read, laugh. tell stories, pull one anothers' hair, swear, rip and tear, kick, roll and tumble, play poker, casino, dominoes, whist, old sledge, eucher, whistle jack, and muggins, with various other amusements too numerous to mention, from "early morn till dewy eve."

Their time off was fun, but Hoosier boys still chafed for action, especially after receiving news of the Union victory at Fort Donelson on February 16th.[17]

Although their only battles were against depression and homesickness, the Indiana boys were quick to assure folks at home that they were still in high spirits. Sergeant Major Snider could write home that the gloomy winter camp was "very apt to give one the *Blues,*" but he quickly pointed out, "I pass the time very pleasantly; and am Satisfied where I am." Austin Conyers, Company C, explained his sentiments by declaring, "I dont want you to think that I am home Sick by any means for if [I] was at home i would not Stay thare See[ing] so many of my friends gone." Allen W. Galyean of Company K was more interested in reassuring one particular segment of the community when he wrote, "Tell the girls that ant married that they had better wait until we soldiers gits back and then they might mary some boy that is some body."[18]

Celebrations held throughout the army on George Washington's birthday, February 22nd, were designed to inspire the enlisted men in preparation for a forward movement. A grand event was planned for King's brigade at the Arlington House, a spot calculated to heighten the inspiration because of its connection with the beloved Washington. The day began ominously with a rainstorm. After breakfast, King's men brushed their clothing, scoured their brass plates until they shone, and cleaned the rust from their muskets. They then fell into line and waded off through the mud toward the Arlington House, but before the regiments could be assembled, orders came postponing the ceremony until that afternoon. The Western boys turned about and waded back to their camps, "swearing a hearty oath."[19]

General King formed his brigade on the steep slope in front of the broad portico of Arlington House at three o'clock that afternoon. The four regiments were aligned in a hollow square in column of division, although the hill's pitch and the mud made the formation look more like a semicircle. The boys then spent an hour listening to patriotic airs from a brass band, the reading of Washington's Farewell Address and a speech by General King. Soldiers in the front ranks could enjoy the show, but those to the rear heard nothing and spent sixty minutes "exerting every nerve to keep from sliding suddenly to the ground" in the mire. Following King's remarks, the regiments deployed into four lines and fired several volleys of blank cartridges. At least that was the order. According to a boy in the 7th Wisconsin, the brigade actually "fired blank cartridges and Ram Rods." Forgetting to remove a ramrod after loading a musket was a dangerous mistake, since the ramrod became a whirring projectile when the weapon fired. In this instance, a soldier in Company F of the 7th Wisconsin was wounded by an errant ramrod, allegedly fired by one veteran of the Ragged Ass Second.[20]

Sergeant Tom Benton missed the birthday bash on Arlington Heights. On February 21st, Tom had been ordered to Washington, where he joined seven other sergeants in a handpicked group of flag bearers. On the morning of Washington's birthday, these eight sergeants assembled at the War Department and each man was given a captured rebel flag. This elite detachment then marched down Pennsylvania Avenue to the Capitol, where the trophies were to be presented to the United States Congress by the War Department. However, the Congressmen balked at accepting the standards. They reasoned that, since Congress had not recognized the Confederacy as a nation, it could not acknowledge rebel battleflags that symbolized Southern independence. After being rebuffed by Congress, the disappointed sergeants marched their flags back to the War Department and Tom Benton returned to Fort Craig on February 23rd.[21]

Losses from the careless handling of muskets continued to mount in King's brigade. One day in February, the 7th Wisconsin returned from picket duty and, following common practice, fired off their loaded muskets prior to reaching camp. In this instance, one bullet glanced off a tree and hit a Company I boy in the shoulder. On February 11th, Colonel Meredith noted in his diary, "Barney Six of Company A shot off his two front fingers on right hand while on picket." While accidental wounds were fairly common occurrences, the death of a comrade in regimental camp was a rare event. One such death was that of Private Andrew J. Reeves of Company C. He had been detailed as a nurse in the regimental hospital at Fort Craig on November 8th, but developed a fever and died of an abcess on February 9th. Reeves was buried in the brigade cemetery near Fort Craig on the following day.[22]

Most deaths occurred in far distant hospitals, but a man who died in camp could count on friends interring him with suitable ceremony. One officer described the military ritual:

> The regimental field music, in front, with muffled drums, playing an appropriate air. Next, eight men, rank and file, with arms reversed; next the ambulance with the deceased; next six pall bearers; next the company in two ranks, without arms; and lastly, the chaplain. On arriving at the grave, the eight men selected from his comrades presented arms to their late brother soldier, then rest on arms, which is done by placing the muzzle of the gun upon the left toe, both hands on the breech and head bowed on hands, while the funeral service was being performed. They then shouldered arms, loaded and fired three volleys over the grave, meaning Peace to his ashes, Peace to his soul and spread wide his fame.

By one count, sixteen soldiers from King's brigade were interred on Arlington Heights during the period October 1, 1861, through March 10, 1862. The brigade cemetery was close to the burial lot of the Custis family, but soldiers who were buried there are not listed on the records of the National Cemetery, which now covers Arlington Heights. One veteran offered a plausible explanation for the oversight, "Soldier tombstones were not in fashion then and I presume their graves were not properly marked so that by the time the headstones were set, their names and the location of their graves was lost."[23]

Although he was not a member of Company B, the death of Sergeant Andrew J. Addleman, Company K, on January 12th was deeply lamented by the boys from Hillsboro (now Whitewater). Andrew was a cousin of Joseph and Jacob Addleman, privates in Captain Dudley's company, and was living in Fairview, Randolph County, when he enlisted. Sergeant Addleman was an active member of Whitewater Lodge No. 159, Free and Accepted Masons at Hillsboro and that organization was quick to extend its sympathy to his bereaved parents and relatives. The Richmond press published a set of resolutions, adopted by that lodge, which included the following statement, "That as Masons we will cherish the memory of brother Addleman, and will endeavor to emulate his virtues as a just and upright Mason friend." The death of Andrew Addleman was the first of four such sacrifices that the Addleman clan would make before the advent of peace.[24]

Private William H. Ford left Company B on February 17th for a glamorous new assignment. Along with a few other disillusioned infantrymen from King's brigade, he was detached as a seaman to Mississippi River gunboat service. Assigned to the U.S.S. *Mound City,* he received an ugly wound on the inner side of his left leg on June 17, 1862, in action at White River, Arkansas. Seaman Ford later developed remittent fever and dropsy "by exposure to climatic influences" and was discharged from the hospital ship *Red Rover* on February 18, 1863.[25]

First Lieutenant Davis Castle had also left Company B, having been detailed to the Signal Corps on January 9th, in compliance with Special Order No. 52, Headquarters, McDowell's division. Colonel Meredith apparently selected Castle for this assignment because it suited his delicate health following the bout of fever that nearly killed him. Castle, officially only detailed to the Signal Corps, would never again serve with Company B in the field, although he would command the Wayne County company on paper for almost two years following the battle of Antietam.[26]

Lieutenant Castle reported for duty at the Signal Camp of Instruction, located near Georgetown, where he spent two months learning the "wig-wag" system of signaling. During daylight hours, messages were sent by signal flags attached to a four-sectioned hickory pole. At night, torches were attached to the signal poles in place of flags. At short range, signal messages were read by officers using field glasses, while the Signal Corps telescope was used at greater distances.[27]

A board of officers recommended Castle for signal duty on March 5th, but active duty was postponed after an accident in which he was crushed by his horse. Assigned to General William B. Franklin's headquarters, Castle's signal detachment rendered an important service by coordinating the fire of gunboats during the battle at West Point, Virginia, on May 7, 1862. A recurrence of typhoid fever forced Castle to miss much of the Peninsula Campaign, although he was again under fire at Mechanicsville. After a period of convalescence, Castle participated in the withdrawal of the Army of the Potomac from the Richmond front. On August 19th, while escorting a signal party from Fortress Monroe to Newport News, he was accidentally shot in the left shoulder by Lieutenant Joseph Gloskoski of the 29th New York and hospitalized until mid-September. Lieutenant Castle's career in the Signal Corps showed him to be an officer of high caliber and his name will be mentioned prominently in later pages.[28]

On January 18th, Colonel Meredith assembled a recruiting detail and sent it back to Indiana with orders to scour the state for volunteers to replace the dead and discharged fever victims. This detail was composed of the following soldiers: Captain Valentine Jacobs, Chaplain Lewis Dale, Lieutenant Samuel Hindman, Sergeant Julius Waldschmidt, Corporal John W. Jack, and Private Isaac R. Blair. Sergeant Tom Benton wrote about Sam

8. Samuel Hindman.
From the Mick Kissick Collection.
Used by permission.

Hindman's good fortune at being sent home and confessed, "I tried to get to go with him but they would not send two from the same company." In order to reassure his father of his intentions, Tom also wrote, "I wish this war was over so that I could come home but I do not want to come until every thing is settled."[29]

Lieutenant Hindman began operations in Wayne County and signed up two volunteers on February 8th at Chester, just north of Richmond. Expanding his search into Henry County, the lieutenant signed up two more men at New Castle on February 20th. One of the latter recruits, William F. Shelley, was already a veteran, having previously enlisted for service in Fremont's Body Guard. He was assigned to Company B, Benton Cadets, United States Reserve Corps Infantry, a Missouri organization, where he served from September 15, 1861, until mustered out January 8, 1862.[30]

Lieutenant Hindman took his recruits to Indianapolis on the day they enlisted. Each new volunteer was examined by an inspecting surgeon, who asked a series of questions that probed his medical history:

1. Have you ever been sick? When, and of what diseases?
2. Have you any disease now, and what?
3. Have you ever had fits?
4. Have you ever received an injury or wound upon the head?

5. Have you ever had a fracture, a dislocation, or a sprain?
6. Are you in the habit of drinking? Or have you ever had the "horrors?" [delirium tremens]
7. Are you subject to the piles?
8. Have you any difficulty in urinating?
9. Have you been vaccinated, or had the small pox?

After these inquiries, the surgeon conducted a detailed physical examination and Sam Hindman was obliged to certify that each new recruit was "entirely sober when enlisted."[31]

9

Spring Advance

The advent of March brought renewed hopes for an advance against the rebels. Sergeant Tom Benton had spent the last two days of February copying four sets of muster rolls, "quite a religious job" according to his own admission, and he was more than ready to take the field. Tom wrote optimistically to his father that the winds were finally beginning to dry the roads and rumors of a move had increased with the issue of new tents to the Hoosiers. The soldiers viewed their portable D'Abri tents (dog tents) with curiosity. According to Sergeant Benton:

> we have got new tents and have to carry them in our knapsacks. one tent to two men and they are so made that they can be divided and each take half of it, which only weighs four (4) pounds. they are only to keep off the dew and some rain and will be a good deal better than nothing. they are about six feet long and four broad shaped

> both ends are open and are fixed so that the tents can be buttoned together.

At first some of the soldiers experimented with one man carrying both sides of the tent and his partner packing the pins and poles. But this arrangement left the pins and poles man in a bad spot if his tent-toting comrade should be detained in rainy weather. After a few days on the march, tents were divided fifty-fifty.[1]

The Indiana regiment was shocked by the sudden death of Sergeant Major John M. Snider on March 4th from congestive pneumonia. Members of the Independent Order of Odd Fellows held a meeting that evening, chaired by Colonel Meredith, and adopted the following preamble and resolutions:

> Whereas, Through a dispensation of Almighty God we are called upon to mourn the loss of our worthy brother, John M. Snider, of ———— Lodge, Sergeant Major of this Regiment, who departed this life in camp at Fort Craig, Va., on the morning of March 4, 1862. Kind and manly in his intercourse with the officers of the regiment, and all others with whom he came in contact, prompt in the discharge of his duty, he had won the esteem of all, both above and below him in command. "After life's fitful fever he sleeps."
>
> *Resolved,* that in this sad bereavement the relatives and friends of the deceased share our true and sincere sympathies, as do the brethren of the Lodge of which he was an honored member.
>
> *Resolved,* that we will, in conjunction with a committee from Co. B, of which he was formerly a member, attend his remains to Washington City, for the purpose of having them embalmed and sent for interment, to his relatives in Indiana.
>
> *Resolved,* that the Indianapolis and Richmond papers be requested to publish the foregoing proceedings, and that a copy of the preamble and resolutions be sent to the family of the deceased.

The document was written out by Lieutenant John A. Cottman, acting secretary, and witnessed by Major Isaac May, Captain Alonzo Makepeace, Captain Robert W. Hamilton, Captain Samuel J. Williams, and Lieutenant Benjamin C. Harter. They sent John home for burial in Crown Hill Cemetery, at Centreville, where the funeral was conducted by members of Hoosier Lodge No. 23.[2]

The first week of March was rather dreary except for a few days when Adjutant Wood claimed the right to run the regiment during Colonel Meredith's absence. Wood's tantrum ended with the colonel's return, but the enlisted men had been amazed by his ranting and storming through camp. Meredith was called to brigade headquarters at 10 P.M. on March 9th, when General King cautioned him that an advance seemed imminent. Positive orders to that effect arrived about midnight and Adjutant Wood was immediately yelling to the various captains, "Prepare two days' rations, and be ready to march at four o'clock!" As the men rolled out of their blankets and formed into line, their officers passed the news—the Army of the Potomac was taking the field! Drills, inspections, and reviews were over! One visitor to the Hoosier camp noticed that "such an outburst of joy, throwing of hats, and terrific yells that went up from as brave men as ever shouldered a musket were truly a grand sight."[3]

One of the Wisconsin regiments took to the road first, but it was halted so that Colonel Meredith's regiment could lead the brigade column.

Theater of Operations - 1862

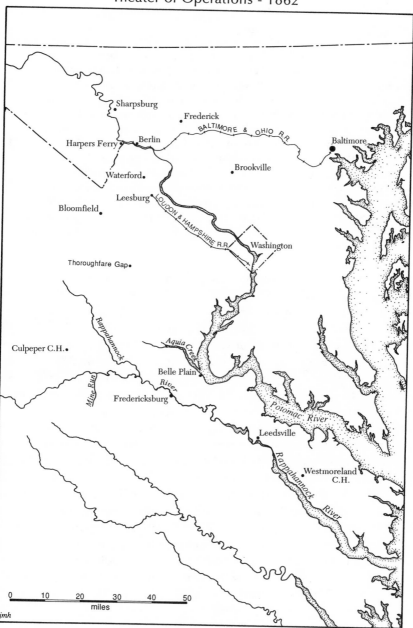

Sharpsburg

Frederick

BALTIMORE & OHIO R.R.

Baltimore

Harpers Ferry   Berlin

Waterford

Brookville

Leesburg

LOUDON & HAMPSHIRE R.R.

Bloomfield

Washington

Thoroughfare Gap

Rappahannock

Aquia Creek

Culpeper C.H.

Belle Plain

Mine Run

River

Fredericksburg

Potomac River

Leedsville

Rappahannock

Westmoreland
C.H.

River

0   10   20   30   40   50

miles

jmh

Earl M. Rogers would later write a history of King's division and he successfully captured the spirit of that first movement:

> It was a grand sight. The morning of March 10th 1862, was bright and clear; one hundred and seventy thousand enthusiastic men enroute, with banners unfurled, bands playing, bugles sounding, men singing; cavalry in their showy yellow trimmings galloping to the front, artillery with red trimmings going into park and pulling out. The infantry uniforms were well fitted and new, their arms polished bright, the unfurled flags inspiring as they waved in the morning light. Well might the commander be proud of that grand army and its equipments; well might the corps commanders be proud of their corps and the discipline; the division commanders are proud of their divisions and the esprit de corps; brigade commanders are jealous of their brigades, and well they might be; colonels are proud of their regiments, and deservedly so; captains are well pleased at the perfect deportment of their companies, and it is merited; the file closers closed up, the men sang joyfully, and none so proud of their commander as the soldiers of King's division.

Many years later, Rufus Dawes would get closer to the truth when he wrote that "our men were in that verdant and idiotic frame of mind, which was then termed 'spoiling for a fight.'"[4]

Captain Dudley's company had returned from picket duty late Saturday night and had just gotten to bed when they were roused for the march. Marching was difficult in the darkness and over muddy roads, but improved as King's brigade turned west on the turnpike that led from Alexandria to Fairfax Court House. Although the sun shone briefly in the early morning, scattered showers fell most of the day. The Hoosiers kept on until about 1 P.M., when Colonel Meredith halted his regiment about a mile west of Fairfax. Sol remembered that his soldiers "marched in fine order" on that eighteen-mile trek, although Sergeant Jeff Crull swore that he had "never seen a more tired set of boys than was in this army on Sunday night."[5]

While encamped near Fairfax, the Western soldiers heard that their enemies had abandoned Centreville and Manassas Junction, taking up a new position south of the Rappahannock River. Lieutenant Orr wrote joyously to his father, "Centreville & Manassas is Ours. Our troops occupy the whole Country from Fairfax to the Junction." Inquisitive soldiers walked down to Manassas Junction to view the rebel fortifications and were amazed by the scene. Sergeant Crull explained:

> the roads are strewed with guns knapsacks and clothing of every kind at manassas. they left almost every thing. Whole stacks of meat and tents and clothing that had never bin opend. thay are hundreds of dead horses run to death and killed by the rebels. Worked to death. there is any a

mount of Blankets and every thing. Thay had a perfect panic the men
throwed a way every thing so as to run faster.

Having a horse to ride, Dr. Calvin Woods turned souvenir hunter and
returned to Fort Craig packing a musket, sword, fearsome bowie knife, and
secesh spear. Although there was great jubilation over this bloodless victory
of General McClellan's, some men felt cheated because there had been no
decisive battle that would have crushed the rebellion then and there.
Corporal James Stine explained the undercurrent of frustration, "Great
disappointment ensued, as the larger part of the army had sacrificed comfortable homes, and left lucrative business to go to ruin for the sake of defending
the Union."[6]

The Western brigade had outmarched its quartermaster wagons and
soldiers were forced to seek contributions from neighboring farmers. According to James Perry, a Wisconsin soldier, "Genl King requested us not to
steal but said boys do not go hungry which in the English language & in the
time of war means take what you want wherever you can find it." Lieutenant
Orr described how the Hoosiers obeyed orders, "The Boys are well an
jubilant. The boys have killed every chicken hog sheep & cow for 3 miles
round & eat it." Food was not the only thing in short supply in the bivouac
near Fairfax. The demand for postage stamps was so high that men offered
twenty-five cents apiece for a three-cent stamp.[7]

While encamped near Fairfax, McClellan's army was organized into
corps by order of President Lincoln. Generally, each corps would contain
three divisions, each division would contain four brigades and each brigade
would contain four regiments. General McDowell was assigned to command
the new First Corps, General King was appointed head of the First Division
and Colonel Lysander Cutler, as senior colonel, took over King's old
brigade. While these new commanders inspected their men and arranged
staff assignments, General McClellan began a bold amphibious campaign
against Richmond, Virginia.[8]

At 10 A.M. on March 15th, Cutler's brigade marched in the rain for
Alexandria. After a long hike, Colonel Meredith halted his regiment a few miles
from town and the Indiana boys waited their chance to board transports for a
trip south. Camp guards who had been left with the baggage at Fort Craig were
ordered to immediately rejoin the regiment at Alexandria. The guard detachment set off for that city, but stayed overnight at the Marshall House when they
were unable to locate the Hoosier camp. Meanwhile General McDowell's
corps was detached from McClellan's army and ordered to protect Washington, so the 19th Indiana marched back to their old quarters at Fort Craig on
March 16th. The guards caught up with their regiment on the following day.
A week of campaigning had been spent marching in a circle.[9]

King's division returned to Alexandria on the morning of March 18th with the expectation of boarding transports. The Western brigade camped about two miles from town and started campfires with fence rails stolen from an irate farmer who "swore & defiantly shook his fist at the whole Brigade." Just after these fires were kindled, the command was ordered to Fairfax Seminary. This latest movement was terribly mismanaged by both General King and Colonel Cutler. Although the Wisconsin regiments went into camp after a march of about eight miles, the Hoosiers received confusing directions and covered about twenty miles before rejoining Cutler's brigade.[10]

Lieutenant Orr declared that this was the hardest march ever made by the 19th Indiana. The regiment marched until about 11 o'clock that night and the officers swore "like mad men" to keep their men from straggling. Even so, Company G arrived at Fairfax Seminary with just five men. Part of that loss may have been occasioned by a "traffic accident" at the rear of the regiment. At one halt, soldiers sprawled in the dusty road to rest when a team following the regiment "took fright & started to run away." Captain Dudley's company, at the rear of the regiment, quickly jumped aside and yelled a warning to those ahead. Companies G and K likewise tumbled off the road, but the team and wagon crashed into Company E and ran over John Harter and the three Collins brothers. The Collins boys were seriously injured and it was feared that one might die.[11]

The campsite near Fairfax Seminary had no wood, so the Hoosiers marched a mile or so into the hills, where they pitched their little tents, christening the spot "Camp Meredith." This new camp had very little wood, but water was plentiful and the regiment was allowed to rest for about two weeks. The Hoosiers were depressed at their marching for no apparent purpose and most agreed with Sergeant William Murray when he wrote, "Soldiering, by nearly all, considered a very hard and killing occupation." Liquor made its appearance again and Murray recorded one result in his diary, "Great excitement in Co. B, one man knocked down with a stone, the man who did it shaken by the Col. and bucked. All occasioned by too much whiskey." Much to the men's dismay, drills and reviews also reappeared, by order of General McDowell. Gloomy spirits in Camp Meredith were lifted by the arrival of the paymaster on March 28th. Long Sol's Hoosier boys had previously voted to purchase Short's Patent Knapsack, demonstrated in camp by a company salesman, for two dollars each, so some 200 of them plunked down their money and paid off the bill in full. Others took advantage of a liberal payment plan that spread the cost over a four-month period.[12]

Meanwhile, Sol Meredith had been passed over for promotion again. The Indiana Congressional delegation had met on March 26th for the purpose of selecting six brigadier generals allotted to the Hoosier state. As might be expected, Sol was there working the crowd, ably assisted by his Wayne County cronies from the Department of the Interior—David P. Holloway, R. O. Dormer, and W. T. Dennis. Despite this "broadside of influence," Meredith was not selected and the coveted positions went to Colonels Thomas T. Crittenden, 6th Indiana; William P. Benton, 8th Indiana; Jeremiah C. Sullivan, 13th Indiana; Pleasant A. Hackleman, 16th Indiana; Alvin P. Hovey, 24th Indiana; and James C. Veatch, 25th Indiana.[13]

The month of April began inauspiciously with yet another division drill at Bailey's Crossroads on the 1st. Camp Meredith had become fouled after two weeks of use, so the tents were moved on April 2nd to a new site, where sanitary conditions improved dramatically. But the Hoosiers packed up again on April 4th in obedience to an order sending King's division south to Catlett's Station on the Orange and Alexandria Railroad. The 19th Indiana started at 3 P.M. and marched by way of Fairfax Court House, Centreville, Manassas Junction, and Bristoe Station, reaching the latter place at 5 P.M. on April 6th. Before halting, the entire division crossed a temporary bridge over Broad Run that allowed but one man to pass at a time, a bottleneck of significant proportion. The Hoosier camp was swept by a combination of rain and snow over the next three days that resulted in mud fully six inches deep. Colonel Meredith called April 9th "the most disagreeable day I ever saw." General King's division finally reached Catlett's Station on April 10th and the 19th Indiana camped on the banks of Cedar Run.[14]

The brief stay at Catlett's was notable for three things, according to Sergeant Tom Benton. First of all, the 16th Indiana was encamped less than a mile away and "it seemed like being at home seeing so many Richmond boys." Another reminder of home came with the arrival of Lieutenant Hindman and his four recruits for Company B, each of whom had stories to share of acquaintances from Wayne and Henry counties. Lastly, the boys spent all of their leisure time angling in Cedar Run for game fish and eels, the latter an odd delicacy that delighted the Hoosiers. After watching the success of friends and smelling the aroma of fried fish, one Delaware County boy wrote home, "I want you to send me some fish hooks and line for I want to ketch some fish and eat."[15]

The fishing ended on April 21st with arrival of orders for King's division to march to Fredericksburg. That movement was marred by the death of Jacob Pierpoint, a private in Company E. William R. Moore described how the unfortunate soldier was killed by a guard belonging to the 16th Indiana:

the way it happened the fellow was cooking for Captain Wilson and was
a going a long with the regiment so he went to this house while we was

there and picked up some old clothes which laid there and started of with them when the guard haulted him and told him that he could not allow him to take them. so the fellow took them back and got in to a quarrel some way and as he started and turned a round to shut the gate the guard shot him through the breast. I heard the gun Crack and heard the fellow hollow. he died in a short time. they put him in an ambulance and allowed to fetch him to Fredricksburgh but before they could get here he would smell so bad they concluded to burry him.

Colonel Meredith recorded the incident in his diary and noted that Private Pierpoint lived but one-half hour after being shot. The deceased was a nephew of Francis H. Pierpoint, the provisional governor of Western Virginia.[16]

General McDowell had issued an order, as most generals do, against straggling on the march, insisting that men would be allowed to fall out only to answer calls of nature. According to one soldier, "Nature had many calls." In the opinion of hungry infantrymen, "the bleating of sheep, squealing of pigs, the lowing of cattle, crowing of roosters, the quacking of ducks" were all classified as calls of nature that needed to be answered immediately. If soldiers dined on rebel mutton, pork, beef, or fowl, they did so proudly, satisfied that they had strictly obeyed McDowell's order to answer calls of nature on the march.[17]

Colonel Cutler's brigade arrived near Falmouth on April 23rd and the Hoosiers camped in a nice grove of pines. Sergeant Benton wrote that "Falmouth is a small place only about twenty houses and two or three stores in it one mill and one cotton factory which is still in full blast." Across the Rappahannock River lay the city of Fredericksburg, which the mayor, intimidated by Yankee cannons, had already surrendered to Union forces. The retreating rebels had destroyed both bridges across the Rappahannock, set fire to some twenty boats on the river and burned hundreds of bales of cotton from the factory at Falmouth. A few of the gray-clad demons could still be seen performing picket duty on the south bank, safely outside of musket range. On April 27th, the regiment moved its camp back to where the Richmond and Potomac Railroad crossed Potomac Creek, about four miles north of Fredericksburg. Duty was easy and Jeff Crull could write, "We have onely to keep our arms in good order and our self clean."[18]

Cleanliness helped to keep the men healthy and ready for duty. Those fevers which had scourged the 19th Indiana during its first months at Camp Kalorama and Camp Advance had abated and would reappear only in isolated cases. The medical staff would now be challenged by another disease that would plague the regiment, indeed the entire army, for the remainder of its service. Bluntly stated, the problem was chronic diarrhea. Christopher Starbuck of Company C explained:

I am well all excep the bowel complaint. there is more than one half of the reg got it. it appears to be the prevailing disease at the present. it is the watter that gave it to us.

Bad water was only partly to blame and Joshua Jones, Company E, offered two other causes—exposure and bad food:

I am not well half of my time any more. it Raines So much and we have to lay on the cold and wet ground and nothing that I like to eat. we was 5 days with 2 days Rations and 4 of them days we was marching. hard Crackers and old tuff beef and no Salt and we had to Roast it on the fire.

After diligently examining the subject of diarrhea and dysentery during the war, one modern writer has concluded that "constipation was a luxury."[19]

Colonel Meredith's doctors did what they could, but treatments were limited. Private Starbuck recorded a confrontation with a surgeon that occurred when he protested the prescribed treatment at sick call:

A man may go to the doctor to get medicine and it is 10 grains of quinine and 1 grain of leftander [laudanum] or 10 grains of quinine and 1 grain of morphene. I told him I never volunteered to take quinine and morphene and that was the dose he ordered for me. I told him I would not take it. he said he thought by the time I got good and sick I would be willing to take it. I did not want to be sick was the reason why I did not take it.

When William Murray began to suffer from hemorrhoids, he consulted Captain Robert Hamilton, a physician in private life. All Hamilton could do was advise the sufferer "to bathe the parts in the creek." This advice may have helped Murray, but the bath must have been somewhat detrimental to those who obtained drinking water downstream.[20]

10

Arrival of Gibbon

During their retreat beyond the Rappahannock River, the rebels had virtually destroyed the Fredericksburg & Potomac Railroad, a fifteen-mile stretch of track between Fredericksburg and its terminus at the confluence of Aquia Creek and the Potomac River. It was imperative to rebuild this line in order to provision General McDowell's corps around Fredericksburg. The War Department assigned this task to Herman Haupt, a West Pointer who had resigned after his graduation in 1835 in order to pursue a career in railroad engineering. Haupt was commissioned a colonel and assigned to General McDowell's staff as an aide-de-camp, where he was ordered to open the railroad to Fredericksburg. In addition to his engineering experience, Haupt had authored a work titled *General Theory of Bridge Construction* in 1851. His new assignment would allow him to test his theoretical knowledge.[1]

The most formidable obstacle on the railroad line was at Potomac Creek, where the bridge had been burned. On May 1st, ten men from each company in the 19th Indiana, the whole commanded by Lieutenant Benjamin Harter of Company K, reported for duty as bridge builders. Similar details were furnished by the 6th and 7th Wisconsin regiments. Colonel Haupt was unimpressed with his construction crew and he complained that:

> many of the men were sickly and inefficient, others were required for guard duty, and it was seldom that more than 100 to 120 men could be found fit for service, of whom a still smaller number were really efficient, and very few were able or willing to climb about on ropes and poles at an elevation of eighty feet.

Despite his untrained crew, lack of tools, and several days of wet weather, the Potomac Creek bridge was completed in less than two weeks.[2]

Haupt's bridge was an engineering marvel. It spanned a chasm nearly 400 feet wide and towered 80 feet above the creek's surface. Built of unhewn trees and saplings cut in the neighboring woods, the bridge would carry ten to fifteen trains a day for several years. One engineer estimated that if all the timber were laid end to end it would stretch nearly seven miles. When President Lincoln saw the bridge while visiting McDowell's command, he declared it to be "the most remarkable structure that human eyes ever rested upon." He also said that it appeared to be built entirely of "bean-poles and cornstalks."[3]

Another construction crew, under the direction of Daniel Stone, who had been selected by the Secretary of War, rebuilt a railroad bridge over the Rappahannock River. This construction effort would, however, be different than the Potomac Creek assignment. Instead of detailing soldiers at random, this time men were carefully selected and organized into what was styled "McDowell's Construction Corps." The new organization contained ten officers and 200 men, each officer commanding a squad of twenty men. There were three squads of framers, two of hoisters, two of hewers, one of picks and shovelers, one in charge of railroad ties, and one to lay track. Soldiers of the Construction Corps camped together, traveled as a unit, and had printed passes that allowed passage back and forth through the lines. They also wore engineer insignia on their caps and adopted an attitude of "live high and work hard." Company B's contingent in this elite unit consisted of Corporal Jesse Jones and Privates Gardiner Lewis and James Wine.[4]

The first bridge constructed at Fredericksburg was simply a line of old canal boats that were anchored parallel to shore, connected with stringers and planks laid on top. The railroad bridge was assembled some 200 yards upstream from this string of canal boats. Colonel Haupt reported that the railroad structure was to be about 600 feet long and 43 feet above the water, which was about ten feet deep at that point. The Federal builders quickly took advantage of abandoned rebel property. Construction began from the south bank, where a small shipyard provided pine and oak logs. The "Lady Washington," an old worthless locomotive left behind by the rebels, was repaired and used for hauling timber from the surrounding hills. Sections of framing were assembled at the shipyard and then towed into position by an old ferryboat.[5]

Bridge construction began on May 9th and Haupt's crew from the Potomac Creek "bean-poles and cornstalks" site arrived in time to begin work from the Falmouth side of the river. Trains began running over the bridge on May 22nd, just fourteen days after work had begun. The project would have been concluded much sooner, but a heavy rain had raised the water level and swept away much of the framing. Despite that setback, soldiers were proud of their engineering feat and one Wisconsin man wrote, "The Western boys know how to build bridges, as you would admit could you have seen the railroad bridge *walk* across the river." One Hoosier volunteer boasted, "A finer body of men were never seen together, or better qualified to do this kind of work, and no organization in the army was required to do harder service than were they."[6]

Ever since General King's promotion to division command, the Western brigade had been led by Lysander Cutler, the senior colonel. On May 2nd, the 19th Indiana marched up to the Rappahannock and camped near Falmouth, although the brigade soon moved to the Lacy House, directly across the river from Fredericksburg, where their new general issued the following order:

> Head Quarters, 3d Brigade
> Camp near Fredericksburg, Va.
> May 8, 1862
>
> General Orders
> No. 52
> In conformity with Special Orders No. 46, from the Head Quarters of Dep't of the Rappahannock, the undersigned assumes command of this Brigade.
> He trusts that the command, on going into action, will emulate the gallant deeds of their brave Statesmen in the West, and prove to them that the heroism displayed at Fort Donelson and Pittsburg Landing, can be rivaled by their brothers, who have come East, to fight the cause of the "Union."
> All existing orders in the Brigade will, until abrogated or modified, be strictly and rigidly enforced.
> 1st Lieut John P. Wood, 19th Indiana Vol. is announced as Act'g Ass't Adj't Gen'l of this Brigade.
>
> > John Gibbon
> > Brig Genl

This was the same John Gibbon who had served with the brigade as captain of Battery B, 4th United States Artillery, until his promotion to brigadier general of volunteers on May 2nd. The Hoosiers had little contact with the captain during his tenure as division chief of artillery, but now they would become intimately acquainted.[7]

John Gibbon spent the first few days getting to know his new command, while the Western officers and enlisted men sized up their new commander. Neither liked what they saw. On May 9th, Gibbon reviewed the Indiana regiment and Colonel Meredith recorded that his men "did not march very well at common time," although they had "done well at quick

9. Charles Sponsler.
From the Mary Bowman Collection.
Used with permission.

time." The general inspected the Hoosier camp on the 10th and professed to be pleased. But after Gibbon had finished, Captain Wood returned and ordered the camp to be aligned "in Columns By Compass," instructions that gave "great disatisfaction." According to one enlisted man, the Hoosiers "Spent the day [11th] in pitching and striking tents, trying to get a straight street in line when finally we moved by Company into Column and succeeded in pitching to the satisfaction of our Brigadier Gibbon." It was little wonder that William Murray would write, "The impression in relation to our new Brigadier, on first sight, is rather unfavorable."[8]

These men of the Western brigade disliked this West Pointer who intruded into the baseball season with drills and inspections. The Wisconsin and Indiana boys laughed at the general behind his back—mostly because his long legs looked silly while riding his short horse, and called him "The Southern Renegade" because his brothers were in the Confederate army. This nickname was applied behind his back since the general was extremely sensitive regarding his North Carolina relatives, particularly after he had been reported to the Committee on the Conduct of the War as a potential Confederate sympathizer.[9]

General Gibbon was unimpressed with his new command, which had apparently gone to seed under Colonel Cutler's administration. The new commander immediately changed affairs in his brigade. After discovering that most officers routinely failed to attend reveille, Gibbon directed that henceforth the regiments would form on the colors under arms. The general and his staff would then gallop through the camps and, after ensuring each regiment had been properly formed, dismiss the men. Privates were elated when they saw the officers roused from their beds along with everyone else.[10]

Gibbon could not help but notice that some of his Western boys were extremely dirty. He quickly ordered company officers to see that their men all bathed "at least once a week." Another order demanded that the regimental camps be thoroughly policed twice each day. In an effort to ward off fevers, Gibbon took a two-step approach. First, he insisted that every soldier drink a cup of hot coffee immediately after reveille. Second, he ordered all brigade officers to grant passes to *every* soldier who desired to gather blackberries. The coffee and blackberry formula had no clinical value, but the general's therapy at least allowed the soldiers an opportunity to leave camp at their convenience.[11]

John Gibbon immediately found himself thrust into the role of a military schoolteacher with several thousand pupils. He was impressed with "the quick intelligence of the scholars," noting that they easily learned complicated battalion movements when properly instructed. These Western volunteers were proud men and the general shrewdly observed that "the hope of reward was far more powerful than the fear of punishment." He soon learned that a single word of praise to his soldiers was worth more than a hundred threats. Slowly but surely, discipline and proficiency in drill increased until Gibbon could claim, "The *habit* of obedience and subjection to the will of another, so difficult to instill into the minds of free and independent men became marked characteristics in the command."[12]

Of course, Gibbon encountered a number of obstacles in his attempt to train the brigade. Perhaps the greatest irritation to his Regular Army soul was the volunteers' neglect of duty while on guard. The duties of a sentinel required him to walk his beat until relieved, keep alert and salute all officers who might pass by his post. The general described the situation when he assumed command:

> Men who had been working hard all their lives for a purpose could see no use in pacing up and down doing nothing. Hence logs of wood, a convenient rock or camp-stool, were frequently resorted to as resting places, and often I would ride by a sentinel without any attention being paid to me whatever, the man on post being entirely too much occupied enjoying his ease, perhaps even smoking a cigar, to notice my approach.

In addition to these breaches of military etiquette, many soldiers spent their time reading books and writing letters, while others simply wandered off. Gibbon devised a novel solution to the problem. Henceforth, any sentinel found deficient would "be at once relieved from duty, placed under charge of the guard as a prisoner, compelled to walk in charge of a sentinel the usual number of hours, and be marched on guard the next day to perform over again the duty he has neglected to perform." No one wished to repeat the dull routine of guard duty, so the Western boys began to pay more attention to their instructions.[13]

Gibbon also tangled with his Western boys over the destruction of fences. Well-seasoned Virginia rails made wonderful fuel and the fences around Fredericksburg had begun to disappear with an amazing frequency. Although the soldiers saw no reason to respect property of rebel sympathizers, there was a standing order in McDowell's division to protect civilian property. Gibbon refused to debate the wisdom of the order, saying simply, "It is an *order* and must be obeyed." The general's solution was simple—whenever a fence was destroyed the nearest regiment must be compelled to cut timber, split rails and rebuild the fence.[14]

One Saturday a fence mysteriously disappeared and, as luck would have it, Colonel Meredith's boys were closest to the scene. Gibbon rejected Hoosier protests that some sneaky New Yorkers had been guilty of the deed and an entire company spent Sunday replacing the missing fence. Hoosiers cursed their new commander with vigor, although they had probably taken the fence, and if not that fence then certainly some other fence at some other time.

Since it was senseless to appeal Gibbon's apparent cruelty through military channels, the Hoosiers sought sympathy at home. An officer contacted the Washington correspondent of the *Daily Journal,* who "railed" against McDowell's order and Gibbon's enforcement of it:

> Such an order is infamous, almost justifies mutiny, and ought to bring its author beneath the feet of the poorest private, and to the contempt of every loyal man. It is a burning shame to make the brave men of our army hold sacred guard over the property of those who are struggling to bury the edifice of our liberties in the grave of perished nations.

After the story was confirmed by Colonel Meredith, the correspondent advised, "Let the Governor lift his voice against these crimes and outrages, if there is none other to do so." Governor Morton was too busy with other matters to intrude into a fence controversy, so the Hoosiers would have to confront General Gibbon in their own way. The mutiny alluded to by the Indianapolis reporter was only weeks away.[15]

Gibbon wanted his brigade not only to act like soldiers, but also to look like soldiers. One obvious problem was the variety of uniforms in the four regiments and even within individual regiments. On dress parade, the brigade displayed a ragtag assortment of hats and caps, coats and blouses, dark trousers and sky-blue trousers, a lack of uniformity that annoyed Gibbon. His solution was simple. The quartermaster must issue enough clothing to assure that each man had a complete outfit, according to army regulations. Every soldier was to be supplied with the following articles: one black (Hardee) hat with regulation trimmings, one blue dress coat, one blue blouse or jacket, two gray woolen shirts, two pairs of light blue wool trousers, two pairs of cotton drawers, two pairs of shoes, two pairs of gray wool stockings, one pair of white leggings, one gray wool blanket, one rubber blanket, one-half of a shelter tent, one knapsack, one canteen, and one haversack capable of holding three days' rations. In addition to these items, each man had his musket, cartridge box with forty rounds of ammunition, cap box, leather belts and brass plates. One man in each company carried a pick, another man a shovel and one of every ten men toted an ax. William Murray summed up the clothing issue with a single word: "Gehosophat!" A rumor circulated through the brigade that when Colonel Meredith turned in his clothing requisition, he had also included a request for "four extra mule teams to transport the extra baggage."[16]

As clothing wore out, quartermasters continued to issue black hats and uniform coats to Gibbon's regiments even though other volunteer organizations received caps and jackets. This distinctive appearance became an important part of the Iron Brigade legend and the Western men could be readily identified by friend and foe alike. But despite the new clothing, Gibbon did not achieve his goal. The brigade still lacked a uniform appearance, especially since the 2nd Wisconsin received dark blue trousers instead of the standard sky blue issue.

Diversity was most evident in the customized black hats, which reflected a determination by men to display their independence. A fully equipped hat contained the following accessories: hat cord and tassels, a brass eagle to pin the brim, a brass horn that signified an infantryman, a brass regimental number, a brass company letter and a black ostrich plume. The brim was supposed to be pinned to the crown on the left side, but some wore it up on the right while others chose to wear the brim flat. Although the hats came fully accessorized, individual items were "lost" until the desired combinations were attained. During spring and summer, men sported flowers on their hats. Many soldiers even fiddled with the basic shape of their headgear, often creasing the crown so that it resembled what is now known as a "cowboy hat."[17]

The 19th Indiana received new clothing in mid-May and the Hoosiers nearly burst with pride when they marched in review for President Lincoln on May 23rd. According to Lieutenant Orr, "the whole regt was dressed as follows: new Blouse, new skye blue pants, new *fine* shoes, new Hats, new leggings & white gloves, and not only some But every last man in the regt was dressed this way." Colonel Meredith gleefully recorded that his regiment "was considered the finest Regiment on review" and Henry Marsh wrote, "the Reg't has new clothes so they look splendid, with new legings on, the best in the Brigade." It was about this time that General McDowell said of his Western troops, "Many times I have shown them to foreign officers of distinction, as specimens of American Volunteer soldiers, and asked them if they had ever anywhere seen even among the picked soldiers of royal and imperial guards, a more splendid body of men, and I have never had an affirmative answer." But veterans of General James Shields's division, including boys from the 7th, 13th, and 14th Indiana, brought Colonel Meredith's men back to reality with taunts of "Bandbox Regiment! Bandbox Regiment!" "You don't look like Hoosiers!" and "You put on too much style for us!" After viewing Shields's ragamuffins, one lieutenant scornfully observed, "They are poorly dressed, dirty looking and very indifferently drilled or disciplined."[18]

On Sunday morning, May 25th, Colonel Meredith paraded his Hoosiers for regimental inspection. At about 11 o'clock the soldiers were startled by "a report louder than a thousand cannon." The Fredericksburg arsenal had exploded, instantly killing a guard detailed from the 23rd New York. At first rumors circulated that rebel spies had sabotaged the arsenal, but investigation revealed that the explosion had resulted from carelessness. This exciting event signaled an advance by General McDowell's division, which began shortly thereafter.[19]

Gibbon's brigade crossed the Rappahannock and started south on the Bowling Green Road at about 3 o'clock. James Perry, of the 7th Wisconsin, described how marches were conducted in Gibbon's brigade:

> When the moment arrives the drum is beat & the order "fall in," is given by the Co. Commanders. When every one able to march is expected to fall in the ranks in proper order, according to heights. The Orderly calls the roll when each one answers to his name. they then number off by 2s then from right to left. When the Co is formed they are permitted to stand at rest and await the orders of the Col. When all is ready he gives the command "attention battalion right face (when the companys form in 4 rank file) forward march["]. then away they go, each one is expected to retain his place in the ranks and preserve order. The battalion generally carry arms at a right shoulder shift. rests are ordered when necessary & opportunities to fill canteens when offered.

Gibbon halted his four regiments at sundown after a fairly easy march of eight miles over good roads. Retreating rebels had left hastily scrawled messages nailed to trees, most simply addressed to the "damned Yanks." One prominent sign boasted a hand pointing southward with the inscription:
"30 MILES TO RICHMOND! COME AND SEE US!"[20]

11
The Legging Mutiny

The Hoosiers had expected to join General McClellan's army at Richmond where they would "be in at the Death" of the Confederacy, but the southward movement was canceled because of General Thomas J. "Stonewall" Jackson's victory over Union troops at Winchester, Virginia. King's division camped near Guiney's Station and spent the next few days repairing the Richmond & Fredericksburg Railroad while they waited for new orders. At 1 o'clock on May 29th, "a sweltering day," Gibbon's brigade retraced its steps to Fredericksburg and headed northwest toward Catlett's Station. This forced march continued on the 30th, which was also described as "excessively warm." During one stretch, the 19th Indiana marched eighteen miles in six hours. A broiling sun, dusty roads and their heavy load of clothing caused many soldiers to collapse by the roadside or straggle along behind the column.[1]

The footsore and weary soldiers, "still waiting to reinforce somebody," rested at Catlett's Station on June 1st, but shortly before noon on the 2nd, Gibbon's brigade was ordered off to Haymarket. The heat was unbearable and after a few miles the boys began to lighten their burdens. According to one Wisconsin soldier, "First would go the coat, then the pants, then the socks, and last of all the shoes, accompanied by the shoe brush and the box of blacking." Some men stopped alongside the road and changed into new coats and pants before pitching their old clothes. Others simply threw away their bulging knapsacks. Many threw away everything but their muskets, cartridge boxes, food and water. One soldier declared that "the sides of the road were literally blue for miles."[2]

General Marsena Patrick, whose brigade followed the Western regiments, observed, "It was terribly hot when we started & Gibbon's Brigade, which started ahead of mine straggled badly & threw away their Blankets, coats etc. before they were three miles out." The march of the 19th

Indiana was described by Captain Robert Hamilton, who wrote that "the weather was extremely warm and the men eager for the fray willingly disencumbered themselves of new cloth coats and pants, and in some cases, Knapsacks and all it contained." Colonel Meredith admitted that his men threw away clothing and knapsacks "to the amount of $4000." Of course, the cast-off clothing was quickly gathered up by the natives and secretly sent off to clothe rebel soldiers.[3]

From Haymarket, Gibbon's brigade tramped to Warrenton, then on to Warrenton Junction and finally back to Falmouth. The campaign to capture Jackson, described as "a big game of 'hide-and-go-seek'" by one Badger, had failed miserably. Sergeant Jeff Crull described the fruitless marching to his mother and then admitted that Jackson was "Pretty cuning." Even though Gibbon drove his soldiers to the point of "complete reckless-ness" on these marches, his soldiers had learned several valuable lessons. Most importantly, they had learned "the possibilities of the situation with a view to economizing everything pertaining to rest, food and shelter." A five-minute halt could be turned into a lunch of boiled coffee and hardtack or a brief nap, no matter if the wool uniforms were soaked by sweat or pelting rain. They had also discovered that improvised songs kept up drooping spirits and Gibbon's brigade marched to such lofty lyrics as these:

> We'll freeze to Old Stonewall,
>   When the Johnnies go to sleep;
> Put 'simmons in his whisky,
>   And mustard on his feet.

It was not exactly "The Battle Hymn of the Republic," but ditties such as this were perfect for marching over dust-clogged roads when it was hotter than hell itself.[4]

Many changes had occurred in the Fredericksburg area during the brigade's brief absence. Yankee occupation had stimulated the local economy and businesses were now operating "full blast." Even more importantly, prices had plummeted fifty percent. The moral character of the town had also improved. A diligent provost marshal set out to remove those distractions that beckoned to lonely soldiers out on the town. Before long, the editor of the *Christian Banner* could report that "hundreds of gallons of liquor have been captured, and prostitution has crept away into more secret places, or been driven out of the city." An 8 o'clock curfew was also instituted and rigidly enforced. On the night of June 11th, the provost guard arrested sixteen soldiers who had violated curfew, including Private James Wine of Captain Dudley's company and Private Thomas Stewart, 1st Pennsylvania Light Artillery, who was "dressed in female dress and very disorderly."

Cavalry pickets even pulled a rebel major from his wife's bed, an act thought to be "pretty cool" by the Hoosiers.[5]

Upon reaching Falmouth at 11 A.M. on June 11th, Gibbon gave his tired soldiers twenty-four hours to prepare for a review. After inspecting his troops on the 12th, the general was completely disgusted with the appearance of his brigade, fully three-fourths of which had discarded their new leggings, along with other clothing. He looked into the matter and learned "that whenever the men wanted clothing a requisition was made out, the clothing being taken and no charges being made against the men." This would not do. Although all were guilty to some degree, Gibbon hurled his wrath at the 19th Indiana in the following fashion:

Head Quarters Gibbon's Brigade
Opposite Fredericksburg, Va. June 13, 1862
General Orders
No. 58
The General Commanding the Brigade was much pleased with the military bearing and appearance of the Regiments on review yesterday.

But whilst commending their appearance as a body, he regrets to be obliged to refer to the marked contrast between the 19th Indiana Volunteers and the other Regiments of the Brigade.

Three weeks ago, when reviewed by the President, every one remarked [upon] the neat and cleanly appearance of this Regiment, and the General noticed with regret, the contrast presented on review yesterday.

It appears that during one of the recent marches, most of the men recklessly threw away the clothing just issued to them. Such foolish waste of Stores provided by the Government can not be tolerated, and would never occur in a properly disciplined body of men. The 38th Art. of War provides a severe punishment for such acts. At the approaching muster, every man of this regiment, who has not now in his possession, the clothing issued to him during the past month will be charged on the muster rolls the cost of such clothing, and have the amount deducted from his pay. The Regimental and Company Commanders will be held strictly accountable that this order is rigidly enforced.
John Gibbon
Brig Genl

The Hoosiers were livid at the general's insult.[6]

Gibbon had never respected Colonel Meredith as a military man and after the war would characterize him as "not being anything of a soldier and too old to be made one." But his testimony before the Congressional Committee on the Conduct of the War was much more harsh. Speaking of Long Sol, Gibbon said:

I found him always opposing every plan of mine to render that brigade more efficient. He had not the first principle of a soldier in him; he was altogether disqualified for his position. I asked that he should be brought before a board of examination, but it was never done.

Summing up Meredith's destructive influence, Gibbon asserted, "This Indiana regiment had the finest material in it in the whole brigade, and yet it was the worst regiment I had." In the general's mind, this reckless squandering of uniforms on the march to Haymarket was simply another manifestation of Meredith's incapacity.[7]

The Hoosier soldiers could not control their anger and Sergeant Jeff Crull put into words what they all must have felt:

We have one of the meanest Brigadier genarls that ever lived. there ant a man in the regt But what hates him. Gibens is his name. he is a regular and if we ever get in a fight he will Be the first to fall. every Body hates his very name.

There is no mistaking the implied threat to kill Gibbon at the first opportunity. Sergeant William Murray recorded in his diary that the feeling was widespread, writing, "Great excitement in Camp on account of Leggins—an insubordination of the 19th threatens."[8]

Sol Meredith responded to General Order No. 58 by going outside of the chain of command. He quickly obtained a leave of absence from brigade headquarters, traveled by train and steamer to Washington, and took a room at the Avenue House. News of Sol's arrival spread among Hoosiers in the capital and many friends dropped by his room to say hello, including Patent Commissioner David P. Holloway, an old Wayne County political ally. The two men apparently devised a scheme to get the 19th Indiana transferred from Gibbon's brigade. On June 16th Sol stopped by the Patent Office, where he borrowed Holloway's carriage in order to call on Indiana's two senators, Joseph Wright and Henry Lane. The following day, Secretary of the Interior Caleb Smith accompanied Wright, Lane, and Long Sol to the office of Edwin Stanton, Secretary of War. Colonel Meredith, supported by his political delegation, presented his case against Gibbon's administration of the brigade and requested that the 19th Indiana be transferred to a new command. Stanton refused to interfere in the dispute, saying that General McDowell was the proper person to make such a decision.[9]

Rebuffed by the Secretary of War, this distinguished group of Hoosier politicos retired to formulate a new plan. Instead of appealing their case to President Lincoln, Sol and his allies decided to put some political pressure on General Irvin McDowell in order to force a transfer of the 19th

Indiana. On June 19th, John G. Stephenson, Librarian of Congress, left Washington bearing letters to Generals McDowell and King from Sol's influential friends.[10]

In one of those letters, Caleb Smith, after referring to a "want of cordial feeling and harmony between Genl Gibbon and the 19th Regiment Indiana Volunteers," explained the situation to McDowell:

> The officers of the 19th Regiment are my personal friends and I should regret extremely if anything should occur which should detract from the good standing which our volunteers have already acquired. Colonel Meredith is one of the leading public men of our state and is regarded by our people as a gentleman of high character and an earnest friend of Government. Although he has not received a military education I think he understands his duties well enough to keep his Regiment in such a state of discipline as to do no discredit to the service, and if placed before the enemy I am sure that he and the Regiment will do their whole duty.

Secretary Smith closed his letter by stating that, if the transfer could be made, he would "esteem it as an important personal favor."

Senator Joseph Wright addressed a similar letter to McDowell on behalf of his "personal friend":

> No braver or truer man is to be found in our Army; none more willing to obey the orders of his Superiors. I shall regard it as a personal favor if you shall feel it consistent with your duties to place the Col. and his men in such a situation as that they may with heart and energy distinguish themselves in maintaining the flag of our glorious Union.

Commissioner Holloway, in the interest of "protecting harmony in the army," gave McDowell his own assessment of Long Sol:

> He is a man of great energy of character, and I think I speak with truth when I say there is not a Colonel in the army who has devoted himself more closely to his Regiment than has Col. Meredith. He is a farmer and not a military man—but he is a gentleman of fine administrative abilities, and deservedly popular with his officers and men, as he is with the people of Indiana.

These letters from Secretary Smith, Senator Wright and Commissioner Holloway were just the first steps in Colonel Meredith's plan to escape Gibbon's overbearing administration.[11]

From his headquarters at the Avenue House, Sol assembled another set of letters, these addressed to General King and seeking the brigade commander's assistance in his application for transfer. On June 20th, Captain Hamilton carried this set of dispatches to General King, who tried to smooth Meredith's ruffled feathers by responding, "I greatly regret the existence of the misunderstanding to which you refer, and, for myself, am most unwilling to part with the 19th Indiana. The first opportunity I have of talking with Gen. McDowell, I will see what can be done to remedy the grievance you speak of."[12]

Meanwhile, Long Sol continued his lobbying efforts in Washington and won the support of a bi-partisan group from the Hoosier congressional delegation. Four congressmen added to the pressure on McDowell. James A. Cravens, a Democrat, wrote on June 20th:

> I have known Col. Meredith for many years, and most cheerfully commend him and his request to your kind consideration. He is a gentleman of strict integrity and a faithful officer, and has done his duties promptly.

William McKee Dunn, a Republican who had served in the state legislature with Meredith, obliged his friend by stating:

> I have many personal friends in this Regiment and have a great interest in its welfare. I learn that they feel they are not properly treated by the general, and from some facts that have come to my knowledge [courtesy of Colonel Meredith, no doubt] I am not surprised they should so *feel*.

Another Democrat, John Law of the First District, pointed out the, by now, obvious point that "there is no cordiality or good feeling between the officers and men of the 19th and their Commanding Brigade officer, and they do not wish to serve under him, if they can avoid it." William Mitchell, a Republican from Kendallville, added in a final letter, "I have quite a number of Constituents in that Regiment. I would not ask you to make the change only for the fact that I am aware that there is quite a feeling in that Regiment against the General Commanding."[13]

Despite this overwhelming display of support from powerful political allies, Meredith was unsuccessful. General McDowell refused to be bullied by these meddling civilians and rejected the colonel's application to transfer the 19th Indiana. Chagrined at his failure, Sol returned to Falmouth with the news that the Hoosiers were stuck with their new commander.

If Sol could not have his way, he could at least be a thorn in Gibbon's side. Upon his return to camp, Meredith requested a clarification over a technicality in the enforcement of General Order No. 58. Cleverly implying that his Hoosier volunteers operated under a different set of regulations, Sol wrote to Gibbon's adjutant on June 26th:

Under the act of Congress which authorizes the calling into the field of the present Volunteer force, their yearly allowance of clothing is fixed at $42, and all excess of that amount is to be charged and deducted from their pay, at the expiration of each fiscal year (June 30th). At least this is the view I take of it, which differs from the yearly allowances of the regular service.

The order referred to seems to contemplate a different construction, but requires the commanding officers to *charge* certain clothing mentioned therein.

You will please explain the order and also what course I shall pursue in making out the present muster Rolls.

Gibbon rejected this claim and responded by stating that men who had lost clothing "should be charged with its cost at the approaching muster, no matter whether he had drawn his full yearly allowance or not." The general could have stopped there, but he taunted Sol by continuing, "Col. Meredith will see that this order is rigidly enforced by holding the Co. commanders responsible to the end that clothing issued by the Govt may not hereafter be recklessly squandered as has recently been the case in his Regt." Meredith gave up in exasperation.[14]

Although their colonel had admitted defeat, the Indiana soldiers continued to defy General Gibbon and his infamous general order by refusing to wear their leggings. A soldier in the 7th Wisconsin wrote that "the 19th stubbornly persisted in a declaration that they would be damned if they would take the leggings, or words to that effect, sympathized with and seconded by the other regiments." Another soldier remembered, "This fretted the General, who, with numerous dress-parades and orders and lectures to the officers on parade, sought to carry his point. The officers exhorted, pleaded, threatened, swore, but the boys would not take the leggings." Finally, Gibbon published an order that if the Hoosiers did not appear in their leggings the next morning, *he would order his battery to open fire on their camp*. Meredith's men returned to their tents considerably "out of sorts," but unanimous in their determination not to wear those damned leggings.

The following morning, Hoosier soldiers, minus leggings, gathered in the company streets, daring Gibbon to carry out his threat. Suddenly, the roar of cannon fire burst upon the still morning air and startled soldiers fell flat on the ground. Cries went up simultaneously from various parts of camp: "Lay down, boys, lay down! We'll take the leggings!! We'll take the leggings!!!" As they cowered on the ground, the Indiana boys soon noticed that no one had been hurt. A few adventurous souls investigated and quickly discovered that a nearby battery was drilling with blank rounds. As the Hoosiers sheepishly regained their feet, Wisconsin boys howled with laughter.

Meredith's men laughed right along with the Badgers. The "Great Legging Mutiny" was too good a story to let die, so the enlisted men turned it into a game. According to one Badger:

> When the artillery are out practicing, with the discharge of every gun, it is a common question to ask "Will you take the leggings now?" A negative reply, succeeded by another discharge from the cannon brings out the solemn, mock compliant answer, "Yes, yes, I'll take the leggings."

The new game remained popular all summer. Thirty years later, Corporal Robert Patterson would recall the Legging Mutiny in verse for his comrades:

> But when that little fighter, General Gibbon,
>   Began to pull the regular army ribbon,
> Every one of you got down and went to begging,
>   But he couldn't make you take the leggings.

Although Gibbon insisted that the government be reimbursed for all missing clothing, he did realize his mistake in forcing a confrontation with the 19th Indiana. Thereafter the hated leggings were not reissued and those lost or worn out were not replaced. This was a workable compromise, although the enlisted men viewed it as a victory and later claimed that Gibbon "acknowledged that his brigade made a volunteer of him."[15]

Following their abortive mutiny, the Hoosiers settled into the familiar camp routine at Falmouth. In their leisure time, men strolled the historic fields around Fredericksburg, where they occasionally stumbled upon items of interest. One officer sent home this curious inscription from a tombstone in an old burying ground outside the city:

> Here lies the body of Edward Helder, practitioner in Physic and Chirurgery. Born in Bedfordshire, England, in the year of our Lord, 1542. Was contemporary with, and one of the pall-bearers to the body of William Shakespeare. After a brief illness, his spirit ascended in the year of our Lord 1618 — aged 76.

Gullible soldiers even claimed to have seen the stump of the cherry tree chopped down by a young George Washington, although that famous story is totally fictional.[16]

Aside from the Legging Mutiny, the biggest regimental news in June was Thomas Gilbert's attempted suicide on the 20th. Gilbert, who was acting as Colonel Meredith's hostler, tried unsuccessfully to cut his throat. Henry Marsh wrote of the incident, "Tom Gilbert did try to cut his throat but the knife was not sharp enough, he was drunk and tired of the service. he wants to go home was the reason." He was patched up by Surgeon Jacob Ebersole, who had replaced the recently departed Calvin Woods. Ebersole's former partner, Abraham B. Haines, would soon join the regiment as an assistant surgeon.[17]

Three days after the Gilbert affair, a violent thunderstorm swept over the Hoosier camp. Sergeant William Murray used a long-winded style of prose to capture the event:

> In the evening the sky became overcast with heavy rolling clouds overfreighted with "*Aqueous Kindness*" and overcharged with Electric fluid, which, in its passage from cloud to cloud seemed to burn great gaps in the condensed atmosphere producing a concussion of the Elements causing the deep-toned thunder in terrific peals to manifest itself to our acoustical organs as an accompaniment to the terrifically grand, august and sublime optical manifestation of forked glaring of lurid sheets of seething electricity.

He concluded by exclaiming, "Oh the ecstacy of the 'tented field' under such felicitous circumstances." It must have been one hell of a storm![18]

On June 26th, the War Department combined a number of independent organizations, including General McDowell's corps, into the Army of Virginia. General John Pope, a promising officer who had gained prominence with victories on the Mississippi, assumed command of this new army. Pope immediately appointed Rufus King to command his First Corps and the division commander said goodbye to his men on June 27th, amid heartfelt congratulations and numerous serenades. King concluded General Order No. 60, dated June 28th, in the following fashion:

> With these few parting words; with fervent good wishes for the individual well being of the officers and privates; with the earnest hope that victory may attend the cause of the Union and glory crown the banner of the division, the General commanding bids farewell to his comrades, fellow-citizens and friends.

King, however, declined the post after being fully informed of his responsibilities and he returned to the division, "to the great joy of all."[19]

12

Campaigning under Pope

During the first days of July, the Hoosiers exhibited considerable excitement and an intense anxiety over news coming from McClellan's army in front of Richmond. The appearance of their Virginia neighbors seemed to indicate a victory for the Federal army, at least according to some careful observation by Sergeant Tom Benton:

> there is no doubt but what there has been a great battle fought at Richmond. we judge as much from the effect it has upon the prominent secessionists of Fredericksburg. they get the news through private resources much quicker than we can and that it has been successful to our forces we judge by seeing the secesh ladies weeping throughout the city and the men are collected in squads with faces about a foot longer than usual.

Meredith's boys did not like being stationed in their quiet backwater while McClellan led his men in glorious battles just a few miles to the south. Letters home from Company G described Fredericksburg as an "out-of-the-way hole" and Private Hawk grumbled that King's division had lost more men to desertion than to any other cause. But newspapers would soon confirm that, instead of capturing the rebel capital, McClellan's army had been forced back on an inglorious retreat to a new base. The ambitious Richmond campaign had failed.[1]

If the Western boys could not be a part of the fighting, they could at least have a grand celebration on the Fourth of July, and what better day to celebrate their victory over General Gibbon and his damned leggings. Independence Day began with a battery firing a thirty-four gun national salute at sunrise, kicking off "a day of general festivity and hilarity." Although regulations specified only one salute at noon, General King's artillery fired one at sunrise, the prescribed salute at noon and a third at sunset.[2]

Late that afternoon, squads of privates confronted their officers, compelling them to remove their hats, coats, and swords. These emblems of authority were eagerly taken up by volunteers from the ranks, who thereupon arrested their own officers. With only a few exceptions, lieutenants, captains and even field officers submitted graciously and performed police duty under the close supervision of expertly trained privates. One officer who claimed to be too sick to work was ordered off to a surgeon, who excused him from duty after an impromptu sick call. When the drums beat to assemble for dress parade, police call ended and the officers equipped themselves with privates' uniforms and muskets and accouterments. The self-appointed officers marched their companies to the brigade parade ground where newly-commissioned colonels assembled their regiments.[3]

It was then that General John Gibbon received his special surprise. Every soldier who still retained his leggings wore them to dress parade. But to show their contempt for the general order that had prompted the Great Legging Mutiny, soldiers wore their leggings—strapped to coats, hats, belts, accouterments, and muskets. This incredible spectacle was a not too subtle reminder to Gibbon that the brigade, and especially the 19th Indiana, at least symbolically refused to take the leggings. The sight was so ludicrous that even the crusty general had to smile.[4]

That evening was devoted to fun. Some soldiers competed in sack races, while others chased a greased pig around camp. Many drank contraband whiskey and roughhoused with friends. But the highlight of the celebration was a strange revival of the old Olympic games. First came mule races, each winner to receive $40 from a sum collected from the officers. Soldiers from the four regiments formed a huge circle around some forty men who had procured mules. At the tap of a drum the race commenced and riders began to whip one another's mules, the last man across the finish line being the winner. A Badger boy described the end of the first race:

> Every mule had a rider when the start was made, not so when the "home stretch" was reached. Many were riderless, and came jogging along in an approved style of their own. The discomfitted riders were to be seen picking themselves up in different parts of the ring, and came savagely walking around, giving vent to their feelings by heaping curses upon the mules.

In a second race, "some flew the track, others broke through the wall of human beings around the circle, others became tired and legged down, some threw themselves, and others came around at breakneck speed." A third race had similar results and for several days "lame men were quite numerous." Private George Williams of the 2nd Wisconsin eventually collected the purse for being the best mule rider.[5]

The mule races were followed by foot races. Between thirty and forty men signed up to race for the purse of $40 and "they all worked hard for it." Captain Hollon Richardson won the final race and could claim to be the fastest man in the Western brigade. The games concluded with two horse races, with the officers betting heavily on their favorites. "Bet," a gray mare belonging to Adjutant John Russey of the Hoosier regiment, won both races. Colonel Meredith shrewdly backed his adjutant's mare and won $140. Despite the almost total absence of women, no money to speak of, and the prospect of army rations for supper, the Hoosiers would still have agreed with their comrade who wrote that "we had a gay old time."[6]

Shortly after this day of festivity, Robert K. Beecham, of the 2nd Wisconsin, gave a candid description of General Gibbon's command:

> Gibbon's brigade, composed entirely of Western men, is more lively by far than the other troops that are with us. We have more music, more dancing, more athletic sports and more real fun and good humor than the Eastern boys, and it is generally admitted that we are not bad on a march. Still there is noticeable difference between each regiment of our brigade. The 2d is probably the hardest set of boys, but good natured and easy to get along with. They wear an air of fearless carelessness wherever found. The 6th is more stately, and distant and march to slower music than we do. The 7th puts on the least style of any and crow the least. It is now the largest regiment in the brigade and well drilled. It is the truest friend the 2d ever found. The 19th Indiana is an indifferent, don't care regiment. They pride themselves on their fighting pluck—which is undoubtedly good—more than their drill.

Despite the differences between individual regiments, Beecham concluded, "As a brigade we get along finely together."[7]

The Hoosiers wanted nothing more than to be led into battle and their choice for a commanding general would almost unanimously have been George B. McClellan. Despite his failure at Richmond, soldiers still loved the man and despised those "vipers" in the press who hounded their hero. Lieutenant William Orr expressed the common sentiment in a letter home:

> if McClellan was so disposed, he could in two weeks, lead his armies, with shouts to Washington; and then prorogue that miserable abortion of a congress, that too long has disgraced the nation. But thanks be to God, I believe McClellan to be a patriot as well as a General, and that he will not abuse the unbounded confidence his soldiers have in him—even to gratify a great, a Laudable thirst for revenge.

Denied the honor of fighting under McClellan, the Hoosiers still wanted a chance, although under their present circumstances they could not be sure since "where we are going, or when, or whether at all or not, is just a great mystery."[8]

Wherever they might be ordered, the Western boys had no desire to go there under the command of General Irvin McDowell. Major Dawes of the 6th Wisconsin wrote of their commander, "There is a strong feeling among the soldiers against McDowell. He is considered incompetent, if not disloyal." Captain John Marsh furnished some specifics:

> Theoretically, McDowell was an accomplished soldier, but he seemed to always lose his head in an emergency. I have seen him attempt to handle a division, simply in practice, only to get his brigades and regiments so divided and twisted that he completely lost control of his command; his horse was such a frequent blunderer over fences and into ditches that there was a general impression that couldn't be shaken, that this man who never tasted wines or liquors was a drunkard.

Camp gossip claimed that McDowell communicated with the enemy and that he wore a conspicuous straw hat so the rebels could recognize him as a friend in battle. The charges of drunkenness and disloyalty were unfounded, but McDowell could no longer inspire his troops.[9]

Sol Meredith's boys hoped that John Pope, their new army commander, would prove to be as worthy as McClellan. General Pope quickly won their approval with two general orders published on July 18th, both of which outlined the procedure by which the army would subsist on the country during future movements. According to these orders, supplies would be taken for army use and vouchers given for the market value of seized goods. At the conclusion of the war, the government would honor vouchers of those Virginians who could prove their loyalty. Although Pope's orders would lead to many unauthorized acts of plunder and robbery, the Union boys looked forward to living off the secessionists instead of standing guard over their property. By the end of the month, Sergeant Crull would write of Pope, "He is the man we was looking fer all summer."[10]

Pope's foraging orders merely formalized a system of petty thievery that had existed for months around Fredericksburg. As previously mentioned, Gibbon had given blanket permission for his men to wander about in search of blackberries and many took advantage of these excursions to bring in a few "extras." Tom Benton related how he and Sam McCown had gone after blackberries a few days before Pope's orders and "while I was throwing a stone very carelessly I happened to strike a turkey which made us a fine dinner." Nearly everyone did it and officers either looked the other way or winked at the hijinks, often in exchange for a share of the loot. Some of the boys still preferred to wander into Fredericksburg, which had reverted to its original character after a series of provost marshals eased former restrictions. According to General Marsena Patrick, "the town is full of Brothels &

Prostitutes & drinking saloons & all sorts of vile institutions," an attractive haven for soldiers.[11]

In mid-July Meredith's Hoosiers cheered the arrival of wagons to haul their knapsacks on the march, a change that would prove to be "a great blessing to the boys." However, there were no marches planned and the boys continued to tote their knapsacks for reviews and drills. Brigade drills were conducted from 7 to 9 A.M. and battalion drills took place at 6 P.M., these times sensibly avoiding the scorching mid-summer heat. Gibbon's brigade was considered "the flower of the army in this department" and, unfortunately, its camp was near division headquarters. Whenever General McDowell would entertain visitors at Fredericksburg, he had Rufus King trot his famous Western brigade around in the sun for a few hours. Even General King began to sympathize with his suffering soldiers. According to Sergeant Jeff Crull, "he thinks we know enuf with out drilling this hot weather." The Hoosiers even began to appreciate John Gibbon's skill at maneuvering his brigade in these seemingly endless reviews and one of them confided, "Feeling toward him has softened a little recently."[12]

While Gibbon's infantry marched around and around, the brigade medical officers practiced caring for make-believe wounded. The medical corps consisted of four regimental surgeons, their assistant surgeons, hospital stewards to assist the doctors, and the ambulance corps, this latter composed of nurses, stretcher-bearers and ambulance drivers. The 19th Indiana had a small one-horse ambulance and a much larger wagon pulled by a four-horse team. The brigade medical officers had the capability of hauling about fifteen wounded men in the various regimental ambulances.[13]

In the 19th Indiana, Dr. Ebersole battled an outbreak of disease in camp, while Dr. Green supervised the Fredericksburg hospital, which had been established in a woolen mill. Illness in camp was simply the result of improper sanitation. General Gibbon attempted to correct the problem by ordering twice-daily police calls, during which "the camps of the several regiments of this Brigade will be thoroughly policed." When that failed to halt the spread of disease, lime was spread all over the campgrounds "to neutralize acids and prevent Malaria." Finally, on July 29th, the brigade moved to a new location a little over two miles east of Fredericksburg.[14]

Seriously ill soldiers were sent to Dr. Green's hospital and several Hoosiers passed away there during this outbreak, among them Sergeant William Kauselmier of the color guard. Joseph Dolph, Company D, died of dysentery on July 7th, and Captain Jacobs described the private's last hours in a letter of condolence to his widow:

> he Died last night at 9 oclock at the Hospital in Fredricksburgh Va., he had been Complaining for the past Ten Days of not being very well but

still he keeps a moving around thinking he would be well in a Day or two, untill night befor last he was taken worse & was sent to Hospital wher he remained untill he Expired. I was over to se him last Evening when he told me he was a going to Die & wished me to write to you & Say good Bye for him, he was Decently Buried this Evening & Much Respect Paid to him by the Company & others.

Without detailing the cruel injustice of Gibbons's General Order No. 58, Jacobs told her that the deceased soldier had "only some Six or Seven Dollars a coming to him as the whole Company is in Debt to the Government for their yearly Clothing which is to be Settled this pay Day." He also advised that Dolph had loaned out money to his friends, but collecting it would be difficult because "they are all in Debt."[15]

Indiana soldiers sent to general hospitals in the Washington area were soon contacted by agents from the Indiana Relief Association, a branch of the Indiana Military Agency. The Military Agency supervised the distribution of food and clothing that had been collected by the Indiana Sanitary Commission. W. T. Dennis reported on the work of distribution:

> The visiting committees all report excellent care and attention, comfortable accommodations, cleanliness, and general good management on the part of those having the active charge of the hospitals, and up to this time our relief has been extended mostly in the way of linen coats and pantaloons, shirts and undershirts, drawers, socks, pocket handkerchiefs, combs, brushes, &c. Fruits and delicacies are furnished when the Surgeon in charge will allow it. Our fund is larger than that of any other State for these purposes, and our committees are industrious and thorough in the discharge of their duties.

But the distribution of sanitary goods was just one of many important duties performed by the Indiana Relief Association.[16]

Probably the most important function of the Relief Association was its dispatch of accurate lists of sick and wounded soldiers "for the benefit of their friends and relatives throughout the State." These lists, many of them published in the *Indianapolis Daily Journal,* contained each patient's name, place hospitalized, company, regiment, type of disease or wound, and home address. Although Governor Morton wanted semi-monthly reports, the great number of Hoosiers scattered in dozens of hospitals throughout Maryland, Virginia, and the District of Columbia made compliance impossible. This problem was evident in Alexandria, where the general hospital served as headquarters for about twenty different hospitals in that city, not including large facilities in nearby Fairfax Seminary and Falls Church. Despite the workload, members of the Indiana Relief Association assured their fellow Hoosiers that all inquiries "will be promptly responded to."[17]

Hoosier boys had quickly learned that disease could strike anyone at any time. Sergeant Benton had accepted the various threats posed by military life and willingly accepted his fate, no matter what that fate might be. He expressed his philosophy in the following manner, "to day we are well and doing well. tomorrow a bullet may end our career in double quick time, but life is no more uncertain here than at the home fireside." Even while peacefully in camp, lives remained in jeopardy. This was never more apparent than on July 17th, when George Johnson, a private from Company A who acted as Major May's hostler, drowned in the Rappahannock. When the tide was out, the river could almost be waded across, but when the tide rushed in the water quickly became deep, rapid, and treacherous. While swimming a horse, Johnson and the animal began to struggle and both went under several times. Then Johnson was struck by the frightened horse and he drowned almost immediately. This sudden death of a soldier in perfect health was a shock to the Hoosiers and underscored Tom Benton's message.[18]

In order to prepare the boys for their afterlife, the brigade chaplains sponsored a series of church meetings. A committee of arrangements, composed of one man from each regiment, scheduled meetings for Tuesday, Friday, and Sunday evenings, in addition to regular Sunday preaching. The committee solicited volunteers to build a proper chapel and the boys responded by building a shelter of poles covered with pine boughs. Although relatively few attended these meetings, religious soldiers vowed to continue the meeting schedule "when practicable."[19]

With their souls prepared for eternity, Gibbon's Western boys were eager for a fight. A Wisconsin officer wrote that they all wished to be "something more than ornamental file closers." Speaking for the Hoosiers, Henry Marsh asserted, "We have a brigade that is spoiling for a fight, composed of excelent men." As for himself, Henry declared, "Father, if I had a thousand lives I would rather loose them all than for our cause to be lost."[20]

On July 24th General Gibbon started on a raid toward Orange Court House, but the Hoosiers were left behind. Gibbon's force consisted of the 2nd and 6th Wisconsin, 23rd and 30th New York, two companies of the 3rd Indiana Cavalry, two companies of Berdan's Sharpshooters, and Battery B, 4th U.S. Artillery. This expedition marched to within two miles of its destination, but retired on the 26th when enemy reinforcements arrived from Gordonsville. As the raiders were returning to camp, Gibbon was eating a picnic lunch when rebel cavalry suddenly scattered the rearguard and charged up to within thirty yards of the general. Horses were unbridled and the infantry sprawled on the grass, so Gibbon was in a tight spot until his Sharpshooters fired a volley and saved him. The Hoosier cavalrymen quickly mounted and drove away the attackers, leaving the column to return to Fredericksburg unmolested.[21]

As the month changed, Sol Meredith's boys spent their time laying out their new camp on a gentle slope. The officers' tents were pitched on top, with the company streets running in straight lines down the slope. Tents were actually small huts with walls of woven pine and cedar boughs, many having doors and windows. Tables and chairs bordered the walkways in front of their huts. Brush piled on top of poles, like enormous open sheds, shaded the company streets. Cook tents and a hospital completed the new Hoosier home. The latter boasted a carpet of pine and cedar, raised beds, mosquito bars and a fabric tent fly to increase circulation. To complete their hospital, the Hoosiers landscaped the exterior with small trees.

Two visitors to Gibbon's brigade interrupted the work in camp. The first guest was the father of General Rufus King, who, in a now too-familiar routine, showed off his Western troops by trotting them around their parade ground. A second caller was much more welcome—the paymaster arrived on August 2nd and he paid off the boys for the months of May and June. General Order No. 58 had required that the boys be docked for lost clothing and many were consequently in debt for more than their pay, remaining penniless after the paymaster's departure.[22]

The Hoosiers finally got their chance at the rebels on August 5th, when General Gibbon led his brigade on a raid to destroy the Virginia Central Railroad. Gibbon split his command, sending the 6th Wisconsin, some cavalry, and two guns toward Frederick's Hall Station, while he headed for Beaver Dam Station with his other regiments, a detachment of the 3rd Indiana Cavalry, and Battery B. The Hoosiers were up at 2 A.M., crossed the pontoon bridge at daylight, and marched south on the Telegraph Road toward their objective. The boys were "stripped for a race," carrying only blankets in addition to their food, water, arms, and accouterments.[23]

The march continued unabated for eight miles until Gibbon halted his men for an hour so they could fix breakfast. According to one of Sol's soldiers, "The day was oppressively hot, the dust completely enveloped the moving mass; water scarce, and many fell out of ranks by the way side, from sheer exhaustion." Soldiers willingly obeyed General Pope's orders and "'confiscated' prety strongly," taking fruit, vegetables, beef, mutton, poultry, honey and whatever else they could find. As a group of Hoosiers rummaged through a secesh house, the offended citizen spoke to an officer, "You used to protect our property, why do you not do it now?" The response was a laconic, "That is played out." At Thornburg's Mill, the boys ground all the corn stocked there and then destroyed the building. They also cleaned out a country store and continued on, loaded down with coffee, sugar, and molasses.[24]

Later that day, the regiment halted at a small stream, where the boys were given permission "to bathe and cool their heated blood." Suddenly, cannon shots announced that the cavalry advance had met the enemy. Sol's boys scrambled out of the creek, took their places in the column, and started south at a rapid pace. Gibbon's infantry hurried forward about four miles in the 100° heat generated by a broiling August sun. Lieutenant George Finney remembered, "Many fell in the road; others, less exhausted, sought the shade of some friendly bush or fence." James Stine, Company C, wrote that "the roadside was strewn with those who had fallen as if dead, beneath the rays of a scorching sun." Less than 100 men of the 500 Hoosiers who had started that morning managed to follow their colors to the scene of the skirmish. The enemy withdrew, but Gibbon saw that his men were "completely prostrated," so he concluded to halt and allow them to rest instead of pushing on to the railroad.[25]

General John P. Hatch's brigade of New Yorkers reinforced Gibbon, who left his worn-out men behind and pushed forward with his diminished column early on the 6th. The Indiana cavalry had picked up a few rebel stragglers by noon, when the infantry halted for dinner, but information that rebel cavalry had gained his rear frustrated Gibbon's plan. Rumor had it that one of Gibbon's orderlies had been killed while carrying a dispatch to Hatch, but, more importantly, several wagons filled with lame and exhausted soldiers had been captured. The brigade countermarched and reopened the Telegraph Road, but it was too late. The rebels, commanded by J. E. B. Stuart, had already withdrawn, taking with them fifty-nine men from Gibbon's brigade.[26]

Many of Gibbon's broken-down men had been loaded into empty commissary wagons and sent back to Fredericksburg by General Hatch. He was faulted by some for not providing an adequate guard, but pointing fingers of blame could not recover those who had been lost. Although Gibbon's cavalry managed to retake a few of the wagons, he lost seven men from the 7th Wisconsin, eighteen from the 2nd Wisconsin and thirty-four from the 19th Indiana. In the latter regiment, Company I lost nine men and Company G lost seven more. Company B had two men taken prisoner, Sergeant Thomas J. Crull and Private Jacob Hunt. Additionally, James Wine, recently returned from the Construction Corps, was thought to have broken his leg by stepping into a gully in the hurried advance of August 5th.[27]

On the 7th, Gibbon marched his force from the Po River toward Spotsylvania Court House to support the 6th Wisconsin, which was returning after successfully cutting the railroad at Frederick's Hall Station. Gibbon's reunited brigade started home and the Hoosiers reached their Fredericksburg camp at 4 P.M. on August 8th, after marching some seventy-five miles in the terrible heat. Sergeant William Murray admitted that he and his comrades were "very much fatigued and were glad to rest our tired limbs after so arduous a march, with so little rest." Henry Marsh treated many of those who returned and recorded that "some boys have thier backs and arms all in blisters, from the heat." He also found that "many just fell frothing at the mouth from over heating." Dr. E. W. H. Beck, a surgeon with the 3rd Indiana Cavalry, had accompanied Gibbon's column and gave a medical opinion of the raid: "Men cant walk in the dust & hot sun & carry the load they have to carry—full one half the men are lost to active service."[28]

Colonel Meredith's boys had precious little time to rest their legs before starting off on another tramp across northern Virginia. Stonewall Jackson had fought an engagement with a portion of Pope's army at Cedar Mountain on August 9th, so all available troops had been ordered to assemble there at once. Reveille sounded at 2:30 A.M. and, after a brief breakfast of coffee and crackers, Gibbon's brigade packed up, sent the sick off to Washington and headed westward along the Rappahannock River. Like every other march, this one was lined by discarded knapsacks and clothing, but a Pennsylvania officer noticed that even though the Western boys sometimes threw away their Bibles, they always managed to hold onto their muskets, ammunition, and playing cards.[29]

Long Sol always watched out for his boys and tried to halt his regiment wherever shade and water were plentiful. Occasionally, he would summon the musicians and command, "Toot up a little, it makes the boys feel lively." At one point he halted his regiment near an apple orchard close by a fine country estate. The colonel and his staff took seats on the mansion's porch, while the enlisted men went as a body into the orchard after harvest apples. An excited matron came running out and complained that the soldiers were stealing her fruit. A bystander remembered the following conversation:

> The old man quietly contemplated the scene for a moment, and turning to the matron said, half apologetically:
>
> "So they are, madam, so they are; but the fact is the boys have a pretty hard time of it down here, and we have to allow them to do pretty much as they please. They have apples at home but they can't get them. The actions of your men have made it necessary for us to leave our home comforts, and we have to pick up such small comforts as we can as we go along."
>
> "But," she replied, "they are not only taking my fruit, but they are ruining my trees; I shall never have any more fruit."
>
> "Well, my dear madam," said the colonel, "if this war resulted in no greater loss than the destruction of a few apple orchards, we would be a happy people at its close."

Seeing his men returning with haversacks and pockets stuffed full of apples, Colonel Meredith rose, thanked the lady for her hospitality and marched away with his regiment.[30]

After tramping about twenty-five miles, the Hoosiers crossed the Rappahannock at Ellis's Ford, "wading up to our middle." This crossing took place by moonlight and the boys were permitted to remove their trousers, slinging them from their muskets. After stripping, the 19th Indiana looked like a militia regiment outfitted in dark coats and bleached pants, although many had no drawers, the moon making their pale legs appear white. As they waded into the water, one wag asked Meredith how he liked the new uniforms. The colonel responded that they were the cleanest he had seen since leaving Indiana. When a half-naked man bragged about the perfect fit and durability of his trousers, which he had worn for twenty-two years, Long Sol leaned over the pommel of his saddle and laughed out loud. The levity briefly masked their fatigue and, after reaching the opposite shore, the boys lay down "too tired to prepare their supper."[31]

The Hoosiers were awakened at 2 A.M. on August 11th and, after their "usual light breakfast," started for Stevensburg. It was another severe march, but many of the boys struck off from the column to forage. Colonel Meredith encountered one such squad as the regiment marched along and asked them to which regiment they belonged. The foragers responded, "To the fighting 19th Indiana, colonel." Sol chastised them by saying, "Get back into your places, you young rascals; you will soon be as bad for straggling as the 7th Wisconsin." The boys resumed their places in the ranks, but foraging was so widespread that one sergeant would write, "Oh jemany how the chickens potatoes and fruit suffered today." There was a stop at Stevensburg so the soldiers could cook some plunder, then the column moved on and joined the army beyond Culpeper Court House, after a day's march of nearly thirty miles.[32]

While everyone expected a huge battle on August 12th, the boys in Company B "did not care anything for that, all we wanted was to stop and rest." But Stonewall Jackson had withdrawn and there would be no battle. All the Western boys could do was picket the battlefield, but even that duty meant an encounter with ghosts. John O. Johnson, of the 6th Wisconsin, described the "singular experience":

In making the rounds of the picket line, one of the guard, Dennis Kelly, said, "Sergeant, I have seen ghosts or spirits." I knew the man to be truthful, and told him to be still and I would examine the causes, being afraid that some of the men would raise a false alarm. I started in the direction of the field, and marched directly to the nearest point. There I found a dead body, interred very shallow, and a phosphorescent light oscillating from the head to the foot of the corpse. And so it proved in every instance. It being a very warm, sultry night and dark, must have been the reason of it, or some gas from the decaying bodies.

Not all visits to the battlefield were of this mystical variety. One important, but highly disagreeable task, assigned to Gibbon's brigade was to build fires and cremate dead horses that littered the landscape.[33]

In their spare time, the Hoosiers wandered all over the battlefield and were horrified by the sights they beheld. Lieutenant John Shafer walked over there on the 13th and wrote home that "the piles of dead horses upon both sides, the remnants of arms, accoutrements and clothing, the fresh soil covering the remains of the fallen, were silent but melancholy evidences of the deadly conflict." Joshua Jones of Company E confided to his wife, "I Seen lots of hair & blood & bloody clothes with bulet holes in them & dead horses any amount of them." Buzzards swarmed overhead and the air was poisoned by the decomposition of bodies so that the stench was "almost suffocating." Burial trenches moved "like gentle waves with living corruption." This was their first visit to a battlefield and it was a ghastly experience that could never be forgotten. Two weeks later, Meredith's boys would visit another battlefield, but this time it would be their own.[34]

13

Brawner Farm

The disappearance of Stonewall Jackson from the Cedar Mountain battlefield meant that Gibbon's Western boys could rest for a few days. Generals Pope and McDowell reviewed King's division on August 14th, but there would be no more fighting at Cedar Mountain. On the 18th, word came that the enemy had crossed the Rapidan River and Pope's army must fall back behind the Rappahannock, where it would await reinforcements from McClellan's army.[1]

Reveille sounded at 12:30 A.M. on August 19th, but King's division had to wait for the wagon trains to pass before it could begin the retreat. Gibbon's brigade did not move until 7:30, but then marched slowly northward until 10 P.M., when it bivouacked a mile south of Rappahannock Station. The brigade crossed in the morning and took "a strategic position on the banks of the Rappahannock." In anticipation of desperate work, the boys tossed their knapsacks into empty wagons, which immediately set off for Catlett's Station, where the army trains had assembled. Gibbon's brigade guard, about 100 men detailed from the various regiments and commanded by Lieutenant Charles K. Baxter of the 19th Indiana, accompanied the wagons.[2]

The Western boys remained along the river for several days without losing a man, although the brigade was occasionally subjected to long-range artillery fire. The only loss in the 19th Indiana occurred when a shell wounded Lieutenant Colonel Bachman's horse and killed "Bet," Adjutant Russey's fast mare which had won so handily on July 4th. During one period of shelling, General McDowell rode up and exchanged pleasantries with Colonel Meredith. The general pulled off his forage cap and beckoned to an aide, who produced the infamous "dishpan" hat. Wearing his "basket cockade," McDowell rode to the crest overlooking the Rappahannock. Private Anthony P. Carr remembered the incident:

10. Charles K. Baxter.
Used by permission of the Indiana State Library.

We actually held our breath, expecting every minute to see him fall, as he was in pointblank range in an open field. He coolly took in the river with a glass, turned to his right, rode up the river by the batteries, in front of the 16th [Indiana Battery], some 300 yards in distance, then wheeled again to his right, rode back to the 19th and 13th Mass., took off the "dishpan," put on the forage-cap, and galloped away. In 15 minutes there was such a storm of iron came over the brow of that same part of the hill that all hands had to "git."

Although McDowell was not a traitor, incidents such as this one bolstered the enlisted men's belief that their general just might be in cahoots with the enemy.[3]

While on the Rappahannock, the boys in King's division quickly learned that shell fire produced more fear than casualties. Artillery projectiles were said to sound "like half a dozen locomotive whistles" or "whizzing like a prairie chicken" or like "little devils screeching and howling in every direction." Shell bursts produced "a puff of smoke, a bang, a whizzing sound, and bits of shell and spherical case would drop like hail-stones all around." After suffering through a few rounds of artillery fire, most soldiers would have agreed with the Badger who declared, "I felt like crawling into the ground, and then pulling the hole in after me."[4]

King's division retired to Warrenton on August 23rd and remained there until the 26th, when it again moved to support batteries on the

Rappahannock. The 19th's regimental historian described the strange strategic situation:

> While these events were transpiring, Jackson marched through Thoroughfare Gap, laid Manassas Junction—immediately in rear of Pope—in ashes. . . . Stuart had attacked many of our wagon trains—among them the train of the Nineteenth, which was saved by the bravery of the guard and teamsters. The army was cut off from its base, and only one corps of the promised aid from McClellan had arrived.

The best description of the opposing forces was the one that simply stated that "the two armies were oddly mixed together."[5]

Pope had concentrated his baggage trains, described by Captain John Clark as "*stupendous,*" near Catlett's Station on the Orange & Alexandria Railroad. Gibbon's brigade train, composed of twenty-one wagons, had been parked some two miles from Catlett's Station in an angle between the railroad and Cedar Run, a short distance from Pope's headquarters train. A storm, punctuated by vivid streaks of lightning, swept over the wagons on the night of August 22nd and the soldiers huddled in their tents.

Suddenly and without the least warning, rebel cavalry rode into Pope's wagons from the north. Lieutenant Baxter, assisted by a couple of Wisconsin officers, quickly formed his men—the brigade guard, teamsters, and some invalids—to defend Gibbon's train. The officers formed three squads, put their boys under the wagons and repulsed three separate charges by a strong force of rebel cavalry. Occasional flashes of lightning revealed "the horses of the invaders rearing and plunging in unmanageable confusion." One of the defenders was cut on the hand by a saber, the only Federal casualty in Baxter's skirmish, but Stuart's cavalry left one dead and several wounded behind. Not everyone, however, acted heroically. Baxter remembered, "One of these, a Corporal of Co. A, 19th Ind., had to be assisted into the wagon when we moved, he was so feeble. When the attack came he made his way to Manassas in remarkably short time, on foot." Although many other wagons had been plundered and burned, the Western boys had "saved all of the baggage under their charge."[6]

On August 27th, McDowell's corps left Sulphur Springs and marched east on the turnpike toward Centreville. Each soldier carried one hundred rounds of ammunition, forty in his cartridge box and sixty on his person, usually in the haversack. In order to reduce straggling, captains marched at the rear of their companies and colonels rode at the rear of their regiments. Exhausted or lame men needed a surgeon's written permit to leave the ranks. The 19th Indiana marched at the head of Gibbon's brigade that day, but, following common practice, would rotate to the rear of the column on the following morning.[7]

Gibbon's brigade marched through Warrenton, where vast piles of Federal rations were being destroyed for lack of transportation. Although Gibbon's soldiers had little food in their haversacks, they were ordered to keep marching and kept on until 10 P.M., when they halted near the small town of New Baltimore. The 19th Indiana camped in a clover field that proved to be alive with grasshoppers. A rooster happened to crow when the regiment halted, so soldiers quietly slipped out of camp to search for poultry, corn, apples, or whatever else might turn up. A mess from Company C returned with an abundant supply of chickens and stayed up past midnight to cook their plunder. Other boys came in with green corn that they roasted before going to sleep.[8]

Although they were nearly exhausted, the boys were "worked up to the battle fever." Sergeant William W. Macy remembered that the Hoosiers were cocky and "we were rather looking for trouble." A New York officer in General Abner Doubleday's brigade summed it up best when he declared, "The very air seemed to whisper, 'danger! danger!'" This tension was too much for Captain Valentine Jacobs, who devised a plan to avoid the impending battle. Lieutenant William Campbell explained how the captain "had his coffee made a little sooner than any of us, and he poured a cupful in his shoe, and charged it onto me; and he got to howling a good deal, and we had to take a little care of him." Corporal James H. Stine was startled when Jacobs "squalled out" and was afraid that "the man would have his foot scalded off of him." Lieutenant Campbell claimed that Jacobs "had that coffee made on purpose; we knew we had to run into the rebels pretty soon."

Captain Jacobs missed the impending battle and soon obtained a furlough. He returned to Indianapolis and looked up his friend, Dr. Kendrick, formerly the 19th Indiana's assistant surgeon. Kendrick listened to Jacobs's explanation that he had been wounded by the explosion of a shell, examined the injured foot and diagnosed "a wound in the foot inflicted by the bursting of a shell." Unless Indianapolis was a terribly dangerous place to live, Kendrick had never seen a shell wound during his practice and simply repeated the captain's story. Jacobs then took the doctor's statement to Henry Vandegrift, his former lieutenant, who verified that Kendrick was a physician "of good standing." Jacobs sent off the paperwork in an attempt to gain a discharge, but the captain's deception failed and he was dishonorably dismissed from the service on October 13, 1862.[9]

After Jacobs's scalded foot had been tended to, the boys settled down for some much-needed rest. A year later, Lieutenant George Finney wistfully remembered the night at New Baltimore: "Many of these brave men, who, in the prime of life, and manly vigor, wrapped their blankets around them that night, and 'lay down to quiet slumber,' were destined soon to sleep their last, long sleep."[10]

The boys were roused at 4 A.M. on August 28th and shuffled forward about a mile before halting for breakfast. Some suspected that the short march had been conducted only as a pretext to get the tired soldiers up and moving, but actually the stop was ordered to allow the passage of an immense wagon train. At Buckland Mills, King's division found several hundred rebel stragglers who had been captured and confined in a church. One soldier observed that they appeared "more worn out than the worst fagged of our men, and it didn't seem possible for men of their appearance to be effective in a fight." The capture of more rebel stragglers on the road to Gainesville seemed to indicate that a fight was imminent.[11]

In the afternoon, King's division left the Warrenton Turnpike and halted on the road to Manassas Junction while it awaited new orders. Lieutenant Shafer wrote that the Hoosiers "had been led to suppose that Jackson and Ewell were surrounded by our forces here, and that his army would soon be captured." Unaware of Pope's strategy, the enlisted men did know that they were again chasing Jackson and they had to defeat him before General Robert E. Lee arrived with the remainder of the rebel army. "While McDowell was fooling around counting the wagons and making maps of the country," Gibbon ordered that fresh beef be issued. An ox was slaughtered for the Hoosiers, but they were ordered to march before all of the meat could be distributed. Their hunger was overpowering and, according to Abe Buckles, "many of us cut off chunks and ate them warm and raw."[12]

Regaining the Warrenton Turnpike, King's division started eastward. Hatch's brigade went first and scouted north of the road before passing out of sight toward Groveton. Gibbon came next, followed in turn by the brigades of Abner Doubleday and Marsena Patrick. Artillery fire sounded in the distance as the 19th Indiana, the last regiment in Gibbon's column, passed into the shade of a piece of woods.[13]

Suddenly, the peaceful summer evening was shattered by the crash of shells in the trees overhead. Colonel Meredith halted his regiment and formed a line of battle in the road. Lieutenant Finney described those first tense moments:

> The unearthly sound of these fearful missiles struck terror to the stoutest heart; yet cool and collected stood that line, obeying with alacrity every command, and waiting impatiently for the order to advance. The order was given; shells burst in front, above, and behind, crashed through the branches of the trees, plowed up the ground, and yelled demoniacly through the air, yet steadily forward pressed the line.

As the battleline moved north into the woods, the Hoosier musicians stepped aside to allow Battery B to gallop ahead up the turnpike. Just then a shell exploded and Henry Gordon, Company B's drummer, was knocked to the ground by its concussion. The shock had partially deafened Gordon, but he stumbled back and reported for duty to the regimental surgeons, who put him to work as a nurse.[14]

Gibbon had already sent the 2nd Wisconsin after the rebel guns and volleys of musketry from beyond the woods announced the commencement of a more serious clash. The 19th Indiana advanced in line of battle through the trees some 300 yards and emerged into open ground that sloped up to a crest another 300 yards ahead. Colonel Meredith pushed his regiment forward at a double-quick to the left of the 2nd Wisconsin's smoke-shrouded position. As his boys crossed a fence at the crest, Long Sol cried out, "Boys, don't forget that you are Hoosiers, and above all, remember the glorious flag of our country!" After the Indiana boys had advanced a few yards, a rebel regiment concealed behind a fence and some haystacks fired a volley into their ranks. Because of the unique configuration of the landscape, Meredith's regiment had been unable to see the enemy until within about seventy-five yards of their position. The battle was fought at that range. According to Lieutenant Finney, "The reply was quickly given—gun answering gun—flame flashing to flame—yell echoing to yell." The Hoosier boys had finally found their long-sought battle.[15]

The Union line of battle stretched from the John C. Brawner house, where the Hoosiers held the left flank, eastward beyond the woods in the following order: 2nd Wisconsin, 7th Wisconsin, 76th New York, 56th Pennsylvania, and 6th Wisconsin. For about ninety minutes, these six regiments (four of Gibbon's and two of Doubleday's) held in check four brigades from Stonewall Jackson's force. Federal troops within hearing of the battle thought that the musketry sounded "like that of hailstones upon an empty barn." One New Yorker observed: "Sometimes the firing would slacken a little as if both sides were losing heart, but then came a wild cheer and a yell and the rattle of musketry would become louder and more fierce than ever." The roar of battle meant only one thing: "bright young lives were going out at every instant like tapers in a wind."[16]

There was little maneuvering in this battle. Regiments marched into place and began to fight. Near the Brawner house and its outbuildings, the 19th Indiana traded musketry with regiments from the famous Stonewall Brigade. Twice the rebels crossed their fence and half-heartedly tried to charge Meredith's line, but twice the Hoosier fire forced them back. As one Company K private put it, "Like two dogs fighting with a fence between them we fought that battle."[17]

The Hoosiers behaved well in their first fight. In his report of the battle, Colonel Meredith boasted:

During the whole time the officers and men of my command behaved
with great gallantry. When the ranks were thinned out by the deadly fire
of the enemy, they were closed up with as much promptness as if on drill.

Captain Dudley reported that his Company B boys "stood to the work nobly
till ordered off the field." Captain Hamilton, who had not been in the fight,
conversed with those who had and concluded that his Randolph County
boys had "fought like demons." Captain Clark reported for Company G:
"Each man seemed eager to meet the foe, unflinchingly they stood to a man
the terrible cross-fire which the regiment was subjected to." Early in the
fight, Corporal Stine glanced to his left and noticed that "Capt. L. B. Wilson,
of Company E, had no sword, but he led his company into action—standing
there with his arms folded, he looked every inch a soldier."[18]

 Although Meredith's boys had twice shot down those red battleflags,
they still waved defiantly from behind the rail fence. In the 19th Indiana,
their State flag "was completely cut up with balls and shell." The National
Colors were "completely riddled—barely enough of it to hold together—
and the staff shot through near the 'union.'" Another observer mentioned
that "it was riddled with bullets, the stars being all shot out of it."[19]

 Completely unaware of what was occurring elsewhere, Hoosiers
hugged the ground and fired until their muskets became clogged with black
powder deposits. Then they either slammed their ramrods into stones and
trees and farm buildings to drive home the minie balls or picked up new
muskets that had been dropped by the dead and wounded. George Finney
described the climax of the fighting:

> The demoniac yells of the belligerants, the piercing screams of the
> wounded, and the deep groans of the dying, could be heard above the
> din of battle. Men in the agonies of death and men already dead, lay
> thick along the line.

Deepening twilight did not halt the fighting and for probably thirty minutes
"the men were guided in their aim by the flash of the enemy's guns."[20]

 At one point, Captain John Pelham placed two rebel cannon so as to
enfilade the 19th Indiana and "grape, canister and shell, whistled through
and screamed above it." Major May had already been shot from his horse, so
Lieutenant Colonel Bachman ordered two companies to drive off this new
threat. Captain Dudley wheeled Companies B and G at right angles to the
battleline, ran them toward the rebel position and "opened a deadly fire on
it, and soon the fire ceased." But the gunners had simply changed location.
Dudley reported, "I then threw back my right, and directed all my fire on
these two guns, and finally silenced them altogether."[21]

When Dudley's men turned to fire on the rebel guns, Colonel Alexander Taliaferro's three Virginia regiments reinforced the Stonewall Brigade and put increased pressure on Meredith's left flank. Sol promptly withdrew his regiment a few rods to the shelter of the fence it had crossed earlier, where a slight offset in the ground would give added protection. General Gibbon spied this new threat to the 19th Indiana and rode over to help. He tied his horse to a tree limb in the Brawner orchard while he examined the field, but the animal became frightened, broke free and ran off. Now on foot, Gibbon ran over and helped Dudley extricate his small command from its perilous position. The Virginians began yet another bayonet charge, but the reunited regiment gave them "hail Columbia with a yell." Captain Patrick Hart wrote later, "The rebels could not stand it, and broke and ran like dogs."[22]

Near the end of the battle, Meredith's horse, "Old Roan," was struck in the neck by a minie ball and the colonel was crushed beneath his mount when it fell. Captain Dudley and Lieutenant Colonel Bachman pulled Sol free and carried him back down the hill a short distance, where doctors found him to be badly bruised with a couple of broken ribs. Bachman took command until Sol recovered from the shock and "exhibited great coolness and courage" in leading the regiment. The soldiers missed their colonel, but he remained on the field just down the hill from their position at the fence. Captain Hart called Meredith "a brick and a fine officer," then concluded his account of the incident by writing, "Bully for Sol." It was a bad day all around for the Meredith family. Samuel Meredith, Sol's son, who was serving as a lieutenant in Company A, went down with a serious neck wound just ten minutes before the firing ended.[23]

After the Hoosiers had ignored three orders to retire, Gibbon finally got their attention and began a systematic withdrawal. The general described the delicate situation:

> As the darkness increased and the fire on both sides slackened I gave orders to the left of the 19th Indiana to fall back obliquely to the rear so as to protect the flank. To do this, the men ceased firing and before we had formed in the new position the enemy threw forward some men into the yard of the Douglas [Brawner] House and in the darkness opened fire upon us. Here some confusion took place but the men readily responded to the voices of their officers and formed line again on the edge of the woods behind them and everything except the groans of the wounded quieted down. The fight was over.

Due to heavy casualties among officers and sergeants and confusion in the darkness, Company C was taken off the battlefield by Corporal Nelson Pegg.[24]

After stumbling into the Brawner woods, those Hoosiers who still remained with the colors sat down for a few minutes' rest. Patrick's brigade, which had taken no part in the battle, now advanced and spread a line of pickets out toward the farmhouse. J. Harrison Mills described his experience on a picket post that night:

> It is my lot to be among the watchers, and as I pace my beat I must guard my uncertain steps, for here in solemn state lie two of our dead heroes, and yonder are more of them, and out in front they are lying thick as forest leaves where they fell; and anon I hear that awful sound, the cry of some abandoned sufferer dying in agony alone.

Volunteers went out to bring in their injured comrades, though many seriously wounded had to be left untended because the rebels now occupied the ground where the Hoosiers had fought. One searcher recalled the pathetic nature of the task: "The cries, moans, and calling for water and help of the wounded and dying comrades was heartrending."[25]

While General King conferred with his brigade commanders, Captain Dudley tried to assemble his shattered company. There were not many of the Richmond company left. Lieutenant Hindman had been severely wounded in the leg during the first minutes of the fight and lay on the ground cheering the men until assisted to the rear by Sergeant Tom Benton, who had been slightly wounded in the thigh. Hindman implored Tom to stay with him, but the young sergeant insisted that he "would go back and fight as long as he could stand." Tom limped back up the hill and joined his comrades, but he soon fell, shot through the breast. Henry Hiatt saw him fall and started back to help him, but was ordered to return to the company. Glancing around, Hiatt saw that Tom had crawled to an apple tree and was sitting with his back against it. Minutes later, Hiatt himself went down with a shattered thigh.[26]

With Lieutenant Hindman gone and Orderly Sergeant Samuel Schlagle also wounded, Sergeant Sam McCown filled in at the post of lieutenant. A minie ball inflicted a painful wound that bled profusely, but he kept at his post and helped drive off Pelham's cannon. However, shortly after he rejoined the regiment, a piece of shell pierced his lungs and Sam was left behind in the withdrawal. Sergeant Charley Davis had been shot in the leg, but worse than that he had lost his shoes. Two boys, Corporal Charley Petty and Private Jeff Wasson, had been shot in the arm and knee, respectively, but both remained in the ranks. Wasson described his experience:

> We fought in an open field at a distance of fifty yards. The balls fell like hail, but I saw no man run. Every one stood up and fought like men, but it was no use; they had too many men for us.

11. Charles Davis.
From the Mick Kissick Collection.
Used by permission.

Including McCown, Benton, and Hiatt, more than a dozen of Dudley's men were missing and about a dozen others had been shot. According to one account, Captain Dudley could only locate sixteen unhurt men after the battle. Nearly every survivor could point to bullet holes in his hat or clothing.[27]

After a brief consultation, the generals decided to abandon their battlefield in order to avoid reopening the engagement against an overwhelming force in the morning. The withdrawal began after midnight and King's division marched for Manassas Junction, taking as many wounded along as possible. Several hundred injured soldiers had to be left behind under the care of two surgeons, Dr. Andrew J. Ward of the 2nd Wisconsin and Dr. Green of the 19th Indiana, and a few medical attendants. Every wounded man who even thought he could make the journey tried to hobble along because they "*would not* be taken prisoners." There was a critical shortage of water for the wounded, for whom there was no relief. Groans from the ambulances guided the way, since the marching men could see nothing but the dim outline of those ahead as they trudged along country roads in their escape.[28]

King's division finally reached Manassas Junction at sunrise. After arranging for the issue of ammunition and food, John Gibbon rode off to give General Pope some details of the fight and subsequent withdrawal. Lieutenant Frank Haskell, Gibbon's aide, paid close attention to the condition of the soldiers on the morning of August 29th and penned this description of the Western boys after their first battle:

> As the daylight came on the next morning, none of us could look upon our thinned ranks, so full the night before, now so shattered, without tears. And the faces of these brave boys as the morning sun disclosed them, no pen can describe. The men were cheerful, quiet, and orderly. The dust and blackness of battle were upon their clothes, and in their hair, and on their skin, but you saw none of these,—you saw only their eyes, and the shadows of the "light of battle," and the furrows plowed upon cheeks that were smooth a day before, and now not half filled up. I could not look upon them without tears, and could have hugged the necks of them all.

Gibbon's soldiers were proud of their performance and all would have agreed with the Hoosier lieutenant who declared, "We have not yet disgraced our flag."[29]

In the daylight, Colonel Meredith finally had an opportunity to count his losses, although it was still impossible to determine who had died. Sol's company officers reported a loss of forty-six killed, 150 wounded and thirty-three missing, a total of 229 out of an aggregate of 423 engaged. But there was still a great deal of confusion and when the surgeons compiled a nominal list of casualties, their numbers added up to thirty killed, 137 wounded and forty-three missing (some of them wounded and left on the field), for a total of 210. Other officers confirmed this range of figures. In a private letter, Surgeon Ebersole noted that some 200 had been killed or wounded out of about 450 in the fight. Lieutenant Orr mentioned that the Hoosiers "lost 227 out of about 450 or 500 who went into the engagement." Lieutenant Shafer related a total loss of 202. In addition to Colonel Meredith's injury, at least nine other officers had been shot: Major Isaac May, mortally in the head; Captain Luther Wilson, by debris in the groin; Captain John Lindley, leg; Lieutenant Samuel Meredith, neck; Lieutenant Hindman, thigh; Lieutenant Joseph Cook, thigh and hand; Lieutenant Joel Newman, both legs; Lieutenant John Jack, thigh; and Lieutenant George Finney, arm.[30]

Company B sustained the following casualties:

KILLED

Sgt Samuel McCown
Pvt Randolph Fort
Pvt Joseph Pike

WOUNDED

2nd Lt Samuel Hindman, leg
1st Sgt Samuel Schlagle, leg
Sgt Thomas Benton, breast and thigh (prisoner)
Sgt Charles Davis, leg
Cpl Benjamin Jewett, leg (prisoner)
Cpl Charles Petty, arm
Pvt William Bennett, both legs (prisoner)
Pvt Joel Curtis, hand
Pvt Hugh English, shoulder
Pvt Henry Hiatt, thigh (prisoner)
Pvt Jefferson Kinder, ankle and groin
Pvt William Locke, leg (prisoner)
Pvt Samuel Lutz, leg (prisoner)
Pvt George Marquis, leg (prisoner)
Pvt Edward Morse, knee (prisoner)
Pvt Alexander Walker, head (prisoner)
Pvt Thomas Wasson, knee (prisoner)
Pvt James Whitlow, foot (prisoner)
Pvt Richard Williams, face

It is obvious from this list that those unable to walk had been left behind.
Four privates—William Hill, James Palmer, John Rariden, and Horace
Wharton—were listed as missing, but all turned up unhurt, except for
Palmer, who had developed a hernia while lugging the wounded off the
battlefield.[31]

While at Manassas Junction, the Hoosiers had a chance to learn what
other regiments had done during the previous night's battle. The 2nd
Wisconsin had gone in first, chasing off the artillery that had shelled the
Indiana boys. After brushing away a line of rebel skirmishers, these Badgers
collided with several regiments of the Stonewall Brigade. Major Thomas Allen
described the result, "Their fire was terrific, bullets came thicker than rain and
it seemed as if our whole regiment must soon be annihilated." Lieutenant
Alexander Hill explained that the Badgers "never flinched, but stood up and
were shot down like sheep, until the men had all fallen in their tracks." As if to
illustrate his claim, Hill reported that he entered the fight with fifty-one men
and came out with only eight! Major Allen saw the entire center of his regiment
shot down: "Every one of our color guard was killed or wounded and a
corporal of C Co. seized the colors and stood erect with them and not a man
on either side of him for 10 or 12 yards." The 2nd Wisconsin lost nearly two-
thirds of its force, 276 out of 430 engaged, including Colonel Edgar O'Connor
killed and Major Allen wounded in the neck and wrist.[32]

On the right of Colonel O'Connor's regiment, the 7th Wisconsin had exchanged musketry with several rebel regiments. According to one member of the 7th: "We advanced within hailing distance of each other, then halted and laid down, and, my God, what a slaughter!" Captain Alexander Gordon described what happened to the regiment's field officers:

> Col. Robinson had his horse killed and was wounded in the leg and had to leave the field early. Lt. Col. Hamilton led the charge and rode right into the face of the enemy. He was shot about the middle of the action, the ball passing through his left thigh and lodging in the right groin; but he brought the regiment from the field. As soon as he got to the hospital his horse dropped dead. Major Bill stood gallantly upon the field until struck by a ball in the left temple, dropping him instantly from his horse.

In the charge referred to by Captain Gordon, his regiment pivoted forward on the flank of a rebel regiment that was advancing against the 2nd Wisconsin. An accurate fire by the 7th Wisconsin "perfectly annihilated the rebels and but few escaped." One of the Badgers might have spoken for all when he confessed, "I stood square and threw cold lead without a shake of nerve."[33]

Two of Abner Doubleday's regiments, the 76th New York and 56th Pennsylvania, advanced to Gibbon's aid and filled a large gap between the 7th and 6th Wisconsin. Their brigadier reported that the Eastern boys "held the position with such determined obstinacy that it is difficult to single out individual merit." The New Yorkers poured in an oblique fire on the force assaulting their Badger friends and one of them described the result:

> We gave the rebs a cross fire, thinning their ranks and prostrating their color bearer. Another picked up the colors—but he soon tumbled too. The Rebels finding they were getting the worst of it turned their backs and pointed for the woods.

The Pennsylvanians endured "a withering fire from the enemy" that hit Colonel Sullivan A. Meredith (an officer occasionally confused with Long Sol) and four captains. E. P. Halstead, Doubleday's adjutant, related that "the battle raged with indescribable fury" and these two regiments lost over one-third of their numbers in less than an hour.[34]

Colonel Lysander Cutler's 6th Wisconsin anchored the right of the Federal battleline. Cutler's regiment had marched into position virtually unmolested by the enemy, who apparently mistook it for one of their own. The Badgers eliminated that confusion with "a fire by battalion on the flank of the Rebels." But the rebs regrouped and came back. Captain John Marsh described the repulse of one attack:

> The sun was sinking behind the horizon, when I saw a Confederate officer form his command as if for a final effort to break our line; . . . recklessly placing himself in front of the lines, he gave the command to charge; down they came at double-quick over that green slope, their gallant leader waving them on; men drop from the ranks by scores, but the line sweeps bravely forward until it seems as though half their number are bleeding on the ground; the living hesitate, and the bold leader rides furiously along in front to urge them on, but the leaden hail is too potent, and they fall back, but with the steady pace of veterans.

Although the rebels made three distinct charges, "there was no confusion, no faltering" in the 6th Wisconsin, even after Cutler had been shot in the leg, the fifth colonel to fall on the Union side.[35]

When Gibbon finally rejoined his brigade on August 29th, he called in the regimental adjutants to receive their casualty reports. His reaction won the hearts of every Western soldier:

> General John Gibbon, in speaking of his losses, fought against an unsteady voice and welling tears, but they mastered him, and his cheeks were wet and his voice was so full of tremble that he put his begrimed face in his hands and cried. "My brave boys, it is too bad," said Gibbon, as he straightened up in his saddle and rode away.

After seeing the tenderness exhibited by their gruff commander, those battle-hardened veterans would have followed him anywhere.[36]

Both officers and enlisted men searched for some meaning to their first real combat experience, but there was none to be found. Their sacrifice had gained nothing for the cause. Consequently, indignation and ill will toward their generals, who had abandoned the Brawner Heights and allowed the enemy to occupy that position, became widespread. Major Rufus Dawes wrote bitterly, "The best blood of Wisconsin and Indiana was poured out like water, and it was spilled for naught." Captain Patrick Hart called the affair "a useless slaughter of brave Indianians." After listening to numerous tales by the Hoosiers, W. T. Dennis declared that Gibbon's losses were "damning evidences of the treachery or stupidity of McDowell." The soldiers expressed their own displeasure on the morning of August 29th, when they greeted General King with a chorus of groans and boos.[37]

After the intimate savagery of their first fight, Western soldiers found the Second Battle of Bull Run to be a strange anticlimax. The division, now commanded by General Hatch because of Rufus King's ill-health, marched to that battlefield on the afternoon of August 29th. Although the balance of Hatch's division got into a sharp fight along the Warrenton Turnpike that night, Gibbon's brigade had been detached to support some batteries and did not participate. That was fine with Gibbon's men. According to one Badger, their experience on the previous evening "had eradicated our yearning for a fight."[38]

In order to fill his depleted ranks, Gibbon had ordered all of the extra duty men (wagon guards, cattle guards, headquarters clerks, etc.) to rejoin their companies. Due to heavy losses, the 2nd and 7th Wisconsin had been consolidated into a "joint regiment," commanded by Lieutenant Colonel Lucius Fairchild, the only uninjured field officer in both regiments. In this new organization the 2nd Wisconsin formed four companies and the 7th Wisconsin was consolidated into six companies, but Fairchild's "joint regiment" still numbered less than the 6th Wisconsin.[39]

On the afternoon of August 30th, General Pope ordered a pursuit of the rebels, whom he mistakenly presumed to be retreating on the Warrenton Turnpike. In reality, General Lee's entire army was waiting for him. Hatch's division participated in this brief "pursuit" and advanced westward into the heavy woods north of Groveton. For this assault, Gibbon formed his brigade in a single line with the 6th Wisconsin on the right, the 19th Indiana in the center, and Fairchild's "joint regiment" on the left. Upon entering the woods, the Westerners came under a heavy shell fire that roared and crashed through the trees. A battle raged fiercely ahead, where Federal infantry vainly assaulted rebel lines partially sheltered in a large railroad cut. This Union attack ultimately failed and Colonel Meredith watched helplessly as a "large number of disorganized troops" ran back and disrupted Gibbon's line. Even the Western bayonets could not stop these fugitives and Gibbon's three regiments began to drift apart in the thick woods.[40]

Pope's pursuit had been smashed and, in a matter of minutes, Gibbon's three regiments moved from a supporting position to the advanced line of the Union army. Unable to see through the trees and underbrush, Colonel Meredith ordered Captain Dudley to deploy Company B as skirmishers. He had advanced only a short distance before discovering large bodies of rebs marching forward to follow up their advantage. After Dudley's skirmishers came running back with that unwelcome news, Meredith received orders to retire. He reported, "The 19th Indiana fell back under fire in perfect order. I halted the regiment several times, and awaited the approach of the enemy." Fifteen Hoosiers had been wounded by the time they left the woods.[41]

In the open fields, Meredith rejoined Fairchild's Badgers and, after what seemed like hours, General Gibbon finally emerged from the woods with the 6th Wisconsin. The brigade then fell back to a hill and supported batteries. During Gibbon's advance into the woods, an overwhelming force had fallen on Pope's left and the rebel success there left Pope no choice but to order his army to retreat to Centreville. As the left continued to give ground, General McDowell ordered the Western brigade to act as rearguard for Pope's army. Gibbon's three small regiments retired from position to position, their pursuers being kept at a respectful distance by Battery B and other Federal artillery. While covering the withdrawal, one Badger noticed that "the jamming of wagons and smash of things showed what style of retreat we had." The brigade reached Bull Run after dark and crossed that stream while engineers chopped away at the bridge supports, tumbling the structure after Gibbon's passage.[42]

In a report on the Second Bull Run battle to Governor Morton, Long Sol boasted, "During the whole engagement the officers and men of my command behaved with great coolness and courage." Meredith's loss totaled one killed, eighteen wounded and eleven missing. Captain Dudley reported that his company behaved with "much bravery" and noted he had lost two privates wounded. King Whitlow received a wound in the knee and Anthony P. Carr was seriously injured by a shell burst that broke his arm in three places, dislocated a shoulder and gashed his hip. This Hoosier loss was again suffered in a defeat, and Sol's men placed the blame squarely upon Eastern troops. According to one lieutenant, "Whole regiments of New York and Pennsylvania troops broke and ran like sheep. Had the Eastern troops stood nobly to the mark, like good soldiers, our defeat would have proven a glorious victory."[43]

Gibbon's brigade bivouacked at Centreville on August 31st. One Wisconsin soldier described the scene:

> On the Heights of Centreville were generals, colonels, captains, and all other rank officers of all the branches of the service, looking for their commands and mobs of men looking for their organizations. Infantry, artillery, cavalry, ambulances, wagons and all the impediments used in an army all mixed up in dire confusion.

Lieutenant William Orr summed up that confusion:

> I do not know what has been the result of the fighting. I dont know whether we were whipped or whipped them. I have no idea how many men were engaged on either side or how many were lost on either side, nor when we are to fight again or how or where.

Orr concluded his message with a plea for his family to send newspapers so the Hoosiers could make some sense out of the last few days.[44]

14

Aftermath

Many wounded men from the battle of August 28th thought that they had been left to die. After darkness ended the fighting, survivors carried their injured friends south of the Warrenton Turnpike. There surgeons had established two makeshift hospitals—one behind the Brawner woods and the other in and around the Cundiff farmhouse—where they tended patients by the light of lanterns and candles. When King's division withdrew to Manassas Junction, Drs. Ward and Green were left to care for several hundred men, each of whom was dreadfully wounded. The doctors were assisted by the 2nd Wisconsin's ambulance corps and a few volunteer nurses. Henry Marsh was one such nurse at the Cundiff house and he remembered that "we had to work as hard as we could."[1]

The story of King's wounded men begins with their removal from the battlefield. Every soldier had his own tale to tell. Corporal James Stine, Company C, related his experience with would-be rescuers:

> There were some New York troops coming along, and my left arm was so palsied with the shot that I could not use it much. I took my hat down and took off the "19," and I got a New York man to take care of me, under the impression that I was a New York man; each regiment took care of their own wounded. He met some of his comrades, who told him he was not very smart to carry off one of those big broad-brimmed hat fellows for a New Yorker, and he threw me down across a log and after a while I was taken back to the field hospital.

Stine was placed in an ambulance belonging to Doubleday's brigade and started for Manassas Junction about 3 A.M. on August 29th. The driver promptly got lost and after sunrise drove aimlessly about in search of the general hospital depot. Stine remembered that they stopped once for water, but "he kept us running over the field till some time near four o'clock before he found the way to Manassas Junction."[2]

Sergeant William Murray, also of Company C, received a serious wound in the left ankle and three other balls passed through his clothing, one of which struck and mutilated his pocket diary. Although in great pain, he faithfully recorded events of the next few days in his ruined book:

> *August 29th* — Having been conveyed off the field the previous evening by H. Knight and R. W. Linton—a great many of us were placed in the ambulances and taken to the Hospital near Manassas Junction.
>
> *August 30th* — Well here I am yet surrounded by scores of wounded Soldiers, whose groans and cries are caused by deep wounds of various kinds—some of them minus an arm or a leg—Some are very cool others are raving desperately. The doctors want to take my leg off.
>
> *August 31st* — Almost a panic—Arrangements made to get away immediately—I left in an ambulance about 10 A.M. Arrived at Fairfax Station at 9:15 P.M. Had a good night's sleep.
>
> *September 1st* — Waked this morning and could see all over the ground wounded soldiers by the acre—suppose there are from 1400 to 1600—more arriving all the time—Left on a train for Washington at 12:30 P.M. Arrived at Trinity Hospital at 6 P.M.

Several months later the sergeant's leg was still swollen and painful. On November 12th, Murray would write, "Two pieces of bone and a piece of lead were taken from my wound today." Murray received treatment at several hospitals until his discharge on March 3, 1863.[3]

Jeff Wasson, although wounded in the knee, limped along with the brigade to Manassas Junction. He went in search of a hospital shortly after sunrise on August 29th:

> I walked two miles to the hospital at the celebrated Weir House, Beauregard's head quarters. There I found all the boys from our company. I stayed there over night and walked the next morning to Bull Run, going to the general hospital; there stayed over night. The next morning I started for the cars at Fairfax Station, which was about ten miles. I walked part of the way and gave out and got into an ambulance and rode the balance of the way. We got to the station at dark; the train was loaded, and hundreds lying on the ground waiting till morning. I got up on an old cart and rode to Washington, arriving there next morning.

Washington hospitals were overwhelmed with casualties from Pope's battles, so the less seriously wounded were sent north to other cities. Wasson journeyed by rail to Baltimore, then on to Wilmington, Delaware, where citizens came to the depot with baskets of pies, cakes, and fruit. The hungry Hoosier warrior confessed, "I filled my haversack with these delicacies." Wasson finally reached Philadelphia, where he became a patient at the Christian Street Hospital on the afternoon of September 3rd. Many of his Hoosier comrades were not so lucky.[4]

Back on King's abandoned battlefield, the glaring sun illuminated a ghastly spectacle on the morning of August 29th. The Brawner farmhouse and its outbuildings, now quite perforated with musket balls, sat as quiet sentinels overlooking the bloodstained land. Hundreds of bodies, clothed in both blue and butternut, lay scattered across the Virginia fields. In some places, a person could walk for several yards on the corpses. At a fence near the house, the bodies of several Hoosiers, now riddled with lead, hung on the rails where they had died. Even farm animals had been shot to death in their pens, while the bodies of rabbits and birds lay in the grass, innocent victims of the relentless musketry. Hundreds of wounded, overlooked during the night, groaned in pain and cried constantly for water. The stench of gunpowder and blood and human waste hung like a cloud over the battlefield. The sight was enough to sicken one's soul.[5]

Shortly after sunrise, a line of rebel skirmishers, supported by a company of cavalry, advanced along the turnpike and informed the Federal wounded that they were now prisoners. This small enemy force retained possession of the area for several hours, but retreated before an advance by Robert Schenck's Union division. Some rebs found temporary shelter behind the Cundiff house and scores of wounded found themselves caught in the middle of a brisk skirmish. Schenck's men, thinking the rebs were also hiding inside the building, fired at it, while the wounded "lay hugging the floor under two fires." One soldier who had been shot twice the previous night was hit again.[6]

Isaiah B. McDonald, a Hoosier serving on the staff of General Robert Milroy, followed the Federal advance until he discovered the dead and wounded from King's division. McDonald related how he assisted one of the survivors:

> Among the wounded I found one a nice intelligent looking corporal, who told me that his name was William R. Barnes, of Co. I, 19th Indiana Volunteers. I think he said that his wife lived in Owen county, Indiana. I had him and others cared for with food and drink as best I could from haversacks and canteens. I ordered an ambulance up to take these noble boys to some hospital. Soon afterwards our Brigade (Gen. Milroy's) was attacked by the enemy a little to the right, which caused some of the

ambulances to turn back, but I think Barnes was got off the field—he was badly wounded but not mortally. When the fight fully began he asked "who was fighting the rebels." I answered, "General Milroy's Brigade." "He'll give them all they want."

Although the Indiana press would list Corporal Barnes as killed in battle, he would recover from his wound and serve out his enlistment in the Veteran Reserve Corps.[7]

McDonald was only able to assist a few individuals before Milroy's brigade retreated. However, several other wounded prisoners, including Abe Buckles, managed to make their escape during Milroy's distraction. Buckles had received a flesh wound in his thigh, but hobbled through some woods and into a ravine as he headed for the Union lines. He continued his story:

Our troops were then falling back to a new position, and I had to use every exertion to keep out of the way until I came to an ambulance. At a field hospital my wound was dressed again, and I rested until the next day, when the army again fell back. As the ambulances were all out on the field, I started once more on foot. Night overtook me, and I slept on the banks of Bull Run, under a drenching rain. In the morning I pursued my way with great difficulty to Centreville.

One can only imagine the "great difficulty" encountered in trudging all the way to Centreville on a thigh with a bullet hole in it.[8]

By 11 A.M. of August 29th, the remaining wounded were firmly behind enemy lines and many of the rebels came by and conversed with their helpless captives. Even Stonewall Jackson rode up and asked, "What troops were those with the black hats, and how many of them?" When informed that six regiments had thwarted his attack, the mighty Stonewall rode off in disbelief. Other rebel officers grudgingly admitted that "those black-hatted fellows fought like tigers." The reb privates were not so cordial. They stripped usable clothing from the dead and waited like harpies for uniforms of men in their death throes. Stragglers scavenged "everything not absolutely a fixture to the body of a live soldier."[9]

Wounded men from King's division anxiously listened to the roar of battle as it faded off to the east on August 30th and September 1st. This battalion of wounded men, with Surgeon Ward in command, was now alone. Unable to forage for themselves, King's soldiers faced an imminent threat of starvation. Although their captors were generally kind and gave them water, the rebs had little food to spare. Some men, like William Locke, who purchased two ears of corn and a hunk of bacon for $2.75, had enough money to buy a few mouthfuls of food. Those without cash crawled to where the cavalry horses had been fed and dug kernels of corn from the dirt.[10]

Drs. Ward and Green performed more major medical procedures in a week than they would ever have encountered in a lifetime of civilian practice. Both men amputated limbs and probed for balls, even though they had no chloroform and could only caution their patients to hold still while they sawed bones and dug into jagged flesh. For a short while on August 29th, a rebel surgeon assisted with operations, including the extraction of a ball from Eli Peck's hip. After cutting out the lead ball, one of the doctors handed the battered slug to Peck and told him, "Take that and show your sweetheart." In many cases, simple dressings were the only option. Such was the case with Major Isaac May. Dr. Green cleaned the wound in May's head and bandaged it, but the major received no additional treatment before his death from exposure and neglect.[11]

The only hope of Ward and Green was to keep as many men alive as possible until their removal to established hospitals. On August 31st, Green started off to meet ambulances combing the battlefield for casualties under a flag of truce. While the Hoosier doctor engaged in this mercy mission, General A. P. Hill accosted him. Apparently reluctant to allow unattended Union officers to walk around at their leisure, Hill ordered the hapless Green placed under arrest and sent him back to Gainesville with other prisoners. After being thus confined for three days, Green finally pleaded his case before a sympathetic officer who gave him an unconditional release. Because of Green's arrest, he had been unable to alert the ambulance parties and they missed Dr. Ward's open-air hospital on the extreme western edge of the Bull Run battlefield. Wounded soldiers from King's division would remain there until the last of them were paroled on September 6th, the ninth day after receiving their injuries.[12]

By that time the Bull Run battlefield was a horrid place. Looking out from the ambulances as they passed along, King's men could see hundreds of unburied Union soldiers lying stark naked or stripped to their underclothing by the rebs. Ten days before they had been brave and jaunty soldiers. Now they lay "swollen, blistered, discolored to the blackness of Ethiopians in most instances, and emitting odors so thick and powerful that it seemed that they might have been felt by the naked hand." Maggots crawled in their eyes, ears, mouths, noses and hideous wounds. Wounded Hoosiers must have considered themselves lucky indeed to have avoided such a fate.[13]

An examination of sketchy surgical records reveals that rebel musketry took a terrible toll on Hoosier bodies. A few case histories will serve to illustrate how badly large caliber lead balls could mangle human flesh. William H. H. Cooper, Company K, had his right femur shattered by a ball. Dr. Green amputated the leg near the hip and Cooper was discharged after nearly a year of hospitalization. Dr. Ward amputated the right arm of J. L.

Dean, Company D, near the shoulder on August 29th. The private recovered quickly and received his discharge on November 18, 1862.[14]

Many operations should have been conducted immediately, but were of necessity postponed until the wounded had been returned to Union hospitals around Washington. With their injuries compounded by exposure and lack of food, some men were too weak to survive major surgery. Samuel McNees, Company C, suffering from a shattered femur, underwent an amputation of his right thigh, but died on September 25th. Sidney Cobb, Company H, had been struck by a ball that broke his radius and ulna near the elbow. When the wound refused to heal, a surgeon removed sections from both bones, but the private died on October 8th. Private Richard May, Company D, was struck in the left shoulder by a ball that fractured the head of his humerus. A section of bone was removed and Surgeon Charles Page, noting May's total disability, recommended his immediate discharge. Private May died on November 22nd, the day before his discharge was approved.[15]

Several wounded soldiers had been left for dead, but would eventually be rescued and nursed back to health. Sergeant Samuel Bonar, Company G, was struck by a ball that entered his left breast, fractured a rib, continued on through his chest and lodged in his right arm near the shoulder. Comrades reported Bonar as killed, but he eventually reached a Washington hospital. Complications of his wound included inflammation of the lungs, followed by anemia and general weakness. Long-term problems consisted of constant pain in the right shoulder, arm and hand, with the arm and hand noticeably smaller than his left ones. Private Henry Jones, Company D, had also been left for the burial parties. He was hit by a musket ball that entered below his right eye and came out through the ear. Permanent injuries included loss of sight in his right eye, impaired hearing, constant tinnitus in the right ear, and a stiff jaw.[16]

A number of Captain Dudley's men were badly wounded while holding the left flank of Gibbon's line. Lieutenant Hindman was carried from the battlefield and taken directly to Willard's Hotel in Washington, where he remained for several days. After receiving a leave of absence, Hindman headed home to heal. Surgeons in Indianapolis regularly examined the wound and reported on Hindman's chances of returning to duty. On December 9th, a doctor examined him and found a gunshot wound on the outer side of the right leg, midway between the ankle and knee. The ball was still in the wound, which remained unhealed. By January 3, 1863, the surgeon observed that "several portions of bone have already come away and one piece is now approaching the surface." The wound healed later in the month and Hindman began to regain use of the limb, although he could never again serve in the field.[17]

Corporal Benjamin Jewett was struck in his left leg by a ball that damaged the nerves so severely that he was thereafter unable to flex his foot. Private Richard Williams was shot in the left cheek and his facial muscles contracted so badly that he was unable to open his mouth. The rebels inflicted a most dreadful wound in Henry Hiatt's right thigh. A ball struck the center of his right femur and caused a "compound comminuted fracture," medical jargon which means that the bone had been pulverized and fragments blown out through the skin. Young Hiatt could never again walk without a crutch and after eighteen months of convalescence a doctor reported that "the limb is three inches too short and two thirds deficient in power." The injury produced constant pain and resulted in his untimely death at the age of twenty-nine.[18]

Samuel Lutz also became a cripple as a result of his wound. A ball struck in the middle of his left thigh, traveled upwards, scraped the top of the femur and penetrated the pelvis, where it remained. An abscess formed around the minie ball and continually discharged large quantities of pus. His leg muscles became atrophied and contracted so that the lower leg was drawn up towards the thigh. Lutz died of his wound on March 22, 1864.[19]

William J. Bennett's injury was perhaps the best documented of all those in Company B. He fell when a ball inflicted a flesh wound in his left leg, smashed into and fractured the right tibia before exiting near the knee. At his discharge the following January, Bennett's wound was still sloughing off pieces of bone. When he needed assistance with a pension claim, Bennett contacted some comrades who agreed to examine his wound. Frank Huff testified, "I found his leg a running sore and he had to keep it bandaged all the time. The leg is black and colored and has the appearance of mortification." Samuel Hill stated that "it looked sickning one young man actually fainted at the sight of it," and concluded by saying, "I dont see how he can walk." Grear Williams stated emphatically, "I know his condition is worse than a man with the loss of one leg." The startling fact about these descriptions of Bennett's condition is that they were made in the early 1890's, *nearly thirty years after he had been shot.*[20]

Hoosier families waited anxiously for news of their loved ones in the wake of Pope's defeat. Some got word of their sons through newspaper accounts and casualty lists, which often contained erroneous information. Such was the case with Sergeant Crockett T. East, Company K, who was first reported to be mortally wounded. A Delaware County resident described the scene when that report reached Selma:

> The Friends of C. T. East was throwed into mourning and sadness when we got the first Report of the killed and wounded of Co. K. . . . his Friends had collected at B. Harters House, and was in great Trouble. the

> Report was that he [was] Mortely wounded and a prisoner. I told the friends there was a faint Ray of hope—his mother imploreingly asked me where. I told her that the Terms Mortaly wounded and a prisoner was conflicting. that the Enemy would not take a Man who was Mortaly wounded a prisoner. the idea gave comfort and a ray of hope.

A day or two later a letter arrived from the wounded man informing his parents that he had received a flesh wound and was in the Georgetown Hospital. His father immediately set out to bring the wounded sergeant home.[21]

Thomas and Zezia Benton heard the mournful news about their boy from R. O. Dormer, a friend employed at the Interior Department who participated in the Indiana relief effort. Dormer advised them: "It is my melancolly duty to inform you, from the best information I can get, that your son Thomas was killed in the battle of the 30th ult." Dormer could only furnish a few meager details:

> His comrads say that he was wounded twice; once through the hips and bowels, and the second and probably the most fatal shot was through the lungs. They were compelled to leave him on the field. He was most likely buried by the Sesecionists, as they still hold that portion of the battle field.

The elder Benton caught the next train for Washington and arrived in the capital on Wednesday night, September 3rd.

He searched through at least ten hospitals during the next two days, but could learn only that Tom and his friend, Sam McCown, had been badly wounded and left on the field. The heartsick father confessed to his wife, "I have mad up my mind that my poor boy is dead and in some ditch on the battle field." Mr. Benton then concluded his letter home with some dispassionate advice: "dear wife try to be resigened to the will of the lord and not let it worry you to much." The determined father, however, did finally manage to locate his son and removed him to the boardinghouse at 417 12th Street West run by Mary Roche. Dr. John G. Stephenson agreed to tend the wounded sergeant. Although Tom's chest wound was still quite painful and continued to discharge large quantities of foul-smelling pus, the doctor seemed to think that he would recover. After making arrangements for his son's care, Benton returned home.

Tom seemed to improve and exhibited a cheerful attitude and good appetite until Thursday, September 11th. After writing a brief letter to his parents, he began to breathe heavily and Dr. Stephenson thought his lungs may have become inflamed from lying untended on the battlefield for so long. Tom rallied briefly, but became progressively worse, as Mrs. Roche described:

on Saturday I began to feel a little more anxious and the Doc staid the most of the day with him. he sleep calmly only waking to take his medicine. his mind wandered in his sleep. he appeared to think he was on the field giving orderes to his comrades and fighting the enemy. Let me assure you he had every attention. Dr. Stephenson dressed his wounds three and four times a day was with him from Saturday afternoon until he died which was at half past one on Sunday, noon. at 11 o clock in the morning he said "Tom" I am afraid this will prove fatal. the only answer he made was "Well." a few moments after he called Mrs Roche give me a drink. he said to me I dont want you to hold the tumbler give it to me. he drank hearty and died very soon after without a struggle.

After his death, Dr. Stephenson used the money in Benton's purse to pay for the room, laundry expenses, and medicine. The young sergeant's uniform, along with two carpet sacks of personal items, was forwarded to his parents in Richmond.[22]

For Sergeant Tom Benton and, indeed, every soldier in the regiment, their first battle had not gone the way they had imagined it would. The Hoosiers had discovered that being a soldier was no longer fun. All had heard the sound of lead balls tearing through human flesh and many had felt the searing pain of disfiguring wounds. The melancholy experience of this first battle had made every one of them sadder, wiser, and older beyond their years. No matter what their actual ages, all trace of boyhood disappeared forever on that hot August night on John Brawner's farm. Hereafter, they will only be referred to as men.

15

Battles in Maryland

On Monday, September 1st, Pope's army continued its retreat from the Bull Run battlefield toward the safety of the forts surrounding Wahington. Soldiers in Gibbon's brigade marched along and listened to the sound of battle as Stonewall Jackson got into another fight near Chantilly during an evening rainstorm. But the Western soldiers, "wearied, footsore, and hungry," happily avoided involvement in this latest battle and bivouacked near Fairfax Court House that evening. On the following morning, Colonel Meredith led his Hoosiers through Falls Church and on to Upton's Hill, where the regiment encamped in line of battle under the protective guns of Fort Buffalo. During the month since leaving Fredericksburg, Long Sol figured that the 19th Indiana had been under fire nineteen days, ten in succession during the last stage of the campaign. His Indiana soldiers were ready for some well-deserved rest.[1]

During his campaign, John Pope had managed to lose every foot of ground gained since McClellan's advance the previous March. That fact did not go unnoticed among the soldiers, who openly sneered at their inept commander. According to Lieutenant John Shafer, "Gen. Pope, in the estimation of the army, has proved a failure. He has advertised more than he could perform." A Hoosier surgeon summed up the common feeling by writing, "*Pope* is sunk lower than Hell—where he belongs."[2]

Even their generals had given up on Pope. When John Gibbon first heard that McClellan had assumed command of the army, he could hardly wait to share this joyful news with his brave Westerners. The general remembered:

> Facing about, I rode towards the head of my brigade which was slowly approaching, and on reaching the leading regiment, called out, "Men, General McClellan is in command of the army!" The announcement was

all that was necessary. Up went caps in the air and a cheer broke out which, as the news travelled, was taken up and carried to the rear of the column and the weary fagged men went into camp, cheerful and happy to talk over their rough experience of the past three weeks and speculate as to what was ahead.

Farther on, a Wisconsin officer noticed, "General John P. Hatch who was commanding our division, swung his sword and called for cheers, which were given with an uproarious good will and repeated." When McClellan chanced to ride by the Indiana camp late that night, Long Sol's men greeted their reinstated commander with "three hearty cheers."[3]

The exhausted troops, "many sick from fatigue of the late marches & Battles" according to Colonel Meredith, rested all day on September 3rd and waited for a Confederate attack that never developed. Meredith spent most of the following day composing reports for the battles of August 28th and 30th. Late in the evening, W. T. Dennis, the Indiana Military Agent, came into camp where he wrote a synopsis of Meredith's reports and carefully compiled a list of Sol's casualties. Both were dispatched to Governor Morton. Colonel Meredith also gave Dennis the regiment's two shot-riddled flags, with instructions to return them to Indiana as evidence of Hoosier courage. Sol's regiment needed a replacement flag, so Captain Dudley dug to the bottom of Company B's baggage and retrieved the Stars and Stripes that had been presented to the City Greys by the citizens of Richmond. For the remainder of 1862, the 19th Indiana would march and fight under their Wayne County flag.[4]

On September 5th, a large group of recruits joined the regiment at Upton's Hill. One of the newcomers was William N. Jackson, Company E, who on that day began keeping a diary of his military experiences. Jackson's first entry included the following observation: "We found the boys wore out and in poor health, they having been doing some hard marching & fighting lately." Two circumstances promised much more marching and fighting. First, all but five of the regimental teams had been turned over to the quartermaster department, a certain indication of swift marching after the enemy. Second, the rebels had crossed into Maryland, a state they would not leave without a fight.[5]

In a hasty army reorganization, General Joseph Hooker replaced McDowell and assumed command of his corps, now designated the First Corps, Army of the Potomac. General Hatch retained command of the First Division, reinforced by the 7th Indiana, which had been assigned to Doubleday's brigade. The Hoosiers were glad to see reinforcements, especially seasoned veterans from their home state.[6]

Gibbon's brigade, commanded by Long Sol in the general's temporary absence, left Upton's Hill after dark on September 6th and crossed into

Maryland over the Georgetown aqueduct. The Hoosiers "marched slowly through the silent streets of the capital," heading north on 7th Street. Some of their Wisconsin comrades claimed to have seen President Lincoln that night, but the story was probably wishful thinking. The Indiana men saw nothing but empty streets and silent buildings.[7]

Colonel Meredith recorded in his diary that it was "one of the most terrible marches ever performed by this or any other reg," surpassing even those that had preceded the Legging Mutiny. Lieutenant Finney remembered: "As the day advanced the heat became almost insupportable, and the men, fatigued with their long night march, sank down in the road by files." William Jackson, the new recruit, saw nothing to remind him of the Sabbath, just "long lines of soldiers, weary and faint, traveling along through heat and dust." There were but ninety men with the regiment when the brigade finally halted a few miles beyond Leesborough, Maryland, after a march of over twenty-five miles.[8]

In the 7th Wisconsin, Surgeon D. Cooper Ayres noticed "an almost ungovernable lassitude" among the men, who straggled worse than ever before. He explained in more detail:

> The men had rested four days at Upton's Hill, but did not recruit physically, and their energy and ambition were so much depressed that they fell out by the wayside in scores, exhibiting the appearance of general exhaustion, without symptoms of corporeal disease.

The whole division was affected by this depressed spirit. When the 7th Indiana's colonel halted his command that night, only a dozen men were still with the colors. The 80th New York fared no better, but its commander felt relieved when still other regiments halted without colors or men enough to form a single stack of arms. Thousands of exhausted men, many unwilling to exert themselves as they had in the past few months, lined the route from Washington. This army was in no condition to push the rebels out of Maryland.[9]

General McClellan's pursuit of Lee's army was delayed a day to allow thousands of stragglers to rejoin their regiments. Colonel Meredith promptly sent the regimental wagons back for rations and baggage left behind at Upton's Hill. Before the teamsters left, Sol considerately advised his recruits to lighten their loads by sending their knapsacks back to Washington. After that first march, the new men readily accepted. Company commanders used this brief lull to finally begin work on the muster rolls for July and August, although they still could not accurately account for their losses.[10]

Orders came to march on September 9th and Gibbon's brigade advanced from Leesborough into northern Maryland by way of Mechanicsville, Brookville, Triadelphia, Cooksville, Lisbon, Poplar Springs, and New Market. The Western brigade finally camped on the Monocacy River, some two miles east of Frederick, on the afternoon of September 13th. Despite the marching, morale had risen sharply since leaving Washington. The column had passed through some perfectly beautiful country on the way north, where delicious peaches and pears beckoned from well-tended orchards. Long Sol's men happily purchased some of the fruit (and swiped much more) to supplement their regular rations. The Monocacy gave them an opportunity to bathe and wash their dirty uniforms.[11]

Creature comforts were important, of course, but the most significant improvement in their morale came from Marylanders who waved flags and voiced Union sentiments, a welcome change from those surly Virginians. One Indiana officer described the delight of campaigning in a loyal state:

> The march of the army thus far, had partaken of the character of a triumphal procession; everywhere the men were cheered and feasted, flags were displayed, and on every hand the most unbounded enthusiasm was shown at the sight of Union soldiers. The veterans began to forget their late hardships; demoralization disappeared; order began to appear where confusion had reigned supreme; discipline resumed its wonted sway; and once more the army felt, that, under its favorite leader, it was equal to the herculean task before it.

Another Hoosier described the passionate display by residents of the Old Line State: "We found the stars and stripes floating from nearly every housetop, little children, young ladies, old men and women were found at nearly every house door or yard gate to join in a word of good cheer on our way." It was again fun to be a soldier.[12]

On September 14th, the 19th Indiana left the Monocacy promptly at 6 A.M. and marched westward through the village of Frederick. Morning sunlight glistened off the spires where Sunday church bells rang out their greetings for McClellan's army. Lieutenant George F. Noyes described the scene as it appeared to the soldiers that morning:

> Our march through the pretty city of Frederick was a perfect ovation— one continuous waving of flags, fluttering of handkerchiefs, tossing of bouquets, and cheering by our men, who grew fairly hoarse before they had passed through its main street.

One circumstance marred the triumphal entry into Frederick. General King, his reputation ruined during Pope's campaign, had returned to field duty and assumed command of the division on September 13th. Much to everyone's delight, King was relieved about noon on the 14th and ordered back to Washington, once again turning the division over to General Hatch.[13]

Hatch's division moved westward on the National Road, crossing Catoctin Mountain and passing through Middletown toward the sound of cannonading. Gibbon's brigade was soon detached from the division and given the unenviable task of attacking Turner's Gap, where the National Road crossed over South Mountain. This rugged mountain gorge was studded with woods, stone fences and other cover for Confederate defenders. Lieutenant Frank Haskell surveyed the terrain and noted it was "an ugly looking place to attack."[14]

Gibbon placed the 7th Wisconsin on the right of the turnpike, supported by the 6th Wisconsin. The 19th Indiana occupied the left of the road, supported by the 2nd Wisconsin and preceded by two companies from that regiment, deployed as skirmishers. Two guns from Battery B held the road. Fighting raged to the right and left of the National Road, but Gibbon's brigade remained stationary until about 5 P.M.[15]

Finally, orders arrived to send forward the skirmishers. On the left of the turnpike, Captain Wilson Colwell directed his two Badger companies in "a deadly game of 'Bo-peep'" with rebel outposts. The Hoosiers, pulling their hat brims down as they marched toward the setting sun, followed in line of battle. Gibbon soon became concerned about an ominous piece of woods on the left and dispatched word for Colonel Meredith to send a couple of companies to investigate. Long Sol misunderstood the instructions and wheeled his entire regiment to face the woods. Gibbon was appalled to see the movement bungled at its outset and halted the brigade's advance until Lieutenant Haskell could gallop over to correct the mess. Haskell finally got the 19th Indiana faced in the proper direction and Sol sent Captain Dudley's company out to protect his flank. The advance then resumed.[16]

Colonel Meredith reported that his regiment advanced "slowly, cautiously, but steadily, forward." Concealed rebels kept up "an annoying fire into the line from every fence, building or bush which lay in their way" and one shot killed Captain Colwell while he directed the skirmish line. Sol's command soon discovered an enemy stronghold on the left, where rebels fired from the shelter of a house and its outbuildings. Lieutenant James Stewart, commanding Battery B's two guns on the road, remembered what happened next:

> Just about that time a son of Colonel Meredith came to me; and I think he was the youngest and tallest, as well as the thinnest man I ever saw. He said: "Father wants you to put a shot in that house; it is full of rebel sharpshooters." I said, "Who in thunder is your father?" He said his father was Colonel Sol Meredith, of the Nineteenth Indiana. I said: "You go back with my compliments to your father, Colonel Sol Meredith, of the Nineteenth Indiana, and tell him I will require him to give me a written order to shell that house." In a few minutes Colonel Meredith came up

and said: "I want you to shell that house." I told him I wanted a written
order. He said: "By Jinks, I will give you a written order."

Stewart told the colonel to rejoin his regiment and he would fire a shell into
the second story of the house. Meredith watched with approval as Stewart
did just that, "causing a general stampede of their forces from that point." As
the rebels scampered away, Sol admired the way his men advanced up the
mountainside: "It was a most magnificent sight to see the boys of the
Nineteenth going forward, crowding the enemy, cheering all the time."[17]

Rebel skirmishers rallied at a stone fence, where they again opened
an annoying fire. Men began to fall more frequently. Captain Patrick Hart,
Company H, received a serious wound in the leg, but "dropping his sword
he picked up a rifle and fought with that while he remained on the field."
Sergeant Isaac Branson, Company E, was struck behind his left ear by a round
ball that knocked him senseless. Branson soon regained consciousness and
tried to walk back down the mountain, but he had little control over his limbs
and constantly stumbled and fell. At one point, the disabled sergeant
"introduced his little finger into the wound for more than an inch, and could
feel the brain substance."[18]

Colonel Meredith ordered Captain Clark to take Company G and
quickly get astride the stone wall so as to drive off those enemy marksmen.
Clark got his men behind a fence that ran perpendicular to the rebel line and,
assisted by some of Captain Dudley's flankers, crept forward and opened fire.
The Hoosiers were on lower ground and aimed up towards the pike, "so that
if a bullet missed one it took another." Clark screamed for his men to charge
and an impetuous attack, "accompanied by the *inimitable Hoosier yell*,"
rounded up a dozen prisoners, including two officers. The rebels fled in
confusion, "retiring with more haste than military precision," and all firing
ceased south of the turnpike.[19]

But the battle still raged on the right where the 7th Wisconsin had
encountered a strongly posted enemy force. Gibbon sent the 6th Wisconsin
to the right of the 7th and advanced the 2nd into the gap between Meredith's
Hoosiers and the National Road. After Captain Clark's successful charge
cleared the enemy south of the road, the 2nd Wisconsin fired by wing into
the enemy north of the turnpike. When that regiment had expended its
ammunition, the 19th Indiana advanced and opened an enfilade fire that
lasted until well after dark. The shooting ended about 9 o'clock and, "pursuit
being considered dangerous," Sol's men were relieved by other troops near
midnight.[20]

Compliments poured in after the battle. Reporting casualties of nine
killed, thirty-seven wounded, and seven missing, Meredith expressed his
pleasure with the regiment's performance: "The boys of the Nineteenth

12. George H. Richardson.
From the 20th Century History of Delaware County, Indiana.

Indiana behaved most gloriously. Too much praise cannot be bestowed upon them for their courage and gallantry." General Gibbon, charitably omitting any reference to Long Sol's mistaken maneuver, wrote: "The conduct of the officers and men was during the engagement everything that could be desired, and they maintained their well-earned reputation for gallantry and discipline acquired in the engagements of the 28th and 30th of August." Unknown to the Western troops, General McClellan had personally witnessed their assault on Turner's Gap. The army commander would later write: "General Gibbon, in this delicate movement, handled his brigade with as much precision and coolness, as if on parade, and the bravery of his troops could not be excelled."[21]

The fighting at South Mountain had not been kind to the new recruits in Company E. Of the eleven men who had joined the regiment at Upton's Hill, three had been shot. James Love and William J. Brinson, who would not live long enough to see his newborn child, were both mortally wounded. A third man, George H. Richardson, was killed instantly by a shot in the left eye. His comrades searched the body for some mark to explain his death, but could not locate any wound until one of them chanced to open his eyelid. Prior to his enlistment, Richardson had been principal of the Muncie public school and was considered "highly efficient, and fully competent." The editor of the *Delaware County Times* lamented Richardson's death with a curse upon his killers: "May God send a fearful retribution upon the accursed traitors who thus fill our land with sorrow and wailing."[22]

After the battle, a squad of Hoosiers took their prisoners down the mountain to General McClellan's headquarters. The corporal in charge searched for someone to whom to give his captives and chanced to blunder into the general's office. McClellan asked the corporal what he wanted, who he was and where he came from. When informed that he came from Gibbon's brigade, McClellan complimented the brigade and its fight in Turner's Gap. The Hoosier responded: "Well, General, that's the way we boys calculate to fight under a general like you." McClellan sprang from his chair, shook his hand and said: "My man, if I can get that kind of feeling amongst the men of the army, I can whip Lee without any trouble at all." The proud corporal returned to his regiment and repeated the story, which quickly spread throughout the brigade. God, how they loved Little Mac.[23]

The enemy had disappeared by morning, so the first task was to bury the dead. Battlefield burial was made without ceremony. Mementoes and locks of hair were removed from the slain, then shallow graves were hacked out of the stony ground. Friends wrapped the bodies, still clothed in blood-clotted uniforms, into blankets, lowered them into the ground and covered them over with rocks and dirt. There was no coffin, no minister to read a burial service, and no firing squad to fire a farewell volley. Headboards with rudely carved names marked each grave. With heavy hearts the Hoosiers began their pursuit of the rebels shortly after 11 o'clock on the morning of September 15th.[24]

Some adjustments in the command structure became necessary after the South Mountain battle. John Hatch had been wounded in fighting north of Turner's Gap, so command of the division devolved upon General Abner Doubleday. This promotion was the latest in a series of changes which saw four men command the division in two days. First there had been Hatch, then King on the night before the battle, Hatch again on September 14th, and now Doubleday, an untried commander, on the eve of another important battle. Stability was at a premium. At the regimental level, Colonel Meredith was hurting badly from broken ribs suffered in his fall on August 28th and would soon relinquish command of the regiment to Lieutenant Colonel Bachman. Captain Dudley filled in as acting major. So many other officers were worn down by fatigue and illness that at least four companies— A, B, C, and E—were led by sergeants.[25]

After crossing South Mountain, the 19th Indiana marched through Boonsborough, then turned southwesterly toward Sharpsburg. Somewhere along that day's march, John Gibbon encountered a Western soldier trudging along with one arm in a sling and the other holding his musket. The general had a brief conversation with the soldier:

"My man, where are you going?"
"Back to my regiment, sir."
"But you can't handle your musket in that fix."
"Yes, I can, sir."

The latter remark was so emphatic that Gibbon could do nothing more than ride away impressed with the man's determination.[26]

The Western brigade halted after passing through Keedysville and the men quickly went to sleep. About 10:30 P.M. Doubleday ordered Gibbon to send one of his regiments out on picket. Lieutenant Haskell rode over to awaken the unlucky Hoosiers:

> They had little sleep the night before, were weary with the day's march, and were sleeping soundly in their bivouac in a plowed field:—it may well be supposed the order was not agreeable to them,—they swore worse than the "Army in Flanders."

The whole affair was a ludicrous example of military folly, since other picket lines already guarded the army. Haskell spent most of the night wandering around trying to locate anyone with information about where the pickets should be placed. The Hoosiers, thoroughly mad by this time, were finally posted at 3 A.M. on September 16th.[27]

Firing commenced about 10:30 that morning, but General Hooker spent most of the afternoon getting the First Corps across Antietam Creek and arranged for battle. Colonel Meredith, unfit due to injuries, turned command of the 19th Indiana over to Lieutenant Colonel Bachman. Shortly after crossing the creek, Bob Patterson, Company E, had a startling experience:

> In passing where the enemy had killed some cattle, some of our boys had detached strips of fat from the intestines of the animals which they applied to their guns to prevent rust. I had unconsciously raised the hammer of my gun and was applying the grease about the tube as the regiment halted, when I rested the muzzle of the gun against my left shoulder, and in drawing the string of fat through the guard the gun was discharged, and the ball passing through the rim of my hat.

Patterson was nearly deafened and those standing nearby thought him injured by a shell burst. After this bit of excitement, Bachman's regiment bivouacked on the left of the Hagerstown Turnpike, within 400 yards of enemy pickets, who, along with their Federal counterparts, "kept up a lively, though comparatively harmless fire" all night.[28]

Every man in the ranks knew that there would be a battle on September 17th and the Hoosiers were ready, each "feeling that that was the day, and that the place, and they the men, who were to decide the destinies of the nation." There was no need for reveille since jittery pickets began firing even before it was light enough to see clearly. Gibbon's brigade left its bivouac north of the Joseph Poffenberger house about 5 A.M. and advanced in column of division. Artillery shells crashed in and around the Western regiments as Gibbon led them south along the Hagerstown Turnpike toward the farm of D. R. Miller. The first Hoosier casualty occurred in the Miller peach orchard.[29]

Gibbon deployed the 6th Wisconsin into line of battle before reaching a large cornfield south of the Miller house. The 2nd Wisconsin formed its battleline to the left and both Badger regiments advanced against rebels concealed in the corn. When Gibbon saw another force of rebels threatening to flank his brigade on the right, he sent two guns from Battery B and his remaining regiments into action across the turnpike. The 19th Indiana followed a little brook that ran between the Miller house and barn, beyond which it formed a line of battle on the right of the 7th Wisconsin. Lieutenant Colonel Bachman sent Company B forward into the timber as skirmishers. Thus Gibbon's brigade was aligned, from right to left, in the following manner: 19th Indiana, 7th Wisconsin, Lieutenant James Stewart's two guns from Battery B (all west of the road), 6th Wisconsin, and 2nd Wisconsin (the latter two in the cornfield east of the road).[30]

At this time, the 19th Indiana held the extreme right flank of the Union Army. Captain Dudley discovered this fact when his skirmishers saw an enemy column:

> I sent one of my brightest sergeants off up to our right & rear to find and notify our friends. He travelled over a mile & returns without finding any, except some stray Rebels who were scouting evidently.

General Patrick's brigade came up shortly thereafter, while the Hoosiers continued to spar with Confederates intent on reaching Gibbon's right flank.[31]

The battle had intensified so quickly that the mighty struggle in the cornfield across the road sounded like so many popguns amid the thundering artillery. An enemy assault against Stewart's guns, now reinforced by the rest of Battery B, sent the 2nd and 6th Wisconsin reeling back toward the Miller house. Captain John Callis, commanding the 7th Wisconsin, swung his regiment parallel with the road and aligned it behind a limestone outcropping which the Badgers used as a breastwork. Canister from Battery B, enfilading musketry from the 7th Wisconsin, and scattered fire from survivors of the 2nd and 6th Wisconsin crushed the attack. One Texan later recalled: "There were shot, shells, and Minie balls sweeping the face of the earth; legs, arms, and other parts of human bodies were flying in the air like straw in a whirlwind." From a distance, the Hoosiers saw that the rebels broke and began to retire with considerable speed."[32]

When he spotted the charge upon Battery B, Lieutenant Colonel Bachman recalled his skirmishers and wheeled his regiment into line on the right of the 7th Wisconsin. Hoosiers fired some long range shots at the rebs, whose shattered regiments soon fell back "in great disorder" along the turnpike and through the cornfield. This half of Gibbon's brigade charged to the road, where they hauled in "many prisoners." Bachman's advance into open fields from the woods attracted the attention of rebel gunners, who began to fire shells at the Indiana regiment. As his soldiers climbed the post and rail fence beside the turnpike, a well-aimed shell burst beneath Bob Patterson and sent him flying amidst a cloud of splinters. He later recalled:

> The concussion and injuries received was so paralyzing that all seemed a blank to me for some time. I know not how long. On regaining consciousness I found I could not move my right hand or foot, with sensations of numbness indicating partial paralysis of [my] right side from the concussion or injury or both.

Clint Anthony, Company E, was struck on the neck by a chunk of iron that threw him head over heels. Anthony was left for dead, but later recovered his senses and discovered only a bruise inflicted by a stray piece of spent shell.[33]

As the enemy began to disappear beyond a small hill in the cornfield, some abandoned cannon were left on the crest. Hoosiers began to point and shout at their commander to follow up the advantage. One soldier watched as Bachman, yielding to their urgent cries, "pushed himself through our ranks and drawing his sword, his deep bass voice rang out, 'Boys, the command is no longer forward, but now it is follow me!'" With hat and sword in hand, Bachman gave the order to double-quick and his Indiana men sprang forward with a cheer into a spirited bayonet charge. Some of the 7th Wisconsin men joined in on the left and most of the 21st New York, reinforcements from Marsena Patrick's brigade, advanced on the right. It was a bold maneuver, but William Jackson wrote that "we got into a hornet's nest."[34]

The attackers quickly reached the brow of the hill, where they came face to face with a rebel line of battle, apparently waiting in reserve. George Finney described the climax of this impetuous charge:

> As the regiment gained the top of the hill they were greeted by a terrible volley of musketry from a full brigade of rebel infantry. For a moment the line staggered. The clarion voice of Bachman was heard urging his men to hold the hill until reinforcements could come up. The men

> rallying to his call began to fire into the dense mass of rebels in front; for
> five minutes they held the hill. . . . In those five minutes, one-third of the
> line had fallen. Still Bachman cheered on his men. A rebel bullet struck
> him, and he fell to rise no more.

One ball struck and shattered Bachman's elbow, the force turning him partially around, when another ball went through his body. Private Joseph Addleman received a mortal wound and stumbled into the arms of Captain Dudley. Lieutenant William Orr fell with a bullet through his lung. Private Joshua Jones dropped with a wound that shattered a leg bone. Rebel musketry knocked over dozens of other Hoosiers on that little hilltop.[35]

Captain Dudley took command and saw instantly that he could not hold that isolated position. While some Company C men carried their dying commander to the rear, Dudley ordered all survivors to fall back out of the cornfield. During Dudley's withdrawal to the turnpike, his Wayne County flag fell three times. One stricken color-bearer raised himself up and waved the flag defiantly a few times, but finally had to give it up. After it fell the third time, Lieutenant David S. Holloway, Company D, saw the banner lying among the cornstalks, ran back amid a storm of musketry and carried it safely from the field. Several fallen enemy standards had been spotted in the cornfield (an Indiana man claimed to have shot a rebel officer while standing on a fallen flag), but all were left behind except for one toted back by an unidentified Hoosier.[36]

Just before reaching the turnpike, a new rebel line fired into the Hoosiers from the south, hastening their retreat. Three men from Company C—John Yost, Henry Kirby, and Thomas Kirby—had carried back Lieutenant Colonel Bachman, while Sergeant William W. Macy cared for him in his dying moments. During the withdrawal, Macy received a wound in the head and he reached the turnpike drenched with blood. General Patrick, who had gotten the 21st New York back to its proper place, saw Macy's return and cried out to his men: "Make way and let that brave man through!" Unhurt but with his clothes pierced in several places, Dudley finally reached safety behind Patrick's line of battle. The grizzled general rode up to the young officer and exclaimed, "Captain, I shall mount you on a horse and call you Major after this."[37]

The 19th Indiana, along with the rest of Gibbon's brigade, was now withdrawn into the woods north of the Miller farm. Gibbon could only assemble about 400 soldiers from his four regiments, some sixty of them Hoosiers. Bachman's charge had cost the regiment over one hundred casualties (only 200 had gone into action that day) and had brought no reward. Henry Marsh was not in the fight, but his friends told him "the chance looked so good" that it could not be overlooked. Dudley would later

13. Company C's Thomas Kirby (left) and Henry Kirby (right).
From the Bob Willey Collection. Used by permission.

refer to the attack as a "foolhardy charge" and one Hoosier veteran described it as "a gallant ill-advised charge." General Patrick probably came closest to the truth when he wrote that the 19th Indiana and 21st New York had dashed forward after forgetting their orders during the excitement.[38]

After spending that afternoon stopping stragglers from other commands, the Hoosiers bivouacked north of the woods. Captain Dudley remembered, "We remained in this bivouac until the morning of the 20th, resting, cleaning guns, and sending details to recover and bury our dead, and remove the wounded to the field hospitals." Trips to the late battlefield revealed a landscape of unbelievable carnage and Sol Meredith, now back in command, confessed, "it makes my heart sicken to see the awful sight." Along the turnpike where the 19th Indiana and 7th Wisconsin had fought, forty-two dead secesh lay in the space of a dozen fence panels. William Jackson saw places where rebel bodies covered the ground for many yards. Other soldiers marveled at a strange sight along the turnpike "where a union soldier & a confederate soldier died on each others bayonets with the fence between them."[39]

The Hoosier dead were gathered together for burial and Sol "directed that boards should be placed at the head & names placed on them." Seventeen men had been killed outright. Thirteen more would die from their wounds after a few weeks of tortured suffering. The dead were a varied lot.

Barton Harter, who some had considered a coward, was killed instantly when a shell crashed through his chest. William Haney had the right side of his skull smashed to fragments by a ball, but somehow managed to live until November 21st. Ephraim Eager, the sole provider for his widowed mother, had enlisted in Company A as a recruit on December 1, 1861. He quickly rose to the rank of sergeant and commanded his company at Antietam before being shot dead in the cornfield.[40]

Many seriously wounded soldiers were carried to shelter behind Miller's brick farmhouse, where they received scant medical attention. Some died there, but a few Hoosiers demonstrated how resilient the human body can be. Bob Patterson, still partially paralyzed from the shell burst, was alert enough to observe one seemingly hopeless case:

> A boy about my age on my left was moaning piteously, and I thought myself luckey when I saw the blood oozing from a bullet wound in his breast with every breath. I tried to incourage him, and when he turned his palid face toward me, I saw he was Andrew Ribble of Company K of our regiment. He could only whisper "Oh, Bob, I'll soon be gone."

Despite his grievous wound, Ribble recovered and was discharged in December. Another Hoosier, Albert Bryant, received a disfiguring facial wound when a minie ball struck the right side of his face, fractured his lower jaw, cut through his tongue, and lodged in the angle of the left jaw. Doctors dug out the missile, treated the injury for a few months and sent Bryant back to duty.[41]

Following their futile charge, Captain Dudley's Hoosiers were unable to carry off their badly wounded comrades. Those left to their fate remained in rebel hands, without medical attention, for two days. Joshua Jones was one such captive. By the time help arrived, Jones could not bear to ride in an ambulance, so friends carried him on a stretcher some three or four miles to a barn at Keedysville. Some time before, Bob Patterson had arrived at the same barn and he was appalled by Joshua's condition. One of his legs was almost severed, being held on by a mere fragment of skin, and maggots crawled through the decaying flesh. Doctors feared that Jones could not survive an operation in his weakened condition, but there was no other option, and Patterson watched a surgeon remove the ruined limb. The diagnosis had been correct and Private Joshua Jones died on September 28th.[42]

So many valuable officers and men had been lost in the past three weeks that the 19th Indiana had almost disappeared. Meredith was injured, Bachman and May were dead, most of the company officers were shot or too sick to command, and there were only enough enlisted men to form one-half of a single company. Despite these appalling losses, the Hoosiers had two prized possessions that they would never lose. First, they still carried their Wayne County flag, now "shot all in strings" by rebel musketry in the Antietam cornfield. Second, they had helped Gibbon's brigade win a nickname that even now had begun to circulate among the rest of the Army of the Potomac, a name given to soldiers by soldiers. For the rest of time, the 19th Indiana and their Badger comrades would proudly bear the name of "The Iron Brigade."[43]

16

The Iron Brigade

On September 26th, an officer from the 3rd Indiana Cavalry described how he had ridden over to see friends in the Western brigade. He was shocked at the dramatic changes wrought by events of the last few weeks:

> Three days ago I visited Gibbon's brigade and was surprised at its appearance. . . . The brigade now musters but four hundred effective men. and the 19th less than one hundred. Their loss in commissioned officers has been heavy, three companies at this time being commanded by corporals.

Despite cries by leading politicians and editors for McClellan's army to follow up its advantage, the 19th Indiana, like so many other regiments, was in absolutely no condition to begin or maintain active operations.[1]

Colonel Meredith had left for Washington to get some much needed rest on September 21st. Before he departed, Long Sol gathered the pitiful remnants of his regiment together and addressed them for a few minutes. He reviewed the regiment's history, praised their courage, and concluded by exhorting them to "maintain the honor of the 'old flag,' and the reputation of the Regt." The Hoosiers sent him on his way with three cheers.[2]

Meredith made good use of his time in the capital and naturally visited many political friends. His lobbying efforts bore fruit when Sol received a copy of the following letter on October 2nd:

> Hon. C. B. Smith, Secretary of the Interior:
> Dear Sir—I have it very much at heart that Col. Meredith should be promoted to the rank of Brigadier General in the Volunteers and take the liberty to request that you will give me the aid of your influence in securing that object.

Col. Meredith is a noble soldier, and will exercise the duties of that office with great credit to himself and the country. He is devoted, of high character, and capable, and I should esteem it a great favor to have him receive this preferment, and then be assigned to my command.

Very truly yours,

Joseph Hooker,
Major Gen.

The Lincoln administration approved Hooker's request and issued a commission to Solomon Meredith as Brigadier General of United States Volunteers on October 6, 1862.[3]

Colonel Meredith's political friends were overjoyed at his good fortune. R. M. Hall, writing from Washington, pointed out that his devotion to the country had led Sol into military service only after having "left the ease of an elegant home, the attractions of a lucrative office, and amidst the jeers and despite the opposition of some sapient friends." The editor of the *Indianapolis Daily Journal* boasted:

It affords us pleasure to be able to state that this officer does not owe his promotion to political influences. He won his promotion fairly, by his undoubted valor on fields of battle, and by his constant and devoted attention to his duties as an officer and soldier.

Of course, that statement was total nonsense. Long Sol had campaigned for his general's star almost from the moment he had received his commission as colonel of the 19th Indiana. He finally found in Hooker an officer ambitious enough to trade his military influence for some of Meredith's considerable political backing.[4]

John Gibbon was livid at what he considered the obvious political promotion of an incompetent officer. A protest to "Fighting Joe" disclosed that "the pressure from very high authority was so strong that General Hooker could not refuse." Hooker also confessed, "the officer had so many strong friends that he could not resist their solicitations." Disgusted with Hooker, who had no firsthand knowledge of Meredith's military career or ability, Gibbon continued to complain. He wrote directly to the Adjutant General and explained that Meredith "was totally disqualified for any such position." That effort also failed and Gibbon, frustrated by the system, had to content himself with the knowledge that at least *he* understood that Long Sol "was in no way fitted to fill" the office of brigadier general.[5]

The wounding and subsequent promotion of Solomon Meredith were just two of many disruptions in the Hoosier command structure during the sixty days following their battle on August 28th. Lieutenant Colonel Bachman and Major May had been killed. Three captains—Luther Wilson,

John Lindley, and Patrick Hart—and eight lieutenants had been wounded. Captain Samuel Williams had been promoted to lieutenant colonel and Captain Dudley became the new major. Captain Robert Hamilton, long suffering from "disease of the heart attended with palpatations and partial paralysis of the left side" finally took his discharge on October 23rd. Captain William M. Campbell resigned on October 15th. Captain Valentine Jacobs had finally been dismissed on October 13th for his cowardice on the eve of the Brawner Farm battle. During this two-month period, all three field officers and eight of ten captains had either been killed, wounded, promoted, discharged or dismissed, a dramatic indication of the cost of campaigning under Pope and McClellan.[6]

Non-combat casualties continued to mount among the enlisted men as well. Captain Hamilton reported the death of Thomas H. Parker on September 21st from the kick of a horse. Parker was serving as a teamster at the time and died a few hours after being struck in the head. William B. Heath, Company E, had been admitted to an Alexandria hospital on July 20th with a case of chronic diarrhea and was later transferred to Portsmouth Grove Hospital in Rhode Island. Bill's father came for him and they started back to Muncie on September 29th. Being home cheered the patient, but doctors had pronounced the case hopeless and friends could easily see that the end was near. He died shortly after midnight in the morning hours of October 5th.[7]

Reorganization in Gibbon's brigade commenced less than a week after the battle. To fill the decimated ranks of Battery B, Special Order No. 131, dated September 22nd, detailed five men from each of the already depleted Western regiments to artillery duty. Reinforcements drifted into the brigade as the slightly wounded and convalescent sick returned to duty. However, a significant reinforcement arrived during the first week of October, when Captain Alonzo Makepeace swelled the Hoosier ranks with fifty men from Alexandria. Makepeace's party included thirty-six newly-exchanged soldiers captured during Gibbon's August raid, some convalescents, and a few new recruits. These recently freed prisoners had been confined together as a group during their captivity and reached Annapolis under the command of Sergeant Charles Watkins, Company A, and Sergeant Jeff Crull, Company B. Crull admitted that he was "not so overly fond of the People in the South" because they had treated the prisoners "Very bad." From Annapolis, Watkins's squad had gone to Alexandria, where the men received new uniforms and, finally, orders to rejoin their regiment. Sergeant Crull was amazed to see that "the company is very small now since the fights. there is no commissioned oficers at all."[8]

Despite their losses, Indiana soldiers were proud of their record and the reputation they had earned in four memorable battles. Jesse Potts explained that the few surviving Richmond City Greys had all conducted themselves honorably:

> You may assure the Richmond folks that the reputation of the city is safe in the hands of Major Dudley and the few remaining Greys. Our flag will be returned without any stains of dishonor. It was carried triumphantly through the battles of South Mountain and Antietam, and carries honorable marks. We look on it with pride, and pleasant recollections of the occasion of its presentation.

The real reason for Jesse's letter to the *Quaker City Telegram* was to send a copy of an endorsement that General McClellan had made on a letter from Gibbon to Governor Morton, asking for volunteers to fill up the 19th Indiana. McClellan's comments read as follows:

> Glorious as has been the record of Indiana in this war, you will pardon me for saying that the career of the 19th Indiana has been such as to add still higher lustre to the reputation of your State. I have watched this regiment, with its Wisconsin comrades, under the hottest fighting in the most dangerous position, and I am glad to say that there is no better regiment in this or any other army. I ask of you as an official and personal favor that you will take the most prompt means to fill the ranks of this noble regiment.

Despite this glowing compliment from Little Mac himself, only a handful of volunteers signed up.[9]

If McClellan could not drum up recruits for individual regiments, he could at least reinforce Gibbon's brigade by bolstering it with a new regiment. John Gibbon had requested another Western unit and McClellan promised that he should have the next one to join the Army of the Potomac. McClellan, who seems to have taken an interest in this particular brigade after the South Mountain affair, kept his word and assigned the 24th Michigan to Gibbon on October 8th.[10]

The general inspected his Michigan troops the following day and then formally introduced them to the brigade. Gibbon quickly saw that the 24th Michigan would be "a worthy member of the 'Black Hats,'" but the veterans were not so sure. Colonel Henry Morrow's Wolverines outnumbered the other four regiments combined and their new uniforms contrasted markedly with the ragged Indiana and Wisconsin clothing. These new men would have to prove themselves in battle before they would be accepted into the veteran fraternity. Major Rufus Dawes noticed that these new men were "crazy to fight," but veterans no longer shared that desire. Noting that their fame had been "dearly paid for," Cornelius Wheeler of the 2nd Wisconsin, declared, "We have had quite glory enough now." Writing a couple of weeks later, a Hoosier private admitted, "We have had no trouble for some time and I hope that we never may have again." Even the new squad of recruits in Company E had seen enough. At first they felt "rather cheap" as old soldiers boasted about fighting at Brawner Farm and Bull Run, but now they could feel "as good as any."[11]

It was not until mid-October that the Quartermaster Department began to issue new shoes, and uniforms to replace the army's worn out rags. Issues to Company B, now commanded by Sergeant Dick Jones, on October 15th included canteens, haversacks, tents, shirts, drawers, trousers, socks, shoes and hats. On the 21st, the company received coats and more hats, drawers, trousers, tents, shirts and shoes. The quartermaster also issued chevrons and lace for use on the trousers of corporals and sergeants. More socks and drawers were issued later in the month. While the government never re-issued leggings and only occasionally handed out frock coats, it always managed to find black hats, complete with all the trimmings, for the Hoosiers. That one distinctive feature of John Gibbon's prescribed uniform would be worn by soldiers of the 19th Indiana long after their commander had gone.[12]

Those black hats, unique in the Army of the Potomac, contributed to the Iron Brigade mystique by identifying what were perhaps the best fighting men in the war. Soldiers quickly embraced their new designation. On September 18th, Major Rufus Dawes boasted that his men had "stood like iron." Writing on September 22nd, Lieutenant Frank Haskell bragged, "I am three fourths iron and the rest is oak." By October, soldiers had become quite comfortable with referring to themselves as "Gibbon's Iron Brigade."[13]

Coincidentally, the same name had been applied to another brigade in the division some five months earlier. Impressed with the marching of Christopher C. Augur's brigade, General Marsena Patrick supposedly remarked, "General, your men must be made of cast-iron, to march so rapidly all day yesterday and all night too." Augur instantly replied, "Yes, sir; this is the Iron Brigade." Augur's soldiers were delighted at their general's response and bought medals with "Iron Brigade" emblazoned on them. They even painted "Iron Brigade" on some of their regimental flags. Commanded successively by General John Hatch and Colonel Walter Phelps, Jr., the brigade would be broken up after the Chancellorsville campaign in 1863.[14]

New Yorkers from Augur's brigade never forgave those upstart Westerners who had stolen their distinctive name. A debate over which brigade really deserved the title raged off and on for over fifty years. The New York argument was presented by Sergeant Edward Sherman, 22nd New

York, who wrote, "I do not know that I can blame those Western kids for taking up our name after we were mustered out; but they should have added jr., making it the 'Iron Brigade, jr.'" Sergeant Jesse Jones, of Captain Dudley's company, argued that their claim did "not rest upon our ability to perform wonderful leg-work and have a Colonel [*sic*] christen us 'The Iron Brigade,' but the title was applied to us while we were in the seething cauldron of battle, by Gen. Geo. B. McClellan, at South Mountain." When veterans appealed to General Gibbon for his opinion, he responded that the name was first applied to his brigade shortly after Antietam. He then wisely advised, "To attempt to *prove* the right to a name applied by general consent, is calculated to throw doubt upon its legitimacy." Rejecting Gibbon's advice, Badgers and Hoosiers continued their fight over the Iron Brigade name, showing the same determination against the New Yorkers as they had against rebels during the war years.[15]

It should not be assumed that every soldier in the brigade was a hero. Field returns on September 18th and 22nd showed that Gibbon's brigade had increased by eighty men during that period. A careful examination disclosed that every soldier returning to the brigade had come from hospitals or returned from detached service. Gibbon would proudly write, "I had no stragglers." But a general order published on the 22nd seemed to indicate otherwise. General Order No. 74 read:

> Hereafter, during an action, no man will be allowed to leave the ranks of this Brigade, unless he is wounded.
>
> Any unwounded man therefore found in rear of his Reg't during a battle will be considered and treated as a coward skulking from a duty bravely faced by his comrades.

This order indicates a problem that Gibbon claimed did not exist in the brigade, but it certainly did. Captain Dudley alluded to it in his official report on Antietam when he confessed, "the men of this regiment are all brave men, if we except the few who found their way to the rear when danger approached." Perhaps General Gibbon should have taken another look at his numbers.[16]

The Hoosiers remained in their camp near the Dunker Church, which they christened the "pepper box," until September 29th, when Doubleday's division moved down to the Potomac River. This change of bivouac was necessitated by the wells becoming tainted "from the multitude of human bodies, many buried in a state of putrefaction, and the carcasses of dead horses deposited a little below the surface of the earth." Medical men had warned of dire consequences not only for this reason, but also because the sinks and waste from slaughtered cattle had poisoned the atmosphere.[17]

President Lincoln came to the Antietam battlefield in October and the First Corps, now commanded by General John F. Reynolds, assembled for review on the 2nd. Gibbon's brigade arrived in position about 2 P.M. and "lay in line on an open field, where the stench of dead horses and offal of butchered cattle were hardly bearable." The sun beat down on the troops all afternoon and they remained in line until after dark without seeing the president. Reynolds reassembled his divisions at 9 the following morning, but it was not until five hours later that Lincoln, McClellan, and his staff came trotting by to review the corps. There was little cheering and that mostly reserved for Little Mac. Private Jackson got a close look at the president and wrote in his diary: "Mr. Lincoln does not look as old as his pictures make him look, he seemed sunburnt as though he took much outdoor exercise, his beard unshaven gave him a rough camp look, altogether he is the man to suit the soldiers." Despite having had an opportunity to see the president, most of the soldiers felt that the review was simply "damn *foolishness!*"[18]

After Lincoln's departure, Lieutenant Colonel Samuel Williams began the task of rejuvenating his regiment. But he apparently began his new duties without the support of General Gibbon, who had recommended Captains John F. Lindley and William Dudley for promotion. However, Meredith endorsed Williams and Dudley, so Governor Morton obliged his old friend. The new lieutenant colonel was described as "cool, cautious and brave," a man whom the soldiers could respect and obey. His foremost problem was the veterans, whose endurance and courage had been rewarded with special treatment by their company officers. Williams felt that such favoritism had undermined discipline, so he began drilling his men at every opportunity in an effort to restore efficiency.[19]

On October 20th, Gibbon's brigade marched up the Potomac River to Bakersville, where it remained until 3 P.M. on the 26th. One observer watched the men of Doubleday's division as they came slogging by in the mud:

> I have noticed that the rougher the day and the more horrible the marching, the more jovial and exhilarated are the troops. As they came plunging along through the deep mud, almost staggering under the torrents of rain, past my tent on the roadside, I have rarely seen them in better spirits.

Passing a tent from which a stove pipe projected prominently, the drenched soldiers shouted out, "Don't shoot!" and "'Lay down, boys, lay down!" and "We've got to charge that battery!" This good humor departed when the march continued until long after dark. Halting somewhere beyond Keedysville, soldiers kindled large fires to dry clothes and cook supper. Next morning the brigade continued on through Burkittsville and Petersville to Berlin, where Gibbon's column crossed back into Virginia on October 30th.[20]

As the Indiana men marched south, a unique recruit was already en route to reinforce the Wayne County company. Francis M. Huff had been born on December 27, 1842, in Harrison County, Virginia. His parents were dirt poor, so Frank spent his youth performing farm labor instead of schoolwork. Disgusted with that rough life, the youngster began his academic career at the age of thirteen and, starting with his ABC's, learned his lessons quickly. By August of 1860, Frank had accumulated $10 and resolved to travel west as far as that sum might take him. He reached Richmond in September, worked for a few months, and began winter classes "under the good influence of the Society of Friends." By the end of this term, war was imminent.

Frank Huff was one of the first Wayne County men to answer the country's call, enlisting in Company B, 16th Indiana, on April 23, 1861. His one-year enlistment was spent on the Upper Potomac, near Harpers Ferry, until his muster out on May 23, 1862. He quickly rejoined the army, this time enlisting in Company E, 87th Ohio, on June 2nd. This regiment was assigned to the garrison at Harpers Ferry, remaining there until that post surrendered to Stonewall Jackson on September 15th. The 87th Ohio was paroled and speedily discharged at Delaware, Ohio, on October 3rd. Frank just had to be in the army, so he enlisted in the 19th Indiana on October 21st at Indianapolis. He was mustered into service on October 31st and would join the regiment after a series of interesting adventures.[21]

17

South to Fredericksburg

After crossing back into Virginia, McClellan's army paralleled the Confederates south by southwest along the Blue Ridge Mountains. For their part, the Hoosiers and Badgers celebrated a return to the Old Dominion by plundering orchards, henhouses, and barns. Jealous Michigan soldiers confessed that the veterans had become experts at stealing fowl, while they still had much to learn. As his Wolverines practiced the fine art of chicken stealing, Colonel Henry Morrow gave them important advice on what to expect and how to act on the battlefield. The regimental surgeon even offered instructions on how to stop the flow of blood if they should happen to be wounded. There was so much for the Michigan soldiers to learn and the veterans laughed at their mistakes, making sport of any miscue.[1]

As the Western troops neared Bloomfield, Gibbon was summoned to corps headquarters, where John Reynolds offered him command of the division formerly led by James Ricketts. This was too important an opportunity for an officer to pass up, so Gibbon somewhat reluctantly agreed to the promotion. With feelings of regret, Gibbon composed his final order to the Iron Brigade:

Brigade Head Quarters
Camp near Bloomfield Va. Nov 4th, 1862
General Orders
    No. 80
    Special Orders No. 44 from the Head Quarters 1st Army Corps relieves the undersigned from command of this Brigade.
    On relinquishing a command which for the past six months I have held with so much pride and gratification I cannot refrain from expressing my high appreciation of the distinguished valor, discipline and efficiency exhibited on so many occasions by this gallant Brigade.

> Though separated from it now, its welfare and reputation will ever remain dear to me, and I leave it fully convinced that men who have commenced so well, can never do anything to tarnish the renown gained by the blood of the many gallant comrades who have fallen. My greatest pride shall always be that I was once the Commander of this Brigade.
>
> John Gibbon
> Brig Genl.

The words in that last order had been chosen carefully and its message was no stylized military jargon. Gibbon meant every word of it because he was damned proud of those Western men. On the morning of November 5th, the general sat by the road and watched the Iron Brigade, his "children" as he now referred to them, march out of his military career.[2]

Opinions of Gibbon had changed over the six months he commanded the Iron Brigade and the Western soldiers would miss their former antagonist. Captain Philip Plummer, 6th Wisconsin, explained:

> We were all sorry to lose him for two good reasons: In the first place we lose our identity, we shall never more be called "Gibbon's Brigade," but will be called by the name of his successor; and because all the battles we have fought have been under him. and he proved himself an able and gallant commander, and won the respect and good wishes of us all.

Major Rufus Dawes admitted, "We are sorry to lose him, for a brave and true man, tested as he has been, is a jewel here." Jewel or not, Gibbon was now gone and his permanent successor could hardly wait to fill the vacancy.[3]

Gibbon's departure created a problem in the brigade, because his veteran regiments were now temporarily placed under Henry Morrow, an untried colonel. Fortunately that arrangement did not last long. Lysander Cutler, still suffering from his Brawner Farm wound and no doubt unfit for duty, returned to assume command of the brigade on November 9th. Cutler was a tough old man and the soldiers felt much safer under his leadership.[4]

One of Cutler's first acts was to inform General Doubleday of the condition of burials on the Brawner Farm battlefield. Soldiers rejoining his brigade brought word that rain had already washed away the soil, exposing the bones of slain soldiers. Colonel Cutler wrote, "As a matter of respect to the brave men who there fell, and in justice to the feelings of their living comrades and friends, I ask permission to make a detail of men to proceed to that battlefield and suitably and decently inter the remains of their comrades." Cutler's humane request was shelved and no action was taken to properly bury the Brawner Farm dead.[5]

The Army of the Potomac was stunned on November 7th by the report that General McClellan had been relieved of command and replaced by General Ambrose Burnside. Reaction in the 6th Wisconsin to that "thunder clap" of news bordered on mutiny:

> On the impulse of the moment the line officers assembled and signed a paper resigning their commissions. We took this to our Colonel, Lysander Cutler, afterwards a general. He begged us to withdraw it, as such action would have a very marked effect among the men, and if disaffection started among the officers of the Iron Brigade, no one could tell where it would stop. We withdrew and talked the matter over.

After much animated discussion, the captains and lieutenants finally agreed that they were fighting for their country, not their commanding general, and the resignations were withdrawn.[6]

McClellan had always been immensely popular with his soldiers, who took every opportunity to express their enthusiasm. His farewell order stirred their souls one last time:

> In parting from you I cannot express the love and gratitude I bear to you. As an army you have grown up under my care. In you I have never found doubt or coldness. The battles you have fought under my command will proudly live in our nation's history. The glory you have achieved, our mutual perils and fatigues, the graves of our comrades fallen in battle and by disease, the broken forms of those whom wounds and sickness have disabled—the strongest associations which can exist among men—unite us still by an indissoluble tie. We shall ever be comrades in supporting the Constitution of our country and the nationality of its people.

To his credit, Burnside graciously allowed McClellan an opportunity to review the army one last time before his departure.[7]

At noon on November 10th, the entire Army of the Potomac, except for men on guard or picket, assembled on Warrenton Heights to say goodbye to Little Mac. Brigades either cheered wildly or stood mute, the silence somehow speaking louder than the cheers. Charles Wainwright described the scene as McClellan, accompanied by Reynolds and a host of staff officers, passed by a portion of the First Corps:

> Not a word was spoken, no noisy demonstration of regret at losing him, but there was hardly a dry eye in the ranks. Very many of the men wept like children, while others could be seen gazing after him in mute grief, one may almost say despair, as a mourner looks down into the grave of a dearly loved friend.

In every previous review, McClellan had rapidly ridden along the lines, smiling at every regiment and waving his jaunty little cap. This time the pace was slower, the cap hung by his side and his face displayed a deeper emotion.[8]

Lieutenant James Stewart, of Battery B, intended to call for three cheers when McClellan passed, but his heart failed him and he felt more like crying than cheering. It was a sentiment repeated over and over on a day that seemed more like a gigantic funeral. In the 2nd Wisconsin, the bravest men shed tears and formerly stoic soldiers voiced loud complaints over Little Mac's removal. In the 19th Indiana, one soldier wrote that "there is considerable of dissatisfaction expressed both rank and file" and Lieutenant Orr remarked that the Hoosiers were "*very very* sore about the removal of McClellan." One Badger even went so far as to predict that McClellan would be the next president "if it is at the point of the bayonet."[9]

Despite Colonel Cutler's success at stopping mass resignations in the 6th Wisconsin, grumbling continued among both officers and enlisted men of the Iron Brigade. Fearing that the situation might still get out of hand, Cutler reacted by publishing General Order No. 82 on the day after McClellan's last review:

> The Colonel Commanding the Brigade is sorry to learn that many of the officers in some of the Regiments of this Brigade are openly expressing dissatisfaction at the recent change of Commander-in-chief of this Army.
>
> However strong their attachment may have been to Gen'l McClellan, it is plainly their duty as good soldiers and patriots, to give to the tried and able Commander who succeeds him, a hearty and earnest support.
>
> The Colonel Commanding appeals to every officer and man in this Brigade not to allow any feelings of disappointment to swerve them from their duty, or betray them into any act which will tarnish the bright and glorious name which the Brigade now sustains.

Heeding Cutler's message, the Western men confined themselves to verbal insubordination and steered clear of any organized rebellious acts. Time would eventually heal the wounds of McClellan's dismissal, but the war changed forever on November 10th, because "when the chief had passed out of sight, the romance of war was over for the Army of the Potomac."[10]

While McClellan and Gibbon made news in Virginia, one of Company B's boys became somewhat of a celebrity in an Indiana lawsuit. Private Luther Montgomery Hall had deserted near Falmouth on May 29, 1862, and returned home to Richmond. After several months, Luther was apprehended, taken to Camp Morton, and held as a deserter until he could be returned to the regiment. His father, William Hall, hastened to Indianapolis and petitioned Judge Charles A. Ray, Common Pleas Court, for a writ of *habeas corpus* for the release of his son. Hall's petition claimed that Luther was unlawfully restrained by Captain Thomas W. Newman, post commander, and Captain Wilcox, his agent, under the pretense that he was a lawfully enlisted soldier. The father swore that Luther had enlisted fraudulently, being "under the age of eighteen years, and without the consent of his said father and against his expressed protest made to the officer recruiting him." Luther had left the regiment prior to his eighteenth birthday, thereby repudiating the contract between himself and the United States Army.

The military responded to Hall's petition by citing the second section of Abraham Lincoln's General Order No. 141, dated September 24, 1862, which read:

> That the writ of habeas corpus is suspended in respect to all persons arrested, or who are now or hereafter during the rebellion shall be imprisoned in any fort, camp, arsenal, military prison or other place of confinement, by any military authority, or by the sentence of any court martial or military commission.

According to this order, if Luther Hall were indeed a deserter, he would be liable for trial before a court-martial and civil courts would have no jurisdiction.

Judge Ray had to determine whether Luther Hall was a soldier, subject to a military court, or whether he was a private citizen with rights in a civil court. The whole case revolved around this important decision because a military officer obviously could not restrain a private citizen on a charge of desertion, but could detain a properly enlisted soldier on such a charge. While admitting the right of President Lincoln to suspend the writ of *habeas corpus* for deserters, Judge Ray ruled that civil courts retained the right to determine whether an individual should be considered a soldier or a private citizen. The justice ruled that since Luther Hall had been fraudulently enlisted, he retained the right to a writ of *habeas corpus* and released him from his enlistment contract.

When ruling on a later lawsuit, Judge Ray cited the case of *Hall vs. Newman* and explained the reasoning behind his decision:

> If the person is under the age of 18 years, and enlisted without the consent of his parent or guardian, as this petition avers, then the enlistment was void, and he was illegally held, without any authority of law, and had a right at any moment to quit the service, and if he has done so and has been arrested as a deserter, is it to be contended that he who is not a soldier and therefore not liable to be tried by military law, but a citizen entitled to have his rights protected by the civil courts, should be refused the writ of Habeas Corpus, and turned over to a military court to be tried for an offense that he, a civilian, could not be guilty of? If he had remained in the military service, and applied for the writ of Habeas Corpus he would have been discharged under the writ, because the

14. Francis M. Huff.
From the Combination Atlas of Huntington County, Indiana.

enlistment was void. How, then, has he forfeited the protection of the writ by leaving a service that was voluntary, and in which he was under no obligation to remain?

In other words, Captain Dudley had illegally enlisted Luther Hall, an underage recruit. Since his enlistment was unlawful, he could have left the army at any time by invoking the writ of *habeas corpus*. Luther's mistake came when he simply walked away from the 19th Indiana, instead of following established legal procedures.[11]

As Luther Hall tried to resolve his desertion from the 19th Indiana, Frank Huff was deserting to join that regiment. After accepting money to serve as a substitute for a drafted man, Frank chose to join some of his neighbors in Company B, 19th Indiana. Being "anxious to get to the regiment," he traveled from Camp Carrington to Washington by way of Richmond, Cincinnati, Columbus, Wheeling, Clarksburg, Pittsburgh, Philadelphia, and Baltimore. He stopped briefly in western Virginia to visit his mother, whom he had not seen in eight years, and gave her a portion of his substitute pay. In Washington, Huff looked up Bill Bennett in Ebenezer Hospital, where he had been taken after the Brawner Farm fight. The two had been classmates at the Chester school during the winter of 1861, so Frank gladly obliged friends and relatives by checking on Bill's recovery. He found the wounded man lying on his cot, still suffering greatly from wounds in both legs.

After a lengthy conversation with Bill, Frank started for Harpers Ferry, where rumor said the 19th Indiana was stationed. Arriving at that post, where he had been taken prisoner less than two months earlier, the recruit learned that the Army of the Potomac had moved south to Warrenton. Dressed in civilian clothes and with only two dollars in his pocket, Frank shouldered his "pretty well stored portmanteau of clothing" and set out on foot. Private Huff had not gone far before Federal cavalry warned him that rebel scouts had blocked the roads in that direction. Returning to the Potomac, Frank crawled into a fodder rick and scrawled a letter, advising a friend that he intended to cross guerrilla country and asking him to tell the regiment of the circumstances if he should fail to arrive.

Bearing east toward Catoctin Mountain, Huff met a squad of cavalry south of Waterford. The officer advised Frank that rebel scouts were gobbling up all stragglers ahead, but he was determined to continue. A mounted civilian accompanying the soldiers said he would go along with Frank. At Philomont the pair came face to face with a real rebel, who was loaded down with pies and cakes and was heading for a camp close by. Frank described how he bluffed the reb:

> I approached the man in gray and confidentially told him he had better return to camp, for we were on our way home, and had seen about 7,000 Yanks camping not more than a mile north. He took me at my word and hurried away.

Frank and his partner pushed on, ignoring inquiries from ladies of the town who wanted to know to which army they belonged. Once out of sight, the two men made their escape by running and riding the horse, exchanging places as the runner got tired. The pair finally encountered a Union picket post where they surrendered and established their identity. After a good night's sleep, the men, "stiff and sore" from running, walked to Warrenton, where Private Frank Huff reported himself for duty with the Wayne County company.[12]

Huff's arrival coincided with a period when the brigade's diet had been restricted to meat and coffee. For some reason supplies of hardtack had dwindled, so that the men were given half rations of that staple on November 7th and quarter rations on the 8th. When no crackers at all were issued on the 9th, veterans took it in stride. But the new Michigan men, back with the brigade after a stint as wagon guards, shouted for bread all day. Badgers and Hoosiers, every one of whom had experienced much worse hardship than a few missing crackers, looked on the carpers with outright contempt. The situation was resolved on November 10th, but the old hands wondered what kind of reinforcements they had received.[13]

This portion of northern Virginia had been passed over so often by both armies that it was a virtual desert to soldiers looking for something to eat. When William Jackson asked for food at a farm near Fayetteville, he was told that they had only a peck of corn meal. The family had no corn, wheat, or flour and had not even seen coffee or tea for more than three months. On top of that, soldiers had dismantled every fence for firewood. Jackson described the encounter in his diary, concluding, "Thus the work of desolation goes on."[14]

From Fayetteville, Cutler turned his brigade eastward and followed a course roughly parallel to the Rappahannock River until November 22nd, when it halted near Brooks Station on the railroad between Aquia Creek and Falmouth. Frank Huff, still enamored with a soldier's life, characterized his arrival in glowing terms:

> The evening was clear and the Autumn rays of the sun fell sweetly upon the little brook that flowed southward to the pleasant Rappahannock; while the trees lifted their green crowns to the skies and waved to and fro and saluted the whistling wind as it sped onto the East.

Although the army seemed to be gathering for an attack in the vicinity of Fredericksburg, Western soldiers prudently built shanties as protection against wind and snow. They remained at Brooks Station until December 9th, being joined there by Long Sol.[15]

Brigadier General Solomon Meredith was assigned to the Fourth Brigade, First Division, First Corps, on November 25th and assumed command the following day. Sergeant George H. Legate, 2nd Wisconsin, described Long Sol as "being 6 feet 7 inches high & well proportioned, and his heart is as big as his body." Legate continued his assessment of the new commander:

> As to his military abilities I cannot say much for he is not much of a tactician, but he will be right part of the time. He is very friendly and sociable & will stop and shake hands with a private soldier & enquire as to his rations, clothing &c. So you see if he does not become distinguished as a military leader, he will become distinguished as a gentleman and kindhearted man. His reputation for bravery has been proven on many a battlefield and is doubted by no one.

Camp scuttlebutt claimed that either Sol was a distant relative of the president or had once worked on the same flatboat with Abe Lincoln and owed his promotion to that close relationship. These rumors had absolutely no foundation. Sol Meredith's promotion had resulted from his war record, combined with tireless political lobbying by powerful friends. One of his first official acts was to appoint Lieutenant Jacob M. Howard, Jr., 24th Michigan, to his staff. Young Howard just happened to be the son of United States Senator Jacob M. Howard of Michigan and his appointment may have been connected to Sol's own advancement.[16]

With time on their hands at Brooks Station, many Hoosiers wandered about and marveled at the impenetrable thickets of pine and cedar trees, with branches so thickly interlaced that birds could scarcely squeeze through them. Deserted farms and untended fields were visible in every direction. Occasionally, rambling soldiers encountered elegant houses that had been hastily abandoned as their inhabitants fled before the Union army's advance. Frank Huff related a visit to one such home:

> There stand the neatly arranged furniture—the silk curtains are still hanging in the window while the sides of the wall are filled with life-sized pictures of the family and relatives—in the parlor is the sweet-toned piano, with many noted ballads lying on top. But a few yards from this beautiful mansion, is situated an old log shanty in which his slaves dwelt. All the old negroes that are not worth any thing, are left to do the best they can.

One old Negro came out and exclaimed, "I neber seen so many sogers in all de days ob my life—why, I tinks you all enuft to eat up de sofe." Of course, Frank and his friends tried their best to do just that![17]

Many of the men desperately needed shoes, some being almost barefoot, and new footwear was issued on December 4th and 5th. The refitting after Antietam had seriously drained army resources and some regiments had need of many items. The adjutant of the 76th New York reported that his regiment lacked spades, paper, clothing, and forage for regimental teams. The regiment also urgently needed manpower, numbering only 126 men present for duty, but thirty-five New Yorkers had no guns. While most supply deficiencies had been corrected in the 19th Indiana, one item was often missing and seldom replaced. Veterans of Brawner Farm and Antietam who had witnessed the accuracy of rebel musketry promptly "lost" the brass eagle plate on the cartridge box belt. This plate was supposed to be worn in the center of the breast, where it served no purpose other than to act as a target for rebel marksmen. Smart soldiers discarded this dangerous ornament at the first opportunity.[18]

Officially, the 19th Indiana was now in the Fourth Brigade, First Division, First Corps, Left Grand Division of the Army of the Potomac, commanded respectively by Generals Sol Meredith, Abner Doubleday, John F. Reynolds, William B. Franklin, and Ambrose Burnside. In addition to its warlike title of Iron Brigade, Meredith's soldiers still answered to the more common nickname of "Big Hat Brigade."[19]

For Wayne County boys in the Big Hat Brigade, two wonderful events occurred on December 6th. That morning there was a total eclipse of the moon and that afternoon the paymaster arrived and commenced passing out greenbacks. Both events were greeted as welcome diversions, since the army would very soon advance against the rebels at Fredericksburg.[20]

At 11 A.M on December 9th, the 19th Indiana, each man supplied with sixty rounds of ammunition, moved from Brooks Station toward Fredericksburg, where Burnside planned to cross the Rappahannock on pontoons. The Hoosiers awoke on December 11th to the sound of cannonading, then advanced close enough to observe smoke from the burning town. There the regiment halted, separated from the river by some woods, while it waited to cross. Many of the men were "a little backward" about the impending battle. Although he was sick and should not have gone along, Sergeant Oliver Carmichael thought he could inspire the hesitant recruits by staying with Company E. This bold gesture failed when he dropped his musket, discharging it and shooting off a finger. Carmichael was sent back to the surgeons where faint-hearted soldiers were already angling to be excused from duty.[21]

As this new battle loomed, some of the Iron Brigade seemed to be a little more human than their reputation might imply. Reverend Samuel Eaton, 7th Wisconsin, shared some of his observations just before the Fredericksburg fight:

> On the eve of battle a soldier will sometimes put his pocket book into the hands of the Chaplain with a word and a tear, or a manner which expresses more than both. At such a moment hearts touch that had hardly recognized their kindred humanity before. Refinement does not separate itself from rudeness; even the pious and the profane have some heart throbs which are similar.

Sergeant George Legate, 2nd Wisconsin, expressing the despondent feeling of soldiers who had no confidence in General Burnside, wrote, "I thought that we were marching to defeat, and this feeling was shared with me by the whole army." Everyone thought that too much time had been wasted and the rebels were too strongly entrenched. Defeat seemed inevitable.[22]

Meredith's Iron Brigade crossed to the south bank on the afternoon of December 12th and marched some two miles downriver, where it camped in a chestnut grove near the imposing Bernard house. The brigade had been shelled just after crossing, but the only casualty in the Hoosier regiment was the wounding of a Negro servant. Mr. Bernard vehemently protested the use of his home and property by Federal troops, but he was quickly hustled away under guard by order of General Reynolds.[23]

While other troops vainly assaulted entrenched rebel positions on other parts of the battlefield, the Iron Brigade held the army's left flank on December 13th. Although subjected to sometimes vicious shell fire all day, the brigade's only significant movement was an advance to drive some rebel cannon from a piece of woods. Lieutenant Orr remembered that it was "a terrible day" when "the shot & shell ploughed the fields on which we stood, like Defenceless sheep." The brigade's small loss was attributed by one soldier to "good fortune and ditches, together with the enemy's bad firing." Shell fragments killed Leander Jarnagin of Company K and sliced open the hand of George Stockhoff of Company H. The only casualty in Company B was Patterson McKinney, who was "hit on the leg with a bullet but not hurt much." Well after sunset, "the men stretched themselves on the ground, without fires, and many without blankets, to rest."[24]

General Meredith was also a casualty of sorts. He had been relieved by General Doubleday, who deemed Long Sol tardy in carrying out an order to place his brigade in position after the battle. Major William Dudley, temporarily detached to Sol's staff, explained the situation:

> Gen. Meredith was ordered, through an aid of Gen. Doubleday, to change his line so as to protect the left flank of the army from an expected attack that eve., and the words of the order as delivered in my hearing were these: "Gen. Meredith, Gen. Doubleday desires that you place your Brigade in line facing down the river, the right to rest at and behind the embankment of the fence running to the river and your left resting on the piece of woods skirting the river bank, and after your line is formed you will put one regiment on picket in your front."

This order was obeyed, but the aide had garbled his message and Doubleday found the line in the wrong position. He promptly relieved a stunned Meredith who remained without a command for several days until the matter could be straightened out. Lieutenant J. D. Wood, lately Gibbon's adjutant, quickly assured folks in the Badger State that as long as Wisconsin troops remained under General Meredith, "the reputation for gallantry they now possess will not be tarnished."[25]

General Burnside would keep his army defiantly in position for another two days, although he had been soundly beaten at Fredericksburg. The only successful attack had been made by two divisions of the First Corps, commanded by Generals George Meade and John Gibbon. When Gibbon's troops finally broke, he tried unsuccessfully to rally them and "swore that he had rather have two regiments of his old Iron Brigade, than the whole division he then commanded."[26]

Gibbon, however, did not realize that his old Iron Brigade had changed. The Michigan troops, still looking to prove themselves, "were exceedingly anxious to go always to the front," but veterans were more than

happy to be left behind. Sergeant George Legate described his own experience under fire with the 2nd Wisconsin:

> As for myself I kept my place, but when it was the hottest, beads of sweat
> stood out upon my forehead and rolled down my face. There was no
> loud talking, but now and then as a shot fell in the Regt. of us a
> smothered ejaculation of "My God." It was the first time I ever heard
> men cry out with so much anguish and horror—horror does not express
> it—terror comes nearer to it.

Legate confessed that some men in the 2nd Wisconsin—veterans of every
previous engagement—could not stand this latest test of courage and simply
"broke and ran."[27]

In the 19th Indiana, at least two dozen soldiers deserted their posts
in the period from December 8th to 13th. Christopher C. Starbuck, Company C, had first deserted on September 24th, went home to Randolph
County and remained at large for a month. Upon his return, Starbuck was
tried before a general court-martial, which removed the desertion charge but
found him guilty of absence without leave. While waiting for his sentence, he
speculated that going home would probably cost him six months pay and
declared, "I dont care if it is so." Starbuck's forecast was right on target. He
was fined six months pay, $78, and conceded it was "quite A small sum for so
large an offense." Undeterred by this punishment, Private Starbuck avoided
the Fredericksburg disaster by running away again on December 8th.[28]

Private Othniel J. Gilbert, a recent recruit for Company E, took an
even more extreme step. Thoroughly scared during his first battle, Gilbert
took sick every time the regiment was shelled. He would be sent to the
doctors, who continually refused to give him a pass to the rear. Desperate to
get across the river, Gilbert finally went behind a hill on the riverbank on
December 15th and reappeared with a severe wound in his left forearm. At
first, he contended that a bursting shell had wounded him, but soon
disclosed that he had accidentally shot himself, although other soldiers
thought the wound had been inflicted intentionally. Doctors tried to save the
shattered wrist, but finally amputated his damaged arm on January 3, 1863.
Gilbert received a discharge and would never again hear the crash of a
bursting shell.[29]

December 14th was strangely quiet. Abram Buckles remembered,
"Everything this day seemed as if hushed and mourning over the slaughter of
the day before." The 2nd Wisconsin established a truce on the division picket
line, with each side agreeing to warn the other before opening fire. When the
24th Michigan men relieved their Badger comrades on the 15th, they eagerly
shot at unsuspecting rebels lounging about their posts. This breach of

common courtesy "irritated" the rebs, who nearly brought on a general engagement with their response. Musketry raged most of the day until a soldier from the 6th Wisconsin challenged a rebel to a fist fight in the middle of the Bowling Green Turnpike. This well-attended match ended in a draw, the result celebrated by an extensive trading of coffee for tobacco and whiskey. Apologies were offered for the new men's lack of etiquette and a cease-fire was reestablished.[30]

This new truce may have helped to save the 19th Indiana from annihilation in the early morning hours of December 16th. The Hoosiers went on picket at dusk on the 15th and "strict orders were given to the officers of the pickets, to keep the line quiet, and allow no firing, unless attacked." The brigade picket line was some three miles from the nearest pontoon bridge, with its left on the Rappahannock and its right connecting with other units more than one-half mile to the west. The night was "black as a stack of black cats," with a gusty wind blowing rain from the rebel lines toward the three-man Hoosier picket posts. Soldiers in the five reserve companies were only slightly more comfortable than those alertly watching the front. Although these Indiana men were completely ignorant of the fact, Burnside had already started to withdraw his army and had decided to sacrifice his pickets to shield the movement. The 19th Indiana had unwittingly become the Army of the Potomac's "forlorn hope."[31]

Long lines of infantry and artillery snaked toward the pontoons until "long before daylight not a soldier's cap nor a mule was left" of that great Union army. Colonel Cutler, still subbing for General Meredith, felt compelled to at least try to rescue Long Sol's regiment. He finally obtained permission from General Reynolds to withdraw the "forlorn hope" after his brigade had crossed the river. The Iron Brigade joined the exodus at 11 P.M., but before he left, Cutler sent word to Lieutenant Colonel Williams to withdraw his Hoosiers at 4:30 A.M. The evacuation proceeded ahead of schedule, so Lieutenant Clayton Rogers of the 6th Wisconsin was sent back to bring off the division pickets.[32]

Captain George F. Noyes, one of Doubleday's staff officers, recounted Rogers's mission:

> Splendidly mounted, he takes ditches and fences at a flying leap, and rushes down to the extreme left with no regard to the roads, but straight as the bee flies. The left once gained, he moderates his pace, and coolly whispers into the ear of each astonished officer his orders. "Order every man in your command to fall back steadily, and very silently; gradually close up your ranks, and move swiftly to the bridges. Whisper these directions into their ears man by man." So quietly but rapidly he speeds down the picket-line; the propitious storm howls with unabated fury; not a rebel sentinel gives the alarm; one by one our drenched boys are

falling back and drawing in together. The last officer has notified the last man; silently as shadows the whole picket-line steals across the plain. And now, as the ranks close up, now for rapid marching. Double-double-quick is about the pace.

To the amazement of anxious spectators, Williams's five reserve companies marched up to and across the pontoon bridge before it was cut loose. Men from the outposts did not form on the reserve, but came back "each man to care for himself" and crossed the river in small boats. Unsuspecting rebel pickets had given the Hoosiers a good head start, but finally detected their withdrawal and launched a half-hearted pursuit. It was too late—the 19th Indiana had escaped and recrossed the Rappahannock without losing a man.[33]

The Hoosiers celebrated their good fortune. Private Allen Galyean, Company K, rejoiced, "We have gust recrossed the river and a happier child you never saw, to think that I was alive." Jeff Crull admitted that "they came very nigh Capturing the 19th." It had been a critical situation. Unaware of Burnside's retreat, the Indiana soldiers would have stubbornly defended the picket line against any enemy attack. Unsupported and isolated, the result would have been predictable: "a wiping out of the old 19th." Even though he was a fellow Hoosier, Indiana soldiers had lost all confidence in Ambrose Burnside, as well as in the Lincoln administration which had promoted him to replace the popular McClellan.[34]

Fredericksburg had been a terrible tragedy for the country, but the death of Jacob Addleman on December 19th brought deeper sorrow to the Wayne County men. His brother John had deserted from Company B in order to stay with the dying man, nursing him in the final hours of his illness and taking the body home for burial. The tombstone over Jacob's grave reads:

> No "Battle Cry" now shall arouse thee from slumber
> "No more" marching shall "burden" thy day
> Thy comrades and friends all of worth will remember
> Thy Duty was done, Heaven called thee away.

A third brother, Joseph, had been killed in the cornfield at Antietam and his body buried on the battlefield. Three months after Jacob's death, Joseph's remains were disinterred, shipped home and buried next to his brother. Joseph's gravestone contains the verse:

> Sleep on my brave boy for thy warfare is ended,
> Thou art resting at last in the land of thy birth,
> Tho fire of battle claimed thee bright angel
> And sent thee beyond all the sorrow of earth.

The two brothers were buried near the grave of their cousin, Sergeant Andrew J. Addleman, who had died the preceding January.[35]

After a few days spent staring down rebels across the river, the Iron Brigade, now back under General Meredith's command, marched off to Belle Plain Landing on Potomac Creek, where it went into winter camp. Depression was rampant. Jeff Crull confided to his folks, "i Whish that the War was over so We could all go home. the men are tired of it and wont fight much any more." Speaking of Fredericksburg, Lieutenant William Orr grumbled, "It is the foulest stain that has ever happened to our arms & the *whole army* is almost mutinous about it." Adam Smelser, Company K, became so despondent that he walked into the woods with an ax and chopped off the thumb on his right hand. His comrades thought he did it deliberately, although Smelser claimed he had done it accidentally while cutting kindling for a fire.[36]

The only upbeat event in the Iron Brigade came following the arrival of several boxes of sanitary stores from Cambridge City. Sol Meredith's neighbors had celebrated his promotion by sending large quantities of canned fruit, dried apples, onions, and other delicacies to the 19th Indiana. Sol wisely insisted that the goodies be distributed as rations, "so that each got his share." The officers addressed a thank you note to "Mrs. S. Meredith and Lady-friends of the 19th," concluding with the pledge, "Be assured, dear ladies, that wherever the tattered banner of the old 19th floats, there cluster hearts, loyal, true and warm, whose lives will willingly be given in protection of *your* firesides."[37]

Two Company F men, John DeBay and John O'Connor, provided a temporary diversion for the morose camp on Christmas day. The two got into a row that ended when DeBay struck O'Connor over the head with a musket, bending the barrel so badly as to render the weapon unserviceable. O'Connor received an ugly wound and DeBay was eventually hauled before a court-martial and fined $50. Despite this brief entertainment, Christmas was hard. No one wanted to be in that bleak, godforsaken corner of Virginia. Everyone thought of home and decorated trees and lighted candles and holiday trimmings and hymns in church. Homesick soldiers sat around smoking fires and wondered if the war would ever end. It was indeed, as Major Rufus Dawes wrote, "the Valley Forge of the war."[38]

18

Valley Forge

On January 1st, General Meredith hosted a celebration at his headquarters during which Iron Brigade officers toasted the New Year with mugs of whiskey. There was much to discuss, but most of the conversation must have centered on President Lincoln's Emancipation Proclamation. According to the proclamation, effective January 1, 1863, all persons held as slaves in rebel-occupied territory "are and henceforward shall be free; and that the Executive government of the United States, including the military and naval authorities thereof, will recognize and maintain the freedom of said persons." Another provision of the proclamation declared that these newly-freed black men were to be accepted into the army and navy, where they would perform duty as soldiers and sailors.[1]

Long Sol was "terribly opposed" to Lincoln's emancipation policy, especially that section which allowed Negroes to enlist as soldiers. He thought it a damned shame to "call in an inferior race to help in fight[ing] our battles." Nearly all of the Hoosiers shared these sentiments with their first colonel. Consider the remarks of Captain William Orr:

> I have just read the presidents proclamation. I dont like it. I dont want
> to fight to free the Darkeys. If any body else wants to do so, They are
> welcome to come & do so. I am not willing to stay in the army much
> longer, unless a different policy is inaugurated.

One Hoosier enlisted man stated bluntly, "I came to fight for the old flag in stead [of] fighting for the negroes." These volunteers of 1861 had enlisted to save the Union, but now it seemed as though the Lincoln administration had changed the focus of their war, much like changing rules in the middle of a game. After their narrow escape at Fredericksburg, these disgusted

Indiana soldiers would now begin to question every new order from army headquarters or the White House.[2]

Cavalry pickets spread the proclamation's "freedom" news to the slave population in St. George's County, thereby stimulating an exodus northward. Lieutenant George Breck, one of the division's artillery officers, described the amazing variety of newly-freed citizens who flocked past Yankee camps:

> A comical sight they present wending their way on foot, on mules, in old carts drawn by oxen—one small cart often carrying a family of half a dozen or more of the female class, with handkerchiefs tied about their heads or their black "tresses" exposed to full view—and stowed away in the two wheel vehicle amid a conglomeration of household furniture, clothes, and blankets of varied hue and texture, may be seen, peering, little faces black as charcoal, relieved by white eyes; Uncle Toms and Aunt Dinahs, Sambos and Topsys—a complete representation of the colored population, of the "poor slave," passengers for Freedom—swarming northward in response, we suppose, to the emancipation edict.

As these caravans passed by the Indiana camp, soldiers would greet them with cries of "you black devils! Some more of the Presidents proclamation!"[3]

On January 6th, a soldier from Company K wrote, "There is no good news, everything is sad, soldiers discouraged, tired of the war and dont like the proclamation freeing the damed negroes." With the abolition of slavery now a political issue, some soldiers were suddenly forced to justify their support of Lincoln and the Republicans, while still opposing equality for blacks. Elisha B. Odle tried to explain his feelings to a friend:

> . . . the African race should be a separate nation from the fact that their cullor is not as ours. nether should we associate with them as have thousands of our race, yet as a true republican I believe slavery to be a great evel and should bee glad to see them immencipated set out of the United States first, then freed, colonized afterward kept as a nation to themselves to make laws and regelations of their own.

Odle acknowledged that the freed slaves were human beings, though he thought them not fit to be "intimate associates of ours," and he would support the Emancipation Proclamation only if it meant "the abolishment of the slaves entirely out of the United States."[4]

A correspondent from the 7th Wisconsin observed that sentiment against the proclamation was widespread throughout the brigade. He wrote:

> Ask almost any soldier what he thinks of the war; he will answer, "I don't like to fight for the damned nigger. It's nothing but an abolition war,

and I wish I was out of it." You can hear it everywhere, let those deny it who may. It is the truth, and why hide the truth. That is the sentiment, go where you will.

There were, of course, some soldiers who supported Lincoln's policy. Corporal Jeff Wasson explained his own personal feelings: "there is a great deal of Hard feeling in the army about freeing the niggers and having them to Shoulder arms and fight. I wish every one of them had a gun and was down here in Virginia fighting for their freedom." After a few months of thought and debate, supporters of emancipation began to gain ground until sentiment became "about equally divided." Soldiers still considered blacks to be social inferiors, but even the dullest private could see that employing black soldiers could shorten the war and save white lives in the process.[5]

Lincoln's Emancipation Proclamation stimulated discussion on the intellectual level, but the soldiers' favorite topic remained their monotonous army rations. Food was indifferent at best, but the biggest complaint was reserved for regimental sutlers who sold items to round out the diet. Jeff Wasson listed the prices for the most popular groceries: butter, sixty cents a pound; apples, thirteen dollars a barrel; cheese, fifty cents a pound; and tobacco, one dollar and fifty cents a pound. Boots that would cost five dollars in Wayne County sold for at least twice that in Virginia. Officers did not receive rations, but formed into messes and purchased their food at the brigade commissary. They paid four cents a pound for flour, ten cents a pound for sugar and twenty cents a pound for coffee, "all ground and ready for use." Contrasting commissary prices and sutler charges, Wasson noticed that the former sold molasses for forty-four cents a gallon, while the latter retailed the same amount for seventy-five cents a pint. Enlisted men could not purchase articles from the commissary, so they complained constantly about the seeming inequity of the situation.[6]

Another complaint by enlisted men was that officers at regimental or brigade headquarters had ready access to whiskey. On January 11th, Lieutenant Colonel Williams felt compelled to write Governor Morton in defense of Quartermaster John A. Cottman. Prompted by Private John Rariden, who had been sent back to Company B for laziness while acting as a teamster, some enlisted men petitioned Morton to dismiss Cottman. The Hoosiers cited Cottman's "too frequent use of the bottle" as grounds for dismissal. Williams did not deny the charge and lamely supported Cottman by saying, "I can say I never called on him to do any thing that he was not fit ready and willing to do it." A few months later, Colonel Morrow would recommend that his Michigan quartermaster be dismissed for "habitual drunkenness" after several episodes of appearing "beastly intoxicated" in camp. Despite efforts to clamp down on alcohol abusers, whiskey would continue to flow and disrupt discipline throughout the Iron Brigade.[7]

Many of the enlisted men spent their off-duty time gambling in a small grove near a stream that provided the brigade's drinking water. At any time from dawn till dusk, as many as 100 men could be found shuffling cards or throwing dice. Wagers of $50 on a single dice roll were commonly seen. Peddlers flocked to this gamblers' grove and offered cigars, tobacco, cakes, pies, apples, and other goodies at prices higher than those charged by regimental sutlers. As Meredith's brigade settled into winter camp, one soldier wrote that this grove proved to be "the most popular place in our vicinity." Private John Hawk offered the observation that "the grand army of the Republic has one third playing cards, the other doing the duty, and the last third deserting as fast as they can."[8]

Soldiers of the Iron Brigade quickly slipped into their winter routine of picket duty, guard duty, police duty, company drill, battalion drill, brigade drill, chopping wood, cooking, and eating, all this varied by rumors of marching orders. Drill was boring and onerous, but picket duty provided a welcome diversion from camp life. That section of picket line occupied by the Hoosiers was far removed from the enemy, so their main duty consisted of watching for spies and arresting smugglers. When not standing watch, soldiers made fires from fence rails, boiled coffee in their tin cups, roasted meat over the coals, and enjoyed the fine January weather. At night they would roll snugly in blankets to keep off the frost and dream of home.[9]

Rumors of a movement surfaced again on January 19th, when orders to cook three days' rations arrived at Meredith's headquarters. But this time it was more than rumor. Burnside planned to embark on an unexpected winter campaign, cross the Rappahannock at Banks's Ford, attack the rear of an unsuspecting enemy and defeat Lee's army. The Iron Brigade, minus the 2nd Wisconsin, which had been detailed as the army's rearguard, left Belle Plain about noon on January 20th and marched toward Falmouth. The day was delightful until about dark, when it began to storm. A cold, driving rain, "almost a herricane" according to one soldier, quickly turned the roads to mud. Private Phraortes Humphreys, Company G, described that miserable night:

> At dark it began to rain. The teams did not arrive, consequently I had no tent. I made a fire, seated myself on a log, threw the cape of my overcoat over my head, and in that manner passed the night. The rain poured down in torrents and the air was very cold. God alone knows how much I suffered. But the longest night will have an end, and when day dawned a more miserable looking wretch than myself never was permitted to move on the face of the earth.

Daylight on the 21st brought no relief. Rain continued to pour down, washing out every attempt to kindle a fire.[10]

After a cold breakfast, General James S. Wadsworth's division "continued their *wade* to glory." The storm had turned low spots into lakes and ditches into raging rivers. Few men had boots and the mud, "awfully awful" according to one soldier, was so deep that shoes submerged at every step. Grear N. Williams spoke for many when he called the route "mudy as hell." After floundering along some five miles that morning, the brigade halted in a pine forest beyond Falmouth and made camp in the rain. Cannons and wagons mired so deep that "horses were no more to them than flies to an ox waggon." Following some Herculean effort, Lieutenant James Stewart came forward with one gun to support the Iron Brigade. Normally a Napoleon gun required only a four-horse team, but Stewart's single cannon could only be dragged along through the ooze by eighteen horses.[11]

Soldiers swore that one pair of mules had disappeared from sight, only to be spotted later pulling a plow for a Chinaman on the other side of the world. Joking aside, the fact was that guns, wagons and pontoons could not be moved, the river was swollen and rebels had discovered the movement (possibly tipped off by the volume of Federal cursing). On the morning of the 22nd, some Southern joker had posted a sign at Banks's Ford: "*BURNSIDE STUCK IN THE MUD.*" Surprise was now impossible and Burnside's plan had obviously miscarried. The only thing to do was turn about and march back to Belle Plain. Meredith's Iron Brigade started back on January 23rd, marching some fifteen miles, and arrived "tired as we can Be." On the return march, Jeff Crull overheard one general say that the army had 50,000 stragglers.[12]

General Wadsworth earned himself an affectionate nickname on this retrograde movement. When the head of his division came upon a deep ditch, now running swiftly with rushing water, Wadsworth turned to the 7th Indiana and shouted: "Men, shall we go around or put down a foot bridge?" Unwilling to waste time on a detour, the soldiers shouted back, "Build a bridge!" Wadsworth promptly dismounted, hung his sword on the pommel of his saddle and gave the reins to an orderly. Then this millionaire general waded into the mud and worked with Hoosier privates to construct a passageway. One of the workers later remembered that "no other officer or man carried and placed more rails" than Wadsworth. Later on he personally superintended necessary road repairs, slogging through the mire to lead by example. Soldiers were so pleased at General Wadsworth's willingness to share the work that they christened him "Old Corduroy" and fondly referred to him in that manner until his death.[13]

Upon reaching their camp at Belle Plain, the Hoosiers found their comfortable log cabins occupied by soldiers from the Eleventh Corps. The Western men "were just a bit hot" at this unexpected invasion of their homes while they were gone on Burnside's ill-fated "Mud March," but gracious men from Ohio and Connecticut offered to share their suppers and thus averted a physical confrontation. The strangers packed up and moved out the following morning, leaving many huts damaged and others torn down for firewood. The whole camp needed several days of rebuilding.[14]

President Lincoln promptly replaced Burnside with Fighting Joe Hooker on January 26th and relieved several other malcontent generals in an effort to rebuild the Army of the Potomac. Jeff Wasson was not impressed:

> Burnside [Edwin V.] Sumner & [William B.] Franklin are out of command and Hooker is going to run the machine awhile and see how he likes it. I think that the Idea is to let all the generals have a trial of their Skill in the army of the Potomac. probably we will get one after while that will Suit us.

A Wisconsin soldier agreed with Wasson's sentiments, then added a few bitter comments of his own:

> Well, perhaps it is best to give them all a trial—it only costs fifteen or twenty thousand lives to take each one on trial; so we may as well try them all, while we are about it. Only four or five months are thrown away on each for nothing; and then we have plenty of men in the North. who can just as well be spared as not, to be killed off in experiments.

Spirits had lifted briefly during the first hours of the Mud March, but its dismal failure resulted in an even more overwhelming depression. No matter what the soldiers would do, the generals always seemed to let them down.[15]

Although Hooker was popular among the troops, standing second only to the beloved McClellan in the Iron Brigade, he had a great deal of work ahead of him. Even after Hooker had improved the quantity and quality of rations, one skeptical Hoosier wrote, "Like a herd of poor oxen they are fattening us for the slaughter." Sergeant George Legate bluntly described affairs as the soldiers saw them:

> They are dissatisfied with the conduct of the war, say that they will not stay and be led by imbecile generals to be butchered. They say better desert and be shot if taken than to lead the life of a dog and then be butchered.

Speaking for himself, Jeff Crull confessed, "i am tired of these old hills and Pine fires and hope to get out of Va Prity soone."[16]

A reminder of home came on January 31st when Mrs. Meredith arrived at brigade headquarters for an extended visit with Long Sol. Other

Hoosier wives were stuck in Washington because they had been repeatedly denied passes to Belle Plain. On the 31st, Colonel Williams, Captain Makepeace, and Captain Orr wrote directly to President Lincoln in order to break the impasse. These officers offered the president a pledge: "We will not falter on the day when it 'rains lead and iron' because the kisses of our wives are still warm upon our lips, instead of 20 months old and we trust that they yet may be permitted to visit us." Congressman George W. Julian discovered this plight of residents from his district and promptly asked the Secretary of War to expedite passage of the women to Belle Plain to see "their sick husbands." Edwin Stanton approved the request and the three ladies, accompanied by Major May's widow, who hoped to retrieve his body, reached camp on February 4th. Although no friend of the congressman, Captain Orr confessed, "This is the 1st thing Julian has done for the last six years that I approve of and I cheerfully give him the credit for it."[17]

The arrival of these Hoosier ladies coincided with mass desertions by disgruntled soldiers. Shortly after the Mud March, the 2nd Wisconsin went on picket for two days, during which time the Badgers arrested over sixty deserters, almost half of whom were from the Iron Brigade. On January 31st, Lieutenant Colonel Mark Flanigan, 24th Michigan, took a detail of fifty men in search of absentees, but after a broad sweep returned with only ten prisoners. At least twenty-five Wolverines remained on the rolls as deserters during the month of January. The most popular means of escape was to build a raft and paddle across the Potomac to Maryland, then go home disguised as a civilian. Crude rafts were captured nearly every day, including a large one carrying sixteen deserters. Picket lines were strengthened to curb runaways, the numbers of which were "alarmingly prevalent of late," but the men's determination and ingenuity kept desertion rates high.[18]

Unable to prevent desertions, the army took a hardline position on punishment for those apprehended by military authorities. Privates Bill Hill and Ben Duke had deserted from Company B on November 4, 1862, near Purcellville, Virginia. Duke remained a fugitive, but Lieutenant Hindman, while at home recuperating from his Brawner Farm wound, spotted Hill in Hagerstown and arrested him. Returned to the 19th Indiana on January 4th, Hill was held in custody until his court-martial on January 29th. The court assembled at 9 A.M. with Colonel Lucius Fairchild, 2nd Wisconsin, presiding. Captain Hollon Richardson, 7th Wisconsin, acted as judge advocate, an assignment that gave him the dual role of prosecutor and defender of the accused man's rights.

Hill had no objections to any member of the court, so he was arraigned on the charge of desertion, with a specification giving details of the charge. The accused pleaded not guilty to both charge and specification. First Sergeant Dick Jones was called as a witness by the judge advocate and testified that Private Hill had left the company after it had arrived at Purcellville and remained absent until he returned in January. Jones also indicated that Hill had been listed as a deserter on every morning report until his return. Asked of Hill's whereabouts during his absence, Jones responded, "He told me he was back home at Hagerstown, Wayne County, Indiana." Describing how Hill returned to the company, his sergeant said, "He came back alone voluntarily and was dressed in citizens clothing." In response to a court member's question about the private's reputation as a soldier, Jones replied: "He has never taken part in but one engagement, the battle of Gainesville [Brawner Farm]. He went in that battle with the Company but was not with it when we came out of it." The judge advocate closed without calling any other witnesses.

Bill had no testimony to offer, but Colonel Fairchild gave him permission to offer an oral statement. His defense consisted of the following narrative:

> I went home to stay a few days with the intent of coming back. I saw my Lieutenant in Indiana. He detained me there two weeks, then arrested me and sent me to Indianapolis. Governor Morton furnished me transportation and I came back of my own accord and not under guard.

After deliberation, the court found William Hill guilty of both the charge and specification. He was sentenced to "forfeit to the United States all pay and bounty due or to become due to him from the United States, that he have his head shaved, the buttons torn from off his clothing, and that he be drummed out of the service of the United States, all in the presence of his brigade." General Wadsworth approved the proceedings on January 31st and ordered Hill held in confinement until his sentence could be carried out.[19]

In the guardhouse, Bill joined three other prisoners, all from Company D, who had previously received the identical sentence. These soldiers had been found guilty of misbehavior before the enemy at Fredericksburg in trials held on January 14th. Privates William St. Clair and Richard Padget had slipped away on December 11th while the 19th Indiana marched forward in anticipation of crossing the Rappahannock. William St. Clair had never been in battle and did not wish to experience one at Fredericksburg, so when the regiment halted for a few minutes to rest, he walked away with the bombardment ringing in his ears. At his trial, St. Clair explained his disappearance by saying:

> The reason I fell out was I was not able through sickness to keep up with my Company. I had a tickling and pain in my breast. I have been so ever since last summer at which time I had a fever.

In Padget's defense, Captain David Holloway testified that he had been in the Brawner Farm fight, where "he behaved himself very well," although he had not been in any subsequent battles. First Sergeant George W. Huntsman admitted, "His conduct as a soldier has been good up to this time so far as I know." Padget offered no explanation for his absence.[20]

Private Isaac Redout walked away from the regiment after it had camped in the woods around the Bernard house on the night of December 12th. When Sergeant Huntsman called the roll next morning, Redout had vanished, but "his arms and accouterments were all there." Captain Holloway could not remember him being in any of the regiment's battles. One soldier assigned to guard these prisoners later described them as "a hard set of scamps."[21]

While these punishments might seem harsh, court members seemed to look for mitigating factors before imposing sentence. From available records, it appears that a soldier's previous good behavior, coupled with a plausible excuse for his absence, would result in a lighter penalty. Private Charles L. McRoberts, Company D, ran away on the morning of December 13th, was arrested and brought back under guard the next evening. He was brought before a court-martial on January 15th and tried on a charge of misbehavior before the enemy. During questioning, Sergeant Huntsman admitted that McRoberts had been under fire with the regiment at Rappahannock Station. The accused also stated: "I have been sorely afflicted with diarrhea for the last four or five months making it difficult for me to march." The court had its two mitigating factors and found him guilty, fining him $10 per month for five months.[22]

The court was most lenient with the best soldiers. Private Minor Berry, also of Company D, had left his company about noon on December 13th and was charged with misbehavior before the enemy. Captain Holloway testified that Berry had been in every battle and he had been sick in Maryland for quite a while. Holloway called him "a good soldier" and pointed out that he had returned to Company D on his own the day after his disappearance. Sergeant Huntsman concurred with the captain's assessment and swore that Berry was "a very good fighting soldier." Private Berry offered a statement in his defense:

> At the time I left the Company or rather the Company left me I had the diarrhea very bad and the double quick from off the field caused me to use my clothes in a very bad way. I asked permission of my Captain or Lieutenant I don't remember which if I might go and wash. They refused and I went of my own accord.

The court showed sympathy in its deliberation and found Berry guilty of absence without leave, fining him only $10.[23]

The judge advocate had a strong case against Private John P. Woods, Company F, who had been charged with misbehavior and cowardice before the enemy on December 13th at Fredericksburg. On December 12th, Woods had been issued a Springfield musket with a distinctive piece of brass fixed to the butt by pins and he carried that weapon into battle. Woods was discovered to be missing in the forenoon of the 13th and he did not return to his company until January 31st. By chance, Lieutenant Chauncey B. Patrick found Woods's musket, identified by the distinctive brass mark, lying on the south bank of the Rappahannock two days after his disappearance. Evidence presented by the judge advocate seemed to indicate that Woods tossed aside his musket while running away from the enemy.

Woods confounded the officers by presenting an able defense. The accused called Patrick Dever, who testified that he and Woods had been hospitalized together, the pair returning to their regiment just a few days before the battle. Dever also stated that Woods had been hospitalized for a long time prior to his release. Private Woods then offered two exhibits to the court, the first of which was a personal statement which read in part:

> there was heavy shelling by the enemy and one of there shelles struck the tree I was leening against and shocked me so as to unable me to travel for some time. So after I come to anuf to travel I started and went down to the brick hospital. there I remaned till morning then I started to hunt the regiment. I got as far as the 2nd Wisconsent regment. there I was asked by some officere I dont know his name what was the matter with me. I told him. he then told me I had better go down the hill for they was expectng a battle soon. I took his advice and went down the hill. after remaning thare a short time I fell in with to friends which helped me to the hospital. on our way we over took a colerd mn which consented to cary my gun and accutriments. he was to take them to the hospital but failed to do it. what he did do with them is more than I am able to Say. now you have heard my sentiments. I throw my self on your mercy trusting you will do me justice.

Woods's second exhibit was an official certificate discharging him from Hammond General Hospital at Point Lookout, Maryland, on December 27th, 1862. After considering this evidence, the court found Private John P. Woods not guilty and restored him to duty.[24]

After this round of court-martials had concluded, a sizable number of Hoosiers still remained at large. In a document dated January 31st, Colonel Williams listed forty-eight deserters from the 19th Indiana who had not yet been apprehended. Eleven of those soldiers had deserted at Fredericksburg and eight more had run away since that battle. In order to stop this alarming trend, General Meredith planned a ceremony that he hoped would put an end to desertion and disobedience of orders in the Iron Brigade. Long

Sol chose the date of February 21st and saved up his captives until he had enough to stage an impressive show.[25]

Meredith called out his five Western regiments under arms in mid-morning and assembled them in a hollow square to witness the execution of sentences for William G. Hill, William St. Clair, Richard Padget, and Isaac Redout of the 19th Indiana; Lewis E. Conklin and Patrick Dunn of the 2nd Wisconsin; and James T. Newington of the 24th Michigan. All were mere boys, except for Newington, who was twenty-seven years old. The young-sters acted cocky and mocked the proceedings, while only Newington "seemed to feel bad and realized the depth of his disgrace." General Meredith addressed a few remarks to the miscreants as they stood in the middle of the square under guard. Jeff Wasson remembered that Sol told them that "he would rather go back to his home a honered Corpse than to be Disgraced for all time to come." Adjutant General James D. Wood read the findings of the court-martial as each man stepped forward: Hill, St. Clair, Padget, Redout, and Conklin were to forfeit all pay and bounty, have their heads shaved and be drummed out; Newington was to forfeit all pay and bounty and be drummed out; Dunn was to be simply drummed out.[26]

Barbers came forward and closely trimmed the hair on five men, lathered their heads well and shaved them "smooth and bare" so that they resembled mammoth white turnips. After these tonsorial duties had been performed, the buttons were torn from their coats. Then the regiments marched away and formed into two long lines, facing inward, along the road to Pratt's Landing. The guard formed into two ranks, the front carrying their arms reversed and the rear marching at a position of charge bayonets. All seven prisoners marched between the guards with bayonets pointing at them from front and rear. All the brigade fifers and drummers formed behind these disgraced soldiers. General Meredith and his staff fell in at the rear of the column.[27]

Adjutant Wood commanded the prisoners to remove their hats, then gave the order, "Forward, March." Musicians began to play "The Rogue's March" as the guards urged their former comrades through a gauntlet of verbal abuse along the road. Some soldiers sang a little ditty in time with the music:

> Poor old soldier,
> Poor old soldier,
> Give him a kick & send him to Hell,
> Because he wouldn't soldier.

Hoosiers, Badgers, and Wolverines jeered and laughed and joked at the turnip-heads as they marched toward the landing. But Patrick Dunn had the last word. After the parade had ended, Dunn turned to the Iron Brigade and yelled out: "It's all right, boys. Ye can squeak the fife and bate the drum, and fight and fight, but I'd rather be a live ass than a dead lion." Guards turned the ex-soldiers over to the Provost Marshal, who sent them to Washington for final banishment. Meredith's "entertainment" had its desired effect. Jeff Wasson thought "it was a Sad Sight to see them, poor fellows, Disgraced forever." William Jackson reflected, "It was a ludicrous scene, and a humiliating punishment on the poor wretches. I hope it may prove a warning to all cowards."[28]

The last few days of February found the Hoosiers stuck in the familiar routine of camp life. Grear Williams recorded the daily highlights of life in Company B during that period:

> *February 25th* — Nice day over head some snow on the ground. cut a load of wood for the company.
>
> *February 26th* — Rainy al day nothing of importance in camp. camp Near Bellplain Landing Va
>
> *February 27th* — a nice day this after noon. went on picket. mudy as hell. nothing of importance. Camp Near Bellplain.

Mud was a constant annoyance and the Indiana men sang a ditty about it: "On 'Dixie Land' we would like to stand, if it was not mud, instead of land."[29]

Men wounded during Pope's campaign began returning to Company B after extended periods of hospitalization. One such soldier was Alexander Walker, who had been shot in the face. Jeff Crull was amazed to see that "it has not disfiguered him a tall. one could hardley tell that he had bin wounded." An unofficial network kept soldiers in touch with wounded friends in Eastern hospitals. Some, like Walker, Joel Curtis, James Whitlow, and William Locke, returned to the ranks as quickly as possible (oftentimes before their wounds had completely healed), but others "Stay in the hospittle as long as they can." The campaigns and battles of 1862 had revealed which men had the courage and stamina to become dependable soldiers and which men failed to measure up in some respect. Letters home told the story eloquently. Jeff Crull wrote that Orderly Sergeant Richard Jones, who had commanded Company B for months after Antietam, was "a very good young man and bin through all the fights and is a good soldier." Jeff Wasson mentioned two other tried and true comrades: "Grear Williams is very well. he makes a good Soldier and never flinches when it comes to a fight. him and george Beetley has been in every fight and never got a Scratch." These were the kind of men who would quietly see the war through to its conclusion, no matter what the cost. They had given their word to do so.[30]

19

Fitzhugh Crossing

General Hooker instituted a series of important changes in order to prepare the dispirited Army of the Potomac for a spring offensive. The army diet no longer consisted primarily of salt pork and hardtack, but now contained such items as fresh beef, fresh bread, potatoes, and onions. To combat desertions, a system of granting furloughs was established so that at least some soldiers could visit their homes. Discipline was tightened and disrespectful or treasonable language outlawed. Paymasters had arrived and brought accounts up to date, ensuring that families were properly supported. In short, Fighting Joe had made exactly those changes that the soldiers wished to be made and they liked him for it.[1]

Despite these improvements, Hoosiers remained skeptical about the future. Lieutenant William Orr stated emphatically, "If this rebellion is to be crushed it must be done this summer." He reasoned that prolonging the rebellion would encourage antiwar sentiment and bring about "a season of terror at home." But Orr had little hope for what lay ahead. As he sadly put it, "I have seen too many failures to be sanguine." The core of Hooker's army remained faithful in spite of repeated failures by its previous commanders. When urged by his father to apply for a furlough, Jeff Wasson responded, "when I left home I made up my mind never to go back till my time was up and I will Stick to it."[2]

Army officers and civilian authorities continued to track down and apprehend soldiers who lacked Wasson's determination, but it was an expensive and time-consuming business. The job often had to be repeated. After receiving a tip where John Yost and Henry Knight, two Fredericksburg deserters from Company C, could be found, Isaac LaFlesh, 1st Indiana Cavalry, and an assistant took a train for Randolph County. They hired horses at Farmland, rode seven miles south and arrested the absentees. After stopping overnight at Anderson, LaFlesh delivered the fugitives to Indianapolis. Yost and Knight escaped, but two weeks later Nathaniel W. Garrish arrested them a second time. Garrish ensured their good behavior by chaining and padlocking their legs. Charges for the two arrests totaled nearly $25, almost two months' pay for a private, not counting the cost of transportation back to the regiment. The whole system of capturing and returning deserters could not keep pace with the number of men who ran away.[3]

President Lincoln gave Hooker and other commanders a windfall of sorts on March 10th when he proclaimed an amnesty for any deserter who would turn himself in by April 1st. This bold stroke would return thousands of trained soldiers to the ranks, where they were desperately needed, hopefully lessening the threat of forced conscription. Responsibility for enforcing terms of the proclamation in Ohio, Indiana, and Illinois rested on General Milo Hascall, who published details in Midwest newspapers:

> All deserters and absentees from the Army in either of the three States above specified are hereby notified that they may deliver themselves up agreeably to the Proclamation of the President at any time between this date and the 1st of April, subject to no other punishment than the forfeiture of their pay and allowances during the time they may have been absent. . . .

Lincoln's amnesty seemed to have a beneficial effect in Hooker's army, where one officer estimated that thousands of men had returned to the ranks.[4]

One fugitive who took advantage of Lincoln's leniency was Ben Duke, who had left for home with Bill Hill on November 4th. As previously related, Hill had been captured and suffered the indignity of having his head shaved, the buttons torn from his coat and being drummed out in front of his brigade. By eluding detection and coming back under Lincoln's proclamation, Duke was welcomed back as if he had been on an extended vacation. By promising to again take up his musket, Ben's past was forgiven and forgotten. He was accepted without prejudice by comrades in Company B and restored to his place in the ranks. The irony of this situation is that by remaining a fugitive some three months longer than Hill, Duke avoided any punishment whatsoever.[5]

Many changes had occurred in the Wayne County company during Duke's absence. One was the loss of First Lieutenant Samuel Hindman. When it became obvious that Sam would resign because of his Brawner Farm wound, Long Sol wrote to Governor Morton and recommended that "he be appointed to some office, in the service, where he will either have the use of a *horse,* or to some 'Post' duty." Meredith did this so that an "able, brave and patriotic officer" would not be "cast aside." When Hindman's resignation was accepted on March 14th, Sol again wrote to the governor and argued that "his Gallantry upon the field of battle and faithfulness in the Camp and on the march certainly entitles his claims to favorable consideration." Apparently such faithfulness did not count for much, because Sam Hindman was cast aside. The ex-lieutenant went back to Wayne County and remained a civilian until he finally received a commission in the Veteran Reserve Corps in October of 1863.[6]

One of Hindman's last official acts in Company B was to add his name on a list of officers recommending two Wayne County sergeants, Allen W. Ogborn and Thomas C. Henderson, for promotion. Each man was presented to Governor Morton for "his undaunted Bravery and good Qualities as a Soldier and gentleman," with the hope that they be commissioned as lieutenants in new regiments then being formed. Twenty-six prominent citizens from Richmond and Abington bolstered Henderson's candidacy when they petitioned Morton to make him a lieutenant. His friends pointed out that he had been in every battle and had always acted with "coolness and bravery."[7]

Henry Zook got ambitious about this time and sought testimonials from Lieutenant Colonel Dudley and General Meredith. Dudley referred to Henry as "a good and faithful soldier always ready to do his duty." Sol painted a glowing picture of Zook, who "has been a faithful and brave soldier passing through all the battles of Virginia and Maryland with great credit. He has been at my Head Qrs some time enabling me to judge of his qualifications for the position he desires." Henry's comrades would have laughed at Sol's words, since they considered Zook nothing more than an officer's servant or headquarters waiter. Despite such glowing recommendations, Governor Morton paid no attention to these letters.[8]

Chaplain Lewis Dale had resigned. Just two weeks before he left his post, Dale wrote a long letter to the *New Castle Courier,* in which he explained his stand on civilian opposition to the war:

> There are two classes at home, who have done more to discourage and dishearten the soldier than all others put together. . . . The first are those who contend that the negro should not be used in any way by the authorities in putting down this rebellion. The second party referred to contend that nothing else will do, and unless the President frees and arms the colored man, they will not lend their influence in this war.

In his letter of resignation, Chaplain Dale stated that he "should be at home to look after the interests of my family." The minister's value to the 19th Indiana had obviously deteriorated, since Lieutenant Colonel Dudley approved and forwarded his resignation with the endorsement, "for the good of the service." Shortly after leaving the regiment Dale acted on his political beliefs and ran for office as a Democratic candidate. Thomas Barnett, one of Colonel Williams's friends from Selma, replaced Dale as chaplain.[9]

Considerable antiwar sentiment existed in Indiana, where the Republican-dominated press characterized anyone opposed to Lincoln, Morton, or the war effort as a "copperhead." This pejorative term was first applied to militant opposition groups, but soon spread to include all classes of opponents, no matter how slight their dissent. Quite naturally, most soldiers wanted a vigorous prosecution of the war and had little use for those who stood for anything less than total victory. A Henry County soldier boasted that the Army of the Potomac was ever ready to shoulder arms "till the last traitor is exterminated," then clarified his point: "When we say traitors, we do not confine ourselves to rebels in arms, but mean all, whether they be in open rebellion, or as the sneaking copperhead traitors of the North, who are too cowardly to meet us on the battle field."[10]

Hoosier soldiers loved Governor Morton, who they saw as the "Soldier's Friend," and Elihu M. Parker, Company C, lashed out at those who would oppose him. Dismissing the Democratic party as a bunch of "poor, illiterate, God-forsaken cusses," Parker declared: "If we succeed in putting the rebellion down, and are spared to get home without being mangled by the steel of the Graybacks—God have mercy on the Northern croakers—I know very well the soldiers will not." He also suggested that if disloyalists resisted conscription, veteran regiments, such as those of the Iron Brigade, should be sent home to enforce the law. Despite his poor judgment in selecting generals, President Lincoln remained popular, although Parker admitted, "if left to the soldiers of our army, little Mac would be the next President."[11]

The widespread gloom after Burnside's fizzle had started rumors that soldiers in the Army of the Potomac favored "peace on any terms." In order to refute such "base and slanderous reports," the Iron Brigade adopted a series of six resolutions that expressed its collective view of war policy. The first resolution disputed those rumors and stated that every soldier would "sacrifice all for the maintenance of our constitution, the integrity of our country, and the crushing out of this rebellion." The second resolution pledged that the Army of the Potomac "will be true to its flag, and does not desire peace until the last rebel in arms has vanished from our soil." Warning of copper-headed "wolves in sheep's clothing," the Iron Brigade then urged the "submission of all little, petty, personal, political, and social interests to the great common cause." After other statements that urged a "vigorous prosecution" of the war and support for the Enrollment Act of March 3rd, the Western men concluded their manifesto with approval of the Lincoln administration and its war policy.[12]

Some soldiers displayed a more physical manner of dealing with anti-Lincoln sentiment. On March 15th, a group of paroled Union prisoners passing west by train took advantage of a layover and trashed the office of the *Richmond Jeffersonian*. Wayne County residents took offense at this destruction of private property, but Republicans rather enjoyed the temporary suspension of this Democratic organ. The *Quaker City Telegram* explained:

> The sole object and aim of the paper seems to have been to gather into its columns all that could be said against the administration, to denounce Union men as "abolitionists," and to take advantage of any and every untoward circumstance that could by any means be brought to bear against the Government, and by this wholesale fault-finding to advance its own political purposes.

Speaking of the *Jeffersonian*, the *Telegram* regarded its destruction "as but a natural consequence of its own course."[13]

March 10th was the first anniversary of McClellan taking the Army of the Potomac into the field. One 7th Wisconsin soldier remembered the occasion:

> A year ago we started forth, full of buoyancy, eager for the fray and expecting a speedy termination of the war. A year has passed—mark the change. That buoyant eager army has melted away, and the few that still remain have settled down into a moodiness that has no parallel.

Fighting Joe needed to rekindle the spark that had flickered at Fredericksburg and been doused in the deluge of the Mud March. The army was still there, but it needed a good dose of inspiration.[14]

With an eye to future movements, Hooker decreed that all mounted officers would carry on their own horses whatever supplies they would need for a ten-day campaign. Two pack mules would transport tents and rations for each regiment's company officers. Baggage for the enlisted men would be limited to greatcoats, blankets, and knapsacks, the latter containing one shirt, one pair of drawers, one pair of stockings, and extra rations. Fighting Joe then sent his brigades out on practice marches, regimental commanders being directed to prevent straggling.[15]

In order to correctly identify stragglers and foragers, General Hooker's staff devised a series of flannel badges to identify the corps and division to which any soldier belonged. Each corps was designated by a different design: First, sphere; Second, cloverleaf; Third, diamond; Fifth, Maltese cross; Sixth, Greek cross; Eleventh, crescent; and Twelfth, star. Red, white, and blue indicated either first, second, or third divisions within a particular corps. According to this system, men in the Iron Brigade wore a red sphere securely fastened to their big hats. The Hoosiers received their badges on April 13th and would wear them proudly until the war ended.[16]

To promote temperance and decrease alcohol-related disturbances, Hooker, himself no teetotaler, decreed that after March 30th no army sutler could sell, give away, or even keep in stock any intoxicating liquor. The provost marshal enthusiastically enforced this order and offenders were fined, banished from the army, and had their goods confiscated. Informants received a reward for turning in lawbreakers. In one noteworthy case of enforcement, two citizens were arrested, tried, fined, saw their goods seized, had their heads shaved, and worked at hard labor for thirty days. Shortly thereafter, one Wayne County soldier told how it was now rare to see imbibers "reeling around under the heavy loads of the essence of corn."[17]

With their whiskey supply drying up, the soldiers spent more and more time playing baseball. The hills around Belle Plain precluded drill, but there were plenty of spots suitable for a ball diamond. Baseball became the rage and men played in an effort to relieve their boredom. Challenges flew back and forth between the 19th Indiana and the 7th Indiana, but it remains unclear just which regiment won the Hoosier championship that spring. The 14th Brooklyn, however, had many fine players from New York City and quickly formed "a nine which whitewashed the nines of all the country regiments with which we were brigaded," including the 7th Indiana.[18]

The arrival of Governor Morton canceled all baseball games scheduled for March 29th. The cry "Governor Morton is here!" swept through Hoosier camps like fire on a dry prairie and soldiers raced to Long Sol's headquarters to see their distinguished visitor. Morton gave a brief speech to each of the Iron Brigade regiments, his theme being "War to the knife—no compromise with traitors—the Union, the whole Union, and all for the Union." Jeff Wasson remembered that the governor "Said he was going to fill up the 19th with Conscripts but it did not Suit the boys very well." Another Wayne County soldier explained why: "We fear to see the drafted or conscript men come here, for we know that we will have to drill." Morton's visit was a welcome diversion, but he had some hefty competition from another favorite visitor. After noting that the governor had spoken to his regiment, Grear Williams wrote in his diary, "the pay master is here too."[19]

Despite distractions provided by baseball and important visitors, General Hooker continued his plan to re-energize the army. Wadsworth's division received an unusual order setting aside Saturday, April 11th, as wash day and demanding that soldiers should appear for Sunday inspection "with a *clean* shirt." Other orders dealing with health, grooming, and appearance followed in rapid succession. For the first time men were compelled to air their bedding and extra clothing on alternate days. Police details swept company streets, alleys, and grounds every day. Daily inspections meant that shoes and brass had to be cleaned and clothing kept in good order.[20]

Of course Hooker had to see the effect of his changes and that meant reviewing the troops. On April 2nd, Wadsworth assembled his four brigades in a line one-half mile in length and five ranks deep. But miracle of miracles, Hooker was already there and waiting, a most unusual circumstance in the Army of the Potomac, where soldiers always waited on generals. When Fighting Joe rode along the line, he received a mixed reception:

> The new troops cheered Hooker tremendously. But the old troops wouldent open their mouths. *They* remember the days when McClellan or McDowell used to review and to use their own language they aint round cheering everybody now.

The message was clear. Hooker's changes, meant to improve morale and increase efficiency, were all well and good, but the real test would come with successful leadership in battle. The old volunteers of 1861 now insisted on winning first and cheering later.[21]

Lincoln came down from Washington to check on Hooker's progress and was guest of honor at a review on April 9th. Long Sol's Iron Brigade was the last to march past the reviewing stand and Hooker introduced it as "the famous 4th brigade." Lincoln supposedly responded, "Yes, it is commanded by the only Quaker General I have in the army." Meredith no longer worshipped with the Society of Friends, but Old Abe knew his outspoken general well from previous contacts. A correspondent for the *Indianapolis Daily Journal* witnessed this review and reported:

> There is a solidity of appearance and steadiness of movement about this brigade that says distinctly, "get out of our way unless you wish to get hurt." As the brigade passed, a murmur of approval ran through the crowd around the President—and the waving handkerchiefs of Mrs. Lincoln and the other ladies told of their admiration.

A member of the 19th Indiana reassured Hoosiers at home that, although less than 400 men remained present for duty, their regiment was ready for the next campaign:

> The men are in high spirits, and have entirely shaken off every thought and feeling of doubt and discouragement. They feel that God has committed a trust to their keeping. They are determined in God's name to stand fast by their plighted honor, their heroic State, and great and glorious country.

Lincoln rode back to Washington and gave his blessing to the changes that Hooker had wrought.[22]

Although not demonstrative about their affection, the soldiers had developed a fondness for Fighting Joe. One Wayne County corporal wrote that "he has confidence in him Self and the Soldiers have confidence in him." Another Company B man stated, "We have the greatest confidence in our leaders, from General Hooker, down to our Brigadier General, Sol Meredith." Elihu Parker said that if an outsider should come into the army and speak disrespectfully of their generals, he "would not give a shilling for his cranium." Healthy individuals still enjoyed military life:

> Joe Curtis of Newport Said he a had a notion of Getting up a petition and Sending it in to old Abe Lincoln to prolong this war but that is camp talk. you know I believe that if this war was over a good many would join the Regular Army rather than work for a living.

Jeff Wasson noticed that only those men whose health had broken down were likely to grow tired of the war. Strong men wanted another crack at the rebels.[23]

While the Wayne County company waited for Hooker's offensive, a scandal swirled around the family of one of its best soldiers. George Bunch's father, Calvin, had been spending more and more time away from the family home in Greensfork Township, Randolph County, and, during one such absence, his wife Eliza fell sick. A physician dropped by, examined her and left some medicine. The husband returned home that night and a nurse happened to notice that Calvin gave her some white powder, instead of the dark powder the doctor had prescribed. When the physician returned, he found Eliza suffering from completely different symptoms. She rapidly grew worse and died on April 13th.

Following Eliza's death, Calvin sent someone into Winchester to purchase burial clothes for the funeral. He also gave the man a sealed letter with instructions to deliver it to a woman at the hotel in Winchester. The messenger easily found this woman, a new arrival in town, who claimed to be Mrs. Calvin Bunch. The suspicious messenger thereupon opened the letter and read its contents. A brief note mentioned the death and cautioned the newcomer to keep quiet until "the dead woman was put away." After Eliza had been buried, Calvin took the mysterious stranger home, where she remained overnight. Nosy neighbors alerted the authorities, who arrested Calvin and threw him in jail.

The prosecuting attorney charged Calvin Bunch with being criminally implicated in the death of his wife. Questioning revealed that the mystery woman was a resident of Dayton and had married Mr. Bunch the previous December. The accused man had assured her that he was single, "although he had a woman keeping house for him that some people supposed to be his wife." Testimony by the doctor and nurse hinted at poison, possibly arsenic. To bolster his case, the prosecuting attorney had Eliza dug up and he personally took her stomach and intestines to Cincinnati for chemical analysis. The *Palladium* described the case as one "so revolting to every impulse of humanity, that the blood runs cold in its contemplation." In September a jury found Calvin Bunch guilty of murder and he was given a life sentence in state prison. George Bunch never publicly revealed his feelings about his mother's murder.[24]

Aside from gossiping about the Bunch family, Wayne County men enjoyed the spring weather in a number of ways. Grear Williams noted that he returned from picket on April 3rd and had several "Chickins for dinner." On the 19th Williams went fishing and boasted that he "got lots of em." But best of all was the diary entry for April 26th that read, "got some ale to drink." Thus did Grear Williams enjoy three of the four "F's" dearest to the heart of a soldier—foraging, fishing, and firewater. The fourth "F" was in short supply, although this lack of female companionship was eased somewhat by reading those racy books which enjoyed wide circulation in the army.[25]

Active operations would commence soon, so on April 26th the 19th Indiana endured a detailed inspection designed to uncover any lingering deficiencies. A detail of 100 men had been made that morning, so only 21 officers and 209 enlisted men were available for inspection. Lieutenant Edward Carrington, one of Wadsworth's staff officers, found that the arms and ammunition, sixty rounds per man, were all in good order. The only shortcomings noted were that one man needed a musket and another was missing a bayonet. Although some items of clothing were needed, nearly every man was now "well supplied with shoes." The Hoosier camp was neat and its hospital tidy. All seriously ill men had been sent off to general hospitals. The result of Carrington's inspection showed that Colonel Williams had his regiment well prepared for Hooker's new campaign.[26]

The long anticipated order to move came at noon on April 28th and General Meredith started the Iron Brigade toward the Rappahannock. His brigade marched west until within two miles of the river, where it was halted until midnight. Lieutenant Finney explained the tactical situation:

> It had been planned to approach the river before daylight, cross in pontoon boats, surprise, and, if possible, capture the picket line, and establish a force on the opposite bank, before it should get light enough for the enemy to execute any counter movements.

No fires were allowed, so the soldiers' supper consisted of "hardtack and raw pork diluted with water." The pontoons, each pulled by six mules, rolled toward the river at a spot called either Fitzhugh Crossing or Pollock's Mill.

Theater of Operations – 1863

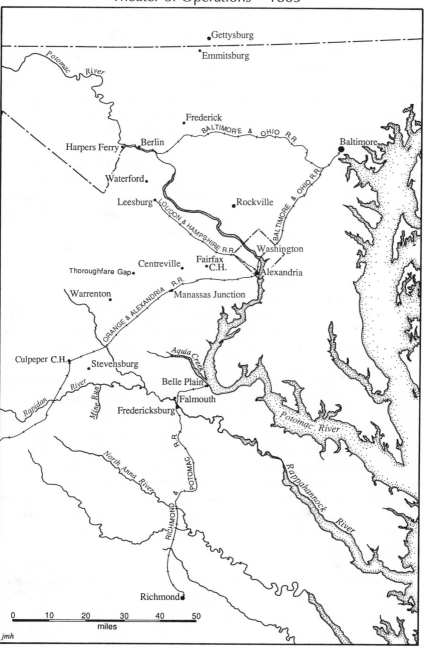

Gettysburg

Emmitsburg

Potomac River

Frederick

BALTIMORE & OHIO R.R.

Baltimore

Harpers Ferry · Berlin

Waterford·

Leesburg · LOUDON & HAMPSHIRE R.R.

Rockville·

BALTIMORE & OHIO R.R.

Washington

Centreville· Fairfax

Thoroughfare Gap· C.H.

Alexandria

Warrenton· ORANGE & ALEXANDRIA R.R.

Manassas Junction

Culpeper C.H.· · Stevensburg

Aquia Creek

Rapidan River Mine Run

Belle Plain

Fredericksburg· Falmouth

North Anna River

RICHMOND & POTOMAC R.R.

Potomac River

Rappahannock River

Richmond·

| 0 | 10 | 20 | 30 | 40 | 50 |
miles

jmh

The mud was terrible, but Wadsworth had insisted on strict silence, so drivers could not swear at their mules. Teamsters plied their whips so loud and so often that it sounded like a skirmish to nearby listeners.[27]

Fog shrouded the Rappahannock when the first pontoons arrived. Twenty boats were in the river before sunrise, but surprise was out of the question. Fitzhugh Crossing was located in a narrow section of the river, where rebels had dug rifle pits atop the bluffs on their side. Despite Wadsworth's ban on noise, rebs from Harry Hays's Louisiana brigade had heard the racket as the column approached. Graybacks taunted their Yankee counterparts and promised to fill them full of lead when it became light enough to see. Engineer troops unsuccessfully attempted to connect the boats into a bridge before sunrise, but rebel musketry from the opposing heights stampeded them. In preparation for "an aggressive movement," Meredith advanced his brigade to the shelter of a slight crest parallel to the river, while the 14th Brooklyn deployed as skirmishers under cover along the river bank.[28]

Reynolds and Wadsworth were discussing their options when General Henry Benham rode up and transmitted an order from Hooker for the First Corps to cross immediately and "at all hazards." Reynolds passed the order to Wadsworth, who instructed Lieutenant Colonel John Kress, his inspector general, to carry out Hooker's order by crossing Meredith's brigade. As he galloped over to the Iron Brigade, Kress formulated a plan for an amphibious assault. Three companies of the 2nd Wisconsin would launch those pontoons still on shore, while the remainder of that regiment, the 7th Wisconsin and 19th Indiana, would open fire on the rebel riflepits. Under cover of this musketry, the 6th Wisconsin and 24th Michigan would cross the river and assault the bluffs. Rowers would then bring back the boats and ferry across Meredith's other three regiments. It was a desperate plan, but Hooker needed this diversion in order to confuse Lee and outmaneuver the rebel army.[29]

Communicating instructions and arranging the regiments took almost an hour. Soldiers piled up their knapsacks and haversacks, retaining only their canteens, and glumly joked about their prospects for survival. Rufus Dawes remembered, "To be shot like sheep in a huddle and drowned in the Rappahannock appeared to be the certain fate of all if we failed, of many if we succeeded."[30]

Soldiers from the 2nd Wisconsin sprang forward and dragged heavy, bulky pontoons to the river's edge. Some men from the 6th Wisconsin ran forward and jumped into boats abandoned earlier by the engineers. Others hopped into those being carried forward, filling them "as soon as they touched the water." To the left, Colonel Morrow's Wolverines did likewise. The 19th Indiana followed the 24th Michigan to the river, the 7th Wisconsin supported the 6th Wisconsin, and the 2nd prolonged Meredith's line to the right. Bullets skipped across the water and crashed into the boats, but a savage fire from men on shore kept many rebs huddled in their rifle pits.[31]

All the regiments seemed to arrive at the river simultaneously. Staff officers gave confusing orders. Formations were broken up and "every man worked on his own hook." Soldiers were ordered into the boats "without regard to regiments or companies" and Colonel W. W. Robinson recalled, "As near as I could see, every boat had representatives from every regiment in the brigade." Once afloat, men rowed with oars or muskets or used poles to get their clumsy craft across the water. Covering fire from the Yankee side seemed to confuse the enemy, who "devoted the most of his attention to this annoying and noisy fusilade, overlooking the quiet fellows in the boats."[32]

Once ashore on the far side, "without waiting for any formation," the first wave "clambered up the bluff bank, in the very face of the opposing force, under a deadly fire." As Wisconsin and Michigan men scrambled upwards through brush and vines, the boats returned for reinforcements. Old Corduroy and Long Sol crossed with a second wave that reinforced the beachhead. Robert K. Beecham, of the 2nd Wisconsin, rode across with his division commander:

> We stood side by side in the bow of the boat, and when we reached jumping distance we both jumped. I was a younger man than Wadsworth and out-jumped him, lighting with one foot upon solid earth and one well out into the water, while the general stuck both feet in the water, but he was out in a moment and to the top of the hill about as quick as any of us. . . .

After watching the attack, one New Yorker wrote, "It was a splendid sight to see the little blue-coated crowd rush up the bank along with the white-headed general, and a few moments afterwards to see the rebels swarm out of their rifle pits into the open, chased hotly by the vigorous boys from the west."[33]

The hurry and confusion of this bold charge resulted in a number of Badgers being hit by friendly fire. Men from the 6th Wisconsin scrambled up the bluffs so fast that they ran right into the musketry sweeping the rifle pits. For a few minutes the situation was exceedingly perilous, fire from the 7th Wisconsin being "nearly equal with the enemy in front." Just as they reached the enemy works, an officer saw Corporal G. A. Ruby shot dead by a ball fired from across the river. One 2nd Wisconsin soldier admitted that the 7th had fired into the 6th, "killing and wounding several." Official reports failed to mention the incident.[34]

Badgers and Wolverines shot down those rebels who refused to surrender and captured many more who were less courageous. Several dozen fugitives barricaded themselves in a barn, but some well-aimed Federal shells compelled them to wave a white flag. Companies and regiments had scattered and intermingled during the attack, but the veterans sorted themselves out "with a kind of instinct, as bees gather, into their separate organizations." The whole affair was over quickly. Colonel Robinson wrote, "From the time of receiving the order to cross over, till the enemy's line of works was carried, prisoners taken, and our line of battle formed with every man in his place in his own regiment, was about twenty minutes."[35]

General Meredith later reported that the Iron Brigade had killed some thirty rebs, wounded many others and captured almost 200. Estimates of rebel prisoners varied widely, probably because there was no standard for counting wounded prisoners. Some placed these men in the wounded category, some lumped them in with unwounded prisoners, while others obviously counted them in both categories. Lieutenant Colonel Joseph Hanson of the 6th Louisiana was the highest ranking captive. Lieutenant Colonel Kress reported that ninety rebels had been taken, while the provost marshal received eighty prisoners. These were, no doubt, unwounded men. No one furnished estimates of rebel wounded. Casualties in the Iron Brigade totaled fifty-seven, killed and wounded.[36]

Hoosier participation in the assault had been limited. Although some Indiana men surely crossed in Michigan boats during the first wave, most of them kept up a lively fire that distracted the enemy from these boat parties. Before he crossed, one private heard Long Sol "hollouring go in boys go in!" As the empty pontoons returned, each Indiana soldier "tried to be the first one in," many wading out into waist-deep water to meet the boats. Colonel Williams reported only four casualties during the operation: John Waller, Company F, killed; Sergeant Charles Petty, Company B; David Green, Company H; and Milton N. Goff, Company K, wounded. Waller's body was carried back to the Fitzhugh house and buried in the orchard. Two other Wayne County soldiers, John Rariden and Charles Sponsler, were also wounded, but not included in Williams's total. Both men received gunshot wounds in their fingers, perhaps an indication of carelessness while engaged in rapid firing during the assault.[37]

Colonel Williams formed a line of battle on the bluffs, then advanced a short distance to the left into an open meadow, with Company B posted out front as skirmishers. Meredith's Iron Brigade guarded Fitzhugh Crossing until the pontoon bridge was completed, then moved to the left and took shelter for the night in a ditch. On the morning of April 30th the brigade shifted position slightly into a small piece of timber, where the men began to build entrenchments. There were no entrenching tools, so soldiers raided the Bernard plantation and brought back mowers, reapers, plows, and anything else that would stop a bullet or shell. Logs, rocks, earth, and other handy material filled in gaps between the farm implements. Picket lines had been quiet since the crossing, but the rebels shelled these entrenchments in the evening. One shell exploded in front of Company F, but the improvised defenses prevented any injury except for jangled nerves. During this shell fire, Colonel Williams mustered the regiment, "rather a cool proceeding under the circumstances."[38]

20

North Again

May Day brought balmy spring weather and continued quiet on the picket line. Entrenching tools had finally arrived the night before, so Grear Williams celebrated the pre-dawn hours of his twentieth birthday by building infantry breastworks and artillery emplacements with his friends. By dawn, a formidable line had been completed, stretching almost two miles around the pontoon bridge. Despite the urgent amphibious attack on April 29th, this movement by Wadsworth's division was nothing but a feint to confuse the enemy while Hooker crossed part of his force farther upstream at Kelly's Ford. Another portion of the army, commanded by General John Sedgwick, advanced from Fredericksburg as Fighting Joe tried to overwhelm the Army of Northern Virginia. Wadsworth held his bridgehead until the morning of May 2nd, when his division was recalled and ordered to rejoin the army. Rebel gunners shelled the troops as they withdrew, causing little harm, although one shell sank a pontoon boat and temporarily closed the bridge. Company K, commanded by Captain William Orr, deployed as skirmishers and covered the withdrawal.[1]

The First Corps marched along the river toward United States Ford and listened intently to the sound of a battle being fought near Chancellorsville. Sergeant Major Asa Blanchard asserted, "I never, in all my life, heard such firing." Meredith's brigade halted that night some two or three miles short of the ford and camped. Reliable rumors told that the army's right flank, held by General Oliver O. Howard's predominantly German Eleventh Corps, had fled in panic before a surprise flank attack. Despite warnings of this enemy movement, Howard had neglected to properly protect his front. One man who alerted Howard to the impending attack was Captain Davis B. Castle, commanding the Eleventh Corps' signal detachment. Castle had established a signal station at Little Wilderness where he could observe "the movements of the enemy, who were moving westerly on [a] road running parallel with Plank road." The captain sent constant reports of this movement to corps headquarters, but they were all ignored. At 4:30 P.M. Castle signaled that the flanking force had encountered Howard's pickets. One-half hour later, Captain Castle and his detachment packed up their equipment and fled just ahead of Stonewall Jackson's attacking infantry. Castle's warnings had been in vain.[2]

This assault on May 2nd had crushed the Eleventh Corps, imperiling Hooker's force, but Stonewall Jackson was mortally wounded that night. Although deprived of his valuable lieutenant, General Lee skillfully maneuvered his army, first stopping Hooker then repulsing Sedgwick. The Iron Brigade crossed a pontoon bridge over the Rappahannock before dawn on May 3rd and formed a line of battle behind General George Sykes's division of the Fifth Corps. By noon earthworks had been completed and the brigade held this position untouched by shot or shell until May 6th. The First Corps took no significant part in the battle of Chancellorsville, laying in reserve during this whole period. By the evening of May 7th, the brigade had returned to the high ground overlooking Fitzhugh Crossing and encamped. In closing his report of the campaign, Colonel Samuel Williams praised the Hoosiers: "Their courage and coolness under fire, the promptness with which they obeyed my orders, the way the men kept closed up on the march, and the assistance rendered me by my officers, was all a commander could ask." Lieutenant Finney noted the regiment's light casualties, then reported, "It had been kept well in hand, and required but little time to be placed again in fighting trim." Expressing a view from the ranks, Jeff Crull had a slightly different perspective of this latest Federal defeat: "we can slip out of any tight Place with out much trouble as we had got usted to doing such things." This was the voice of a soldier who had become accustomed to losing.[3]

Although it had not fought at Chancellorsville, the Iron Brigade was occasionally cheered by regiments familiar with its reputation. One such incident occurred on the return march, when Berdan's Sharpshooters, carrying a distinguished reputation of their own, shouted boisterous approval of these "giants with their tall black hats." One Sharpshooter remembered "that famed body of troops marching up that long muddy hill unmindful of the pouring rain, but full of life and spirit, with steady step, filling the entire roadway, their big black hats and feathers conspicuous." In his opinion, they were the finest representation of the "model American volunteer."[4]

Upon returning to the Fitzhugh plantation, John G. Stephenson, Congressional Librarian and occasional Hoosier staff officer, wrote to Governor Morton and urged him to commission a third field officer "without delay." Samuel Williams and William Dudley had finally been promoted colonel and lieutenant colonel, respectively, so the librarian recommended elevating Captain Lindley to the vacant post of major. As for himself, Stephenson assured Morton that there was "probably no man outside of this Regt that knows its history and present condition or the quality of its officers better than I do." Apparently relishing this active life, Stephenson sought to take advantage of the Congressional recess and advised the governor, "I expect to remain with this Corps during the campaign."[5]

On May 13th, the Hoosiers received orders to fix up their camp by ditching and grading streets. William Jackson thought this looked "like staying around." Gray awnings began to appear over the tents, serving the dual purpose of providing shade and airing musty wool blankets. Men took advantage of the lull to write letters advising family and friends that they had safely passed through yet another campaign. Asa Blanchard began his letter to the *Quaker City Telegram* as a way to enliven "the dull monotony of camp life." Many men chose to break this monotony by wagering on chuck-a-luck, a dice game that always drew a larger crowd than church services. When Wadsworth learned "with regret" of this widespread gambling, he ordered a crackdown. Brigade commanders received instructions to send out special patrols "at least twice a day, changing the hours from day to day," with orders to arrest gamblers and send them to their colonels under guard. Old Corduroy's proscription stopped nothing; it merely forced the dice throwers and card shufflers to keep a sharper eye out for the patrols.[6]

Western men took their turn at picket duty along the Rappahannock after returning from Chancellorsville. Guarding the river, which was only fifty yards wide at this point, proved to be more of a social function than a military assignment. A truce remained in effect by mutual consent, so that Private Jackson could take out his diary and write that "a Squad of Rebs are bathing within a stones throw of our line & many others are fishing." This disregard for regulations was apparent to any officer who visited the picket line. After Rufus Dawes spent two days in charge of the division pickets, he wrote down his observations: "There is no hostility and the men sit dozing and staring at each other, and when there are no officers about, they exchange papers and communicate with each other in as friendly a manner as if there was no cause for enmity." Hoosier soldiers shared the popular feeling that picket firing should never be conducted "by properly disciplined armies of civilized nations." As different detachments rotated out to the river, they would first strike up trade by sailing wooden boats back and forth. Soon men began swimming out to meet the enemy for trade, generally Yankee coffee for rebel tobacco, until a few bold ones would eventually crawl out of the water and play cards on the opposite shore. After talking and trading newspapers with one group of rebs, C. C. Starbuck admitted that "they were good looking fellows."[7]

Fraternization kept pickets from being shot, but it led to other serious problems. One trading session ended when a Yankee swimmer had exchanged his load of coffee for whiskey, resulting in one-half of the division pickets becoming pie-eyed. On another occasion, Northern and Southern pickets indulged in a friendly swim. But a quarrel ensued over some trivial matter and the adversaries climbed out on their respective banks, grabbed their muskets and began shooting. This sudden outburst caused army headquarters to assume that a force of rebels had attempted to cross the Rappahannock. Orders came for the First Corps to tear down their tents and await instructions. Soldiers in regiments that carried out these orders were mad as hell when they learned that the whole affair was simply an outrageous false alarm.[8]

When Iron Brigade pickets rotated off duty, their grayclad enemies bade them goodbye. The rebs knew those black-hatted fellows and respected their hard-won reputation, having little use for the average cap-wearing Yankees. One incident will serve to illustrate why the Southerners felt that way. A rebel swam the river to trade and was taken prisoner by a green Connecticut soldier, who proudly marched his naked captive to General Lysander Cutler's headquarters. After listening to an explanation by the New Englander, Cutler barked: "It's a damned piece of treachery to take a man prisoner in that way. Give him a suit of clothing and send him to me." Clothed in a blue uniform, the rebel corroborated the story. After asking a few pointed questions of the captive, Cutler sent him back to his own lines. No Iron Brigade picket would have conducted himself in such a high-handed manner. After all, it would be a breach of picket-line etiquette.[9]

The insanity of this picket situation was not lost on those who guarded the shores of the Rappahannock. Private William Jackson mused:

> What a proof here is of the inconsistancy of human beings, one day seeks to take each others lives, the next all is quiet, and we spend days and nights within a stones throw of one another in peace and I might say sociability.

It all made no sense, this shooting at rebels one day and playing cards with them the next. No wonder that Jackson would exclaim, "O, when will this cease—when will men learn wisdom?"[10]

On May 21st, four regiments—19th Indiana, 24th Michigan, 2nd and 6th Wisconsin—set out on a forced march to rescue the 8th Illinois Cavalry, which had supposedly been cut off while operating against smugglers. Colonel Morrow commanded the expedition and he had his men on the road by daylight. Morrow's column marched briskly down the Northern Neck, a peninsula between the Potomac and Rappahannock Rivers, despite the still, sultry air and dust "near shoe mouth deep." A rapid pace forced many men to drop out before noon, but Morrow kept his men moving until the column had passed King George Court House and they did not bivouac until after covering over thirty miles. The colonel detached a reserve of 160 men, commanded by Lieutenant Colonel Rufus Dawes, at a crossroads to guard the line of retreat, then continued on the next morning to Mattox Creek. Dawes had a hard time keeping his men in camp. So many wandered off to forage that he impulsively sent out a patrol "with strict orders to arrest every man or officer found." The patrol's most important captive was Captain Patrick Hart of the Hoosier regiment, who had gotten a pass from Dawes to go purchase chickens.[11]

Morrow's main body rebuilt a bridge over Mattox Creek, then continued eastward, zigzagging across the peninsula in search of the cavalry. Near Leedsville, the Federals captured Lieutenant Colonel John Critcher, 15th Virginia Cavalry, who was trying to escape by means of a small boat secreted along the Rappahannock. On May 24th, Morrow's column met the 8th Illinois Cavalry about one mile from Westmoreland Court House, some fifty-five miles from Belle Plain, although the men had marched eighty miles to get that far. The cavalry had ridden all the way to Chesapeake Bay, destroying over 100 boats of various sizes, along with their contents. Their force had been swollen by the addition of many wagons, 500 horses and mules, and upwards of 800 Negroes who were determined to follow the horsemen to freedom. There was now nothing to do but return to camp and Morrow's soldiers covered the fifty-five miles in just over one and a half days. Six days of marching had left the participants "stiff and crippled," a needless agony since the cavalry had never been in any danger.[12]

A series of inspections in late May revealed that the First Corps' best brigade failed to keep its paperwork in order. Meredith's brigade was cited for the following lapses: "Regmt and Co. Books incomplete," "Chaplains fail to make quarterly reports to Colonels," "Sutlers establishments not inspected," "Sutlers goods not tariffed and lists exposed," and "Sutlers keep articles not allowed by Regulations." Long Sol had no time for such trivial red tape: he had an extremely important general order to prepare. Meredith had carefully bided his time and on June 2nd, the anniversary of the march that had precipitated the Great Legging Mutiny, he exacted his vengeance on John Gibbon with General Order No. 17:

> The General Commanding the Brigade feels it is his duty to the gallant dead who in defence of their loved country bedewed the fields of Gainesville, Bull Run, South Mountain, Antietam, Fredericksburg and Fitzhugh Crossing with their life's blood and the few brave officers and men who yet survive their fallen comrades to rescind Genl. Order No.

58 HdQrs Gibbon's Brigade, dated, opposite Fredericksburg, Va. June 13, 1862. . . . He feels it his duty to state that the circumstances under which the waste complained of occurred, were as follows. The troops were compelled to each have two full suits of clothing. Early in June the command was ordered on a forced march to Haymarket via Catlett Station to intercept Genl. Jackson in the Shenandoah valley; the weather being oppresively hot, the march long and load heavy, through exhaustion the men of the entire command were compelled to throw away much of the clothing. In this all the Regts. of the command acted alike. The waste was occasioned through physical incapacity to perform the march imposed and not through recklessness, foolish waste or want of discipline as alleged. So much of the order as orders the clothing charged on the coming muster roll was never enforced, for the reason the order was a strict violation of law. Genl. Order no 58 HdQrs Gibbon's Brigade is hereby rescinded.

So many important events had transpired since June 2, 1862 that everyone except Sol had forgotten the legging affair. Soldiers had even stopped playing their "Lay down, boys! Lay down!" game. But Meredith would not be denied the last word and finally his victory over Gibbon was complete.[13]

Most soldiers were more interested in liquor than in General Meredith's vendetta. Drinking provided an escape for a variety of reasons. One Hoosier thought it gave drinkers a false sense of courage:

Too many men who wish to be called brave invariably fortify themselves before going into battle by partaking freely of the vile liquor that is sold here—and their insane rashness is mistaken for bravery and heroism.

Private Jackson sadly confessed that "many of our best officers are fast becoming slaves to the demon of alcohol." As if to reinforce the private's claim, Adjutant Finney mentioned one particular episode that occurred on May 16th. After riding to a nearby signal station, Finney "Ret'd and found all drunk. The officers carried on their debauch until late in the night. Dudley got particularly tight."[14]

Alcohol played a major role in ending the military career of Lieutenant Benjamin F. Hancock. On May 29th, Hancock, "grossly intoxicated," stumbled into Company D and tried to pick a fight with Abram J. Oliver, a noted brawler. Attracted by the quarrel, Captain David Holloway walked over and heard Hancock call the private a "son-of-a-bitch." Holloway told Hancock to get out of his company and leave his men alone. Hancock said he would obey orders and left, but stumbled back a few minutes later. Private Oliver refused to fight an officer, so Hancock took off his coat and yelled, "You are a Damned Son-of-a-bitch, a Coward, and a liar. I have taken off my Straps and am now your equal, in rank, and can whip you." To emphasize his point, Hancock drew a line in the dirt and dared him to cross. This time Lieutenant Lewis Yeatman spoke to Hancock and convinced him to depart, but he returned once again. By now Oliver had lost patience with the drunken officer and punched him. Such conduct could not be tolerated, so Lieutenant Hancock was court-martialed on June 5th for conduct prejudicial to good order and military discipline and conduct unbecoming an officer and a gentleman. The court found Hancock guilty of both charges and sentenced him to be dismissed from United States service. His sentence took effect on June 24, 1863.[15]

Two important changes in the brigade occurred about this time. On May 27th, the 24th Michigan finally received their coveted black hats, standardizing the brigade headgear and making the Wolverines feel that now they really belonged with the veterans. A second addition was the arrival of a new stand of colors for the 19th Indiana. Company B took back its Wayne County flag and the color guard accepted the new Stars and Stripes. This new flag bore inscriptions of the 19th Indiana's previous battles: Lewinsville, Battles of the Rappahannock and Gainesville, Battles of Bull Run, South Mountain, Antietam, and Fredericksburg. Shortly afterwards several men volunteered for the color guard, among them Abe Buckles, Company E, and Burr N. Clifford, Company F. Buckles explained his motivation: "I had always had a great anxiety to carry the flag of my regiment, and did not know how I could get the place of color-bearer, unless by serving in the guard until I could see a proper chance to pick the flag up, should the color-bearer be killed or wounded." These new volunteers filled the color guard to its maximum: two flags, Stars and Stripes and regimental colors, two bearers and eight guards. Members of this elite group differentiated between their two flags by referring to their national colors as the banner and their state colors as the flag. Other soldiers made no such distinction.[16]

Finding himself with some time on Monday, June 1st, Jeff Wasson wrote a letter to his mother. He mused about the fate of a comrade so seriously wounded at Brawner Farm that he still required medical treatment:

> I cant help but think about Henry H. Hyatt of our company who was wounded at Gainsville. he was wounded with the Same Ball that Struck me and is lying in the Hospital yet at Washington. Poor fellow he has Suffered a good deal but I believe he would a had to have his leg taken off if the bullet had not a went through my leg first. he was Standing behind me when it was done.

Wasson also passed on some information about his friend, Sergeant Charley Petty, who was lying wounded about a mile from the Hoosier camp:

he is at the Fitzhugh Hospital a Splendid place. our boys Some of them
are there most every day. they take him Oranges and any thing that he
wants to eat. they will not let him Suffer. I was down there to See him
the other day and Seen a good many others at the Same time.

Jeff then gave his mother some advice: "I dont want you to be alarmed on my
account every time you hear of a big battle going off in this army. I have been
Shot at So often that I am used to it." But maybe Jeff realized that his luck
might be running out, for he closed his letter by writing, "them that lives to
See the end to this war ought to be thankful and think them Selves lucky for
being alive." Corporal Thomas Jefferson Wasson would not be one of the
lucky ones. At the time he concluded this letter, Jeff had exactly one month
to live.[17]

So many regimental enlistments had expired by June 1st that
Wadsworth's division had been reduced from four brigades to two. In the
resulting realignment, Meredith's Iron Brigade became the First Brigade,
First Division, First Corps, a designation that put just a little more swagger
into their stride. Marching orders had arrived and were as quickly countermanded several times during the first ten days of June. Soldiers were content
to continue their camp life, but General Wadsworth had a pet scheme he
wished to inaugurate.[18]

Ever since the Mud March, hundreds of Negro refugees had
streamed past the Belle Plain camps. Many left their carts and wagons behind
after reaching freedom. When a large number of vehicles had accumulated at
division headquarters, General Wadsworth conceived a novel plan. These
carts and wagons, drawn by trained oxen, could be loaded with rations and
dispatched to the front. After their loads had been issued, the oxen could be
slaughtered for fresh beef and cooked over fires that used the wagons for fuel.
It seemed a very practical scheme, so Captain Charles Ford, 6th Wisconsin,
was assigned the task of making draft animals out of some fifty oxen.[19]

A slight setback occurred when these "stall fed" cattle were given
unsoaked hardtack, which caused several to bloat up and die. Then Old
Corduroy took a personal interest in the training and one of his soldiers
wrote later:

> I well remember Gen. Wadsworth, with pants in the top of heavy boots.
> mud shoe-top deep in the corral, among the cattle, helping to mate
> them. He would point to an ox and say, "That is an off ox," or "This one
> works on the nigh side, don't you see his left horn," or "His right horn
> is worn on the yoke," and in this way spent many hours with the men.

Soldiers from the division always gathered at the pens of this "bull city" to
watch their general, whip in hand, wade through the manure in an effort to

train his stubborn cattle. They said Old Corduroy was "whispering to his calves" or drilling them in "ox tactics," a system of instruction not covered by contemporary military manuals.[20]

Hooker's Chancellorsville campaign had not presented an opportunity to test the "Bull Train," as the plan had come to be known. But when the First Corps left camp on June 12th, Captain Ford's bulls fell in behind the corps wagon train. Much to Wadsworth's chagrin, men, horses, and mules all marched away from the plodding Bull Train. Lashing and cursing could not speed up the column. By nightfall Ford's command was miles behind and became easy prey for rebel guerrillas, so supplies were issued, cattle returned to the herd, and wagons set afire. Old Corduroy's ox tactics had failed.[21]

The victorious rebel army had started north, perhaps contemplating another invasion of Maryland, so the 19th Indiana was up and marching before daylight on June 12th. Despite the urgency of their march, after lunch the entire division formed up to witness an exceptional sight. Private John P. Woods, Company F, 19th Indiana, was to be shot to death with musketry. He had been found guilty of desertion for running away on the morning the Iron Brigade charged across the river at Fitzhugh Crossing. This was his third such offense. He had deserted first at Rappahannock Station on August 20, 1862, and remained absent until November 17th. His second absence occurred at Fredericksburg, but he had managed to convince a court-martial of his innocence. He would not run away again.[22]

On April 29, 1863, Woods divested himself of his honorable Iron Brigade uniform and dressed instead in a United States cavalry jacket, butternut civilian trousers, and a black slouch hat. When captured by Federal pickets about two weeks later, he attempted to pass as a rebel deserter. Woods was taken to First Corps headquarters, where the provost marshal interrogated him and wrote down his statement:

> I am a deserter from the 19th Tennessee. under command of Genl A. P. Hill. It was never brigaded. Col. Eager of the 19th had command of the brigade when I left. It was over to Fredericksburg when I left on the right. The Regt was never together always detached—different companies standing about guard. I am not acquainted with much of the Regiment. I was raised and born in Brown Co Ohio. I have been in service a year and nine months. I enlisted in Memphis Tenn. I know the 7th and 9th Tenn of the brigade. The 7th is in Jacksons corps. We were encamped about three miles from Fredericksburg. I was here the first fight. We were never in any particular brigade. I had been in Memphis 4 months before the war broke out. I was overseeing about 30 niggers when I enlisted. Our Regt went to Richmond from Memphis then to the James river. I know Genls Lee Longstreet Jackson Brekenridge and most of them on the other side of the river.

This rambling narrative raised doubts about his identity, so the provost marshal checked descriptions of deserters and tentatively ascertained that Woods belonged to the 19th Indiana. A clerk at First Corps headquarters confirmed his identity.[23]

Woods was tried in a court-martial assembled on May 29th. The judge advocate introduced the above statement and called two witnesses, First Sergeant William P. Wilson and Sergeant Zachariah Coffin, both of whom testified that he had been absent without permission. Private Woods offered no testimony in his defense, although he did make an oral statement:

> The reason I left the regiment before crossing the river near Fredericksburg was because I did not want to go in a fight. I cant fight. I cannot stand it to fight. I am ashamed to make the statement, but I may as well do it now as at any other time. I never could stand a fight. I never could bear to shoot any body. I have done my duty in every way but fight. I have tried to do it but cannot. I am perfectly willing to work all my lifetime for the United States in any other way but fight. I have tried to do it but cannot. I went to my doctor when I left the regiment and wanted him to give me a pass and I would go and work and wait on the wounded in the hospital. he told me that he guessed he had enough. I had better go on and try to do my duty. he said he would see about it. I could not find out where the hospital was. he had not stationed it. then after a while I came to the conclusion I would try to go home. I started to go to Aquia Creek landing and got lost on my way and got outside of our picket lines, out by Stafford Court House. I met the pickets there and came on to our own pickets and gave myself up. I had been acquainted in Tennessee and I gave myself up as a rebel. I made the statement for fear they would think I was a bushwhacker. then I was sent on under arms until they received me here. I am willing to do all I could for my country. I like it as much as anybody does. I was always willing to try to fight for my country, but I never could. I am willing to try to fight for it again. I am ashamed of my conduct and will always try to do better hereafter.

After deliberation, the court found Private John P. Woods guilty of desertion and sentenced him "to be shot to death with muskets at such time and place as the Commanding General may direct." General Hooker approved the sentence and directed that the execution take place on Friday, June 12th, between the hours of noon and 4 P.M., in the presence of Wadsworth's entire division.[24]

The prisoner was turned over to Clayton Rogers, Wadsworth's provost marshal, who found Woods to be "a simple-minded soldier, without any force or decision of character." Chaplain Samuel Eaton, 7th Wisconsin, spent June 11th with the condemned man and found him to be holding up well. Eaton wrote, "His firmness, composure and naturalness is astonishing.

He does not complain or whine or cry; says he is not afraid to die." The chaplain kindly gave Woods seven small tracts to read, so that his father and each of his brothers and sisters could have a memento after his death. While Reverend Eaton talked with Woods, the provost marshal assembled a guard detail, put together a twelve-man firing party and had a rude coffin constructed.[25]

When Wadsworth's division marched on the 12th, Woods, handcuffed and with shackles on his feet, rode behind in an ambulance. After completing their noon meal, the Iron Brigade and Lysander Cutler's brigade marched into position around a hastily dug grave and the soldiers stacked arms. General Wadsworth and his staff, all mounted, waited for the prisoner, while curious men from other commands collected outside the formation. His coffin was placed by the grave, then Woods stepped down from the ambulance and knelt in prayer with the chaplain for a few minutes. Moving with a "sturdy step" to his coffin, he took off his hat, placed it upon the ground and sat down on the rough wooden box. Woods asked that he not be blindfolded, but Lieutenant Rogers said it must be done and tied a handkerchief around his head. The condemned man's last view of this world was of twelve stern-faced men with muskets, his executioners.[26]

This firing party "manifested more uneasiness than the criminal." The twelve men were addressed by Wadsworth, then received their muskets, one of which contained a blank charge. This would, in theory, allow each man to imagine that he had fired a blank round, but experienced troops could easily tell the difference. As they filed into line thirty feet in front of their target, the firing party must have been impressed with Woods's composure. Others certainly were. Jeff Wasson said "he took it very cool" and a 7th Indiana man remembered, "He seemed to be as calm as though his end was not so near." A Badger noticed that Woods sat on his coffin "as one would take a seat before a camera." Sergeant Sullivan Green, 24th Michigan, thought he detected a slight shudder after Lieutenant Rogers tied the blindfold, but no other soldier mentioned any similar reaction.[27]

As Rogers gave the command, "Ready!" one Badger imagined, "What a moment it must have been to the unfortunate victim who heard that awful click, the prelude to the last sound he was to hear on earth!" At the command, "Aim!" Woods did not move a muscle. When Lieutenant Rogers commanded "Fire!" eight muskets on the right of the line roared an answer and Woods toppled backwards over his coffin. But the firing party had aimed low, only four bullets hitting him, and he still lived. The next two men advanced to within three feet and administered the *coup de grace*. Wadsworth's medical director examined Woods and pronounced him dead. The lifeless corpse was lifted into its coffin, placed in the hole and covered over with dirt.[28]

There was strong reaction to Woods's execution. Lieutenant George Breck, an officer in the division artillery, wrote: "Better a thousand times that he should have fallen on the battlefield than have fallen in this ignoble way." A 7th Indiana man meditated: "In perfect health and with his friends and the next minute in eternity. What a warning, let us hope that not very many of those who witnessed the execution needed such a warning." Another Hoosier wrote that it was a "very useful" example since desertions were so common. Jeff Wasson prefaced his description of the event by stating, "I hope never to witness the like again while in the service."[29]

Rumors about the affair began circulating almost immediately. One of the 14th Brooklyn boys remembered:

> It was said that Wood had a wife at home, back in Indiana, who was lying desperately ill. As he marched he brooded over the probability of her dying without seeing him again. He applied for a furlough, but the furlough was refused to him. The more he brooded, the more he determined to see her at all costs. He therefore deserted, expecting to return to his duty afterwards.

Orville Thomson of the 7th Indiana heard a different story: "The sympathetic part came in an hour later when his aged father came to head-quarters bringing a pardon signed by President Lincoln." Another version of this story told of an officer and citizen arriving just five minutes after the execution with a message from Lincoln commuting the sentence of death to life imprisonment. Yet a third variation claimed that an officer arrived with a reprieve just as Woods had expected to hear the command to fire. He fell back upon his coffin, "apparently dead," but the great strain and instant release had left him "a hopeless maniac." This last version claimed that the whole event, "a fearful ordeal for the deserter," had been staged to make an impression upon the brigade. These rumors seemed to exonerate Woods, making his death some sort of huge mistake by army bureaucrats.[30]

Corporal Thomas Jefferson Wasson wrote the best account of the campaign that had been interrupted by Woods's execution. His narrative picks up just after that gruesome event and concludes on June 28th:

> We started again on our march and stopped at dark to stay all night and again started at daylight and marched to Bealton, a station on the Orange and Alexandria railroad. Roads very dusty and hot—water very scarce; we drank most of the time out of mudholes along the road. The next morning was Sunday and we were on the march early. We marched to Warrenton Junction—stopped an hour for dinner—and kept on in the direction of Washington—passed Catlett's Station and stopped close to Bristoe Station, about 9 o'clock at night, but only long enough

to make coffee. We marched only five miles from that till daylight. We stopped on Manassas Plains about daylight to get breakfast, but most of the boys were too tired to eat, and in less time than you could imagine they were all asleep. We stayed there about three hours and started on our journey to Manassas Junction, about one mile off—dust six inches deep and no water of any kind for several miles around. It is one of the most desolate countries I have ever seen; but we have been here before. We only marched five miles again, stopped at noon and made coffee out of the sacred Bull Run water—just the color of clay. We started again towards Centreville in the hope of getting some water to drink and got there in about three hours—three miles, and actually did get some good cold water to drink, the first we had that was fit to drink since we left Falmouth.

We put up tents and stayed there the balance of the day and all the next day. Wednesday morning we started again in a northerly direction and stopped 2 nights and one day at Herndon Station, Fairfax county, on the Alexandria & Leesburg railroad. General Meredith arrived while we were there and took command of the brigade, which pleased us very much. We went from there to Guilford Station, in Loudon county—distance 4 miles and camped on a stream called Broad Run. Our regiment went on picket and stayed 48 hours. We left here on Thursday morning, the 25th, and crossed the Potomac River at Edwards' Ferry, and took dinner in "my Maryland" on salt pork, hardtack, and coffee without sugar; but bright prospects ahead for warm biscuits, fresh butter, ham and sweet milk.

We marched very hard the balance of the day and passed through Poolsville about 8 o'clock—the flags were flying from the houses. We camped for the night in the outskirts of a town called Barnesville. It rained all that night, the next morning we were on the march. It rained all day and we took the road toward Frederick City; but left it before noon. We crossed the Monocacy river about noon—we also crossed the Baltimore & Ohio railroad at Adamstown and took the road to the Kittocton Mountains, and crossed them about 6 o'clock in the evening, and camped for the night close by the town of Jefferson; we were then about ten miles from Harper's Ferry. We marched through Jefferson yesterday morning, bands playing and colors flying, and passed thro' Middletown before noon. There were several flags waved at us by the young ladies—everybody was glad to see us, even the dogs looked like they were glad to see us come. We can buy anything we want to eat in Maryland at a very low price. I am sorry to say that there are a good many men in this army that will steal from the Union people—so we have to have a guard around our camps when we stop to keep the men from scattering over the country. To-day is Sunday, and the young men for miles around have been visiting our camps. They all pretend to be Union men, and I guess the most of them are.

We are now lying in camp 2 miles from where the battle of South Mountain was fought in September last. We are in the Middletown valley—the finest country I have ever seen in my life. The farmers are cutting their wheat—it looks well. Corn looks beautiful. It looks like a pity to camp on their farms and burn their fence rails, but if they prove themselves loyal to the Government, they can get pay for all damages done by the army.

We can buy all the bread and butter we want cheap. Get good milk for 5 cents a canteen full; butter 25 cents per pound; bread 25 cents per loaf—large ones, weighing 4 or 5 pounds; good warm biscuits 1 cent apiece. I think we will be up in Pennsylvania in a few days, and possibly the Army of the Potomac may give Indiana a call. We are changing our base this time, I hope for good.

When will this war close? Echo answers never—not unless the whole rebel army invades the North, and then it will wake them up. They have been asleep long enough—we want the rebels to get North just as far as possible, and then I think the people will not wait to be drafted.[31]

Wasson's comprehensive letter did leave out a few details. He did not mention the men's sore feet, blistered from long hours on the march, or their aching shoulders from toting heavy, awkward knapsacks. Neither did he mention the sense of dread or the inward shudder that many felt as they passed near battlefields where their friends had died. General Meredith and Lieutenant Colonel Dawes rode over the South Mountain battlefield, where grass covered the graves, now marked by barely legible headboards. Long Sol described how George H. Richardson had given up his career only to be killed in his first fight. Dawes later mused, "What could be more unselfish and noble than the sacrifice this man has made for his country."[32]

There were light-hearted moments, too, especially when it rained and the men became "hilarious and jolly." On June 19th, after reaching Guilford Station, Phraortes Humphreys composed a little rhyme for Sergeant Major Asa Blanchard:

> With joy and delight
> I will try to indite
> A nice little poem for you:—
> At the close of this tramp
> I got hold of a stamp,
> The amount I believe is your due.
>
> I hope you will write
> Sometime tonight
> And let me know if you got this letter
> And if not why not.

Songs and ditties often broke the monotony, but smiles broke out on every face at the sight of cherry trees that bowed under the weight of their fruit. However, the biggest smiles were reserved for mail. The postal system had broken down during this northward march, but on June 20th nine large sacks of long-awaited letters arrived for the eleven regiments in Wadsworth's division. Two days later the Iron Brigade's postal clerk reported that he had mailed 2,041 letters, along with various larger envelopes, books, papers, ambrotypes, and other miscellaneous material.[33]

On June 28th, the men struck their tents and marched through Frederick, remaining there overnight after being greeted enthusiastically by the populace. The column marched next day through a drenching rain to Emmitsburg, a small village near the Mason-Dixon Line. On the morning of June 30th, the 19th Indiana became the first infantry unit from the Army of the Potomac to enter Pennsylvania. A short march brought the Federals to Marsh Creek, where the Iron Brigade camped for the night. Williams's Hoosiers were selected to picket the road ahead, so they crossed the creek and moved up to the tiny village of Green Mount, where the reserve encamped. Companies A, B, C, and E established outposts farther north, where the men could see the outline of a bold prominence, known locally as Round Top. Officers and sergeants began work on the muster rolls and clothing accounts, but much paperwork remained undone and tucked away in pockets for completion later. But it was not all work. According to Lieutenant Finney, "We lived high here. People brought in everything in the way of eatables. Had lots of good fresh milk, a luxury not often indulged in by the soldier." Residents of the vicinity generously filled the Indiana haversacks with turkey, chicken, fresh bread, and pie. Rebels were rumored to be ahead, but no one cared. For that one night it was again fun to be a soldier.[34]

21

Gettysburg

Pennsylvania citizens had warned the Hoosiers that rebels were camped less than ten miles to the northwest, beyond the village of Gettysburg. Early on the morning of July 1st, Colonel Williams received word that Wadsworth's division would march at 8 A.M and his regiment should fall into line as the column marched past. After Williams called in the outposts from his three-mile picket line, the Indiana men got ready to march with "full haversacks and canteens, and with well satisfied appetites." Soon Cutler's brigade and a battery marched by, followed at some distance by the Iron Brigade. The 2nd and 7th Wisconsin passed, then the Hoosiers joined the column in front of the 24th Michigan and 6th Wisconsin. Shortly afterwards, soldiers watched General Reynolds and his staff ride northward toward Gettysburg, where Federal cavalry screened advance elements of the First Corps.[1]

By 9 A.M. cannon fire could be heard ahead. The pace quickened and word passed from officer to officer that the infantry should hurry to assist General John Buford's hard-pressed cavalry. About a mile south of town Meredith halted his column, had the men pile up their knapsacks, and ordered all non-combatants to fall out. According to Lieutenant Colonel Dudley, "The regiment never went into action in such good spirits as it did that morning, and when the battlefield was reached the cheerful songs of the men and the sincerity with which they stripped for action betokened ill for any force of Confederates whom we might meet."[2]

Meredith's Iron Brigade then veered left through gaps in a fence opened by the pioneer corps. Double-quicking to a ridge immediately west of the Emmitsburg road, Meredith's column slowed to quick time and advanced north, crossing the Fairfield road. Moving into a hollow between ridges, the 19th Indiana halted directly west of a large brick structure that proved to be the Lutheran Theological Seminary. Here mounted aides brought word that rebel infantry was advancing along both sides of the road ahead, driving Buford's cavalry and threatening his artillery. Cutler's brigade had already deployed, but now Reynolds ordered the Iron Brigade to attack those rebels south of the Chambersburg road. Lieutenant Colonel Kress galloped to each of the Western regiments, ordered them to fix bayonets and shouted, "You have not a second to lose—the enemy are upon you!"[3]

The 2nd Wisconsin quickly formed into line of battle and charged up McPherson's Ridge into the woods at its crest. Meredith's remaining regiments, except the 6th Wisconsin, which was held in reserve, formed their lines, then advanced in succession to assist the 2nd. The Badgers had struck General James J. Archer's brigade of Tennesseans and Alabamians, commencing a vicious musketry fight. Just as the 19th Indiana finished its deployment from column into line, news arrived that Reynolds had been fatally wounded while urging the 2nd Wisconsin forward. Reynolds was popular with his men and this was a crushing blow, but "the men set their faces resolutely to meet the foe and avenge his death." The Hoosier line swept forward to McPherson's Ridge, followed by a lone corporal, limping along as fast as his blistered feet could carry him. Corporal Conn McGuire, Company G, was so lame that he had been ordered to fall to the rear, but he would not leave and hobbled along to join his comrades.[4]

Rushing forward "with great spirit and celerity" through wheat fields and over fences, the 19th Indiana soon halted under the crest of McPherson's Ridge on the left of the 7th Wisconsin. Buford's cavalry had withdrawn, so the rebels came rushing up the opposite slope "howling like demons." As soon as their heads and shoulders appeared over the crest, the Indiana men fired a surprise volley into the rebel ranks. Then as the enemy recoiled down the slope, Colonel Williams ordered his men forward. Archer's Tennesseans opened fire on the Hoosiers as they crossed a fence on the ridge. "A shower of bullets rained about the colors," more than a dozen minie balls tearing through the new banner. Color bearer Burlington Cunningham fell, shot in the side, and guard Patterson McKinney was hit in the ankle.[5]

Suddenly, there was a loud roar in Company C and Corporal Andrew J. Wood flew three feet into the air. A rebel minie ball had struck his cartridge box, tearing it apart and igniting his cartridges. Wood was rendered unconscious, his hands and face burned black, his eyelashes and eyebrows singed off. Lieutenant Macy jumped forward, stripped off Wood's accouterments and extinguished his burning uniform. This rough handling revived the corporal and Macy ordered him to the rear, then raced after the battleline.[6]

When Cunningham fell with the flag, someone shouted, "Abe, drop your gun and take the flag!" Corporal Abram Buckles, finally realizing his dream to carry the Stars and Stripes, sprang forward, grabbed the flagstaff, and raced down the hill. All at once, the 7th Wisconsin, 19th Indiana, and 24th Michigan gave a yell and rushed forward into the ravine. Not more than seventy-five yards distant from the Hoosiers, the 1st Tennessee, "partly hidden from view by the low shrubbery," held the wooded ravine along Willoughby Run, a knee-deep, pebbly-bottomed stream. Before the rebs could rally, the Iron Brigade had overrun their position. One Alabama soldier recalled that "it seemed to me there were 20,000 Yanks down in among us hollowing surrender." All along the creek, Southern men threw down their muskets and ducked through the Federal battlelines. Without slackening their pace, the Hoosiers smashed the 1st Tennessee, splashed across the run and dashed up the opposite bank.[7]

Organization in the Indiana regiment fell apart during this impetuous charge. Abe Buckles led the attack, waving his banner so far in front that Lieutenant Colonel Dudley had to yell repeatedly, "Come back with that flag!" From his position on the left flank of the 19th Indiana, Frank Huff and other Hoosiers chased fleeing rebels all the way across the front of the brigade. Huff did not stop until he reached a stone quarry on the far bank, to the right and front of the 2nd Wisconsin. There he was struck by a minie ball and fell into the pit, being wounded, bruised, and stunned all at once. William H. Murray boasted, "Our Regiment took the 1st Tenn. Regt except a very few stragglers and the colors." The Tennessee color bearer "broke through the lines and ran up a slope, and when he reached the top he turned and shook the flag at our troops and disappeared from sight." Murray shot at the reb twice, as did others eager to capture a Confederate flag, but the Tennessean eluded his pursuers and escaped.[8]

After their successful charge, the Hoosiers spent about an hour in disarming "most of the officers and men of the 1st Rebel Tennessee Regiment," who had surrendered as prisoners of war. Side arms of the field officers were handed to Dudley, who gave Sergeant Major Asa Blanchard the sword and belt formerly worn by Lieutenant Colonel Newton George. Adjutant Finney and Blanchard headed a detail that took reb captives to the rear, where they were turned over to the 9th New York Cavalry. Returning to the battle ground, Finney's detail then collected rebel muskets that lay seemingly everywhere. Dudley estimated that this detail "destroyed at least 400 stands of arms within the space of an hour and a half." While the prisoners and muskets were being disposed of, Colonel Williams re-formed the regiment and sent his wounded to the Seminary, where brigade surgeons set up their hospital.[9]

Losses in this attack on Archer's brigade were heaviest in the 2nd Wisconsin, which repeated its Brawner Farm feat by attacking a concealed enemy force, then holding its ground until the other regiments could arrive.

The Badgers received the brunt of Archer's fire, which cut down Colonel Lucius Fairchild, Lieutenant Colonel George Stevens, and over one-third of the regiment. Private Patrick Maloney avenged these Wisconsin casualties by grabbing hold of General Archer after his line collapsed. He was the first general officer from Lee's army to be captured in battle. The 7th Wisconsin had arrived quickly on the ridge to Fairchild's left, but Colonel William W. Robinson hesitated. When he finally spotted a rebel flag along the run, Robinson moved his line forward, fired a volley, and charged down the slope. The 19th Indiana and 24th Michigan arrived in turn, producing an avalanche of blows from right to left. The latter two regiments drove off the force in their front, swung to the right, and enfiladed the remainder of Archer's line. While Colonel Williams reported only two or three wounded in this dash to Willoughby Run, the Wolverines met heavier resistance. Colonel Morrow lost his color bearer, several of the color guard, and many good men.[10]

There was never an adequate accounting of the casualties in Archer's brigade on July 1st. Lieutenant Colonel S. G. Shepard, 7th Tennessee, who wrote the official brigade report, stated that only seventy-five of the brigade were captured. Federal accounts suggest a much higher figure. General Wadsworth reported that Archer and "several hundred" of his men were prisoners. Lieutenant Colonel Kress wrote that the Iron Brigade captured Archer and "nearly 800 of his men." Two Wisconsin men, Sidney Mead and Cornelius Wheeler, writing just after the action, suggested a loss in Archer's brigade of 300 and 600 prisoners, respectively. Lieutenant Finney recorded that the 19th Indiana "got about 200 prisoners." Lieutenant Potts, Company C, wrote that "we captured near 600 rebels, breaking their entire line." Combining these accounts with Dudley's statement that the Hoosiers disabled "at least" 400 muskets, leads to the inescapable conclusion that significantly more than seventy-five rebels had been captured along Willoughby Run.[11]

Confederate testimony is even more compelling. An Alabama captain wrote that the Yankees had captured their general, "a considerable portion of the 13th Alabama Regiment, and many from a Tennessee Regiment." One member of the 7th Tennessee recalled that the Iron Brigade captured "nearly the entire right wing of the Seventh Regiment." At one point the 14th Tennessee was nearly surrounded, its colors shot down twice and, according to one veteran, "some of our best men were captured." Chaplain Jaquelin Meredith, 47th Virginia, watched Archer's attack and was shocked when "in a few moments I saw General Archer and two-thirds of his brigade captured." He estimated that the Federal troops took from 600 to 700 prisoners. After considering the evidence from both sides, it is still impossible to arrive at an accurate figure for the number of men captured by the Iron Brigade. But no one could argue with William Barnes's claim: "We went down at them pretty lively and captured a good many, the rest ran away."[12]

After this initial clash, Colonel Williams formed the 19th Indiana on ground recently occupied by Archer's brigade. After chasing off rebel survivors, the Hoosiers and their Michigan comrades traded places, with the former now holding the brigade's left flank. One officer pinpointed this new Indiana line, which "extended from near the edge of the timber skirting Willoughby Run on the left across the level space in the south west corner of McPherson's woods—northward about two hundred and seventy five feet part way up the rising ground until it joined the 24th Michigan, being within the woods but on ground sparsely covered with trees." Colonel Williams sent Sam Schlagle's Wayne County company forward to the creek, where it deployed as skirmishers and commenced sharpshooting at rebels lurking in the distance. About this time men from the brigade guard returned with stories of how the 6th Wisconsin, assisted by 100 men from the guard, had captured a Mississippi regiment north of the road.[13]

The Iron Brigade remained stationary until 3 P.M., kept on the alert by exploding shells and minie balls fired by distant reb skirmishers. An ever-increasing force of Confederates could be seen marching into position during the afternoon, enemy lines extending far beyond the Iron Brigade's left flank. Colonel Williams and Colonel Morrow thought their position untenable should the enemy advance, so they both repeatedly requested permission "to retire to the crest of the hill behind us, and throw up rail barricades." Sergeant Major Asa Blanchard carried the last request to General Meredith, who, "pleased with the clear statement of the situation made by Mr. Blanchard," sent him on to General Doubleday, who now commanded the First Corps. Doubleday listened to the earnest young man, then remarked that he considered the woods the critical point on his line, since it acted as a redoubt on the left flank. The general concluded by saying that "he hoped it would be held." Asa Blanchard responded emphatically: "General, if that is what you want, and the Iron Brigade can't hold it, where can you find troops who can?" Doubleday replied, "Present my compliments to General Meredith and say to him that with the Iron Brigade in possession of McPherson's Woods I have no fear for our left flank."[14]

Doubleday's only order to Long Sol was that he "expected that the Iron Brigade would hold the woods at all hazards." General Meredith requested Wadsworth to send reinforcements to bolster his left flank, boldly proclaiming that the Iron Brigade could then hold their position "until the army arrived, or hell froze over!" Wadsworth promptly sent three regiments of Colonel Chapman Biddle's brigade to strengthen this exposed flank. Aware that an overwhelming force would soon descend upon them, the

Hoosiers clearly saw the wisdom of fortifying a line atop the ridge. According to Adjutant Finney, "The men saw the immense host bearing upon them; they looked along their own thin line, and felt that, though they had been often tried in battle, and had won high honors for their bravery before the foe, anything they had ever done, was nothing, compared to the work now before them." After all their appeals had been exhausted, Colonel Williams grimly announced: "Boys, we must hold our colors on this line, or lie here under them."[15]

At 3 o'clock the storm broke. Colonel Williams shouted to his men, "Fall in!" Hoosier soldiers saw two lines advancing rapidly to attack their front and what seemed like a whole rebel brigade marching to attack the left flank. These attackers were North Carolinians from James J. Pettigrew's brigade of General Henry Heth's division. William Dudley observed that the rebels "moved forward upon us in splendid style, advancing across the oat fields which lay between us in a perfect line." He also noticed Lieutenant Schlagle's skirmishers, recently reinforced by details from Companies D and E, being driven back. Every man would be needed in line, so Sergeant Major Blanchard was sent out to bring them back at once. But it was too late. The skirmishers had been posted in a wheat field to the left front, with orders to hold out as long as possible. They fought bravely, but the North Carolina advance quickly overpowered and captured a dozen men from the skirmish line, including Ben Duke, George Bunch, William Locke, John Markle, and William Castator from Company B.[16]

It seemed as if the Hoosiers were outnumbered by at least four to one and according to one private, "Total annihilation stared us in the face." Officers passed the word to aim low and conserve ammunition. When the rebels reached Willoughby Run, Colonel Williams gave the command to fire. An Indiana volley blasted into rebel faces and their first line disappeared. This musketry, "delivered at such short range and with such terrible effect," kept the enemy at bay. Dudley could later report that "for one hour no Rebel crossed that stream and lived." Minie balls from North Carolina muskets responded in kind. Captain Hollon Richardson, of the brigade staff, watched the fighting on this line and remembered, "Like dew before the morning sun our men wilted away."[17]

Burlington Cunningham had been thought killed during the charge on Archer, but he had his wound patched up and returned to carry the Stars and Stripes that afternoon. Now he went down with a second wound in the right leg, Abe Buckles being hit in the shoulder by the same volley that felled his friend. Sergeant Murray described the carnage: "The slaughter in our ranks now became frightful, beyond description. The dead lay piled up on the ground, and the shriek and groans of the wounded was too horrible for contemplation." One North Carolina officer wrote that "the fighting was terrible—our men advancing, the enemy stubbornly resisting, until the two lines were pouring volleys into each other at a distance not greater than 20 paces." General Heth alluded to the vicious fighting along Willoughby Run when he wrote, "I struck the Iron Brigade and had a desperate fight. I lost 2,300 men in thirty minutes." The general himself was wounded by a minie ball that cracked his skull.[18]

The Hoosier line, along with its Michigan neighbors, held the 26th North Carolina at bay along the stream, but the 11th North Carolina exploited a gap between Colonel Williams's regiment and Colonel Biddle's brigade. Flanking fire from this latter regiment almost annihilated the Indiana men. Williams reported, "My regiment held its position until we had suffered severely from the column on the left and until twenty men lay dead and one hundred wounded along the line." No troops could stand the terrible crossfire that had virtually destroyed all organization in his Hoosier regiment in less than an hour. It became obvious that to stay any longer would be a useless sacrifice, so Colonel Williams ordered his men to fall back from Willoughby Run. His lieutenant colonel proudly remarked, "The line was held as long as there were men left to hold it."[19]

All the dead and badly wounded were necessarily left behind. Colonel Morrow commended the neighboring Hoosiers, who "maintained their first line of battle, until their dead were so thick upon the ground that you might step from one dead body to another." By now the entire color guard had been killed or wounded. As the regiment began to fall back, someone yelled to Lieutenant Macy that the flag was down. He shouted back, "Go and get it!" The reply was, "Go to hell, I won't do it!" Macy and First Sergeant Crockett East, Company K, ran back and tried to put the blue silk flag in its case, but East was shot dead and fell on it. Macy pulled the stained silk from under East's body and started up the hill. Burr Clifford, Company F, threw down his musket and accouterments and took the flag, noticing that the banner had also fallen. He started back, but stopped to furl the colors so that "they would not make so conspicuous a mark." Holding the state flag in his left hand and turning sideways to minimize his exposure, Clifford became the target for rebel muskets:

> almost instantly a Bullitt struck the staff below my hand an other struck my hat an other the left leg just cutting my pants below my knee, an other the right leg just above the knee cutting the pant, also two others cut the tail of my Blouse in the rear.

Seeing no officer nearby, Clifford prudently started back up the hill with the state flag.[20]

15. Battleflag of the 19th Indiana carried at Gettysburg. On the fiftieth anniversary of that battle, the Indiana Battleflag Commission reinforced the torn silk with new backing and, so that the bullet holes might be photographed, marked the white stripes with red dots and the red stripes and blue field with white dots.
From the Carroll County *Citizen-Times.*

Sergeant Major Asa Blanchard had requested and been assigned the duty of detailing replacements from the ranks as color bearers fell, killed or wounded. The lieutenant colonel saw this desperate situation and the "almost impossibility of getting men from the decimated ranks to discharge the fatal duty as fast as necessary" and ran to help. While Blanchard went after another volunteer, Dudley held the Stars and Stripes "long enough to meet the fate of all who touched it that day." A minie ball struck Dudley's right leg midway between ankle and knee, shattering the fibula. In a letter to Blanchard's sister, Dudley described what followed:

> As I lay there with the staff in my hand your brother, his voice trembling with feeling, took the staff from my hand, and giving it to a soldier he had detailed, assisted me back from the line a few feet and said: "Colonel, you shouldn't have done this. That was my duty. I shall never forgive myself for letting you touch that flag." He called to two slightly wounded soldiers and bade them get me out of the fire, and as he left he turned and smilingly said, "It's down again, Colonel. Now it's my turn."

Two men dragged Dudley back over the crest, leaving a bloody smear from his leg in their wake. While removing the crippled officer, one of his bearers was struck by a ball that had glanced off Dudley's side.[21]

When Blanchard saw Burr Clifford walking up the ridge, he ran up, demanded to know why he was running away with the colors and snatched them from his hands. Asa unfurled the flag and began waving it vigorously. Private William R. Moore, Company K, now had the Stars and Stripes, but a bullet took off the index finger of his left hand. He looked about and saw most of the remaining men higher up the ridge, firing over the heads of those lagging behind. He then spotted Blanchard with the regimental flag and yelled that they had better get up the hill. Blanchard, whom Moore considered "a pompous kind of a fellow," ignored the suggestion. Colonel Williams saw Moore's finger gushing blood "about like a chicken's having its head chopped off" and ordered him to give up the banner. He tried to give it to Joe Carder, who was loading and firing vigorously from behind a pile of fence rails, but Carder declined the honor. Corporal David Phipps, Company I, finally took the standard.[22]

Blanchard was waving his flag and crying out "Rally, boys," when a minie ball severed an artery in his groin. Burr Clifford stepped aside to avoid blood spurting from the wound and William Jackson, who stood next to Blanchard, watched in horror as his life gushed away. When Clifford reached for the flag, Blanchard managed to blurt out, "Don't stop for me. Don't let them have the flag." Then with his dying breath, Asa murmured, "Tell mother I never faltered." Clifford glanced back and saw that Corporal Phipps had the banner, then he headed for the crest. The new Stars and Stripes and its staff had been "literally shot to pieces" by the time Phipps fell. Someone ran back, rolled him off the banner and carried it away. Phipps remembered, "I crawled a piece into the wheat field and tried to go into the ground, as there seemed to be no place for me. The earth was all torn to pieces as I lay between the two fires."[23]

A second line had been established 100 yards to the rear, where as many as two or three men took cover behind a single tree. While Meredith was organizing this line, fragments from a shell fractured his skull, an injury that "affected the brain very seriously," and also killed his horse. The dead animal crushed Sol's leg and side, breaking several ribs and tearing them from the breastbone. Captain Henry C. Holloway, of the brigade staff, received a severe wound in the hip while helping to form this second line in the woods. After Colonel Williams abandoned his first line, Colonel Morrow bent back the left of the 24th Michigan to avoid a vicious enfilading fire. The 151st Pennsylvania marched into the gap between Biddle's brigade and the Iron Brigade, but could not stop the rebel onslaught, despite losing over 250 men in forty minutes.[24]

This new line could not hold, so the Hoosiers fell back to a fence near the 7th Wisconsin. Colonel Morrow's Michigan men now occupied a salient, or bulge, in the brigade line, which had now been bent back upon itself. Sergeant Thomas Winset was killed here. Sergeant Murray described the incident:

> I was standing within two feet of him at the time. He fell like a log of wood, and the blood spouted from the bullet hole in his forehead in a stream as large as your finger. He never moved hand or foot but died instantly.

By now Lieutenant Colonel Dudley was being carried to the Seminary building and had lost sight of individuals, but he continued to watch as the Indiana line "gallantly withstood the terrific front and flank fire of the enemy."[25]

On the firing line, sweaty hands slipped off the rammers, so soldiers jammed them against trees or rocks or the ground as they loaded their muskets. Cartridges were almost gone. Survivors had already searched the dead and wounded for ammunition, but there was no more to be found. Suddenly, ordnance wagons rumbled up behind the Iron Brigade and men began to throw out wooden boxes full of cartridges. A few blows from an ax split the boxes open and within minutes three wagon loads, some 75,000 rounds, had been issued. Then the wagons were sent off to safety in the rear, by way of the Chambersburg road, although subjected along the way to a vigorous shelling by rebel batteries. Here occurred one of the few ludicrous incidents during the day's battle. Bert O'Connor, 7th Wisconsin, was driving one of these ordnance wagons when he happened to glance back:

> The team next behind me was driven by an Indiana man. A solid shot struck his saddle mule, cutting off both of its hind legs. I shall never forget the look given by old "Indiana," as we called him, when the poor mule fell down on those stumps of legs. He was ordered to cut the harness and haul his load with the remaining three mules. One of the extra men shot the wounded animal. Before he did so, however, another shot made a flesh wound on the other wheel mule and still another shot away both hind wheels of the wagon. Just then a retreating regiment came along and took the ammunition from the disabled wagon, and "Indiana" drove into town with three mules hauling the front wheels and box of his wagon.

Two other wagons had been hit and badly damaged, but no ammunition was lost. Three ordnance men were wounded. This timely arrival of a new supply of cartridges allowed the Iron Brigade, unlike its Southern counterparts, to continue fighting.[26]

The Hoosiers had ammunition, but the regiment, "now reduced to a mere squad" according to Colonel Williams, had been so reduced that it was forced to abandon the crest of McPherson's Ridge. Hoosier survivors quickly formed on the right of the 151st Pennsylvania and these Federals delivered "a deadly volley" into the Tarheels as they gained the crest. This defiant act halted the rebs, who had exhausted their ammunition and could not finish off the badly battered Yankees. Colonel Williams and the remnants of his once mighty regiment withdrew, "loading and firing," to yet another defensive position at the Seminary.[27]

Pettigrew's Tarheels were content to let them go. The 26th North Carolina, which had fought opposite the 19th Indiana and 24th Michigan, had eleven men shot down with the colors and reported losing all but 216 men out of over 800 who advanced to Willoughby Run. The 11th North Carolina suffered almost as severely while turning the Hoosier flank, its Company C having two officers killed and thirty-four of thirty-eight enlisted men shot down. No matter whether he be Black Hat or Confederate, every man would have agreed with Sergeant William Murray when he wrote, "Oh Maggie, I pray God that I may never witness such another slaughter."[28]

22

Last Stand

When its line on McPherson's Ridge collapsed, the First Corps scrambled for the high ground at Seminary Ridge like a wounded old bear fleeing a pack of dogs. Fragments of the Iron Brigade streamed back to a barricade on the western slope, "semi-circular, convex to the enemy," that had been thrown together earlier by troops from another division. Colonel Williams reported, "I placed the remnants of my command behind a barricade of logs and rails," then added, "here was made out our last and hopeless stand." The rebs did not advance from McPherson's Ridge, seemingly "content from that position to peg away at the boys as they skedaddled toward the Seminary." After retreating about halfway to the Seminary, Major John Mansfield noticed the absence of pursuit, faced the 2nd Wisconsin about and boldly started back for the woods. But when the Badgers spotted a fresh enemy brigade advancing onto McPherson's Ridge, they scattered "as a flock of birds are seen to quit their tree at the same instant" and ran back to the barricade.[1]

To the left of the Iron Brigade, Biddle's brigade fell back from its exposed position in the open fields south of McPherson's Woods. On the right, a shattered brigade of Pennsylvania Bucktails, torn apart during a series of bayonet charges along an unfinished railroad, came running back. Soldiers from all three brigades crouched behind the barricade, got behind trees, or lay on the ground between cannon. The Iron Brigade had no commander after General Meredith fell, because no one had informed Colonel Robinson that he should assume command. Men from different regiments and brigades intermingled, improvising a line out of sheer habit. Despite the shelter provided by their barricade, it was still a dangerous place, where bullets smacked against trees, plowed into the ground or tore through flesh. Corporal Jeff Wasson raised his head over the pile of rails to see what had become of the rebels and fell dead when a minie ball pierced his brain.[2]

Federal staff officers ran upstairs to the Seminary cupola, where they eagerly scanned the southern horizon for any hint of reinforcements. But there were no columns of glittering bayonets, no jangling cavalry following jaunty guidons. To the south and east they saw only the town of Gettysburg and neatly tended fields, albeit dotted here and there with wounded men, stragglers, wagons, and cast-off equipment. There would be no help. Unknown to officers in the cupola, however, mounted couriers were already carrying orders across northern Maryland for the army to assemble. Their message was always the same: "The enemy is at Gettysburg. Reynolds is dead. Get there fast."

Like a coiled spring that has been suddenly loosened, the Army of the Potomac marched toward the sound of the guns. Brigades and divisions instantly started north at a rapid pace, not the herky-jerky, stop-and-start McClellan march, but a get-the-wagons-off-the-road-and-let-us-by gait that left men gasping for breath along the roadsides. Collecting that vast army would take time and that time would have to be won with the blood of men on Seminary Ridge. Lieutenant Earl Rogers saw those soldiers who huddled behind the barricade with the weight of the nation upon their shoulders: "The faces of the men were grim with smoke of powder, dust and perspiration; their canteens, haversacks, blankets, shelter tents, caps and clothes perforated with bullets." These exhausted soldiers must somehow hold the Seminary, whose lower story and grounds were already crowded with dead and dying comrades. If this line at the Seminary could not hold against Lee's next attack, the Army of the Potomac was doomed and "Pennsylvania, New York and New England lay helpless at his feet."[3]

Union defenders had an unobstructed view of the valley between the Seminary and McPherson's Ridge. With shells exploding, minie balls whistling overhead, and officers shouting to rally their commands, suddenly men began to point. Confederate battleflags appeared along the opposite crest and before long the western horizon was filled with ranks of butternut and gray. This was General William Dorsey Pender's division, sent forward to sweep away that pesky remnant of resistance south of the Chambersburg road. General Alfred Scales's brigade of five North Carolina regiments advanced with its left flank near the road. Colonel Abner Perrin's four South Carolina regiments extended the line southward. Far off in the distance, General James H. Lane's brigade advanced around the critical left flank. After passing Heth's division and clearing the woods, Pender's men responded to the order, "Charge bayonets!" Their "flaunting banners" moved forward, the rebs "yelling like demons."[4]

Three batteries had been placed to defend this last Union line and gunners frantically waved infantry away from in front of their guns, now loaded with shell and case shot. Across the road, Iron Brigade gunners shifted three of Battery B's guns so they could blast solid shot lengthwise down the rebel lines. As Pender's division appeared, "Seminary Ridge blazed with a solid sheet of flame." N. B. Prentice, 7th Wisconsin, wrote, "We cut great gaps in their lines which were instantly closed up, yet their columns never faltered." Scales reported that his brigade "encountered a most terrific fire" which "made sad havoc in our line." Colonel Perrin encountered "a furious storm of musketry and shells from the enemy's batteries." Officers behind the barricade screamed at soldiers to hold their fire, these commands being heard by attackers over the roar of cannon.[5]

Carolinians watched helplessly as Yankees behind the barricade "took as deliberate aim as if they were on dress parade." When the rebels reached a fence some 200 yards distant, the "breastworks in front became a sheet of fire and smoke." According to a Wisconsin officer, "their ranks went down like grass before the scythe." Colonel Perrin saw Scales's brigade come to "a dead halt" at the fence, survivors lying on the ground and feebly returning fire. General Scales, now wounded himself, admitted, "Our line had been broken up, and now only a squad here and there marked the place where regiments had rested."[6]

In front of the South Carolinians, Colonel Perrin confessed that "the brigade received the most destructive fire of musketry I have ever been exposed to." Perrin's 14th South Carolina was staggered at the fence and it seemed "as though this regiment was entirely destroyed." The right of Perrin's brigade was stung by Buford's cavalrymen, who had filed behind a stone fence south of the barricade with breechloading carbines and revolvers. Buford's men opened fire "at a range of 50 steps" and the rebs fell "frightfully fast." Behind the barricade, soldiers "used their muskets until by fast firing, they became so hot they were compelled to drop them, when they would take the one nearest them on the ground."[7]

For a minute it seemed that the Federal line would hold, but Perrin ordered the 1st South Carolina to exploit a gap between the barricade and the stone fence. Success in this movement allowed his brigade to penetrate the Union line, then fire north into the infantry and south into the cavalry. To counter this threat, Captain James Cooper, Battery B, 1st Pennsylvania Artillery, fired blasts of double canister, but to do so he caused his immediate front to be cleared of infantry. Other troops on the left, mostly Biddle's men, interpreted this movement from the barricade as a retreat and began to fall back. Dog-tired men simply followed the crowd to the rear and no one could stop them. The end had come and, according to Captain Hollon Richardson, "Further resistance was suicidal."[8]

Troops farther north began to fall back, exposing the right of the Seminary line. Colonel Williams could not see Perrin's successful maneuver on the left, but the general withdrawal north of the Chambersburg road was quite apparent. He reported, "I saw our retreat would soon be entirely cut off, and gave the order to fall back." The retreat was anything but orderly and Williams confessed that "I found it impossible to form my command and we retired, each to care for himself through the town." But the few surviving Hoosiers, "after having started to the rear, returned again to the barricade to pay the enemy one more compliment." Lieutenant Finney summed up their defense of the Seminary with the statement, "In all history there is no parallel to that heroic charge, so desperately made, so determinedly met, so tragically ended."[9]

Pender's charge had lasted perhaps fifteen minutes, but his two brigades had been smashed to pieces. General Scales reported a loss of 545 during the charge, leaving the Tarheel brigade in a "depressed, dilapidated, and almost unorganized condition." The colonel who succeeded Scales could gather only 500 men that night, with "but few line officers, and many companies were without a single officer to lead them." The worst loss occurred in the 13th North Carolina, which lost 150 killed and wounded out of 180 who began the charge.[10]

Colonel Perrin's brigade had likewise been hard hit, taking 1,100 men into the attack and losing about 600. Each of his regiments had lost at least one-third of its number. Every one of the original color bearers was killed, four men being killed and two wounded while carrying the flag of the 12th South Carolina. One participant stated that Company K, 14th South Carolina, entered the fight with three officers and thirty-six men, losing thirty-four killed and wounded. He continued, "Our regiment, the night of the first day's fighting at Gettysburg, stacked 82 guns out of the 472 that went into the fight."[11]

The 7th Wisconsin, which had suffered less than its Iron Brigade comrades, was last to abandon the barricade. Covering the Union withdrawal from the Seminary, these well-disciplined Badgers fought back rebels on their front, right flank, and left flank, losing heavily all the way into town. Sergeant Daniel McDermott was carrying the regimental banner when a charge of canister shattered his ankle and damaged the flagstaff. Comrades placed him atop a caisson and McDermott defiantly waved his flag at the foe as he rode into Gettysburg. Soon the sergeant became separated from his regiment, saw that capture was imminent, and wrapped the banner underneath his shirt and trousers. The regiment thought its banner captured after rebels occupied the town, but McDermott kept his secret hidden while a prisoner. After the battle concluded, McDermott reappeared and the 7th Wisconsin reclaimed its missing flag.[12]

Many First Corps regiments followed the Chambersburg road into town. Lieutenant Colonel Kress described the general trend of the retreat:

> The corps passed through streets, traversing the southern side of
> Gettysburg, under lively musketry fire from the enemy, who then
> occupied a large portion of the town, having driven the Eleventh corps
> into and through it. We inclined to the left after getting through the
> village. Wadsworth's division halted in the fields opposite the main
> entrance to the cemetery on the turnpike to Baltimore.

Rufus Dawes wrote, "There was much confusion; the streets were crowded
with retiring troops, batteries and ambulance trains." Men who failed to keep
up or ducked into buildings quickly became prisoners.[13]

Soldiers were "almost dead with thirst." Sergeant Murray described
one incident when thirsty men stopped to drink:

> At one place, perhaps a hundred were crowded around a well, trying,
> but mostly in vain, to quench their raging thirst. A shell came bursting
> into the midst of the crowd; several were killed outright and many were
> wounded, but the rest scattered like birds from a tree, and in ten seconds
> more not a living soul was there.

William Jackson recalled stopping at a rain barrel, when a shell struck
overhead and scattered bricks on the heads of those assembled below. He
confessed that they moved on "rather *briskly*." Jackson continued his narrative of the retreat:

> As we passed along, the shells were flying so thickly that some dodged down
> into cellars and were captured. I could hear the shot whizzing through the
> air from behind us. One seemed to pass very near my head. It struck not
> many yards ahead of me, plowing up the walk and killing several men.

At several points, women left the safety of their homes to carry pitchers of
water out to soldiers as they hurried to the rear.[14]

Union troops streamed south to high ground around the town
cemetery, where generals attempted to rally fugitives and re-form broken
brigades. The 6th Wisconsin arrived in the midst of this chaos and Lieutenant
Colonel Dawes was dismayed at the sight:

> When I got my regiment to the hill, I found everything in disorder.
> Panic was impending over the exhausted soldiers. It was a confused
> rabble of disorganized regiments of infantry and crippled batteries.

Adding to the confusion was General Thomas Rowley who "had become
positively insane." Dawes watched him "raving and storming, and giving
wild and crazy orders," then gladly furnished a squad of muskets for
Lieutenant Clayton Rogers when he arrested Rowley. This bold act by

Rogers was later approved by the corps commander and Rowley would eventually be convicted of drunkenness on the battlefield.[15]

Upon arriving at the cemetery with his rear guard, Colonel Robinson was directed to take command of the brigade by General Wadsworth. As the regiments gradually sorted themselves out, General Doubleday ordered the Iron Brigade to occupy a neighboring hilltop, known locally as Culp's Hill. Cutler's brigade moved to that point soon afterwards and Wadsworth's division built breastworks on the brow of the hill, remaining in that location throughout the battles of July 2nd and 3rd. When the 7th Indiana reached the front that night, after guarding trains for several days, officers found General Wadsworth nearly prostrated by grief. His despair was understandable, considering that Reynolds was dead, the First Corps had lost well over one-half its numbers and his First Division had been "almost wiped out of existence." One Hoosier remembered, "The General greeted us warmly, adding, 'I am glad you were not with us this afternoon;' and, in response to a remark of General Cutler, 'If the Seventh had been with us we could have held our position,' said, 'Yes, and all would now be dead or prisoners.'"[16]

On July 2nd, Lieutenant Jesse Potts wrote to the *Winchester Journal* on behalf of the Randolph County company and boldly asserted: "We are confident of holding our present position. We have nine men present this morning, ready and willing to revenge the death of their fallen comrades." Although "the shells shrieked fiercely overhead, and the minnie balls from the sharpshooters whistled uncomfortably close," the Hoosiers were not engaged in the battles of July 2nd and 3rd. Old Corduroy's division held Culp's Hill, a relatively quiet section of the Union "fishhook" line, while other units from the Army of the Potomac finished the battle. Devil's Den, the Wheatfield, the Peach Orchard, and Cemetery Ridge would be scenes of bloody carnage, but the 19th Indiana would not be called upon again. Enjoying this change from participant to spectator, Adjutant Finney described the battle's climax on July 3rd:

> Over 300 pieces of artillery were belching forth their missiles of destruction. At the same time the rebel infantry advanced, massed, assaulting our works with a vehemence unparalleled even at Malvern Hill. They were repulsed, and the day closed upon the greatest and most complete victory ever gained by the army of the Potomac.

Decisively defeated at Gettysburg, Lee's army began a long, slow retreat back to Virginia.[17]

Although the 19th Indiana had not been involved in any fighting on July 3rd, one of its officers displayed great courage that day. Captain L. B. Norton furnished details:

On July 3, when the enemy made their furious attack upon our center at Gettysburg, Captain Castle occupied a signal station at General Meade's headquarters, near Cemetery Hill, and remained there on duty after all others had been driven away. His flagmen had also left with his signal equipments, under the impression that their officer had gone with the rest. Having occasion to send a couple of important messages to the general commanding, then at General Slocum's headquarters, Captain Castle quickly cut a pole, extemporized a signal flag from a bed sheet procured nearby and sent his dispatches through under a most galling fire.

Among those dispatches to Meade was one from Gibbon that read, "The enemy is advancing his infantry in force upon my front." This was the first word Meade received about the attack that would forever be known as "Pickett's Charge." Colonel John Stephenson came upon Captain Davis Castle on the night of July 3rd and found him completely prostrated by his exertions.[18]

The 19th Indiana suffered only two casualties while occupying its trenches on Culp's Hill. Sergeant Henry B. Reeves, "a man universally respected," had been detailed to the quartermaster department, but took a musket and rejoined Company H, which had been reduced to two men on the afternoon of July 1st. Mortally wounded by a fragment of shell that broke his skull, he left behind a son, born in October of 1861, who bore the proud name George B. McClellan Reeves. Lieutenant William Macy, who had emerged unscathed from the battle of July 1st, was asleep at daylight on July 3rd when a spent ball struck his forehead, "producing a severe concussion of the brain, but not fracturing the skull."[19]

Upon concluding his report of operations at Gettysburg, Lieutenant Colonel Dudley had great praise for the conduct of Colonel Samuel Williams: "It is due to him and his memory to say that no more courageous or faithful officer ever drew sword than Col. Williams, and his conduct throughout was that of a coolheaded, brave man fully aware of his responsibility for the lives of those under him." Although he emerged uninjured, Williams had two narrow escapes. One ball passed through his hat and another pierced his coat, striking a map in his pocket and lodging in the last fold. The colonel did not extract the minie ball, preferring to keep it as a reminder of his brush with death.[20]

Colonel Williams praised the conduct of his second-in-command:

> Lieut. Col. William W. Dudley was active and fearless in the discharge of his duty rendering most important service at the critical juncture in preserving the integrity of our line, and fell struck by a minnie ball while holding up the colors of the Regiment after their guard had all been killed or wounded.

On July 3rd, while behind rebel lines, Surgeon Jacob Ebersole operated on

Dudley's right leg and removed three inches of the shattered fibula. Gangrene appeared and the leg was removed below the knee on July 9th at Littlestown, Maryland, where Assistant Surgeon H. F. Garver attended to Dudley's care. Colonel Williams also commended the "cool and courageous" Major John M. Lindley, who offered invaluable assistance "in reforming the lines at different times and in cheering on the men." During the retreat through town, a ball struck his hand and saber, resulting in amputation of a finger. Another missile struck his cheek, but just grazed the skin. Dudley eulogized the fallen sergeant major, Asa W. Blanchard: "No braver men fell that day in all the Union lines. Neither the regiment nor the brigade, nor yet the division, could furnish a man to fill his place with equal valor. If it was his fate to die in battle, no grander field nor greater battle, nor more decisive victory could his blood have bought."[21]

Colonel Williams reported that the 19th Indiana went into action with 27 officers and 261 enlisted men, and came out with 9 officers and 69 men, experiencing a loss of 73 percent. Survivors compiled lists of casualties that were sent home to the various Indiana counties and published by local newspapers. These rosters of woe gave the home folks only an inkling of what had happened, but it was enough to plunge entire communities into mourning. Lieutenant Jesse Potts reported a loss of 27 out of a total of 39 engaged in Company C. Of the Delaware County companies, E went in 39 strong and lost 32, while K lost 28 of 39. Lieutenant Julius Waldschmidt listed 16 wounded and missing of 26 in Company G. Colonel Williams finally sent his regiment's official casualty list to Governor Morton on July 30th and included the following message:

> To the friends and relatives of those who have given their lives a willing sacrifice upon the altar of our common country, I tender my heart-felt sympathy. In the hour of their country's need, like *men* they flew to arms, and amid the battle's din and the clash of steel like patriot soldiers died!

Hoosier casualties mirrored those of the Iron Brigade, which reported a loss of 1,212 out of 1,883 engaged.[22]

Corporal Bob Conley wrote to the *Quaker City Telegram* that Company B entered the fight with thirty-two officers and men and lost twenty-seven. The losses were as follows:

KILLED

2nd Lt Richard Jones
Cpl Thomas J. Wasson
Cpl William O. Williams
Pvt John McKinney

DIED OF WOUNDS

Sgt Allen W. Ogborn, arm, died July 18th
Pvt Lot Enix, not specified, died July 5th
Pvt Gardiner Lewis, right knee, died December 23rd
Pvt James W. Whitlow, not specified, died December 12th

WOUNDED

1st Lt Samuel B. Schlagle, both thighs
1st Sgt Thomas J. Crull, right hand
Sgt Charles C. Sater, right arm and shoulder
Cpl Robert G. Conley, face
Cpl Patterson McKinney, left leg
Pvt Joseph B. Bennett, left thigh
Pvt Samuel Bradbury, face
Pvt Joel B. Curtis, left leg
Pvt Francis M. Huff, head
Pvt John Motz, right ankle
Pvt Ambrose Swain, head
Pvt William Sykes, not specified
Pvt Grear N. Williams, right thigh

CAPTURED

Cpl Jefferson Kinder
Pvt George W. Bunch
Pvt William H. Castator
Pvt Benjamin B. Duke
Pvt William M. Locke
Pvt John Markle

Lists of men and their wounds cannot do justice to the injuries inflicted. A few examples may serve as explanation. Charles Sater had his right arm raised when a minie ball struck the middle of the humerus, passed behind the shoulder blade and exited near the spine. While defending the barricade at the Seminary, one of the Pennsylvania Bucktails fired his musket when the muzzle was only three inches from Bob Conley's face. The blast injured Conley's ear and eye and turned the left side of his face black. Samuel Bradbury's facial wound was more serious. A minie ball fractured the upper jaw on the left side of his face and, according to his mother, "the jaw bone came out." The ball that wounded Grear Williams passed through the inner surface of his right thigh, through the left testicle and damaged the penis.[23]

Life-threatening wounds were commonplace on July 1st and surgeons struggled to keep pace with their work load. By necessity, the Lutheran

16. William O. Williams.
Hazzard's History of Henry County, Indiana.

Seminary had been turned into a makeshift hospital, the halls of learning now awash in blood. Assistant Surgeon Abraham Haines was left in charge at the Seminary when other doctors from the Iron Brigade went into town and established hospitals in the railroad depot, court house, and other large buildings. Military Agent Isaac Montfort described the primitive conditions confronting Haines after the First Corps abandoned its line at the Seminary:

> Under his charge were several hundred wounded. He was left without supplies of any kind. Calling upon the Medical Purveyor [of Lee's army] for supplies, he was told that there were none. Finding in the cellar of a deserted house a crock of lard, he filled an empty fruit can with lard—took a sheet from a bed, and tearing off a strip a wick was prepared and soon a lamp was burning. By this light he dressed wounds for the first evening. Having no bandages he went into the town, and entering a house, took from the beds fine sheets, which were soon converted into bandages and lint for his patients.

Haines's patients included the most seriously injured of those wounded on July 1st. His lack of medical supplies was compounded by a shortage of food, leaving the Seminary Hospital destitute in every respect.[24]

Drs. Jacob Ebersole, 19th Indiana, D. Cooper Ayres, 7th Wisconsin, A. W. Preston, 6th Wisconsin, and Alexander Collar, 24th Michigan, treated patients at the railroad depot and in surrounding warehouses. When the Eleventh Corps gave way on the afternoon of July 1st, Hospital Steward

Henry Marsh, who greatly wished to avoid being made a prisoner, excitedly asked Ebersole if he should flee or stay with the wounded. The doctor replied, "Do as you think best, but whatever you do, act quickly." As Marsh grabbed his hat and dashed downstairs, Ebersole yelled for him to ride to safety. Glancing out a window, the doctor noticed his horse, loaded down with saddlebags and blankets, tied to a fence in the street. Just before Marsh arrived, a blue-coated fugitive sprang into the saddle and galloped away. The hospital steward started south on foot. Ebersole saw that seconds later the rebels "were enveloping the town from that side, sweeping past the hospital, and completely filling the streets."[25]

Enemy troops soon invaded the hospital, aimed muskets at the doctors and demanded their surrender. A rebel captain quickly saw that their captives were medical personnel and allowed them to resume treating the wounded. Soon another squad of rebels burst in and demanded again that the officers surrender. When informed that they had captured surgeons, the disappointed rebs ordered them to put up a hospital flag and demanded that the attendants give up their weapons. Overwhelmed by work, the doctors responded, "Give us time!" Although deprived of medical supplies, the hospitals in town at least had food. One warehouse contained twenty-seven barrels of flour, "a bonanza to the wounded soldiers." At one time, General Jubal Early sent his compliments to Dr. Ayres and inquired whether the Yankees would like some whiskey for their patients. Ayres responded, "Does a duck like to swim?" Early sent in two pails full of whiskey, which revived many of the wounded.[26]

Doctors dressed flesh wounds, probed for bullets or amputated limbs, depending upon the severity of injury. Several Hoosiers ended up on the operating table. Corporal Conn McGuire, who had hobbled into the fight against Archer's brigade, lost his left leg below the knee. William P. Wilson was a Wayne County boy, but served in Company F, where he had reached the rank of first sergeant. His military career was cut short when a Badger doctor removed his left leg midway between ankle and knee. Isaac Hughes, Company E, lost his right arm. Perry Rowe had enlisted in Company G, but served as a detached volunteer in Battery B after October 1861. While acting as a cannoneer on the No. 1 gun in the right section, Rowe received a severe flesh wound in the right leg, but remained at his post. A few minutes later, another bullet shattered both bones in his lower left leg, rendering amputation necessary.[27]

Among all of the Hoosier casualties, John Miller's wound seemed somehow a little special. Frederick Miller, who lived on Bear Creek in Randolph County, had seven sons, four of whom enlisted in Company C of the 19th Indiana and one who joined the 69th Indiana. His eldest son had a family of three children and chose not to enlist, while another boy had been crippled as a child. Fate was not kind to the Miller family. Daniel, serving in the 69th Indiana, was shot in the left shoulder at the battle of Richmond, Kentucky, on August 30, 1862. Of the sons in Company C, William died on September 7th of wounds received at Brawner Farm. Jacob was killed at Antietam and left a widow and two orphaned children. Christian was wounded in the right arm at Antietam. John, the last Miller brother in uniform, had just been wounded in the right shoulder at Gettysburg. Thus the Miller family sent five brothers off to war, burying two and welcoming home three crippled veterans.[28]

After Henry Marsh left the railroad depot just ahead of the rebels, he found the 6th Wisconsin on Washington Street. Marsh remembered, "I followed them out of town with the rebels firing at us from each side of the street." He then told how he rejoined the regiment:

When we arrived at Cemetery Ridge, General Wadsworth was sitting on his horse, on the slope. Seeing "Nineteenth Indiana" on my hat, he said: "There is your flag," pointing to Burr N. Clifford and the flag. When I came up to Clifford he showed me the bullet holes in his clothing and hat, but he had no flesh wounds. The flag staff was splintered and the flag punctured with bullets.

Marsh was sent south on the Baltimore road to where the slightly wounded from Wadsworth's division were being assembled at a white church. A neighboring house and barn, supplemented by thirteen large tents, completed the hospital.[29]

The arrival of hospital wagons allowed medical personnel to make these patients relatively comfortable. They were placed on straw ticks and a small supply of clothing was handed out to men who "had nearly all their clothing torn off, being covered with blood." On July 7th, Isaac Montfort and a party of assistants arrived at Gettysburg with clothing, medical supplies, and wine, the first such stores to reach the battlefield. Supplies began to pour in when the railroad was finally repaired on July 8th and Montfort returned with "almost everything that could be wished for or needed—socks, shoes, drawers, handkerchiefs, towels, jellies, wines, vegetables, fruit, bread, butter, &c." Henry Marsh distributed all these sanitary stores and witnessed "the change from blood-clotted, filthy garments to clean and white, from 'hard-tack' to fresh light bread, from salt pork to fresh mutton." He believed that these sanitary stores had saved hundreds of lives.[30]

Wounded men were shipped off to general hospitals as soon as they were able to endure a train ride, but sometimes they strayed outside of military channels. Lysander D. Trent, Company I, had been shot three times, but remained lying on the battlefield until July 5th. He was found by the ambulance corps and carried to the home of the Harper family, where he received his first food since being wounded. Trent was then taken to the court house, a First Corps hospital, on July 10th, but was shipped to Baltimore the next day. In Baltimore, a kindly passer-by arranged to take Trent into his home, where his wounds were finally treated:

I was placed on a bed upstairs and soon a lady came with water, sponges, soap and towels, and I was thoroughly cleansed. I had three wounds, one in the hip, one in the limb, and one in the knee. My pants were matted with blood and had been on for twelve days, as my wounds had not been dressed till this time. That woman dressed them every six hours for weeks. When she had first dressed them and was leaving the room she said, "You be a good boy and I will be a mother to you." When she closed the door I cried like a child.

Trent remained with his benefactors until December 3rd, enjoying better care than his comrades ever experienced in army hospitals.[31]

Many of the First Corps prisoners, some of them slightly wounded, had been assembled near where the Chambersburg road cuts through Seminary Ridge. Early in the afternoon on July 3rd, General A. P. Hill rode up and addressed some 200 of these men. He offered them the option of accepting a parole or being sent south to prison. Captain Robert Hughes of the 2nd Wisconsin spoke up and pointed out that the offer might be invalid on technical grounds. But no one wanted to see the inside of a rebel prison, so the captives unanimously agreed to accept a parole and wait to be regularly exchanged. Captain Hughes took command of the parolees and was instructed to march them to Carlisle, where he would report to United States authorities.[32]

This "Limpy Brigade," supplied with a worn-out wagon to carry the most seriously wounded, began its long tramp to Carlisle that same afternoon. Along the road, these paroled men met numerous Pennsylvania militia organizations hurrying toward Gettysburg to fight the rebels, who had already abandoned the battlefield. Corporal Robert Patterson remembered, "Our souls were gladdened by the sight of 'Old Glory,' when we arrived at the quaint old town of Carlisle." After supper, the men were placed aboard hog cars and shipped across Pennsylvania to West Chester, where an improvised hospital had been fixed up for the men from Gettysburg. Bob Patterson was amazed by this strange civilian world that he had not experienced for two years: "I recall my fear and shame on meeting the neat and natty little female nurses, one of whom seated herself by my cot, finally bringing my dirty and swollen foot with a soft thud into her snow-white lap."[33]

After an investigation, Federal authorities declared that the paroles given on July 3rd had indeed been invalid and the men were simply returned to duty without being exchanged. But many soldiers went their own way, either never reporting to the West Chester Parole Camp as ordered or deserting shortly after their arrival. Over thirty of the 24th Michigan prisoners headed for Detroit without waiting for the formality of a furlough. Of the six Wayne County boys captured on the skirmish line July 1st, at least three—Bill Locke, Bill Castator, and Ben Duke—went home. Jeff Crull, Company B's orderly sergeant, wrote of them: "thay had better come back as soone as posible or thay will be arrested and treated as deserters. thay had not the least business to go home from their not any more than to leave the company."[34]

All Federal prisoners had been offered a parole by the rebs, but most refused, having the attitude that those who accepted were "foolish." Many thought that the only honorable course was to remain in enemy hands. So thousands of captured Yankees marched to Williamsport, Maryland, where they crossed the Potomac on July 10th. The column reached Staunton, Virginia, on the 17th and on the 19th the rebs began to ship their captives to prison camps in Richmond. Some soldiers from the 19th Indiana were among this crowd, including seven men from Company K. Of these seven, six were paroled after staying just one night at Richmond. Elijah Brewington was accidentally separated from the rest and left behind. Samuel Dickover wrote of their abandoned friend: "It is a pretty hard place to live down there. I dont suppose that Lige will ever get away before the war is over. If he will, he will be a lucky boy. We was lucky boys for getting away as soon as we did." Indeed they were lucky. Not only had they emerged unharmed from the battle at Gettysburg, but they escaped unscathed from a captivity that would kill more of their comrades.[35]

23

Back to Virginia

The surviving Hoosiers spent their Fourth of July holiday doing nothing, lying behind their breastworks on Culp's Hill and thanking God they were still alive. A few officers started off to visit the battlefield of July 1st, but were stopped in Gettysburg and ordered back by the provost guard. In Indiana, citizens of Cambridge City, Long Sol's hometown, celebrated an old-fashioned holiday, complete with an over-long oration by Governor Morton. During his speech, Morton pointed to the platform where hung the Stars and Stripes riddled by rebel musketry at Brawner Farm and declared: "Look at that battle shattered flag. The sad news comes to us today that more than half of what remained of that gallant regiment have met a soldier's and a patriot's death in the battle now going on." Questions about the slain would not be answered until July 5th, when Hoosiers went to the battlefield to bury their dead. After four days of decomposition in a hot July sun, the bodies were in a horrid, offensive condition. First Sergeant Crockett East had swollen so badly that he could be identified only by his chevrons. Published accounts refer to Lieutenant East, but he technically was an enlisted man during the battle. Although commissioned second lieutenant in Company K on April 24, 1863, his army paperwork did not arrive until July 3rd, two days after his death.[1]

The Iron Brigade was not idle for long. On July 5th, it left the Culp's Hill line and marched to a large open field south of town. Then it was off in pursuit of the rebel army, retracing its route south into Maryland through Emmitsburg and Middletown, where the brigade turned west toward South Mountain. This road over the mountain was little more than a bridle path, so narrow in spots that only two men could march abreast. The Hoosiers marched "up, up, up for a long time" until they reached the summit, where they had a magnificent view of the valley to the west. Halting on the western slope, Indiana men built breastworks to protect their camp, a practice that would now become almost routine. Much like the ancient Roman legionnaires, the Iron Brigade had learned that its most important weapon was a shovel. Soldiers quickly discovered that tearing down a rail fence and covering it with earth made a solid defensive line with only a minimum of effort. Officers and senior noncoms took advantage of this halt in the pursuit to begin work on the June 30th muster rolls, a task greatly complicated by the fact that many records had been carried on the persons of men now dead or prisoners.[2]

The Indiana soldiers were not far from the enemy, as two Company K men soon discovered when they went foraging. After wandering some two miles from camp, they spied a house across a stream. William Murray swam across, leaving behind his friend, who could not swim. He walked boldly into the house and sat down at the table where the family had gathered for dinner. A few minutes later four armed men, either rebel stragglers or guerrillas, burst in and sat down at the same table. After a lady gave him some bread and butter, Murray, who was not armed, promptly paid her for the food, "then sprang suddenly from the door, quick as thought, round the corner of the verandah, and was off for the creek like a shot." The startled rebs ran for their horses. The swift-footed Murray recalled, "By that time I was at the creek, and jumped in, and swam and waded across, managing to keep hold of my bread and butter." The horsemen reached the stream, but hesitated because Murray had said Federal troops were camped nearby. When the pursuers turned back, Murray and his comrade ran back to camp, huffing and puffing between bites of fresh bread and butter.[3]

The Army of the Potomac had cornered Lee's army at Williamsport, Maryland, a few miles northwest of the Antietam battlefield, so the 19th Indiana marched through Boonsborough to Funkstown in the rain. Private William Jackson wrote that "the water fairly came down in torrents but still we moved on over muddy fields and through rapid running brooks." Heavy rains raised the Potomac River, effectively trapping the rebs in Maryland. The Pennsylvania campaign had left Wadsworth's division "ragged and shoeless." On the pursuit to Williamsport, Old Corduroy gathered shoes from houses along the road and passed them out to needy soldiers. At one point he halted at a blacksmith shop where a farmer had taken his horse. Addressing the farmer, Wadsworth said, "My men are without shoes; we can't stop to get them now. Won't you give your boots to one of them?" The civilian refused, whereupon the general declared that he must take the place of a soldier without shoes. Wadsworth directed a passing man to give up his musket and accouterments. A grinning soldier unslung his knapsack, but the disgusted farmer suddenly saw wisdom in Wadsworth's demand

and handed his boots to the barefoot man. How the soldiers loved that old general![4]

Everyone expected a battle at Williamsport, but on July 14th news arrived that the enemy had escaped over the river into Virginia. Turning south, the Iron Brigade marched through Crampton's Gap and halted near Berlin in a familiar spot. One veteran recalled that they "encamped on the same farm and within one hundred yards of our last camp in Maryland last fall." Twice rebels had invaded the North and twice the 19th Indiana had lost heavily in repulsing those offensives. But no matter what their sacrifice, the war continued to drag on.[5]

After Antietam, Little Mac had acknowledged the Iron Brigade's special status by assigning the 24th Michigan to reinforce it, thereby retaining a distinctive Western organization. After Gettysburg, General George G. Meade, who had succeeded Hooker immediately prior to the battle, showed no such sympathy. He, too, assigned a new regiment to the brigade, but his choice could not have been more discordant. On July 16th, the 167th Pennsylvania reported for duty. These reinforcements, 800 strong, "nearly as many as the entire brigade previously," had no place in the Iron Brigade. The new arrivals were *Easterners* who had been *drafted* into a *nine months regiment*. While the Black Hats were thrown into a meat grinder at Gettysburg, these Pennsylvanians sat on their butts in a safe and comfortable Virginia camp. The veterans had absolutely nothing in common with these new members of the brigade and spoke of them only with contempt.[6]

The brigade was up early on July 18th, crossed the Potomac at Berlin and marched to Lovettsville, then on to Waterford. Here the Hoosiers had a wonderful surprise. Rebel sympathizers had held a grand dance for soldiers in Lee's army when it passed through a few days earlier, but now Union citizens responded by throwing a party for the Iron Brigade. Cut off from the real world for two years, soldiers had become accustomed to stag dances, but at Waterford "they enjoyed the novelty of a real dance, with real, live girls for partners." One happy participant recalled, "Those who could trip the light fantastic fixed themselves up in fine style and had a most enjoyable time." This merriment was tempered by the loss of Old Corduroy. Depressed over the progress of the war and commanding a division now reduced to less than a brigade, Wadsworth had asked to be relieved. His request was granted, effective July 17th, and he started for Washington.[7]

Leaving Waterford and its pleasant memories, the brigade continued on to Hamilton, where fifteen Hoosiers were assigned to the picket detail. Poultry stealing had commenced in earnest after reentering Virginia and that night was no exception. One of the picket detail promised that "the chickens will suffer tonight." On the 18th Colonel Williams's regiment marched over what Lieutenant Finney called "the crookedest road I ever saw." One enlisted man agreed that it was indeed "the roughest and most crooked road imaginable." After dinner the Indiana soldiers "again moved off zigzag to almost every point of the compass over hills, through fields, and fording Goose Creek where it was waist deep to the men." Thoroughly tired out, they halted near Middleburg, "one of the rankest rebel towns" in Virginia. A trooper from the 3rd Indiana Cavalry dropped by for a chat, but came away in a depressed mood:

> Yesterday I visited the "Iron Brigade" and found that gallant command but a sorry remnant of its former self. On inquiry for two acquaintances belonging to the 19th Indiana, I was told they were both killed at Gettysburg. Peace to the ashes of Lieutenant Dick Jones and Sergeant-Major Asa Blanchard.

The column did not move next day, so the men celebrated their layover by picking blackberries.[8]

Continuing south, the brigade passed through White Plains, George-town, and New Baltimore, where the Hoosiers had camped the night before their Brawner Farm fight. Memories came rolling back as they turned west to Warrenton, stopping just short of that town on July 24th. This pleasant Virginia countryside had changed dramatically during the past year. Accord-ing to Private Jackson, "the curse of rebellion is laid heavily on town and country, no sign of improvement, no growing crops but briars and bush are overrunning field and farm, desolation has taken the place of prosperity." The regiment, about eighty present for duty, marched to Warrenton Junc-tion on the 25th and encamped. On the 28th a work party of forty men began building block houses along the Orange & Alexandria Railroad, a task that kept them busy for three days. July 29th marked the second anniversary of the 19th Indiana's muster into Federal service, leaving the men with but twelve months to serve on their enlistments. There was no celebration by the "tired, ragged and dirty" soldiers, only a wish that "we had our nice 'Sunday ("go to meetin") clothes.'"[9]

There was no healthy water at Warrenton Junction, only "pond or Bog water," so the brigade was ordered to march to Rappahannock Station early on the morning of August 1st. But the Pennsylvania conscripts refused to fall into line. With the connivance of their officers, soldiers claimed that their enlistments had expired and they should be discharged. General Lysander Cutler, who had succeeded Wadsworth, was in no mood to bargain with mutineers. He ordered his three Wisconsin regiments into line, had them load their muskets and gave the commands, "Ready!" and "Aim!" Then Cutler instructed the 167th Pennsylvania to fall in. Quite sure that the steely-eyed veterans would kill them where they stood, the conscripts fell into line "with great alacrity." As the Pennsylvanians marched away, no-nonsense Cutler ordered the 6th Wisconsin to follow them and shoot anyone who straggled. After describing the despicable affair, Lieutenant Finney wrote with disgust, "They should be sent home."[10]

The weather at Rappahannock Station was described as "Hot.—Hotter.—Hottest." On Sunday, August 2nd, Private Jackson wrote, "O how warm, the sun beams down warm enough to roast one alive—the men are lying around in the shade, panting." Work was curtailed during the heat wave, much to the soldiers' delight. Jackson described their simple lifestyle: "Well, this is a real gypsey way of living. We occupy a small grove, have nothing to do but lay around, sleep, cook and eat." Picket duty south of the Rappahannock was the only distraction from camp life. Naturally, a truce prevailed on the Iron Brigade front. Jeff Crull explained why:

> our Picketts and the rebel picketts are with in two hundred yards all the time and do not fire on one another at all for there is no use in it, it is only a waiste of amunition to no purpose whatever. at least I never could see any good from it.

On August 10th, Colonel Williams received a letter written by Captain George W. Greene from Libby Prison in Richmond, Virginia. Greene wished to inform the regiment that he, Captain Alonzo Makepeace, Captain Patrick Hart, and Lieutenant Harland Richardson had all been captured at Gettysburg and taken south. This news brought a collective sigh of relief since none of these four officers had been seen since the retreat and many thought at least some of them were dead. Joy again swept through camp on August 12th when the 167th Pennsylvania was mustered out and marched away for good.[11]

August 13th was a busy day for the Indiana soldiers. Activities began early when a pre-dawn cloudburst inundated the camp, forcing men to crawl from their tents in search of high ground. Across the river, sunrise disclosed that foragers had been busy under cover of the storm. An ox belonging to Mrs. Mary Jameson had been stolen and butchered, the thieves making off with both hindquarters. Since the brigade picket line ran through Jameson's yard, immediate suspicion centered on members of the picket detail. A quick search disclosed a Hoosier, Corporal William H. Green of Company D, frying beef in a skillet as another man watched. Green was promptly arrested and held for trial. He wisely asked Captain Orr to represent him at his court-martial. Orr called Lieutenant Lewis Yeatman and Corporal Milton Blair as witnesses for the accused. Both men testified that Green had not left their tent during the night. Faced with this ironclad alibi, the court had no choice but to find Corporal Green innocent. If not guilty, Green probably was at least involved in the outrage, but veterans would do anything to protect their comrades, even if it meant lying to officers at a court-martial.[12]

August 13th also marked the appearance of a handsome piece of sheet music. H. N. Hempsted, composer of the "Light Guard Quickstep," which honored a Milwaukee militia unit, had been contacted by Wisconsin officers and urged to compose a tune that would similarly glorify the Iron Brigade. Hempsted seemed agreeable, but he insisted on selling advance copies at fifty cents each. When the officers agreed, Hempsted created the "Iron Brigade Quickstep." A "brilliant title" page contained engravings of General Meredith and Colonels Williams, Fairchild, Bragg, and Robinson. Michigan men were miffed that Colonel Morrow had been slighted, but the order had been placed before the 24th Michigan was accepted into the brigade and that omission could not be corrected. One Badger officer commented, "The music was not so pleasing to the ear as the Light Guard Quickstep, but the name sold it, and I understand that it has the second best record on sales of all of Hempsted's compositions." Lieutenant Colonel Dawes dismissed the piece as "not worthy of its name." Nevertheless, hundreds of copies were sent back to Indiana and Wisconsin, where families listened proudly to the patriotic march.[13]

On August 17th, the 19th Indiana held its first dress parade in more than two months, a ritual the men had not missed since it required appearing with clean clothing and equipment. Soldiers were most concerned with serving out their time and speculated on their chances of doing so uninjured. Jeff Crull pondered that he had just over eleven months and weighed his odds:

> Probably the most of that time will be in winter quarters so I think that I will get along very well. we may have to fight some hard Battles this fall yet but I think not. I hope not any ways.

About this time Henry Gordon returned from Gettysburg where he had been tending the wounded. Gordon brought word that Gardiner Lewis was doing well and that "when the rebs had him prisner he saw a good manney of his old north carlina friends." It is quite possible that one of his Tarheel friends fired the ball that shattered Lewis's knee, then stopped by to chat about the good old days back in North Carolina. What a senseless war![14]

Up to this point, Indiana citizens had followed the 19th Indiana's illustrious career through newspaper accounts and private correspondence. Now the regiment had an opportunity to write its own history. The Indiana General Assembly, during the 1862–1863 session, had passed a resolution that instructed the state librarian to collect and arrange the names of Hoosier soldiers who had died or would die during the war, along with any details surrounding those deaths. This collection would be called *Indiana's Roll of*

17. Jesse N. Potts.
From the Craig Johnson Collection. Used by permission.

Honor. On March 6, 1863, David Stevenson announced to Indiana's citizens that he proposed publishing a volume by that name, including accounts of the various regiments and "a complete list of our brave soldiers who have died from sickness or fallen on the battlefield." Stevenson then stated, "My aim shall be to do *justice* to the *living,* and to embalm in the hearts of Indiana's sons the memory of the *patriotic dead* who have fallen in defense of our national Government."[15]

On March 23rd, Stevenson announced that he would gladly receive "truthful statements" of Indiana valor and gallantry. He emphasized his determination "to avoid *fiction* and adhere to *fact*" and promised to donate a large share of the profits to benefit the widows and orphans of Hoosier soldiers. Adjutant George E. Finney was selected to prepare a historical sketch of the 19th Indiana and he began work on August 23rd. Lieutenant Jesse Potts acted as Finney's assistant. Work on the regiment's history continued off and on, as other duties allowed, through October. When published in 1864, Stevenson's *Indiana's Roll of Honor* contained Finney's history of the 19th Indiana from its organization up to August 1, 1863. Minor errors in the text seem to indicate that some editing by a person not familiar with the regimental officers had occurred. Finney's narrative was supplemented by biographies of Lieutenant Colonel Alois Bachman and Captain James Drum. A brief sketch of Major Isaac May appeared later in the volume.[16]

As the first anniversary of their Brawner Farm battle approached, the celebrated Iron Brigade was but a pathetic remnant of its former self. A soldier from the 7th Wisconsin described the four veteran regiments as they came into line for Sunday inspection:

> There was the prompt and clock-like *Sixth,* in its best apparel, burnish and bright, looking as it always does, well, with less than two hundred men. Then look! there is the old *Second,* at the tap of the drum! You see the same saucy, jaunty happy tread but less than one hundred men, dressed in line, and ready for inspection. As far as they go, they never looked better.
>
> Then at the call comes the *sturdy Seventh,* moving steadily into line, *firm* as a rock, *stalwart men,* with *iron hands* and will, who look and act *defiance.* Less than two hundred bristling bayonets are all that remain of the *eight hundred* a year ago to-day. Then the 19th Indiana Volunteers showed less than one hundred and fifty of their handsome Springfield rifles. *And there it is!*

The first division had been so reduced that it took nearly all the men left to perform routine duty.[17]

Quoting an article from the *Indianapolis Daily Journal,* a Richmond editor presented the following commentary on a hard-won reputation:

> The 19th Regiment, of which General Meredith was the first Colonel, has been nearly all shot away, literally shot to pieces. It has now less than 100 men for duty, not quite a single company, of 1,046 who went out at the start, and 200 recruits added since. If all the wounded and absent were in camp it would still number less than 300. No regiment in the service, from any State, can boast of more battles or more gallantry than it. No regiment in the world has seen more deadly perils or met them more bravely.

Despite the terrible ordeal through which they had passed, the Hoosiers were determined to finish the job they had undertaken. Charles W. Hartup expressed the common sentiment: "The remaining 'Corporal's Guard' of the old 19th are in good health and spirits, and ready for any emergency."[18]

Adjutant Edward P. Brooks, 6th Wisconsin, estimated the fighting strength of Gibbon's brigade on August 15, 1862, to be about 2,500. The 24th Michigan brought another 600 men to the battleline after Antietam. Small detachments of recruits added a few more men to the brigade total, a sum that could not have surpassed 3,500 soldiers. From Brawner Farm through Gettysburg, nearly 3,000 Black Hats had been either killed, wounded, or captured. Hundreds more had been discharged, their bodies broken down by disease and exhaustion. Brooks estimated that "of those hit in action twenty out of every hundred were killed." If the mortally wounded were included, he figured that over thirty percent died as a result of enemy fire. Referring to a long string of Union defeats and tarnished victories, Brooks declared proudly: "We claim to be as good fighting material as this country affords, and if the army to which we are attached has not always been successful, we have the satisfaction of knowing that we have *always* whipped the line in front of us."[19]

Another Wisconsin soldier proclaimed his belief that the Hoosiers and Badgers "have killed and wounded a rebel, or Johnny, as they call them, for each and every man that left the State within their ranks." Anyone who disputed the assertion was advised to go to the battlefields where they could "see the 'graybacks' laying loose around." While the Iron Brigade had "a record beyond reproach," no veteran longed for the "awful experience" of combat. Such nonsense was rookie posturing and newspaper bravado. But if another clash should become necessary, the old hands knew exactly what to do. Gone was the impetuous recklessness of their youth, now replaced by hard-won knowledge that "safety is best had by steadiness, persistence in firing, and most of all by holding together." Any lingering doubts they had about the importance of John Gibbon's training had now vanished.[20]

24

Along the Rapidan

 The Iron Brigade remained in camp near Rappahannock Station, "doing picket and fatigue duty, constructing rifle pits and earthworks to command the approaches to the railroad bridge." This lull in active campaigning as both armies recuperated after their Gettysburg losses brought a return of the old army vices. There were but few recreational activities that the chaplains could endorse and "nothing to read in the army but trash and newspapers." Boredom meant that drinking and gambling reappeared in earnest, with officers arranging high-stakes horse races as occasional diversions. Although there was a truce on the picket line, shells and minie balls still screeched and whined through Iron Brigade camps. There was no danger, however, because pranksters had learned to perfectly imitate the sounds of projectiles after having heard them so often.[1]

Gentlemen from Indiana, Michigan, and Wisconsin who resided in Washington had decided to honor the Iron Brigade by presenting it with a distinctive flag. Noting that this magnificent flag was on display in the store of Tiffany & Co., the *New York Times* described it as "a fit and elegant tribute to the heroism of one of the most glorious organizations in the entire army." One man offered the following description of the Iron Brigade flag:

> It is of heavy blue silk, regulation size, and surrounded by a yellow fringe. The staff is of ash, stained brown and is surmounted by a spear. In the centre of the flag is an eagle with outstretched wings, bearing in his talons a scroll with the motto, "E Pluribus Unum." Above the eagle, in golden letters, are the words, "Iron Brigade," while in graceful scrolls appear the names of "Gainesville," "Antietam," "Bull Run," "Fredericksburg," "South Mountain," "Gettysburg." In the corners are inscribed "Second Wisconsin," "Sixth Wisconsin," "Seventh Wisconsin," "Nineteenth Indiana," and "Twenty-fourth Michigan." The embroidery is the finest ever done in this country, and shows as plain on one side as the other.

A committee of officers assembled at Colonel Robinson's headquarters on September 6th and made plans for a ceremony suitable for accepting this generous gift. They decided that September 17th, the first anniversary of their Antietam battle, would be a suitable date for the presentation. A finance committee solicited funds for a grand festival, while invitations went out to high-ranking government officials and generals associated with the brigade's service in the Army of the Potomac.[2]

Construction began immediately. A work party erected a large arch, decorated with evergreens, and signs which read "Iron Brigade" and "Welcome Guests." Behind the arch and in the midst of a grove of trees carpenters built a 100-foot-long banquet hall, complete with plank floor. Tables, benches, and a speaker's stand completed the interior arrangements. A nearby level space was converted into a track suitable for racing horses. Among the guests who had promised to attend were Secretary of the Interior John P. Usher, Commissioner of Patents David P. Holloway, and Alexander W. Randall, Wisconsin's first war governor. Arrangements had been made for a special train to carry distinguished guests from Washington to Rappahannock Station for the jubilee.[3]

Lieutenant George Breck was an interested observer of all this hustle and bustle. He expressed his opinion that no organization deserved such an honor more than the Iron Brigade:

> Their record is eloquent of the highest courage, the most heroic deeds, the most patriotic devotion. They have been first and foremost in the hottest and most sanguinary conflicts, going in some instances, where other troops who were supporting them, did not dare to go, charging the enemy at the point of the bayonet, up steep banks and rugged hills, in strong entrenchments and formidable rifle pits, routing and discomforting the foe, capturing flags and whole regiments of the rebels. But all this has not been done without a terrible sacrifice of life, as the diminished ranks of the brigade give plain and sad evidence.

Breck noted that the Iron Brigade "has been associated with the Army of the Potomac since its organization, has grown up with it, and as one of its officers remarked, will probably expire with it."[4]

Army headquarters made no concessions for such special ceremonies and orders came for the brigade to march at 5 A.M. on September 16th. The men broke camp at the appointed hour and, although "considerably provoked" at missing the presentation, marched past Stevensburg and halted near Culpeper Court House. When W. Y. Selleck, Wisconsin Military Agent, arrived with the flag, he was shocked to discover that the brigade had marched away. Undeterred, Selleck continued on to Culpeper, taking along with him food prepared for the party and, most importantly, the liquid refreshments. Since everything was on hand, the committee on arrangements determined to hold their program at 4 P.M. on September 17th, as originally scheduled. Several wagons were dispatched to Culpeper to pick up the food and drink, while some 200 men hastily constructed tables in a grove near camp. Although the excursion of prominent guests from Washington had been canceled, they were not really missed. At the appointed hour, the five Western regiments and their comrades in Battery B formed three sides of a square, inside of which stood Generals John Newton, commanding the First Corps, James C. Rice, commanding the First Division, and John C. Robinson, commanding the Second Division, along with a large number of staff officers.[5]

After some introductory remarks on the distinguished career of the Iron Brigade, Agent Selleck handed the flag to Colonel William W. Robinson with the following remarks:

> In behalf of the citizens of Wisconsin, Indiana, and Michigan, resident in Washington, I present to you this flag. Take, protect and preserve it; may your future be like the past, brilliant and glorious, and may you be spared by God in his providence to once again witness a united and happy country, enjoying peace, happiness and prosperity.

Robinson responded to Selleck's brief speech with a much longer oration that first recounted the sacrifice of the 19th Indiana and the three Wisconsin regiments:

> During the past thirteen months these regiments have stood shoulder to shoulder more than twenty days under the enemy's fire; in one stream has mingled the blood of their comrades slain—poured out like a willing sacrifice in the cause of our suffering country.

He then alluded to the 24th Michigan, with its "disposition common to the younger boys of a family to imitate the feats of the elder brothers." After acknowledging the splendid career of Battery B, staffed primarily by Iron Brigade volunteers, Robinson observed: "The feeling existing in the several regiments is that of mutual confidence in each other; perhaps no body of troops ever possessed this feeling to a greater extent.[6]

At one point in his address, Colonel Robinson alluded to a band of ghosts who also had gathered to witness the flag presentation:

> If it be true—as we trust it is—that the spirits of the departed have cognizance of the affairs of this life, then the balance of our brigade, the commander we miss, whose life-blood moistens the sods of Virginia,

Maryland and Pennsylvania, are now marshaled near us in the bright uniform of the heavenly corps to which they have been transferred, witnessing with approving smiles the ceremonies of this occasion.

After concluding his speech, Robinson handed the new flag to the 2nd Wisconsin's color sergeant and that regiment escorted it to brigade head-quarters. Then officers rallied on the tables and enjoyed a "sumptuous feast" suitable for a first class hotel. After their meal, toasts and speeches followed in rapid succession.[7]

W. Y. Selleck read letters of regret from several generals who had been invited to attend, but could not accept for various reasons. Fighting Joe Hooker proclaimed, "I have seen and heard nothing but good of them. Ever valiant in their encounters with the enemy, and faithfully and devotedly loyal in preparing for them." Hooker concluded his letter by stating, "With a clear apprehension of the principles involved in the pending struggle, they have been as true to them as the Old Guard ever was to Napoleon." If there was polite applause for this message, imagine the wild response to General McClellan's letter, which had been written on September 14th:

It happens to be precisely one year to day since I first saw them in action, at South Mountain, and with the recollection of their superb bearing brought thus freshly to my mind, I feel renewed in my heart, the pain of separation from them and their comrades.

But say to them that my heart and prayers are ever with them, and that, although their new colors can witness no more brilliant acts of patriotism and devotion than those which the old torn flags have shared in, I know that on every future field, they and the whole Army of the Potomac, will maintain on their part, the honor of their country and their colors.

Even after many months of official banishment, Little Mac still had the power to reach out and touch the hearts of soldiers who had worshipped him while he commanded the Army of the Potomac.[8]

Captain Eminel P. Halstead, one of General Rice's staff officers, started the toasts by proposing, "The Iron Brigade," which was drunk to loud cheers. Selleck offered a toast, "The non-commissioned officers and privates of the Armies of the United States," which was responded to by General Rice, who said:

To the non-commissioned officers and privates we owe every-thing. To the First Corps alone at Gettysburg, do we owe the result of that battle; to the rank and file of that corps who stood so many hours, beating back the tremendous odds thrown against them, holding the enemy in check until the troops came up and formed in position on the field; to that corps and its indomitable pluck, the nation owes its most grateful thanks.

Other toasts were given to the president, invited guests, and Generals McDowell, McClellan, Hooker, Meade, Newton, Rice, Robinson, Wadsworth, Meredith, Gibbon, and King. Then General Robinson stood up and offered the toast, "To the memory of that brave and gallant soldier, Major General John F. Reynolds." Every man within earshot rose, removed his black hat, and drank in silence.[9]

After their catered supper, enlisted men crowded around and listened to the speeches, but kept an eye out for alcohol. One man remembered that "the rank and file got what they could swipe, which was no small amount." No one noticed that it began to rain shortly after the meal. Lieutenant Colonel Dawes wrote that, with only a few exceptions, "the officers of this brigade and the Generals and staff officers within any convenient distance of us were almost unanimously drunk last night." Lieutenant Finney agreed, writing, "Everybody nearly was drunk." Another man called the ceremony a "drunken spree." Soldiers from other commands graciously pitched in to help the Iron Brigade celebrate, with the result that "there was scarcely a sober man in the Second Brigade." Sutlers had obtained special permits to sell whiskey for the evening and nearly everyone participated in the debauch. No one protested; the Iron Brigade had earned its party.[10]

Later that evening, some drunken men from the 14th Brooklyn tried to exact some revenge for a long-forgotten boxing match. While Rufus King's brigade had occupied Arlington Heights, Private John H. Bowman, Company C, 6th Wisconsin, had challenged any man in the Army of the Potomac to whip him in the ring. Some Brooklyn boys brought forth a professional fighter, but Bowman thrashed him soundly and embarrassed the New Yorkers, who undoubtedly had bet heavily on their champion. Now, almost two years later, flowing whiskey rekindled old memories and brought the matter to a head. Taunts and curses flew back and forth between drunken Iron Brigade men and their inebriated comrades in the Second Brigade. Finally, Black Hat privates fell into line of battle "with no arms, but bent on a fist fight" to protect the brigade's honor. A brawl was averted when the 7th Indiana deserted their Eastern comrades and fell into line with the Iron Brigade. New Yorkers and Pennsylvanians "felt discouraged and quietly retired."[11]

Incredibly, the stock of liquor had not been exhausted by this all-night binge, so September 18th was also marked by "a great deal of drinking," accompanied by several fist fights. Two days later, after everyone had presumably sobered up, wagons loaded with the Hoosiers' winter gear, which had been stored in a Washington warehouse, arrived in camp. It was a timely arrival, one private recalling that the "overcoats feel quite comfortable" in the crisp autumn air. But there were far more knapsacks and blankets than there were men to carry them, a none too subtle reminder of the losses sustained in 1863.[12]

Soon after this flag presentation, General Rice tried to correct some obvious deficiencies in his division. He first tackled a problem that had dismayed General Gibbon some sixteen months earlier—improper etiquette by men on guard duty. According to Rice, "The general notices that the guards of some of the Regiments do not face correctly in saluting and do not present arms correctly, while many of them do not salute at all." Emphasizing that soldiers needed to conform to Army Regulations, Rice declared that "no commissioned officer should pass a soldier who fails to properly salute him without at once correcting the failure." This lax attitude resulted from a blurring of the line between commissioned officers and enlisted men. Colonel Williams and Major Lindley had both been captains when they entered the service, but nearly every other officer present at this time had risen from the ranks. Of the eighteen line officers, two had started as second lieutenants, one as hospital steward, two as first sergeants, nine as sergeants, one as a corporal and three as privates. Having served in the ranks, these veterans had experienced firsthand the army's fascination with insignificant details and overlooked much after having been promoted to positions of authority.[13]

General Rice also discovered that these iron men were slobs. He still found it necessary to issue basic sanitary guidelines. Rice commanded each colonel "to thoroughly inspect his Camp daily and see that the sinks are made deep, that they are properly masked from view, and that they are covered at least twice a day with Earth, also that all offal, refuse meat and filth of all kind in the vicinity of the Camps be at once destroyed by fire." A medical inspector reported that policing of the Hoosier camp was only fair and their sinks were bad. Hoosier surgeons, whose duties included overseeing sanitary affairs, came in for additional criticism when the inspector discovered that medical supplies were missing, records were incomplete, and even the surgical instruments were in "bad condition." Of course, temporary improvements were made, but no permanent change in behavior resulted from such inspections and the same problems would reoccur.[14]

On September 24th, the Iron Brigade marched to the Rapidan River and occupied some old camps between Raccoon Ford and Morton's Ford. The rebels were so close that Indiana pickets could hear drum calls and bands of both armies. On the 29th, the tents were moved back a mile or so to near Pony Mountain. Encouraged by an absence of hostilities, Federal foraging parties began to harvest the standing Virginia crops. One party offended the reb picket line when it began to gather corn from a field close to its position. The rebels, who "did not like to see their corn taken so unceremoniously," persuaded a nearby battery to fire some shells at these Yankee thieves. Exploding shells created a panic among the teamsters, who lashed their mules in an effort to escape. No lives were lost, but one wagon was smashed during the stampede. A Hoosier concluded that "this will learn our boys better manners."[15]

Affairs in early October centered around the veteran question. In an effort to keep the various armies staffed with trained soldiers, the War Department had published General Order No. 191 on June 25, 1863. Under its provisions, any soldier between the ages of eighteen and forty-five who had served at least nine months and could pass a physical examination was eligible to reenlist as a "veteran volunteer." This new enlistment would be for three years or during the war. Every veteran volunteer would receive one month's pay in advance, plus $400 in bounty and a $2 premium, the bounty being paid at intervals over his enlistment period. If the veterans were not required to serve their full term, they would still receive the entire sum. A service chevron would be issued to each veteran and would be worn as "a badge of honorable distinction." Every man who reenlisted would also be granted a thirty-day furlough.[16]

With no end to the war in sight, administration officials began a serious push to reenlist those soldiers whose three-year terms would expire in the spring and summer of 1864. They wished to avoid a repetition of 1863, when many two-year regiments left the service, some in the weeks just previous to the battle at Gettysburg. By offering the twin "flattering inducements" of a large bounty and a furlough home, the government hoped to keep their best men in uniform. A test vote taken in the 19th Indiana on October 5th revealed that four-fifths of the eligible men would reenlist. That same day, Chaplain W. R. Jewell of the 7th Indiana explained why Colonel Williams's regiment should be sent back to Indiana to recruit:

> The 19th has fought itself nearly all away, and had better be sent home, for as long as there is a live piece of it, that piece will be found fighting when there is any fighting to do. The live piece that is left now is small, but better material is not to be found in the army.

While the bounty money was a small fortune to most men, the government's insidious lure of a trip home after an absence of almost thirty months was overwhelming, especially when rumor claimed that they might remain "two, three or more months." So many men seemed inclined to reenlist that the common salutation in Hoosier camps became, "How are you, Veteran?"[17]

This veteran question caused many soldiers to gravely consider their options. None pondered them more seriously than did Captain William Orr. Although he had shared the universal depression that followed the battles of Fredericksburg and Chancellorsville, the Gettysburg victory had given him hope. By September 28th he could write:

> But, I now believe that we will yet *Conquer*. It will take time, *perhaps a long time*. We will meet reverses. But we will eventualy reestablish the Government.

Orr's optimism did not extend to his own regiment. He confessed, "The 19th is played out. We can never again muster 200 men for duty." As senior captain present, Orr had acted as a field officer since July 1st but saw no chance of advancement. Despite his valuable experience, two captains— Makepeace and Hart—outranked Orr, although they were confined in Libby Prison, and could expect to be promoted ahead of him. Whenever Makepeace and Hart returned, Captain Orr would resume command of the dozen men in Company K, no fit position for an ambitious and talented young officer. But he still felt compelled to see the war through to its conclusion and wrote to his wife, "I know you would not want a man who would Back Out, and leave the gallant boys who had followed him to so many Bloody fields."[18]

Everything remained quiet along the Rapidan until October 10th, when the First Corps advanced as if to cross the river. But a new rebel offensive had been discovered and that night soldiers built large fires to deceive the enemy, then marched back to Pony Mountain. This retrograde movement continued on the 11th and at sundown the Iron Brigade crossed the Rappahannock at Kelly's Ford. The 19th Indiana left Kelly's Ford at 12:30 A.M. on the 13th and marched until 10 o'clock that night, when it finally halted at Bristoe Station. Colonel Williams had the men on the road again by 6 A.M. and his column crossed a portion of the Bull Run battlefields before wading across Blackburn's Ford. The brigade halted near Centreville at noon on the 14th and occupied entrenchments that commanded the Warrenton Turnpike.[19]

General Solomon Meredith, who had been absent since Gettysburg, returned to the Iron Brigade on October 16th to officially relinquish his command. No longer physically able for duty in the field, Meredith was relieved by Special Order No. 273, Headquarters, Army of the Potomac, dated October 17, 1863. To mark the occasion, Long Sol received the following testimonial:

> It would be an affectation of stoicism that we do not possess, to permit the severance of the ties which have existed between us, without

an expression of the sentiments of affection & esteem which we entertain towards you.

It was our fortune to enter the service at nearly the same period, to
be joined in the same organization, and to do battle as comrades on
many a bloody field. Casual acquaintance has ripened into esteem &
affection, and the ties, which bind us, have been cemented by the blood
of the brave.

It has been your good fortune Sir, to receive from the Government
a recognition of the services of yourself, and your gallant 19th Ind., and
it has been our good fortune, to be placed under the leadership of our
comrade in arms.

While this latter has existed, harmony has prevailed among us, we
have been cared for, as by a paternal hand, yet discipline has not
slackened, nor has the lustre of our arms been dimmed.

We fought beside you in the bloody campaigns of 1862, and under
you in the campaign of 1863. Our affection has not been weakened, but
strengthened, and our confidence in your ability & capacity has grown
firmer & more abiding, as each new emergency has proven that it has not
been misplaced nor imprudently given.

We shall deeply feel your loss, and whatever may betide you in life's
journey, you may carry with you, the pleasing assurance, if it be one,
that you have the respect, confidence & affection of the Iron Brigade
of the West.

Sol's testimonial was signed by all the brigade's officers, every one of them a
combat-hardened veteran. This was not empty flattery, but a genuine
expression of love for a man who had left a comfortable situation to serve his
country. Despite John Gibbon's harsh assessment of Long Sol's capabilities,
he had grown into the office of brigadier general. Never given an opportunity
to distinguish himself with an independent command, Meredith nevertheless
provided the Iron Brigade with solid, consistent leadership throughout his
tenure. All things considered, Meredith had developed into a fairly competent commander.[20]

Centreville was in the middle of a once prosperous, but now utterly
depressing region of Virginia. One writer described the sights visible along
the retreat:

Many desolate homesteads marked the way, through fertile fields rich in
nothing but luxurious weeds. Black ruins and naked chimneys pointed
out the desolating track; decaying head-boards and nameless heaps of
fresh-piled earth told their tale along the way.

Centreville itself, "a desolate looking place," contained but a dozen old
houses, only a few occupied, and a stone church crumbling to ruins. Blackened
chimneys marked the spots where other buildings had once stood.[21]

General Lee's flanking maneuver had been thwarted, so now it was Meade's turn to chase the rebel army. The Hoosiers struck their tents at 4 A.M. on October 19th, packed up and ate breakfast in a rainstorm. Marching at daylight, the Iron Brigade headed west along the Warrenton Turnpike, passing over the battlefields of Bull Run and Brawner Farm. The latter was of particular interest to veterans who had fought there, as well as to recruits and Michigan men who had listened to tales of the battle ever since joining the brigade. As they went by, "many of the officers and men could not resist the temptation to fall out and view the ground whereon they fought their first battle."[22]

Discipline was forsaken while soldiers wandered the fields where they had lost their boyhood so long ago. They were nauseated and horrified to discover "scattered about on the ground, the bones of human beings who not many months since were living, acting mortals, possessing reason, intelligence, and all the attributes of an immortal being." One man remembered:

> On coming upon the field where the battle was fought, the sight was indeed sickening. Lying about in every direction were the bleaching bones and ghastly skulls of the men who fell in that memorable fight. The rebels had but slightly covered the dead with earth, which was quickly washed off by the heavy rains, leaving the bodies fully exposed to view.

Here could be seen the protruding skeleton of an arm and hand, "the upper part of the fleshless arm covered with an old tattered sleeve which fluttered in the breeze." There could be seen "a human skull in all its ghastliness," near where "legs and arms lay dried and bleaching in the sun." But these were not just any bones, they were the mortal remains of friends, buddies, tentmates, and euchre partners. They had drunk from the same canteen, slept under the same blanket, shared their pilfered food, and laughed at the same stupid jokes. Then on the night of August 28, 1862, whizzing rebel minie balls came and randomly took some of them forever, leaving only these bones and scraps of rotten wool. Veteran enlistments lost their luster when men realized that this, too, might be their own fate if they chose to stay in the army.[23]

Their morbid curiosity satisfied, Hoosiers regained the turnpike and marched on to Gainesville, where the column turned right to Haymarket. Halting in open fields near that small village, the Western men had just finished supper when they were ordered to fall in at once. A force of rebels had slipped past General Judson Kilpatrick's cavalry at Buckland Mills and the division seemed to be surrounded on three sides by a lively skirmish fire. When the commander of the Federal picket line gathered up those men conveniently nearby and retreated, one of the Iron Brigade detachments was overlooked. Unaware that the line had withdrawn, Lieutenant Christian M. Prutsman and forty men from the 7th Wisconsin continued a vigilant watch. Seeing some rebs stealing sheep, the Badgers went after them and, of course, disclosed their presence. An overwhelming line of grayback skirmishers advanced and Prutsman prudently withdrew, "disputing the way from tree to tree." When the Wisconsin men tried to rally on their reserve, they ran into more rebels and had to surrender.[24]

Jeff Crull told how the Hoosiers went to the rescue, only to miss a fight and spend an uncomfortable night in the woods:

> I was then sent out with our company but they skedaddled. I saw several of them but did not get to shoot any of them. I Stayed out all night with my Company and did come very nigh freezing for when we went out we expected to have a cavelry fight and Left our Knapsacks In camp so we had to do with out our Blankets that night and It was very frosty and we could not build any fires until daylight and then we found all the rebels had gone.

While the Iron Brigade marched through Thoroughfare Gap on the 20th, the Hoosiers stayed behind and acted as rear guard for the First Corps. Sergeant Crull offered a terse view of the campaign's strategy: "Old Lee tryed to flank us and get In the rear of us but Meade beet him and then we went out to fight him but he retreated too fast so we Lay In the bull run mountains at Presant."[25]

On October 24th, the Iron Brigade marched at 7 A.M. "through heavy rain, wading flooded streams and deep mud." From Thoroughfare Gap the route led through Haymarket, Gainesville, and Bristoe Station to Brentsville. Soon after they halted, the soldiers were urged to hurry supper because orders had come to retrace their steps to Bristoe. That news resulted in a torrent of curses directed at those fools at headquarters who had misdirected them. They had already waded Broad Run and Kettle Run, now they would have to wade them again on the return march, but orders had to be obeyed. According to one Badger, "When we camp at night the Iron Brigade is about played out." Coupled with their shocking discovery at the Brawner Farm battlefield, this stupidity had a "decidedly unhealthy" effect on reenlistments.[26]

Black Hat veterans were fed up with taking all of the risks and making all of the sacrifices. Private John Parshall, Company D, explained that they had not wavered from their original intention: "We have stained nearly every farm in this part of Virginia, with our blood, for peace. We do not beg or plead for peace; but, by force of arms, *demand* it." But Parshall asked if the old soldiers were to be left in the field to carry on alone:

> The question now arises from the army to all friends, brothers and countrymen: shall we fight five years more, or will you come and help us to get through in one year? Shall we, who have come out to defend our homes, lives, rights, and property—shall we all die martyrs before your faces and in your sight, and you never raise a hand to help us out?

He then assured potential recruits that the veterans would willingly share their secrets of survival, an advantage the volunteers of 1861 had never enjoyed. Parshall concluded his appeal with a challenge: "So come out and join our little band—make hundreds of our tens; then we will show the rebel graybacks, that Yankee boys are MEN!"[27]

25

The Veteran Question

 By November 1st, much work had been completed on the new National Cemetery at Gettysburg. Robert Corson, one of Indiana's military agents, had visited the site and discovered it to be "beautifully situated in the rear of the present Cemetery, commanding a splendid view of the valley, the town and the battle-field." Graves had been located, bodies disinterred and placed in new coffins, then carted to the cemetery where they were reburied, with the government contractor receiving $1.59 for each set of remains thus moved. The new graves were arranged in a vast, tastefully landscaped semicircle, soldiers from each state being buried together. Elaborate plans had already been made to consecrate the cemetery and the next day President Lincoln would be invited to speak at the November 19th ceremony.[1]

The Brawner Farm dead, however, received no special attention. On Sunday, November 1st, General Cutler sent to the old battlefield a detail from each regiment that had fought there in 1862. All exposed remains were carefully interred. By diligent search, survivors could identify many of the dead, either by where they fell or by unique marks on rotted clothing and leather gear, thereby removing all doubt as to the fate of some of those still listed as missing. What now seems to be a grisly task was actually a coveted honor for the burial parties. A Wisconsin man explained why: "With loving hands they were given decent sepulture, and we knew that they would thereafter sleep more peacefully, and felt a comfort in having been able to perform for our dead this kindly office which had so long been neglected."[2]

What did the soldiers think of these contrasting burials? Lieutenant Frank Haskell, one of General Gibbon's aides during the brigade's first four battles, strongly objected to moving the Gettysburg dead to where they would be "wedged in rows like herrings in a box." But his greatest criticism

was that the soldiers were buried "on a spot where there was no fighting."
The lieutenant offered his opinion on the proper burial place for a soldier:

> But what so appropriate for the soldier's rest as the spot where he died
> nobly fighting the enemies of the country—where perhaps the shout of
> victory went up with his spirit to Heaven—where his companions in
> arms, his survivors, had lovingly wrapped him in his blanket, and wet
> with brave men's tears, had covered him with the earth his blood had
> consecrated.

Another Iron Brigade man asked the simple question, "Is it not just as well
to remain where first we are placed at rest?" Old soldiers certainly thought so.
But the establishment of national cemeteries was just one of the first steps in
tidying up the war. Civilians understood cemeteries and needed those orderly
rows of graves to help them cope with their loss. On the other hand, soldiers
understood battlefields and would have been content to wander where each
footstep might have trod on a comrade's grave.[3]

Lysander Cutler's concern for the dead at Brawner Farm was only
matched by his outrage at the living. On November 2nd, the old general raged
against Iron Brigade marauders who had stolen hogs and chickens from Mrs.
Mitchel Rosebury at Brentsville on the stormy night of October 24th. The
offense particularly irritated Cutler because Mitchel Rosebury was confined in
a Richmond prison for voicing Union sentiments and his wife was seriously ill.
The brigade commander demanded to know who was responsible:

> The property stolen and taken was of the value of at least one hundred and
> fifty dollars. Unless within the next twelve hours from the receipt of this
> order, that sum is furnished at these Head Quarters, to be paid to Mrs
> Rosebury, and the guilty parties arrested and turned over for punishment,
> with the evidence necessary to their conviction, proceedings will be
> instituted against the officers to whose commands the men are known to
> belong. It is a shame and disgrace to the service and the men, that such
> acts are committed, and still more disgraceful to the officers, that they
> occur in their commands. The plea sometimes raised by officers that they
> cannot detect the guilty, is only an evidence that they connive at the
> marauding, or are entirely unfit for the commands they hold. It is an
> admission that they have no control over their men or do not choose to
> exercise it. They deserve more severe punishment than the men and will
> receive it if any efforts on my part can procure it for them.

Mrs. Rosebury told the general that the men who carried off her chickens
and hogs wore a "6" on their black hats. This was a personal affront to Cutler,
who had been the 6th Wisconsin's first colonel, and he set out to identify and
make an example of the offenders.

The 6th Wisconsin immediately came "under a cloud." Guilty Badgers tried to shift the blame onto their Hoosier friends, who would "remove the figure 1 from their hats and by inverting the 9, were able to pass as the old 6th and make themselves the terror of the country." Cutler was not fooled by this defense, nor by an unsatisfactory explanation from Colonel Edward Bragg. He continued to pound away: "It is not possible that so much plunder could come into the camp and all the officers and men be ignorant of the fact." In an effort to ferret out witnesses, Cutler threatened: "If there are men or officers who do know and choose to remain silent, they become parties to the crime and have no cause of complaint if they are made to suffer therefor."

When no one confessed, Cutler decided to play detective. He sent for Private E. C. Jones of Company E, 6th Wisconsin, and questioned him about the Rosebury theft. Although Jones claimed not to know the thieves, he did admit that he had seen a man carrying half of a pig into camp. Cutler pounced on this information and commanded Jones to identify the culprit. After some hesitation, Jones confided that it was Pete, Cutler's Negro servant, who had carried off the purloined pork and cooked it for the general's supper. Cutler was so stunned by this revelation that he abandoned his investigation. The affair blew over without a man being punished or a cent being paid to the Roseburys. Years later, an officer of the 6th Wisconsin admitted that "the dare-devils of that regiment killed the hogs, cooked and ate them almost under the general's nose, and what was left was smuggled into Col. Bragg's headquarter wagon."[4]

After this embarrassing conclusion to the Rosebury affair, Cutler worked himself into a towering rage. He lashed out at an easy target on November 3rd:

> The degrading and disgraceful habit of gambling among the officers and men of this command prevails to an alarming degree. The General Commanding has no desire to prevent any proper amusement among those under him but on the contrary desires to encourage it. Gambling is not of that character. If officers forget themselves and lose their self respect, so far as to become gamblers, they have no right to set the evil example before the men entrusted to their care. The indulgence in the practice has become so habitual that officers neglect their duties, remain away from their camp and quarters to indulge in it, and in some instances it is found do not hesitate to indulge in the lowest tricks of Blacklegs.

Cutler promised that if officers continued their gambling, offenders would be charged with "conduct prejudicial to good order and military discipline," a court-martial offense. He promised to suspend quartermaster and subsistence officers found gambling and to report them to the War Department.

Cutler's attempt to stop "the demoralization of those under him through the influence of this vice" was admirable, but he might just as well have tried to stop the sun from rising.[5]

Ten Hoosiers sidestepped General Cutler's wrath by being sent home on November 2nd to recruit for their companies. The soldiers in this recruiting party and their destinations were:

Company A 1st Sgt James L. Mitchell, Anderson
      "   B 1st Sgt Thomas J. Crull, Hagerstown
      "   C 1st Lt William W. Macy, Winchester
      "   D 1st Lt Lewis M. Yeatman, Plainfield
      "   E Sgt Edwin O. Burt, Muncie
      "   F Sgt David M. Fisher, Indianapolis
      "   G 1st Lt Charles K. Baxter, Waterloo
      "   H 2nd Lt Joseph W. Scarborough, Seymour
      "   I 1st Sgt Clinton Johnson, Freedom
      "   K 1st Lt Joseph P. Carder, Selma

Everyone else was jealous of these lucky men, who would undoubtedly stay home in Indiana at least through the holidays. Arrival of these recruiters was usually noticed by local editors. The *Palladium* mentioned that Sergeant Crull would accept recruits in Hagerstown and urged, "Now is the time to enlist in a regiment that has on every field of battle so gallantly bore up the Old Flag of beauty and of glory." Despite such encouragement, few men signed up. Prospective volunteers thought their chances of survival were better in regiments with less glorious histories.[6]

The Hoosiers sustained one casualty while camped at Bristoe Station, but it was not due to enemy fire. A Company C private was badly wounded by the explosion of an artillery shell he was playing with and his recovery was thought doubtful. On November 5th, the Iron Brigade marched down the railroad to Catlett's Station, a pleasant little village the Western men had once guarded while serving under McDowell in 1862. The 19th Indiana acted as guard for the corps wagon train, its march delayed by wagons bogged in the mud or broken down in the road. At dawn, the Hoosiers were shocked by the transformation at Catlett's Station:

> Now nothing but charred ruins and ghostly looking chimneys mark the places of those pretty cottages. Not a fence, barn, nor scarce a vestige of timber remains.

The "horrid desolation" at Catlett's Station was just one example of how geographical landmarks had simply disappeared from the Virginia countryside.[7]

Their march resumed at sunrise on November 7th and the Iron Brigade headed for Kelly's Ford. Troops ahead had allowed campfires to get into the grass and trees, so both sides of the road were lined with smoking fires that added to the discomfort. After Meade's army crossed the Rappahannock, Lee's army had taken up a new defensive position south of the Rapidan River. So the First Corps recrossed the Rappahannock, camped at Beverly Ford, and began to build winter quarters.[8]

Troops worked at repairing the Orange & Alexandria Railroad or rebuilding forts along its right of way. But the officers had the toughest job of all. One Hoosier captain confessed that "the hardest duty an officer has to do is to keep these 2 year veterans at *work*." On November 19th, the regimental sutler brought much-needed relief in the form of a whiskey shipment. He could legally sell alcohol only to officers, but through their generosity the whiskey successfully trickled down to many enlisted men. Typical sights of drunken soldiers and fist fights ensued.[9]

November 19th also brought the dedication of the National Cemetery at Gettysburg. Although no living members of the 19th Indiana attended this ceremony, Governor Morton, the "Soldier's Friend," represented his Hoosiers. General Gibbon and Lieutenant Frank Haskell represented the Army of the Potomac and had with them the Iron Brigade flag. Despite a vast array of dignitaries, Gettysburg's great cemetery was yet unfinished and many of the dead still lay in their original graves. Only thirty-one Hoosiers, nine of them from Colonel Williams's regiment, had been reburied in the Indiana section.[10]

Berry Sulgrove, editor of the *Indianapolis Daily Journal,* had journeyed to Pennsylvania to cover the dedication for his paper, but he found "the great surging crowd . . . made it impossible for anybody but those closest to see or hear." Although probably unheard, one stanza of a hymn written for the occasion by B. B. French explained that the civilians needed a shrine where they could mourn:

> Here, where they fell,
> Oft shall the widow's tear be shed,
> Oft shall fond parents mourn their dead;
> The orphan here shall kneel and weep,
> And maidens, where their lovers sleep,
> Their woes shall tell.

Soldiers were not particularly interested in the cemetery. While Edward Everett's classical oration roared and crashed over the crowd, Gibbon and Haskell got bored and wandered over to Cemetery Ridge. After reliving their parts in the battle for a small group of avid tourists, the two officers walked back just in time to hear President Lincoln's little speech.[11]

18. Samuel B. Schlagle.
From the Craig Johnson Collection. Used by permission.

Gettysburg's legacy continued to impact the 19th Indiana long after the fighting. Lieutenant Samuel Schlagle had been shot through both thighs and lay on the field for four days, during which time the rebels stripped him of his blanket, shoes, and hat. After a period of hospitalization in Philadelphia, he went home to heal. When Long Sol finally agreed to vacate his position as Clerk of Courts, influential Wayne County citizens urged Schlagle to run for that office. Although barely able to get about on crutches, he accepted. The *Richmond Palladium* endorsed his candidacy:

> The soldier has fought for us, he has been disabled from further service in the field, and cannot again resume the occupation followed by him before the war, and now let us show him that his sacrifices are not to be forgotten, and that the reward of bravery and devotion to the cause of the Union, is to be commensurate with the services he has rendered the country in the hour of her trial.

Thinking his candidacy had been announced too late, Meredith at first advised Schlagle against seeking the office. But support for the lieutenant mounted quickly and Sol cheerfully offered his endorsement, writing, "The brave men of the 19th regiment have never deserted me, and while life lasts I will not desert one of them." No viable alternate candidate emerged and Lieutenant Schlagle was elected in the October 13th election. He tendered his resignation from the 19th Indiana on October 20th and it was accepted

November 23rd. Schlagle was sworn into office as Wayne County Clerk on March 19, 1864, but he never regained his health and died of consumption on January 21, 1866, at the age of twenty-nine.[12]

A unique communication arrived in late November from Gettysburg prisoners confined in Richmond. On November 22nd, some 19th Indiana enlisted men locked up on Belle Isle sent a letter to the Hoosier officers in Libby Prison:

> There is three of us here on the Island, Brasier, Brewington & Stockoff, and we wish you to do us a favor, that is by sending to the Regt for a Box of hard Bread a few lbs of Pork Coffee Sugar Salt Peper Soap Tea Rice & Tobacco and oblige and we will pay you well for your trouble and oblige us.
>
> P.S. Also Please send 1/2 of a Chease

Next day, Captain George W. Greene wrote to Colonel Williams and enclosed the above letter. Greene's message read:

> We have just rec'd the within enclosed note from men of the 19th now on Belle Isle. And in conformity with their request—forward for your action. Of their necessities we have no doubt and believe that the circumstances demand our approval and best endeavors for their relief. We therefore submit the matter for your consideration—believing that your action in the premises will be much as will render perfect satisfaction to all concerned. There are yet eight—in all—of our Regt. on the Island. Viz. S. P. Brasier "I." Elijah Brewington "K." Geo. Stockhoff "H." Jas. Denver. Jno. O'Conner. Danl McKerin. & Frank Ford. "F." Jack Oliver, "D." We recommend that all be included in the articles that may be sent. Hard Bread, Pork, Coffee, Sugar, Soap, and Tobacco are the most essential, others if convenient. Direct to either of us and we will use our best endeavors to see that a proper distribution is made of all the articles.
>
> P.S. Give compliments to all friends, and let us hear from you soon.

Packages sent south for Hoosier captives had to be marked, "For ———, Prisoner of War, Richmond, Va." on the lid. Each side of the box had to be marked, "For Indiana Prisoners of War, From Gov. O. P. Morton, of Indiana, Care Major J. E. Mulford, Fort Monroe, Va., and Hon. Robt. Ould, Agent of Exchange, Richmond, Va." All packages thus marked and sent by express, with charges prepaid, would have receipts indicating delivery returned to the Indiana Military Agent in Washington.[13]

November 26th was Thanksgiving, but soldiers of the Iron Brigade did not celebrate the holiday. They left Beverly Ford at 6 A.M. and marched all day until halting at Culpeper Ford on the Rapidan River. Crossing on a pontoon bridge before dawn the next morning, the brigade started off toward Chancellorsville, but soon turned to the right and headed for Orange Court House. Fear of rebel guerrillas resulted in a new marching formation on this campaign. In order to provide better protection, wagon trains followed their own corps instead of being strung out for miles behind the army. But this new tactic did not keep the rebs from making at least one attempt at capturing a train.[14]

Just before reaching the plank road from Fredericksburg to Orange Court House, General Cutler heard firing to the front of his column. Sensing that guerrillas might have pounced on the unguarded trains of the Fifth Corps marching just ahead, he rushed forward the 2nd and 6th Wisconsin. The enemy had indeed made a dash and had gotten in among the baggage, ambulance, and ammunition wagons. They were shooting teamsters and cutting mules loose when the 6th Wisconsin came running up. A brisk skirmish ensued, but the rebs soon ran off with some twenty wagons. Before their retreat, they set fire to some ammunition wagons, which blew up with terrible explosions, "scattering shot, shell and wagon wheels all over the country." Cutler believed the entire train might have been lost if he had not sent timely assistance.[15]

One reason for this successful attack on the Fifth Corps train was the country through which the army was marching. This vast section of second growth Virginia timber was called the Wilderness, and rightly so. One Badger veteran described the terrain:

> There are absolutely no landmarks. The roads are narrow. With the exception of here and there a small clearing the country is covered with timber beneath which is a compact tangle of undergrowth, sometimes so dense as to be almost impenetrable.

The Iron Brigade had been in the Wilderness twice before, first on its raid to Orange Court House in 1862 and then during the Chancellorsville campaign. The Western men would go back a fourth time in May of 1864.[16]

General Newton's First Corps camped overnight near Robertson's Tavern, but the men were up and in line before daylight on November 28th. The corps advanced through tangled thickets and underbrush until the enemy was discovered in position behind Mine Run, a stream that drains part of the Wilderness. While General Meade planned an attack on the rebel line, Iron Brigade soldiers thought that the situation was reminiscent of Fredericksburg. A tangle of felled trees threatened to hold up any attacking force, but worst of all, artillery posted on high ground to the rear had a clear field of fire against any attacking force for at least 2,500 yards.[17]

On November 29th, General Newton ordered a detachment from Cutler's division sent across the stream so that the ground could be thoroughly reconnoitered for the impending advance. Cutler selected the 1st Battalion of New York Sharpshooters, a unit recently transferred to the Iron Brigade as replacements for Gettysburg losses, and 200 men from the 7th Indiana. The attacking party waded across Mine Run, breaking through ice and sinking to their shoulders in water and mud. One Indiana officer described the attack as "charging rifle pits with a raking fire of iron hail, coming full into the face for six hundred yards, and wading water to the arm pits in the bargain, when it is cold enough to freeze every garment on the body in a few moments." These near-frozen Hoosiers and New Yorkers quickly dislodged enemy skirmishers along the stream, capturing some fifteen rebs and advancing a picket line far enough forward to cover the construction of two bridges. From the picket line, Cutler's men observed a deep ravine, now filled with water, that made their newly-won position a virtual island. This ravine, under the rebel guns, was not visible from the north bank and could have turned into a murderous trap had the First Corps unwittingly advanced into it.[18]

Cutler's men held their bridgehead until 3 A.M. on the 30th, when General Newton ordered the detachment recalled and the bridges destroyed. Cutler's detachment lost three killed, thirty-three wounded, and seven missing during its reconnaissance, but the losses had been worth the price. After receiving a detailed report of the topography of the far shore, General Newton concluded, "Success at the best was only probable, and must have been attended with heavy sacrifice of life." General Gouverneur K. Warren, commanding the Second Corps, had reached a similar conclusion about the defenses on his front, so Meade reluctantly abandoned his planned assault. According to Colonel William C. Talley of the Pennsylvania Reserves, "Had the two armies fought at Mine Run the result would have been the greatest slaughter recorded in the history of the United States." In referring to this Mine Run position, one Hoosier confided, "Meade did wisely in letting it alone." When newspaper editors complained about the army retreating without forcing a battle, soldiers solidly backed Meade and his corps commanders. Lieutenant Orr wrote indignantly, "If any body aint satisfied with the way *we* carry on this war, let *him* come and carry it on his own way."[19]

The two armies stared at each other across Mine Run until Meade began a withdrawal on December 1st. Cutler's division marched for Germanna Ford on the Rapidan at 4 P.M. and on the 2nd "recrossed to the *safe* side of that *classic* river." Passing through Stevensburg and Paoli Mills, the division finally halted near Kelly's Ford on the Rappahannock's south bank. On December 5th, the Hoosiers, "bound to build whether they use the houses or not," began cutting logs for winter quarters. William Jackson, the regiment's new ordnance sergeant, noticed how inconsistently his friends observed the first Sabbath in December: "It seems strange to hear preaching and swearing and see worship & work going on at the same time." While the

19. Julius Waldschmidt.
Used by permission of the Indiana State Library.

enlisted men cut timber and built cabins, their officers tended to long-neglected paperwork. Lieutenant Julius Waldschmidt was now assigned to command Company B, which had been without officers since July 1st. He spent many long hours filling out endless forms, which included inventories of the effects of men killed at Gettysburg.[20]

After the Mine Run campaign, there was a general rush by officers to apply for furloughs. Colonel Williams, Chaplain Barnett, and Surgeon Ebersole all went home between the 14th and 16th, followed by three lucky enlisted men on the 18th. Three Company K men—James M. Campbell, Joseph Helvie, and James Goings—imposed upon Colonel Williams's good nature and persuaded him to arrange for shipping a package from their families to Kelly's Ford. Then the soldiers wrote home and instructed their parents to fill "a ten bushel box" with delicacies, such as twenty-five pounds of butter, five gallons of apple and pear butter, pies (preferably mince), sausage, roast chicken, turkey, dried beef, a few sweetcakes, canned fruit, biscuits, and chewing tobacco (preferably plug), any extra space to be filled with green apples. As for personal items, Campbell wanted a pair of boots (size 7), two pair of socks, a towel, a military vest, and "a small box of cigars if you have a mind to." After the Helvie and Goings families added some personal items for Joe and Jim, that box must have been crammed to the lid.[21]

Officers and veteran volunteers were not the only ones trying to get home for the holidays. William Sykes and two comrades, writing from Camp Convalescent in Alexandria, asked for assistance from a military agent on December 23rd:

we the members of the 19th Ind having been wounded at the Battle of Getiesburg, and since that time we have been in Hospital at Baltimore Md. untill 21st inst. we was sent here where they told us we could get transportation to our own state. but we are to late they tell us as the Ind. men left here the day before we came. we are not any of us able to do any duty and are very anxious to go home and ask your assistance.

There is no indication whether these men got Christmas furloughs, but no organization was better at untying knots in the army's red tape than the Indiana Military Agency.[22]

Back at Kelly's Ford, the 19th Indiana got a little Christmas present of its own when orders came for Cutler's division to leave their cozy cabins and march to Culpeper Court House. After a night as "cold as Greenland," they marched at daylight on December 24th and reached their new camp at 2 P.M., bitching constantly about being "turned out on the woodless plains of Virginia in the dead of winter." The Hoosiers spent Christmas Eve trying to weatherproof their tents. Christmas Day was devoted to filling out discharge and reenlistment forms for veterans. On the 27th, the division packed up again and moved about a mile to a new camp on the road between Culpeper and Sperryville. Although the Army of the Potomac had spent the year marching across northern Virginia, through Maryland, into Pennsylvania, back again and then round about northern Virginia a couple more times, Cutler's division ended up 1863 just a few miles south of its previous winter's camp at Belle Plain.[23]

The prevailing topic of conversation in December was the debate over reenlisting as veteran volunteers. Recruiters back in Indiana found few volunteers to fill old regiments, one officer remarking that it was "an up-hill business to recruit for infantry." The country desperately needed its veterans to make another major commitment. A Hoosier officer described the 19th Indiana's response:

> The regiment responded almost unanimously to the call, and forgetting past hardships, and ignoring the fact that one fourth of their original number lay in their graves, and one half had been sent home maimed and disabled for life, the remaining one fourth promptly veteranized, saying: "We came out to put the rebellion down, and we will do it or die in the attempt."

Peer pressure had much to do with this show of patriotism. After being away for almost two and one-half years, Indiana seemed as far away as Australia. The soldiers' world had now become the regiment, which provided them employment, a home, a family, a circle of close friends, and a set of customs and traditions. These bonds between combat veterans were closer than those between wives, parents, and siblings and they would never leave comrades to carry on without them. Teamsters, clerks, guards, cooks, and other men on detached duty had not been admitted to this elite fraternity and found it much easier to decline reenlistment.[24]

The veteran question had been a muddled mess ever since its inception. November 24th seemed to be a watershed day for the 19th Indiana. Samuel Dickover wrote home that "We have but eight months to stay then we are a coming home to have a big time." Ominously, William Jackson later recorded in his diary, "Col. Dennis arrived from Washington today & is stirring up the veteran arrangement again." Colonel Dennis's visit was undoubtedly to inform Hoosiers of a new interpretation of the original veteran order. Effective November 21st, veterans would receive furloughs in their home state prior to the expiration of their original enlistment, transportation being furnished by the quartermaster. If three-fourths of the soldiers reenlisted, the regiment would be sent home in a body. Those individuals who refused to accept another three-year term would be assigned to other regiments until the expiration of their enlistment. A special report for the Iron Brigade listed the number of men present and absent for each regiment eligible for reenlistment:

	OFFICERS		ENLISTED MEN		
	Present	Absent	Present	Absent	Aggregate
19th Ind.					422
2nd Wis.	22	7	159	237	425
6th Wis.	21	10	225	216	472
7th Wis.	24	12	189	245	470

These totals indicate dramatically that the Iron Brigade had not recovered from its Gettysburg losses.[25]

Officers began the task of reenlisting veterans on December 20th at Kelly's Ford. In Company B, each man signed a standard enlistment form and one duplicate, swearing before Adjutant Finney that the personal information was correct. Finney then signed the form. A surgeon examined the man and certified him "free from all bodily defects and mental infirmity" that would disqualify him as a soldier. The doctor then signed the form. Captain Joseph Hartley, acting as regimental recruiting officer because of a long-standing medical condition, also signed the form. On the back, the veteran signed a declaration that was witnessed by Lieutenant Waldschmidt, who also signed his name. Of the seventeen veterans from Company B, Joel Curtis and James Grunden were the only ones who could not sign their names, both men using an X instead. Grunden, who had served as a teamster since shooting off a finger in 1861, reenlisted with the explicit understanding that "he should drive [an] ambulance instead of using his gun."[26]

A new interpretation of the veteran order was issued on December 21st. If three-fourths of a regiment reenlisted, the men would now be allowed to take their arms and equipment with them on furlough so they could make an imposing appearance at home. A regiment not reaching the three-fourths goal would turn its arms and equipment over to the quartermaster department during its absence. Recruits and non-veterans would be temporarily transferred to another unit from their home state or formed into a battalion until the veterans returned. Furloughs would not be granted until the corps commander had supplied headquarters with a statement of strength and number of men reenlisted. A later directive cleared up some confusion by stating that three-fourths of a veteran regiment meant three-fourths of men from that regiment within the limits of the Army of the Potomac. Soldiers in prison and hospitals would not be counted in the total.[27]

Ordnance Sergeant Jackson recorded the frustrating progress of recruiting veterans in his diary. On December 21st, he thought there might be "some probability of success this time." On the 22nd Jackson noted that "Col. Dennis is out here again, from Washington," whipping up patriotic fervor. The plan was to try and go home by New Year's Day and prospects looked good that "the 19th will go as a regiment." By the 23rd, three-fourths of the regiment and "12 men over" had signed up for a second enlistment and the regiment had been reported to corps headquarters as ready to go home. But the 26th brought another disappointment and it appeared that the "Reg't cant go home, so the veteran is played out again, for good this time." This complicated process of veteran recruitment, after causing much resentment, had left the soldiers "impatient and suspicious." Some Iron Brigade regiments had voted to reenlist three times, but had been turned down on technicalities. Hopeful Indiana officers spent New Year's Eve changing the enlistment forms originally signed at Kelly's Ford, crossing out the date December 20th and inserting December 31st.[28]

26

Veteran Furlough

New Year's Day was bitterly cold and blustery, but the veteran question remained in doubt. Men continued to step forward and it appeared that the 19th Indiana might yet meet the magic goal of three-fourths, although a question still remained about whether recruits from 1861 could be counted. A big snow storm hit the Hoosier camp on January 4th, but weather would not deter potential veterans and reenlistments continued at a lively pace. It appeared that a few more days would see the men on their way to Indiana. On January 7th, William Jackson proudly wrote in his diary, "The 19th were mustered in today as veteran volunteers to serve for three years from Jan. 1st 1864." First Lieutenant Harry C. Egbert, Commissary of Musters for the First Army Corps, signed each of the veteran enlistment forms, backdating his declaration to January 1st. On January 8th, Egbert would write: "I certify on honor that I have mustered over three fourths of the 19th Regt. Indiana Volunteers (including men who have fifteen months to serve) into the service of the United States as Veteran Volunteers." Amid the euphoria of going home, there were hints of bitterness by recruits who could not tag along. Samuel Dickover was not eligible to reenlist and vented his frustration in a letter dated January 7th, "I wish this war was over so we could come home, live a white man's life once more."[1]

Preparations commenced on January 8th for the return to Indiana. These mostly involved paperwork, since the soldiers could have been ready to leave at a moment's notice. Sixty-five enlisted men would be left behind, temporarily assigned to the 7th Indiana in the Second Brigade. Of those men, forty-three had declined the veteran offer, twenty-one were ineligible recruits, and one man would eventually reenlist. Despite Lieutenant Egbert's assertion that he had mustered over three-fourths of the Hoosier regiment as veterans, some headquarters clerk did not accept those figures. As a result, the army refused to officially acknowledge the 19th Indiana as a "veteran regiment."[2]

After turning over their arms and equipment to the ordnance department, excited men boarded cars at Culpeper Court House on the evening of January 10th. They wore their best soldier clothes and distinctive black hats, but their best was often tattered and torn. Some men's shoes were so badly worn that they had to tie them together with twine. Despite a worn appearance, one man wrote with understatement of "how glad we were and happy in anticipation of again meeting our friends & loved ones." The regiment arrived in Washington on the night of the 10th and left for Indiana on the 13th, each man's pocketbook bulging with greenbacks. Colonel Williams and his men reached Indianapolis on the morning of January 17th and were fed at the Soldiers Home before marching to quarters in Vajen's building on Meridian Street. The *Indianapolis Daily Journal* announced that the regiment would be honored at a public reception at three o'clock on the 18th and issued an appeal to citizens of the city:

> The men are happy to get home again; they want to see their friends; they expect to see them; let them not be disappointed. Turn out, citizens! Let the old 19th see and feel that you are glad to see them. Ladies, let your presence and smiles cheer the hearts of the brave defenders who have been so long from home and families, from wives and sweethearts. In short, let the welcome be such as it is our duty to give the returning braves, fresh from the din and strife of battle for a little rest in the quiet and comfort of home.

Lieutenant Colonel Dudley had already rejoined the veterans and a telegram alerted General Meredith, who was at Cambridge City recovering from his wounds, of the regiment's arrival. Long Sol, "the father of the regiment," was expected to speak at the reception.[3]

Despite inclement weather, citizens packed Masonic Hall to witness a heartfelt welcome-home ceremony. The program began when color bearers carried the national and regimental standards to the speaker's platform amid cheers from the soldiers. Applause swelled when Governor Morton made his entrance, but the appearance of Long Sol brought pandemonium. Soldiers jumped to their feet and roared out cheer after cheer, crowding around him, shaking his hand and embracing the general "as children would a father." When order was restored, the regiment's officers took seats upon the stage, soldiers cheering loudly when Lieutenant Colonel Dudley limped forward on his crutches. Hahn's Band played "The Star Spangled Banner" and Chaplain Barnett offered a prayer. Governor Morton then stepped forward and officially welcomed the regiment, saying that his joy was tempered by sadness at the large number of missing friends. After recounting the regiment's battles, Morton said that "it had fought another, and distinguished itself above all others—had re-enlisted for the war." By becoming veterans, the soldiers "had said to the nation, we will not lay down our arms until the rebellion is crushed and the country restored."

General Meredith acknowledged the governor's compliments, then remembered how the regiment had first stood in line for inspection on Washington Street. One listener reported, "He said the regiment had sworn never to give up the struggle until the Stars and Stripes should wave over all the traitor's land; they would keep that oath; nearly every man had reen-listed." After recounting some anecdotes of South Mountain, Antietam, and Gettysburg, Long Sol proudly proclaimed that the regiment's history "has been written in blood." He related how the 19th Indiana had shared in all honors won by the Army of the Potomac, honors largely ignored by the country. But Sol assured the audience that "the welcome they receive at the hands of friends at home compensates for all they have endured."

Colonel John T. Wilder spoke briefly and said that "the fame of the 19th was known all over the country," and its reenlistment was "another nail in a sure place." General Alvin P. Hovey had arrived late, but made a short speech, saying "his command had gone to the west, the 19th had gone to the east; yet Indiana soldiers, east and west, had watched each other with longing eyes, and rejoiced when each had shared in victories." After Adjutant General Lazarus Noble spoke on some technical aspects of recruiting, the veterans stood up and gave cheers for the Union, Abraham Lincoln, Governor Morton, and Long Sol. The guests of honor then marched back to their quarters as Hahn's Band played a stirring march.[4]

Members of the regiment received thirty-day furloughs on January 19th and individual companies dispersed across the state as quickly as railroad schedules allowed. In each hometown there was generally a public dinner, complete with speeches and dancing, for the returning soldiers. Friends and families proudly crowded around their heroes, filling them with food and drink. It was all wonderful for a few hours, but then the old soldiers began to slip away with their wives and girlfriends for a more intimate welcome. Those first few days must have seemed strange as veterans rediscovered a long-forgotten lifestyle which included beds with honest-to-goodness sheets and food that boasted ingredients other than hardtack and pork grease. Each of the 218 Hoosier veterans spent his furlough as he chose. Some passed the time quietly with families, while others loitered in taverns and traded war stories for drinks.[5]

Although men in the 19th Indiana found many reasons for reenlist-ing, James Rigby, a private from Company G, had perhaps the most compelling reason to become a veteran volunteer. He came home to save a woman's honor. Previous to his enlistment, Rigby had romanced Catherine Cronk of Waterloo. Their farewell must have been especially amorous, because Catherine gave birth to a bouncing baby boy on March 16, 1862. James came home specifically to rectify this situation, confessing to Lieutenant Baxter that "because it was his he was going to take care of it." James married Catherine before a justice of the peace on January 26th, thereby legitimizing the birth of little Edwin Ellsworth Rigby.[6]

Company B, "or what is left of it," according to one editor, arrived in Richmond on Tuesday, January 19th, and citizens hastily organized a reception for that evening. Despite such short notice, Starr Hall was well filled with ladies and gentlemen who had come to honor what remained of the Richmond City Greys. Lieutenant Colonel Dudley, the original captain, now commanded a squad of seventeen men:

Sgt Thomas Henderson	Pvt James Bradbury
" Jesse Jones	" Thomas Davis
" Charles Davis	" Benjamin Duke
Cpl Daniel Curry	" James Grunden
" Jefferson Kinder	" Jacob Hunt
" George Beetley	" John Markle
" George Bunch	" Joseph Sykes
" Joel Curtis	" Grear Williams
" David Fort	

The highlight of this impromptu ceremony came when Dudley returned the flag that had been given to the City Greys previous to their departure for Indianapolis. John Yaryan, father of one of the original company, accepted the flag on behalf of the ladies, then made "a feeling and appropriate speech" that was greeted by enthusiastic applause. When John Bridgland had originally presented the flag back in 1861, he said: "May God help you to honor and protect it; and when you return, may it come back to the fair hands that gave it, unstained, unless by the blood of your enemies." There was no enemy blood on the standard, but it did bear indelible stains and bullet marks from the carnage that had swirled about it in the cornfield at Antietam.[7]

While at home, veterans found interesting news in the Richmond newspapers. An appeal for volunteers by Commissioner John F. Kibbey noted that Indiana had avoided a draft during the last call for troops only because of veteran credits. That news was probably worth a few more free drinks in county taverns. *Indiana's Roll of Honor,* "an excellent and important history of Indiana's part in the war," had finally been published and was selling very well. Veterans could point with pride to Adjutant Finney's extensive history of the 19th Indiana in the book. William P. Wilson, formerly a sergeant in Company F, had recently returned from Gettysburg minus a leg, but a whirlwind political campaign resulted in his election as city collector. In other political news, General Meredith had announced his candidacy for the congressional seat held by his archrival, George W. Julian. Each issue of the *Palladium* proudly proclaimed its support for Long Sol in what would prove to be a bitter primary campaign.[8]

The *Palladium* also published a melancholy announcement of the death of Lieutenant Samuel Meredith, Long Sol's eldest son, on January 22nd. At Brawner Farm, Sam had been wounded in the neck by a minie ball that had just missed his windpipe and jugular vein. Shortly after Fredericksburg, Long Sol appointed Sam to a safer position as acting aide-de-camp on his staff. Both father and son were wounded at Gettysburg and they returned to Washington to recuperate. An officer of the provost marshal's department had approved of Sam going with Sol, but failed to record his decision, so technically the lieutenant was listed as absent without leave. Congressman Julian exploited the provost's error and insisted that Sam's case be examined by a military commission, which obliged and recommended that he be "dismissed the service of the United States, for being in the City of Washington without proper authority, and failing to report at Headquarters Provost Marshal, under arrest, as ordered."[9]

Before the paperwork could be corrected, Lieutenant Meredith fell ill with lung fever on January 19th. While on his deathbed, Sam told Sol, "Father I feel that I have given my life to my country." He died at home, aged twenty-five years and seven months. The funeral was conducted on January 27th, with four ministers participating in the service. One of the ministers was Reverend Lewis Dale, first chaplain of the 19th Indiana. A correspondent of the *Indianapolis Daily Journal* said of Dale's sermon, "The discourse of the chaplain was a tribute to the military character of the deceased—his fidelity to duty and his bravery and efficiency as an officer by which he had secured the esteem of both his superiors and subordinates in command." Sam was interred in the family burying ground on Oakland Farm at Cambridge City. Richmond's *Palladium* referred to Sam as "brave, generous and truly loyal," being eminently qualified for military life. The editor concluded, "Let us drop a tear over the brave soldier, not forgetting that such are the saviours of our country."[10]

After burying his son, Sol was confined to his room with fever and exhaustion and was spitting up blood from his Gettysburg injury. He corresponded with Colonel Samuel Williams about correcting the muster rolls "that Samuel might stand right" and assumed that the proper changes had been made. Later that year, Sol visited President Lincoln and asked that the order dismissing Sam be revoked. Lincoln wrote to Secretary of War Stanton on April 27th, "I know from Mr. Usher that the son was severely wounded in one of the battles, and I desire to extend this small favor to his memory." The War Department obliged and rescinded Sam's dismissal on May 18th. Colonel Williams, however, would be killed before he could correct Sam's record and the Indiana Adjutant General still listed the younger Meredith as having been dismissed from the army. Sol experienced "great pain" when he learned in 1867 that this error had been perpetuated in the published roster of the 19th Indiana.[11]

Furloughs passed much too quickly and eventually the sumptuous dinners and late-night dances had to end. Comfy feather beds at home had to give way to contraptions of poles and pine boughs in drafty army cabins near Culpeper. Colonel Williams's scattered companies rendezvoused at Indianapolis on February 18th and their thirty days of freedom now began to fade into history. It had been a gay old time for the veterans. One old soldier confessed, "I find out there is better company with girls." Allen Galyean noticed of his comrades that "some are crazy because they have been away two or three years" and went "hull hog" into marrying their girlfriends. For his part, Galyean stated that his friend Martha began referring to him in her letters as "my dear intended" and added, "that is all I am supposed to tell." The absolute worst part for the veterans was saying goodbye to their families. Galyean admitted, "I never hated any thing in my life as bad as I did to leave my dear old mother. I had to keep whistling, singing, all the way to Selma to keep it off my mind." Allen Galyean was just one of several hundred Hoosier veterans who hid their heartache with false bravado to keep back tears as they again headed to the front.[12]

In addition to a few new recruits, Company B also snagged John Addleman. The eldest of the Addleman brothers had enlisted and joined Joseph and Jacob before the Antietam campaign. Following their deaths, John lost interest in military service and deserted. He apparently took advantage of Lincoln's amnesty to deserters in April of 1863 and returned to the company, but then deserted again almost immediately. Returning home, John married Elizabeth Bunnell on February 2, 1864. The veterans took him back to stand trial for desertion. At a general court-martial held on May 2nd, he was found not guilty of desertion, but guilty of absence without leave, the reduced charge undoubtedly an acknowledgment of the family's sacrifice. John was sentenced to the loss of all pay and allowances while absent, forfeiture of all pay and bounty due him and dismissal from the service.[13]

Mustering in of recruits and other military red tape kept the 19th Indiana in Indianapolis until February 24th. The regiment departed on that date, taking along about fifty recruits and leaving twenty-five unmustered men behind. Everyone was a little homesick on the "tiresome trip" to Washington, but most were proud to be on the way "to again battle for our country & our country's flag." They had fun, but not quite so much as on the trip home because the greenbacks had given out. Since everyone was out of sorts, it did not take long for trouble to develop. Shortly after the train left Selma, a brakeman tried to collect a fare from Absalom Shroyer's father. Silas Stonebreaker promptly kicked the brakeman off his own train and when last seen the railroad man was rolling along the roadbed. The regiment passed peacefully through Crestline, Ohio, at 2 P.M. on Thursday, the 25th, and reached Pittsburgh at 10 A.M. the following day.[14]

Several severely ill veterans had been left behind to recuperate with their parents, including Private James Goings, one of the three Delaware County boys who had written home for the "ten bushel box" of food. Goings never rejoined his comrades and died at home on April 5, 1864. Captain Joseph Hartley, unable to perform any active duty during the preceding twelve months because of chronic rheumatism of the right knee joint, tendered his resignation on February 20th. He remained in Indianapolis on recruiting duty until his resignation was accepted on April 4th.[15]

The regiment lost another man at the town of Beaver, Pennsylvania, near the Ohio state line. The trainload of Hoosiers had been sidetracked to allow a westbound train to pass. Since there were no toilets aboard the cars, Colonel Williams and nearly all of his men took advantage of the halt and got off. Robert Patterson and David Whitney ducked behind a lumber pile to relieve themselves. As the westbound train chugged past, scores of Hoosiers in various states of undress rushed to reclaim their seats.[16]

When their engine started off, platforms were crammed with men pushing to get inside the cars. Suddenly, the train passed close by some burning piles of railroad ties and debris. Curious soldiers leaned forward to see the fire, then instinctively surged away from its intense heat. Bob Patterson lost his grip and fell, striking his abdomen against the station platform. He bounced off the platform and almost onto the tracks, where his clothing caught on an axle box. Patterson was dragged a considerable distance before the engineer could be alerted. The unlucky soldier was seriously injured and Henry Marsh, the hospital steward, found him suffering from large bruises, an abdominal blister and "severe cramping in his bowels." Patterson was taken along with the regiment, not being sent to a hospital until it reached Culpeper. Doctors could do little for him. Patterson was never able to do much duty afterwards and his internal injuries eventually resulted in a discharge on September 9th. His diagnosis was "Chronic Hepatitis (result of a Contusion); attended by general debility & dispesia; of long standing; resisting all approved treatments."[17]

Colonel Williams and Adjutant Finney left the 19th Indiana at Pittsburgh, going ahead to Baltimore where they made arrangements for transportation on the last leg of the regiment's journey. Captain Orr brought the men through with but one more casualty. Somewhere between Pittsburgh and Harrisburg, Corporal David Fort leaned out of the car and received a face full of cinders thrown out by the engine. Fort's eyes were injured, but not so badly that he needed hospitalization. The regiment reached Baltimore at 11 P.M. on February 27th and marched two miles to the Soldiers Home. There the men ate supper and bedded down to sleep, their officers staying overnight at the Eutaw House. Leaving Baltimore at 11 A.M. on the 28th, the regiment reached Washington at 3 P.M. Officers saw their men settled into barracks, then booked rooms at the Clarendon Hotel. Lieutenant Macy was not feeling well and would soon be diagnosed as having a severe case of smallpox. It would take six weeks in a hospital and four more weeks at home before he could resume the field.[18]

Lieutenant Colonel Dudley "burned again to return to active service," but he was left behind to finish up recruiting matters. Dudley and Colonel William T. Dennis canvassed Wayne County's northern townships, giving notice of their appearance with posters. One of Dudley's recruits was Colonel Dennis's son, Frank, although he never served with Company B. Probably due to his father's influence, Frank was detailed as a mounted orderly on the staff of General Henry B. Carrington, supervisor of Indiana's recruiting service. It was a cushy job and the young Dennis kept at it until his discharge in May of 1865. Hatch Squires, another of Dudley's recruits, also never served a day with Company B. Eighteen years old and a native of Guilford County, North Carolina, Squires had been presented by Sergeant Charles Davis and duly enlisted by Dudley. But the young man took the first installment of his bounty money, walked away, and simply disappeared.[19]

Lieutenant Colonel Dudley had promised Nathan S. Williams a twenty-day furlough immediately after his enlistment so that he could make personal arrangements. Specifically, Williams had a case in court that involved transferring his property to his mother so that "in case of accident to himself" she would be provided for. When the case dragged on longer than Williams's leave, Dudley wrote directly to General George W. Morell in Indianapolis and, on behalf of his new recruit, asked for an extension. Dudley concluded his letter, "I hope you will grant his & my request, so that I can deal in good faith with him." As events unfolded, Nathan Williams suffered no fatal accident so the precautionary legal work proved unnecessary.[20]

New recruits for the regiment came from a variety of places and a wide array of backgrounds. Private Enoch T. Neal went home to Jasonville, Greene County, and personally recruited Joseph B. Warrick and John R.

Morgan for Captain Shafer's Company G. Friends and relatives usually enlisted so that they could serve together. One example was a trio of young men—Nathaniel Cary, Silas Hiatt, and Michael Ryan—from New Burlington who signed on with Company K. Letters written by Cary and Ryan routinely kept those three families informed of the men's health and movements while they remained together. Some recruits already had military experience, such as John Thompson, Company K, who had served just over eighteen months in the 34th Indiana.[21]

A few men had less than honorable service before their enlistment in the 19th Indiana. Charles O. Rider had been captured at Lexington, Missouri, while serving in Company A, 1st Illinois Cavalry. Ignoring his parole, Rider enlisted in the 39th Illinois, but left before his company's organization was complete. He went to a St. Louis hospital, took the money and effects of his dead brother, stole a horse and headed for Ohio. In 1864 Rider was living in Lynn, Randolph County, and declared himself ready for another stint in the army.[22]

The recruits of 1864 were a different type of men from those who had volunteered earlier in the war. Young, healthy, single men were now seldom seen in Indiana cities or rural areas. So many men had enlisted that recruiters now concentrated their efforts on farmers and tradesmen with families. Appeals to patriotism and waving the Stars and Stripes did not work on these older men. The only thing that could lure them into military service was money, and lots of it. This fact caused bounties to increase dramatically from the $100 given to the volunteers of 1861 (and that given retroactively!). Shrewd recruits would credit themselves to counties where lagging enlistments raised the threat of a draft. Those communities usually added generous local bounties onto the Federal money. Men struggling to make ends meet could make two or three years' wages just by signing their names on an enlistment form. Such a windfall was hard to turn down and economics, rather than patriotism, brought men into the ranks during 1864.

27

Arrival of Grant

Hoosier soldiers spent the first two days of March "running around" the nation's capital. Places of special interest included a sanitary fair being held in the Patent Office and the House of Representatives, where one soldier made the startling discovery "that congress men look like other men." The only criticism during these last days of freedom came from Captain Orr, who complained that expenses at the Clarendon Hotel were too high, $3.50 a day. The 19th Indiana finally left Washington on the morning of March 3rd, crossing the Potomac to Alexandria by boat. Lodging overnight at the "clean and comfortable" Soldiers Rest, the men left Alexandria next morning aboard a train bound for Brandy Station. From there they marched about five miles to Culpeper Court House. According to one officer, the Hoosiers received a splendid reception, "All the soldiers in the neighborhood were out and quite a cavalcade of Officers and Ladies rode out, accompanied by the Band, to meet the Returning Braves of Indiana."[1]

Officers were put up in a suite of rooms and the enlisted men spent the night in an old church. On March 5th, everyone was busy drawing arms, accouterments, and ammunition from the ordnance department, along with tents, haversacks, canteens, and other essentials from the quartermaster. After being outfitted for the field, Colonel Williams marched his regiment two miles out on the Sperryville Pike to its campground. There the Iron Brigade was finally reassembled, the 6th and 7th Wisconsin having arrived a week or so earlier from veteran furlough. If the Hoosiers brought a mixed bag of recruits along with them, the 7th Wisconsin had an even odder assortment. Their volunteers included over a dozen Chippewa Indians, some of whom could not speak English. Arrival of the Indiana soldiers at Culpeper signaled a return to military discipline. The men had enjoyed "a gay old time" on their return trip, with only a minimal amount of supervision. One

20. Officers of the 19th Indiana in Washington on Veteran Furlough.
From the Mick Kissick Collection. Used by permission.

private remembered, "The boys were running the machine. Officers had not a word to say." Now the officers were back in charge and the official chain of command was reestablished.[2]

In compliance with an order from Meade's headquarters, the Hoosiers furnished a complete accounting of their losses and gains on the trip home:

	OFFICERS	MEN	TOTAL
Strength on leaving	19	214	233
Gain while absent	4	80	84
Loss while absent	5	35	40
Total number returned	18	259	277
Veterans returned			179
Recruits left behind			25

On March 7th, Colonel Williams reported to Indiana's Adjutant General that the 19th Indiana had received a total of 190 recruits from July 29, 1861, to its return from veteran furlough. Hundreds more men were still needed to fill the regiment's ranks, leading one veteran to declare, "Uncle Sam has a Spring field rifle layed up rusting for all that will use one."[3]

The first order of business was "manufacturing soldiers out of raw recruits." That meant drilling as often as weather would permit, an oppressive burden to the old soldiers but one that was absolutely necessary to make the regiment ready for battle. Nathaniel Cary, one of the recruits, remarked, "we hafe to drill a while evry day" and "we have to shoot at target," the latter an important element in their training. Unfortunately, new arrivals had the same casual attitude toward firearms as did the volunteers of 1861. Shortly after joining the regiment, Levi Chalfant was fooling around with his revolver and shot himself in the right hand, the ball entering beneath the thumb and exiting through his wrist.[4]

In addition to self-inflicted wounds, the newcomers also had to endure their share of communicable diseases, including an outbreak of smallpox. The trio of friends from New Burlington had their share of physical maladies. Silas Hiatt had been left at Alexandria with a case of measles. Shortly afterwards, he began to have nightly fits so bad that three or four men had to hold him down. Hiatt was discharged in April, never having served a day in the field. Nathaniel Cary got the mumps and spent the month of March in a hospital. Michael Ryan remained healthy a little longer and on April 7th could boast, "I hant ben sick a day sence i left you. i am gitting fat as a hog." Alas for boasting! Ryan became so seriously ill in May that he was sent to the general hospital at Madison, Indiana.[5]

Before commencing a spring campaign, General Meade proposed to reorganize the Army of the Potomac. His plan was to reduce the five army corps to three, thereby eliminating the First and Third Corps. Meade's reorganization became effective on March 23rd. The old First Corps was consolidated into two divisions, which were transferred to the Fifth Corps as its second and fourth divisions. The Iron Brigade thus became the First Brigade, Fourth Division, Fifth Corps. General Gouverneur K. Warren, the hero of Gettysburg's Little Round Top, became their new corps commander. Young-looking, with black hair and eyes, Warren was described as a "keen-looking fellow of small stature." Old Corduroy returned to command the Fourth Division, thereby demoting General Cutler to command of the Iron Brigade. Although long contemplated at army headquarters, this radical change struck the rank and file "as if by lightning."[6]

Captain Orr described the change with bitter words, "We are now 1st Brig 4th Div 5th Corps and we do not like the change a bit." Another soldier was more emotional on the subject:

> It is no more; the deed is done; the fiat has gone forth, and the First Army Corps has ceased to exist. The corps that was first formed—it seems to us a long time ago—in the early days of this unholy rebellion, the nation's first and greatest hope after the sun went down in dark and threatening clouds at the First Bull Run; that band that prided themselves upon being the first in thorough organization; the corps that has fought in a score of battles, losing over twenty thousand men, has been sacrificed and parcelled out to another. We weep. Is it unmanly? Is it womanly? We may have the woman's heart; she weeps over her lost idol;

we weep over ours. We were of the First Corps; its history is our history.
Its glory ours; we were it and it was us. Unmanly?

Of course not, but the consolidation did cripple morale for a while.[7]

Referring to the loss of the First and Third Corps, General Andrew
A. Humphreys wrote, "The history and associations of these organizations
were different, and when they were merged in other organizations their
identity was lost and their pride and *esprit de corps* wounded." One Badger
officer agreed, arguing harshly that the First Corps "deserved something
better than obliteration." General Meade eased the pain somewhat by
allowing the men to retain their old corps badges and thus the Iron Brigade
retained its distinctive red circular insignia, an emblem that would never be
worn by any other United States soldiers. The Western men were also
permitted to retain their characteristic black hats.[8]

On March 25th, General John Newton issued General Order No. 9
as the last official communication of the First Corps:

> Upon relinquishing command I take occasion to express the pride
> and pleasure I have experienced in my connection with you and my
> profound regret at our separation. Identified by its service with the
> history of the war the First Corps gave at Gettysburg a crowning proof
> of valor and endurance in saving from the grasp of the enemy the strong
> position upon which the battle was fought. The terrible losses suffered
> by the corps in that conflict attest its supreme devotion to the country.
> Though the corps has lost its distinctive name by the present changes
> history will not be silent upon the magnitude of its services.

One historian would later write, "No prouder record was ever made in the
military history of the world than the First Corps had."[9]

Shortly after losing their corps organization, the Hoosiers learned of
the political vilification of their beloved commander, Solomon Meredith. On
March 24th, the *Delaware County Free Press* published a scathing attack on
Long Sol by Isaac W. Witemyre, formerly a first lieutenant of Company K,
19th Indiana. Supporters of George W. Julian, Meredith's political enemy,
presented Witemyre's statement in an effort to discredit Sol's military career.
According to Witemyre, Lieutenant Colonel Bachman commanded the 19th
Indiana at Brawner Farm and "should have the credit of whatever honor may
attach to the commander of that regiment." At Second Bull Run, Colonel
Meredith "was not seen until late in the evening," the credit again belonging
to Bachman.

Witemyre than related Sol's mistake at South Mountain, recounting
how he mistakenly faced his regiment the wrong way, exposing the men's
backs to the enemy. Although Meredith had never claimed to have led the

19th Indiana at Antietam, some newspapers had erroneously given him credit for doing so. Witemyre dredged up those old stories and correctly claimed that Meredith "was not upon the field." Witemyre continued his attack on Sol's career after his promotion to command the Iron Brigade. The former lieutenant related that Meredith was removed from command for blunders committed at Fredericksburg. His supposed incompetence extended to Gettysburg, where Meredith had disappeared in the afternoon of July 1st, leaving his brigade without orders. Witemyre concluded, "To this cause alone is attributable the heavy losses sustained by the brigade, and the 19th regiment, in that battle."

Reaction from Hoosier veterans at home was immediate. Lieutenant Colonel Dudley, Lieutenant Walter Jack, Lieutenant Samuel Schlagle, Sergeant Major Elihu Parker, and Sergeant William P. Wilson prepared "The Military History of I. W. Witemyre," which was printed along with other material by the *Palladium*. Addressing his "utterly false and slanderous" statements, these veterans pointed out four instances of Witemyre's misbehavior under fire. They then explained to voters of the Fifth Congressional District that the lieutenant had finally been dismissed from the army for cowardice.

While refuting many of the incredible allegations against Sol, Dudley's group indulged in a bit of untruth when it claimed that Meredith had "handled his regiment with great skill and bravery" at South Mountain. After presenting a pro-Meredith statement by five members of Company K from Delaware County, Dudley and his friends asked:

> Now, fellow citizens, this is the statement of the boys of the old 19th, who did not run away—who did not skulk—who did not play the coward—who were NOT DISHONORABLY DISMISSED for deserting in the face of the enemy! What more do you require to convince you that this most iniquitous and damnable tirade against Gen. Meredith is only for the purpose of abusing your minds, and defeating your honest preference for Congress? Could fiends incarnate exceed this kind of malignity?

Meredith's supporters then took a swipe at Julian, who had "never raised a soldier for the army—never visited one that was sick, or relieved one that was wounded." For good measure they reminded voters that Julian's son had finagled a job "in a fat office at Washington for $1200 per annum, only six hours a day," while other sons from the district were earning $13 a month in the army.[10]

From Virginia, officers of the 19th Indiana confessed that they "had concluded to remain silent in regard to his military history and the manner in which he retired to civil life," but Witemyre's ambush of Sol ended their silence. Referring to Witemyre as "a loafer, a gambler, a liar and a coward," the officers listed some highlights of his military career. He first gained notoriety on January 14, 1862, when a general order announced that Orderly Sergeant I. W. Witemyre had been detected gambling with a Negro, "thus lowering his dignity and the respectability of the soldiers he is placed over." Soon after he was promoted to lieutenant, but quickly fell into his old habits of gambling and loafing, generally being regarded as a nuisance by his fellow officers.

At Second Bull Run, Witemyre commanded Company E, but was found hiding behind a tree some 400 yards behind the regiment by Lieutenant Haskell. Gibbon wanted him court-martialed, but Meredith begged leniency since it was his first offense. After South Mountain, his men found him safely tucked behind a rock, complaining of a "belly-ache." Witemyre was not present at Antietam and did not rejoin the regiment until several days after the battle. At Fitzhugh Crossing, he did not cross the river until long after firing had ceased. While the 19th Indiana was at the front during the Chancellorsville battle, Lieutenant Witemyre was in the rear gambling with stragglers. On July 1st he went into battle, but "was severely wounded in the hat, and beat a hasty retreat," not reappearing during the rest of the Gettysburg fight. When the regiment anticipated going into action at Mine Run, the lieutenant "sought congenial company in the stragglers of the 3rd corps wagon train, and remained for five days, until the army recrossed the Rapidan." Enough was enough. Lieutenant Isaac W. Witemyre was court-martialed, found guilty on the charges of absence without leave and misbehavior before the enemy, and dismissed from the army.

Having explained to *Palladium* readers what sort of man had attacked Long Sol's record, the Hoosier officers also took a swipe at the Julian faction, "Witemyre is too grossly illiterate to write a single sentence, and we have no doubt, has merely signed this paper at the instigation of others whose literary attainments are, perhaps, better, but whose hearts are fully as black as Witemyre's."[11]

Officers of other Iron Brigade regiments jumped to support their former commander. Emphasizing their "esteem for, and confidence in, our soldier comrade," they wrote of Meredith:

> Parlor knights may affect to despise him. Radical politicians may raise hue and cry against him, but the heart of Solomon Meredith is sound as oak and as true to the Union—the State of Indiana and its interests, as the needle to the pole.

Repulsed by "*the covert attack of the coward and the base insinuations of the slanderer*," nearly every Iron Brigade officer commended Sol to the voters of his district. One-legged William Wilson gathered up some back issues of a Julian sheet that had attacked Sol, then sent the bundle to the regiment at

Culpeper. He quickly received a letter that expressed their sentiment: "The editor of the *Broad Axe* had better not come out here, for the boys will hang him higher than Haman!"[12]

One of the *Broad Axe of Freedom* editors wrote to Isaac Kinley, Provost Marshal of the Fifth Congressional District, and asked if his records disclosed whether Lieutenant Witemyre had been dishonorably dismissed from the service. Kinley responded that after searching in back issues of the *Army and Navy Gazette,* he was unable to locate any mention of Witemyre's dismissal. Kinley did, however, add: "The only name on the list of dismissed officers of the 19th Ind., is that of 1st Lieut. S. H. Meredith, son of Gen. Sol. Meredith." Julian supporters gloated over the "vindication" of their source and the unexpected jab at Sol's family.[13]

Attacks on his military record may have cost Meredith some votes, but his biggest liability was an opposition to anti-slavery sentiment in the Fifth District. Sol had always stigmatized anti-slavery men as abolitionists and was personally opposed to freeing the Negroes. When Lincoln first proposed to emancipate the slaves, Meredith wrote to the president in opposition to the plan. After Lincoln signed the Emancipation Proclamation, Long Sol openly declared that he "did not want to fight by the side of the niggers." This attitude offended the Fifth District's Quakers, who were overwhelmingly anti-slavery. They also had strong reservations about Meredith, who, although raised a Quaker, had ridden off to war in contradiction of church teachings. After a spirited mud-slinging campaign, Julian prevailed at the polls and Meredith was sent off to command the post at Cairo, Illinois.[14]

Coincident with Long Sol's congressional race, Lieutenant General Ulysses S. Grant moved his headquarters to Culpeper. Many soldiers had credited the demise of the First Corps to Grant, saying that he had "lieutenant generalized" them out of existence, but that restructuring had been Meade's idea. When working near army headquarters, individuals from the Iron Brigade occasionally caught glimpses of the famous general, from whom so much was expected. But Western men were no longer inclined to hero worship. One officer quietly, but emphatically, explained that "the army can fight no more heroically under General Grant than it did under General McClellan at Antietam, or General Meade at Gettysburg. There is a measure of human achievement." Despite their reservations, everyone wanted to see their new commander. Twice the division had been ordered out for review and twice the lieutenant general had failed to make an appearance, leading jokesters to refer to him as "Un Seen Grant."[15]

On March 29th, Grant, Meade, and Warren held their long-anticipated review of the old First Corps, now the second and fourth divisions of the Fifth Corps. Grant, exhibiting "a sort of shy, half-embarassed, half-bored look," slowly rode along the lines, solemnly doffing his hat before each torn regimental color. One Hoosier wrote of him, "He is a plain unassuming looking man, medium size, sandy hair and whiskers, very well dressed. But dont look half as much like a General as Meade or Warren and he dont know how to have a review." Regiments displayed little or no enthusiasm, partly due to the rain, but primarily because of their attitude. One First Corps veteran wrote, "He rode slowly, in a business like, quiet manner, along the front of the massed battalions, looking critically as he passed, not at the buttons, but at the faces, which, in turn, looked critically at him." Grant and the army were sizing each other up. Both would reserve judgment until the fighting began.[16]

Despite his generally unenthusiastic reception, Grant had impressed one Hoosier soldier. Shortly afterwards, Private Grear N. Williams composed a song about Grant and wrote it down in his new diary. According to the author, "Ulysses Leads the Van" was to be sung to the tune of the popular song "A Little More Cider Too":

> We['ve] Sung the praises of many [a] Brave
>   While marching on to Battle
> Whose deeds and words have served our arms
>   Amid the muskets rattle
> But now a nother leader com[e]s
>   who ever[y] doubt dismisses
> with shout and song we welcome him
>   the nation['s] hope Ulysses
>
>   Chorus:
> Ulysses leads the van
> Ulysses leads the van
> We['ll] ever dare
> to follow whare
> Ulysses leads the van
>
> the west has seen his flashing steel
>   on many field[s] of glory
> His soldiers tell round thare fiers
>   the never w[av]ering story
> of victorys won and ever Bo[a]stes
>   with order undiminished
> that when Ulysses does a job
>   He leaves no work unfinished
>
>   Chorus
>
> the east extends a welcome hand
>   and loads him with caresses
> she's made [his] name a household word

    that aged and childhood blesses
and now she stands with Beating heart
    along his war path gazing
while at her alters, morn and night
    her prayers for him she[']s raising

        Chorus

her soldiers know bey heart the fields
    whareon his flag was planted
and whare the Bo[a]sting traitors found
    thare right to yield was granted
and now they long to here his word
    and onward tramp togather
and richmond[']s spairs [spires] th[e]y hope to greet
    ear [ere] summer blossoms wither

        Chorus

they tell of vicksburg whare too years
    the r[e]bble flag was floating
how uncle sam was in a fix
    a Bout his western Boating
till once he thought he had one lad
    whose rifle never misses
and so he gave the ugly job
    to his Brave Boy, Ulysses

        Chorus

this plan had fail[e]d and so had that
    and worthless wer[e] the ditches
he saw he[']d got to run thare fire
    and take them By the Breeches
so tiger like he made a spring
    and siesed them in the tender
hold on sed [t]hem "I[']ve got enough
    I might als well surrender["]

        Chorus

the ware will soon Be over Boys
    and then in countless number
we[']ll go whare drum and Bugle note
    will not invade our slumbers
and when our dear on[e]s greet us home
    and give thare long Kept Kisses
with them we[']ll talk and sing the deeds
    of modest Brave Ulysses

        Chorus

One can almost imagine Private Williams composing these lyrics in his log shanty and trying them out on his bunkmates Dan Curry, Bob Conley, and Jacob Hunt.[17]

One of Brave Ulysses's top priorities was to clean up Culpeper Court House. Provost guards flushed hundreds of stragglers from the village "like a lot of wharf rats driven by high tide." Pioneer squads were set to work cleaning what a Hoosier chaplain declared "had become one of the most filthy, loathsome towns that I ever saw in every way." The pioneers graded roads, cleaned stables, built fences and repaired fortifications under the watchful eye of General Warren, "the Boss workman."[18]

Weather at the end of March was wildly unpredictable, "one day cold, one wet and the 3rd warm and pleasant." Hoosiers had good times huddled in their quarters, speculating on the hot times ahead in the next campaign and bragging about how they would show Grant what they could do. That was mostly empty boasting. One Iron Brigade soldier explained:

> The boys are always hoping that the fighting may be done by someone else. That something may happen to prevent a battle &c but never express a wish showing any impatience—have all learned to be very patient upon that point.

Veteran Allen Galyean joked about the issue when he wrote, "I have more fun in battle but we dont have any preserves." Old timers would have chosen preserves over combat every time.[19]

April began with a mixture of rain and snow that continued off and on for nearly a week so that "a man Cant go out of the house without he gets his fiet weat." A medical inspection of the Hoosier camp on April 8th disclosed that the officers and men still ignored basic sanitation. The inspector's report read, in part, "The 19th Indiana is in a poor condition owing to the recent rain, the camp not being sufficiently ditched. Their policing in general is poor, especially between their huts." As a result of this unfavorable report, no passes were granted to Indiana men until their camp had been properly put in order.[20]

By April 9th the ordnance sergeant could report that he had issued 130 muskets to recruits and convalescents in the month since the 19th Indiana had returned from Hoosierland. Recruits continued to arrive, but learned nothing about proper sanitation from slovenly veterans who could not even dispose of their own garbage. Newcomers also learned to appreciate the culinary "ability" of army cooks. John W. Modlin explained the variety of military rations to his mother and father:

> we have for breakfast coffee meat and bread. at dinner we have meat bread and coffee. at supper we have bread coffee and meat and none of the above mentioned victuals are fit for a dog to eat and not enough of that.

While sniping at cooks and the army's "hurry up and wait" mentality, Modlin reserved his harshest comments for a rascal back home who had tried to buy his enlistment bond at less than face value. Calling the man a "mean sneak low lifed sheepkilling coward," Modlin advised his parents to ignore the offer.[21]

Signs of a spring campaign increased as the month progressed. On April 9th Colonel Williams sent to headquarters a list of men in his regiment who did not carry arms. Unarmed men included the quartermaster sergeant, commissary sergeant, two principal musicians, six company musicians, two prisoners under arrest, one stretcher-bearer and the adjutant's clerk. This list, of course, did not include men on daily, extra, or detached duty.[22]

Lieutenant Colonel William W. Dudley would not be with the regiment during its next campaign. Although he had stubbornly insisted upon rejoining the 19th Indiana at Culpeper, the unhealed stump of his leg kept him from traveling. Dudley finally admitted his inability to command and resigned so that Major Lindley could be promoted to his place. His resignation became effective on April 9th and Dudley accepted a clerkship in the Pension Office, working there until March of 1865 when he entered the Veteran Reserve Corps as a captain. He received a brevet as brigadier general of volunteers for "gallantry at the battle of Gettysburg" and was mustered out June 30, 1866. Dudley succeeded Sam Schlagle as Clerk of Wayne County Courts, served as United States Marshal for Indiana, and was appointed Commissioner of Pensions in 1881. This latter position allowed him to assist former comrades and several pension applications by Company B men contain handwritten notes indicating his personal interest in those cases. The general later formed a law partnership and practiced in Washington, D.C., until his death on December 15, 1909. He is buried in Arlington National Cemetery.[23]

Dudley's discharge left a vacancy and resulted in a spirited contest among the remaining Hoosier officers. They unanimously nominated Major Lindley for lieutenant colonel, but then the scramble began. After four ballots and some lively campaigning, an informal poll of the officers produced nine votes for Adjutant Finney and seven votes for Captain William Orr. But when Finney asked his supporters to sign a recommendation, only six were willing to do so. Lieutenants Baxter and Waldschmidt lobbied for Captain Shafer's promotion and proposed that the enlisted men should vote for their new major. Friends of Captain Orr urged Colonel Williams to simply recommend the senior officer present with the regiment, who just happened to be Orr. Thirteen officers supported this latter plan, including three former supporters of Finney who became "fast friends" of Orr after sensing the eventual outcome. On April 19th, Colonel Williams wrote to Governor Morton and recommended the promotion of Lindley and Orr. However, this whole affair was pointless. Since the 19th Indiana was well below the minimum regimental strength and already had two field officers, the army refused to muster in a new major, no matter who his friends might be.[24]

While the Hoosiers argued over their phantom major, the army was clearly getting ready to campaign. Leaves were halted, baggage allowances reduced, and sutlers sent to the rear. By the 17th William Jackson could write that "all camp followers have been ordered to leave, sutler, picture takers, peddlers &c are all gone." Every man able to bear arms was in the ranks and the first rumors of marching orders began to circulate on April 26th. Two days later the 7th Indiana was transferred to the Iron Brigade, their veterans being a welcome addition to General Cutler's under-strength command.[25]

Despite all that had transpired since their enlistment, a few men still believed (or wanted desperately to believe) in that Sir Walter Scott nonsense of knights and chivalry and valiant conduct. Because he had served in the construction corps and ambulance corps, Sergeant Jesse Jones had only experienced combat from a distance. Perhaps that would explain how he could compose the following story, entitled "Sleeping Comrade":

> I sit beside a comrade, who is wrapt in the mantle of slumber, doubtless dreaming of dear ones many hundred miles away, far beyond the grim Blue Ridge, and lofty Alleghanies, upon the fertile and beautiful plains of the distant West, with whom he associated in the dawn of his day of existence, when peace and prosperity blessed the lovely land of his nativity, and War was a thing of history.
>
> When he floated in the merry dance with the fairest daughters of the west and heard not the bugle call to battle, nor was disturbed by the thundering voice of the hoarse-mouthed cannon, the rushing of frantic steeds, or the clash of small arms crossed with deadly aim. Little did he then think that War would ever wage its wide desolation, and threaten our land to deform. But the dark and ghastly clouds of treason gathered in the horizon and burst forth as a mighty flash of lightning shaking the foundation of our Union, and creating a fearful commotion in the elements of government. The dreadful omen nerved his arm, and aroused him to deeds of valor that eclipse in splendor and brilliancy, the chivalrous deeds performed by the redoubtable Knights of the past ages of gallantry.
>
> He still sleeps, and in all probability is now dreaming of that happy day when our country is free from the polluted tread of traitors, and he, as one of our noble band of its defenders, returns to the home of his youth, and offers the hand of a true American soldier to the gentle and queenly lady who smiled upon him in the gay and festive circles of the elite of the land, and dropped a tear at that last parting. She who possesses his heart. But hark! The drums are sounding the assembly call, the call that has aroused him so oft, fails not to awake him from even so pleasant and happy dreams. He springs from his rough couch; buckles on his armor, and again goes forth to duty.

All too soon, drums in the Army of the Potomac would again sound the long roll. The Iron Brigade would make its fourth visit to the Wilderness and, within six weeks, well over 200 of the Hoosiers would be dead, wounded, or missing. The coming campaign would smash to atoms all lingering notions of medieval nonsense. Unaware of what the future held, the Hoosiers spent their last days at Culpeper innocently playing baseball.[26]

Into the Wilderness

May 1st was a Sunday and offered the soldiers a quiet day of relaxation from their preparations for a forward movement. A storm blew up on Monday, drenching Culpeper with a heavy rain in the evening. Well-informed sources quoted rumors that Grant would move on May 3rd, so soldiers got up one last baseball game before marching orders arrived. Shortly after shagging fly balls and chasing grounders, the Hoosiers learned that the army would move at midnight. Men loaded haversacks with three days' rations, stowed three days' rations in their knapsacks and jammed fifty extra rounds of ammunition into coat and pants pockets. They were ready for anything when Old Corduroy led his division from the bivouac near Culpeper and marched toward Germanna Ford on the Rapidan.[1]

Two incidents illustrate the fighting men's confidence and determination. Just after his division left camp, General Wadsworth spoke to Chaplain Samuel W. Eaton and said, "If any man doubts that we are going to Richmond this time, I doubt his loyalty." Shortly after this exchange, Surgeon Ebersole approached Color Sergeant Abram Buckles, who was still suffering from his Gettysburg wound. The doctor told him bluntly, "Abe, you are not fit to go into battle." Abe responded simply, "I can't stay out if the boys have to go."[2]

The road was dry and dusty and, as the sun rose on May 4th, it began to beat down upon soldiers whose marching muscles had grown soft in winter camp. But recruits, "burdened with prodigious knapsacks," suffered the most. Blankets and overcoats were cast aside by the thousands as the Army of the Potomac hurried toward the Rapidan. Wadsworth's division crossed the river about noon and halted on the far bank for coffee and a bite of long-delayed breakfast. After about an hour of rest, Old Corduroy got his division back on the road for what Grear Williams thought was "the hardest

Theater of Operations – 1864 and 1865

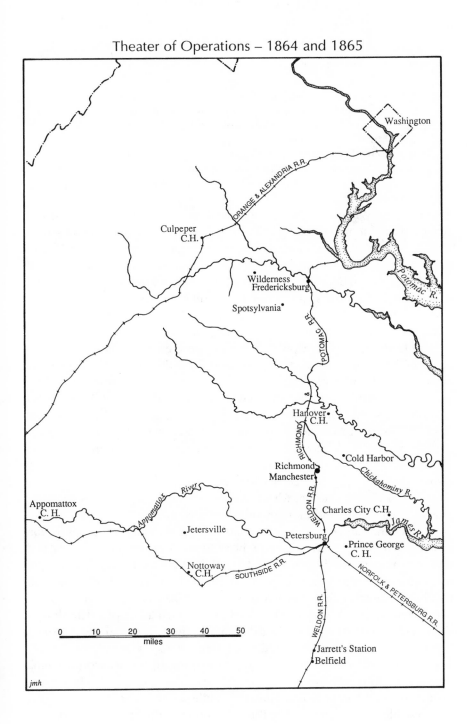

Washington

Culpeper C.H.

ORANGE & ALEXANDRIA R.R.

POTOMAC R.

Wilderness
Fredericksburg

Spotsylvania

POTOMAC R.R.

Hanover C.H.

RICHMOND &

Cold Harbor

Chickahominy R.

Richmond
Manchester

WELDON R.R.

Appomattox C. H.

Appomattox River

Charles City C.H.

James R.

Jetersville

Petersburg

Prince George C. H.

Nottoway C.H.

SOUTHSIDE R.R.

NORFOLK & PETERSBURG R.R.

WELDON R.R.

0   10   20   30   40   50
miles

Jarrett's Station
Belfield

jmh

march that I ever was on." Lieutenant John V. Hadley described the latter stages of Wadsworth's movement:

> Many were overcome and fell by the way side, and many more were discouraged and sullen, so that before we reached our bivouac at Wilderness Tavern, the straggling was alarming. Our staff was ordered out to drive all stragglers to the ranks, and for one, I have spent few afternoons when my duties were more fatiguing. It was one continuous command of "move on!" and forcing up with the sword or revolver worn out soldiers, whose very countenance depicted extreme suffering.

After reaching Wilderness Tavern, an old two-story stage house, Wadsworth's division turned southwest along Wilderness Run and bivouacked about 4 P.M.[3]

The Wilderness was a dreary, menacing place, unlike any forest of the Old Northwest. The original timber had been cut down years before and now the sandy soil boasted a crop of saplings, "fifteen to thirty feet high and seldom larger than one's arm." One Badger officer described the region as "a dense undergrowth of low-limbed and scraggy pines, stiff and bristling chinkopins, scrub oaks and hazel." Spring foliage cut visibility to less than fifty yards. Except for a few isolated clearings, there were no landmarks once a person left the narrow roads that bisected the Wilderness. On the ground, blooming wildflowers contrasted starkly with rotting and rusting debris from the Chancellorsville battle of 1863. It was no wonder that one of Wadsworth's staff officers would later write, "It is a region of gloom and the shadow of death." This funereal atmosphere quickly affected the troops. Before going to sleep on May 4th, Colonel Samuel Williams penned a final note to his wife, "Whether we shall be permitted to meet again in this world or not, my earnest prayer is that you may live long and happily, and that we may at last meet in our Father's home, where there is no war to separate his children. May God bless you, and mother, and our little children."[4]

Grant had crossed the Rapidan River without meeting opposition and he had hoped to march through the Wilderness before the rebels realized that the campaign had started. Wadsworth had his men up and moving at dawn along the faint, grass-covered trail that led toward Parker's Store, but they halted shortly after 7 A.M. when skirmishers from another division of the corps came upon the enemy. Old Corduroy formed a line of battle along a slight ridge with the Iron Brigade on his right, Colonel Roy Stone's Pennsylvania brigade in the middle and General Rice's brigade on his left. The Western men immediately began "throwing up breast works, felling trees and digging trenches, using the little axes and spades with which every man who could had provided himself." While soldiers labored to construct a formidable line of defense, Abe Buckles sat down and removed his coat and shirt. Taking a small pair of pincers from his pocket, the color sergeant calmly proceeded to pluck bone fragments from the unhealed wound in his right shoulder. A few minutes later, the order came to advance. Abe dressed quickly, hoisted the furled battleflag onto his healthy shoulder and led the 19th Indiana deeper into the Wilderness.[5]

General Warren had ordered Wadsworth to advance into the area between the Parker's Store Road and the Orange and Fredericksburg Turnpike, instructing him to march due west "by the compass." He was to keep in contact with General Samuel Crawford on the left and General Charles Griffin on the right. According to a staff officer, Warren's order was ludicrous:

> The first one hundred yards of underbrush, and then one of those briar-tangled ravines, and all reliance on the compass was gone. Self-protection, if nothing else, called on the regiments and brigades to try to keep in touch with each other, whatever the compass might say.

Undergrowth so thick that men were sometimes compelled to crawl on their hands and knees broke up every line of battle. Officers re-formed their regiments into columns, so that "all semblance of line of battle was gone and there were gaps everywhere between regiments and brigades."[6]

General Cutler originally formed his brigade in two lines, but accounts vary as to the order in which the regiments were arranged. The 7th Indiana was undoubtedly on Cutler's right, with skirmishers from that regiment well to the front. When Cutler moved forward, his brigade suddenly encountered the Maryland Brigade, from the Second Division, which had been ordered to support Wadsworth. As they searched for Wadsworth, these Marylanders had unwittingly blundered into the gap between the Iron Brigade and the Hoosier skirmish line. Cutler's command had the right of way, so Maryland men obligingly opened intervals for their Western comrades. The Iron Brigade swept through the gaps and disappeared.[7]

After an advance of a half-mile, the Iron Brigade struck the rebel lines about noon. Colonel Ira Grover's 7th Indiana became engaged first, followed by other regiments as they stumbled onto enemy positions. Colonel Williams got his men into a sort of a battleline just before the 19th Indiana ran into the Confederates, who fired a ragged volley from short range. Abe Buckles instinctively looked toward his friends in Company E and was shocked to see that nearly every man had fallen. But they quickly scrambled to their feet, having "gone down out of force of habit, trying to dodge the bullets after these little missiles of death had gone by." As the Hoosiers returned fire, Buckles saw Spence Richardson, a drummer who was "a little wild but as faithful to duty as any," come striding along with a musket. As he passed the colors, Richardson said, "You know what I told you Abe." Buckles recalled that the drummer had vowed to kill Adjutant Finney because he had preferred charges for some misconduct while at Culpeper. He yelled back, "Spence you have no business here, go to the rear where you belong." Richardson ignored him and resumed his hunt for the adjutant.[8]

Cutler's men had initially been staggered by rebel resistance, but the Black Hats struck back at General John M. Jones's rebel brigade and crashed through it in "Iron Brigade fashion." Not stopping to attempt an alignment, the Western men raced after fleeing Virginians. Samuel Shirts, Company G, was so intent on capturing a rebel that he forgot to duck. While running forward, a tree limb snapped back, striking him in the left eye and blinding him on that side. Still able for limited duty, Shirts escorted rebel prisoners to the rear, but he had the further misfortune to catch smallpox from one of the captives. An officer described the impetuous rush of the Hoosiers: "Over rocks and underbrush, through woods and through thicket, our boys dashed in pursuit, charging them over the river [Wilderness Run], through an open field, and upon a little hill, when they received heavy reinforcements." This wild chase netted three battleflags, including those of the 48th and 50th Virginia, one colonel, and hundreds of prisoners.[9]

The 19th Indiana halted at this small clearing so the men could re-form and catch their breath. On the opposite side of the open space was a dense thicket filled with rebs who kept up a withering fire against the panting Yankees. Sergeant Buckles instinctively knew what had to be done:

> The thought came to me that the thing to do was to make a dash across this clearing, and [I] looked around for some field officer to direct the charge and seeing none, determined I would lead and knowing the boys would follow the colors, I unfurled our tattered and torn flag the best I could, waved it over my head and started, the line moving after me, but almost instantly I was pierced through the body with a rebel bullet; the ball passing entirely through my body.

Abe planted the staff on the ground and leaned against it until Corporal Seth Peden, Company A, took the flag. Then, "being in intense agony," Buckles turned and staggered to the rear. Peden was killed a few moments later. Sergeant Jesse Jones, author of "Sleeping Comrade," grabbed the standard, but was hit by a minie ball that shattered the middle finger of his right hand.[10]

Private James Marquis, Company G of the 7th Indiana, was killed at the farthest point of the Federal advance. A comrade wrote of him:

> Jim had just captured one rebel and turned him over to the guard who were going to the rear with a squad and was pressing forward after another. About this time Some of our troops on the right, gave way and

let the enemy flank us. Come in behind us and fire into our rear, this was when Jim was shot.

When Cutler realized he was isolated far from any supporting troops, he ordered an immediate withdrawal. It was nearly too late. Being almost surrounded, the Iron Brigade had to fight its way back a short distance before the Western men took to their heels. All was confusion. Colonel Grover rallied about three dozen men from the 7th Indiana and promptly walked into a rebel regiment, which captured the whole lot. After its lieutenant colonel and major were wounded, the 2nd Wisconsin nearly lost its flag. The bearer had not received an order to retire the colors, so he stubbornly maintained his position, "bolt upright in the woods," until the adjutant found him and ordered him back. Sergeant Major Cuyler Babcock saved the 6th Wisconsin's flag by tying it about his body and running through the woods.[11]

In the 19th Indiana, Richard T. Henderson, Company D, and a few others found themselves alone when the brigade withdrew. While Henderson dodged and ran through the trees, he stumbled upon Colonel Joseph Hayes of the 18th Massachusetts. As the blood streamed down his face from a bad head wound, Colonel Hayes, who was unable to get away, implored the Hoosier to save his sword and revolver, both gifts from friends at home. Henderson took the colonel's weapons and hurried off, but had not gone more than a hundred yards before he sank to the ground completely exhausted. After resting about fifteen minutes in some thick underbrush, Henderson soon reached safety. He located the 18th Massachusetts and, keeping his battlefield promise to a stranger, turned Hayes's treasures over to the regimental surgeon.[12]

During Cutler's advance and repulse, the Maryland Brigade had remained motionless. Soldiers watched approvingly as captured flags and prisoners came streaming in, but then the tide of battle turned. Wounded men came limping back assisted by too many able-bodied helpers. Stragglers returned with tales of disaster at the front. Staff officers galloped up with news that Wadsworth's division had caved in. Old Corduroy himself rode about, shouting, "Where is my second line? Bring up my second line!" Broken Iron Brigade regiments streamed back with screaming rebels right on their heels. The Marylanders held their fire until the rebs were almost onto their muzzles, then began "a hot and bloody duel at close range" that allowed the Iron Brigade to escape. More than half of the supporting brigade was swept away, but the enemy had been checked and recoiled toward its original line.[13]

General Wadsworth's other two brigades had also been thrown back after a spirited fight. Confusion on that front can best be illustrated by a single occurrence. When General Rice's skirmish line was attacked in both front and rear, some fifty officers and men found themselves trapped deep behind rebel lines. These Federals were completely lost and drifted aimlessly in the woods. Unsure of directions, this isolated squad found rebels wherever they turned, but, incredibly, they remained at large until the morning of May 6th.[14]

Upon reaching open ground near the Lacy plantation, Western soldiers encountered General Warren rallying Wadsworth's fugitives. Once in the clear, fragmented regiments quickly re-formed around their colors. Despite heavy losses the division still retained its combat efficiency, so at 4 P.M. Warren ordered Wadsworth to support the Second Corps along the Orange and Fredericksburg Plank Road. Officers pulled out compasses, shook their heads and headed their commands due south. Dr. Charles K. Winne watched one of Old Corduroy's men march off:

> When Wadsworth's demoralized division was reforming at the Lacy house, I saw a wonderful example of the triumph of mind over matter which I have never forgotten; and I can almost see the boy's face yet. The shattered division was just moving back to the line when I noticed the youngster in his place going to what may have been his death, with pallid face and trembling lips, yet with his head erect and eyes to the front, going to meet Fate like a gentleman and soldier.

Warren's order took the Iron Brigade away from its Wilderness battlefield and, mercifully, shielded them from the fight's ultimate horror. In the afternoon, fire began to creep along the forest floor and wounded men tried to drag their crippled bodies toward safety beyond the turnpike. One wounded Hoosier from the Iron Brigade saw the gruesome result: "The ground, which had been strewn with dead and wounded, was in a few hours blackened, with no distinguishable figure upon it."[15]

Great attention had been devoted to removing the wounded from the battlefield. The Fifth Corps ambulance train contained 171 ambulances, with one driver and two stretcher-bearers assigned to each. Two of these ambulances were assigned to the 19th Indiana. In an attempt to avoid parochial assistance, stretcher-bearers were ordered "to assist all sick and wounded men who came within their reach, without reference to the corps, division, or brigade to which they might belong." Surgeons established division hospitals near some springs located one mile east of Wilderness Tavern on the Fredericksburg Turnpike. The first wounded arrived about noon on May 5th and by 9 P.M. 1,235 injured men had made their way to that point.[16]

The 19th Indiana had marched into the Wilderness with 332 officers and men present for duty. By nightfall on May 5th, the regiment had lost twelve killed, forty severely wounded, thirty-one less seriously wounded and thirteen missing, including Adjutant Finney. Color Sergeant Buckles had staggered to the rear until he met two men who agreed to help him. They first took off his belt that held the flag socket and two small boxes that held Abe's Bible and diary. Then the Samaritans supported the wounded man between them and began a hasty withdrawal. A few moments later, a volley of minie balls rattled through the trees overhead and Abe's helpers dropped him and ran off. Stretcher-bearers later found Buckles and carried him to a hospital, where a doctor examined his wound and pronounced it mortal. He was then taken back to the Fourth Division hospital. Henry Marsh found him there in a tent, sitting on the ground and leaning against a branch nestled between two forked sticks. A hasty search disclosed that a minie ball had penetrated his right lung and passed out his back. Marsh remembered, "Lint was stuffed in the holes, but the air was passing out of them with each breath." After another examination, a chaplain informed Abe that he had been mortally wounded and must prepare to meet his Maker. Several days later, Sergeant Buckles was mistakenly reported to have died in a wagon on the way to Fredericksburg.[17]

Wounded men unable to get away were taken prisoner and carried to temporary hospitals along the turnpike between the battlefield and Robertson's Tavern. Most had appalling wounds. The right femur of Sergeant Matthew Duckworth, Company H, was shattered, leaving that leg two inches shorter than his left one. Sergeant John W. Dittemore, Company I, was reported killed, but he had been injured when a minie ball crashed into his right knee, leaving a wound that would compel him to forever walk on his toes. Ralph Coats, Company G, and James Miller, Company K, were reported killed, although both captives were still alive in June. One soldier from the 6th Wisconsin extracted two buckshots with his own knife, but could do nothing about the wound in his thigh that would eventually yield more than sixty bone fragments. Rebel surgeons attended the Yankees as best they could, but food and shelter were in short supply. At one hospital, all the cooking for 150 prisoners was done in a single fourteen-quart kettle.[18]

Back in the Wilderness, Wadsworth had advanced his division to support the Second Corps on the night of May 5th, taking his direction from the sound of battle. When that firing ceased after dark, Old Corduroy had nothing to guide his movement, so he prudently halted his command to await daylight. Although he would not know it until morning, Wadsworth had gotten his division to within one-half mile of the Orange and Fredericksburg Plank Road and parallel to it. Weary soldiers dropped to sleep "on the dead leaves and among spice-bushes, spring beauties, violets and dogwoods in bloom." Generals and staff officers spent the night preparing to attack next

21. Samuel J. Williams.
From the collection of the author.

morning and Wadsworth did not allow himself to sleep until 3 A.M., when 20,000 rounds of ammunition arrived on muleback.[19]

After soldiers grabbed cartridges and gulped down a breakfast, Wadsworth attacked at 5 A.M., pushed across the Plank Road and linked up with the Second Corps. Rebel artillery opened fire and shells began to explode "thick and fast" overhead. Colonel Williams yelled above the noise that the shells had been fired too high and the men should ignore them. Just then a projectile (some said a solid shot and others thought it an unexploded shell) struck Williams in the right breast, killing him instantly. In reporting the colonel's death, Major Lindley wrote, "In him the Regt. has lost an able and loved Commander, and the Country a zealous patriot and true soldier."[20]

In response to this heavy shelling, Wadsworth changed his deployment, but the division was suddenly scattered by an enemy attack that first struck the Iron Brigade. When Cutler's men broke, they ran back in the direction from which they had come. The general and his staff tried to rally the fugitives, but they could not restore any semblance of order until nearly back to the Lacy house. Morris Schaff, one of Warren's staff officers, first encountered "swarms of stragglers," then met Cutler with 700 or 800 of Wadsworth's men. Schaff remembered that the old general "was bleeding from a wound across his upper lip, and looked ghastly, and I have no doubt felt worse." When asked what had happened to Wadsworth, Cutler replied grimly, "I think he is dead." Seeing Wadsworth's flag and mounted men rallying disheartened soldiers, Cutler rode over thinking he might find Old

Corduroy there, but discovered only two aides and the division orderlies. At this point, General Meade rode up and ordered Cutler to organize a line. He managed to assemble almost 1,300 men from every brigade in the division and held the position pointed out by Meade.[21]

Despite reports to the contrary, Old Corduroy was still very much alive, although thoroughly worn out and sorely depressed. Lieutenant Earl Rogers recalled that the terrible losses, the gloomy battlefield and lack of victory greatly saddened his white-haired commander. After Cutler's repulse, Wadsworth had plunged into the fighting along the Plank Road, personally leading his remaining force to blunt the enemy attack. His gallant example would have been inspiring on any other battlefield, but it was lost amidst the smoky jungle of the Wilderness. Captain Robert Monteith remembered a brief conversation with the general during a lull in the battle: "He told me that he felt completely exhausted and worn out; that he was unfit to command, and felt that he ought, in justice to himself and his men, to turn the command of the division over to General Cutler."[22]

Two horses had already been shot from under Wadsworth by the time another Confederate assault smashed into his new line. As regiments crumbled, the old general, "in an almost frantic state of mind," hurried reinforcements forward. He started to wheel some fragments of Rice's brigade, which had stuck with him, so they could fire into rebels across the road. Leading the movement in person, Wadsworth cried out, "I have told you to go, but now I say come!" and galloped forward. Old Corduroy, accompanied only by Lieutenant Rogers, was in among the rebels before he could turn his horse. Cries of "Surrender!" were ignored as the two officers turned to escape. Rebs "not three yards distant" fired at them, one minie ball striking Wadsworth in the head and splattering his brains all over Rogers's coat. Another ball killed the lieutenant's horse, so he jumped into the saddle of Wadsworth's mount and raced off with the news that Old Corduroy had been killed.[23]

Wadsworth's loss was a personal blow felt deeply by every man in his division. One soldier in the 7th Indiana said of him, "Many pure and noble lives went down amid the smoke and thunder of those eventful days, but none more worthy of a grateful remembrance than this white-haired patriot." But Wadsworth still was not dead. Old Corduroy was carried to a rebel hospital where he remained, beyond medical help, until his death on May 8th. A captured Confederate officer's diary described his last hours, "uncared for and unconscious, with a gaping crowd staring at his prostrate carcase." The reb officer concluded his account with the terse observation, "So much for fame."[24]

In addition to the loss of Colonel Williams, the 19th Indiana lost one man killed, two seriously wounded and five slightly wounded on May 6th. In its announcement of the colonel's death, the *Palladium* concluded with a familiar remark, "The old 19th displayed its usual bravery and has added glory to glory, but has lost heavily." For once, Company B emerged relatively unscathed, with a loss on May 5th of only five men: Sergeant Jesse Jones and Private William Pitman, wounded; Sergeant Bob Conley, Privates Ben Duke and Bill Sykes, captured. Private Charles Sponsler was listed as missing in early reports, but he had actually taken to his heels after throwing away his shelter tent, knapsack, haversack, and canteen. Lieutenant Thomas J. Crull reported that Company B expended 860 rounds (500 of .58 caliber and 360 of .574 caliber) during the Wilderness battles.[25]

Fighting in the thickets and ravines had been a new experience for the Hoosiers. There had been little artillery firing, the battle being fought almost exclusively with deadly musketry at close range. But what of the results? One Iron Brigade officer bitterly expressed the common opinion: "The battle continued two days, but decided nothing and its only result appeared in the tens of thousands of dead and wounded in blue and gray that lay in the thick woods."[26]

29

Grant's Campaign

On May 7th, the army rested. General Warren got the Fifth Corps behind defensive positions and spent the day sorting out scattered fragments of his command. Cutler now headed the Fourth Division, reuniting a detachment along the Plank Road with his main body at the Lacy house. Colonel William W. Robinson, 7th Wisconsin, took over the Iron Brigade. Stragglers were swept from the woods and sent back to their regiments. Then at 9 P.M. the Army of the Potomac started for Spotsylvania, Warren's Fifth Corps leading the way. Marching by way of the Brock Road and Todd's Tavern, Warren's advance was hindered by cavalry trying to open the road ahead. The horsemen gave up at 6 A.M. on May 8th and Warren, distressed by the long delay, sent forward his Second Division, old First Corps troops commanded by General John C. Robinson. Warren's order was succinct: "Never mind cannon, never mind bullets, press on and clear this road." Robinson found the rebels at Laurel Hill and attacked their entrenchments, but his troops fell back after the general received a wound that would cost him a leg.[1]

Cutler reached Laurel Hill in mid-morning and attacked the rebel position on a densely wooded range of hills crowned with earthworks and strengthened by artillery. Robinson's Iron Brigade advance first encountered a smaller elevation, "partly wooded and formed like a hog's back," which became the scene of bitter fighting. A soldier from Cutler's Third Brigade recounted the battle's progress: "We took the ridge; the enemy rallied and drove us back; we rallied and retook it; the enemy again rallied and pushed us back a short distance; but we went for them again, and drove them away beyond the ridge." A last rebel attempt to recapture the ridge fell particularly heavily upon the 19th Indiana. This charge forced the Hoosiers back up the slope some thirty or forty yards, but their color bearer refused to yield and held his ground. Confederates pushed to within thirty steps of the colors where they took shelter in a slight depression.[2]

Two soldiers from the 143rd Pennsylvania, Sergeant DeLacy and Private Engle of Company A, rushed to rescue the Indiana colors. They found the bearer kneeling behind a broken-down rail fence, so DeLacy instinctively went to his right and Engle to his left. Soon after the rescuers opened fire, a minie ball struck the flagstaff and tore into the Hoosier's arm. He fell against DeLacy, both men being shrouded by the flag. The sergeant propped up the injured man, who raised the broken staff with his good arm and, groaning with pain, cried out, "Stay with me, boys." These three men held their isolated position for perhaps fifteen minutes, the 19th Indiana firing over their heads during the whole time. To their front, the color squad could see ramrods glisten in the sun every time the rebs turned over to load their muskets. When Federal reinforcements arrived, the rebs ran back across an open field to the woods beyond. Major Lindley then moved the Indiana regiment forward and offered his thanks to the Pennsylvanians who had saved his colors. Sergeant DeLacy never learned the color bearer's name.[3]

After failing to reach Laurel Hill, the Iron Brigade constructed a line of entrenchments in the valley facing the high ground. To their front was a large open field and beyond lay tangled thickets of "low cedars, the long bayonet-like branches of which interlaced." Opposing skirmish lines confronted each other in the cedar jungle. This position would be the brigade's base of operations for the next few days.[4]

Fighting on May 8th on the Laurel Hill line resulted in five casualties in Major Lindley's regiment. Four men were wounded and Sergeant Amos H. Sparks, a native of Elizabethtown, was killed. Sergeant Sparks, who possessed a "pleasant demeanor, high toned intellect and unexceptionable moral qualities," had enlisted in Company H and served in every one of the 19th Indiana's battles. When the veteran question arose, "his soul was too strongly fired with patriotism to remain in scenes pleasurable to himself while yet there was need of another arm to be raised against tyranny and oppression." Sparks was struck down at the age of twenty-three, his body being left on the field and the location of his grave unmarked.[5]

Dawn on May 9th revealed that the rebs still held Laurel Hill. Although the night had passed quietly, preparations had been made in anticipation of an attack. Soldiers slept with their cartridge boxes strapped on and their loaded muskets leaning against the breastworks with bayonets fixed, ready for instant use. Alarm guards had been posted along the breastworks just in case the enemy slipped by the skirmishers. During the day, men raced back and forth across the open field as new detachments relieved portions of the skirmish line in the cedar tangle where Yanks and rebs hunted one another. In the evening, Colonel Robinson strengthened his skirmishers and started a lively little fight when he attempted to drive back the reb line, a maneuver that ultimately proved unsuccessful. The 19th Indiana's loss during the day was three men killed and four soldiers slightly wounded.[6]

Captain Davis Castle, commanding the Fifth Corps signal party, rendered important service on this day. At about 3 P.M. he spotted some dismounted rebel cavalry making their way toward the corps hospital and signaled that intelligence to headquarters. One staff officer raced to the scene with two regiments and quickly drove off the attackers before they could do any damage.[7]

The morning of May 10th was relatively quiet as Meade moved troops from the Second Corps into line on Cutler's right in preparation for another attack. General John Gibbon commanded the newly arrived troops and rode over to examine the ground with Warren before this new assault. Gibbon recounted what happened during his ride:

> As we rode forward, we passed along a line of troops who sprang to their feet and commenced loud cheering. At first I did not realize what it meant but on looking around I discovered the smiling faces of the men of my old brigade, who took this method of testifying their feeling for their old commander. The demonstration, however, was somewhat inopportune and drew upon us a heavy artillery fire from the enemy.

Despite Gibbon's objections to the proposed attack, Meade ordered it to be carried out. The Iron Brigade advanced at 12:30 P.M. and plunged into the cedar woods past their skirmishers.[8]

Portions of Robinson's brigade unexpectedly stumbled upon the main reb line, a vicious volley disclosing its location. Troops from the Second Corps broke and exposed the Iron Brigade's right, compelling the Western men to retire after suffering a heavy loss. Most of Colonel Robinson's men established a temporary line a few hundred yards from the enemy earthworks where they witnessed one of the war's ultimate horrors. Heavy rebel musketry had ignited fires and soon portions of the woods were aflame. One Badger officer remembered that they could smell burning woolen clothes and charred human flesh. Any rescue attempt would have been suicidal. All the survivors could do was hug the ground and listen to the piteous cries of the wounded. Lieutenant Earl Rogers heard one dying soldier recite the Lord's Prayer, "From the strong, full voice, it lessened to a moan: 'Forgive us as we forgive those that trespass against us.'" Rogers continued, "They went to the presence of their Maker in the agonies of bleeding bodies, burning clothes and crisping flesh." The Iron Brigade held the woods until 4 P.M., when it retired to its breastworks in the valley. Another assault that evening was mercifully canceled. The 19th Indiana lost one man killed, one seriously wounded, and five slightly wounded in the attack against Laurel Hill on May 10th. In addition to those casualties, Captain John Shafer was sunstruck in the afternoon and carried insensible from the field.[9]

General Warren reported that on May 11th the Fifth Corps "mostly lay quiet, straightening matters out and preparing for next day's operations." If one discounts the heavy shell fire and constant picket firing, the day really was mostly quiet. Grant's campaign had already put great stress on the remnants of the old First Corps. By nightfall on May 10th, both division commanders, James Wadsworth and John C. Robinson, had been shot down, along with three brigade commanders. In discussing the campaign, Gouverneur Warren concluded, "General Cutler was the only general officer belonging to the old First Corps remaining with us when we left Spotsylvania Court-House." Losses among regimental officers were similarly tragic: Colonel Ira Grover, 7th Indiana, captured; Colonel Samuel Williams, 19th Indiana, killed; Colonel Henry Morrow, 24th Michigan, wounded; Lieutenant Colonel John Mansfield, 2nd Wisconsin, wounded and a prisoner; Colonel Edward Bragg, 6th Wisconsin, transferred to command another brigade; and Colonel William Robinson, 7th Wisconsin, promoted to command the Iron Brigade. However, the most significant casualty was the 2nd Wisconsin, which had been reduced to a skeleton regiment with less than one hundred men present for duty and no field officers. On May 11th, Cutler assigned this pitiful remnant of the once proud organization to duty as division provost guard. Although still exposed to occasional shellfire in the rear, the 2nd Wisconsin would no longer march into battle with the Iron Brigade.[10]

General Cutler had his division under arms at dawn on May 12th and launched another uncoordinated and unsuccessful attack on Laurel Hill at 8:30 A.M. After some four hours, Cutler withdrew his division and led it to the left, where desperate fighting raged over Confederate trenches captured that morning by the Second Corps. Regiments from the Iron Brigade took up positions within thirty yards of the enemy's line and kept up a constant musketry fire until well after midnight. Some men remembered firing almost 300 rounds per man that hellish night. Regiments relieved one another as muskets fouled from constant use, men standing in trenches whose bottoms were filled with water, mud, and corpses. In the morning it was discovered that bodies between the opposing lines had literally been flattened, simply "shot to shapeless masses." Cutler pulled out his division and returned to his original position before dawn, relieving a thin line of skirmishers who had held his line all afternoon and evening.[11]

The 19th Indiana had missed this terrible fighting on the Second Corps front, having been left behind as skirmishers to hold Cutler's vacant

22. Nathan S. Williams.
From the Mick Kissick Collection. Used by permission.

line. During the assault and skirmishing phases of May 12th, Major Lindley's regiment lost one killed, seven severely wounded, and six slightly wounded. Among the injured were two recruits from Company B, Augustus C. Gill and Nathan S. Williams. Gill was struck while charging the enemy breastworks, a musket ball shattering his left shoulder joint and rendering the arm completely useless forever. Williams, also hit in the attack, received a deep wound in the left thigh that would keep him in a hospital for nine months. Two soldiers, Sergeant Thomas Banfill, Company C, and Private James M. Keaton of Company D, received wounds in the left thigh that struck the femoral artery. Banfill eventually succumbed to pyemia, an infection characterized by pus in the blood, and Keaton died after surgeons amputated his leg, both men expiring on June 12th, exactly one month after being shot. About the only positive thing that happened to the Hoosiers at Laurel Hill was when Orderly Sergeant Thomas Henderson picked up an officer's field glass that had been dropped by its owner. Henderson sent the glass home as a battlefield trophy (there being no indication which army its owner had served) and friends in Richmond delighted in climbing to rooftops and scanning the city with it.[12]

Cutler started his division to the left at 8:30 P.M. on May 13th, even though the men were "so completely exhausted by two days' continual marching and fighting, that it would have been utterly impossible to charge the enemy." The route lay over unfamiliar roads through swamps and forests, all shrouded in darkness. General Warren reported that many Fifth Corps men, "from exhaustion and weariness, gave out; the line became disjointed and parts lost their way." At 4 A.M. on the 14th, Warren had only 1,000 men up and ready for duty. The rest of his command straggled in at all hours that day, Cutler's division being assigned to a position between the Ny River and Fredericksburg Pike.[13]

Letters written by Iron Brigade soldiers after Laurel Hill all have a depressing tone. The 2nd Wisconsin's Cornelius Wheeler wrote on May 13th, "We have had terrible fighting, and more of it than ever before crowded into so short a time." Noting that the enemy had been strongly entrenched wherever found, Sergeant Samuel List jotted down, "Boys are very much worn out. Scarcely able to get along." Chaplain Eaton of the 7th Wisconsin noticed that, after just ten days of fighting, officers who had appeared young and healthy were now "older by years than before the campaign." Eaton said of Lieutenant Rogers that "he has sunken cheeks and can but just hang on his horse." Lieutenant Colonel Rufus Dawes, 6th Wisconsin, confessed, "I can never tell, if I live through it, the sufferings of this campaign." In his official report, Dawes observed that operations around Laurel Hill and Spotsylvania had been "perhaps most trying to their morale of anything in the experience of the oldest in service." After stating that the 19th Indiana had charged rebel breastworks on eight separate occasions, Captain Shafer wrote with cautious optimism, "No great mistakes have been made, and we are actually crowding the enemy toward Richmond."[14]

The period from May 15th through May 20th was relatively quiet. Soldiers built earthworks, brought up stores and rested, trying to shake the melancholy of Brave Ulysses's campaign. Spirits lifted in the 19th Indiana on the 17th when prisoners captured at the Wilderness returned after their escape with news that Adjutant Finney had been captured, not killed, as many had believed. After the Wilderness fight, Abe Buckles chanced to meet young Spence Richardson, now wounded in the calf, who had vowed to kill the adjutant. Buckles knew that Finney was missing and asked, "Spence, what have you done?" Richardson replied sternly, "You know I told you I would kill him." Abe was in no condition to argue, so let the matter drop, but he would later declare, "I am satisfied he went to his grave believing he had killed the Adjutant in the battle of the Wilderness."[15]

The Army of the Potomac left a sea of misery in its wake as Grant continued his march toward Richmond. At the field hospitals, wounded men judged fit to survive the trip were loaded into ambulances and springless army wagons which had been emptied of rations, ammunition, and fodder. Henry Marsh accompanied one such train to Fredericksburg, walking and running all night to keep up with the wagons. This train came in on the Plank Road and, wherever planks were missing, Marsh remembered that he "could hear the groans of the wounded as the wagons struck." By May 11th,

Fredericksburg had been turned into one vast hospital, where every church, shop, factory, store, and many private homes sheltered wounded soldiers. Slightly wounded men were given coffee, meat and bread, then sent on nine more miles to Belle Plain for shipment to Washington. Severely injured men were kept at Fredericksburg. One Wisconsin inspector said of those in the city, "Many of them must die—and more still must die of disease than of wounds, for the whole city is a filthy hole."[16]

Steamers from Belle Plain docked at the Sixth Street Wharf in Washington, where immense tables loaded with coffee, sandwiches, and delicacies awaited new arrivals. In two weeks, more than 15,000 men were thus greeted at the wharf before being dispersed to twenty-two general hospitals in the Department of Washington. Like Fredericksburg, Washington had turned into "one vast receptacle of the mangled heroes, who have bled and died for the republic." Military Agent Isaac W. Montfort began to forward stores as soon as word of the Wilderness fighting reached Washington. A sub-agent was dispatched to Fredericksburg with orders to "keep his room open, so things can be had at any hour," whether for Hoosier soldier, nurse, or friend. Perhaps the Indiana Agency's greatest contribution was its register, which daily updated the location and condition of every wounded Indiana soldier in that particular theater of the war. Family members and friends had only to stop at the Agency to obtain directions on how to find their loved ones.[17]

During their May 15th to May 20th hiatus, the 19th Indiana lost two men slightly wounded. On the 21st William Jackson went to the front from the brigade train and found his friends "generally well." After strengthening his picket line, Cutler withdrew the division that afternoon and started his rested troops for Guiney's Station. The Iron Brigade marched at 3 A.M. on May 22nd and halted at Thornburg's Mill on the Po River. There the men built breastworks and watched a large enemy force, which totally ignored the Western brigade, marching along across the river. Camping that night near Harris's Store, Cutler got his men moving by 5 o'clock next morning and by 1 P.M. on May 23rd the Fourth Division was in position to force a crossing of the North Anna River at Jericho Mills. Cutler held his ground until the rest of the corps arrived, then covered Griffin's division as it waded across. Warren's engineers arrived shortly after 3 o'clock and had a pontoon bridge erected in an hour's time. Cutler's division walked over the river and, since no enemy had appeared, halted on the open bank, stacked arms, and prepared to cook supper.[18]

When a few rebels were spotted off to the right, Cutler was ordered to prolong Griffin's line. The men were unprepared for a movement, but quickly hurried off toward their assigned positions. One New York officer remembered:

> The men had their traps off or straps loosened to rest, and they had to pick them up and fix them as they went. The coffee was too hot to drink, so I went along with my cup in one hand and stick with a piece of ham on it, about half cooked, in the other.

Cutler's advance had more the appearance of a picnic than a military movement as it crossed the open field to some woods beyond. The 6th Wisconsin had just joined the right of Griffin's works and the rest of Colonel Robinson's regiments were still moving into line when the rebs sprang an ambush. Volley after volley roared from the woods, then regiment after regiment sprang forward "with great fury." Artillery shells exploded in the rear, creating pandemonium among non-combatants and driving many back into the river.[19]

The 7th Indiana was on Robinson's right and Major Merit Welsh reported that his men were forced to retire by "overwhelming numbers." One of Welsh's soldiers admitted that the enemy "suddenly fired a volley which caused the old iron brigade to waver a little." The brigade collapsed from right to left, men dropping their suppers and taking to their heels. Other observers were not so charitable in their descriptions. L. A. Hendrick, correspondent for the *New York Herald,* called it a "temporary panic." One New York artillery officer watched as the Iron Brigade "began to retire in great haste and confusion." Recalling the brigade's proud history, he continued, "But there are times when scarred and war-worn soldiers cower before the 'leaden rain and iron hail' of battle, particularly when such a furious storm bursts upon them at an unlooked for moment." For a few minutes it looked like the Fifth Corps would be driven into the North Anna, duplicating the Ball's Bluff disaster of 1861.[20]

Until the infantry could rally, artillery would have to hold back the attackers. Fortunately, three batteries had crossed the river just before Cutler's First and Third brigades dissolved. They immediately went into position and commenced firing canister. The 6th Wisconsin, last of the Iron Brigade regiments to retire, rallied behind Captain Charles Mink's Battery H, 1st New York Artillery. Captain Orr, with a portion of the 19th Indiana, and Captain Volney Shipman and his sharpshooters joined the Badgers and hastily formed a line to protect Mink's guns. Captain Wood of the brigade staff rallied about fifty fugitives and put them into line nearby. This hastily formed force near the guns was reinforced by John Truitt, who had come to Virginia in a vain attempt to recover Colonel Williams's body. He had stayed on to visit with friends in the regiment, but now took up a musket in the emergency and joined the line defending the New York battery.[21]

The 19th Indiana lost one man killed and seven wounded during this fight. Corporal Andrew J. Wood had carried the 19th Indiana's flag back to the batteries and stood there with the colors at the bottom of a slight elevation. Wood remembered that "a rebel came on top of the hill & drew bead on me and I about faced and recd the ball in [my] left hip." Corporal William Small, Company D, was struck by a ball that entered his left elbow, shattered the bones of his arm and exited through the wrist, leaving the arm twisted and the hand unable to grip. Sergeant Samuel Goodwin, detailed to the Ambulance Corps from Company I, ran forward from the river with some stretcher-bearers to remove wounded. Goodwin fell when a bullet shattered his ankle, later resulting in amputation and his eventual death in November. At Gettysburg, Private Zacharias Hancock, Company I, had received a gunshot wound in the head that left him hard of hearing, unable to chew food, and subject to blindness and dizziness whenever he bent over. Hancock had received a discharge on December 2, 1863, and promptly applied for a disability pension, but then inexplicably returned to his company. Hancock was shot dead during the fighting on May 23rd, just four days before the Pension Bureau approved his application.[22]

The batteries, supported by fragments from several Iron Brigade regiments, fired double (some said triple) charges of canister and soon stopped the rebel advance, but not before artillery officers had considered either spiking their guns or running them into the river if they were overrun. Cutler's Second Brigade came up beyond the guns and "poured in its murderous volley and the havoc was awful." The astounded attackers, now facing canister in front, Cutler's Second Brigade on their left, and Griffin's men on their right, found themselves trapped and fled in confusion. One Iron Brigade soldier confessed that the batteries had "saved us [from] a disaster most direful." Artillerymen rightly took credit for what turned out to be a Federal triumph, one officer writing that their arm "decided the fight in our favor, and turned, what appeared to be a defeat, into a victory." Another officer stated that the artillery "saved the 5th corps, or changed what was likely to prove a terrible disaster to our army into a victory."[23]

The battle on May 23rd found the Iron Brigade completely surprised and totally unprepared for combat. According to Colonel Charles Wainwright, corps chief of artillery, General Cutler "lost his head entirely when his men behaved so badly." Speaking of the Iron Brigade, Wainwright said:

> The bad behaviour of Cutler's first brigade is a strong instance of how panic at times seizes a whole command. No brigade in the whole army had a higher reputation than the 'Iron Brigade.' Its pre-eminence in the old First Corps was very generally acknowledged, yet one-half of it ran clear across the river without firing a shot, and two-thirds of the other half were brought back with difficulty by their officers to support the batteries, a service in which they have always taken especial delight.

Colonel William W. Robinson was severely criticized for his brigade's rout on May 23rd. Two weeks later, General Warren would write to army headquarters that Robinson "is not a satisfactory commander in battle, and neutralizes the efficiency of one of our best brigades." Warren hinted that Robinson might be detailed to some other duty, but his suggestion was ignored by Grant's adjutant general. Replacing Robinson became a moot point, however, because he resigned on July 9th after his Brawner Farm wound reopened, thereby disabling him.[24]

Henry F. Young, one of Colonel Robinson's officers, alluded to another reason for the brigade's embarrassing performance when he confided, "I never knew how much I could stand before." Captain William Orr predicted that "men can not endure such exposure & fatigue much longer." The Iron Brigade was simply worn out. Previous battles had tested their courage, but Grant's campaign, where every foot of ground had been contested, tested their endurance. Officers had not changed clothes since leaving Culpeper and their men were so exhausted that they often fell asleep in line of battle under artillery fire. Fatigue may have been a factor, but courage had not dimmed. One example will serve for illustration. Private Melvin Starkweather, Company D, 7th Wisconsin, had been wounded at the Wilderness, but was absent only a few days. He was again wounded in action on May 12th, but returned shortly thereafter, only to be mortally wounded on May 23rd.[25]

On May 25th, Cutler's division moved several miles down the river and his skirmishers found the enemy strongly entrenched. The Iron Brigade skirmish line lost heavily, particularly the 7th Indiana, which had one officer and six men killed. Casualties in the 19th Indiana were limited to one man killed and another missing. Although not wounded, Private William Balch, Company G, had a close call. A spent ball penetrated his blanket roll, but only inflicted a severe bruise when it struck in the pit of his stomach.[26]

Unwilling to assault the entrenchments found by his skirmishers, Warren withdrew the Fifth Corps across the North Anna on May 26th and started south again. Major Lindley's regiment did not cross until the following day, losing Sergeant John Hiatt, Company A, during the withdrawal. Crossing the Pamunkey River about noon on the 28th, Warren's corps advanced and took up a position near Bethesda Church. While fighting raged on the front near Cold Harbor, Cutler's portion of the line was relatively quiet, subject only to "a very galling fire" from rebel batteries and sharpshooters. Loss in the 19th Indiana during this period was one killed and three wounded. Among the wounded was Lewis Eller, Company G, who was injured when a cannon ball struck a tree behind the regiment, throwing tree limbs and debris onto his head, neck and shoulder.[27]

A veteran from the old First Corps described how this new campaign had depleted the ranks, then explained what surely must have weighed upon the minds of every soldier in Grant's army:

> Every day some comrades fell in battle, little noted by the world, but greatly missed by their companions as well as by the loved ones at home, and yet the handful of survivors—a mere fragment of a regiment marched and fought, wondering who next would fill a soldier's grave or be carried to the hospital disabled and incapacitated from making a living in the future. [28]

30

Nadir at Petersburg

On the night of June 5th, the 19th Indiana moved to the rear far enough to be away from bursting shells and whizzing bullets for the first time in a month. General Warren reported that the Fifth Corps, moving in the darkness over rough and unfamiliar roads, marched "little better than the crowd that walks the streets, as far as organization is concerned." The general's first concern was to bring up his corps baggage wagons so that officers could get a change of clothing and send back luggage belonging to officers who had been killed and wounded. Captain Alexander Pattison, 7th Indiana, went back to get fresh clothes and took a swim, his first opportunity to wash in thirty-five days. All of the officers were in the same fix. Captain Young of the 7th Wisconsin, confessing that he finally got a chance to change his drawers after more than a month of campaigning, remarked, "talk about being lousy & dirty!"[1]

On June 7th, Cutler's division marched to the railroad bridge over the Chickahominy River and camped, spreading pickets along the north bank from Bottom's Bridge to Sumner's Bridge. In typical fashion, the Iron Brigade quickly concluded a truce with their opponents on the opposite shore. Then the Western men went for a swim, diving in fully dressed and soaping up their uniforms in an effort to remove accumulated grime, having found this the most efficient way to wash clothes during Grant's campaign. After walking around in the sunlight to dry off, they felt and smelt much better. The freshly scrubbed Western men then constructed miniature boats and began to float them across the river to their trading partners. At any one time, as many as fifty of these vessels could be seen floating across the Chickahominy, only thirty feet wide on the Iron Brigade front.[2]

General Cutler was appalled by the fraternization between the two sides when he went down to the river on June 10th:

Upon an inspection of the right of my picket line this forenoon, it was found that our men and the rebels were mixed up promiscuously—on one log crossing the stream six rebels and five of our men were sitting, and a Lieut laying within twenty feet of them in a state of perfect indifference. The orders to hold no intercourse with the rebels were the most stringent kind, and if there had been none, the officers should have known their duty better.

After describing the incident to Grant's adjutant, Cutler recommended that two Hoosier officers, Captain Chauncey B. Patrick (in charge of the picket line) and Lieutenant William W. Macy (the indifferent lieutenant), "be dismissed the service with loss of all pay, for gross neglect of duty on the picket line." A second letter from Cutler to army headquarters offered proof of Patrick's culpability in the crime: "The captain had written orders in his pocket which he had not read or tried to execute." But veteran officers were now too scarce and Cutler's recommendation was ignored. Besides, fraternization did have some benefits, such as when six rebs from the 49th North Carolina gave themselves up the same night that Cutler reprimanded Patrick and Macy.[3]

The Army of the Potomac had been along the banks of the Chickahominy once before, and scattered everywhere along the river was grim evidence of McClellan's unsuccessful advance against Richmond in 1862. Several graves near the Hoosier camp were still marked by headboards that bore the date of June 11, 1862. When a *New York Herald* correspondent tired of walking through the two-year-old debris of Little Mac's campaign, he talked of going to a lookout post for a glimpse of Richmond. Captain Davis Castle obliged his curiosity and took him to a Signal Corps station. But when the newspaperman heard "the speedy little whistling of several bullets," he suggested cutting short their visit. The only response from Captain Castle was the remark, "Let them blaze away—they can't hit us in all day." Considering Castle's recent experience, his disdain for danger was understandable. Just five days earlier, a solid shot had shattered the table at which he and three other officers were eating supper, thereby creating "a curious confusion of crockery, vibratory motion of viands and derangement of digestions." Instantly jumping aside, the officers cautiously returned just as another bolt destroyed one of the chairs. Inaccurate, long-range sniping failed to inspire fear in men who had come so close to death on many occasions.[4]

June 11th brought the end of an era. The day began with an order from brigade headquarters designed to stop a simple, but successful, confidence scheme. Apparently when the wagons finally came up on June 6th, commissary officers were besieged by crowds of enlisted men bearing orders authorizing them to purchase goods for their company officers. But the officers, who had their accounts debited, never received any goods and the orders turned out to be fraudulent. In order to halt such deception in the future, any enlisted man who attempted to obtain supplies from the commissary was to have his name listed upon muster and pay rolls as a servant. Commanders had finally learned that pride was still the best weapon to use against those incorrigible veterans.[5]

One can only hope that soldiers from the 2nd Wisconsin were somehow involved in this cunning bamboozle as one last defiant gesture against military authority. The 2nd had always set the standard for theft, debauch, and courage for other regiments of the Iron Brigade ever since its organization. Now that proud old regiment was going home—few men had reenlisted and its three-year term of enlistment had now expired. Cutler said goodbye to them with the ultimate compliment, "You have never failed in any duty required of you." Then on June 11th, 133 officers and men (many of them unfit for duty) left camp and started for Wisconsin. Other Badgers joined the main body from hospital beds in Alexandria and Washington and Philadelphia until there were 173 old soldiers on the train when it arrived in Madison. A huge procession escorted the regiment through city streets to Capitol Park, where an official welcome awaited. Sick, wounded, and enfeebled convalescent soldiers followed behind their marching comrades in ambulances. At the edge of the park, Captain George H. Otis halted his column. Men were helped down from the ambulances and took their places in line, many either leaning on friends or struggling awkwardly with their crutches. Then with every man at his post and every face to the front, the 2nd Wisconsin marched into history. The American army would never see its equal again.[6]

As the 2nd Wisconsin started north, the Iron Brigade headed south. Under cover of darkness, Cutler's division marched to Long Bridge and crossed the Chickahominy at 5 A.M. on June 13th. One Hoosier noticed that here the river had two channels with a marsh between, the river resembling a bayou and "forming a fit habitation for reptiles frogs and musquetoes." On the far shore, the division turned to its right and guarded the crossing until nightfall, when it fell in behind trains bound for Charles City Court House. Cutler camped on the Coleville plantation, about one mile from Wilcox's Landing, at 3 A.M. on June 14th. The following day men passed their time either cooking, eating, or sleeping. Charles City Court House had once been a small village, but now all that remained unburned were the court house and jail. The home of former president John Tyler, now dead some two years, stood relatively unscathed nearby. The frame building, "neither extensive in its dimensions nor palatial in style," failed to impress Northern visitors.[7]

Grant's army had been repulsed in every attempt to reach Richmond, so now the general decided to bypass that city, capture Petersburg, and attack from a new direction. Cutler had his division ready to cross the James River at dawn, but it was not taken aboard steamers until 10:30 on the morning of June 16th. Shortly after 3 P.M., Cutler started his column for Petersburg. After seven hours, the men were allowed to stop and make coffee near Prince George Court House, but then moved on to within a few miles of Petersburg and halted. At daylight Cutler moved forward, located the enemy, and entrenched within 600 yards of their line. Rebel shells exploded about the new line of works all day, but inflicted few casualties. Although a few projectiles struck the Hoosier works, no one was hurt in the 19th Indiana. One Hoosier confessed, "It is no trouble for a man to lay close during shelling." Grant's new movement had created an opportunity, but instead of pressing forward immediately the generals squandered their advantage. By nightfall, veterans from the Army of Northern Virginia had arrived on the field and replaced the ragtag original defenders of Petersburg.[8]

After a reorganization at Cold Harbor, Cutler's division had been reduced to only two small brigades, basically old First Corps regiments with a few recent additions. Heavy details for picket duty along Blackwater Creek further reduced the command. At daylight on June 18th, Cutler's depleted division crossed its own works, sent forward skirmishers, and advanced upon the enemy line. Skirmishers walked unopposed into the enemy works, which had been abandoned overnight, waited for Cutler's main line to arrive, and started forward again. A second line of enemy works, also empty, was taken along with a few sleeping rebels. The enemy had not abandoned the field, but had merely withdrawn to a better position beyond the Norfolk & Petersburg Railroad. To hinder pursuit, retreating rebs had burned the bridge over a deep cut in the railroad that lay in the path of Cutler's advance. Crossing one portion of the infantry at a time, Cutler finally got them all across the cut, then had his pioneer corps rebuild the bridge so that he could bring across his artillery. After passing through a strip of woods, a third enemy line was discovered, this new position being on a ridge about one-half mile beyond the railroad.[9]

At 2:50 P.M. Cutler received an order to attack with his division, another message received ten minutes later announcing that there would be a general assault along the entire line. It was not until 3:20 that his Second Brigade, supported by the Iron Brigade, began the assault. Cutler's report of the operation reads:

> My command suffered severely both by direct and flank fire of both infantry and artillery, and though a part of both brigades got within about seventy-five yards of the enemy's works they were unable to carry

them. My men held the ground gained until dark, when, in obedience
of orders, I withdrew the most advanced portions of my command and
intrenched, connecting with Griffin on my right and Ayres on my left.

Admitting that he had lost one-third of his division in the attack, Cutler
glossed over the fact that it was "a horrid massacre," hopelessly mismanaged
and doomed from its inception.[10]

Colonel J. William Hofmann had formed his brigade behind the
crest of a hill in preparation for the charge on rebel entrenchments on
another crest some 700 yards distant. One member of the brigade wrote,
"Believing that the final blow to the rebellion was about to be struck, the line
moved forward with spirit." As Hofmann's regiments appeared and de-
scended into the valley between the lines, Lee's veterans opened fire with
musketry, case shot, and canister from their front and both flanks. This
Federal line broke as it approached a large ravine about 200 yards from its
objective. A few hundred men reached the far slope of this ravine where they
took shelter, while the remainder ran for the rear, their flight disrupting the
Iron Brigade's advance. Of Hofmann's seven regimental commanders, two
were dead and four others wounded.[11]

By the time Colonel Robinson's Iron Brigade passed over the
protective crest, Hofmann's attack had collapsed. Cutler doomed the reinforcements when he ordered them to change direction after they came under
fire. On the right, Lieutenant Colonel Mark Finnicum reported that the 7th
Wisconsin began to double-quick and raced through Hofmann's fugitives,
some of whom turned about and joined the new attack. Finnicum's men got
beyond the ravine and within one hundred paces of the enemy before coming
to a halt. The ground at this point ascended at an angle of about fifteen
degrees before leveling off toward the reb breastworks. This topography
protected the Badgers in front, but cannon fire and musketry continued to
tear into men from both flanks. Soldiers began to dig rifle pits in their
advanced position beyond the ravine, five shovels being augmented by
bayonets and tin plates. Batteries in the rear fired shells overhead to keep the
rebs from coming out of their works and capturing the attackers, some of
these rounds exploding just twenty feet in front of the Wisconsin men.
Finnicum sent Major Hollon Richardson, the brigade's fastest runner, racing
back with a request for assistance. Headquarters could do nothing, so
Finnicum held out on his own, losing fifty-one killed, wounded, and missing
during the day.[12]

As the 6th Wisconsin passed the crest, it was greeted by what seemed
to be "a bushel of small shot" from enemy artillery and "a heavy and killing
musketry fire" from Lee's infantry. In response to Cutler's command, this
regiment turned to its right under a murderous fire that forced it still farther

to the right and over a slight rise of ground. The Badgers had lost forty-four men, including their color sergeant, and never fired a shot. Experiences of other regiments fell somewhere between those two extremes. The 7th Indiana got to within one hundred yards of the rebels in what Captain Pattison wrote was "the most severe charge that we have yet made." Pattison's regiment lost thirty-three men out of less than a hundred that began the assault. The 24th Michigan listed thirty-six casualties and, although it too got men forward into the ravine, had no better success than other units. General Cutler emerged unscathed from the battle, although an aide, Lieutenant Seril Chilson of the Michigan regiment, was killed.[13]

During the 19th Indiana's charge, Captain Orr remembered that "for about 15 minutes the Bullets flew as thick [as] I ever seen them." After getting to within seventy-five yards of the crest, the Hoosiers broke and fell back to the ravine. Jesse Waidley of Company F described conditions there:

> We had to lay in the ravine until dark exposed to a flank fire all the time, both of artillery and infantry. They killed a great many of our boys. They threw 12 pound solid shot—it would make dreadful havoc. I never want to get into a place like it again. We had to lay and take it—what hurt me the most was the groans and sighs of the wounded and dying. It was awful and we did not know how soon we would be enduring the same. We could not do anything for them, for to raise up was sure and certain death. We dug holes with our bayonets and hands, which sheltered us from the infantry fire,—but not the artillery. We thought that night would never come—hours that passed seemed days; but at last night came; oh, I never thought men could be so glad. I will remember that night as long as I live.

Cutler and other officers rallied broken regiments on a small rise about halfway across the valley, where soldiers hastily entrenched. Besides waiting for nightfall, they could do nothing but drive back rebs who attempted to dislodge Iron Brigade men huddled in the ravine. After dark, Cutler withdrew his men from the ravine and got everyone behind his newly constructed line of earthworks. Then at 5 P.M. the general dispatched the results of his division's assault: "Every regimental commander in the Second Brigade is killed or wounded, and a very large number of line officers. The First has suffered most as badly."[14]

The attack had been a stunning failure. Colonel Wainwright called it "a fiasco of the worst kind" that even the stupidest private knew could not succeed. Lieutenant Colonel Dawes complained of the "suicidal manner" in which the assault had been carried out and asserted that the Iron Brigade had been used as "simply food for powder." Lieutenant Henry Young, 7th Wisconsin, could not believe that they had been ordered to capture "fortifi-

23. James Grunden.
From the Frances M. Vander Weide Collection. Used by permission.

cations that we could not take and we could not have held them if we had succeeded in carrying them." His conclusion was succinctly stated, "About one more charge on Rebble fortifications and our Regt will be out of Service entirely." Generals had failed them again, from Cutler to Warren to Meade. The Army of the Potomac was the most experienced, best-trained, and best-equipped army on the planet, but the inept generals, even after three long years of fighting, still could not coordinate an assault. Staff work was atrocious. No time was left for proper preparations. It was little wonder that an Iron Brigade soldier could write, "My hopes of getting out of the service with the regiment grows fainter every day and thoughts of my fate from the perfidy of authorities makes my feelings more and more bitter every day."[15]

A line of pickets advanced over the battlefield that night and screened the stretcher-bearers as they carried wounded men back to waiting ambulances. Cutler's pioneer corps put down their shovels and axes to lend a hand. Whenever searchers found a casualty, they stripped off his equipment and dragged him back to the stretchers. As he drove his ambulance back and forth to the division hospital, James Grunden was surprised to discover that his patients included three comrades from Company B—Dan Curry, Dave Fort, and Jake Hunt. A portion of the Hoosier regiment had been on picket, so Lieutenant Crull led only seven enlisted men from the Wayne County company into action. Six of them had been shot. Private Levi Purvis, one of the 1864 recruits, had been struck in the head and killed. In addition to those listed above, the wounded included Orderly Sergeant Tom Henderson and

Frank Huff. Crull had been struck by a ball that glanced off his boot. These casualties and the lieutenant's report that his company had expended 700 rounds indicate the severity of combat on June 18th.[16]

The 19th Indiana reported a loss of eight killed and thirty-two wounded for the day, leaving but about 125 muskets for duty. Among the dead was Private James Rigby, who had gone home to make an honest woman of his sweetheart while on veteran furlough. One of the wounded was David Norris, an ill-fated 1864 recruit from Company K. Norris had suffered through the typical diseases of new arrivals, having come down with remittent fever, acute diarrhea, and mumps during the month of April alone. It was no wonder that he did not feel well during his last days at Culpeper. When John Moore went to see Norris in early May, he could see that something was wrong. Moore asked what had happened and later recalled the conversation:

> He said he dident know, he never felt so strange in his life, he believed he was going to die. I helped him up and he walked around and said he felt better. He was excused from the ranks the remainder of the march but was always up in a short time after we would make halt. He was with us all through the battle of the Wilderness but was reduced to almost a skelleton by camp diarreah.

Although obviously unfit for duty, Norris kept with the regiment until his bad luck flared up again on June 18th, when he received a gunshot wound in the right shoulder. During his hospitalization, gangrene set in and ate away so much of the shoulder that an apple could be placed in the hole.[17]

The litany of broken health and broken lives continued apace. John Fitzsimmons, Company E, lost his right leg and succumbed to complications of gangrene. Seventeen-year-old Isaac Cherry, Company C, had his right leg amputated at the thigh. Dr. Ebersole took off the left leg of Corporal John Smock, Company F, but the stump failed to heal properly and left him incapable of wearing an artificial limb. James Denton, Company C, was struck while in the ravine, the ball entering in front of his left shoulder, passing through the lung and exiting from his back. He would never be able to raise his arm again. Corporal Carson Andrews, Company G, lost all but the middle finger on his left hand. The list goes on and on, mute testimony to the incompetence of generals who should have known better. But these soldiers were no strangers to suffering. Over thirty percent of the 19th Indiana's casualties during Grant's campaign had been wounded or captured in previous battles.[18]

After its disastrous charge, the Iron Brigade held that slight rise in the valley about 300 yards from the enemy's works. Rebs occupied the higher ground, thus allowing them to shoot down at the Western men almost at will.

June 19th seemed like an exceptionally long day, with bullets striking the works almost every minute. Men rigged tents for shade, but the Johnnies kept filling them with holes. There was little room, one of Company B's men remarking that he occupied "a space of about six inches square and about four men on top, I dont know now which is my feet." It was certain death to leave shelter. Captain Orr wrote, "If one steps out in the daytime Zip Zip the Balls come." John Dotson, one of Orr's men, was killed that day while innocently making coffee. Another casualty occurred in the pioneer corps, Grear Williams writing in his diary that "old rocksy the mule was killed." Firing finally ended after dark and the Hoosiers were careful to avoid showing any lights that could be used as targets by eager sharpshooters.[19]

Darkness on June 19th allowed one soldier from the 7th Indiana to perform a debt of honor. Lieutenant David Holmes, Company F, had been killed in the charge, but his body was too far forward to recover safely that first night. Benjamin Turner was determined to recover the lieutenant's corpse, explaining, "After the battle of Port Republic he swam the Shenandoah twice and saved me from capture, perhaps death in prison. I for one will try to get his body." Sergeant Abner Hardin offered to help. Crawling to within fifteen feet of rebel pickets, the two men found Holmes and crept back on hands and knees, dragging the body along behind them. After reaching their division skirmish line, they made a litter from their muskets and a tent, carried Holmes back, and made sure he was decently interred with a proper headboard.[20]

The 19th Indiana held its portion of the line until the end of July, digging trenches and improving conditions as much as possible. But sharpshooters continued to shoot up the Hoosiers as they went about their day-to-day activities. Nathaniel Rigsby, Company A, lost a leg when a rebel spotted him filling his canteen as he got ready to cook a meal. William Balch's arm was so shattered by a ball that Dr. Ebersole had to amputate it near the shoulder. Ebersole had plenty of work. In addition to one man killed, the 19th Indiana had thirteen men wounded between June 20th and June 30th. One of these was Thomas P. Davis, Company B, shot on June 27th while on the skirmish line. A ball entered his left forearm, causing permanent contraction of his ring and little fingers and paralysis of the thumb.[21]

On June 26th, a captain in the 7th Indiana would record those questions asked by everyone, "When will this end. Oh, God. Have we not suffered enough." Writing from a hospital bed at Satterlee Hospital in Philadelphia, Allen Galyean, Company K, thought it useless to say anything about his wound since so many had been hurt worse during Grant's campaign. For his part, Galyean confessed, "I am glad that I got shot, I git to live with the Sisters of Charity."[22]

It had been reported that Color Sergeant Buckles died on the way to Fredericksburg, but "being of a very strong constitution, and temperate in his habits," Abe managed to pull through. He was eventually taken to Lincoln Hospital, but Abe wished to recuperate back in his home state. The wounded sergeant wrote to Dr. Isaac Montfort on June 4th to ask for assistance in being transferred to Indiana, declaring that "a private soldier can do nothing for himself in a case of this kind." Abe declared his intention to return to the ranks "so that our old flag may once more float on the breeze from every fort and city of the South." Unsure whether patriotism was enough to convince Montfort, he added a postscript, "Judge Buckles of Delaware County is my uncle."

By June 30th, Buckles was in the Convalescent Hospital at Annapolis, but had just missed a mass transfer of Hoosier patients to Indianapolis so he wrote again to Montfort for help. After waiting another month, Buckles wrote directly to Governor Morton and pleaded his case:

> I was wounded in action at the Battle of the Wilderness May 5th \ 64 and at Gettesburg July 1st \ 63 and at Gainesville August 28th \ 62. I have suffered but little in comparison with some others though I think it no more than fair and just that I should be transfered to my own state while I am unfit for duty.

Sergeant Buckles's persistence finally paid off and he did obtain a transfer to Indiana before returning to duty in November.[23]

Confusion over the death of Abe Buckles was just one of many such instances during the campaign. General Cutler explained why when he admitted that "the losing of nearly every original brigade, regimental, and company commander, render it impossible to make anything like an accurate report as to details." Cutler continued:

> One thing I think may safely be claimed for the division—that it has endeavored to discharge its duties as promptly and cheerfully as any command in the army. If in common with the army it has not achieved any brilliant victories its list of casualties shows that it lacked not in its endeavors nor shrunk from its duties.

Iron Brigade men, along with their division comrades, had done everything within their power for three long years to end this war. However it was beyond their ability to influence the war's outcome, although Grant finally seemed to be heading in the right direction.[24]

Despite the terrible losses thus far, General Grant remained popular with the enlisted men. Private Elliott Winscott explained why:

He is a servant in which his country can safely confide, energetic, honest and faithful. The tender sympathy of kind humanitarians is not a trait to characterize a great General. It is his place to do and not to feel, and suffering should be of no consideration when a great object is to be accomplished. The country demands the accomplishment of a purpose in the prosecution of the war, at every cost, and sacrifice of life necessary, and he acts as the High Priest of the carnival. I make no pretentions to military genius, and do not profess to judge of military competence in men but I believe Grant to be the ablest General on our catalogue.

Although General Meade still commanded the Army of the Potomac, his men gave Grant credit for their success and seemed willing to endure still more for Brave Ulysses if he could finally stop the war.[25]

31

Weldon Railroad

 There had obviously been many changes during the last two months. General Edward S. Bragg, formerly colonel of the 6th Wisconsin, now commanded the Iron Brigade. John Lindley still led the 19th Indiana, but with the new rank of lieutenant colonel. As of July 1st, the following number of officers and men were listed as present for duty in Lindley's regiment:

Field & Staff	3 officers	5 enlisted men
Company A	1 "	19 " "
" B	1 "	8 " "
" C	2 "	14 " "
" D	2 "	17 " "
" E	– "	11 " "
" F	– "	14 " "
" G	3 "	11 " "
" H	2 "	7 " "
" I	1 "	21 " "
" K	2 "	20 " "
Total	17 officers	147 enlisted men

Including those either sick, on daily duty or in confinement, there were twenty officers and 172 enlisted men present with the regiment. At the company level, that meant a ratio of one officer to ten enlisted men instead of the full-strength ratio of one officer to over thirty enlisted men.[1]

July opened with the Iron Brigade still pinned down in the Petersburg trenches, although it would rotate with Hofmann's brigade, one holding the division line while the other rested in comparative safety to the rear. Time passed slowly in the trenches, where there was little to read and nothing to do but talk and write letters, letters that must have been rather hard to read at times. Jesse Waidley explained his odd handwriting to one-legged Billy Wilson, saying that "whenever you see queer letters, that is where or when a minnie passed pretty close, and where there is a big mistake, that was caused by a shell passing over." A battery of mortars was stationed nearby and the men enjoyed watching its shells throw dirt around in the rebel works all day. Every night the Hoosiers enjoyed a fireworks display, courtesy of the neighboring artillerymen.[2]

When the mortars were silent, there were two main topics of conversation. First, those soldiers who had not reenlisted were constantly talking about how few days they had left to serve. The second topic was a recent decision by the War Department to raise a private's pay from $13 to $16 per month, with other ranks compensated accordingly. Now men could have fun, see the country, *and* get rich in the army.[3]

After three days in the trenches, the Iron Brigade was rotated back on the night of July 1st. There had been constant skirmishing since the June 18th attack, except for an hour's time shortly before the Hoosiers were withdrawn. Christian Hearst heard the firing die down, then saw rebels waving papers and asking for an exchange. Hearst described the brief truce:

> Some of our men agreed to the offer, and one of the graybacks came over their works and offered to come half way if he would meet him. One of our men that was talking to him went over our works and met him half way; they exchanged papers and returned to their places. By that time, both sides commenced talking to each other quite friendly; they called over, saying, "Let's go home, and quit fighting." Our men told them an unconditional surrender would settle that. By this time, the conversation became quite sociable; but it was not long until one of our mortar guns sent a shell over to them, which burst directly in their works, and caused quite a commotion among the Graybacks.

After that shell exploded, Hearst noticed that the rebs lost interest in any further negotiation.[4]

When out of the trenches, soldiers spent their time singing, rough-housing, playing cards, pitching quoits, and playing tenpins with solid shot that could be found lying about. Rations and good water were plentiful, along with the luxury of ice from an icehouse a scant half-mile distant. Surviving officers spent most of their time on paperwork, returns relating to casualties, ammunition expenditure, and lost equipment adding to the normal stack of forms. There was a brief break for the July 4th holiday, when it seemed that everyone in the army was drunk. The celebration could have been more extensive, but everyone, officers and men alike, was out of money.

The 19th Indiana went back to their trenches that night and July 5th turned out to be relatively quiet, the hot weather and widespread hangovers discouraging skirmishers.[5]

Chaplain Thomas Barnett had written a letter of resignation on July 2nd, giving his reasons for wishing to leave the service:

> Out door speaking has so impaired my vocal organs that I am unable to speak loud enough to be heard by even a small congregation in the open air. I can not continue to perform the duties of a Chaplain longer with any degree of benefit to the Regiment.

After examining Barnett, Dr. Ebersole concluded that he was "unable to speak or sing so as to be heard by a congregation" and expressed fear that the chaplain might lose his voice entirely. Barnett's resignation was accepted on July 5th, leaving the Hoosiers without a minister for the remainder of the regiment's history.[6]

Aside from another battery of mortars moving into position nearby, there was no news of importance for about a week. Even the mortars were not important news since one Hoosier thought they already had "Artillery enough here to Shell the whole Southern Confederacy, if it was in range of our guns." Real news came in mid-July when Mrs. G. W. New, wife of the 7th Indiana's chaplain, forwarded stores to the regiment from the Indiana Agency at City Point. The three boxes of "house luxuries" and a large package of paper and envelopes were "equitably distributed" among the Hoosiers. In writing to express his appreciation to Mrs. New, Lieutenant Colonel Lindley said, "Allow me to say, after returning thanks through you, to the ladies of the Association, that the Hoosier soldiers cannot help but fight well, when they sensibly feel they are never forgotten by the ladies at home." Mrs. New forwarded Lindley's note to the *Indianapolis Daily Journal* for publication, hoping that the ladies might learn "how the brave soldiers feel about their donations." She also appealed for additional gifts so that all Indiana soldiers could be taken care of "in the rifle pits or in the hospitals."[7]

Delicacies from home were especially welcome, given the general upward spiral of food prices since the war's first year. Brown sugar had risen from nine to sixteen cents a pound, white sugar from thirteen to twenty-four cents a pound. Coffee that had once sold for twenty-eight cents a pound had almost doubled in price. Tea had risen from forty cents to $1.05. Of course, the largest price jumps occurred in the most desirable items. Prices of whiskey and tobacco had increased fivefold, but the largest increase was for pickles, which rose from twenty cents to $1.25 a gallon. Even the price of the common army hardtack had risen twenty-five percent. It was no wonder that the War Department had to increase military pay.[8]

By mid-July everyone had given up hope for Iron Brigade soldiers who had left camp on a mysterious secret mission four weeks earlier. Lieutenant E. P. Brooks had lived in that section of Virginia before the war and was quite familiar with the countryside south and west of Petersburg. Using this knowledge, Brooks formulated a plan to cut the Confederate supply line with a small mounted force of picked men. After his scheme had been approved at army headquarters, the lieutenant selected thirty Iron Brigade volunteers who were purposely kept in the dark about details of the expedition. On June 19th, Brooks gathered his squad and went to army headquarters for sealed orders. Then it was on to City Point, where they drew horses, equipment, and Spencer rifles. After being outfitted for mounted service, Brooks's party rode to Bermuda Hundred for supper and camped overnight with General James H. Wilson's cavalry division at White Pine Church. That night Lieutenant Brooks revealed that his force had been ordered to strike at the Weldon Railroad, to burn the bridge over Nottoway River and escape toward North Carolina. Upon hearing of their destination, most of the men considered it "a dangerous, if not a foolhardy undertaking."[9]

The bridge burners accompanied a brigade of Wilson's cavalry that passed through the lines near Reams Station, following along as far as Dinwiddie Court House. While the cavalry continued west, Brooks turned his party south. The raiders encountered no enemy troops for two days and two nights, but Confederate units all over the region had been alerted to their presence. At sunrise on the third day, just as the exhausted riders were about to eat breakfast, a rebel officer rode forward and demanded that the Yankees surrender. He quickly assured Brooks that his little command was surrounded and the Iron Brigade detachment gave up without firing a shot, a scant eleven miles from its objective. Brooks and his men were sent south into captivity along the railroad they had set out to destroy. As far as their Iron Brigade comrades were concerned, the raiders had simply dropped out of sight and it would be many months before their fate became known.[10]

Back at Petersburg, the fate of Cutler's command was unsettled. Reduced to only 2,000 men present for duty, the Fourth Division was less than one-half the size of other divisions in the Fifth Corps. General Warren proposed to eliminate his smallest division, but first consulted Cutler, who objected that to do so would break up what little remained of the old First Corps. As "the only general officer left in what was the First Corps," Cutler felt compelled to remind Warren of what his Fourth Division had accomplished: "I believe its history will show that its losses are greater in killed and wounded and less in prisoners than any body of men of its size in the army." Speaking for his men, the old man then stated bluntly, "They will not consider it just and what was promised." Meade rejected Warren's proposed reorganization, but did indicate that he would consider any plan that would place all the old First Corps regiments into a single division. That idea proved impractical, but the Fourth Division was obviously on borrowed time.[11]

On July 22nd, General Lysander Cutler wrote an extraordinary letter to President Lincoln. The general confessed that for the first time since the war had commenced, he was "seriously apprehensive for the result," not for lack of proper leadership, but for want of proper soldiers. Speaking of the troops then being sent to the army, Cutler explained:

> I take it for granted that a large proportion of the new men are to be substitutes furnished by those able to do so. They will get the cheapest they can, and unless some thorough, radical change is effected among provost marshals, examining surgeons, and superintendents of recruits, we shall, as heretofore, receive a batch of aged paralytics, scorbutics, imbeciles, &c., to be sent to hospitals or discharged—an element of weakness instead of strength. All these men are credited to the States, charged to the army, paid by the Government, and only do immense harm, by filling up the hospitals, requiring the time of surgeons and officers and of well men to take care of them and get them out of the army again, to say nothing of the immense drain upon the Treasury without any equivalent. I am most firmly convinced that not two-thirds of the conscripts and substitutes ever reached the army, and I think a thorough investigation would show that not half of those who did were ever available as soldiers for the field.

Cutler's letter was politically motivated. He thought that if tougher standards could be established, "the peace Democracy may not prevail" in the upcoming fall election.[12]

Good men were needed for the army because many good men were leaving. Terms of service for regiments organized in 1861 had already started to expire, reducing depleted battalions still further. The 2nd Wisconsin had already gone, leaving behind only two small companies of veterans. Non-veterans of the 6th Wisconsin, "nearly wild at the prospect of seeing once more their long separated families and their homes," departed on July 16th. Soldiers who had not reenlisted in the Hoosier regiment would leave next, their term expiring on July 28th. It is a safe assumption that these men did nothing that would needlessly expose themselves to risk in their last few days of army life.[13]

As might be expected, there were a few details that needed to be worked out. Lieutenant Adam Gisse explained the problem to Cutler's adjutant general:

> There are two men in my Co (Co A 19th Ind Vols) who Deserted their company and were arrested and returned to the Regiment. One (Eli Pearsol Private) had a trial but the sentence was not made public. the

other (George M. Conger Private) had not been tried. I was ordered by Col. S. J. Williams comdg the Regt to release the above named men from arrest, providing that they agreed to go into Battle. They Both agreed and behaved well and were both wounded on the 5th day of May at the Battle of the Wilderness. They are now in hospital. Their time of enlistment expires July 28th 1864. I would respectfuly ask the General what I am to do in the case.

Lieutenant Colonel Lindley added an endorsement that these facts were correct and that "the men spoken of above behaved well." General Cutler apparently approved of the men's good conduct and both were allowed to go home without punishment. Pearsol had deserted on December 14, 1862, and remained at large until March 12, 1864. After his death on May 16, 1866, Eli's widow asked Conger for an affidavit to bolster her claim for a pension. Conger obliged by swearing that, after Pearsol got sick in the summer of 1862, he "continued with the command until he was discharged in 1864." Pension investigators must have enjoyed the outlandish situation of one deserter swearing that another deserter was present with the regiment when both were actually hiding from the provost marshal.[14]

On July 28th, 104 men from the 19th Indiana were mustered out of Federal service. Many of them were in hospital beds or on detached service and could not actually leave for Indiana until later. Captain Orr was selected to accompany the non-veterans back to Indianapolis, but only fifty-six men could be assembled for the journey. The rest came along later as they recovered and became strong enough to travel. According to one Hoosier veteran, "thare will Be som glad lads when they get home." Among those going home was Samuel Smith, Company H, who had been given a discharge on October 11, 1861, when the regiment had been stationed at Fort Craig, Virginia. Smith, however, refused to accept the discharge and remained with his company until his enlistment expired. He was wounded in the head at Brawner Farm and in the right leg at Gettysburg prior to his muster out.[15]

Captain Orr used this opportunity to plead for promotion. On July 6th, Lieutenant Colonel Lindley had written to Governor Morton recommending once more that Orr be promoted major of the regiment. Lindley reminded Morton that Orr had been the only captain remaining after Gettysburg and that Colonel Williams had appointed him acting major. Since then Captain Orr "frequently had command of the Regt. Both in Camp on Drill and in *Battles*." Lindley concluded his appeal to the governor by saying that "Justice demands that he should have the Rank of Major." In a letter to his father, Captain Orr explained how he wished to end his military career: "I would like to see the war ended in our Triumphant Victory, I would like to march at the head of the 19th Ind. through the city of Richmond, in triumph, and then when the war is done to take back the Remnants of this gallant Regt. to their homes." Orr was determined to do all this as a major.[16]

At the request of Hoosier officers, General Bragg urged the governor to commission Orr a major. Writing that two field officers were absolutely necessary "for the proper efficiency of a command in the field, subject to the casualties of climate and combat," Bragg noted that the War Department had provided for two such officers "regardless of the strength of the command." The general then expressed his fear that the 19th Indiana would "sink in discipline and all that makes one organization better than another." Speaking of Orr personally, Bragg wrote, "He is a good soldier, quiet and unassuming, attentive to duty, respected by his command, as well as by his superiors, and of unflinching courage." General Cutler also wrote to Morton and concluded by saying, "I think Capt Orr should be appointed for the benefit of the service." Upon reaching Indianapolis, Orr obtained a personal interview with Morton on August 4th and presented the letters from Bragg and Cutler. His commission as major was issued that same day.[17]

By the end of July, the Petersburg line had undergone a considerable change. When the Iron Brigade first occupied this position, men who crouched in shallow trenches were at the mercy of rebel sharpshooters. Now, one Badger claimed, "a six mule Government team and wagon could have been driven up to the first line without becoming exposed to the enemy's fire in any part of the way." Picks, shovels, and axes proved to be an important part of the Federal arsenal. This section of the line remained quiet, but there was constant skirmishing on the front occupied by the Ninth and Eighteenth Corps, undoubtedly due to the hatred of the rebels toward Negro troops in those commands.[18]

The Iron Brigade was in the trenches on July 30th when the great Petersburg mine exploded on the Ninth Corps front. Everyone waited anxiously for the mine, whose scheduled detonation was well known to Union troops. Shortly after sunrise, one Wisconsin soldier watched in awe as a Confederate fort disappeared. He described the event: "A great volume of gas and smoke rose heavenward; the air surrounding the column of smoke was filled with pieces of boards, timbers, knapsacks, guns, gun-carriages and the bodies of those who occupied the fort." As guns and muskets opened fire along the entire Union line, the Ninth Corps charged into a huge crater left by the blast. After hours of fighting, the attackers were repulsed. During this assault, Cutler strengthened his picket line (a series of pits about ten yards apart and 150 yards from the rebel entrenchments), but made no other offensive movement. In the Hoosier regiment, Sergeant Henry Cain, Company K, was killed and Privates James Keith and Theodore Ward wounded. A minie ball shattered Keith's right hand, rendering it useless, although doctors thought he might one day be able to grasp small objects between his thumb and forefinger.[19]

On July 31st, the Iron Brigade moved to a new camp on the extreme left of the army, "almost out of hearing of the shooting." There the Western men enjoyed the quiet monotony of camp life for about two weeks. Lieutenant Colonel Lindley had been seriously ill for some time and finally received a twenty-day furlough on the morning of August 5th, leaving Major Orr to command the regiment. Major William P. Gould, "Old Greenbacks" to the Iron Brigade, finally made an appearance in camp and paid off the Indiana regiment on August 12th. Next day Grear Williams scribbled in his diary, "I am on a drunk." Williams had prudently sent some money home, but by the 16th he found himself broke. Hoping to restore his finances, he borrowed $15 but lost it all playing chuck-a-luck.[20]

The 19th Indiana lost the last of its young trio of 1864 recruits from New Burlington in August. Silas Hiatt had already been discharged because of his nightly fits. Michael Ryan, the likeable young Irishman who had ended his letters by writing "yours truly untill deth," had been killed in the badly bungled charge on June 18th. Now Nathaniel Cary was dead. After becoming dangerously ill, he had been sent to Methodist Church Hospital in Alexandria, where a family friend found him on August 3rd. P. W. Lewellen wrote of Nathaniel:

> He is as well taken care of as it is possible for a person to be in hospital. His clothes and bed clothes are changed two or three times a day and he is kept clean and comfortable all the time. The Hospital is a large Methodist Church, well vemntilated and kept as clean as a parlor, you cant find a bit of dirt any place about the house. The Officers of the hospital are gentlemen, from the Surgeon down to the nurses.

Although Cary seemed to be better than previously reported, Lewellen advised his father, "He is taking no medicine now except stimulants, whiskey and wine, he also takes beef tea, but does not eat anything." W. H. Ferguson attended the dying soldier in his last days and shared some details:

> He said that he want[ed] to talk with me. I told him to express himself freely. Said he I should like to see some of my folks but I feel as though I never shall in this world. I asked him if he was prepared to meet them in annoather. He said he was that he was ready to go at any time the lord saw fit to call on him

Ferguson concluded his letter by saying, "your son died happy & seemed perfectly willing to go to that blessed land where parting is no more." Nathaniel Cary passed away on August 17th, one month short of his seventeenth birthday.[21]

The Iron Brigade changed its camp on August 14th, again on the 16th, and struck tents at 12:30 A.M. on the 17th in preparation for yet another move. After waiting for orders until noon, the Western men gave up and pitched their tents. Bragg's brigade was up at first light on August 18th and marched to Yellow House (or Globe Tavern) on the Petersburg & Weldon Railroad, the direct rebel rail link to North Carolina. The Fifth Corps cut the railroad and repelled an attempt to retake it, but the Iron Brigade did nothing more than skirmish that day. Before dawn on August 19th, General Bragg was ordered to report to General Crawford, who gave him an important assignment. The Fifth Corps' movement had lost connection with the army's main line of entrenchments, leaving a dangerous hole that could be exploited by the enemy. Crawford ordered Bragg to deploy his brigade as skirmishers and fill the gap.[22]

Bragg's brigade numbered just 760 officers and men, but was ordered to hold a line nearly one mile in length. He at first failed to occupy the ground pointed out by Warren and Crawford, but after some prodding from his superiors finally got his line established. From the left, the Iron Brigade alignment, stretching through what Bragg called "a dense tangled thicket," consisted of the New York Sharpshooters, 7th Indiana, 24th Michigan, 19th Indiana, and 7th Wisconsin. The 6th Wisconsin, seventy-four muskets, served as brigade reserve. Men could not see over one hundred feet through the undergrowth, visibility declining even more during a pelting rainstorm.[23]

At 4 P.M. General William Mahone's rebel division rushed upon Bragg's flimsy line and cut it effortlessly. Striking the left of the 19th Indiana, the rebs captured Sergeants John Murray and Thompson Williams, Corporal David Whitney, and Privates Henry Marshall and William Parr. Sweeping over the 24th Michigan's advanced line, attackers snared almost two dozen Wolverines. Mahone's impetuous rush next overran the 7th Indiana, which lost two officers and fifty men. The Sharpshooters were next and screaming rebs captured the entire battalion, three officers and fifty men, before attacking the right flank of Crawford's division. The 24th Michigan had tried to hold, but "every man then took care of himself" amid a storm of rebel musketry. The gritty 6th Wisconsin came up quickly, attempted to stop the rebel tide at a few points, but then collapsed and ran for it. Mahone's men continued on and nearly surrounded Crawford's division before retiring with almost 2,000 prisoners. Bragg's Iron Brigade, obviously stretched far too thin, had crumpled like paper in a matter of minutes.[24]

The 7th Wisconsin and some of the 19th Indiana, after capturing forty-five of the attackers, fell back toward the old lines and linked up with Gershom Mott's division of the Second Corps. General Crawford met another fragment of the Hoosier regiment, under a lieutenant, just after the attack began. Unaware of the force confronting him and the danger posed to his division, Crawford directed the Indiana officer to form his men and "at once return to his position and establish his connection to the right and left." Crawford galloped away, leaving the lieutenant shaking his head at the idea of holding the extended line with his small squad. Generals Cutler and Bragg, with their staff officers, set about to rally the broken brigade. That night they could assemble but 170 men of the Iron Brigade.[25]

On the afternoon of August 20th, Bragg's brigade marched to the left, near the Yellow House, and formed a line parallel to and beyond the Weldon Railroad. Undisturbed by the rebels, Western men built a solid line of entrenchments. Sunday morning, the 21st, was dreary and rainy, and according to one observer, "An unmistakable smell of battle was in the air." At 9 A.M. firing burst out on the skirmish line and soon after Mahone's division attacked Cutler's line of entrenchments. As the rebels came into range, the Iron Brigade opened fire, or at least tried to open fire. Muskets had remained loaded since Mahone's previous attack and constant rain had dampened the powder. As a brigade of Mississippians came closer and closer, soldiers furiously tried to dry the wet powder. One soldier remembered, "It was a continuous snapping of caps with here and there a p-i-s-h until the exploding caps had dried the powder sufficiently to burn and generate gas enough to blow the ball out of the gun." It looked like bayonets might decide the day, but finally the charges began to go off and Bragg's men "let them have it right in their faces, mowing them down by hundreds, and in a short time breaking their lines." Some rebs found shelter in a ravine, where they dropped their muskets and waved hats as a token of surrender. Ordered to leave their weapons and come in, they ran for Bragg's line "as if Satan would get the last man."[26]

Fighting behind breastworks was a novel experience for soldiers of the Iron Brigade. They had often assaulted entrenched lines, but now discovered that defending them was awfully easy. Bragg lost only a handful of men, not one of them from the 19th Indiana, but the brigade's musketry, belated as it was, created a field of carnage. Hundreds were shot down and many more simply gave up. The Iron Brigade commander could proudly report, "In this affair my brigade captured 6 field officers, 15 line officers and 101 enlisted men, 2 stand of colors, a number of wounded, and a quantity of small arms." The colors referred to belonged to the 12th and 16th Mississippi, both of whose commanders had also been captured.[27]

On August 22nd, the skirmish line advanced to protect those Union troops engaged in burying the rebel dead, bringing in the wounded, and recovering muskets and equipment in front of the breastworks. The Hoosiers turned in eighty muskets picked up on their front. From the gloom of

Mahone's devastating attack two days earlier, the 19th Indiana had rallied to win perhaps its most satisfying victory of the war.[28]

After August 21st, the Weldon Railroad was securely in Union hands. General Warren's stature had increased tremendously and the Indiana men thought more of him than ever before. Generals Cutler and Bragg both had experienced close calls on the last day of battle. Cutler, who had reached the Iron Brigade front just before the firing ceased, was struck on the upper lip by a ball that inflicted a slight wound. The old man took advantage of his opportunity to obtain a leave of absence and soon left for home, never to return to active duty. Bragg's face had been splattered with blood and brains when a nearby soldier was struck in the head by a shell, but he emerged unscathed and retained command of the Iron Brigade. On the 24th, Cutler's old division was "temporarily" broken up, the Iron Brigade thus becoming the First Brigade, Third Division (Crawford's), Fifth Corps, a reorganization that soon proved permanent. The Weldon Railroad engagement would prove to be the 19th Indiana's last major battle and thereafter its fighting would be confined to picket pits or skirmish lines. Lieutenant Crull estimated that, in this last fling with the rebels, Company B expended 600 rounds of ammunition on August 19th and 400 rounds on the 21st.[29]

The Iron Brigade remained quietly near Yellow House, strengthening its works and building abatis. On August 25th, Bragg's men started off to reinforce the Second Corps at Reams Station, but turned back after marching less than a mile. The remainder of the month followed an old formula. One Badger soldier recalled, "We had marching orders, same countermanded, prepared for an attack by the enemy, made out muster rolls and on the 31st of August, the regiment was mustered for July and August, after which, we packed up and got ready to move, but did not." By the end of August, many Hoosier officers had already served past their three-year term and indicated an intention to leave the army, either by accepting a muster out or by applying for a discharge. Other officers remained on detached service or in prison. Major Orr warned Indiana authorities that, unless new commissions were quickly issued, "we shall not have an Officer to each Company for Duty."[30]

32

Betrayal

Following Warren's successful capture of the Weldon Railroad, the military railroad from City Point that supplied the Army of the Potomac was extended to Yellow House, the first locomotive arriving there on September 11th. By that time, another regiment from the Iron Brigade was gone. The 7th Indiana had been a late addition to the brigade, joining the Western men just in time to march into the Wilderness. These Hoosiers had been welcomed with open arms by veterans of Gibbon's old brigade and had been treated as equals from the very first day. Early on September 6th, thirty-two veterans and eighty-three recruits were officially transferred to the 19th Indiana.[1]

At 8 A.M. on that day, the remainder of the 7th Indiana fell into line for the march to City Point and points north. One last time that regiment's survivors swung their hats and gave rousing cheers for Governor Morton, President Lincoln, and the Union. A band struck up a marching tune and "with solemn gladness" they started homeward. One of them later remembered being "sorry to leave our old army comrades, and yet glad to be 'homeward bound.'" Lieutenant Charles W. Hartup, the 19th Indiana's new quartermaster, offered a eulogy at their departure, "They have served faithfully, and now return to their homes and friends with the full assurance that they have done their part well. No better Regiment ever left the State."[2]

Six of Major Orr's officers left the 19th Indiana during this period. They included Captains David Holloway and Chauncey Patrick; First Lieutenant Lewis Yeatman (twice wounded in Grant's campaign); and Second Lieutenants Adam Gisse, Julius Waldschmidt, and William Murray. Commenting on the departure of Lieutenant Murray, a personal friend, Major Orr sadly wrote, "Thus one by one the 19th melts away." His only consolation was in knowing that Murray would be safe back in Indiana. In previous years, sick and wounded men often left their hospital beds to be with their comrades if a battle threatened. Now soldiers lingered in the hospitals. Writing from Satterlee Hospital in Philadelphia, Sergeant Allen Galyean confessed, "I am going to lay back and see what effect the Draft has before I volunteer for the front again."[3]

As if personifying the 19th Indiana's woebegone condition, the Stars and Stripes had worn out and become unfit for further service. This banner had been carried at Fitzhugh Crossing, Chancellorsville, Gettysburg, Mine Run, Wilderness, Laurel Hill, North Anna, Petersburg, and Weldon Railroad. On September 8th, Major Orr described the regimental standard: "The staff is shattered by balls and the flag itself torn to shreds by balls and by the elements." Orr requested that the state send a replacement, "under whose ample folds we can in the future as we have in the past fight for the integrity of the Country and the preservation of the Government."[4]

The departure of combat-tested veterans was balanced by the arrival of substitutes, convalescents, and conscripts, so the army's strength remained relatively stable. Echoing the sentiments that General Cutler had shared with President Lincoln, Quartermaster Hartup wrote that the army badly needed more men, but only if they were of good quality:

> Oh, that our people would, as becomes American citizens who desire a good and free government, rush to arms, strike the last blow at treason, and victory triumphant would crown and bless us; instead of wrangling, and contending as to who shall go or who shall not go, and running all over the country, buying up old, decripid negroes, refugees, and bounty jumpers, to represent them in our armies.

Hartup continued:

> The army does not want such men. We want good, honest, sober and patriotic men who appreciate and will fight for the noble cause in which we are engaged. The soldiers in the field have endured almost everything that mortals can endure, and are willing and anxious to continue, if the people will support them—will send more men to their support—but they do not like to be, as it were, cast into a den of lions, and left to their fate.

But the 19th Indiana had indeed been cast to its fate and could never recapture those halcyon days of 1862 and 1863 when the Iron Brigade feared nothing in its path.[5]

Having been reduced to only eighty-two muskets, the Hoosier regiment was doomed. Special Orders No. 317, Adjutant General's Office, dated September 23, 1864, signaled the War Department's intention:

> Upon the receipt of this Order by the Commanding General, Army of the Potomac, the reenlisted veterans and recruits of the 7th and 19th Indiana Volunteers, now remaining in service, will be permanently transferred to the 20th Indiana Volunteers, the consolidated force to bear the name of the latter regiment.

On September 27th, Special Orders No. 260, Headquarters, Army of the Potomac, directed implementation of the War Department's directive:

> For the purpose of carrying into effect paragraph 47 of Special Orders No. 317 of September 23d 1864, from the War Department, the battalions of the 7th and 19th Indiana Vols, serving in the 5th Army Corps, will report with as little delay as practicable to Major General Hancock, Commanding the 2d Army Corps, for consolidation with the 20th Indiana Vols.

The 19th Indiana was about to suffer what the soldiers perceived as a terrible indignity after more than three years of distinguished service.[6]

Knowing that they had no chance of successfully appealing the substance of these orders, officers decided to object on a technicality. On September 29th, the Hoosiers carefully crafted their protest and sent it up the chain of command to Colonel T. S. Bowers, Grant's adjutant general. Frustration and pride are evident in their emotional appeal for justice:

> Col. we have the honor to represent that by paragraph 47 Special Orders No 317 from the War Dept, Adjutant Generals Office, dated Sept 23d 1864, and paragraph 2 Special Orders No 260 Hd Qtrs Army of the Potomac, dated Sept 27th 1864, we are ordered to report with our Battalion of the 19th Ind Vols to Major Gen. Hancock for consolidation with the 20th Ind Vols. We would respectfully represent that the 19th Ind Vols is not a Battalion in the strict meaning of the word. It is a *Regiment*. It is true that we have been fearfully reduced in numbers by the casualties of Battle. We number but 303 present and absent, yet we are a *Regiment, A Veteran Regiment,* and not a Battalion. Our men reenlisted with the express understanding that we should not lose our identity as a Regt, and it will be a sad day to us when we are absorbed in any other Regiment. Again: We form a part of the "Iron Brigade" of the West originally composed of the 19th Ind Vols 2nd 6th and 7th Wis Vols.
>
> The Brigade was organized in 1861. Has fought as a Brigade on many bloody fields and the survivors had hoped that we might still be associated together till the *end* which we trust is near at hand and we would esteem it as a great favour; to be permitted to retain our Regimental organization and name, and to remain in our old Brigade. Here we are known and understood. Here we have a reputation and a name; and if it is consistent with the interest of the Service we would like to be permitted to remain as we are, and to be relieved from the necessity of consolidating as provided in the orders above referred to.

General Bragg forwarded the letter after adding his own endorsement, "This Regt is a part of my command & has belonged to the Brig since its first organization in 1861. A separation of the Regt from their old associates in Arms I do not think will operate to the efficiency of the Service." Generals Crawford and Warren forwarded the Hoosier appeal, without additional comment, to Meade's headquarters. Before sending the letter on to Grant's headquarters, Meade added a brief explanation: "In the order from these Head Quarters the 19th Indiana organization should have been styled a regiment and not a battalion. It was supposed at the time that the regiment had been consolidated into a battalion."[7]

While he waited for a response, Major Orr made a cosmetic change in the regiment's appearance. The Indiana men still wore the frock coats and big black hats forever associated with the Iron Brigade, but one uniform item had been generally neglected. Sergeants and corporals had stopped wearing chevrons because the turnover in those ranks had been so rapid. Now Orr had the quartermaster issue new chevrons to all current noncoms, as well as lace for the seams of their trousers. The men were thus suitably attired when the astounding order came on October 12th that the regiment *must* report for consolidation next morning. Their appeal had been denied. One Hoosier soldier remembered that the news resulted in "long faces and much murmuring among our boys."[8]

On October 13th, the Iron Brigade was drawn up in front of Bragg's headquarters to bid an emotional farewell to the 19th Indiana. Lieutenant Mair Pointon spoke for the 6th Wisconsin when he described the "cruel act" that took away the Hoosiers:

> They left us, their hearts filled with sorrow over their forced separation from us. We regretted the separation and felt badly over their being taken away from us. We all gloried in the splendid record of the "Iron Brigade," a record which they helped to make.

Lieutenant Henry Young remembered how the 19th Indiana had served alongside the 7th Wisconsin for over three years, soldiers from the two regiments forming "warm friendships." Young then continued:

> The friendships that are formed in camp and on the field of danger are Stronger than they are in civil life. I seen officers and men of the gallant Old 19th Shed tears this morning in parting with us, and I have Seen those same men Stand firm and Swing their hats and cheer when charging on the enemy amidst a perfect Storm of bullets.

The lieutenant ended his observation with a common refrain, "Thus they go. there will Soon be nothing of our once Splendid Brigade left together."[9]

Major Orr marched his regiment to the Second Corps front and reported for consolidation with an aggregate strength, present and absent, of 408 officers and enlisted men. Of that total, fifteen officers and 288 men had belonged to the 19th Indiana and 105 men had originally been members of the 7th Indiana. While officers began to tackle the mountain of paperwork necessary to consolidate their regiments, the men took in their new surroundings. The entrenchments appeared formidable, built high enough so that a man could walk behind them in safety. A line of picket pits, about 200 yards in advance of the main line, had been dug at twenty-foot intervals, with no connecting trenches. The opposing forces had reached a sensible accommodation that allowed both sides to safely relieve their picket lines. Each night at sundown an unofficial truce went into effect and new squads of rebs and Yanks walked out and replaced the old details. A 20th Indiana soldier furnished a description of this unique arrangement:

> well when the boys begin to halloo to cease firing the whole of both sides raise up and have a jolification and one evening one of our boys went over to their line and Swaped papers with them. well when every thing is ready they call out get in your holes and they lay down and Shoot away all night.

Men on picket took from 100 to 150 rounds for a twenty-four hour tour of duty. The rebel pits were not too far distant and, when men from the 19th Indiana went out on picket the night of October 14th, "the rebs struck a man on the head with [a] Brickbat." Grear Williams went out to the pits on October 21st and recalled that "one Johny com over and we had a kind of a chat." The next night was "Cold as hell" and no one came calling.[10]

Soldiers from the 7th and 19th Indiana were formed into five companies: A, Captain Joseph T. Ives; C, Captain John W. Shafer; E, Captain James Nash; G, First Lieutenant William B. Wilson; and I, First Lieutenant William W. Macy. The 20th Indiana, which had previously absorbed the 14th Indiana, was reorganized into Companies B, D, F, H, and K. Many officers took advantage of this consolidation to leave the service and the Hoosiers said goodbye to Lieutenant Colonel John M. Lindley; Quartermaster Charles W. Hartup; Surgeon Jacob Ebersole; Captain James Nash; First Lieutenants Thomas J. Crull, Isaac Branson, Charles Baxter, and Clinton Johnson; and Second Lieutenants Thomas Henderson, Walter Jack, Joseph Scarbrough, and John Dittemore. Henderson, Jack, and Dittemore had received commissions as lieutenants, but never mustered at that rank and left as sergeants.[11]

Merging of these Indiana regiments resulted in a large surplus of noncommissioned officers, so the excess were discharged as supernumeraries. Forty-one sergeants and corporals from the 19th Indiana took advantage of this opportunity and went home. But they could not leave right away because red tape at corps headquarters kept them waiting until October

23rd. One of the noncoms would write, "It is perplexing to us to be thus delayed, our discharges are dated on the 19th." Their concern was intensified by the death of Corporal William A. Howren, one of the supernumeraries from Company C, who was killed by a stray bullet on October 17th while in bed asleep. Men anxious to get away from the entrenchments had no desire to further imperil their lives while waiting on some lazy headquarters clerk. Company B's supernumeraries were Orderly Sergeant Tom Henderson, Sergeant Charley Davis, Corporal George Beetley, and Corporal Dan Curry. Those remaining in the ranks were jealous of the noncoms' departure and Grear Williams would admit, "I would like to Go a long."[12]

The merger of these two regiments was officially completed on October 18th, but the Iron Brigade men had not yet accepted their fate. Grear Williams expressed the bitterness everyone felt in a diary entry: "Consolidated hell and Damb Nation No more company B any how." Williams was right. Captain Dudley's old City Greys organization had finally passed into history. Seventeen men were transferred from Company B of the 19th Indiana to Company C of the 20th Indiana, but only eight actually joined the new regiment. Nine others were either in hospitals or prison. One man—Sergeant Bob Conley—was cast adrift by this consolidation. Conley had been captured in the Wilderness and, because he had not veteranized, was mistakenly mustered out on July 28th with the other non-veterans. Since he was no longer in the service, at least according to the army's records, Conley could not be transferred to the 20th Indiana. So after October 18th, he was a man without a regiment. Although the sergeant still languished in a rebel prison pen, Robert G. Conley had ceased to exist on the army rolls. It was a interesting way for the government to express its appreciation for his suffering.[13]

Major Orr commanded the new 20th Indiana and his field and staff included a surgeon, two assistant surgeons, a quartermaster, a chaplain and six enlisted men. Strength of the various companies is given below:

	OFFICERS	MEN	TOTAL	PRISONERS
Company A	1	90	91	6
" B	2	95	97	4
" C	1	82	83	15
" D	3	80	83	7
" E	1	82	83	6
" F	2	104	106	9
" G	1	91	92	15
" H	1	94	95	4
" I	1	71	72	14
" K	0	89	89	2

As newly organized, the 20th Indiana listed 903 officers and enlisted men on its rolls. Of this total, eighty-two soldiers were prisoners of war and hundreds more were either in hospitals or on detached service. The number of soldiers actually serving in the ranks was approximately 300. That pitifully small remnant included all of the Indiana infantry troops remaining in the Army of the Potomac.[14]

Failure of the War Department to adopt a policy that would fill up regiments raised in 1861, instead of creating new ones, eventually made a shambles of the army's organization. General Phillipe Regis Denis de Keredern de Trobriand's brigade was no exception. De Trobriand had ten regiments under his command:

> 20th Indiana (7th, 14th, and 19th Indiana)
> 1st Maine Heavy Artillery (converted to infantry)
> 17th Maine (3rd Maine)
> 40th New York (37th, 38th, 74th, and 87th New York)
> 73rd New York (163rd New York)
> 86th New York (70th New York)
> 124th New York
> 99th Pennsylvania (26th Pennsylvania)
> 110th Pennsylvania
> 2nd United States Sharpshooters

Those ten regiments also included fragments, both veterans and recruits, from eleven other regiments, whose designations are indicated by parentheses. With the exception of his converted heavy artillery, De Trobriand's regiments had originally served in the Third Corps. Now what remained of that corps had been merged into a single division. Survivors of the 19th Indiana, still wearing black hats with the First Corps insignia, found themselves in a new brigade, where men proudly displayed red or white diamonds (Third Corps badges) on their caps.[15]

General De Trobriand was one of the army's dependable brigade commanders. The son of a French general and baron, he had lived as a socialite until the Civil War began. Commissioned colonel of the 55th New York, the "Lafayette Guards," De Trobriand fought with his regiment in McClellan's Peninsula campaign, then was assigned to command the 38th New York. He filled in as brigade commander on a number of occasions before being mustered out in November 1863. His nomination as brigadier general was held up in the Senate, but after his confirmation he was assigned to command the defenses of New York harbor. After missing Grant's campaign from the Wilderness to Petersburg, General De Trobriand was finally relieved of other duties and assumed command of the First Brigade, Third Division, Second Corps in mid-July.[16]

Gershom Mott commanded the Third Division. He had entered the service as lieutenant colonel of the 5th New Jersey but was promoted to colonel of the 6th New Jersey in May of 1862. Mott led his regiment in the Peninsula campaign and at Second Bull Run, where he was wounded. Promoted brigadier general, he was wounded again at Chancellorsville. Assigned to division command at the outset of Grant's campaign, Mott was briefly demoted for a poor performance on May 10th. He was soon restored to command of a division and would continue in that capacity until the war's end. The Hoosiers' new corps commander was General Winfield Scott Hancock, one of the handsomest men in the army. De Trobriand penned a description of Hancock:

> He is tall in stature, robust in figure, with movements of easy dignity. His head, shaded by thick hair of a light chestnut color, strikes one favorably from the first by the regularity of his features and the engaging expression which is habitual to him. His manners are generally polite. His voice is pleasant, and his speech as agreeable as his looks. Such is Hancock in repose. In action he is entirely different. Dignity gives way to activity; his features become animated, his voice loud, his eyes are on fire, his blood kindles, and his bearing is that of a man carried away by passion,—the character of his bravery.

Indiana soldiers had first encountered Hancock back at Camp Advance in September of 1861. Hancock's brigade was then camped across the river and the Western men could clearly hear him drilling and cursing his new regiments. Both Hancock and the Hoosiers had come a long way since then.[17]

Hancock's regiments, like those in the Fifth Corps, needed large numbers of soldiers to fill their depleted ranks. But De Trobriand estimated that only sixty to seventy percent of new men ever reached his brigade. As part of a strenuous effort to recruit the 124th New York, nicknamed the "Orange Blossoms," officers appealed directly to Secretary of State William Seward for help. After Seward intervened, the commander at Elmira, New York, was ordered to dispatch 200 recruits to the 124th New York. Writing on October 12th, Lieutenant Colonel Charles Weygant described the result:

> I respectfully report that on the eighth of this month, I received from Col. B. F. Tracy comd'g Draft Rendezvous at Elmira, N. Y., muster and descriptive rolls that had originally contained the names of two hundred (200) men, but from which one hundred and eighteen had been ruled off, leaving eighty-two names yet on the rolls. With these rolls there

came to my regiment but seven (7) men and not one of the remaining number have since arrived.

Two official inquiries failed to discover what had happened to the absentees and Weygant wrote with disgust that "not one of the missing men ever reached the 124th."[18]

With winter rapidly approaching, Grant hoped to reach the Southside Railroad with an expedition launched in late October. Grant's plan was for two divisions of the Second Corps to locate the end of rebel fortifications, probably near Hatcher's Run, move beyond them and push forward to the railroad. On October 27th, Mott's division marched through heavy woods along a muddy country road until it reached the Boydton Plank Road. De Trobriand formed his brigade on the extreme left of the Union line, four regiments deployed as skirmishers and six regiments in line of battle to protect the Federal rear. At 3 P.M., without warning, a rebel attack exploited a gap between the Second and Fifth Corps. One brigade was overrun and lost two cannon, but the remainder of Mott's division turned toward the attackers.[19]

Hancock now ordered De Trobriand to charge the triumphant rebels. On the right, the 20th Indiana, 40th New York, 99th and part of the 110th Pennsylvania sprang forward "with wild shouts." De Trobriand galloped up behind the line just as a guidon bearer fell, his horse disemboweled by a shell. Three staff officers fell around the general during the charge, which caused the rebs to hesitate and give way. An officer from Hancock's staff led forward the Heavy Artillery and the remainder of the 110th Pennsylvania. In its impetuous attack, the brigade recaptured the two guns lost earlier, took one battleflag, and brought back 200 prisoners. De Trobriand's loss came to eighteen officers and 170 enlisted men, the 20th Indiana losing one man killed and one officer and seven men wounded. The general rightly gave credit to his veterans, who proved "a good example to the new men." One officer wrote that De Trobriand recaptured the guns because the rebs "had to run faster than was consistent with hauling away cannon." Anyway, Hancock's movement against the Boydton Plank Road had illustrated the critical importance of Petersburg's formidable defenses. General Lee could hold the trenches with a small number of soldiers, thereby freeing up enough troops to operate successfully against any flanking force.[20]

Men from the old 19th Indiana apparently did not like fighting with their new Second Corps comrades. After returning from the Boydton Road raid, many of the old-timers simply walked back to the Iron Brigade. Lieutenant Pointon remembered, "They swore that they would never go back to their new command and did not until forced at the point of a bayonet." Obviously, the Hoosiers still had not accepted their consolidation.[21]

Conversation during the last days of October centered on the national election scheduled for November 8th. Soldiers debated endlessly over whether Lincoln would be reelected or whether George B. McClellan, the army's favorite "Little Mac," would carry the Democratic party into power. Hoosier troops could only argue among themselves, the Democrat-controlled state legislature deeming it "inexpedient" for Indiana soldiers to vote in the field. But at least one of Major Orr's men managed to vote for the Republican ticket. Private Jacob Hunt had been laid up at Emory Hospital ever since his foot had been amputated on June 18th. He received a furlough and returned to Plainfield, Indiana, where he consulted with Dr. William F. Harvey. The congenial doctor found Hunt's limb swollen and tender, so he wrote out a unique recommendation:

> I would recommend that his Furlough be extended so long as to permit him to remain at home to vote for President of the U. States at the next Presidential Election, for two reasons. 1st The general weakness of his body is such that he can not at this time render the United States much service; and 2ndly, his vote will be of as much or more value in the Presidential Election, in this State, than the service he might otherwise render the Government, I think.

Hunt was permitted to remain at home and he cast a vote for Lincoln, his final contribution to the war effort.[22]

33

20th Indiana

Word reached Federal authorities that the rebs had planned a night attack that would be carried out just a few days before the national election. A night attack was a rare event during the war, so the Second Corps made elaborate plans to defend its sector of the front. Leaving only a few men behind as camp guards, every available soldier in Mott's division was put in the ranks. They slept with their accouterments on and muskets stacked nearby, with orders to be in line and ready for action an hour before daybreak. The 20th Indiana was ordered to hold a section of breastworks near Battery 22. About midnight on November 5th, firing erupted to the right of De Trobriand's brigade and quickly spread to the picket lines in his front. Gunners from both sides opened fire with cannons and mortars, filling the sky with brilliant flashes and streaking projectiles. The enemy attack succeeded only in capturing a minor section of breastworks before the attackers were repulsed. Enemy losses totaled several hundred and a potential embarrassment to the Lincoln administration was averted.[1]

President Lincoln was overwhelmingly reelected on November 8th, McClellan carrying but three states. General De Trobriand estimated that the Army of the Potomac had endorsed Lincoln at the rate of seven to one. Soldiers in his brigade had voted on November 7th, slipping their ballots into ammunition boxes under the supervision of senior officers. McClellan's best showing was in the 40th New York, but he also did well in the 17th Maine. In the old Iron Brigade, Lincoln's majority was 389, every regiment voting its approval. The Hoosiers might have voted against Old Abe if they had been given the chance, but probably not. Major Orr certainly would have opposed the president, since he had recently written, "I do not chose to fight any longer *under* Mr *Lincoln* nor for the object for which *He* is now carrying on this war—I refer to the obliteration of slavery." Following the lead of Sol

Meredith, the 19th Indiana men had always opposed the Emancipation Proclamation.²

Rebel pickets had often cheered for McClellan before the voting, but those demonstrations ceased when election results became known. However, a constant stream of minie balls still punctuated their opposition to the Lincoln administration. One sergeant from Company K was mortally wounded on November 2nd and several other Hoosiers were struck by stray balls that fell into their camp behind Fort Sedgwick or "Fort Hell" as it was commonly known. Occasionally the Hoosiers would return the favor. Grear Williams and Joseph Warrick spent the day together on picket and the former could report with pride that "thare was one of the John rebs wounded and one killed." A camp story made the rounds about this time. According to those "reliable sources," General Grant was touring the front with a large gaggle of civilians when one of them expressed a desire to visit the pickets. Grant supposedly replied, "No, no; if I take a crowd of civilians, the enemy may fire and some of the soldiers might get hurt!"³

It is doubtful whether any of the soldiers would actually have been hurt. Reports indicated that the 124th New York expended over 100,000 rounds of ammunition on the picket line during November, all this from a detail that would not have averaged eighty men per day. Lieutenant Colonel Charles Weygant estimated that the John Rebs must have fired nearly as many rounds as his own men, resulting in but two casualties in his regiment. From this, Weygant concluded, "If put to my oath and asked the question 'How many rounds of this vast amount of ammunition do you think was actually fired at a human being by your men or by the enemy opposite them?' I should unhesitatingly answer—'Not one.'" At least in front of De Trobriand's brigade, it would appear that the pickets inflicted injury only by accident.⁴

Extracts from letters written by Hospital Steward Marsh give some idea of the exposure on the Petersburg front during November. On the 10th he wrote, "It has been very bad picketing lately, there has been so much rain filling the trenches partly with mud and water so that the men had either to stand up and be in danger of being shot or lay in the mud and the nights has been cool and wet, so you may judge of the comfort of soldiering here." Marsh explained the discomfort he experienced on November 21st, "I was busy nearly all day most of the time in the rain getting the sick away medicine wood &c, so when I got in I took off my clothing and rung it." One-third of the 20th Indiana was in the pits each day and Henry hoped that "both sides will draw in their lines so that it will not take so many and will not have to lay in those pits which are so disagreeable in wet weather." Constant exposure finally caught up with Private Joseph Sykes, "a fighting soldier not a hospital bummer" according to Lieutenant Colonel Dudley. Sykes contracted a

24. George W. Bunch.
From the Frances M. Vander Weide Collection. Used by permission.

severe case of bronchitis and was hospitalized on November 18th. After treatment at several different hospitals, Joe returned to duty on March 11, 1865, but Lieutenant George Bunch remembered that he was never able to perform any work thereafter.[5]

After a brief attempt by the commissary department to introduce salted fish into the soldiers' diet, Thanksgiving Day must have seemed like heaven. Contributions from all across the country flowed into the army so that men could enjoy a true holiday meal. General De Trobriand remembered what the Sanitary Commission had done:

> The City Point railroad brought us mountains of eatables, fowls of all kinds, pastry of all sorts, preserves of every nature. Turkeys and the traditional plum pudding figured there above all in sumptuous abundance, many having on them the card with the name of the giver.

Wagons kept distributing the food all day, so that every soldier, sooner or later, got a share of the delicacies. When one sergeant was asked how much the soldiers received, he responded that each man in his squad had gotten one-quarter of a turkey, a piece of pie, and four apples. Upon being told that it seemed like quite a meal, he responded quickly, "Yes, yes, a *small* meal; I could eat half a turkey myself!"[6]

Two days after their Thanksgiving feast, General Hancock relinquished command of the Second Corps and went north to recruit a new veteran corps. The War Department thought that the popular Hancock could tap into the large pool of soldiers who had become exhausted or disgusted, had accepted discharges and gone home. But veterans stayed away from the veteran corps in droves and the scheme proved a dismal failure. To replace Hancock, General Meade chose his own chief of staff, General Andrew A. Humphreys. De Trobriand gave an assessment of the Second Corps' new commander:

> His calm bravery and insensibility to danger left him always in full possession of his faculties. The only thing which could affect his self-possession was an unexecuted order or movement badly carried out in time of action. Then he broke forth so much the more violently in that ordinarily his feelings were restrained. To give vent to it, the general had flaming outbreaks in which all the vigor known or unknown of the English language burst forth like a bomb. After which, manifestly relieved, he resumed his usual calm demeanor.

He concluded his description of Humphreys with the observation that the general always wore a narrow, brilliant red necktie.[7]

Shortly after their new chief took command, soldiers from Mott's division had an opportunity to leave the trenches. Although Warren had broken the Weldon Railroad at Yellow House in August, Confederates still used that supply line. They simply ran trains up close to the Union lines, unloaded provisions from North Carolina onto wagons and carted them overland to the Southside Railroad. On February 7th General Warren took the Fifth Corps, reinforced by Mott's division, on a raid with orders to destroy the Weldon Railroad beyond the Nottoway River. Soldiers carried six days' rations and 100 rounds of ammunition. Annoyance at having to abandon newly constructed winter quarters quickly vanished as men learned that they would be marching into some new territory.[8]

Marching on the Jerusalem Plank Road was easy and the weather pleasant. By nightfall Mott's division had reached the Nottoway River, some twenty miles from Petersburg, without meeting any rebels. The second day Warren's column passed Sussex Court House and struck the railroad near Jarratt's Station. Cavalry had already begun the destruction that afternoon and the infantry continued it all night. De Trobriand's brigade soon became rather adept at railroad wrecking. Pioneer squads would remove some rails, then loosen the ties, or sleepers, along a section of track. Horace Shaw described how the work then proceeded:

> A regiment would file along beside the road, men would take hold of the sleepers at the place where the pioneers started, lift up the track, sleepers and all, and turn it directly over, as a plow does a furrow. Other pioneers

would follow along the overturned track and knock the rails off the sleepers. Another regiment would file along, pile up the sleepers on either side of the track, set them on fire, pile the rails on top of the burning sleepers with the middle directly over the fire. While the sleepers were being consumed the rails were being heated red-hot in the middle. Another regiment would march along, a couple of men would seize each end of a rail, hot in the middle, and start for a big pine tree, bend it around the tree until they came together, shift ends and go back, thus hooping the tree with railroad iron.

The night presented "a weird and queer spectacle," with bonfires seemingly everywhere, some men wrapping heated rails around pine trees and others brewing coffee over the flames, all during a pelting rainstorm.[9]

In less than twenty-four hours, Warren's expedition had systematically destroyed twenty miles of railroad, even though part of the men were kept under arms to guard the rail-benders. Rebel cavalry made an appearance near Belfield, but quickly retired across the Meherrin River to Hicksford, where a sizable force appeared ready to contest any further advance by Warren. The rain had changed to sleet in the pre-dawn hours of December 9th and everything was soon covered with ice. De Trobriand described the icy spectacle:

> The trees bent and the branches were broken under the weight. The wind, cold and damp, groaned amongst the pines like a complaint from suffering nature. The temperature lowered still more before morning, and, finally, a sun pale and as though himself frozen shone over a landscape of sugar candy. It was as beautiful as an opera decoration, and fantastic as a fairy tale, but exceedingly uncomfortable. Those who involuntarily stood around on the ice or sunk in the mud-holes were not much disposed to admire the marvellous delicacy of the twigs under their transparent envelope.

Pleased with the successful completion of his mission, Warren ordered the column back to Petersburg before pursuing enemy forces could reach the scene.[10]

Word spread among the Negroes who had readied themselves to flee with Warren's troop on their return march. After preparing provisions, they dressed up in their finest clothing for a march to freedom. Federal troops were astonished by the display:

> There was the Bolivar hat, with large wings, and the stove-pipe, with almost imperceptible brim; the frock coat of the time of the Restoration, and the coat with the codfish tail, of the reign of Louis Phillipe; the pantaloon *a la hussarde,* and the knee-breeches; boots and pumps; the

wool blouse and the ruffled shirt. Among the women, the hoops of the second empire were displayed alongside the narrow scabbard of the first; printed calico and white muslin. And what hats! and what caps! and flowers, and even feathers! An improvised carnival in the woods of Virginia.

Soldiers mightily enjoyed the circus-like atmosphere, but their attention was soon diverted to more serious matters.[11]

Near Sussex Court House Warren's force learned that farmers had turned into guerrillas, murdering Yankee stragglers wherever they could be found. Captured soldiers were stabbed, strangled, shot, cut to pieces with an ax, or had their throats slashed. Among the victims were two soldiers from Company B of the 20th Indiana, Corporal John Jones and Private Edmund Gainey. The two Hoosiers were traveling along a short distance from the main column when a party of blue-coated strangers walked up and engaged them in conversation. As soon as Jones and Gainey were off their guard, the guerrillas opened fire. Jones was killed instantly and Gainey fell, pierced by four balls. He was shot again while lying helpless on the ground. Jones and Gainey were found shortly afterwards by friends who brought them into camp.

Retaliation for these grisly murders came swiftly. Private property had been respected before these outrages, but now the order was to burn everything. The court house was burnt to the ground, along with every other building in the village. Every structure on fifty plantations was reduced to ashes, along with foodstuffs and haystacks. Near the Nottoway River, outraged Federals torched a tavern when they suspected guerrillas might be hiding in the basement. Nothing was left standing along the route except for now-empty slave quarters, a bitter joke on the county's residents. G. A. Hinon, a Hoosier military agent, wrote that "the people of Sussex county will long remember the swift retribution visited on them for cold-blooded murder."[12]

Upon its return, Mott's division occupied a new section of the Petersburg front between Forts Siebert and Clarke. One dark night shortly thereafter, William Orr was acting as field officer of the picket line. While making his rounds, Orr spotted several fires burning brightly, a clear violation of orders. The following conversation ensued:

Orr — "Put out those fires!"
Picket — "Can't do it."
Orr — "I order you to put them out!"
Picket — "My instructions are to let these fires burn."
Orr — "I shall report you for disobedience of orders."
Picket — "Also report that these fires are on the enemy's line."

Orr finally saw the light, so to speak, and politely apologized for having bothered them.[13]

Nearby another interesting conversation took place on the picket line. A large house had been burned between the lines, leaving only two blackened chimneys. As the nights were getting colder, one picket hit upon a novel idea:

> Yank — "I say, Johnny!"
> Reb — "Aye, aye, Yank."
> Yank — "Rather chilly over here. What say you to getting a few brick from those chimneys? They would make splendid fire places for our shebang."
> Reb — "Guess they would, but how can we get 'em?"
> Yank — "Easy enough. You fellows take one chimney, we will take the other."

Seeing the wisdom of such a proposal, men from both sides threw down their muskets and raced for the ruins, toppling the chimneys and carting useable bricks back to their own lines.[14]

The entire brigade was assembled on December 15th to witness a unique ceremony. On July 12, 1862, Congress had authorized the presentation of Medals of Honor "to the enlisted men of the army and volunteer forces who have distinguished or may distinguish themselves in battle during the present rebellion." The War Department had authorized one such medal for Private Archibald Freeman, Company E, 124th New York for his capture of the 17th Louisiana's battleflag at Spotsylvania on May 12th. His medal also brought a promotion to sergeant. After the presentation, Lieutenant Colonel Weygant recalled that Freeman "became for the time being the envied hero of de Trobriand's command."[15]

Before concluding the narrative for 1864, there must be some discussion of those soldiers from the 19th Indiana who remained in rebel prisons. Captain George W. Greene had been taken prisoner at Gettysburg and was later confined in Libby Prison. From there he wrote, "My health is not very good at present, but hope to be better soon. We suffer not a little for want of a sufficient amount of clothing, blankets &c. but we hope this is not to continue always, and with this hope, make the best of our condition." Except for a brief period at large with other officers who escaped through a tunnel, Greene spent ten months in Libby. He was afterwards confined in prisons at Danville, Virginia; Macon, Georgia; and Charleston, South Carolina. At Charleston, Greene and 1,600 officers shared quarters in the Marine Hospital. During his captivity, he wrote several letters home, but had to carefully avoid any mention of ill treatment to ensure they would be sent north. On December 2nd, Captain Greene finally could speak his mind in a letter that would be carried by another officer scheduled for exchange.[16]

Greene began by mentioning an urgent need for clothing, admitting that he was "entirely *barefoot*, and in other respects shockingly unsightly." He advised folks that letters and packages sent to Union prisoners were generally ripped open and their contents stolen. Boxes often arrived with only one-half of the foodstuffs and clothing intact. After being removed from the Marine Hospital in Charleston, the 1,600 officers were obliged to build their own quarters, sharing a dozen shovels and a few axes. Captain Greene furnished details of one prisoner's murder on December 1st, a scant twenty feet from his hut:

> This officer had an ax on his shoulder, and was starting for wood, the line having been extended to allow us to get fuel, when he was notified by the guard not to cross the line. He remarked that he was not across the line and turned to take another route, when the guard fired upon him, killing him instantly, the ball taking effect in the back and passing directly through the body in the region of the heart. This makes the fifth man of our number who has been killed outright, besides a much larger number wounded.

Many officers had made their escape and the Hoosier captain likened those remaining to an elephant won in a raffle, since the rebels had no idea what to do with them. Being free to express himself, the Hoosier captain lashed out at "this horrible 'bastile,' erected and fostered by a poor, weak, ignorant and relentless enemy, who are absolutely a reproach to our enlightened civilization—they, too, the self-styled, boasted chivalry of America! Oh! shame, shame on such ignorant, self-conceited hypocrisy."[17]

Any mention of enlisted men and rebel prisons in 1864 must center around Andersonville. Opened early in 1864, this new prison was designed to keep Union prisoners penned up in rural Georgia, rather than in any of the South's metropolitan areas. In the summer of 1864, over 30,000 men were confined on twenty-six acres, resulting in horrible living conditions. Lack of sanitation, combined with scanty rations and virtually no shelter, sent the death toll over one hundred a day. The situation in Andersonville was best described by two soldiers captured on the ill-fated Brooks raid, O. F. Tipple, 7th Wisconsin, and Thomas Newton, 6th Wisconsin. Tipple described the sight that greeted them when they first entered:

> The prisoners had gathered in a disorderly crowd on either side to recognize any acquaintance or friends that might be in our company; their faces, hands and naked feet were black with smoke from the pine fires, their clothing hung in tattered strips from their limbs and bodies, their hair, long and matted with tar and dirt, fell in ropes over their eyes,

which glared fearfully upon us as we marched between these living walls. It was like entering the portals of hell, where the gathered demons had crowded to the passage to bid us welcome to their infernal abode.

These men had once been healthy soldiers, but now were mental and physical wrecks. To Newton, they seemed to be "literally rotting alive."[18]

The prison was crawling with lice, which covered everyone and everything. Most of the men had diarrhea so bad that they could not reach the sinks and simply dug holes with sticks into which they relieved themselves. Newton remembered that "every available space was dug and filled up, causing myriads of maggots to be crawling over the ground, more detestable than even the lice." The main source of water was a small brook, downstream from rebel camps, which always had a filthy scum floating upon it. Men preferred to dig into swampy soil along the stream and allow water to filter into the hole, although every cupful also contained a few maggots. There was no soap and no shelter, except what could be rigged together from sticks and blankets. Thus had Union soldiers been shorn of strength and dignity, but their spirit remained remarkably strong.[19]

A few of the Gettysburg prisoners had ended up in Andersonville, including Private James Dever of Company F, 19th Indiana. It is possible to follow Jimmy's life in Andersonville by referring to the diary of John Ransom, a Michigan cavalryman. Ransom described meeting Jimmy on December 18, 1863, while still confined at Belle Isle in Richmond:

> Looked at him for some time and finally thought I recognized in him an old neighbor of mine in Jackson Michigan; one Jimmy Dever, a whole souled and comical genius as ever it was my fortune to meet. Went up to him and asked what regiment he belonged to; said he belonged to the 19th Indiana, at which I could not believe it was my old acquaintance. Went back to my work. Pretty soon he said to me: "Ain't you Johnny Ransom?" And then I knew I was right. He had lived in Jackson, but had enlisted in an Indiana regiment. Well, we were glad to see one another . . . Jimmy is a case; was captured on the 1st day of July at the Gettysburg battle, and is consequently an old prisoner. Is very tough and hardy. Says the Johnny Rebs have a big contract on their hands to kill him. But I tell him to take care of himself anyway, as there is no knowing what he will be called upon to pass through yet.

Jimmy began to spend evenings with Johnny, talking over old times in Michigan so often that they soon offered a reward for a new story. On January 20th, Ransom wrote, "Jimmy Dever comes to our tent every night and sits with us until bed time. Is a jolly chap and keeps us all in good spirits with his sayings."

By April, both men were in Andersonville, where Jimmy Dever was occasionally mentioned in his friend's diary, those relevant passages being given below:

April 10th — I have omitted to mention Jimmy's name of late, although he is with us all the time—not in our mess, but close by. He has an old pack of cards with which we play to pass away the time.

April 11th — Jimmy Dever has evidently sort of dried up, and it don't seem to make any difference whether he gets anything to eat or not. He has now been a prisoner of war nearly a year, and is in good health and very hopeful of getting away in time. Sticks up for our government and says there is some good reason for our continued imprisonment.

April 14th — Jimmy Dever the old prisoner, coming down. Those who have stood it bravely begin to weaken.

June 19th — Jimmy Dever looks and is in a very bad way. Too bad if the poor fellow should die now, after being a prisoner almost a year. Talks a great deal about his younger brother in Jackson, named Willie. Says if he should die to be sure and tell Willie not to drink, which has been one of Jimmy's failings, and he sees now what a foolish habit it is.

June 22nd — Jimmy Dever losing heart and thinks he will die.

June 24th — Almost July 1st, when Jimmy Dever will have been a prisoner of war one year. Unless relief comes very soon he will die.

June 26th — Jimmy Dever is very bad with the scurvy and dropsy and will probably die if relief does not come.

July 1st — Jimmy Dever still lives, with wonderful tenacity to life. To-morrow he will have been a prisoner of war a year.

July 4th — Jimmy Dever regrets that he cannot take a hand [in arresting the Andersonville raiders, a group of cutthroats and thugs], as he likes to fight, and especially with a club.

July 6th — Jimmy has now been a prisoner over a year, and poor boy, will probably die soon.

July 11th — Jimmy thanks God that he has lived to see justice done the raiders [six of whom were hung]; he is about gone—nothing but skin and bones and can hardly move hand or foot; rest of the mess moderately well.

July 17th — Jimmy Dever anxious to be taken to the hospital but is persuaded to give it up. . . . Many old prisoners are dropping off now this fearful hot weather; knew that July and August would thin us out; cannot keep track of them in my disabled condition.

July 18th — Jimmy Dever most dead and begs us to take him to the hospital and guess will have to. Every morning the sick are carried to the gate in blankets and on stretchers, and the worst cases admitted to the hospital. Probably out of five or six hundred half are admitted. Do not think any lives after being taken there; are past all human aid. Four out of every five prefer to stay inside and die with their friends rather than go to the hospital.

July 20th — Jimmy Dever was taken out to die to-day. I hear that McGill is also dead. John McGuire died last night, both were Jackson men and old acquaintances. . . . And so we have seen the last of Jimmy. A prisoner of war one year and eighteen days. Struggled hard to live through it, if ever any one did. Ever since I can remember have known him. . . . Thus you will see that three of my acquaintances died the same day, for Jimmy cannot live until night I don't think. Not a person in the world but would have thought either one of them would kill me a dozen times enduring hardships. Pretty hard to tell about such things.

July 24th — Jimmy Dever is dead.

Ransom's information was incorrect. Jimmy's "wonderful tenacity to life" allowed him to hang on until September 19th, when he finally succumbed to scurvy.[20]

Ben Duke had been captured with nine others from Colonel Williams's regiment at the Wilderness on May 5th and was eventually shipped to Andersonville. There the newcomers found five members of the 19th Indiana who had been captured at Gettysburg, but they all died soon after. In addition to Jimmy Dever, the doomed Gettysburg prisoners included James Edwards, Abram "Jack" Oliver, George Stockhoff, and Simpson Brasier. Duke bunked with two comrades from Company B captured at the same time, Bob Conley and Bill Sykes. Duke remembered, "We had one blanket and that blanket was all we had for shelter and bedding. We had four small poles and we stretched the blanket upon them for a shade in the day time; at night we took it down and slept under it, lying on the bare ground."[21]

A few weeks after his arrival, Duke was selected by a rebel sergeant to work with a squad unloading lumber at the railroad station. Ben took advantage of his good fortune to trade with the rebels. The first day he swapped a friend's cavalry jacket for onions and biscuits. Back inside, he sold the biscuits for twenty-five cents each and the onions from twenty-five cents to $1.25 apiece and made a tidy profit after paying for the jacket. Next day he managed to trade a watch belonging to John Pitman, Company A of the 19th Indiana, for Irish potatoes and biscuits, again making a nice profit. During his business ventures, Duke's rate of exchange for currency was one United States dollar being equal to four Confederate dollars.[22]

The camp commander quickly put a stop to such trading, but the rebel sergeant allowed prisoners to carry in armloads of wood that would sell for up to $3 a load. The sergeant, for a share of the profits, also allowed men to smuggle goods into the prison, as long as they were concealed from view. They did so by either hiding them inside an armful of pine boughs or by slipping them inside a hollowed-out pine log. After a few weeks of brisk trading, Duke had amassed enough money to start a shebang, or store. He would buy staples from the camp sutler at wholesale prices and sell them to fellow prisoners at retail, but not always for cash. Duke explained, "Three-fourths of the prisoners had no money. The blockade made all kinds of goods high; buttons of all kind sold very high; lead pencils, needles, pins, pocket knives were a better medium of exchange than money."

Duke realized that the key to successful trading was being able to convert cornmeal into bread. That meant he needed an oven, pans for baking, and wood for fuel. He described how his plan was implemented:

> Bob Conley said he could build the oven out of the clay that was in the bank on the North side of the prison. He took off his drawers, tied the end of each leg like a sack and carried the clay from the North side to our quarters and he soon had the oven. I bought six canteens, put them in the fire, burnt the cloth off, melted the solder and each canteen made two plates. I could buy the wood of the men who carried out the dead.

Every night he baked several batches of bread, the only ingredients being unsifted cornmeal, saleratus, and corn mush soured in the hot summer sun. Each half canteen yielded a cake of bread that would sell for twenty-five cents.[23]

Ben Duke's resourcefulness allowed him to live better than most Andersonville prisoners. His relative wealth also enabled him to help his friends, one of whom was Calvin S. Engle of the 5th Indiana Cavalry. Duke recalled that Engle "was rotten with the scurvy, had great sores on his body and limbs; his mouth and gums were rotten." Engle gave more details:

> My mouth got so bad my gums turned black and came loose from my teeth and swelled and bled. I could run my fingers over my gums and bring out chunks of black clotted blood. At night I would lay on my face and leave my mouth open so the drool would run out. It stunk so I could hardly bear my own breath. . . . He bought flour and made biscuits and sold to the prisoners that got in with money. By doing so he was enabled to help his friends, which he did as far as he could. I believe he saved several of us from dying, and when I had the scurvy so bad he got me some Irish potatoes which checked it in my mouth. He had five or six men in his tent, and got extra rations enough to keep the scurvy off. If there was ever a whole soul and solid man Ben Duke is one.

Summing up Ben's charity under impossible circumstances, one writer offered a touching tribute:

> It is asserted by those who were with him during this trying time, that his kind and cheering words, his gentle nursing, his trading and trafficking and many times dividing his last ration, although scant, with a weak and sick comrade, and his general activity in their behalf, saved the life of many a disheartened and discouraged comrade.

So Jimmy Dever died and Ben Duke lived, two unlucky Iron Brigade men who, although physically held captive in a loathsome hellhole, never surrendered their spirit.[24]

34

The Last Winter

 Rebel prison pens began to discharge their contents early in 1865 and officers from the 19th Indiana were among those exchanged and sent north to Annapolis. Captain Alonzo Makepeace had last been seen by his men dodging into a barn during the retreat through Gettysburg. He had been captured there and sent to Libby Prison, where he quickly learned not to trust his fellow prisoners. Makepeace bought seven loaves of bread from a boy standing outside of Libby and stowed them on a shelf he made in the rafters of the "Gettysburg Room," so called because most of its residents had been captured in that battle. After a good night's sleep, the captain awoke to discover that all of his bread had been stolen.

One day Makepeace said to fellow prisoner Captain Patrick Hart, "Now, I am going to get out of here if I can." Hart responded, "I don't want you to go off and leave me here. I want to get out, too." Soon afterwards Makepeace began work on a tunnel, a popular means of escape from Libby. Makepeace was downstairs in the cookroom when he heard the news that another tunnel had broken through outside the prison grounds. He raced upstairs to tell Hart he planned to escape, but his friend thought it foolishness and declined to go. By the time Makepeace got back downstairs, the room was packed with other officers willing to take the chance, so he had to wait his turn. One hundred and nine men got out before guards discovered the tunnel. Eventually, forty of these escapees reached Union lines. Makepeace never got into the tunnel, but always thought he might have been one of the lucky ones if he had not wasted time in going after Hart.

Makepeace was transferred to Danville and Salisbury prisons and then to Macon, Georgia. On the journey to Macon, Makepeace resolved to attempt another escape. At one point the train began to run slowly, so he decided to jump from the moving cars. Captain Hart advised him not to make the attempt, but Makepeace found another willing officer and the two men jumped off the prison train near Branchville. Guards fired at them, wounding his partner, so Makepeace surrendered. At Macon, the captain again went into the tunneling business. Two tunnels were due to be completed on July 3, 1864, with a breakout scheduled for the Fourth of July, but an informer tipped off the guards.

From Macon the officers were sent to Columbia, South Carolina, where Makepeace finally got away from his captors. One evening on a wood detail, he and two other Hoosier officers dropped into the weeds without being noticed. Traveling only by night, they remained at large for forty-eight days. Wandering about through thickets and swamps, the officers covered about 400 miles, several times being chased by bloodhounds through dense canebrakes. But the escapees were finally done in by a goose. While walking along a back road, the officers saw a flock of geese, captured one and wrung its neck. When they went into a ravine to cook their plunder, the foragers were spotted and quickly recaptured. Captain Makepeace would remain a prisoner until his exchange on March 1, 1865, exactly twenty months after his capture.[1]

Captain Greene was exchanged along with Captain Hart and Adjutant Finney and was "very much reduced in body and spirit, and was very sick and unable to walk." Greene had also considered an escape, but being shoeless and 250 miles from freedom, determined "to endure yet for a while the miseries to which we are subjected." While in captivity and without his knowledge, Greene had been nominated for the office of Auditor of Delaware County (provided he might reach home before the election.) Another candidate for that office was Benjamin Harter, formerly a lieutenant in the 19th Indiana. This was not a unique situation since Othniel J. Gilbert and William H. Cooper were candidates for Recorder, the former having lost a hand and the latter a leg while serving in the 19th Indiana.[2]

After the fall of Atlanta in September 1864, Andersonville was emptied of all enlisted prisoners fit enough to travel. Most were shipped to Charleston, where conditions were considerably better than in Georgia because the Sisters of Charity and private citizens brought them bread, potatoes, and clothing. This kind treatment was but a brief interlude before prisoners were shipped on to confinement in a new prison at Florence, South Carolina. Although Florence offered more space, better water, and more wood, rations were the same as at Andersonville.[3]

George Banner, one of the Wilderness prisoners, wrote that the sadistic commander at Florence, a red-headed lieutenant named Barrett, made life a living hell. Barrett would walk through the compound with a club in his hand, striking out at exhausted men who did not move fast enough to suit him. George remembered dodging Barrett's club on several occasions. By the time Banner left Florence, his weight had plunged from 156 pounds to eighty-four pounds.[4]

Ben Duke's business operations made him one of the best-fed prisoners, but he lost sixty pounds before reaching Union lines, tipping the scales at 130 pounds in Annapolis. Despite his declining health, Ben continued his benevolence at Florence. Calvin Engle recalled being summoned to Duke's tent one day:

> When I got there he gave me a blanket, and as I had until now been without one, I went back to the shanty feeling pretty good, the boys having a worn out blanket each, we had one to lay on and two to put over us. Now the boys were not at all sorry that they took me in. In a week or two after that Duke sent for me to come down to the Sutler's house and bring my blanket. I could not think what he wanted, but felt that nothing bad was wanted. When I got there he gave me half a bushel of sweet potatoes. It took all the power I had to get them back to the tent.

One of Engle's tentmates, a Hoosier cavalryman named John Fenimore, had already benefited from Ben's largesse. Scurvy had swollen Fenimore's tongue so badly that it stuck out of his mouth about an inch. Duke kindly gave him a chunk of alum, which enabled him to get his tongue back in his mouth.[5]

Ben Duke had lost one of his Andersonville bunkmates while at Charleston. When other prisoners were transferred to Florence, the sickest men were left behind, including Sergeant Bob Conley, who had been reported as killed in the Wilderness. Conley reached home on January 17th and the *Palladium* and *Telegram* both publicized his arrival, the latter noting, "He states that he left Phil. Timmons in prison at Andersonville, sick and not likely to recover." Shortly thereafter, Conley received a letter from Mrs. Phillip Timmons, who was desperate for news of her husband:

> will you be kind enough to drop me a few lines stating at what time you left him and how he was in fact everything you know concerning him. as I have not heard from him since September and then he was at Macon. also let me know if it would be possible for me to write to him.

Unfortunately, Timmons had already died in Andersonville, where Conley said "men were starved, shot, poisoned, and every other cruelty practiced that rebel malignity could invent."[6]

Bob Conley's main concern became obtaining his discharge, normally a simple task, but one that had been complicated by his "man without a regiment" status. He wrote to the 20th Indiana for the necessary paperwork and Lieutenant George Bunch responded:

I made out another Descriptive list to day. the captain will Sign it and tomorrow he will Send it "forth with" to Major L B Hayman Indianapolis Ind. Please find Enclosed A Certifficate which will Bring matters all Right. Should it not please Inform me and I will have all the old 19th Ind to Sign it who were present on the 28th Day of July 1864.

Two weeks later, Conley wrote to Reverend Isaac Montfort that he could "prove beyond doubt that I was not mustered out on the 28th of July, and that I was a prisoner at that time." Bob then offered his opinion, "I have undoubtedly been fraudulently represented on the Muster out Roll supposing I was dead." With assistance from Montfort and the Indiana Military Agency, his muster out date was finally changed from July 28, 1864 to March 22, 1865.[7]

On February 1st, Ben Duke and his friends got to leave the Florence prison on parole. Duke had been working for the rebel sutler, who needed some quarters built near Columbia, South Carolina. Duke was allowed to select some of his friends for the job. Calvin Engle remembered that they got a camp kettle, boiled their clothing, washed themselves thoroughly, and heartily enjoyed the pleasure of being louse-free.

After erecting one building, all construction suddenly ceased when the booming of cannon announced that General William T. Sherman had reached Columbia. Engle recalled, "This put big smiles on our faces." Duke and half a dozen others resolved to escape and join Sherman's army, but one of the other prisoners strode off to tell their rebel boss. The informer was overtaken and soundly thrashed into silence. Duke and a few friends ran off into the swamps and got through to Sherman three days later.[8]

The only reliable information about soldiers in Southern prisons came from friends lucky enough to be exchanged. At least half a dozen men listed on the roster of the newly consolidated 20th Indiana were actually in various prison cemeteries. Among this number was Squire Wood, a Wilderness captive who died at Charleston on September 23, 1864. Soldiers from the 19th Indiana captured at Weldon Railroad had been sent to Salisbury, North Carolina. This was another loathsome prison pen where the diet consisted almost entirely of cornbread and rice. One Iron Brigade soldier gave a brief description of the place:

> There was not enough to drink, and, none at all, for purposes of cleanliness. Our men were reeking in filth, and almost devoured by vermin. The only change of clothes they had were those taken from the dead bodies of their companions.

Henry and William, the only children of widowed Sarah Marshall, had enlisted in the Randolph County company. Sarah lost William to disease in

Indianapolis on December 2, 1863, and now Henry died in Salisbury on February 18, 1865. Both boys had willingly sent part of their pay to their mother, but after Henry's death she became forever dependent upon her own labor and the charity of friends.[9]

Many former prisoners had become so debilitated that they died on their way home after finally being released in 1865. Some expired in general hospitals, like Lewis Garrett, Company I, who died at Annapolis on January 17th, or George Elliott, Company A, who passed away at Wilmington General Hospital on March 7th. Other men, nothing more than living skeletons, managed to hang on to life long enough to see their folks one last time. William Parr, Company I, had been captured with Henry Marshall at Weldon Railroad, and was exchanged on February 28th. He reached Camp Chase, Ohio, in mid-March and went home, but died just sixteen days after receiving his furlough.[10]

Bill Sykes and Calvin Engle, two of Ben Duke's prison friends, remained in the Florence camp until they were paroled on February 28th. The freed prisoners were sent to Annapolis, where they received baths, new clothing, and nourishing food in limited quantities to protect their delicate health. After a few days, Sykes and Engle were sent on to Camp Chase. By this time, Bill was so far gone that he had to be carried in a blanket. Responding to a telegram telling of the alarming state of Bill's health, Jesse Sykes immediately went to get his son. Rallying every bit of his remaining strength, Bill Sykes clung desperately to life until March 25th, dying the day after he got home.[11]

Shortly after the war, Andersonville would come to symbolize all of the Confederate prisons. The burial trenches would be designated a national cemetery and a party headed by Miss Clara Barton fenced it in, erected a flagstaff and generally tidied up the old field where almost 13,000 soldiers lay buried. An Indiana man paid a visit to the site in October 1865 and he quickly noticed that birds did not sing and the wind seemed cold, chilly, and damp despite a bright autumn sun. Walking among the thousands of white headboards, he mused:

> There, in little dark letters, is the name of a patriot who sacrificed his life for his country. Beneath, he slumbers far away from sister, wife or mother. Burning tears have flown for him; anxious hours came to that beloved one at home, when uncertain tidings filled the breast with achings. He starved, or froze or scorched, and died. The story is brief, but woeful.

Summing up his Andersonville experience, the somber visitor wrote, "How very, very lonely it is here."[12]

Unaware of the fate of their captive comrades, soldiers of the 20th Indiana continued with duty on the Petersburg line. Relative quiet on this front during January allowed officers time to drill their men, an activity that the 1864 recruits had done very little of since joining the army in March. One officer recalled that, at least in De Trobriand's brigade, "Drilling by squad, company, battalion, and brigade was resumed, and inspections and reviews were of frequent occurrence." Such drill was an absolute necessity in the 40th New York, which had received a large number of recruits, "many of them being ignorant of the English language."[13]

There was little work on entrenchments, so most activity centered around guard or picket duty. This latter duty was performed by multiple squads, each composed of four privates and a corporal, supervised by a few sergeants and officers. One such picket squad on January 21st consisted of Corporal Grear Williams and Privates Milton Rains, Company A; Eli Washburn and Henry Wilkinson, Company F; and Thomas Fletcher, Company I. They lay in their pits all day and got soaked with rain and covered with sleet. Williams probably did not object to this hardship as much as the others because he had been promoted corporal on New Year's Day and this assignment was one of his first commands.[14]

On February 5th, the Second and Fifth Corps started off on another expedition to extend the army's left flank, their positions being just reversed from the attack on the Boydton Plank Road in October. General Humphreys led the Second Corps toward its assigned objective—the intersection of the Vaughan Road and Hatcher's Run. This day's march showed how much the war had changed; telegraph wires had been strung to Hatcher's Run before the rear of Humphreys's column even got there.

De Trobriand received orders to cross Hatcher's Run, but he found the stream obstructed by felled trees and deep holes that had been dug in the stream bed. He deployed the Sharpshooters in front of the reb defenses, then slipped the 99th Pennsylvania, supported by the 110th Pennsylvania, some 200 yards below near a broken dam. While the Sharpshooters kept the enemy pinned down, De Trobriand personally led the Pennsylvanians across the creek, his men jumping from log to log to effect the crossing. The rebels fled and he crossed the remainder of his brigade, deploying his regiments in an arc-shaped line to protect the crossing, with pickets well out in front.[15]

Other troops came to occupy that sector before dawn on February 6th and De Trobriand withdrew his brigade and held it in reserve. By 9 A.M. the enemy in front had apparently disappeared, so De Trobriand advanced the 20th Indiana, 17th Maine, the Maine Heavy Artillery, and the Sharp-shooters to reconnoiter. During this operation, two companies of the Indiana regiment, commanded now by Lieutenant Colonel Albert Andrews, advanced across a small swamp and located an enemy position with a redoubt containing two guns. De Trobriand reported that the Hoosiers "opened on the rebels visible above the parapet, when their fire was briskly returned, many of the enemy jumping above the parapet to occupy small pits in front of their intrenchments." After a brief skirmish, Andrews withdrew his two companies without loss and the 20th Indiana's part in the fighting was over. Later the brigade started off to reinforce the Fifth Corps near Dabney's Mill, but was recalled before reaching that portion of the battlefield.[16]

After remaining inactive for two days, the Hoosiers began to fortify their new line along Hatcher's Run. Nothing of importance happened until February 17th, when the brigade assembled to witness the execution of a soldier from the 124th New York. He had been convicted of cowardice and desertion, and was sentenced to be shot to death by musketry. Lieutenant Amory K. Allen described the event:

he was marched around with music and his coffin along the lines to his grave and a detail of 8 men Shot him as he Sat on his coffin. he fell back but Still Showed life when 2 other men went close and Shot him through the heart and the Ceremony was over and we come to our quarters and rested.

This orchestrated spectacle must have reminded the old soldiers of another execution back on June 12, 1863, when John Woods had been put to death just as the Gettysburg campaign started.[17]

Although convalescents from Grant's campaign continued to return to the ranks, many Hoosier veterans remained absent in Indiana without authority. John F. Harter, Company E, had gone home on veteran furlough, but was sick with a fever when the 19th Indiana returned to the front. Colonel Williams discussed the case with his doctor, then told Harter to rejoin his regiment when he was fully recovered. The veteran had not left home after more than seven months, so he was arrested, sent to Alexandria, and thrown into jail. After being incarcerated there for nearly two months, Harter was not released until he had enlisted the help of Congressman Julian.[18]

In general, absentees were treated leniently if their cases were brought before a court-martial. Officers seemed almost to be looking for an excuse to reduce a charge or convict on a lesser offense. Such was the case with Patrick Sullivan of Company F. After two months in Mount Pleasant Hospital, Sullivan received a furlough on September 1, 1864, and went home to Indianapolis, where he was apprehended by a detective on November 20th. Taken to Alexandria, he was locked up in the Washington Street Military Prison until his trial in late January on a charge of desertion. Sullivan claimed to have been sick when his furlough expired, so he was found not guilty of desertion, but guilty of absence without leave and fined $20.[19]

Overstaying furloughs was the desertion of choice, since in most cases men were already at home. The stigma of desertion no longer meant anything to soldiers who had suffered for their government and gotten little in return. In their opinion, the army owed them a few extra days with their folks. Consider the actions of two of Company B's best soldiers. In 1862 Frank Huff had deserted from the Indianapolis rendezvous so he could get to the 19th Indiana sooner. Now, after being shot at Gettysburg and Petersburg, Huff arbitrarily added an additional five weeks to his thirty-day furlough. Tom Davis did the same thing. He had served honorably in the battles of Brawner Farm, Second Bull Run, Fredericksburg, Chancellorsville, Gettysburg, Mine Run, Wilderness, Laurel Hill, Cold Harbor, and Petersburg. Furloughed for a wound received on June 25, 1864, Davis took an extra month before returning to Satterlee Hospital at Philadelphia. This cavalier attitude toward extended furloughs was especially prevalent among soldiers who remained unfit for duty, thus giving them a logical justification for their actions. In Tom Davis's case, he returned to his company on December 10th but did no duty at all until his transfer to the Veteran Reserve Corps on February 28th.[20]

Disabled men were a common sight in the ranks during 1865. One such soldier was David Norris, who had been shot during the abortive Petersburg charge. When he returned to duty in mid-March, his wound was unhealed and still discharging. Lieutenant John Moore remembered having words with his captain about Norris's condition:

> the Capt. was on detail duty one day & left me in charge of the Co. and ordered me to draw him a gun. I told the capt. that he wasent able for duty. the Capt. said he was. I told him to come and go with me and look at his wound and he would think different. he examined his wound and he was excused.

It should be remembered that Norris was the man who had a hole the size of an apple in his shoulder where gangrene had eaten away his flesh.[21]

After returning from his self-extended furlough, Frank Huff penned a long letter to the *Palladium* on February 22nd, but there was more to celebrate than just Washington's Birthday in 1865. Frank wrote:

> Then while we honor the hero for what he has done, we have with it the glad tidings of the recapture of Fort Sumter; also, the occupation of the cities of Charleston and Wilmington, by those boys in blue; then long may the Stars and Stripes float over the shattered walls of Fort Sumter that has so long been under the flaunting flag of treason.

Then he confessed, "Could I speak with the eloquence of the Hon. Edward Everett, who now lies mouldering in a patriot's grave, I could not describe the enthusiasm the soldiers possess on such occasions as this." Hospital patients joined with their sturdy comrades in the ranks to look forward to "the speedy restoration of the old Union, and Peace, permanent Peace, once more spread throughout our blessed land."[22]

Corporal Grear Williams celebrated Washington's Birthday by getting shot while on the picket line. He was speedily taken to the rear and furloughed home. It is possible to reconstruct his journey from notes made on blank pages in his 1864 diary:

> *February 23rd* — in washington City D.C. star[t]ed from City Point 22nd 10 a m and Got no pay and 10 a m finds me at the office trying to Get transportation

> *February 24th* — left [H]arper Fary 2 clock p m. laying at St John run 50 mile from Cumberl[an]d and the Bridge washed a way and Bey so Doing we loose 12 hours

> *February 26th* — we landed at Belar [Bellaire] and we haft to lay till 6 o'clock mondy the 27th

> *February 27th* — stayed at Bellair from monday 11 oclock febuar the 26th and stayed till 7 mondy 27th / 65. started from Bellair 7 o clock, monday the 27 Day of febuary and Got Delayed at newark 4 hours. Delayed at Newark account of the train runing of the track

> *February 28th* — they layed at Columbis 8 in the evening. stay in Columbis last night started from Columbis 11 ocolck febuary the 28. Got home the 28th day febuary / 65. on the road one week

> *March 1st* — at Chester in morning and I am going to Richmond. went to Richmond and that is all.

Grear's diary entries indicate just how much the war had changed. He had been wounded on February 22nd and reached home on the 28th. At Brawner Farm, in 1862, many of the wounded had still not been removed from the battlefield in that same amount of time, indicating a distinct change in the type of warfare and a vast improvement in treating the wounded.[23]

35

Appomattox

March passed quietly, with convalescent soldiers swelling the ranks so that the 20th Indiana averaged 520 officers and men present, with about twenty sick each day. Major Orr had finally received a commission as colonel of the Indiana regiment, but shortly thereafter caught a severe cold that settled in the lung that had been injured at Antietam. Pneumonia set in and Orr was briefly hospitalized before being sent home, never to return to active duty. Lieutenant Colonel Albert S. Andrews, formerly of the 14th Indiana, now commanded the regiment. Quiet reigned on the picket line, where outposts were bothered more by rebel deserters than by rebel musketry.[1]

All that changed at first light on March 25th when a roaring cannonade and distant musketry startled sleeping men in De Trobriand's brigade. The general sprang from his bed rushed outside and shouted for the officers to get their men under arms at once. Moments later, an orderly from division headquarters announced that the rebs had attacked and captured Fort Stedman on the Ninth Corps front, pushing their attack forward to the City Point Railroad. Mott's division would leave at a moment's notice. Soldiers pulled down tents, loaded wagons, and rushed into line, where they waited for orders. The firing continued until 9 A.M., when word came that a Federal counterattack had recaptured Fort Stedman.[2]

General Meade was convinced that the enemy had weakened his lines elsewhere to furnish troops for this assault, so he ordered the Second and Sixth Corps to advance and capture the rebel picket lines on their front. Any weakness uncovered would be exploited if an opportunity presented itself. De Trobriand sent forward the 73rd New York and 20th Indiana, the latter on the right of the brigade and division, both regiments under command of Lieutenant Colonel Andrews. With a sudden rush, the two regiments sprang forward. Captain John Shafer reported, "We met with a sharp infantry fire from the enemy's picket-line, strongly posted behind earthworks, but gained the position with but slight loss, capturing a number of prisoners." The Hoosiers sent back one officer and forty-six men as captives; the New Yorkers, assisted by other regiments, capturing three officers and 124 men. After holding their new line all day, with but minor adjustments while responding to reb attacks, the Hoosiers were relieved after dark.[3]

Lieutenant Colonel Andrews had been wounded early in the fighting, but bandaged his bleeding elbow and remained on the field until his regiment withdrew. In addition to Andrews, the other casualties included two men killed and three officers and seventeen men wounded. Eight soldiers from the old 19th had been wounded, including Second Lieutenant Abram J. Buckles. He remembered that "while on the skirmish-line, a rebel sharp-shooter put a ball through my right leg, causing amputation above the knee." John Holbert, formerly of Company K, 19th Indiana, had his left leg amputated after a ball shattered the femur. Other losses included Sergeant William C. Barnes, George W. Taylor, James Lamey, Adam Smelser, Nathan Williams, and William Pitman. The latter two men had joined old Company B in the spring of 1864. Both were hit by shell fragments, with Williams receiving slight wounds in both thighs and his right hand. Pitman's injury was more severe. A shell burst behind him, one fragment shattering his right shoulder and rendering it virtually useless.[4]

A general movement against the Petersburg defenses had already been set and the fighting on March 25th did not ruin that plan. On March 29th, the Second Corps packed up and left its Hatcher's Run entrenchments for one final campaign. But it only moved forward a short distance and occupied a line closer to the rebels. The main thrust of the offensive was to be by the Fifth Corps and cavalry farther off to the left. Despite a promising start, torrential rain on the 30th brought the army to a halt because wagons and artillery could not move in the deep mud. Early on March 31st, the army began to shift left toward what Grant hoped would be the vulnerable flank of the Petersburg earthworks. A rebel attack struck the Fifth Corps, but all De Trobriand's men could do was listen to the fighting at Gravelly Run, "Not a hurrah, not a volley was fired which we did not hear distinctly. But the woods interposed as a curtain, and we could see nothing."[5]

The decisive victory at Five Forks by the Fifth Corps and General Philip Sheridan's cavalry on April 1st resulted in the Confederate evacuation of Petersburg and Richmond on the following day. After scattered fighting that morning, the enemy withdrew and Mott's division advanced almost to the city of Petersburg before halting for the night. On April 3rd, De Trobriand's brigade led the Second Corps' pursuit west along the Appomattox

River, capturing over 300 rebs who had scattered into forests by the wayside. Disheartened rebels surrendered to anyone who happened to be going by, one mounted orderly "capturing" a squad of forty-eight.[6]

The Second Corps' pursuit had gotten far ahead of the artillery and commissary wagons, so most of April 4th was spent patching roads. One can bet that some sections were well corduroyed because, after all, the Hoosiers had learned how to repair roads from Old Corduroy himself. That night, Jacob Young and John Markle wanted to cook a chicken they had confiscated earlier. While splitting kindling with a hatchet, Young accidentally sliced open the big toe on his left foot, inflicting a bad wound. On April 5th the march was resumed "in earnest" and tired soldiers stopped for the night only after reaching Jetersville. Despite his painful foot, Jake Young was still in the ranks.[7]

The chase began again at 7 A.M. on April 6th with De Trobriand's brigade leading the Second Corps. The head of the Second Corps came upon Lee's rearguard near Salt Sulphur Spring about two hours later. General Mott ordered De Trobriand to advance his skirmishers and within ten minutes he had deployed the 110th Pennsylvania and five companies of the 20th Indiana, now commanded by Captain John Shafer. The remaining five companies of Shafer's regiment acted as a reserve. De Trobriand's other regiments formed a line of battle perpendicular to the Deatonsville road. Generals Mott and De Trobriand rode forward to check on the deployment as their advance line engaged "a straggling line of retreating Confederate skirmishers." Just after approving the maneuver, Mott was struck by a bullet in the lower leg. A slight delay ensued while Mott was removed, De Trobriand taking command of the division and Colonel Russell B. Shepherd, 1st Maine Heavy Artillery, assuming command of the brigade. By now the rebels had disappeared from view, pursued closely by the Hoosiers.[8]

Captain Shafer pressed the retreating foe closely, not allowing them time to organize any resistance. At one point during this impetuous advance, John Markle was some fifteen yards from Jake Young when he heard him cry out. Young had grabbed his ankle, so Markle yelled to Jefferson Kinder and asked if he had been shot. Kinder yelled back, "I think he is just 'skelped' a little." (Combat soldiers considered a "skelped" wound as one that just grazed the skin.) Kinder and Markle continued on, the latter remarking later that "at that time a slight wound was not paid any attention to because we had got used to such things." Frank Huff had been wounded in the right thigh and just returned to the company on March 15th. Now he fell again when a minie ball struck the same thigh. Frank remembered, "This paralized my whole limb and I crawled off of the field dragging my leg after me. It cut certain cords in my thigh that turned the toes upward and foot to one side." Three others from the old 19th Indiana received wounds that day—Sergeant

Ephraim Bartholomew, Sergeant John B. Spellman, and Franklin L. Keever, the latter mortally.[9]

After about two miles, Colonel Shepherd's skirmish line ran out of ammunition, so it was relieved by the 124th New York and the five reserve 20th Indiana companies. These new skirmishers spotted a rebel wagon train and soon got close enough to fire into the teams. Whenever one horse fell, the driver and guards unhitched the remaining horses and galloped off. As wagon after wagon was captured, the officers could scarcely contain their excited men. Lieutenant Colonel Weygant remembered, "For miles the boys moved so rapidly that I was obliged to keep my horse on a jog trot to keep with them." A member of the Maine Heavy Artillery noticed something extremely peculiar about this running fight:

> For the first time in the history of our war the stragglers, hunting for plunder, were actually in front of the skirmish line. Sometimes a band of marauding stragglers would come upon a group of the enemy's rear guard near a plantation house, blaze away at them, demand their surrender, pick up what they could find, and race on for the next place.

If any particular point seemed to be held in force, the stragglers bypassed it and left some work for the skirmishers, who pushed rebs from several improvised defensive positions. Whenever a skirmisher would fall, "their comrades would only quicken their pace, yell the louder and load and fire the faster."[10]

It all seemed too easy. Maybe that was because everyone knew what needed to be done. When the First Division was slow to come up on the right, the skirmishers, "every man apparently acting as a general," instinctively prolonged their line to cover the gap. The Johnny Rebs had tried to halt Colonel Shepherd's brigade at three different points, but had been easily brushed aside each time. Suddenly a more formidable position appeared, a hilltop filled with rebs crouching behind felled trees and piles of fence rails. Skirmishers were not enough. The brigade's line of battle had almost mingled with the skirmishers on several occasions, so it was quickly ready for an attack.[11]

De Trobriand formed a line of six regiments: 110th Pennsylvania, 73rd and 86th New York and 1st Maine Heavy Artillery from Shepherd's brigade, and 105th Pennsylvania and 17th Maine (recently transferred) from the Second Brigade. The division commander proudly watched the charge:

> It was a beautiful sight. The six flags advanced in line as though carried by six human waves, which ascended without halting until they had extinguished and submerged the flaming dyke which was raised in front of them.

Taking time only to round up almost 400 prisoners and reorganize, the brigade started again for Deatonsville. Shepherd's skirmish line had again expended its ammunition, so the 1st Maine now led the advance.[12]

Beyond Deatonsville, another charge netted more prisoners, along with flags, artillery, and wagons. Ammunition wagons had not kept up, so Colonel Shepherd yielded the advance to a brigade still well-supplied with cartridges and began to assemble his badly scattered soldiers. He reported proudly on what the First Brigade had accomplished:

> April 6, the enemy was attacked directly in rear on the road by which he was retreating and driven several miles. The brigade captured 1,390 enlisted men, 17 commissioned officers, 5 pieces of artillery, 28 wagons, 1 limber, 1 artillery guidon, and 3 battle flags. The conduct of both officers and men throughout the day was excellent; even the recruits, inspired by the gallantry of the veterans, charged with enthusiasm. I cannot make special mention of any without injustice to others, for all behaved with great gallantry.

During its day's work, the 20th Indiana lost two officers and eleven enlisted men wounded.[13]

While Shepherd's brigade had concluded its part of the pursuit, De Trobriand's division was not yet finished. Racing ahead so fast that the men did not stop to load, the skirmishers would carry positions before their friends even knew an obstacle had been encountered. Near sunset, the soldiers spied a large wagon train whose escape was protected by rebs behind a line of earthworks. According to their commander, "there was no intrenchment which could hold against the determination of our men when they saw the wagons." Eager troops overpowered the rearguard, capturing almost 1,000 men, and bagged some 200 wagons. Over $400,000 in rebel currency was found in the captured wagons, a sum evidently intended as pay for rebel soldiers. The now worthless money circulated freely around the Second Corps and Yankee pranksters often acted as paymasters for rebel prisoners:

> "Hallo! Johnny. When were you paid?"
> "About six months ago."
> "How much do they owe you?"
> "Don't know. Tain't much 'count any how."
> "Here's a couple hundred. Will that cover it?"
> "Yas's. Thank yer."

The end of the Confederacy was clearly in sight, so many soldiers, enjoying the irony, paid for foraged provisions instead of stealing them outright.[14]

The Second Corps continued to follow Lee's army westward for two more days, but the 20th Indiana would never again be under fire. The Army of Northern Virginia finally gave up on the morning of April 9th, when Lee agreed to terms of surrender with Grant. Shepherd's brigade had halted while the negotiations were in progress and an aide from army headquarters came riding by, crying that the fighting was over. But instead of shouting their approval, these war-weary soldiers crossed their fingers, held their breath, and awaited confirmation. It soon arrived when General Meade and his staff trotted along. Behind them, cheering rose into an ear-splitting roar. Meade, smiling for the first time men could remember, assured everyone that Lee had indeed surrendered. Shepherd's brigade went wild:

> Men shouted until they could shout no more, the air above us was for full half an hour filled with caps, coats, blankets, and knapsacks, and when at length the excitement subsided, the men threw themselves on the ground completely exhausted.

During the evening men slipped over to rebel camps in search of souvenirs, then "slept gloriously that night feeling safe."[15]

April 11th was devoted to a surrender ceremony, the rebel regiments marching up to turn in their arms and colors. Colonel R. M. Potter, the last commander of the famous Texas Brigade, described the poignant end of the Army of Northern Virginia:

> No word was spoken except the words of command to stack arms, which was done orderly and quietly, facing the line of federal troops. Human lips were pressed to iron muzzles of guns and the men turned from them as sadly and sorrowfully as if they were moving from the graves of their first born. We passed on, never looking back to that national potter's field, where our young republic was buried.

That very night, Henry Marsh would exclaim, "It seems all like a dream to us, can it be that Peace is declared. Glory to God." After writing a history of the old First Division, First Corps, Lieutenant Earl Rogers would conclude, "In that army at Appomattox stood the remnants and shattered battalions of King's division, that for nearly four years had fought the battles of their country. Many had fallen by the wayside, while others had pressed forward to the end."[16]

Shortly after the surrender, some witty Federal composed an obituary for the Confederate government that proved quite popular among the victorious troops:

Died, near the South-Side Railroad, on Sunday, April 9th, 1865, the SOUTHERN CONFEDERACY, aged four years.

Conceived in sin, born in iniquity, nurtured by tyranny, it died of a chronic attack of Punch. U. S. Grant, Attending Physician; Abraham Lincoln, Undertaker; Jeff. Davis, Chief Mourner.

EPITAPH

Gentle stranger, drop a tear,
The C.S.A. lies buried here;
In youth it lived and prospered well,
But soon, like Lucifer, it fell,
Its body here, its soul in — well,
E'en if I knew I wouldn't tell.
Rest, C.S.A., from every strife,
Your death is better than your life;
And this one line shall grace your grave,
Your death gave freedom to the slave.

On April 11th, the Second Corps marched to Burkeville, arriving there on the 13th. It was a hard march since "the men were under strict orders about keeping in their places and as there was no enemy in front to delay us so moved rapidly." Orders to prevent straggling were meant to protect Virginians from pillagers, private property now being respected as it would be in the North.[17]

Shortly before 2 A.M. on April 15th, a telegram reached Shepherd's brigade that announced the assassination of President Lincoln and Secretary Seward and the probable murder of General Grant. One sleepy officer stumbled from his tent, gazing around in bewilderment:

> Everything about the camp was quiet, and the shelter tents of my men had an unusually uniform appearance; but they were all empty, and the men with heavy hearts and speechless tongues, were gathered in groups about the smoking camp-fires. They all seemed stupified by the terrible news, and were anxiously awaiting the arrival of the next telegram.

Lieutenant Colonel Weygant rode over to division headquarters later that morning to speak with his division commander. General De Trobriand received him cordially, but their conversation quickly turned to France's Reign of Terror and his conviction that the war would now continue "with the dagger and revolver rather than the rifle and cannon." Telegrams announced the safety of Grant and the probable recovery of Seward, but gloom over Lincoln's death remained. It was, according to Lieutenant Amory Allen of the 20th Indiana, "the most terrible of all circumstances that ever happened in the united States."[18]

36

Peace

The Second Corps remained at Burkeville until May 2nd, when it began a march to Richmond. Roads and weather were perfect. Spring had transformed the Virginia countryside into various shades of green, with blossoms and flowers adding swatches of color. Some thought the march leisurely, while others believed it to be some sort of "foolish race" between the Second and Sixth Corps. The first night was spent at Jetersville, the second night eighteen miles farther east near the Appomattox River and the third night just ten miles from Richmond. After enduring a soaking rainstorm, the Second Corps marched to Manchester, across the river from Richmond, where it spent two more nights. Passes were given freely, so curious soldiers flocked into Richmond to see the sights—Libby Prison, Belle Isle, and Castle Thunder—all of which were notorious rebel prison pens and among the top attractions. City streets seemed quiet and there was no indication of opposition to Union occupation. On May 7th, Humphreys's Second Corps marched through the streets of Richmond past ranks of the Twenty-fifth Corps, which had been drawn up in its honor.[1]

The march continued north toward Washington, passing by many sites made famous by the late war. On May 10th, a detachment was sent over to Spotsylvania to retrieve a large oak tree which had been cut down by musketry in 1864. It was carted off to Washington as the war's largest souvenir. Arriving near the capital's forts on May 16th, soldiers had no real duty other than preparing for a grand review of the Army of the Potomac scheduled for May 23rd. Sherman's command was to be reviewed the following day.[2]

The Eastern and Western armies had always argued about which had performed better, killed more rebs, marched better, suffered more, etc., etc. As they marched up from North Carolina, one of Sherman's officers had an opportunity to see where Meade's army had fought at Spotsylvania:

In a thicket near by, where the appalling stillness seems never to have been broken, except by owl or bat, or raven, lie hundreds of skeletons. Some had collected, as they lay wounded, such sticks as were within their reach and had striven to erect a barrier to protect them from further injury. Some had taken the straps from their knapsacks to bind a severed artery, and now the leather lying loosely about the bone told pathetically of the vain effort.

This melancholy scene was duplicated a little farther north:

Some of us visited the Wilderness battle-ground and saw there the same sad scenes. The commingled bones of horse and rider, all the possessions of the soldier, from the envelope with its faint address in a woman's hand, to the broken gun, lie scattered over the ground. Knapsacks, placed together by companies before they made a charge, and for which the owners never returned, remain in decaying heaps. 'Tis a gloomy sepulchre, where the trees, in tenderly covering with leaves the remains of the patriots, alone perform the last sad offices. The wind moans through the pines, tears fall at home for them, but they sleep on, unconscious of a weeping nation.

An old gray-haired man leaned upon his hoe-handle, trying to quiet his trembling head, as he said, "Ah, sir, there are thousands of both sides lying unburied in the Wilderness."

After such encounters, Sherman's men must have shown a greater appreciation for the deeds of the Potomac army.[3]

Three more men from the old 19th Indiana died before the grand review in Washington and all, by coincidence, had belonged to Company A. They were John Tucker, who died May 6th; Jacob Bolen, May 13th; and John Surber, May 16th. Surber, a veteran, died of complications from a wound received June 25, 1864. Tucker and Bolen died of disease, the latter survived by his wife and six children.[4]

The grand review of the Army of the Potomac was led by General Meade and his staff, followed in turn by the provost troops, engineer brigade, Ninth Corps, and Fifth Corps. Then it was the Second Corps' turn. Marching without knapsacks, at route step and in column of companies, the First Division led off, then the artillery brigade, the Second Division, and Third Division. General Humphreys made an immediate impression, having mounted his entire staff on white horses.[5]

Immense, cheering crowds greeted the ragged banners as they moved down Pennsylvania Avenue toward the White House. President Andrew Johnson, General Grant, cabinet officers, senators, congressmen, generals, foreign ambassadors, governors, members of the press, and a multitude of citizens watched with approval as the famous Second Corps passed by, marching with a cadenced step during this portion of the parade. If spectators had been so inclined, they could have spotted some big black hats, still proudly bearing old First Corps insignia, among that multitude of soldiers. Almost four years earlier, on May 31, 1861, the citizens of Richmond had given the City Greys a flag and a speaker had advised them that "the post of danger is the post of honor." Now that flag and most of the City Greys were gone and the danger was over, but the honor would remain forever.[6]

On June 5th all Western regiments serving with the Army of the Potomac were ordered sent to General John A. Logan, head of the Army of the Tennessee, at Louisville, Kentucky. Lieutenant Colonel Andrews and the 20th Indiana left Washington on June 16th and arrived in Louisville five days later. There the Hoosier regiment was assigned to the Second Brigade of what was styled the Provisional Division, commanded by General Henry Morrow, formerly colonel of the 24th Michigan. Indiana men were glad to once again be with their comrades from the 6th and 7th Wisconsin. A few days after its arrival, the 20th Indiana was stationed across the river in Jeffersonville, Indiana.[7]

By that time, Colonel Samuel Williams had been brought home for burial. Because of roving guerrilla bands, the colonel's friends had been unable to recover his body immediately after the Wilderness battle in 1864. Williams's funeral at Selma was held on June 12th and the funeral cortege was reported as "the largest ever known in that section of the country." The *Daily Journal* remarked that his splendid record "entitles him to rank with the loved, the distinguished, and the honored of our country's heroes."[8]

While they waited patiently for muster out, the Hoosiers could think of nothing but going home. But civilian life had not been kind to some of their former comrades. Severely wounded at Brawner Farm, Sam Lutz's shattered thigh never healed and his widowed mother could afford but mediocre medical care. William Dudley, Sam's former captain, advised the *Palladium* that the Lutz family needed "pecuniary assistance with the view of getting him better medical treatment than he has been enabled to procure and to make him more comfortable." The editor urged the Sanitary Commission "to start a subscription for this brave soldier, and to make an effort to save a life that has been periled in behalf of his country." But there was nothing any doctor could do and Sam Lutz died on May 26, 1864. One of Sam's comrades, James Livengood, had lost a leg at Antietam. After a period of convalescence, young Livengood began work in a Centreville machine shop, but in April of 1865 he had the misfortune to cut off three fingers while using a circular saw.[9]

Isaac Hughes, a veteran who had lost an arm at Gettysburg, was murdered in Muncie during August 1864. While drinking with the hired

25. Charles W. Hartup.
From the Mick Kissick Collection. Used by permission.

girls at the Davis House, he got into a row with their employer, Joseph M. Davis. Mr. Davis's son grabbed a revolver and shot Hughes at point-blank range, the ball cutting his windpipe and lodging in his chest. The murderer immediately left town, while Hughes was carried home to die.[10]

Another Delaware County man, Andrew Ribble, was killed January 21, 1865, while working as a brakeman on the Bellefontaine Railroad. As he walked on top of a car, the train went through a bridge and Ribble's head struck one of the timbers, killing him instantly.[11]

Leaving the army did not break the bonds between Indiana soldiers who had shared so many experiences. William Dudley came directly to the point in a letter to Lieutenant Crull, when he penned shamelessly, "Love to Tom & all the boys." Charley Hartup also kept in touch with Jeff Crull, confessing his aversion to hard work and a determination to live somewhere other than in the tiny village of Hagerstown. Referring to Henry Gordon, Company B's drummer, Hartup wrote, "I understand that Harry has not gone to a trade nor has he been going to school. This would seem that after all his parents are not so anxious to have him at home on that account." Hartup inquired about how Jeff was doing with the girls, advising him to look for one that had lots of money.[12]

Daniel Curry was one soldier who had trouble adjusting to civilian life after his war service. Discharged as a supernumerary corporal, he moved to Effingham, Illinois, to buy timber, and got in touch with an old friend when Bob Conley was released from rebel prison. Writing on February 9,

1865, Dan told Bob, "this is a dry place the girles is teaching school" and admitted, "when I get a peace of timber I think I will come back there and try the service one year more." In another letter written on March 12th, Curry mentioned how his social life was faring, "I am well but times is rather dull here I have not been at a party since I came out of the army." Dan finally decided not to enlist, but he did admit, "It taikes a good deel of money to get a long out of the army." He then confessed he missed army life when he said, "Robert I wish you were here and I had my tent. then we would keep back a while."

Writing again on April 23rd, Curry asked for some information, "tell me if you have herd from the oald regiment since the surrender of Lee and the reble army. I have not herd any thing for some time." On August 6th, Dan again asked for news about the old regiment, obviously unaware that everyone had been mustered out by that time. He confessed, "I am well but have got the blews awful bad. I wish that I was in the army a gan. out of money and out of friends which is always the case." By this time, one of Dan Curry's comrades, the oft-wounded Frank Huff, had left the service a bitter man. When applying for a pension, Frank would write, "I left the war a fit subject for the poor farm. Discharged after serving over 4 years for 'Disability.' A Quaker Girl helped to school me after the war and saved the government that disgrace."[13]

A Badger officer in the 6th Wisconsin expressed the sentiment that everyone felt in late June: "Action is what we wanted, action we had; but now that the last important act is passed, the drama closed—there's nothing in our present occupation but idleness and that is our bane." The only good news was that the government had decided to allow soldiers to purchase the weapons they had carried during the war. Men from the old 19th Indiana could now buy a musket, complete with accouterments, for $6, and everyone took advantage of the opportunity.[14]

Finally, on July 12th the 20th Indiana, numbering just seventeen officers and 390 enlisted men, was sent to Indianapolis for muster out. Governor Morton addressed the men at a huge public reception and said of them:

> This regiment has left its bones along the line of its long and toilsome marches—its graves are on the battlefield. You that are here should be truly thankful to a kind Providence for being here. In after years those that read your history will look upon it almost as a wild romance. It has been so daring, so strange, that it will be indeed an eventful history.[15]

Epilogue

Home

After saying their goodbyes to friends from other companies who had gathered at the Indianapolis depot, a pitifully small remnant of the Wayne County company climbed aboard a passenger car for their final journey together. George Bunch, lately commanding the company, was unofficial head of this group of ten veterans, not because a leader was needed, but because four years of military life had taught them to always look to their officers and old habits were hard to break. George must have watched them with pride as they settled into their seats, sitting slightly apart from the other passengers with whom they had so little in common. Still uniformed in worn Union blue and carrying their muskets and accouterments, they were obviously, even to casual observers, veterans of many hard-fought battles.

Like all old companies, this group was top-heavy with rank. George wore the silver bars on his shoulder straps that identified him as a first lieutenant of infantry. Joel Curtis, Dave Fort, and Jeff Kinder each sported the three light blue stripes that designated an infantry sergeant. The sleeves of John Markle and Grear Williams were marked by corporal chevrons. All original officers and noncoms had long since died or left the service and these leaders had won their positions by long and faithful service in the ranks. Four privates—Jim Bradbury, Jim Grunden, Joe Sykes, and Nathan Williams—completed the little band. These ten veterans were the survivors of 115 men who had served in Company B, 19th Indiana Veteran Volunteers.

As their train pulled out of the Indiana Central depot and headed for Richmond, the returning soldiers could not help but think back to when the City Greys started for Indianapolis to save the nation from Southern rebels. What a difference four years had made on them. In 1861 these volunteers had no inkling of what this war would be like. Their knowledge of war was confined to books that had glorified America's previous conflicts, fanciful patriotic engravings, and tales of neighbors who had served briefly in the Mexican War. These naive recruits were stirred by the sight of prancing horses and plumed hats, accompanied by the squeaking of fifes and the beating of drums. The boys were in the prime of their lives, eager to prove themselves in this greatest of adventures. There was glory to be won and the train ride from Richmond to Indianapolis seemed like the beginning of a holy crusade against traitors who sought to destroy the country.

These weary men must surely have smiled at that recollection of their youthful enthusiasm in 1861. Four years later, these veterans of the Iron Brigade were well aware of the cost of winning the war and preserving the nation. They had charged time after time into musketry hotter than a thousand Julys, had spit repeatedly in Death's face and had somehow, miraculously, emerged alive from the trauma that gutted a generation of American youth. They had seen firsthand the waste, the overwhelming waste of human life and property and resources. Historians would later write of glory, but the soldiers, from a unique perspective gained with the burial parties, saw only murder on a massive scale.

Among the survivors there was a sense of fraternity, of comradeship, of sharing something special that would never come again. In fact, for many of them the rest of their lives would be anticlimactic, never able to generate the same intensity as the war had done. Even the specter of death no longer held any fascination because, after seeing hundreds and hundreds of men die in every conceivable fashion, familiarity had bred a sort of contempt for the grim reaper. Besides, their religious faith promised that death would bring about a reunion with those who had gone on ahead as a sort of heavenly skirmish line.

In July 1865 these survivors were prematurely old. They could not explain the change that had come over them, nor could any civilian ever begin to comprehend it. The collapse of the Southern armies had ended the war and muster out had terminated their army service, but, in reality, the war would never be over for these men. It was all jumbled up inside their heads and would be with them until the day they died. There were glimpses of it, though, when the veterans could be persuaded to talk about their experiences. It could be heard in the voices and seen in the eyes—eyes that had seen far too much for their years. Even the abrupt snap of a twig would cause their eyes to glance instinctively to the right, aligning on a battleflag that had been furled for years.

But above all, there would always be memories of comrades dropped from the rolls, dead or disabled, friends burned by fever, torn by shell, or punctured by bullets. Friends, now dead, remembered by a memento, a few letters, or a youthful face, forever young, in a photograph. The boys of 1861 had been thrust into a crucible that had changed them forever and, try as they might, these Hoosier veterans would never be rid of that damned war.

As the train bearing the returning veterans chugged into the Richmond station, these blue-coated civilians roused themselves from their private thoughts. Grabbing their muskets and other gear they sprang down to the platform, where families and friends and well-wishers waited anxiously. After greetings were exchanged all around it was finally time to disband the group. Goodbyes and polite handshakes were not enough. Comrades grabbed one another and hugged and embraced shamelessly, and for one last time those sun-browned cheeks were wet with tears, tears the families could never understand. After their brief emotional farewell, the old soldiers turned and started home.

ROSTER OF COMPANY B, 19TH INDIANA VOLUNTEERS

Information consists of age, place of birth, occupation prior to enlistment, rank attained, and highlights of military service. During the war, 115 officers and enlisted men served in Company B. It must be pointed out that, excluding veteran enlistments and transfers to the Veteran Reserve Corps, these men also enlisted forty-one times in other organizations, either before or after serving in the 19th Indiana. Minute Men regiments referred to below were formed in Indiana to repulse General John Hunt Morgan's invasion of the state in July 1863.

Addleman, Jacob O., 21, b. Wayne Co., Indiana, farmer, died December 19, 1862, of chronic diarrhea.

Addleman, John H., 26, b. Wayne Co., Indiana, farmer, recruit, mustered in August 8, 1862, discharged August 10, 1864, by sentence of general court-martial.

Addleman, Joseph O., 19, b. Wayne Co., Indiana, farmer, killed Antietam.

Allen, Bartley, 18, b. Union Co., Indiana, farmer, discharged April 18, 1862, for accidental gunshot wound, mustered into Company A, 147th Indiana on February 8, 1865, mustered out August 4, 1865.

Barker, Jerome, 19, b. Wayne Co., Indiana, farmer, detached January 4, 1863, as division teamster, mustered out July 28, 1864.

Baughan, Peter, 31, b. Montgomery Co., Ohio, farmer, killed Antietam.

Beck, William, 20, b. Wayne Co., Indiana, mechanic, deserted July 30, 1861, mustered into Company E, 75th Indiana on August 19, 1862, transferred to Veteran Reserve Corps on October 25, 1863, veteran, deserted September 1, 1865.

Beetley, George V., 22, b. Preble Co., Ohio, farmer, veteran, corporal, discharged October 19, 1864, as supernumerary, mustered into Company I, 147th Indiana on February 7, 1865, sergeant, mustered out August 4, 1865.

Bennett, Joseph B., 20, b. Wayne Co., Indiana, farmer, recruit, mustered in February 8, 1862, wounded Gettysburg, transferred to Veteran Reserve Corps, mustered out February 8, 1865.

Bennett, William J., 22, b. Wayne Co., Indiana, farmer, wounded and captured Brawner Farm, discharged March 31, 1863, mustered into Company G, 106th Indiana (Minute Men) on July 10, 1863, mustered out July 17, 1863.

Benton, Thomas H., 20, b. Wayne Co., Indiana, merchant, sergeant, wounded and captured Brawner Farm, died September 14, 1862, of wounds.

Blain, Daniel, 24, b. Queens Co., New York, mechanic, detached September 22, 1862, to Battery B, 4th U.S. Artillery, wounded Gettysburg, discharged September 4, 1863, for heart disease, mustered into Company B, 123rd Indiana on December 24, 1863, mustered out August 25, 1865.

Blanchard, Asa, 17, b. Erie Co., New York, bookkeeper, corporal, sergeant major, killed Gettysburg.

Bradbury, James, 42, b. Wayne Co., Indiana, wagoner, wagoner, veteran, transferred to Company C, 20th Indiana on October 18, 1864, mustered out July 12, 1865.

Bradbury, John W., 18, b. Greene Co., Indiana, farmer, recruit, mustered in September 24, 1864, joined Company C, 20th Indiana, discharged May 31, 1865, for disability.

Bradbury, Samuel, 17, b. Wayne Co., Indiana, farmer, wounded Gettysburg, transferred to Veteran Reserve Corps, died February 19, 1864, of diarrhea.

Bunch, George W., 18, b. Darke Co., Ohio, farmer, recruit, mustered in November 25, 1861, captured Gettysburg, parole invalid, veteran, corporal, sergeant, transferred to Company C, 20th Indiana on October 18, 1864, second lieutenant, first lieutenant, mustered out July 12, 1865.

Burket, Milton M., 20, b. Wayne Co., Indiana, mechanic, corporal, discharged December 31, 1862, for scrotal hernia.

Butler, John P., 19, b. Warren Co., Ohio, student, detached October 21, 1861, as hospital steward, discharged June 26, 1862, to accept appointment as hospital steward, U.S. Army.

Carr, Anthony P., 20, b. Jay Co., Indiana, painter, corporal, wounded Second Bull Run, discharged March 14th, 1863, mustered into Company H, 103rd Indiana (Minute Men) on July 6, 1863, mustered out July 17, 1863, mustered into Company H, 34th Indiana on October 17, 1864, deserted October 16, 1865.

Castator, William H., 20, b. Wayne Co., Indiana, mechanic, captured Gettysburg, parole invalid, transferred to Veteran Reserve Corps, discharged May 14, 1864, for chronic diarrhea and extreme debility.

Castle, Davis E., 25, b. Oswego Co., New York, railroader, first lieutenant, detached to Signal Corps on January 8, 1862, wounded near Newport News, captain, mustered out August 24, 1864.

Conger, Gershom, 20, farmer, discharged April 20, 1862, for chronic bronchitis, mustered into Company I, 3rd Indiana Cavalry on September 24, 1862, transferred to Company M, 8th Indiana Cavalry, mustered out June 8, 1865.

Conley, Robert G., 22, b. Wayne Co., Indiana, nurseryman, corporal, sergeant, wounded Gettysburg, captured Wilderness, discharged March 22, 1865.

Craig, Noah, 22, b. Preble Co., Ohio, farmer, corporal, reduced to private, died June 25, 1862, of pneumonia.

Crull, Thomas J., 18, b. Ohio Co., Virginia, painter, corporal, captured Thornburg's Mill, sergeant, first sergeant, wounded Gettysburg, second lieutenant, first lieutenant, transferred to Company C, 20th Indiana on October 18, 1864, discharged October 25, 1864.

Curry, Daniel, 28, b. Preble Co., Ohio, farmer, corporal, veteran, wounded Petersburg, discharged October 19, 1864, as supernumerary.

Curtis, Joel B., 20, b. Wayne Co., Indiana, mechanic, wounded Brawner Farm, wounded and captured Gettysburg, veteran, corporal, transferred to Company C, 20th Indiana on October 18, 1864, sergeant, mustered out July 12, 1865.

Davis, Charles, 20, b. Wayne Co., Indiana, farmer, sergeant, wounded Brawner Farm, reduced to private, sergeant, veteran, sergeant major, discharged October 19, 1864, as supernumerary.

Davis, Thomas P., 24, b. Wayne Co., Indiana, farmer, veteran, wounded Petersburg, transferred to Company C, 20th Indiana on October 18, 1864, transferred to Veteran Reserve Corps, mustered out July 12, 1865.

Dillon, Ira, 19, b. Kentucky, laborer, discharged April 27, 1862, for chronic bronchitis, mustered into Company C, 5th Indiana Cavalry on August 23, 1862, deserted August 13, 1863.

Dudley, William W., 18, b. Vermont, miller, captain, major, lieutenant colonel, wounded Gettysburg, discharged April 9, 1864, for wounds, commissioned captain in Veteran Reserve Corps on March 25, 1865, mustered out June 30, 1866, breveted major, lieutenant colonel, colonel and brigadier general.

Duke, Benjamin B., 19, b. Wayne Co., Indiana, farmer, captured Gettysburg, parole invalid, veteran, captured Wilderness, transferred to Company C, 20th Indiana on October 18, 1864, mustered out July 27, 1865.

Edwards, William H., 18, b. Henry Co., Indiana, laborer, detached March 1, 1862, as nurse, discharged September 16, 1862, for phthisis pulmonalis.

English, Hugh L., 18, b. Rush Co., Indiana, farmer, wounded Brawner Farm, transferred to Veteran Reserve Corps, mustered out July 28, 1864.

Enix, Lot, 18, b. Darke Co., Ohio, farmer, wounded Gettysburg, died July 5, 1863, of wounds.

Ford, William H., 17, b. Monroe Co., New York, farmer, detached February 17, 1862, to gunboat service, wounded White River, Arkansas, discharged February 18, 1863, for remittent fever and dropsy, mustered into Company A, 42nd Indiana on November 16, 1864, mustered out July 21, 1865.

Fort, David P., 19, b. Henry Co., Indiana, farmer, veteran, corporal, wounded Petersburg, transferred to Company C, 20th Indiana on October 18, 1864, sergeant, mustered out July 12, 1865.

Fort, Randolph, 18, b. Henry Co., Indiana, farmer, killed Brawner Farm.

Franklin, Milton, 20, b. Wayne Co., Indiana, mechanic, fifer, discharged February 22, 1863, as "too small to be a soldier," mustered into Company C, 109th Indiana (Minute Men) on July 10, 1863, mustered out July 17, 1863.

Fulkerson, James C., 19, b. Hamilton Co., Ohio, died September 9, 1861, of remittent fever.

Gill, Augustus C., 33, b. Plymouth Co., Massachusetts, merchant, recruit, mustered in January 6, 1864, wounded Laurel Hill, transferred to Company C, 20th Indiana on October 18, 1864, discharged January 6, 1865, for wounds.

Gordon, Henry, 17, b. Wayne Co., Indiana, drummer, drummer, principal musician, veteran, discharged October 19, 1864, as supernumerary.

Gorgas, Edward W., 23, b. Philadelphia, Pennsylvania, railroader, sergeant, discharged October 25, 1861, for insanity.

Grunden, James, 19, b. Wayne Co., Indiana, farmer, detached September, 1861, to ambulance corps, veteran, transferred to Company C, 20th Indiana on October 18, 1864, mustered out July 12, 1865.

Hall, Luther M., 17, b. Hamilton Co., Ohio, laborer, discharged in November 1862, by writ of habeas corpus, mustered into Company H, 103rd Indiana (Minute Men) on July 6, 1863, mustered out July 17, 1863, mustered into Company K, 124th Indiana on December 19, 1863, corporal, captured Calhoun, Georgia, died April 27, 1865, in the sinking of the *Sultana*.

Hart, Timothy, 23, b. New York, New York, farmer, mustered out July 28, 1864.

Hartup, Charles W., 20, b. Wayne Co., Indiana, teacher, quartermaster sergeant, veteran, first lieutenant, regimental quartermaster, discharged October 19, 1864, as supernumerary.

Henderson, Thomas C., 20, b. Clermont Co., Ohio, farmer, corporal, sergeant, veteran, first sergeant, wounded Petersburg, discharged October 19, 1864, as supernumerary, mustered into Company I, 147th Indiana on February 1, 1865, first lieutenant Company G, 147th Indiana, mustered out August 4, 1865.

Hiatt, Henry H., 19, b. Henry Co., Indiana, farmer, wounded and captured Brawner Farm, discharged October 20, 1863, for wounds.

Hill, William G., 17, b. Wayne Co., Indiana, laborer, discharged February 21, 1863, by sentence of general court-martial, mustered into Company A, 110th Indiana (Minute Men) on July 11, 1863, mustered out July 14, 1863, mustered into Company C, 9th Indiana Cavalry on November 10, 1864, mustered out August 28, 1865.

Hindman, Samuel, 24, b. Montgomery Co., Ohio, farmer, second lieutenant, wounded Brawner Farm, first lieutenant, resigned March 14, 1863, commissioned first lieutenant in Veteran Reserve Corps on October 23, 1863, discharged June 30, 1866.

Huff, Francis M., 20, b. Rockbridge Co., Virginia, farmer, mustered into Company B, 16th Indiana on April 23, 1861, mustered out May 23, 1862, mustered into Company E, 87th Ohio on June 2, 1862, captured Harpers Ferry, mustered out October 3, 1862, recruit, mustered in October 31, 1862, wounded Gettysburg, wounded Petersburg, transferred to Company C, 20th Indiana on October 18, 1864, corporal, wounded Amelia Springs, discharged June 5, 1865, for wounds.

Hunt, Jacob, 35, b. Piscataquis Co., Maine, mechanic, captured Thornburg's Mill, veteran, wounded Petersburg, transferred to Company C, 20th Indiana on October 18, 1864, discharged May 20, 1865, for wounds.

Jewett, Benjamin F., 20, b. Randolph Co., Indiana, mechanic, corporal, wounded Brawner Farm, discharged February 6, 1863, for wounds.

Jones, Jesse E., 18, b. Wayne Co., Indiana, farmer, corporal, sergeant, veteran, wounded at Wilderness, discharged September 15, 1864, for wounds.

Jones, Richard, 21, b. Wayne Co., Indiana, mechanic, sergeant, first sergeant, second lieutenant, killed Gettysburg.

Jordan, Edward, 18, b. Butler Co., Ohio, farmer, discharged February 7, 1863, for heart disease, mustered into Company G, 106th Indiana (Minute Men) on July 10, 1863, as sergeant, mustered out July 17, 1863.

Kemp, George W., 21, b. Wayne Co., Indiana, farmer, detached on October 21, 1861, as nurse, discharged May 26, 1862, for general debility, mustered into Company G, 106th Indiana (Minute Men) on July 10, 1863, as sergeant, mustered out July 17, 1863.

Kinder, Jefferson, 18, b. Rush Co., Indiana, farmer, wounded Brawner Farm, corporal, captured Gettysburg, veteran, sergeant, transferred to Company C, 20th Indiana on October 18, 1864, mustered out July 12, 1865.

Lemon, Homer, 22, b. Cuyahoga Co., Ohio, farmer, recruit, mustered in February 8, 1862, deserted August 10, 1862.

Lewis, Gardiner, 21, b. Randolph Co., North Carolina, farmer, wounded Gettysburg, died December 23, 1863, of wounds.

Livengood, James D., 20, b. Warren Co., Indiana, mechanic, wounded Antietam, discharged March 10, 1863, for wounds.

Locke, William M., 18, b. Wayne Co., Indiana, farmer, wounded and captured Brawner Farm, captured Gettysburg, parole invalid, mustered out July 28, 1864.

Luce, Abraham, 22, b. Wayne Co., Indiana, horseman, corporal, discharged December 5, 1861, for phthisis pulmonalis, mustered into Company A, 110th Indiana (Minute Men) on July 11, 1863, mustered out July 14, 1863, mustered into Company C, 9th Indiana Cavalry on January 15, 1864, corporal, mustered out August 28, 1865.

Lutz, Samuel, 16, b. Virginia, laborer, wounded and captured Brawner Farm, discharged February 10, 1863, for wounds.

McCown, Samuel, 20, b. Preble Co., Ohio, merchant, sergeant, killed Brawner Farm.

McKinney, John, 20, b. Ireland, farmer, recruit, mustered in September 2, 1862, killed Gettysburg.

McKinney, Patterson, 18, b. Albany Co., New York, farmer, corporal, wounded Gettysburg, discharged March 24, 1864, for wounds.

Markle, John, 27, b. Schuylkill Co., Pennsylvania, laborer, captured Gettysburg, parole invalid, veteran, transferred to Company C, 20th Indiana on October 18, 1864, corporal, mustered out July 12, 1865.

Marquis, George, 19, b. Warren Co., Ohio, farmer, wounded and captured Brawner Farm, discharged February 20, 1863, for wounds.

Mills, James H., 22, b. Darke Co., Ohio, farmer, discharged March 4, 1863, for chronic diarrhea, died the same day.

Morgan, John, 25, b. Ireland, laborer, wounded Antietam, died October 10, 1862, of wounds.

Morse, Edward W., 18, b. Franklin Co., Maine, farmer, wounded and captured Brawner Farm, discharged December 27, 1862, for wounds.

Motz, John, 21, "cosmopolite" (so listed on his form), carpenter, corporal, reduced to private, wounded Gettysburg, transferred to Veteran Reserve Corps, mustered out July 28, 1864.

Ogborn, Allen W., 21, b. Wayne Co., Indiana, mechanic, corporal, sergeant, wounded Gettysburg, died July 18, 1863, of erysipelas.

Palmer, James M., 19, b. Mason Co., Kentucky, farmer, discharged September 16, 1862, for varicocele, mustered into Company A, 110th Indiana (Minute Men) on July 11, 1863, mustered out July 14, 1863, mustered into 2nd Indiana Light Artillery on January 28, 1864, discharged May 30, 1865.

Parsons, George W., 17, b. Wayne Co., Indiana, farmer, discharged July 30, 1861, by writ of habeas corpus, mustered into Company I, 57th Indiana on February 5, 1862, corporal, wounded Stone's River, sergeant, veteran, first sergeant, captured Peach Tree Creek, first lieutenant, mustered out December 14, 1865.

Petty, Charles H., 18, b. Long Island, New York, nurseryman, corporal, wounded Brawner Farm, sergeant, wounded Fitzhugh Crossing, died June 9, 1863, of wounds.

Pierce, Daniel, 20, b. Wayne Co., Indiana farmer, discharged November 4, 1861, for phthisis pulmonalis, mustered into Company K, 124th Indiana on December 19, 1863, corporal, reduced to private, mustered out August 31, 1865.

Pike, Joseph, 21, b. Pasquotank Co., North Carolina, farmer, killed Brawner Farm.

Pitman, William H., 22, b. Wayne Co., Indiana, shoemaker, recruit, mustered in January 6, 1864, wounded Wilderness, transferred to Company C, 20th Indiana on October 18, 1864, wounded Petersburg, discharged June 15, 1865.

Pool, George, 23, b. Pasquotank Co., North Carolina, farmer, wounded Antietam, died October 9, 1862, of wounds.

Purvis, Levi, 35, b. Wayne Co., Indiana, cooper, recruit, mustered in February 10, 1864, killed Petersburg.

Rariden, John T., 22, b. Wayne Co., Indiana, farmer, wounded Fitzhugh Crossing, transferred to Veteran Reserve Corps, mustered out July 28, 1864.

Sater, Charles C., 18, b. Fulton Co., Indiana, farmer, corporal, sergeant, wounded Gettysburg, transferred to Veteran Reserve Corps, no muster out date available.

Schlagle, Samuel B., 24, b. Wayne Co., Indiana, brickmaker, first sergeant, wounded Brawner Farm, second lieutenant, first lieutenant, wounded Gettysburg, resigned November 25, 1863.

Shelley, William F., 25, b. Henry Co., Indiana, plasterer, mustered into Company B, Benton Cadets, United States Reserve Corps [Missouri] on September 15, 1861, mustered out January 8, 1862, recruit, mustered in February 20, 1862, discharged April 10, 1863, for chronic diarrhea, mustered into Company G, 139th Indiana on June 6, 1864, as first lieutenant, captain, mustered out August 4, 1865.

Snider, John M., 23, b. Cumberland Co., Pennsylvania, mechanic, corporal, sergeant major, died March 4, 1862, of congestion of the lungs.

Sparklin, Samuel, 36, b. Maryland, mechanic, detached November 18, 1861, as nurse, discharged January 23, 1862, for hydrocele, mustered into Company B, 152nd Ohio National Guard on May 1, 1864, as sergeant, mustered out July 28, 1864.

Sponsler, Charles, 18, b. Wayne Co., Indiana, farmer, wounded Fitzhugh Crossing, mustered out July 28, 1864.

Swain, Ambrose H., 20, b. Delaware Co., Indiana, farmer, wounded Gettysburg, discharged May 3, 1864, for wounds.

Sykes, Joseph, 23, b. Perquimans Co., North Carolina, farmer, veteran, transferred to Company C, 20th Indiana on October 18, 1864, mustered out July 12, 1865.

Sykes, William H., 20, b. Perquimans Co., North Carolina, farmer, corporal, reduced to private, wounded Gettysburg, captured Wilderness, died March 25, 1865, of extreme debility.

Thornburg, Benjamin, 40, b. Tennessee, farmer, discharged April 15, 1862, for scrotal hernia, mustered into Company F, 69th Indiana on July 24, 1862, wagoner, discharged March 6, 1863, for mental and physical incapacity, mustered into Company C, 9th Indiana Cavalry on December 18, 1863, assistant wagon master, mustered out June 6, 1865.

Thornburg, James, 20, b. Wayne Co., Indiana, farmer, discharged October 31, 1861, for phthisis pulmonalis, mustered into Company H, 147th Indiana on February 15, 1865, mustered out August 4, 1865.

Thornburg, John R., 21, b. Wayne Co., Indiana, farmer, corporal, died December 6, 1861, of remittent fever.

Thornburg, William, 18, b. Wayne Co., Indiana, farmer, discharged April 16, 1862, for general debility.

Titus, Joseph W. C., 22, b. Clinton Co., Ohio, mechanic, discharged April 16, 1862, for general debility, mustered into Company D, 79th Ohio on August 20, 1862, corporal, reduced to private, mustered out June 9, 1865.

Walker, Alexander C., 20, b. Ripley Co., Indiana, farmer, wounded and captured Brawner Farm, transferred to Veteran Reserve Corps, no muster out date available.

Wallick, Sanford, 15, b. Wayne Co., Indiana, deserted August 2, 1861, mustered into Company I, 36th Indiana on October 23, 1861, wounded Kenesaw Mountain, died July 17, 1864, of wounds.

Wasson, Thomas J., 17, b. Wayne Co., Indiana, mechanic, wounded and captured Brawner Farm, corporal, killed Gettysburg.

Wharton, Horace, 21, b. Butler Co., Ohio, farmer, corporal, reduced to private, deserted September 14, 1862.

Whitlow, James W., 21, b. Barn Co., Kentucky, farmer, wounded and captured Brawner Farm, wounded and captured Gettysburg, died December 12, 1863, of wounds.

Whitlow, King S., 19, b. Barn Co., Kentucky, farmer, wounded and captured Brawner Farm, transferred to Veteran Reserve Corps, mustered out July 28, 1864.

Williams, Grear N., 18, b. Wayne Co., Indiana, farmer, wounded Gettysburg, veteran, transferred to Company C, 20th Indiana on October 18, 1864, corporal, wounded Petersburg, mustered out July 12, 1865.

Williams, Nathan S., 19, b. Wayne Co., Indiana, farmer, mustered into Company G, 106th Indiana (Minute Men) on July 10, 1863, mustered out July 17, 1863, recruit, mustered in February 27, 1864, wounded Laurel Hill, transferred to Company C, 20th Indiana on October 18, 1864, wounded Hatcher's Run, mustered out July 12, 1865.

Williams, Richard, 18, b. Wayne Co., Indiana, farmer, wounded Brawner Farm, discharged February 25, 1863, for wounds, mustered into Company G, 106th Indiana (Minute Men) on July 10, 1863, mustered out July 17, 1863, mustered into Company H, 140th Indiana on October 24, 1864, as sergeant, mustered out July 11, 1865.

Williams, William O., 23, b. Guilford Co., North Carolina, farmer, mustered into Company B, 6th Indiana on April 23, 1861, mustered out August 2, 1861, recruit, mustered in February 20, 1862, corporal, killed Gettysburg.

Winder, John M., 21, b. Champaign Co., Ohio, clerk, discharged December 6, 1861, for a deformity that existed previous to enlistment.

Wine, James, 18, b. Randolph Co., Indiana, farmer, detached September 22, 1862, to Battery B, 4th U.S. Artillery, mustered out July 28, 1864.

Wisenberg, Joseph, 26, b. Monroe Co., Ohio, laborer, discharged November 26, 1861, for phthisis pulmonalis, mustered into 3rd Indiana Cavalry on October 7, 1862, corporal, discharged May 19, 1863, for chronic inflammation of the stomach and liver.

Woolverton, Charles W., 25, b. Bucks Co., Pennsylvania, mechanic, discharged February 8, 1863, for chronic laryngitis, mustered into Company G, 106th Indiana (Minute Men) on July 10, 1863, as corporal, mustered out July 17, 1863, mustered into Company B, 152nd Ohio National Guard on May 2, 1864, mustered out September 2, 1864.

Young, Jacob, 35, b. Pennsylvania, miller, recruit, mustered in February 10, 1864, wounded Cold Harbor, transferred to Company C, 20th Indiana on October 18, 1864, mustered out August 2, 1865.

Zook, Henry, 15, b. Wayne Co., Indiana, tinner, corporal, reduced to private, mustered out July 28, 1864.

NEWSPAPER ABBREVIATIONS
CITED IN NOTES

BAOF	*Broad Axe of Freedom*	Richmond, Indiana
CCT	*Cambridge City Tribune*	Cambridge City, Indiana
DCFP	*Delaware County Free Press*	Muncie, Indiana
DSS	*Daily State Sentinel*	Indianapolis, Indiana
EWR	*Elkhart Weekly Review*	Elkhart, Indiana
GCH	*Grant County Herald*	Lancaster, Wisconsin
GCW	*Grant County Witness*	Platteville, Wisconsin
IDJ	*Indianapolis Daily Journal*	Indianapolis, Indiana
ITR	*Indiana True Republican*	Centerville, Indiana
JDG	*Janesville Daily Gazette*	Janesville, Wisconsin
MPT	*Mineral Point Tribune*	Mineral Point, Wisconsin
MR	*Missouri Republican*	St. Louis, Missouri
MS	*Milwaukee Sentinel*	Milwaukee, Wisconsin
MST	*Milwaukee Sunday Telegraph*	Milwaukee, Wisconsin
NCC	*New Castle Courier*	New Castle, Indiana
NT	*The National Tribune*	Washington, D.C.
NYH	*New York Herald*	New York, New York
QCT	*Quaker City Telegram*	Richmond, Indiana
RCJ	*Randolph County Journal*	Winchester, Indiana
RDUA	*Rochester Daily Union and Advertiser*	Rochester, New York
REI	*Richmond Evening Item*	Richmond, Indiana
RP	*Richmond Palladium*	Richmond, Indiana
RWA	*Racine Weekly Advocate*	Racine, Wisconsin
RWT	*Richmond Weekly Telegram*	Richmond, Indiana
WDP	*Wisconsin Daily Patriot*	Madison, Wisconsin
WES	*Washington Evening Star*	Washington, D.C.
WJ	*Winchester Journal*	Winchester, Indiana
WSJ	*Wisconsin State Journal*	Madison, Wisconsin

NOTES

INTRODUCTION

1. *Richmond Palladium* [hereinafter cited as *RP*] February 20, 1863, 3.
2. Ibid., June 12, 1863, 3.
3. Ibid., June 19, 1863, 3; *Quaker City Telegram* [hereinafter cited as *QCT*] June 19, 1863, 3.
4. Ibid.; *RP*, June 19, 1863, 3.
5. *RP*, July 20, 1865, 2; *QCT*, June 19, 1863, 3.
6. *RP*, September 18, 1863, 3.
7. Earlham Cemetery Interment Records, Earlham Cemetery, Richmond, Indiana, and letter from Clem Zwissler, cemetery caretaker, to author, April 5, 1978.
8. *Daily Cincinnati Gazette*, August 1, 1863, 1.

1. RICHMOND CITY GREYS

1. John M. Snider Pension File.
2. "Official Program and Souvenir, 32nd Annual Encampment" (Richmond: Indiana Department, Grand Army of the Republic, 1911).
3. Andrew W. Young, *History of Wayne County, Indiana* (Cincinnati: Robert Clarke, 1872), 678–79.
4. *Broad Axe of Freedom* [hereinafter cited as *BAOF*] April 21, 1861, 3; ibid., May 11, 1861, 3.
5. Dean Dudley, *History of the Dudley Family* (Boston: Dean Dudley, 1892), 736–37; *Richmond Weekly Telegram* [hereinafter cited as *RWT*] January 27, 1866, 2; Russell Seeds, ed., *History of the Republican Party of Indiana* (Indianapolis: n.p., 1899) I: 356; *A Biographical History of Eminent and Self-Made Men of the State of Indiana* (Cincinnati: n.p., 1880), I: 24–25.
6. *QCT*, March 5, 1864, 3; *Sutherland & McEvoy's Richmond and Cambridge City Directories* (Richmond: Sutherland & McEvoy, 1860); U.S. Bureau of the Census, *Census of Population* [hereinafter cited as Census], Wayne County, Indiana, 1860; Company Descriptive Book; Henry Clay Fox, ed., *Memoirs of Wayne County and the City of Richmond, Indiana* (Madison, Wisconsin: Western Historical Association, 1912), II, 640–41.
7. John Lee Yaryan, "Stone River," *War Papers Read Before Indiana Commandery, Military Order of the Loyal Legion of the United States* [hereinafter cited as *MOLLUS*] II (1878): 157–58.
8. *RP*, May 23, 1861, 3; *BAOF*, May 18, 1861, 2; *BAOF*, May 25, 1861, 3.
9. Ibid., 4; *BAOF*, June 1, 1861, 3.
10. Ibid.; *BAOF*, June 8, 1861, 3.

11. *BAOF,* June 1, 1861, 3.

12. J. C. Power, *Directory and Soldiers' Register of Wayne County, Indiana* (Richmond: privately printed, 1865), 258, 341, 277, 361, 309, 269, 334; Census, Wayne County, Indiana, 1860.

13. Ibid.; Young, *Wayne County,* 437–38, 502–503; Fox, *Memoirs,* II, 533, 611; Young, *Wayne County,* 218; Power, *Soldiers' Register,* 281, 382.

14. *RP,* June 20, 1861, 2.

15. Solomon Meredith, "Truth Is Mighty and Will Prevail" (Indianapolis: Douglass & Conner, 1866); *RP,* August 8, 1862, 2.

16. *BAOF,* June 29, 1861, 2; *BAOF,* July 13, 1861, 3.

17. Ibid.

2. CAMP MORTON

1. *Indianapolis Daily Journal* [hereinafter cited as *IDJ*] July 8, 1861, 3; William R. Moore Papers, Indiana Historical Society, Indianapolis; *RP,* May 23, 1861, 2; Hattie L. Winslow and Joseph R. H. Moore, *Camp Morton 1861–1865* (Indianapolis: Indiana Historical Society, 1940), 248; Records of the Indiana Commissary General [hereinafter cited as Commissary General], Camp Morton, 1861 Archives, Indiana State Library.

2. *IDJ,* July 8, 1861, 3.

3. Commissary General; *Daily State Sentinel* [hereinafter cited as *DSS*] July 1, 1861, 3; Congress, Senate, *Proceedings and Report of the Board of Army Officers Convened by Special Order No. 78, Headquarters of the Army, Adjutant General's Office, Washington, April 12, 1878, in the Case of Fitz John Porter, Together with Proceedings in the Original Trial and Papers Relating Thereto* [hereinafter cited as Porter Case], 46th Cong., 1st sess., 1878, S. Exec. Doc. 37, 597; Lessel Long, *Twelve Months in Andersonville* (Huntington, Indiana: Thad and Mark Butler Publishers, 1886), 54.

4. Regimental Correspondence, Nineteenth Indiana Infantry, Archives, Indiana State Library [hereinafter cited as Correspondence File, Indiana]; *Memorial and Biographical History of Northern California* (Chicago: Lewis Publishing, 1891), 510–11; Samuel Harden, comp., *Those I Have Met, or Boys in Blue* (Anderson, Indiana: printed privately, 1888), 384.

5. Correspondence File, Indiana; Owen County Historical Society, *History of Owen County, Indiana* (Spencer, Indiana: Owen County Historical Society, 1977), II, 861–62.

6. Correspondence File, Indiana; Theodore T. Scribner, *Indiana's Roll of Honor* (Indianapolis: A. D. Streight, 1866), I, 590; Moore MSS.

7. Henry S. K. Bartholomew, *Pioneer History of Elkhart County, Indiana* (Goshen, Indiana: privately printed, 1930), 289; *History of DeKalb County, Indiana* (Chicago: Interstate Publishing Co., 1885), 335–36.

8. Correspondence File, Indiana; David Stevenson, *Indiana's Roll of Honor* (Indianapolis: A. D. Streight, 1864) I, 633; Harden, *Boys in Blue,* 73–74.

9. Correspondence File, Indiana; John Andis Pension File; Abraham Cly Pension File.

10. *BAOF,* July 13, 1861, 3; Meredith, "Truth," 16; *DSS,* July 8, 1861, 3.

11. D. D. Banta, *A Historical Sketch of Johnson County, Indiana* (Chicago: J. H. Beers, 1881), 99; *History of Johnson County, Indiana* (Chicago: Brant & Fuller, 1888), 534–35.

12. Correspondence File, Indiana; Ebenezer Tucker, *History of Randolph County, Indiana* (Chicago: A. L. Kingman, 1882), 238, 386; *Portrait and Record of Delaware and Randolph Counties, Indiana* (Chicago: A. W. Bowen, 1894), 1251.

13. William J. Hardee, *Rifle and Light Infantry Tactics* (Philadelphia: Lippincott, Graenlof, 1861), I, 3 passim; *Report of the Adjutant General of the State of Indiana*, prepared by W. H. H. Terrell (Indianapolis: State Printing Office, 1869), II, 168–75.

14. Moore MSS.

15. Hardee, *Tactics*, I, passim; Moore MSS.

16. *Indiana True Republican* [hereinafter cited as *ITR*] July 11, 1861, 3.

17. *RP*, June 15, 1864, 2; Scribner, *Roll of Honor*, II, 77.

18. *Richmond Evening Item* [hereinafter cited as *REI*] March 10, 1882, 3; Scribner, *Roll of Honor*, II, 78–79; *Biographical and Genealogical History of Wayne, Fayette, Union and Franklin Counties, Indiana* (Chicago: Lewis Publishing, 1899), I, 271–73.

19. Ibid., I, 272–73.

20. Scribner, *Roll of Honor*, II, 79–80; *Palladium-Item and Sun-Telegraph*, December 21, 1953, 9.

21. Scribner, *Roll of Honor*, II, 79–80; *Genealogical History*, 272; Carl Brand, "The Knownothing Party in Indiana," *Indiana Magazine of History* (December 1917), 18: 267; *The Diary of Calvin Fletcher, 1857–1860* (Indianapolis: Indiana Historical Society, 1978), I, 434; Charles Zimmerman, "The Origin and Rise of the Republican Party in Indiana from 1854 to 1860," *Indiana Magazine of History* (December 1917) 13: 382.

22. Scribner, *Roll of Honor*, II, 81; Murat Halstead, *Caucuses of 1860: A History of the National Political Conventions* (Columbus, Ohio: Follett, Foster, 1860), 146; Letters from Solomon Meredith to Abraham Lincoln, December 31, 1860, January 2, 1861, January 26, 1861, in the Robert Todd Lincoln Papers, Lincoln National Life Insurance Company, Fort Wayne, Indiana; Roy P. Basler, ed., *The Collected Works of Abraham Lincoln* (New Brunswick, New Jersey: Rutgers University Press, 1953), IV, 196.

23. *Genealogical History*, 272; *Richmond Daily Free Press*, October 22, 1875, 2.

24. Scribner, *Roll of Honor*, II, 80–81; *Genealogical History*, 272; *RP*, October 11, 1860, 1.

25. Orr Family Papers, Lilly Library, Indiana University, Bloomington, Indiana.

26. Ibid.; Thomas Davis Pension File; John Winder Military Service Record; Milton Franklin Military Service Record.

27. David B. Floyd, *History of the Seventy-Fifth Regiment* (Philadelphia: Lutheran Publishing Society, 1893), 22–23; Power, *Soldiers' Register*, 337; Harden, *Boys in Blue*, 248; Census, Wayne County, 1860; National Archives, Records of the Adjutant General's Office, Regimental Record Books, Record Group 94 [hereinafter cited as Regimental Records] Nineteenth Indiana Infantry, Descriptive Book.

28. *History of Wayne County* (Chicago: Interstate Publishing, 1884), II, 626; Fox, *Memoirs*, II, 673–74; John Snider Pension File; George Hazzard, *Hazzard's History of Henry County, Indiana 1822–1906* (New Castle, Indiana: George Hazzard, 1906), I, 306–307.

29. Regimental Records, Descriptive Book; Fox, *Memoirs*, II, 622.

30. Yaryan, "Stone River," 157–59; James H. Stine, *History of the Army of the Potomac* (Washington: Gibson, 1893), 721; Jesse Potts Military Service Record.

31. Regimental Records, Descriptive Book.

32. *IDJ*, July 18, 1861, 3, and July 26, 1861, 3; Bartholomew, *Elkhart History*, 288; Helen Hudson, *Civil War Hawks: Story and Letters of Hawk Family in Civil War* (Hagerstown, Indiana: Historic Hagerstown, 1974), 2; Levi Yost Pension File.

33. Terrell, *Adjutant General*, IV, 392–93; ibid., II, 170; Levi Yost Pension File.

34. *Report of John H. Vajen, Quartermaster General of the State of Indiana* [hereinafter cited as Quartermaster, Indiana] (Indianapolis: Joseph J. Bingham, State Printer, 1863), 665; *BAOF*, August 3, 1861, 3.

35. Quartermaster, Indiana, 1861; *DSS,* August 6, 1861, 3; Donald E. Thompson, comp., *Indiana Authors and Their Books 1917–1966* (Crawfordsville, Indiana: Wabash College, 1974), II, 677.

36. Commissary General, Camp Morton.

37. Orr MSS; *Report of the Indiana Arsenal* (Indianapolis: Joseph J. Bingham, State Printer, 1863) [hereinafter cited as Indiana Arsenal] 1861.

38. Ibid., 1348–49 and 1375–77.

39. Ezra J. Warner, *Generals in Blue: Lives of Union Commanders* (Baton Rouge: Louisiana State University Press, 1964), 64; Stevenson, *Roll of Honor,* I, 84; Terrell, *Adjutant General,* II, 20.

40. Stevenson, *Roll of Honor,* I, 381–82.

41. Orr MSS; *DSS,* August 6, 1861, 3.

42. Indiana Battleflag Commission, *Battle Flags and Organizations* (Indianapolis: Commission, 1929), 155.

43. Ibid.

3. CAMP KALORAMA

1. *DSS,* August 19, 1861, 2; Orr MSS; Campbell Family Papers privately owned by James Biltz, Pierceton, Indiana; Hudson, *Hawks,* 3.

2. Campbell MSS; *DSS,* August 19, 1861, 2; Hudson, *Hawks,* 3.

3. *BAOF,* August 10, 1861, 3.

4. *DSS,* August 19, 1861, 2; Orr MSS; Campbell MSS.

5. Orr MSS; *DSS,* August 19, 1861, 2; Campbell MSS.

6. Ibid.; Orr MSS; Julietta Starbuck Civil War Papers, Indiana Historical Society, Indianapolis.

7. Moore MSS; Campbell MSS.

8. Solomon Meredith Papers, Indiana Historical Society, Indianapolis; *DSS,* August 19, 1861, 2.

9. Alan Nolan, *The Iron Brigade* (New York: Macmillan, 1961), 24; Charles King Scrapbook, State Historical Society of Wisconsin, Madison.

10. William R. Holloway, *Report of Indiana Military Agencies to the Governor* (Indianapolis: State Printing Office, 1865), 72; Orr MSS; Crull MSS privately owned.

11. J. Harrison Mills, *Chronicles of the Twenty-First Regiment* (Buffalo: privately printed, 1887), 99; Holloway, *Military Agencies,* 72.

12. Crull MSS; Starbuck MSS; Edwin Quiner, *Correspondence of Wisconsin Volunteers 1861–1865,* State Historical Society of Wisconsin, Madison, I, 245; *Milwaukee Sentinel* [hereinafter cited as *MS*] October 3, 1861, 2.

13. National Archives, *Regimental Correspondence Files,* National Archives, Washington, D.C., Nineteenth Indiana Infantry [hereinafter cited as Correspondence File, National]; *MS,* October 3, 1861, 2; *Wisconsin Daily Patriot* [hereinafter cited as *WDP*] September 20, 1861, 2.

14. War Department, *The War of the Rebellion: A Compilation of the Official Records of the Union and Confederate Armies* [hereinafter cited as *OR*] (Washington: Government Printing Office, 1880–1901), 51: 443, 456, 462; Andrew E. Ford, *The Story of the Fifteenth Regiment Massachusetts Volunteers* (Clinton: Press of W. J. Coulter, 1898), 49–51; Rufus R. Dawes, *Service with the Sixth Wisconsin Volunteers* (Marietta: E. R. Alderman & Sons, 1890), 21.

15. Crull MSS; Quiner, *Wisconsin Volunteers,* I, 140; Dawes, *Sixth Wisconsin,* 21.

16. Quiner, *Wisconsin Volunteers,* I, 140; ibid., I, 247; *MS,* September 11, 1861, 1.

17. *IDJ*, September 6, 1861, 2; Dawes, *Sixth Wisconsin*, 21; Starbuck MSS; Crull MSS; Hudson, *Hawks*, 3.

18. Crull MSS; Charles King, "Army Bands," unidentified newspaper clipping in author's possession.

19. *Cincinnati Daily Commercial*, September 4, 1861, 2; Philip Cheek and Mair Pointon, *Sauk County Riflemen* (Madison, Wisconsin: Democrat Printing, 1909), 18.

20. Correspondence File, National; Oliver Morton Papers and Correspondence, Archives Division, Indiana State Library, Indianapolis.

21. Stine, *Army of the Potomac*, 715–16.

22. Correspondence File, National.

23. Crull MSS; Starbuck MSS.

24. *DSS*, August 19, 1861, 2; *WDP*, August 19, 1861, 2; Moore MSS; Quiner, *Wisconsin Volunteers*, I, 136.

25. Ford, *Fifteenth Regiment*, 49.

26. *Randolph County Journal* [hereinafter cited as *RCJ*] August 29, 1861, 2.

27. Ibid.; Crull MSS.

28. Ibid.

29. *MS*, September 18, 1861, 1; Moore MSS.

30. *OR*, 5: 83; *IDJ*, September 6, 1861, 2.

31. *Revised United States Army Regulations of 1861* (Washington: Government Printing Office, 1863), 49–50.

32. Ibid., 545–46.

4. AFFAIR AT LEWINSVILLE

1. Nineteenth Indiana Infantry Morning Reports, Archives, Indiana State Library, Indianapolis; *Washington Evening Star* [hereinafter cited as *WES*], September 3, 1861, 1; Morton MSS; John Johnson Civil War Papers, Indiana Historical Society, Indianapolis.

2. *MS*, September 17, 1861, 2; *IDJ*, September 14, 1861, 2.

3. *MS*, September 17, 1861, 2; Orr MSS.

4. *MS*, September 17, 1861, 2.

5. Charles King, "Rufus King: Soldier, Editor, Statesman," *Wisconsin Magazine of History*, IV (1920–21): 377–78.

6. *IDJ*, September 14, 1861, 2; *IDJ*, September 11, 1861, 2.

7. George Kemp Pension File; Starbuck MSS.

8. Hudson, *Hawks*, 4; *IDJ*, September 14, 1861, 2; William Todd, *The Seventy-Ninth Highlanders, New York Volunteers in the War of the Rebellion, 1861–1865* (Albany: Brandow, Barton, 1886), 72–73.

9. *IDJ*, September 14, 1861, 2; Todd, *Highlanders*, 72–73; *Delaware County Free Press* [hereinafter cited as *DCFP*] January 2, 1862, 1.

10. *IDJ*, September 14, 1861, 2; Hudson, *Hawks*, 4.

11. Orr MSS; Starbuck MSS; Hudson, *Hawks*, 4.

12. *IDJ*, September 20, 1861, 2; Starbuck MSS.

13. Crull MSS; *RCJ*, September 19, 1861, 3.

14. Stine, *Army of the Potomac*, 101–102; Otis Waite, *Vermont in the Great Rebellion* (Claremont, New Hampshire: privately printed, 1869), 281–83; Theodore S. Peck, comp., *Revised Roster of Vermont Volunteers* (Montpelier: Watchman Publishing, 1892), 105.

15. Moore MSS; *RCJ*, October 3, 1861, 1.

16. Ibid.; Cornelius Wheeler Papers, State Historical Society of Wisconsin, Madison.

17. *OR*, 5: 165–67.

18. Ibid., 169.

19. Ibid., 169–70, 172–73; Moore MSS.

20. *OR*, 5: 170.

21. Ibid., 170, 173, 184.

22. *IDJ*, September 20, 1861, 2.

23. Crull MSS; *OR*, 5: 173; *IDJ*, September 20, 1861, 2.

24. Ibid.

25. *OR*, 5: 168, 173; *IDJ*, September 20, 1861, 2; Crull MSS; Starbuck MSS.

26. *IDJ*, September 20, 1861, 2; Crull MSS.

27. *OR*, 5: 171, 173; ibid., 51, pt. 1: 42.

28. *WES*, September 13, 1861, 2; *IDJ*, September 20, 1861, 2.

29. Asbury Inlow Pension File.

30. *IDJ*, September 20, 1861, 2; Stevenson, *Roll of Honor*, I, 348; Jefferson Kinder Pension File.

31. *Wisconsin State Journal* [hereinafter cited as *WSJ*] September 21, 1861, 2; *IDJ*, September 20, 1861, 2.

32. *OR*, 5: 215–16; *Mineral Point Tribune* [hereinafter cited as *MPT*] October 8, 1861, 1.

33. *BAOF*, October 5, 1861, 2; *OR*, 5: 216.

34. *BAOF*, October 5, 1861, 2; *OR*, 5: 217; *MPT*, October 8, 1861, 1.

35. Stevenson, *Roll of Honor*, I, 349; Starbuck MSS; Hudson, *Hawks*, 5.

36. *OR*, 51, pt. 1: 489; Dawes, *Sixth Wisconsin*, 23; Charles King, "Memories of a Busy Life," *Wisconsin Magazine of History*, 6 (1922): 172–73.

37. *WDP*, October 14, 1861, 1; *Racine Weekly Advocate* [hereinafter cited as *RWA*] October 16, 1861, 2.

38. *WDP*, October 14, 1861, 1; *Grant County Witness* [hereinafter cited as *GCW*] October 17, 1861, 2.

39. Ibid.; Quiner, *Wisconsin Volunteers*, I, 275.

5. INDIANA HOSPITAL

1. *IDJ*, September 16, 1861, 1; Morning Reports.

2. *IDJ*, September 16, 1861, 1.

3. Sylvia G. L. Dannett, *Noble Women of the North* (New York: Thomas Yoseloff, 1959), 82.

4. *IDJ*, September 14, 1861, 2; *IDJ*, September 30, 1861, 2.

5. Morton MSS; Quartermaster, Indiana, 37.

6. *IDJ*, June 26, 1862, 2; *IDJ*, September 14, 1861, 2; *IDJ*, October 25, 1861, 2.

7. *IDJ*, September 16, 1861, 1; Frank Moore, ed., *Women of the War* (Hartford: S. S. Scranton, 1866), 401.

8. Morton MSS.

9. Morning Reports; Regis De Trobriand, trans. George K. Dauchy, *Four Years with the Army of the Potomac* (Gaithersburg, Maryland: Ron Van Sickle Military Books, 1988), 88.

10. Morton MSS; Holloway, *Military Agencies*, 72–73.

11. Morton MSS.

12. Ibid.; Correspondence File, Indiana.

13. Morton MSS.

14. Joseph K. Barnes, *The Medical and Surgical History of the War of the Rebellion* (Wilmington, NC: Broadfoot Publishing, 1990–91) V, 245.

15. Ibid.; National Archives, Quartermaster General Department, *Register of Burials in National Cemeteries,* Record Group 92.

16. Orr MSS.

17. Davis Castle Pension File.

18. Gershom Conger Military Service Record; Randolph Fort Military Service Record; James Fulkerson Military Service Record; Grear Williams Military Service Record; National Archives, Record Group 94, Hospital Registers, Patent Office General Hospital.

19. Edward Gorgas Pension File.

20. Hospital Register, Patent Office; William Kepler Pension File; Eliza Howland, *Family Records* (New Haven: Tuttle, Morehouse, & Taylor, 1900), 248.

21. James Lloyd Pension File.

22. Starbuck MSS; *DCFP,* October 17, 1861, 3; John Keller Pension File; James Franklin Pension File.

23. Starbuck MSS; *DSS,* December 7, 1861, 2.

24. Morton MSS; Hospital Register, Patent Office Hospital.

25. Morton MSS.

26. Correspondence Files, National.

27. Ibid.; Morton MSS.

28. *IDJ,* September 30, 1861, 2.

29. *WES,* November 20, 1861, 1; Hospital Register, Patent Office; Starbuck MSS; U.S. Department of the Interior, *Report of the Secretary of the Interior for 1862,* (Washington: Government Printing Office, 1862), 13–14.

30. *RP,* January 4, 1862, 2.

31. *IDJ,* October 16, 1861, 2; ibid., October 25, 1861, 2; Orr MSS; *IDJ,* January 18, 1862, 2.

32. *IDJ,* June 26, 1862, 2; *RP,* January 4, 1862, 2; *IDJ,* September 16, 1861, 1.

33. Linus Brockett, *Famous Women of the War* (Edgewood Publishing, 1867), 449–50.

34. *IDJ,* September 16, 1861, 1; Dannett, *Noble Women,* 83; *IDJ,* September 30, 1861, 2; Marsh MSS.

6. ARLINGTON HEIGHTS

1. Randall Bond Truett, *Washington D.C.: A Guide to the Nation's Capital,* American Guide Series (New York: Hastings House, 1968), 439–40; Quiner, *Wisconsin Volunteers,* I, 279.

2. Truett, *Guide to D.C.,* 440–41; Crull MSS.

3. George B. McClellan, *Report on the Organization and Campaigns of the Army of the Potomac* (New York: Sheldon, 1864), 453.

4. Michael H. Fitch, *Echoes of the Civil War As I Hear Them* (New York: R. F. Fenno, 1905), 34; *National Tribune* [hereinafter cited as *NT*], August 21, 1902, 3; Quiner, *Wisconsin Volunteers,* III, 274; Hudson, *Hawks,* 6.

5. Quiner, *Wisconsin Volunteers,* I, 149; Crull MSS.

6. Francis Trevelyan Miller, ed., *The Photographic History of the Civil War* (New York: Review of Reviews, 1911), I, 115, 309; *NT,* August 21, 1902, 3; Dawes, *Sixth Wisconsin,* 27; Mark M. Boatner, *The Civil War Dictionary* (New York: David McKay, 1961), 718.

7. Crull MSS.

8. Augustus Buell, *The Cannoneer* (Washington: National Tribune, 1890), 398; John Gibbon, *Personal Recollections of the Civil War* (Dayton: Morningside, 1991), 13.

9. Buell, *Cannoneer,* 17.

10. J. Albert Monroe, "Reminiscences of the War of the Rebellion of 1861–1865," *Rhode Island Soldiers and Sailors Historical Society,* Series 2 (Providence: N. Bangs Williams, 1887), 16–17.

11. Morton MSS; Thompson, *Indiana Authors,* II, 677.

12. Hudson, *Hawks,* 7; Orr MSS; *DSS,* November 8, 1861, 3.

13. Dawes, *Sixth Wisconsin,* 25–26; *WSJ,* October 25, 1861, 2.

14. Benjamin F. Reed Military Service Record.

15. John Johnson Military Service Record; Henry Vandegrift Military Service Record; Theodore Hudnut Military Service Record; James Kilgore Military Service Record; Frederick Hale Military Service Record.

16. Stevenson, *Roll of Honor,* I, 383–84; *DSS,* November 8, 1861, 3.

17. Campbell MSS.

18. Crull MSS.

19. L. Allison Wilmer, J. H. Jarrett, and George W. F. Vernon, *History and Roster of Maryland Volunteers, War of 1861–1865* (Baltimore: Guggenheimer, Weil, 1898), I, 260–61.

7. HEADQUARTERS GUARD

1. *DCFP,* December 5, 1861, 1; Quiner, *Wisconsin Volunteers,* II, 2; *WDP,* November 29, 1861, 1.

2. Stine, *Army of the Potomac,* 103–104.

3. *DCFP,* December 5, 1861, 1; *WDP,* November 29, 1861, 1.

4. Ibid.; Edward S. Bragg Papers, State Historical Society of Wisconsin, Madison; Quiner, *Wisconsin Volunteers,* II, 4.

5. Orr MSS; *WDP,* December 13, 1861, 2.

6. Quiner, *Wisconsin Volunteers,* III, 274; Thomas Crull Letters, privately owned by Thomas R. Pratt, Santa Barbara, California.

7. Quiner, *Wisconsin Volunteers,* I, 280; ibid., III, 274; *Janesville Daily Gazette* [hereinafter cited as *JDG*] October 11, 1861, 2; Orr MSS; *DCFP,* January 2, 1862, 3.

8. Crull MSS; George Beetley Pension File; James Grunden Pension File.

9. Hudson, *Hawks,* 7; Indiana Quartermaster General, Ordnance and Ordnance Stores Received, Archives, Indiana State Library, Indianapolis; Francis A. Lord, *They Fought for the Union* (New York: Bonanza Books, 1960), 154–55; Boatner, *Dictionary,* 766.

10. Morton MSS; Hudson, *Hawks,* 8; *ITR,* December 19, 1861, 1; Crull MSS.

11. *Milwaukee Sunday Telegraph* [hereinafter cited as *MST*] October 16, 1861, 2.

12. Crull MSS; C. A. Woodruff, "In Memory of Major General John Gibbon, USA," *Personal Recollections of the War of the Rebellion,* II, 292.

13. Quiner, *Wisconsin Volunteers,* III, 274.

14. Quiner, *Wisconsin Volunteers,* II, 3.

15. *MS,* November 20, 1861, 2.

16. Campbell MSS.

17. John Winder Pension File.

18. John Snider Pension File; Crull MSS; Correspondence File, Indiana.

8. WINTER CAMP

1. Correspondence File, Indiana.
2. Ibid.; Terrell, *Adjutant General,* II, 173; the Adjutant General mistakenly lists Lee as "Leander Morgan."
3. Correspondence File, Indiana.
4. *IDJ,* January 24, 1862, 2; John Snider Pension File.
5. *RP,* February 1, 1862, 2; John Snider Pension File.
6. *RP,* January 11, 1862, 2.
7. Quiner, *Wisconsin Volunteers,* II, 217, 215.
8. Congress, House, Joint Committee on the Conduct of the War, *Report of the Joint Committee on the Conduct of the War 1863–1866* [hereinafter cited as *Report 108*], 37th Cong., 3d sess., H. Rept. 108, 628–29; Hudson, *Hawks,* 11.
9. Quiner, *Wisconsin Volunteers,* II, 215, 217, 221; George H. Otis, *The Second Wisconsin Infantry* (Dayton: Morningside, 1984), 45; Eugene H. Berwanger, "'absent So long from those I love,': The Civil War Letters of Joshua Jones," *Indiana Magazine of History,* 88 (September 1992): 223; William Murray Diary, privately owned by John W. Green, Livermore, California.
10. Moore MSS; Henry C. Marsh Papers, Indiana Division, Indiana State Library, Indianapolis.
11. *OR,* 5: 708; Regimental Records, Muster Rolls.
12. Terrell, *Adjutant General,* II, 168; Isaac May Pension File.
13. Correspondence File, Indiana.
14. Ibid.
15. Ibid.
16. John Snider Pension File.
17. William Murray Diary; Thomas Benton Letters, Indiana Historical Society, Indianapolis; *MPT,* February 19, 1862, 2.
18. John Snider Pension File; Julietta Starbuck Civil War Papers, Indiana Historical Society, Indianapolis; Hudson, *Hawks,* 13.
19. Quiner, *Wisconsin Volunteers,* II, 235–36; Dawes, *Sixth Wisconsin,* 36.
20. Quiner, *Wisconsin Volunteers,* II, 235–36, III, 283; Dawes, *Sixth Wisconsin,* 35; James Perry Diary, Perry Papers, State Historical Society of Wisconsin, Madison.
21. Benton MSS.
22. Meredith Diary, Solomon Meredith Papers, Indiana Historical Society, Indianapolis; William Murray Diary; Andrew J. Reeves Pension File; Quiner, *Wisconsin Volunteers,* II, 220, III, 279.
23. Ibid., IV, 4–5; *NT,* June 28, 1900, 7; *MST,* May 13, 1883, 2.
24. Correspondence File, Indiana; Campbell MSS; *RP,* February 1, 1862, 3.
25. William H. Ford Pension File; Correspondence File, Indiana.
26. Davis Castle Military Service Record.
27. Francis A. Lord, *Civil War Collector's Encyclopedia* (New York: Castle Books, 1965), 258–59.
28. Davis Castle Pension File; Correspondence File, Indiana; *OR,* 9, pt. 1: 232.
29. Correspondence File, National; Benton MSS.
30. Homer Lemon Military Service Record; Joseph B. Bennett Military Service Record; William O. Williams Military Service Record; William Shelley Military Service Record; Hazzard, *Hazzard's History,* I, 570.
31. Joseph B. Bennett Military Service Record.

9. SPRING ADVANCE

1. Benton MSS; Quiner, *Wisconsin Volunteers,* III, 284.
2. *IDJ,* March 15, 1862, 2; *History of Wayne County,* II, 319.
3. William Murray Diary; Meredith Diary; *New Castle Courier* [hereinafter cited as *NCC*] March 20, 1862, 2.
4. Ibid.; *MST,* February 24, 1889, 3; Dawes, *Sixth Wisconsin,* 36.
5. Crull MSS; *WDP,* March 18, 1862, 3; Meredith Diary.
6. Orr MSS; Crull MSS; William Murray Diary; Stine, *Army of the Potomac,* 108.
7. Perry Diary; Orr MSS; Crull MSS.
8. Otis, *Second Wisconsin,* 47.
9. Ibid.; Stevenson, *Roll of Honor,* I, 350; Dawes, *Sixth Wisconsin,* 37; William Murray Diary.
10. Orr MSS; Sydney Mead Diary, State Historical Society of Wisconsin, Madison; Stevenson, *Roll of Honor,* I, 350.
11. Orr MSS.
12. William Murray Diary; Meredith Diary; Regimental Records, Muster Roll, Co. K.
13. *ITR,* April 3, 1862, 2; Frederick Phisterer, *Statistical Record of the Armies of the United States,* Campaigns of the Civil War (New York: Charles Scribner's Sons, 1886), 275.
14. William Murray Diary; Perry Diary; Meredith Diary; Benton MSS.
15. Ibid.; Hudson, *Hawks,* 20.
16. Moore MSS; Meredith Diary.
17. *MST,* February 24, 1889, 3.
18. William Murray Diary; Benton MSS; Crull MSS; Regimental Records, Muster Roll, Co. G.
19. Starbuck MSS; Berwanger, "Joshua Jones," 227; Stewart Brooks, *Civil War Medicine* (Springfield, Illinois: Charles C. Thomas Publishers, 1966), 114.
20. Starbuck MSS; William Murray Diary.

10. ARRIVAL OF GIBBON

1. George W. Cullum, *Biographical Register of the Officers and Graduates of the U.S. Military Academy* (New York: D. Van Nostrand, 1868), I, 479.
2. William Murray Diary; *OR,* 51, pt. 1: 637.
3. Ibid.; Dawes, *Sixth Wisconsin,* 43; Miller, *Photographic History,* V, 280.
4. *OR,* 51, pt. 1: 637; *RWA,* June 18, 1862, 2; *NT,* October 17, 1895, 2; Regimental Records, Muster Roll.
5. *NT,* October 17, 1895, 1; ibid., 2; *OR,* 51, pt. 1: 637.
6. *NT,* April 26, 1900, 7; *NT,* February 22, 1894, 3; *WSJ,* May 24, 1862, 2.
7. William Murray Diary; Gibbon, *Personal Recollections,* 35; Regimental Records, Letter Book, National Archives.
8. Meredith Diary; William Murray Diary.
9. George Fairfield Diary, Fairfield Papers, State Historical Society of Wisconsin, Madison; *MST,* July 1, 1888, 3; *Rochester Daily Union and Advertiser* [hereinafter cited as *RDUA*] October 24, 1862, 2; U. S. Congress, *H. Report 108,* 436.
10. Gibbon, *Recollections,* 35–36.
11. Correspondence File, Indiana; *MST,* July 1, 1888, 3; Regimental Records, Letter Book.

12. Gibbon, *Recollections*, 30–31, 38, 40.

13. Ibid., 36–37; Regimental Records, Letter Book; *Elkhart Weekly Review* [hereinafter cited as *EWR*] May 24, 1864, 3.

14. Gibbon, *Recollections*, 31–32.

15. *IDJ*, June 10, 1862, 2; *IDJ*, June 23, 1862, 2.

16. See Appendix by Howard Michael Madaus in Lance J. Herdegen and William J. K. Beaudot's *In the Bloody Railroad Cut at Gettysburg* (Dayton: Morningside, 1990) for an excellent detailed description of clothing issued to the Iron Brigade; *WDP*, June 27, 1862, 2; William Murray Diary.

17. Nineteenth Clothing Records; Maudus, Appendix; The individualized treatment given the uniform clothing is perceptible in existing Iron Brigade photographs.

18. Marsh MSS; William Murray Diary; Meredith Diary; Dawes, *Sixth Wisconsin*, 45; Orr MSS.

19. Ibid.; William Murray Diary; Mills, *Chronicles*, 184–85.

20. Orr MSS; William Murray Diary; Stevenson, *Roll of Honor*, I, 351; Mills, *Chronicles*, 185.

11. THE LEGGING MUTINY

1. Stevenson, *Roll of Honor*, I, 351; William Murray Diary; Otis, *Second Wisconsin*, 49; Crull MSS.

2. William Murray Diary; *MST*, July 1, 1888, 3; Fairfield Diary.

3. David Sparks, ed., *Inside Lincoln's Army* (New York: Thomas Yoseloff, 1964), 90; Robert Hamilton Papers, Indiana Historical Society, Indianapolis; Meredith Diary; *MST*, July 1, 1888, 3.

4. William Murray Diary; Otis, *Second Wisconsin*, 50; Stevenson, *Roll of Honor*, I, 351; Crull MSS; *NT*, December 11, 1902, 5.

5. Benton MSS; Marsh MSS; *Christian Banner*, June 14, 1862, 2; ibid., June 18, 1862, 2; Hudson, *Hawks*, 21.

6. William Murray Diary; Quiner, *Wisconsin Volunteers*, IV, 213; Gibbon, *Recollections*, 34–35; Regimental Records, Letter Book.

7. Gibbon, Recollections, 28; *Report 108*, 447.

8. Crull MSS; William Murray Diary.

9. Meredith Diary.

10. Ibid.

11. Correspondence File, National.

12. Meredith Diary; Meredith MSS.

13. Correspondence File, National.

14. Meredith MSS.

15. Quiner, *Wisconsin Volunteers*, IV, 213; *NT*, October 3, 1895, 3; ibid., August 21, 1902, 3; Marsh MSS.

16. *IDJ*, June 10, 1862, 2; Cheek, *Sauk Riflemen*, 26.

17. Benton MSS; Berwanger, "Joshua Jones," 228; Correspondence File, Indiana.

18. William Murray Diary.

19. Nolan, *Iron Brigade*, 61–62; *MS*, July 3, 1862, 1; William Murray Diary.

12. CAMPAIGNING UNDER POPE

1. William Murray Diary; Benton MSS; *EWR*, July 19, 1862, 3; Hudson, *Hawks*, 22.

2. Meredith Diary; *GCW*, July 24, 1862, 1; *Revised Army Regulations*, 43.

3. *WDP,* July 2, 1862, 1; Stine, *Army of the Potomac,* 114; *NT,* October 3, 1895, 3.

4. Ibid.

5. Dawes, *Sixth Wisconsin,* 51; *WDP,* October 9, 1862, 1; Meredith Diary; *GCW,* July 24, 1862, 1; *MS,* August 2, 1862, 2.

6. Fairfield Diary; Dawes, *Sixth Wisconsin,* 51; Meredith Diary; *DCFP,* September 4, 1862, 3; *MS,* August 2, 1862, 2; Hudson, *Hawks,* 22.

7. *WDP,* July 9, 1862, 1.

8. Orr MSS.

9. Dawes, *Sixth Wisconsin,* 51; *NT,* December 11, 1902, 5.

10. Marsh MSS; *Report 108*-I, 111–12; Crull MSS.

11. Benton MSS; Sparks, *Lincoln's Army,* 112.

12. Orr MSS; Crull MSS; Quiner, *Wisconsin Volunteers,* IV, 5; William Murray Diary.

13. Marsh MSS.

14. Ibid.; Regimental Records, Letter Book; William Murray Diary.

15. Ibid.; Joseph Dolph Pension File.

16. *IDJ,* August 14, 1862, 2; Terrell, *Adjutant General,* I, 402–406; *RP,* July 19, 1862, 2.

17. *IDJ,* August 1, 1862, 2; ibid., August 2, 1862, 2; ibid., August 14, 1862, 2.

18. Benton MSS; Orr MSS; Marsh MSS.

19. Ibid.

20. Dawes, *Sixth Wisconsin,* 51; Marsh MSS.

21. *IDJ,* August 5, 1862, 2; Crull MSS.

22. William Murray Diary; Marsh MSS.

23. *OR,* 12, pt. 2: 122–23; William Murray Diary; Dawes, *Sixth Wisconsin,* 53.

24. Stevenson, *Roll of Honor,* I, 352; Marsh MSS.

25. Stevenson, *Roll of Honor,* I, 352–53; Marsh MSS; *Winchester Journal* [hereinafter cited as *WJ*] August 29, 1862, 1; *OR,* 12, pt. 2: 122–23.

26. Ibid.; Stevenson, *Roll of Honor,* I, 353; *IDJ,* August 14, 1862, 2.

27. Marsh MSS; *EWR,* August 23, 1862, 2; *IDJ,* August 14, 1862, 2; *WJ,* August 26, 1862, 1; Regimental Records, Muster Rolls, Co. I; ibid., Co B.; James Wine Pension File.

28. Otis, *Second Wisconsin,* 53; Stevenson, *Roll of Honor,* I, 354; William Murray Diary; Marsh MSS; E. W. H. Beck, "Letters of a Civil War Surgeon," *Indiana Magazine of History,* 27 (June 1931): 140.

29. Stevenson, *Roll of Honor,* I, 354; William Murray Diary; Otis, *Second Wisconsin,* 54.

30. *REI,* August 28, 1884, 3.

31. Stevenson, *Roll of Honor,* I, 354; Benton MSS; *REI,* August 28, 1884, 3.

32. Stevenson, *Roll of Honor,* I, 354; William Murray Diary; *REI,* August 28, 1884, 3; Otis, *Second Wisconsin,* 54; Benton MSS.

33. Benton MSS; *MST,* November 30, 1884, 3; Cheek, *Sauk Riflemen,* 31.

34. *EWR,* August 23, 1862, 2; Berwanger, "Joshua Jones," 231; Abram Smith, *History of the Seventy-Sixth New York Volunteers* (Cortland, New York: Truain, Smith, and Miles, 1867), 101; William Murray Diary; Cheek, *Sauk Riflemen,* 31.

13. BRAWNER FARM

1. Otis, *Second Wisconsin,* 54; Charles King, "Gainesville, 1862," *War Papers, Wisconsin Commandery, MOLLUS,* III, 269; *EWR,* September 13, 1862, 3.

2. Stevenson, *Roll of Honor,* I, 354–55; William Murray Diary; *EWR,* September 13, 1862, 3; ibid., October 25, 1862, 2.

3. Stevenson, *Roll of Honor*, I, 355; William Murray Diary; Sheldon Judson MSS in T. C. H. Smith MSS, Ohio Historical Society, Columbus; *NT*, April 28, 1902, 4.

4. *WSJ*, September 10, 1862, 1; *GCW*, December 10, 1863, 1.

5. *JDG*, September 18, 1862, 2; Stevenson, *Roll of Honor*, I, 355; Catherine Merrill, *The Soldier of Indiana in the War for the Union* (Indianapolis: Merrill, 1866–68), I, 587.

6. Dawes, *Sixth Wisconsin*, 58; Cheek, *Sauk Riflemen*, 31; *Soldiers and Citizens Album of Biographical Record* (Chicago: Grand Army Publishing, 1888), I, 722; *EWR*, September 13, 1862, 3; *NT*, October 11, 1888, 3.

7. *Report 108*-Report of General Pope, pt. 1: 115; Theron W. Haight, "King's Division: Fredericksburg to Manassas," *War Papers, Wisconsin Commandery, MOLLUS*, II, 353; Moore MSS.

8. Dawes, *Sixth Wisconsin*, 59; Porter Case, 586, 592, 595.

9. Ibid., 594, 596–97; Smith, *Seventy-Sixth New York*, 116; Terrell, *Adjutant General*, II, 170; Valentine Jacobs Military Service Record.

10. Stevenson, *Roll of Honor*, I, 355–56.

11. Marsh MSS; Haight, "Fredericksburg," 355.

12. Gibbon, *Recollections*, 49–50; *EWR*, September 13, 1862, 3; Marsh MSS; Merrill, *Soldier of Indiana*, I, 593.

13. *OR*, 12, pt. 2: 378.

14. *IDJ*, September 11, 1862, 2; Henry Gordon Pension File.

15. *IDJ*, September 11, 1862, 2; Moore MSS; *EWR*, September 13, 1862, 3; Stevenson, *Roll of Honor*, I, 356.

16. Alan D. Gaff, *Brave Men's Tears: The Iron Brigade at Brawner Farm* (Dayton: Morningside, 1985), 69–78 passim; Haight, "Gainesville," 361–62; John Byson, *History of the Thirtieth New York Volunteers*, Archives, Manassas National Battlefield Park, Manassas, Virginia.

17. *IDJ*, September 11, 1862, 2; Moore MSS.

18. *IDJ*, September 11, 1862, 2; *RP*, September 12, 1862, 2; *RCJ*, September 12, 1862, 4; *EWR*, October 25, 1862, 2; Stine, *Army of the Potomac*, 133.

19. *IDJ*, September 11, 1862, 2; ibid., October 7, 1862, 3; *RCJ*, September 12, 1862, 4; *RP*, September 12, 1862, 2.

20. Stevenson, *Roll of Honor*, I, 356–57.

21. Gaff, *Brave Men*, 79–80; Stevenson, *Roll of Honor*, I, 357; *IDJ*, September 11, 1862, 2; *RP*, September 12, 1862, 2.

22. Gaff, *Brave Men*, 79–80; Stine, *Army of the Potomac*, 132; *IDJ*, September 11, 1862, 2; *DSS*, September 12, 1862, 2.

23. Stine, *Army of the Potomac*, 132; *DSS*, September 12, 1862, 2; ibid., September 13, 1862, 3; *IDJ*, September 11, 1862, 2; Meredith Diary.

24. *RCJ*, September 12, 1862, 4; Gibbon, *Recollections*, 54; Stine, *Army of the Potomac*, 133.

25. Mills, *Chronicles*, 249; Moore MSS.

26. Gibbon, *Recollections*, 55–56; Benton MSS.

27. *RP*, September 12, 1862, 2; ibid., September 19, 1862, 2; *QCT*, September 6, 1862, 2; ibid., December 13, 1862, 3; Power, *Soldiers' Register*, 284; *IDJ*, September 8, 1862, 3; *RCJ*, September 12, 1862, 4.

28. Gaff, *Brave Men*, 147–52 passim; Marsh MSS.

29. Gaff, *Brave Men*, 152; Frank A. Haskell Papers, State Historical Society of Wisconsin, Madison; Orr MSS.

30. *IDJ*, September 8, 1862, 3; ibid., September 11, 1862, 2; Nineteenth Indiana Hospital Register, Archives, Indiana State Library, Indianapolis; *DSS*, September 13, 1862, 3; ibid., September 19, 1862, 2; Orr MSS; *EWR*, September 13, 1862, 3; Luther Wilson Military Service Record.

31. Nineteenth Hospital Register; *QCT*, September 13, 1862, 2; *IDJ*, September 8, 1862, 3.

32. "Letter from Major Thomas Scott Allen," *Civil War Times Illustrated*, 1 (November 1962): 32–33; *Wisconsin State Register* [hereinafter cited as *WSR*] September 13, 1862, 2; Gaff, *Brave Men*, 157–58.

33. Ibid., 84; *Grant County Herald* [hereinafter cited as *GCH*] September 11, 1862, 2; ibid., September 30, 1862, 1.

34. Gaff, *Brave Men*, 75–77; *OR*, 12, pt. 2: 370, 373; Uberto Burnham Papers, Archives, New York State Library, Albany; *New York Herald* [hereinafter cited as *NYH*] September 14, 1862, 4.

35. Rufus R. Dawes, "Skirmish of the Rappahannock and Battle of Gainesville," in T. C. H. Smith Papers, Ohio Historical Society, Columbus; *NT*, December 11, 1902, 5; *OR*, 12, pt. 2: 382; Dawes, *Sixth Wisconsin*, 62.

36. *MST*, March 22, 1885, 6.

37. Dawes, *Sixth Wisconsin*, 68; *DSS*, September 12, 1862, 2; *RP*, September 19, 1862, 2; Otis, *Second Wisconsin*, 57.

38. *OR*, 12, pt. 2: 367; Dawes, *Sixth Wisconsin*, 70.

39. *WSJ*, September 17, 1862, 2; ibid., September 18, 1862, 2; *GCH*, September 30, 1862, 1.

40. *OR*, 12, pt. 2: 379; Dawes, *Sixth Wisconsin*, 70–71; *RP*, September 19, 1862, 1.

41. Ibid.

42. Gibbon, *Recollections*, 63–65; *RP*, September 19, 1862, 1; *GCH*, September 30, 1862, 1; Dawes, *Sixth Wisconsin*, 73–74; Stevenson, *Roll of Honor*, I, 359.

43. *RP*, September 12, 1862, 2; ibid., September 19, 1862, 1; Power, *Soldiers' Register*, 271; *EWR*, September 13, 1862, 3.

44. Dawes, *Sixth Wisconsin*, 75; Cheek, *Sauk Riflemen*, 44; Orr MSS.

14. AFTERMATH

1. Gaff, *Brave Men*, 171–73; Marsh MSS.

2. Porter Case, 598.

3. Ibid.; William Murray Diary.

4. *RP*, September 19, 1862, 2.

5. Gaff, *Brave Men*, 177–78; William W. Blackford, *War Years with Jeb Stuart* (New York: Charles Scribner's Sons, 1945), 122; *Charleston Daily Courier*, September 23, 1862, 4; Otis, *Second Wisconsin*, 248; Charles A. Moore, *The Story of a Cannoneer under Stonewall Jackson* (New York: Neale, 1907), 112.

6. Gaff, *Brave Men*, 174; Robert U. Johnson and Clarence C. Buel, eds., *Battles and Leaders of the Civil War* (New York: Thomas Yoseloff, 1956), II, 527; Quiner, *Wisconsin Volunteers*, III, 262.

7. *IDJ*, September 8, 1862, 3; ibid., September 22, 1862, 2; Terrell, *Adjutant General*, VIII, 47.

8. Merrill, *Soldier of Indiana*, I, 593–94.

9. Johnson, *Battles and Leaders*, II, 527; C. A. Stevens, *Berdan's United States Sharpshooters in the Army of the Potomac* (Dayton: Morningside, 1984), 178–79; Smith, *Seventy-Sixth New York*, 126.

10. Quiner, *Wisconsin Volunteers*, II, 299; ibid., III, 262; Power, *Soldiers' Register*, 334.

11. Smith, *Seventy-Sixth New York*, 125; *NYH*, September 13, 1862, 5.

12. *NYH*, September 8, 1862, 1; ibid., September 13, 1862, 5; William Locke Military Service Record; William J. Bennett Military Service Record and Bennett Pension File.

13. Haight, "Gainesville," 372; Quiner, *Wisconsin Volunteers,* III, 262.
14. Barnes, *Medical and Surgical History,* X, 703; ibid., XII, 516; Nineteenth Hospital Register.
15. Barnes, *Medical and Surgical History,* X, 547; ibid., XI, 276; Isaac May Pension File.
16. Samuel Bonar Pension File; Henry Jones Pension File.
17. Samuel Hindman Pension File.
18. Benjamin Jewett Military Service Record; Richard Williams Military Service Record; Henry Hiatt Pension File.
19. Samuel Lutz Pension File.
20. William J. Bennett Military Service Record; Bennett Pension File.
21. Orr MSS.
22. Benton MSS.

15. BATTLES IN MARYLAND

1. Meredith Diary; Stevenson, *Roll of Honor,* I, 359.
2. *EWR,* September 13, 1862, 3; Beck, "Civil War Surgeon," 141.
3. Gibbon, *Recollections,* 70; Dawes, *Sixth Wisconsin,* 76; Stevenson, *Roll of Honor,* I, 359.
4. Meredith Diary; Hudson, *Hawks,* 30.
5. Jackson Diary; Meredith Diary.
6. Nolan, *Iron Brigade,* 114.
7. Meredith Diary; Stevenson, *Roll of Honor,* I, 359; Cheek, *Sauk Riflemen,* 46.
8. Meredith Diary; Stevenson, *Roll of Honor,* I, 359; Jackson Diary.
9. *WSJ,* October 25, 1862, 2; *Record of the Movements, Camps, Campaigns, Skirmishes and Battles of the Seventh Indiana Regiment* (Fort Wayne: Fort Wayne Public Library); Theodore B. Gates, *The "Ulster Guard" and the War of the Rebellion* (New York: Benjamin T. Tyrrel, 1879), 288.
10. Gibbon, *Recollections,* 71; Meredith Diary; Jackson Diary.
11. Meredith Diary; Jackson Diary.
12. Stevenson, *Roll of Honor,* I, 360; *EWR,* October 4, 1862, 1.
13. Dawes, *Sixth Wisconsin,* 79; George F. Noyes, *The Bivouac and the Battlefield* (New York: Harper and Bros., 1863), 165; Sparks, *Lincoln's Army,* 143.
14. Stevenson, *Roll of Honor,* I, 360; *OR,* 19, pt. 1: 247; Haskell MSS.
15. *OR,* 19, pt. 1: 247.
16. Dawes, *Sixth Wisconsin,* 81; *Report 108*-Army of the Potomac, pt. 2, 447; *OR,* 19, pt. 1: 249.
17. Ibid., 249–50, 253; Stevenson, *Roll of Honor,* 360; *MST,* January 26, 1895, 2.
18. *OR,* 19, pt. 1: 250; *DSS,* November 4, 1862, 3; Barnes, *Medical and Surgical History,* VIII, 225.
19. *OR,* 19, pt. 1: 250; Marsh MSS; *EWR,* October 4, 1862, 1; Stevenson, *Roll of Honor,* I, 261.
20. *OR,* 19, pt. 1: 248, 250, 252–53; Stevenson, *Roll of Honor,* I, 261.
21. *OR,* 19, pt. 1: 248, 250; George B. McClellan, *Report on the Organization and Campaigns of the Army of the Potomac* (New York: Sheldon, 1864), 372.
22. Correspondence File, Indiana; William J. Brinson Pension File; *DCFP,* August 7, 1862, 3; ibid., September 18, 1862, 3; ibid., October 3, 1862, 2.
23. Gibbon, *Recollections,* 78–79.
24. Noyes, *Bivouac,* 181–82; Marsh MSS; Meredith Diary.
25. Sparks, *Lincoln's Army,* 143, 145; Stevenson, *Roll of Honor,* I, 363.

26. Ibid., 361; Gibbon, *Recollections*, 90.

27. Stevenson, *Roll of Honor*, I, 362; Haskell MSS.

28. Stevenson, *Roll of Honor*, I, 363; *OR*, 19, pt. 1: 251; Meredith Diary.

29. Stevenson, *Roll of Honor*, I, 362; *OR*, 19, pt. 1: 248, 251.

30. *OR*, 19, pt. 1: 248, 251; W. W. Dudley MSS in E. A. Carmen Papers, National Archives, Washington, D.C.

31. Ibid.; Stevenson, *Roll of Honor*, I, 363.

32. Julius Murray Papers, State Historical Society of Wisconsin, Madison; *OR*, 19, pt. 1: 248, 257–58; Quiner, *Wisconsin Volunteers*, IV, 22; "Texans at Sharpsburg," *Confederate Veteran*, 22 (December 1914), 555.

33. *OR*, 19, pt. 1: 251; Marsh MSS.

34. *OR*, 19, pt. 1: 251; Marsh MSS; *EWR*, October 4, 1862, 1; Mills, *Chronicles*, 290; Sparks, *Lincoln's Army*, 148; Jackson Diary.

35. Stevenson, *Roll of Honor*, I, 364; *OR*, 19, pt. 1: 251; *IDJ*, September 27, 1862, 2; *RWT*, January 27, 1866, 2; Berwanger, "Joshua Jones," 235.

36. *OR*, 19, pt. 1: 251–52; Stine, *Army of the Potomac*, 193; Marsh MSS.

37. *OR*, 19, pt. 1: 251–52; Stevenson, *Roll of Honor*, I, 365; Stine, *Army of the Potomac*, 193; *NT*, August 20, 1881, 5.

38. Dudley MSS in Carmen Papers; Marsh MSS; Stine, *Army of the Potomac*, 193; Sparks, *Lincoln's Army*, 148.

39. Dudley MSS in Carmen Papers; Meredith MSS; Marsh MSS; Jackson Diary; *Seventh Indiana Skirmishes*.

40. Meredith Diary; Terrell, *Adjutant General*, II, 168; ibid., IV, 390–408; Marsh MSS; Barnes, *Medical and Surgical History*, VIII, 253; Ephriam Eager Pension File.

41. Marsh MSS; Barnes, *Medical and Surgical History*, VIII, 363.

42. Berwanger, "Joshua Jones," 235; Marsh MSS.

43. Hudson, *Hawks*, 30.

16. THE IRON BRIGADE

1. *IDJ*, October 5, 1862, 2.

2. Jackson Diary.

3. *QCT*, November 1, 1862, 3; Meredith Diary.

4. *IDJ*, October 28, 1862, 2; ibid., October 29, 1862, 2.

5. Gibbon, *Recollections*, 107–109; *Report 108*-Gettysburg, 447.

6. Terrell, *Adjutant General*, II, 168–75; Robert Hamilton Pension File.

7. Thomas H. Parker Pension File; William B. Heath Pension File.

8. Regimental Records, Letter Book, National Archives; Meredith MSS; Crull MSS.

9. *QCT*, October 18, 1862, 3.

10. Gibbon, *Recollections*, 73, 92.

11. Ibid., 92; O. B. Curtis, *History of the Twenty-Fourth Michigan of the Iron Brigade* (Detroit: Winn and Hammond, 1891), 65; Dawes, *Sixth Wisconsin*, 101; Wheeler MSS; Hudson, *Hawks*, 27; Marsh MSS; Jackson Diary.

12. Regimental Records, Clothing Book.

13. Dawes, *Sixth Wisconsin*, 96; Haskell MSS; Wheeler MSS.

14. *NT*, November 24, 1892, 4; *NT*, August 11, 1904, 3.

15. Ibid.; *NT*, September 14, 1889, 3; ibid., January 28, 1886, 3.

16. Gibbon, *Recollections*, 92; Regimental Records, Letter Book; *OR*, 19, pt. 1: 252.

17. Jackson Diary; *RDUA*, October 7, 1862, 2.

18. Jackson Diary; Quiner, *Wisconsin Volunteers*, II, 316.

19. Cullen B. Aubrey, *Echoes of the Marches of the Iron Brigade 1861–1865* (Milwaukee: Privately printed, 1900), 47–48; Stevenson, *Roll of Honor,* I, 365.

20. Jackson Diary; Noyes, *Bivouac,* 263.

21. *Combination Atlas Map of Huntington County, Indiana* (Chicago: Kingman Brothers, 1879), 50; *History of Huntington County, Indiana* (Chicago: Brandt & Fuller, 1887), 813–14; Francis Huff Military Service Record; Huff Pension File.

17. SOUTH TO FREDERICKSBURG

1. Jackson Diary; Curtis, *Twenty-Fourth Michigan,* 74–75.

2. Gibbon, *Recollections,* 95–96; Regimental Records, Letter Book.

3. *Prairie Du Chien Courier,* November 20, 1862, 2; Dawes, *Sixth Wisconsin,* 105.

4. Gibbon, *Recollections,* 95–96; Dawes, *Sixth Wisconsin,* 64–65.

5. Sullivan Green Papers, State Historical Society of Wisconsin, Madison.

6. *MST,* August 7, 1887, 1.

7. George B. McClellan, *McClellan's Own Story* (New York: Charles L. Webster, 1887), 653.

8. Allan Nevins, ed., *A Diary of Battle: The Personal Journals of Colonel Charles S. Wainwright 1861–1865* (New York: Harcourt, Brace & World, 1962), 125; Quiner, *Wisconsin Volunteers,* II, 322; *RDUA,* November 22, 1862, 2.

9. Ibid.; Otis, *Second Wisconsin,* 65; Starbuck MSS; Orr MSS; Quiner, *Wisconsin Volunteers,* II, 321.

10. Regimental Records, Letter Book; Francis A. Walker, *History of the Second Army Corps* (New York: Charles Scribner's Sons, 1886), 138.

11. *IDJ,* November 3, 1862, 3; *IDJ,* December 6, 1862, 2; ibid., 3; Leander Monks, *Courts and Lawyers of Indiana* (Indianapolis: Federal Publishing, 1916), I, 256.

12. *RP,* December 19, 1862, 2; *NT,* March 28, 1889, 3; William Bennett Pension File.

13. Dawes, *Sixth Wisconsin,* 105; Jackson Diary; Curtis, *Twenty-Fourth Michigan,* 79.

14. Jackson Diary.

15. *RP,* December 19, 1862, 2; Jackson Diary; Stevenson, *Roll of Honor,* I, 366.

16. *OR,* 51, pt. 1: 951; Jackson Diary; Quiner, *Wisconsin Volunteers,* II, 322; George H. Legate Pension File; Curtis, *Twenty-Fourth Michigan,* 43; Congress, House, *A Biographical Congressional Directory 1774 to 1903,* compiled by O. M. Enyart, 57th Cong., 2d sess., H. Doc. 458, 198.

17. *RP,* December 19, 1862, 2.

18. Jackson Diary; Regimental Records, Clothing Book; Regimental Records, 76th New York Regimental Returns; Regimental Records, *Summary Statement of Ordnance and Ordnance Stores, 19th Indiana.*

19. *RP,* December 19, 1862, 2.

20. Jackson Diary.

21. Ibid.; Stevenson, *Roll of Honor,* I, 366; Marsh MSS.

22. *WSJ,* December 16, 1862, 2; Legate Pension File.

23. Stevenson, *Roll of Honor,* I, 366; Jackson Diary; Marsh MSS; Curtis, *Twenty-Fourth Michigan,* 90.

24. *OR,* 21, 476; Orr MSS; *GCH,* December 30, 1862, 2; Marsh MSS; Crull MSS.

25. *OR,* 21, 476; *RP,* April 9, 1864, 2; *WSJ,* January 20, 1863, 2.

26. *GCH,* December 30, 1862, 2.

27. Dawes, *Sixth Wisconsin,* 112; Legate Pension File.

28. Regimental Correspondence, Indianapolis; Starbuck MSS.

29. Marsh MSS; Barnes, *Medical and Surgical History,* X, 982; *DCFP,* January 15, 1863, 3.

30. Merrill, *Soldier of Indiana,* II, 64; Johnson, *Battles and Leaders,* III, 142; Hudson, *Hawks,* 29.

31. Stevenson, *Roll of Honor,* I, 368; Orville Thomson, *Narrative of the Service of the Seventh Indiana Infantry* (n.p.: privately printed, n. d.), 144; *OR,* 21, 478; Regimental Records, Muster Rolls.

32. *QCT,* December 27, 1862, 2; *OR,* 21, 464, 478.

33. Noyes, *Bivouac,* 318–19; Marsh MSS; Stevenson, *Roll of Honor,* I, 368.

34. Hudson, *Hawks,* 29; Crull MSS; Jackson Diary.

35. Jacob Addleman Military Service Record; Joseph Addleman Military Service Record; Power, *Soldiers' Register,* 250; Young, *Wayne County,* 218.

36. Crull MSS; Orr MSS; Moore MSS; Adam Smelser Pension File.

37. Jackson Diary; Marsh MSS; *RP,* March 13, 1863, 2.

38. National Archives, *Records of the Bureau of Military Justice, General Court-Martial,* Record Group 153 [hereinafter cited as Court-Martial], DeBay LL58; Legate Pension File; Dawes, *Sixth Wisconsin,* 115.

18. VALLEY FORGE

1. George Edward Finney Diary, Indiana Division, Indiana State Library, Indianapolis; Carl Sandburg, *Abraham Lincoln: The War Years* (New York: Harcourt, Brace, 1939), II, 17–18.

2. Henry A. Morrow, "To Chancellorsville with the Iron Brigade," *Civil War Times Illustrated* 14 (January 1976): 16; Orr MSS; Hudson, *Hawks,* 21.

3. *RDUA,* January 12, 1863, 2; Hudson, *Hawks,* 21.

4. Ibid., 30; Elisha B. Odle Letters, Archives, Fredericksburg National Battlefield Park, Fredericksburg, Virginia.

5. *WDP,* February 4, 1863, 2; *WDP,* March 28, 1863, 2; Thomas J. Wasson Pension File.

6. Ibid.

7. Correspondence File, Indiana; Green MSS.

8. Jackson Diary; Hudson, *Hawks,* 30.

9. Jackson Diary.

10. Merrill, *Soldier of Indiana,* II, 74–75; James I. Robertson, Jr., "An Indiana Soldier in Love and War: The Civil War Letters of John V. Hadley," *Indiana Magazine of History,* 59 (September 1963): 227.

11. Smith, *Seventy-Sixth New York,* 200; *Seventh Indiana Skirmishes,* 40; Grear N. Williams Diary, privately owned by Mick Kissick, Albany, Indiana; Merrill, *Soldier of Indiana,* II, 75; Robertson, "Indiana Soldier," 228; Legate Pension File.

12. Thomson, *Narrative of Seventh,* 147; Legate Pension File; Smith, *Seventy-Sixth New York,* 201; Williams Diary; Crull MSS.

13. *Seventh Indiana Skirmishes,* 41; Thomson, *Narrative of Seventh,* 148; Noyes, *Bivouac,* 324. Nickname "Old Corduroy" refers to the method of road-building employed by the soldiers, which involved the laying of logs transversely in the road producing a "ribbed" or corduroy effect.

14. Cheek, *Sauk Riflemen,* 58; Jackson Diary.

15. Wasson Pension File; *WDP,* February 12, 1863, 2.

16. Ibid.; Robertson, "Indiana Soldier," 229; Legate Pension File; Crull MSS.

17. Green MSS; Orr MSS.

18. Legate Pension File; Curtis, *Twenty-Fourth Michigan,* 113; Green MSS; Crull MSS.

19. Crull MSS; Court-Martial, Hill LL58.

20. Court-Martial, St. Clair and Padget LL58.

21. Court-Martial, Redout LL58; Jackson Diary.
22. Court-Martial, McRoberts LL58.
23. Court-Martial, Berry LL58.
24. Court-Martial, Woods LL58.
25. Correspondence File, Indiana.
26. Green MSS; *WDP,* February 27, 1863, 2; Wasson Pension File.
27. Jackson Diary; *MST,* August 24, 1879, 2; Moore MSS.
28. *WDP,* February 27, 1863, 2; *MST,* August 24, 1879, 2; Nathaniel Rollins Diary, Nathaniel Rollins Papers, State Historical Society of Wisconsin, Madison; Wasson Pension File; Jackson Diary.
29. Williams Diary; Jackson Diary.
30. Crull MSS; Wasson Pension File.

19. FITZHUGH CROSSING

1. Dawes, *Sixth Wisconsin,* 125.
2. Orr MSS; Wasson Pension File.
3. Correspondence File, National.
4. Stine, *Army of the Potomac,* 312; *IDJ,* March 14, 1863, 3; *RDUA,* April 10, 1863, 2.
5. Benjamin B. Duke Military Service Record; Correspondence File, National; Williams Diary.
6. Correspondence File, Indiana; Samuel Hindman Military Service Record.
7. Correspondence File, Indiana.
8. Henry Zook Pension File.
9. *NCC,* March 5, 1863, 2; Lewis Dale Military Service Record.
10. James H. Madison, *The Indiana Way* (Bloomington: Indiana University Press and Indiana Historical Society, 1986), 201–202; *NCC,* March 12, 1863, 2.
11. *RP,* April 3, 1863, 3.
12. *QCT,* April 25, 1863, 2.
13. *QCT,* March 21, 1863, 3.
14. *WDP,* March 23, 1863, 2.
15. Regimental Records, Letter Book.
16. *RDUA,* March 30, 1863, 2; Regimental Records, Clothing Book.
17. Ibid., Letter Book; *RP,* May 8, 1863, 2.
18. Ibid.; Williams Diary; C. Tevis, *History of the Fighting Fourteenth* (New York: Brooklyn Eagle Press, 1911), 194.
19. *IDJ,* April 11, 1863, 2; Curtis, *Twenty-Fourth Michigan,* 117; Wasson Pension File; *RP,* May 8, 1863, 2; Williams Diary.
20. *RDUA,* April 17, 1863, 2; Regimental Records, Letter Book.
21. *RDUA,* April 10, 1863, 2; Orr MSS.
22. *RP,* April 24, 1863, 2.
23. Wasson Pension File; *RP,* May 8, 1863, 2.
24. *History of Henry County,* 469; *RP,* April 26, 1863, 2; *WJ,* May 1, 1863, 2; *WJ,* October 3, 1863, 3.
25. Williams Diary; Sparks, *Lincoln's Army,* 256.
26. Correspondence File, National.
27. Stevenson, *Roll of Honor,* I, 370; *NT,* April 12, 1887, 3; *NT,* July 21, 1887, 5.
28. Ibid.; *OR,* 25, pt. 1: 261; Theron M. Haight, "Among the Pontoons at Fitzhugh Crossing," *War Papers, Wisconsin Commandery, MOLLUS,* 1891, I, 420; *OR,* 25, pt. 1: 267.

29. Newspaper article in the author's possession, n.p., n.d.; *OR*, 25, pt. 1: 267.

30. Quiner, *Wisconsin Volunteers*, VIII, 370; *WSJ*, May 21, 1863, 2; *MST*, September 25, 1887, 3.

31. *WSJ*, May 21, 1863, 2; *MST*, August 7, 1887, 3.

32. *MST*, August 21, 1887, 3; *OR*, 25, pt. 1: 273; newspaper article in author's possession.

33. *MST*, August 7, 1887, 3; Stevenson, *Roll of Honor*, I, 371; *WSJ*, June 2, 1863, 2; *MST*, August 21, 1887, 3; Haight, "Among the Pontoons," 422.

34. *MST*, August 7, 1887, 3; *WSJ*, May 14, 1863, 2; *OR*, 25, pt. 1: 266–74.

35. Haight, "Among the Pontoons," 422; *MST*, August 21, 1887, 3; *WSJ*, May 21, 1863, 3.

36. *OR*, 25, pt. 1: 261, 267; Sparks, *Lincoln's Army*, 238; Nolan, *Iron Brigade*, 214.

37. Starbuck MSS; *QCT*, May 23, 1863, 2; *OR*, 25, pt. 1: 269; Regimental Records, Roster; *IDJ*, May 14, 1863, 2; Charles Sponsler Military Service Record.

38. *OR*, 25, pt. 1: 267, 269; Curtis, *Twenty-Fourth Michigan*, 127; Stevenson, *Roll of Honor*, I, 371.

20. NORTH AGAIN

1. Williams Diary; Stevenson, *Roll of Honor*, I, 371–72; *OR*, 25, pt. 1: 269.

2. *QCT*, May 23, 1863, 2; *OR*, 25, pt. 1: 231, 268–69; Dawes, *Sixth Wisconsin*, 137; Stine, *Army of the Potomac*, 350.

3. *OR*, 25, pt. 1: 268–69; Dawes, *Sixth Wisconsin*, 138; Stevenson, *Roll of Honor*, I, 372; Crull MSS.

4. Stevens, *Berdan's Sharpshooters*, 277–78.

5. Correspondence File, Indiana.

6. Jackson Diary; *QCT*, May 23, 1863, 2; Curtis, *Twenty-Fourth Michigan*, 138; Regimental Records, Letter Book.

7. Jackson Diary; Dawes, *Sixth Wisconsin*, 146; Smith, *Seventy-Sixth New York*, 224; Starbuck MSS.

8. Dawes, *Sixth Wisconsin*, 142; *RDUA*, June 10, 1863, 2.

9. Quiner, *Wisconsin Volunteers*, VIII, 137; *Muncie Daily Herald*, September 16, 1892, 2.

10. Jackson Diary.

11. Stevenson, *Roll of Honor*, I, 372–73; Dawes, *Sixth Wisconsin*, 143; Curtis, *Twenty-Fourth Michigan*, 140; Otis, *Second Wisconsin*, 79; Jackson Diary.

12. Stevenson, *Roll of Honor*, I, 373; Otis, *Second Wisconsin*, 79; Jackson Diary; Abner Hard, *History of the Eighth Cavalry Regiment Illinois Volunteers, During the Great Rebellion* (Dayton: Morningside Bookshop, 1984), 238–40.

13. Regimental Records, Letter Book.

14. Jackson Diary; Finney Diary.

15. Court-Martial, Hancock NN29.

16. Curtis, *Twenty-Fourth Michigan*, 142; Orr MSS; Merrill, *Soldier of Indiana*, II, 97; Marsh MSS.

17. Wasson Pension File.

18. Dawes, *Sixth Wisconsin*, 142; Nolan, *Iron Brigade*, 224.

19. John D. Billings, *Hardtack and Coffee* (Philadelphia: Thompson Publishing, 1887), 369–70.

20. Dawes, *Sixth Wisconsin*, 129; Billings, *Hardtack*, 370; *NT*, June 20, 1895, 3; *RDUA*, April 7, 1863, 2.

21. Billings, *Hardtack*, 370.

22. John Woods Military Service Record. See chapter 18 for details of Woods's other court-martial.

23. Court-Martial, Woods LL434; *MST,* May 24, 1885, 3.

24. Court-Martial, Woods LL 434.

25. *MST,* May 24, 1885, 3; Samuel Eaton Papers, State Historical Society of Wisconsin, Madison.

26. *MST,* May 24, 1885, 3; *Seventh Indiana Skirmishes,* 75; *RDUA,* June 19, 1863, 2; Rollins Diary; Curtis, *Twenty-Fourth Michigan,* 144–46.

27. Cheek, *Sauk Riflemen,* 69; *Seventh Indiana Skirmishes,* 76; *RP,* July 24, 1863, 2; Curtis, *Twenty-Fourth Michigan,* 146.

28. Cheek, *Sauk Riflemen,* 69; Rollins Diary; *MST,* May 24, 1885, 3.

29. *RDUA,* June 19, 1863, 2; *Seventh Indiana Skirmishes,* 76; Thomson, *Narrative of Seventh,* 160; *RP,* July 24, 1863, 2.

30. Tevis, *Fighting Fourteenth,* 76; Thomson, *Narrative of Seventh,* 160; *RDUA,* June 19, 1863, 2; Frazer Kirkland, *The Pictorial Book of Anecdotes and Incidents of the War of the Rebellion* (Hartford: Hartford Publishing, 1866), 174.

31. Wasson's letter has been modified slightly to preserve the chronology. *RP,* July 24, 1863, 2.

32. Finney Diary; Dawes, *Sixth Wisconsin,* 153, 157; Smith, *Seventy-Sixth New York,* 226, 229.

33. Dawes, *Sixth Wisconsin,* 157; Green MSS; Herdegen, *Bloody Railroad,* 109–11.

34. Stevenson, *Roll of Honor,* I, 474–75; Green MSS; Finney Diary.

21. GETTYSBURG

1. Stevenson, *Roll of Honor,* I, 375; Alan D. Gaff, "'Here Was Made Out Our Last and Hopeless Stand': The 'Lost' Gettysburg Reports of the Nineteenth Indiana," *Gettysburg Magazine,* I (Winter 1990): 29–30; Norma Hawkins, "Sergeant-Major Blanchard at Gettysburg," *Indiana Magazine of History,* 34 (June 1938): 214; Dudley MSS in Bachelder Papers.

2. Gaff, "Lost Report," 29–30; Stevenson, *Roll of Honor,* I, 375; William W. Dudley, *The Iron Brigade at Gettysburg: Official Report of the Part Borne by the 1st Brigade, 1st Division, 1st Army Corps,* 1879, 5–6; Hawkins, "Blanchard," 216.

3. Dudley MSS, Bachelder MSS; Gaff, "Lost Report," 29–30; *Missouri Republican* [hereinafter cited as *MR*] December 4, 1886, 9.

4. Dudley, *Official Report,* 6; Dudley MSS, Bachelder MSS; *EWR,* July 25, 1863, 3.

5. Dudley MSS, Bachelder MSS; Hawkins, "Blanchard," 214; Orr MSS; Marsh MSS; Letter from William C. Barnes to Dudley, March 28, 1883, Bachelder Papers.

6. Andrew Wood Pension File.

7. Marsh MSS; Gaff, "Lost Report," 29–30; Dudley MSS in Bachelder MSS; *OR,* 27, pt. 1: 279; W. Bird, *Stories of the Civil War* (Columbiana: Advocate Print, n.d.), 7; *OR,* 27, pt. 1: 279.

8. Marsh MSS; Francis Huff Pension File; Orr MSS.

9. Dudley MSS, Bachelder MSS; Hawkins, "Blanchard," 214; *NT,* December 27, 1892, 4.

10. Dudley, *Official Report,* 6–7; *OR,* 27, pt. 1: 267, 273–74, 279.

11. *OR,* 27, pt. 2: 646; ibid., pt. 1: 266; *MR,* December 4, 1886, 9; Mead Diary; Wheeler MSS; Finney Diary; *WJ,* July 17, 1863, 2.

12. W. F. Fulton, "The Fifth Alabama Battalion at Gettysburg," *Confederate Veteran,* 31 (October 1923): 379; W. M. McCall, "Letter to the Editor," *Confederate Veteran,* 3 (January 1895): 19; John B. Lindsley, *Military Annals of Tennessee,*

Confederate, 1886, 327; Jaquelin Meredith, "The First Day at Gettysburg," *Southern Historical Society Papers,* 24:182–87; Barnes Letter, Bachelder Papers.

13. Gaff, "Lost Report," 29–30; Dudley MSS, Bachelder MSS; Dudley, *Official Report,* 14.

14. Dudley, *Official Report,* 11; Dudley MSS, Bachelder MSS; *OR,* 27, pt. 1: 268; Hawkins, "Blanchard," 215; Abner Doubleday, *Chancellorsville and Gettysburg* (New York: Charles Scribner's Sons, 1886), 130. Doubleday's account of July 1st, although inaccurate in the timing and occasion of this conversation, indicates that Blanchard reported to him, not Wadsworth, as Dudley related in his narrative.

15. Dudley, *Official Report,* 11; *OR,* 27, pt. 1: 268; *Cambridge City Tribune* [hereinafter cited as *CCT*] August 31, 1871, 1; Stevenson, *Roll of Honor,* I, 377.

16. Orr MSS; Dudley MSS, Bachelder MSS; Hawkins, "Blanchard," 215; Stine, *Army of the Potomac,* 719–21.

17. *WJ,* July 13, 1863, 2; Moore MSS; Hawkins, "Blanchard," 215; Dudley, *Official Report,* 12; *CCT,* August 31, 1871, 1.

18. Marsh MSS; Orr MSS; *OR,* 27, pt. 2: 643; James L. Morrison, ed., *The Memoirs of Henry Heth* (Westport, CT: Greenwood Press, 1974), 305. Confederate references to the second line count the skirmish line as a first line of resistance.

19. *OR,* 27, pt. 2: 643; Dudley MSS, Bachelder MSS; Gaff, "Lost Report," 29–30; Stevenson, *Roll of Honor,* I, 377; Dudley MSS, Bachelder MSS.

20. Orr MSS; *RP,* September 11, 1863, 2; Marsh MSS.

21. Gaff, "Lost Report," 29–30; Hawkins, "Blanchard," 215; *NT,* August 20, 1881, 5; *REI,* March 22, 1883, 1.

22. Marsh MSS; Moore MSS; newspaper clipping in author's possession.

23. Marsh MSS; Charles C. Coffin, *Four Years of Fighting* (Boston: Ticknor and Fields, 1866), 273; newspaper clipping in author's possession. This account of the colors is the best possible compilation from the postwar accounts by participants that sometimes do not agree on details.

24. Gaff, "Lost Report," 29–30; Moore MSS; Dudley, *Official Report,* 13; *RP,* August 28, 1863, 2; *OR,* 27, pt. 1: 268; John Nicholson, comp., *Pennsylvania at Gettysburg* (Harrisburg: E. K. Meyers, 1893), II, 762–63.

25. Gaff, "Lost Report," 29–30; Orr MSS; Hawkins, "Blanchard," 216.

26. *MST,* July 30, 1882, 2; *OR,* 27, pt. 2: 643.

27. Gaff, "Lost Report," 29–30.

28. Ibid.; *OR,* pt. 2: 645; Walter Clark, ed., *Histories of the Several Regiments and Battalions from North Carolina in the Great War* (Raleigh: E. M. Uzzell, 1901), V, 131; Orr MSS.

22. LAST STAND

1. *IDJ,* August 11, 1863, 2; Gaff, "Lost Report," 30; Survivor's Association, *History of the 121st Regiment Pennsylvania Volunteers: An Account from the Ranks* (Philadelphia: Burk & McFetridge, 1893), 48; *OR,* 27, pt. 1: 274; R. K. Beecham, *Gettysburg: The Pivotal Battle of the Civil War* (Chicago: A. C. McClurg, 1911), 73.

2. *OR,* 27, pt. 1: 280, 315, 323, 328, 330; Scrapbook, Archives, Wayne County Historical Museum, Richmond, Indiana.

3. *MST,* February 24, 1889, 3; Stevenson, *Roll of Honor,* I, 379.

4. *OR,* 27, pt. 2: 661, 669; Stevenson, *Roll of Honor,* I, 378; Beecham, *Gettysburg,* 73.

5. Ibid.; Stine, *Army of the Potomac,* 487; *OR,* 27, pt. 1: 280; ibid., pt. 2: 661, 670; Daniel A. Tomkins, *Company K, Fourteenth South Carolina Volunteers* (Charlotte: Observer Printing and Publishing House, 1897), 19.

6. Ibid., 20; *OR*, 27, pt. 1: 280; ibid., pt. 2: 662; Varina D. Brown, *A Colonel at Gettysburg and Spotsylvania* (Columbia, SC: State, 1931), 79.

7. *OR*, 27, pt. 2: 661; Milledge L. Bonham, "A Little More Light on Gettysburg," *Mississippi Valley Historical Review*, 24 (March 1938): 522; *NT*, July 30, 1903, 3; Horatio N. Warren, *Two Reunions of the 142nd Regiment Pennsylvania Volunteers* (Buffalo: Courier, 1890), 22.

8. *OR*, 27, pt. 2: 662; Nicholson, *Pennsylvania at Gettysburg*, II, 879; J. D. Cook, "Reminiscences of Gettysburg," *War Talks in Kansas, Kansas Commandery, MOLLUS*, 1906, 327; *CCT*, August 31, 1871, 1.

9. *IDJ*, August 11, 1863, 2; Gaff, "Lost Report," 29–30; Stevenson, *Roll of Honor*, I, 378.

10. *OR*, 27, pt. 2: 670–71; Clark, *North Carolina Regiments*, I, 698.

11. Bonham, "Little More Light," 522; Brown, *Gettysburg and Spotsylvania*, 83; *OR*, 27, pt. 2: 663; Tomkins, *Company K*, 20.

12. *OR*, 27, pt. 1: 280–81; *MST*, September 2, 1863, 2.

13. *MR*, December 4, 1886, 9; *OR*, 27, pt. 1: 277; Henry F. Young Letters in the Warner Papers, State Historical Society of Wisconsin, Madison.

14. *MST*, February 3, 1884, 3; Thomas Helm, *History of Delaware County, Indiana* (Chicago: Kingman Bros., 1881), 118.

15. *MST*, February 3, 1884, 3; Warner, *Generals in Blue*, 655.

16. *OR*, 27, pt. 1: 280; Doubleday, *Chancellorsville*, 151; *MR*, December 4, 1886, 9; Dudley, *Official Report*, 14; Thomson, *Narrative of Seventh*, 161–63.

17. *WJ*, July 17, 1863, 2; Stevenson, *Roll of Honor*, I, 380; Finney Diary.

18. *OR*, 27, pt. 1: 206; Richard Harwell, ed., *Two Views of Gettysburg* (Chicago: R. R. Donnelley & Sons, 1964), 191–92; Davis Castle Pension File.

19. *REI*, October 4, 1911, 1; Regimental Records, Muster Roll; Henry B. Reeves Pension File; Tucker, *Delaware County*, 238.

20. Dudley MSS, Bachelder MSS; *IDJ*, July 13, 1863, 2.

21. Dudley MSS, Bachelder MSS; Barnes, *Medical and Surgical History*, XII, 447, 450, 516; *IDJ*, July 13, 1863, 2; ibid., July 23, 1863, 2; Gaff, "Lost Report," 29; Hawkins, "Blanchard," 216.

22. Gaff, "Lost Report," 30; *WJ*, July 17, 1863, 2; *DCFP*, July 23, 1863, 2–3; *EWR*, August 29, 1863, 2; *IDJ*, August 11, 1863, 2.

23. *QCT*, August 1, 1863, 3; Charles C. Sater Military Service Record; Robert Conley Pension File; Samuel Bradbury Pension File; Grear Williams Pension File.

24. *IDJ*, July 23, 1863, 2.

25. *MST*, September 30, 1883, 3; Jacob Ebersole, "Incidents of Field Hospital Life with the Army of the Potomac," *Sketches of War History, Ohio Commandery, MOLLUS*, 1896, IV, 328–29.

26. *MST*, September 30, 1883, 3.

27. Barnes, *Medical and Surgical History*, XII, 471, 489; ibid., X, 749; *NT*, January 22, 1891, 3.

28. *RCJ*, January 15, 1864, 3; William Miller Pension File.

29. Marsh MSS.

30. *IDJ*, July 23, 1863, 2; *IDJ*, August 1, 1863, 2.

31. Marsh MSS.

32. *NT*, May 27, 1890, 3; *Indianapolis Star*, July 5, 1913, 3.

33. *Indianapolis Star*, July 6, 1913, 2.

34. Stine, *Army of the Potomac*, 719–21; Green MSS; Crull MSS.

35. *WSJ*, September 12, 1863, 2; Orr MSS; Hudson, *Hawks*, 44.

23. BACK TO VIRGINIA

1. Finney Diary; *RP,* July 9, 1863, 1; Orr MSS.

2. Finney Diary; Jackson Diary; Curtis, *Twenty-Fourth Michigan,* 194.

3. Helm, *Delaware County,* 118.

4. Finney Diary; Jackson Diary; Dawes, *Sixth Wisconsin,* 187; *NT,* June 20, 1895, 3.

5. Finney Diary; Jackson Diary.

6. *OR,* 27, pt. 3: 674–75; Dawes, *Sixth Wisconsin,* 194; Green MSS.

7. Finney Diary; *MDH,* September 16, 1892, 2; *Major General James S. Wadsworth at Gettysburg and Other Fields* (Albany: J. B. Lyon, 1916), 90; *OR,* 27, pt. 3: 717.

8. Finney Diary; Jackson Diary; *IDJ,* July 27, 1863, 2.

9. Finney Diary; Jackson Diary; Orr MSS.

10. Jackson Diary; Dawes, *Sixth Wisconsin,* 194; Fairfield Diary; Finney Diary.

11. Ibid.; Jackson Diary; Crull MSS; F. H. Dyer, *A Compendium of the War of the Rebellion* (Des Moines: Dyer Publishing, 1908), 1620.

12. Jackson Diary; Court-Martial, Green LL771.

13. *MST,* January 18, 1880, 2; Green MSS; Dawes, *Sixth Wisconsin,* 199; Finney Diary.

14. Finney Diary; Crull MSS.

15. Stevenson, *Roll of Honor,* I, ix; *IDJ,* March 7, 1863, 3.

16. *IDJ,* March 30, 1863, 3; Finney Diary; Stevenson, *Roll of Honor,* I, 347–85, 633.

17. *WSJ,* August 27, 1863, 2; Orr MSS.

18. *RP,* August 28, 1863, 2; *QCT,* August 29, 1863, 3.

19. Green MSS.

20. *WSJ,* August 27, 1863, 2; Dawes, *Sixth Wisconsin,* 197.

24. ALONG THE RAPIDAN

1. Otis, *Second Wisconsin,* 91; Dawes, *Sixth Wisconsin,* 202–204.

2. Ibid., 206; *RP,* September 11, 1863, 3; Finney Diary.

3. Curtis, *Twenty-Fourth Michigan,* 202; Cheek, *Sauk Riflemen,* 80; Quiner, *Wisconsin Volunteers,* VIII, 154.

4. *RDUA,* September 18, 1863, 2.

5. Finney Diary; Quiner, *Wisconsin Volunteers,* VIII, 154.

6. Ibid., 155.

7. Ibid., 155–56.

8. *WSR,* October 3, 1863, 1.

9. Quiner, *Wisconsin Volunteers,* VIII, 156; Curtis, *Twenty-Fourth Michigan,* 203.

10. Cheek, *Sauk Riflemen,* 80; Dawes, *Sixth Wisconsin,* 205–206; Smith, *Seventy-Sixth New York,* 257.

11. *MST,* January 30, 1881, 2. This account mistakenly identifies the defecting regiment as the 20th instead of the 7th, which was brigaded with the Brooklyn men.

12. Jackson Diary.

13. Regimental Records, Letter Book; ibid., Muster Roll.

14. Regimental Records, Letter Book.

15. Finney Diary; Jackson Diary.

16. *OR,* Series 3, 3: 414–16. A curious thing had occurred in the army. In 1861 the volunteers had looked to the Regular Army as the "rock" upon which the volunteer army would be built. By the end of 1863, these three-year regiments had

supplanted the Regulars and were the backbone of the Federal military. These regiments had to be preserved at all costs, hence the generous reenlistment bounty.

17. *RDUA*, October 13, 1863, 2; Jackson Diary; *IDJ*, October 12, 1863, 1.

18. Orr MSS.

19. Finney Diary; Otis, *Second Wisconsin*, 92; Jackson Diary.

20. Meredith MSS.

21. Curtis, *Twenty-Fourth Michigan*, 207; Jackson Diary.

22. Ibid.; Smith, *Seventy-Sixth New York*, 266.

23. *RDUA*, November 3, 1863, 2; Smith, *Seventy-Sixth New York*, 266.

24. Jackson Diary; Otis, *Second Wisconsin*, 92; C. M. Prutsman, *A Soldier's Experience in Southern Prisons* (New York: Andrew H. Kellogg, 1901), 7–8.

25. Crull MSS.

26. Finney Diary; Otis, *Second Wisconsin*, 93; Jackson Diary; Dawes, *Sixth Wisconsin*, 214.

27. *RP*, November 13, 1863, 2.

25. THE VETERAN QUESTION

1. *IDJ*, October 3, 1863, 2; *Revised Report of the Select Committee Relative to the Soldier's National Cemetery, Together with the Accompanying Documents as Reported to the House of Representatives of the Commonwealth of Pennsylvania* (Harrisburg: Singersly & Meyers, 1865), 15; Sandburg, *War Years*, II, 454.

2. Dawes, *Sixth Wisconsin*, 219–20; *MST*, May 6, 1888, 3.

3. Haskell MSS; Green MSS.

4. Regimental Records, Letter Book; *MST*, August 5, 1883, 2; Dawes, *Sixth Wisconsin*, 222.

5. Regimental Records, Letter Book.

6. Finney Diary; *IDJ*, November 9, 1863, 2; Jackson Diary; *RP*, November 13, 1863, 3.

7. Jackson Diary; Otis, *Second Wisconsin*, 93; Dawes, *Sixth Wisconsin*, 219.

8. Otis, *Second Wisconsin*, 93; Orr MSS; Jackson Diary.

9. Orr MSS; *OR*, 51, pt. 1: 1121; Jackson Diary.

10. *IDJ*, November 23, 1863, 2; Haskell MSS.

11. Ibid.; *Revised Report, Commonwealth Pennsylvania*, 210; Gibbon, *Recollections*, 184.

12. *RP*, September 11, 1863, 2; *RP, Extra*, September 14, 1863; Samuel Schlagle Military Service Record; *RWT*, January 27, 1866, 3.

13. Correspondence File, Indiana; *IDJ*, November 24, 1863, 2.

14. *OR*, 29, pt. 1: 689; Otis, *Second Wisconsin*, 94; *MST*, June 3, 1888, 3.

15. *OR*, 29, pt. 1: 689–90; *RDUA*, December 11, 1863, 2; Dawes, *Sixth Wisconsin*, 226–27.

16. *MST*, June 3, 1888, 3.

17. *OR*, 29, pt. 1: 687; Otis, *Second Wisconsin*, 94; *IDJ*, December 11, 1863, 2; Dawes, *Sixth Wisconsin*, 226–27.

18. *OR*, 29, pt. 1: 687, 689–90; *IDJ*, December 11, 1863, 2.

19. *OR*, 29, pt. 1: 687–88, 690; Stine, *Army of the Potomac*, 590, 592; *IDJ*, December 11, 1863, 2; Orr MSS.

20. *OR*, 29, pt. 1: 690; Orr MSS; Jackson Diary; John McKinney Military Service Record.

21. Jackson Diary; Campbell MSS.

22. Correspondence File, Indiana.
23. Jackson Diary; Smith, *Seventy-Sixth New York,* 267.
24. Dawes, *Sixth Wisconsin,* 231–32, 235; Stevenson, *Roll of Honor,* I, 584.
25. Hudson, *Hawks,* 44; Jackson Diary; *OR,* Series 3, 3: 1084; ibid., 29, pt. 2: 560.
26. Thomas Henderson Military Service Record; Joel Curtis Military Service Record; James Grunden Military Service Record; James Grunden Pension File.
27. *OR,* 29, pt. 2: 573; *OR,* Series 3, 3: 1179.
28. Jackson Diary; Dawes, *Sixth Wisconsin,* 236; Military Service Records of various Company B veterans.

26. VETERAN FURLOUGH

1. Jackson Diary; Correspondence File, National; Hudson, *Hawks,* 46.
2. Jackson Diary; Regimental Records, Letter Book; Dawes, *Sixth Wisconsin,* 235; *OR,* 33: 460.
3. Jackson Diary; *RP,* October 4, 1911, 1; *IDJ,* January 18, 1864, 3.
4. Ibid.
5. *EWR,* January 23, 1864, 2; *DCFP,* January 21, 1864, 2; ibid., January 28, 1864, 3.
6. James Rigby Pension File.
7. *Richmond Jeffersonian,* January 28, 1864, 3; *RP,* January 30, 1864, 3; Regimental Records, Muster Rolls. Corporals Beetley, Bunch, Curtis and Fort had been promoted effective January 1st, the date of their reenlistment.
8. *RP,* January 27, 1864, 2; *RP,* February 10, 1864, 2–3.
9. Ibid.; Samuel H. Meredith Military Service Record; Correspondence File, Indiana.
10. *RP,* February 10, 1864, 2; *IDJ,* January 30, 1864, 3.
11. *RP,* February 17, 1864, 2; Paul Kallina, "Lincoln's Quaker General," *The Lincolnian,* 6 (November–December 1987): 3–4; Correspondence File, Indiana; Terrell, *Adjutant General,* II, 169.
12. Hudson, *Hawks,* 17, 19, 47. The letters in *Civil War Hawks* dated March 6/62 and March 17 were obviously written in 1864, not 1862 as the editors have indicated.
13. John Addleman Military Service Record; Work Projects Administration, *Index to Marriage Records, Wayne County, Indiana* (Work Projects Administration, 1941), I, 5.
14. Orr MSS; Correspondence File, National; Jackson Diary.
15. James Goings Pension File; Joseph Hartley Military Service Record.
16. Robert Patterson Pension File.
17. Ibid.
18. Orr MSS; David Fort Pension File; Tucker, *Randolph County,* 292.
19. *RWT,* January 27, 1866, 2; *RP,* January 30, 1864, 3; Frank Dennis Military Service Record; Hatch Squires Military Service Record.
20. Nathan Williams Military Service Record.
21. Correspondence File, National; Nathaniel Cary Pension File; Michael Ryan Pension File; John Thompson Pension File.
22. Charles Rider Pension File.

27. ARRIVAL OF GRANT

1. Jackson Diary; Orr MSS.
2. Ibid.; Dawes, *Sixth Wisconsin,* 249–50; Hudson, *Hawks,* 19.

3. Correspondence File, National; Correspondence File, Indiana; Hudson, *Hawks,* 17.

4. *WSJ,* April 25, 1864, 2; Nathaniel Cary Pension File.

5. Hudson, *Hawks,* 19; Jackson Diary; Orr MSS; Cary Pension File; Ryan Pension File.

6. *OR,* 33, 638–39; ibid., 717–18; ibid., 42, pt. 2: 750; Wilmer, *Maryland Volunteers,* I, 262.

7. Orr MSS; William H. Powell, *The Fifth Army Corps, Army of the Potomac* (New York: G. P. Putnam's Sons, 1896), 591; Wilmer, *Maryland Volunteers,* I, 262.

8. Andrew A. Humphreys, *The Virginia Campaign of '64 and '65* (New York: Charles Scribner's Sons, 1883), 3; Dawes, *Sixth Wisconsin,* 239; *OR,* 33: 717.

9. Ibid., 735; Stine, *Army of the Potomac,* 597.

10. Meredith MSS.

11. *RP,* April 14, 1864, 2.

12. Meredith MSS; *RP,* March 30, 1864, 3.

13. *BAOF,* April 2, 1864, 2.

14. *DCFP,* March 17, 1864, 2; *BAOF,* April 2, 1864, 1.

15. Wilmer, *Maryland Volunteers,* I, 262; Dawes, *Sixth Wisconsin,* 239–40.

16. Wilmer, *Maryland Volunteers,* I, 262; Orr MSS.

17. Williams Diary.

18. *IDJ,* April 5, 1864, 1; Williams Diary.

19. Orr MSS; *IDJ,* April 4, 1864, 1; Hudson, *Hawks,* 17, 19; Wheeler MSS.

20. Williams Diary; Regimental Records, Letter Book.

21. Jackson Diary; John W. Modlin Pension File.

22. Correspondence File, National.

23. William W. Dudley Military Service Record; Seeds, *Republican Party,* I, 357; Francis B. Heitman, *Historical Register and Dictionary of the United States Army* (Washington: Government Printing Office, 1903), I, 386; *RP,* December 16, 1909, 1.

24. Orr MSS; Correspondence File, National.

25. Dawes, *Sixth Wisconsin,* 243, 247; Jackson Diary.

26. *RP,* May 25, 1864, 1; Williams Diary.

28. INTO THE WILDERNESS

1. Williams Diary; *OR,* 36, pt. 2: 359.

2. William D. Love, *Wisconsin in the War of the Rebellion* (Chicago: Church and Goodman, 1866), 935; Marsh MSS.

3. John V. Hadley, "A Day with Escaping Prisoners," *War Papers Read Before the Indiana Commandery, MOLLUS,* 1898, 7; Williams Diary; Morris Schaff, *The Battle of the Wilderness* (Boston: Houghton, Mifflin, 1910), 96–97.

4. George R. Agassiz, ed., *Meade's Headquarters 1863–1865* (Boston: Atlantic Monthly Press, 1922), 89; *MST,* January 17, 1886, 3; Schaff, *Wilderness,* 97; Merrill, *Soldier of Indiana,* II, 629.

5. *OR,* 36, pt. 1: 610, 614; *WJ,* September 25, 1912, 5; Walter F. Beyer and Oscar F. Keydel, *Deeds of Valor* (Detroit: Perrien-Keydel, 1901), I, 317.

6. *OR,* 36, pt. 1: 614; Schaff, *Wilderness,* 151–52; Stine, *Army of the Potomac,* 722.

7. *OR,* 36, pt. 1: 617; Wilmer, *Maryland Volunteers,* I, 264; Dawes, *Sixth Wisconsin,* 259; Love, *Wisconsin in War,* 934; Curtis, *Twenty-Fourth Michigan,* 230–31. Major Merit Welsh of the 7th Indiana reported on August 7, 1864, that his regiment formed the "extreme right of [the] brigade and of the division," connecting with Griffin's division. In some recollections written in 1874, Colonel Rufus

Dawes remembered that the 6th Wisconsin was on the left of Cutler's second line and the 7th Indiana "was directly in front of us." In an account based on contemporary sources, William D. Love wrote that the 7th Wisconsin was on the left of Cutler's brigade, with the 6th Wisconsin "in reserve." O. B. Curtis's history of the 24th Michigan gets the alignment totally wrong. He erroneously has the 24th Michigan on the left of the Iron Brigade, which was on the left of the division. Curtis then places both the 7th Indiana and 6th Wisconsin "in reserve." At this time there is no source available that will rectify the confusion.

8. *OR*, 36, pt. 1: 614; *WJ*, September 25, 1912, 5.

9. Beyer, *Deeds of Valor*, I, 317; Samuel Shirts Pension File; Scribner, *Roll of Honor*, II, 585; *OR*, 36, pt. 1: 545, 610–11; Love, *Wisconsin in War*, 934; Curtis, *Twenty-Fourth Michigan*, 231; Thomson, *Narrative of Seventh*, 184–85. Other units claimed to have destroyed Jones's brigade, but the fact that Iron Brigade regiments captured two flags from it seems to end any dispute on that point. But controversy did swirl about the flags. Capture of the 48th Virginia standard was claimed by both the 7th Wisconsin and 24th Michigan. The flag of the 50th Virginia was undoubtedly taken by someone in the 7th Indiana, but two men claimed that honor. John N. Opel was recognized as the "official" captor, but others argued that Perry S. Tremain had actually seized it. The third flag has never been identified.

10. *WJ*, September 25, 1912, 5; Beyer, *Deeds of Valor*, I, 317; Jesse Jones Pension File; Congress, Senate, Committee on Veteran's Affairs, *Medal of Honor Recipients 1863–1973*, 93d Cong., 1st sess., October 22, 1973, Committee Print 15, 46. Buckles wrote that he gave the flag to John Divelbuss, who was then killed. But Daniel Divelbuss was the only man with that surname in the regiment and he was not killed until June 18th. Catherine Merrill, in *The Soldier of Indiana in the War for the Union*, II, 621, stated that it was Seth Peden who took the flag. Peden was killed on May 5. Buckles was more intent on staying alive than watching who became the new color-bearer, so Merrill's account, based on contemporary sources, is preferred. December 4, 1893, Abram J. Buckles was awarded a Medal of Honor for his conduct at the Wilderness. The inscription on his medal reads, "The Congress to A. J. Buckles for distinguished gallantry at the Battle of the Wilderness, Va., May 5, 1864." The citation accompanying his medal reads, "Though suffering from an open wound, carried the regimental colors until again wounded."

11. George Marquis Papers, Indiana Division, Indiana State Library, Indianapolis; Thomson, *Narrative of Seventh*, 186; Schaff, *Wilderness*, 158; *MST*, October 6, 1894, 8.

12. *NT*, September 30, 1886, 3.

13. Wilmer, *Maryland Volunteers*, I, 265–66.

14. John V. Hadley, *Seven Months a Prisoner* (New York: Charles Scribner's Sons, 1898), 35–36.

15. *MST*, October 6, 1894, 8; Schaff, *Wilderness*, 158–59, 166; *OR*, 36, pt. 1: 611.

16. William F. Drum, "Work of the Fifth Corps Ambulance Train, Spring and Summer of 1864," *Glimpses of the Nation's Struggle, series III, Minnesota Commandery, MOLLUS*, 1893, 77–86 passim; *OR*, 36, pt. 1: 217.

17. *IDJ*, June 27, 1864, 1; Correspondence File, Indiana; *WJ*, September 25, 1912, 5; Marsh MSS; Stine, *Army of the Potomac*, 722. The numbers for men lost in Grant's campaign are taken from "Report of Casualties 19th Regiment Indiana Veteran Volunteers from the Crossing of the Rapidan May 4th 1864 to July 30 1864," Correspondence File, Indiana, and do not necessarily coincide with other sources.

18. *IDJ*, June 17, 1864, 2; Matthew Duckworth Pension File; John W. Dittemore Pension File; Terrell, *Adjutant General*, IV, 401, 408; *Soldiers and Citizens Album of Biographical Record* (Chicago: Grand Army Publishing, 1888), I, 256; Fielding H. Garrison, *John Shaw Billings: A Memoir* (New York: G. P. Putnam's Sons, 1915), 88.

19. *NT,* December 24, 1885, 1; Schaff, *Wilderness,* 198; *MST,* April 10, 1897, 1.

20. Scribner, *Roll of Honor,* II, 586; *OR,* 36, pt. 1: 615; Correspondence File, Indiana.

21. *OR,* 36, pt. 2: 459, 506; Schaff, *Wilderness,* 235–36; *NT,* June 4, 1891, 3.

22. *MST,* April 10, 1897, 1; *MST,* January 17, 1886, 3.

23. *NT,* December 24, 1885, 1; *NT,* June 20, 1895, 3; Schaff, *Wilderness,* 270.

24. *MST,* April 10, 1897, 1; *NT,* May 20, 1886, 3; *NT,* June 20, 1895, 3.

25. Correspondence File, Indiana; *RP,* May 25, 1864, 3; Crull MSS; *IDJ,* May 24, 1864, 1.

26. Eaton MSS; *MST,* January 17, 1886, 3.

29. GRANT'S CAMPAIGN

1. *OR,* 36, pt. 1: 540–41; Schaff, *Wilderness,* 91.

2. Dawes, *Sixth Wisconsin,* 264; Stine, *Army of the Potomac,* 618–19.

3. Ibid.; Correspondence File, Indiana. James H. Stine conducted an investigation and determined that Corporal Andrew J. Wood had carried the flag that day. But the list of casualties in Grant's campaign shows that Wood was actually wounded on May 23. The author has been unable to positively identify the color-bearer in this incident.

4. Dawes, *Sixth Wisconsin,* 264–65.

5. Correspondence File, Indiana; *IDJ,* July 9, 1864, 2.

6. Cheek, *Sauk Riflemen,* 95; *OR,* 36, pt. 1: 611, 619.

7. *NYH,* May 13, 1864, 8.

8. Gibbon, *Recollections,* 218; *OR,* 36, pt. 1: 619.

9. Ibid., 611, 619; *MST,* February 24, 1889, 3; Correspondence File, Indiana; *EWR,* May 21, 1864, 3.

10. *OR,* 36, pt. 1: 203, 541, 611, 617; ibid., 42, pt. 2: 754; Cheek, *Sauk Riflemen,* 96; Correspondence File, Indiana; Curtis, *Twenty-Fourth Michigan,* 237; Otis, *Second Wisconsin,* 294; *Roster of Wisconsin Volunteers, War of the Rebellion, 1861–1865* (Madison, Wisconsin: Democrat Printing, 1886), I, 431.

11. *OR,* 36, pt. 1: 611, 617, 620; Dawes, *Sixth Wisconsin,* 268–69; Cheek, *Sauk Riflemen,* 97–98; Alexander B. Pattison Diary, Indiana Historical Society, Indianapolis; *MST,* February 24, 1889, 3.

12. Scribner, *Roll of Honor,* II, 587; Correspondence File, Indiana; Crull MSS; Barnes, *Medical and Surgical History,* XI, 47, 261; ibid., XII, 791, 794; *QCT,* August 13, 1864, 3.

13. *OR,* 36, pt. 1: 541–42, 611.

14. Wheeler MSS; Merrill, *Soldier of Indiana,* II, 630; Eaton MSS; Dawes, *Sixth Wisconsin,* 255; *OR,* 36, pt. 1: 621; *EWR,* May 21, 1864, 3.

15. *OR,* 36, pt. 1: 542; Jackson Diary; *WJ,* September 25, 1912, 5.

16. Marsh MSS; *WSJ,* May 25, 1864, 1; *WSJ,* May 30, 1864, 2.

17. *MS,* May 31, 1864, 2; *IDJ,* May 25, 1864, 2; *IDJ,* June 28, 1864, 1.

18. Correspondence File, Indiana; Jackson Diary; *OR,* 36, pt. 1: 542, 612, 617, 621.

19. Ibid., 612, 621; Curtis, *Twenty-Fourth Michigan,* 250; *NT,* May 26, 1887, 3.

20. *OR,* 36, pt. 1: 617; *NYH,* May 30, 1864, 1; *RDUA,* June 21, 1864, 2.

21. New York Monuments Commission, *Final Report on the Battlefield of Gettysburg* (Albany: J. B. Lyon, 1902), III, 1210–11; *OR,* 36, pt. 1: 621; Curtis, *Twenty-Fourth Michigan,* 251; Orr MSS.

22. Correspondence File, Indiana; Andrew J. Wood Pension File; William Small Pension File; Samuel Goodwin Pension File; Zacharias Hancock Pension File.

23. *NT,* May 26, 1887, 2; Elliott Winscott Letter, privately owned by Rick Saunders, Martinez, Georgia; *Final Report Gettysburg,* III, 1211; *RDUA,* June 21, 1864, 2.

24. Nevins, *Diary of Battle,* 386; *OR,* 36, pt. 3: 651; Frederick C. Pierce, *Fiske and Fisk Family* (Chicago: W. B. Conkey, 1896), 428.

25. Young MSS; Orr MSS; *WSJ,* August 17, 1864, 2.

26. Orr MSS; Winscott MS; Correspondence File, Indiana; William Balch Pension File.

27. *OR,* 36, pt. 1: 613; Correspondence File, Indiana; Lewis Eller Pension File.

28. John D. Vautier, *History of the Eighty-Eighth Pennsylvania Volunteers in the War for the Union* (Philadelphia: J. B. Lippincott, 1894), 187.

30. NADIR AT PETERSBURG

1. Scribner, *Roll of Honor,* II, 587; *OR,* 36, pt. 3: 649; Pattison Diary; Young MSS.

2. *OR,* 36, pt. 1: 613; Jackson Diary; Williams Diary; Thomas Chamberlin, *History of the 150th Regiment, Pennsylvania Volunteers* (Philadelphia: J. P. Lippincott, 1895), 260; Young MSS.

3. Correspondence File, National; Jackson Diary.

4. Ibid.; *NYH,* June 10, 1864, 1; *NYH,* June 16, 1864, 1.

5. Regimental Records, Letter Book.

6. Otis, *Second Wisconsin,* 7–8, 100, 126.

7. *OR,* 40, pt. 1: 190, 473; Winscott MS; *QCT,* July 2, 1864, 1.

8. *OR,* 40, pt. 1: 190, 473; ibid., pt. 2: 668; *QCT,* July 2, 1864, 1.

9. *OR,* 40, pt. 1: 473; *OR,* 52, pt. 2: 751; *QCT,* July 2, 1864, 1.

10. *OR,* 40, pt. 1: 473–74; Dawes, *Sixth Wisconsin,* 291.

11. Smith, *Seventy-Sixth New York,* 306; *OR,* 40, pt. 1: 476.

12. Curtis, *Twenty-Fourth Michigan,* 262–63; *WSJ,* June 25, 1864, 2.

13. Cheek, *Sauk Riflemen,* 114–16; Pattison Diary; *OR,* 40, pt. 1: 475; Curtis, *Twenty-Fourth Michigan,* 263–64.

14. Orr MSS; *RP,* July 13, 1864, 3; *QCT,* July 2, 1864, 1; *OR,* 40, pt. 2: 188.

15. Nevins, *Diary of Battle,* 425; Dawes, *Sixth Wisconsin,* 291; Young MSS; Winscott MS.

16. Young MSS; Williams Diary; Crull MSS; Daniel Curry Pension File; *QCT,* July 2, 1864, 1.

17. *IDJ,* June 27, 1864, 1; Orr MSS; James Rigby Pension File; David Norris Pension File.

18. Barnes, *Medical and Surgical History,* XI, 402; ibid., XII, 467; ibid., XI, 234; John Smock Pension File; James Denton Pension File; Carson Andrews Pension File. The 30% figure comes from a comparison of 1864 casualty lists with those from preceding years.

19. *RP,* July 13, 1864, 3; Pattison Diary; *QCT,* July 2, 1864, 1; Orr MSS; Williams Diary.

20. Merrill, *Soldier of Indiana,* II, 676.

21. Nathaniel Rigsby Pension File; Barnes, *Medical and Surgical History,* XI, 253; ibid., X, 700; Crull MSS; Thomas Davis Pension File.

22. Pattison Diary; Hudson, *Hawks,* 49.

23. Stine, *Army of the Potomac,* 722; Correspondence File, Indiana.
24. *OR,* 40, pt. 1: 474.
25. Winscott MS.

31. WELDON RAILROAD

1. Regimental Records, Muster Roll.
2. *RP,* July 13, 1864, 3.
3. *OR,* series 3, 1, 402; *OR,* 4, 448.
4. *IDJ,* July 9, 1864, 2.
5. Ibid.; *IDJ,* August 3, 1864, 1; Crull MSS; Pattison Diary; Hudson, *Hawks,* 50.
6. Thomas Barnett Military Service Record.
7. Hudson, *Hawks,* 51; *RP,* July 21, 1864, 3; *IDJ,* August 2, 1864, 1.
8. *NYH,* July 20, 1864, 1.
9. Dawes, *Sixth Wisconsin,* 294; *OR,* 40, pt. 1: 475; *MST,* October 11, 1885, 7.
10. Ibid. Details of the secret expedition were given by Sergeant O. F. Tipple, 7th Wisconsin, one of the survivors.
11. *OR,* 40, pt. 1: 445; ibid., pt. 3: 470–71; *OR,* 42, pt. 2: 751–52.
12. *OR,* 40, pt. 3: 394–95.
13. Otis, *Second Wisconsin,* 100; Cheek, *Sauk Riflemen,* 121; Dawes, *Sixth Wisconsin,* 300–301.
14. Correspondence File, National; Levi Pearson Pension File.
15. Correspondence File, National; Williams Diary; Samuel Smith Pension File.
16. Correspondence File, Indiana; Orr MSS.
17. Correspondence File, Indiana.
18. Cheek, *Sauk Riflemen,* 122; *IDJ,* August 3, 1864, 1.
19. Cheek, *Sauk Riflemen,* 125; *OR,* 40, pt. 1: 474; Correspondence File, Indiana; Theodore Ward Pension File.
20. Curtis, *Twenty-Fourth Michigan,* 270; Dawes, *Sixth Wisconsin,* 302, 303; Williams Diary.
21. Nathaniel Cary Pension File.
22. Cheek, *Sauk Riflemen,* 129; *OR,* 42, pt. 1: 534; Stine, *Army of the Potomac,* 691.
23. *OR,* 42, pt. 1: 429, 492–93, 535; Stine, *Army of the Potomac,* 691.
24. *OR,* 42, pt. 1: 66, 430, 535–36; Correspondence File, Indiana.
25. *OR,* 42, pt. 1: 493, 534; ibid., pt. 2: 304; Curtis, *Twenty-Fourth Michigan,* 271.
26. *OR,* 42, pt. 1: 536; *IDJ,* August 31, 1864, 1; Cheek, *Sauk Riflemen,* 134; Curtis, *Twenty-Fourth Michigan,* 273.
27. Merrill, *Soldier of Indiana,* II, 671; *OR,* 42, pt. 1: 431, 536; Curtis, *Twenty-Fourth Michigan,* 273.
28. Scribner, *Roll of Honor,* II, 588.
29. *IDJ,* August 31, 1864, 1; Bragg MSS; *OR,* 42, pt. 2: 423; Curtis, *Twenty-Fourth Michigan,* 275; Crull MSS.
30. Cheek, *Sauk Riflemen,* 137; Curtis, *Twenty-Fourth Michigan,* 275; Orr MSS.

32. BETRAYAL

1. Jackson Diary; Thomson, *Narrative of Seventh,* 193–94.
2. *IDJ,* September 15, 1864, 2; *QCT,* September 10, 1864, 2.
3. Terrell, *Adjutant General,* II, 169–75; Orr MSS; Hudson, *Hawks,* 52.
4. Correspondence File, Indiana.

5. *QCT,* September 10, 1864, 2.

6. National Archives, Records of the Adjutant General's Office, Ordnance Reports, Records Group 94; Regimental Records, Letter Book.

7. Correspondence File, National.

8. Regimental Records, Clothing Book; Jackson Diary.

9. Williams Diary; Cheek, *Sauk Riflemen,* 139; Young MSS.

10. *OR,* 42, pt. 1: 64; Correspondence File, Indiana; "Civil War Letters of Amory K. Allen," *Indiana Magazine of History,* 31 (1935): 381; Williams Diary.

11. Jackson Diary; Terrell, *Adjutant General,* II, 168–75; Correspondence File, Indiana.

12. Ibid.; Jackson Diary; Williams Diary.

13. Ibid.; Terrell, *Adjutant General,* IV, 435–36; Robert Conley Military Service Record; William Sykes Military Service Record; Correspondence File, Indiana; Crull MSS.

14. Ibid.; *IDJ,* October 24, 1864, 2. These numbers are based on a tabular statement dated November 10, 1864. The only change since October 18 had been a net gain of three men, so the statement accurately reflects the status of the 20th Indiana at the time of consolidation.

15. Walker, *Second Army Corps,* 610; *OR,* 27, pt. 1: 177–78; ibid., 42, pt. 3: 459; Dyer, *Compendium,* III, 1124, 1127, 1220, 1417, 1418, 1431, 1433, 1439, 1585; Charles H. Weygant, *History of the One Hundred and Twenty-Fourth Regiment, NYSV* (Newburgh: Journal Printing House, 1877), 359.

16. Warner, *Generals in Blue,* 121–22; Boatner, *Dictionary,* 237–38; De Trobriand, *Four Years,* 567–69, 598–99.

17. Warner, *Generals in Blue,* 337–38; Boatner, *Dictionary,* 572; De Trobriand, *Four Years,* 596–97; Dawes, *Sixth Wisconsin,* 24.

18. De Trobriand, *Four Years,* 656; Weygant, *124th New York,* 376–378.

19. Walker, *Second Corps,* 613; De Trobriand, *Four Years,* 659–62; *OR,* 42, pt. 1: 359.

20. Ibid., 154, 359–61; De Trobriand, *Four Years,* 663; Weygant, *124th New York,* 383; Walker, *Second Corps,* 630, 635–36.

21. Cheek, *Sauk Riflemen,* 139.

22. Terrell, *Adjutant General,* I, 318; Jacob Hunt Military Service Record.

33. 20TH INDIANA

1. *OR,* 42, pt. 3: 510; De Trobriand, *Four Years,* 683–84.

2. Ibid., 683; Edwin B. Houghton, *The Campaigns of the Seventeenth Maine* (Portland: Short & Loring, 1866), 245; *NYH,* November 16, 1864, 5; Orr MSS.

3. De Trobriand, *Four Years,* 656; 683; *QCT,* November 19, 1864, 2; James Blake Pension File; Williams Diary; Agassiz, *Meade's Headquarters,* 269.

4. Weygant, *124th New York,* 397.

5. Joseph Sykes Pension File.

6. Frederick C. Floyd, *History of the Fortieth (Mozart) Regiment New York Volunteers* (Boston: F. H. Gilson, 1909), 237; De Trobriand, *Four Years,* 685; Agassiz, *Meade's Headquarters,* 278.

7. Walker, *Second Corps,* 640–41; Lord, *They Fought,* 63–64; De Trobriand, *Four Years,* 686.

8. Horace H. Shaw, *The First Maine Heavy Artillery 1862–1865* (Portland: n.p., 1903), 151; De Trobriand, *Four Years,* 688–89.

9. Ibid., 689–91; Shaw, *First Maine,* 151–52.

10. De Trobriand, *Four Years,* 691–92; Shaw, *First Maine,* 152.

11. De Trobriand, *Four Years,* 692–93.

12. Ibid., 693; *IDJ,* December 30, 1864, 1.

13. Walker, *Second Corps,* 643; *IDJ,* December 30, 1864, 1.

14. Ibid.

15. Weygant, *124th New York,* 403.

16. *Portrait of Delaware and Randolph,* 284; *DCFP,* February 4, 1864, 3; ibid., October 27, 1864, 1; ibid., December 29, 1864, 2.

17. Ibid.

18. Boatner, *Dictionary,* 15; *MST,* October 11, 1885, 7; ibid., September 19, 1886, 3.

19. *MST,* October 11, 1885, 7; ibid., September 19, 1886, 3.

20. John L. Ransom, *Andersonville Diary* (Auburn, New York: By the author, 1881), 19 and passim; James Dever Military Service Record. John Ransom referred to his friend as Jimmy *Devers* and thought that he belonged to the 23rd Indiana. Records of the Indiana Adjutant General and Andersonville burial records indicate that Jimmy Devers could only be Jimmy *Dever* of the 19th Indiana. Ransom's text has been corrected to provide continuity.

21. *Register of Burials; WJ,* September 25, 1912, 5.

22. Ibid.

23. Ibid.

24. Ibid.; C. S. Engle, *Andersonville and Other Southern Prisons,* Union City Public Library.

34. THE LAST WINTER

1. *WJ,* October 3, 1906, 2; *IDJ,* March 16, 1865, 2; Stine, *Army of the Potomac,* 723–24; Harden, *Boys in Blue,* 74–75.

2. *DCFP,* December 29, 1864, 2; ibid., March 2, 1865, 3; *Portrait of Delaware and Randolph,* 284.

3. *MST,* October 11, 1885, 7; *MST,* September 19, 1886, 3.

4. *NT,* September 13, 1883, 2.

5. Engle, *Andersonville; WJ,* September 25, 1912, 5.

6. *RP,* January 19, 1865, 3; *QCT,* January 21, 1865, 3; Robert Conley Letters, Indiana Historical Society, Indianapolis; Terrell, *Adjutant General,* VI, 367; Power, *Soldiers' Register,* 277.

7. Correspondence File, Indiana; Conley Military Service Record.

8. Engle, *Andersonville;* Power, *Soldiers' Register,* 290.

9. Squire Wood Pension File; *GCW,* March 23, 1865, 3; William and Henry Marshal Pension Files.

10. Lewis Garrett Pension File; Correspondence File, Indiana; William Parr Pension File.

11. William Sykes Pension File; Engle, *Andersonville.*

12. *IDJ,* October 31, 1865, 2.

13. Weygant, *124th New York,* 404; *OR,* 46, pt. 1: 231.

14. Williams Diary.

15. Floyd, *Mozart Regiment,* 239; *NYH,* February 8, 1865, 1; *OR,* 46, pt. 1: 226–27.

16. Ibid., 227–28.

17. Ibid., 228; *NYH,* February 12, 1865, 1; Williams Diary; "Civil War Letters, Amory Allen," 384.

18. Correspondence File, Indiana.

19. Court-Martial, Sullivan LL3140.

20. Francis Huff Military Service Record and Pension File; Thomas Davis Military Service Record and Pension File.

21. David Norris Pension File.
22. *RP,* March 9, 1865, 3.
23. Williams Diary.

35. APPOMATTOX

1. *OR,* 46, pt. 1: 692–93.
2. Scribner, *Roll of Honor,* II, 596; De Trobriand, *Four Years,* 705–706.
3. Ibid., 706; *OR,* 46, pt. 1: 229, 232.
4. *IDJ,* April 1, 1865, 1; De Trobriand, *Four Years,* 710; *NT,* December 30, 1886, 3; John Holbert Pension File; Nathan Williams Military Service Record; William Pitman Pension File.
5. De Trobriand, *Four Years,* 714–16.
6. Ibid., 720–27; *OR,* 46, pt. 1: 782–83.
7. De Trobriand, *Four Years,* 720–27; *NYH,* April 10, 1865, 1; Jacob Young Pension File.
8. *OR,* 46, pt. 1: 783; Weygant, *124th New York,* 436.
9. De Trobriand, *Four Years,* 735; Young Pension File; Huff Pension File; *IDJ,* April 25, 1865, 1.
10. *OR,* 46, pt. 1: 783; Weygant, *124th New York,* 437; Shaw, *First Maine,* 178.
11. Ibid., 178–79.
12. *OR,* 46, pt. 1: 778–79, 783; De Trobriand, *Four Years,* 737.
13. *OR,* 46, pt. 1: 784; *IDJ,* April 25, 1865, 1.
14. *OR,* 46, pt. 1: 779–80; De Trobriand, *Four Years,* 738–39; *NYH,* April 14, 1865, 8.
15. Weygant, *124th New York,* 441–43; Marsh MSS.
16. *MR,* July 10, 1886, 1; Marsh MSS; *MST,* February 24, 1889, 3.
17. *GCW,* June 29, 1865, 2; Walker, *Second Corps,* 690; Marsh MSS.
18. Weygant, *124th New York,* 445–46; "Civil War Letters, Amory Allen," 384.

36. PEACE

1. Shaw, *First Maine,* 196–97; Weygant, *124th New York,* 446.
2. Shaw, *First Maine,* 198–99.
3. Merrill, *Soldier of Indiana,* II, 801–802.
4. Terrell, *Adjutant General,* VIII, 458–59; Correspondence File, Indiana; Jacob Bolen Pension File.
5. *NYH,* May 20, 1865, 5.
6. Ibid.; *NYH,* May 24, 1865, 1.
7. *OR,* 46, pt. 1: 1255–56; *OR,* 49, pt. 2: 1037; Field & Staff Muster Rolls.
8. *IDJ,* June 14, 1865, 1.
9. *RP,* April 9, 1864, 3; Samuel Lutz Pension File; *ITR,* May 4, 1865, 3.
10. Ibid.; August 25, 1864, 3.
11. Ibid., January 26, 1865, 3.
12. Crull MSS.
13. Conley MSS; Huff Pension File.
14. William H. Church Papers, State Historical Society of Wisconsin, Madison; *JDG,* June 13, 1865, 1.
15. *IDJ,* July 13, 1865, 4.

BIBLIOGRAPHY

BOOKS

Agassiz, George R., ed. *Meade's Headquarters 1863–1865*. Boston: Atlantic Monthly Press, 1922.

Allan, William. *The Army of Northern Virginia in 1862*. Dayton: Morningside, 1984.

Annals of the War. Dayton: Morningside, 1988. Reprint, Philadelphia: Times Publishing, 1878.

Aubrey, Cullen B. *Echoes of the Marches of the Iron Brigade 1861–1865*. Milwaukee: Privately published, 1900.

Banta, D. D. *A Historical Sketch of Johnson County, Indiana*. Chicago: J. H. Beers, 1881.

Bartholomew, Henry S. K. *Pioneer History of Elkhart County, Indiana*. Goshen, Indiana: n.p., 1930.

Basler, Roy P., ed. *The Collected Works of Abraham Lincoln*. New Brunswick, New Jersey: Rutgers University Press, 1953. 10 vols.

Bates, Samuel P. *History of Pennsylvania Volunteers, 1861–1865*. Harrisburg: B. Singerly, 1869.

Beecham, R. K. *Gettysburg: The Pivotal Battle of the Civil War*. Chicago: A. C. McClurg, 1911.

Beyer, Walter F., and Oscar F. Keydel. *Deeds of Valor*. Detroit: Perrien-Keydel, 1901. 2 vols.

Billings, John D. *Hardtack and Coffee*. Philadelphia: Thompson Publishing, 1887.

Biographical and Genealogical History of Wayne, Fayette, Union and Franklin Counties, Indiana. Chicago: Lewis Publishing, 1899.

Biographical History of Eminent and Self-Made Men of the State of Indiana. Cincinnati: n.p., 1880. 2 vols.

Bird, W. *Stories of the Civil War*. Columbiana, Alabama: Advocate Print, undated.

Blackford, William W. *War Years with Jeb Stuart*. New York: Charles Scribner's Sons, 1945.

Boatner, Mark M. *The Civil War Dictionary*. New York: David McKay, 1961.

Boyd's Washington and Georgetown Directory. Washington: Thomas Hutchinson, 1862.

Brockett, Linus P. *Famous Women of the War*. [Brooklyn]: Edgewood Publishing, 1867.

Brooks, Stewart. *Civil War Medicine*. Springfield, Illinois: Charles C. Thomas Publishers, 1966.

Brown, Varina D. *A Colonel at Gettysburg and Spotsylvania*. Columbia, South Carolina: State, 1931.

Buell, Augustus. *The Cannoneer*. Washington: National Tribune, 1890.

Carter, Constance. "John Gould Stephenson, Largely Known and Much Liked." In *Librarians of Congress 1802–1974.* Washington: Library of Congress, 1977.

Casey, Silas. *Infantry Tactics, for the Instruction, Exercise, and Manoeuvres of the Soldier, a Company, Line of Skirmishers, Battalion, Brigade, or Corps D'Armee,* vol I. New York: D. Van Nostrand, 1862. Reprint, Dayton: Morningside, 1985.

Chamberlin, Thomas. *History of the 150th Regiment, Pennsylvania Volunteers.* Philadelphia: J. B. Lippincott, 1895.

Cheek, Philip, and Mair Pointon. *History of the Sauk County Riflemen.* Madison: Democrat Printing, 1909.

Clark, Walter, ed. *Histories of the Several Regiments and Battalions from North Carolina in the Great War.* Raleigh: E. M. Uzzell, 1901. 5 vols.

Coffin, Charles Carleton. *Four Years of Fighting.* Boston: Ticknor and Fields, 1866.

Combination Atlas Map of Huntington County, Indiana. Chicago: Kingman Brothers, 1879.

Cullum, George W. *Biographical Register of the Officers and Graduates of the U.S. Military Academy.* New York: D. Van Nostrand, 1868. 2 vols.

Curtis, O. B. *History of the Twenty-fourth Michigan of the Iron Brigade.* Detroit: Winn and Hammond, 1891.

Dannett, Sylvia G. L. *Noble Women of the North.* New York: Thomas Yoseloff, 1959.

Dawes, Rufus R. *Service with the Sixth Wisconsin Volunteers.* Marietta, Ohio: E. R. Alderman & Sons, 1890.

De Trobriand, Regis. Translated by George K. Dauchy. *Four Years with the Army of the Potomac.* Boston: Ticknor, 1889. Reprint, Gaithersburg, Maryland: Ron R. Van Sickle Military Books, 1988.

Diary of Calvin Fletcher 1857–1860. Indianapolis: Indiana Historical Society, 1978. 8 vols.

Doubleday, Abner. *Chancellorsville and Gettysburg.* New York: Charles Scribner's Sons, 1886.

Dudley, Dean. *History of the Dudley Family.* Boston: Dean Dudley, 1892.

Dwight, Theodore F., ed. *The Virginia Campaign of 1862 under General Pope.* Boston: Houghton, Mifflin, 1895.

Dyer, F. H. *A Compendium of the War of the Rebellion.* Des Moines: Dyer Publishing, 1908. Reprint, New York: Thomas Yoseloff, 1959. 3 vols.

Fitch, Michael H. *Echoes of the Civil War As I Hear Them.* New York: R. F. Fenno, 1905.

Floyd, David B. *History of the Seventy-fifth Regiment.* Philadelphia: Lutheran Publishing Society, 1893.

Floyd, Frederick C. *History of the Fortieth (Mozart) Regiment New York Volunteers.* Boston: F. H. Gilson, 1909.

Ford, Andrew E. *The Story of the Fifteenth Regiment Massachusetts Volunteer Infantry in the Civil War 1861–1864.* Clinton: Press of W. J. Coulter, 1898.

Foulke, William Dudley. *Life of Oliver P. Morton.* Indianapolis: Bowen-Merrill, 1899. 2 vols.

Fox, Henry Clay, ed. *Memoirs of Wayne County and the City of Richmond, Indiana.* Madison: Western Historical Association, 1912. 2 vols.

Fox, William F. *Regimental Losses in the American Civil War.* Dayton: Morningside, 1974.

Fremantle, Arthur J. L., and Frank A. Haskell. *Two Views of Gettysburg*. Chicago: R. R. Donnelley & Sons, 1964.

Gaff, Alan D. *Brave Men's Tears: The Iron Brigade at Brawner Farm*. Dayton: Morningside, 1985.

———. *If This Is War: A History of the Campaign of Bull's Run by the Wisconsin Regiment Thereafter Known as the Ragged Ass Second*. Dayton: Morningside, 1991.

Garrison, Fielding H. *John Shaw Billings: A Memoir*. New York: G. P. Putnam's Sons, 1915.

Gates, Theodore B. *The "Ulster Guard" and the War of the Rebellion*. New York: Benjamin T. Tyrrel, 1879.

Gibbon, John. *The Artillerist's Manual*. 2d ed. New York: D. Van Nostrand, 1863. Reprint, Dayton: Morningside, 1991.

———. *Personal Recollections of the Civil War*. Dayton: Morningside, 1978.

Gordon, George H. *The History of the Campaign of the Army of Virginia*. Boston: Houghton, Osgood, 1880.

Hadley, John V. *Seven Months a Prisoner*. New York: Charles Scribner's Sons, 1898.

Halstead, Murat. *Caucuses of 1860: A History of the National Political Conventions*. Columbus, Ohio: Follett, Foster, 1860.

Hanson, Joseph M. *Bull Run Remembers*. Manassas: National Capitol Publishers, 1953.

Hard, Abner. *History of the Eighth Cavalry Regiment Illinois Volunteers, During the Great Rebellion*. Dayton: Morningside Bookshop, 1984.

Hardee, William J. *Rifle and Light Infantry Tactics*. Philadelphia: Lippincott, Granelof, 1861. 2 vols.

Harden, Samuel, comp. *Those I Have Met, or Boys in Blue*. Anderson, Indiana: printed privately, 1888.

Hazzard, George. *Hazzard's History of Henry County, Indiana 1822–1906*. New Castle, Indiana: George Hazzard, 1906. 2 vols.

Heitman, Francis B. *Historical Register and Dictionary of the United States Army*. Washington: Government Printing Office, 1903. 2 vols. Reprint, Gaithersburg, Maryland: Olde Soldiers Books, 1988.

Helm, Thomas. *History of Delaware County, Indiana*. Chicago: Kingman Bros., 1881.

Herdegen, Lance J., and William J. K. Beaudot. *In the Bloody Railroad Cut at Gettysburg*. Dayton: Morningside, 1990.

History of DeKalb County, Indiana. Chicago: Interstate Publishing, 1885.

History of Henry County, Indiana. Chicago: Interstate Publishing, 1884.

History of Huntington County, Indiana. Chicago: Brant & Fuller, 1887.

History of Johnson County, Indiana. Chicago: Brant & Fuller, 1888.

History of Wayne County, Indiana. Chicago: Interstate Publishing, 1884. 2 vols.

Houghton, Edwin B. *The Campaigns of the Seventeenth Maine*. Portland: Short and Loring, 1866.

Howland, Eliza Woolsey. *Family Records*. New Haven: Tuttle, Morehouse & Taylor, 1900.

Humphreys, Andrew A. *The Virginia Campaign of '64 and '65*. New York: Charles Scribner's Sons, 1883.

Indiana at Antietam. Indianapolis: Indiana Antietam Monument Commission, 1911.

Indiana at Gettysburg. Indianapolis: Fiftieth Anniversary Commission, 1913.

Indiana Battleflag Commission. *Battle Flags and Organizations.* Indianapolis: The Commission, 1974.

Indiana Historical Society. *Fayette County, Indiana Early Marriages.* Indianapolis: Historical Society, 1956.

Johnson, Robert U., and Clarence C. Buel, eds. *Battles and Leaders of the Civil War.* New York: Thomas Yoseloff, 1956. 4 vols.

Julian, George W. *Political Recollections 1840 to 1872.* Chicago: Jansen, McClurg, 1884.

Kirkland, Frazer [Richard Miller Devens]. *The Pictorial Book of Anecdotes and Incidents of the War of the Rebellion.* Hartford: Hartford Publishing, 1866.

Krick, Robert K. *Lee's Colonels.* Dayton: Morningside, 1984.

Leech, Margaret. *Reveille in Washington 1860–1865.* New York: Harper & Brothers, 1941.

Lindsley, John B. *The Military Annals of Tennessee, Confederate.* Nashville: J. M. Lindsley, 1886. First Series.

Long, Lessel. *Twelve Months in Andersonville.* Huntington, Indiana: Thad and Mark Butler Publishers, 1886.

Lord, Francis A. *Civil War Collector's Encyclopedia.* New York: Castle Books, 1965.

———. *Lincoln's Railroad Man: Herman Haupt.* Rutherford, New Jersey: Fairleigh Dickinson University Press, 1969.

———. *They Fought for the Union.* New York: Bonanza Books, 1960.

Love, William D. *Wisconsin in the War of the Rebellion.* Chicago: Church and Goodman, 1866.

Madison, James H. *The Indiana Way.* Bloomington: Indiana Historical Society, 1986.

Major General James S. Wadsworth at Gettysburg and Other Fields. Albany: J. B. Lyon, 1916.

Maxson, William P. *Campfires of the Twenty-third New York.* New York: Davies and Kent, 1863.

McClellan, George B. *McClellan's Own Story.* New York: Charles L. Webster, 1887.

———. *Report on the Organization and Campaigns of the Army of the Potomac.* New York: Sheldon, 1864.

Memorial and Biographical History of Northern California. Chicago: Lewis Publishing, 1891.

Merrill, Catherine. *The Soldier of Indiana in the War for the Union.* Indianapolis: Merrill, 1866–1868. 2 vols.

Miller, Francis Trevelyan, ed. *The Photographic History of the Civil War.* New York: Review of Reviews, 1911. 10 vols.

Mills, J. Harrison. *Chronicles of the Twenty-first Regiment.* Buffalo: privately printed, 1887.

Monks, Leander J. *Courts and Lawyers of Indiana.* Indianapolis: Federal Publishing, 1916. 2 vols.

Moore, Charles A. *The Story of a Cannoneer under Stonewall Jackson.* New York: Neale, 1907.

Moore, Frank, ed. *The Rebellion Record*. New York: G. P. Putnam's Sons, 1864–1871. 11 vols.

———. *Women of the War*. Hartford: S. S. Scranton, 1866.

Morrison, James L., ed. *The Memoirs of Henry Heth*. Contributions in Military History Series. Westport, Connecticut: Greenwood Press, 1974.

Naisawald, L. Van Loan. *Grape and Canister*. New York: Oxford University Press, 1960.

Nelson, Jacqueline. *Indiana Quakers Confront the Civil War*. Indianapolis: Indiana Historical Society, 1991.

Nevins, Allan, ed. *A Diary of Battle: The Personal Journals of Colonel Charles S. Wainwright 1861–1865*. New York: Harcourt, Brace & World, 1962.

New York Monuments Commission. *Final Report on the Battlefield of Gettysburg*. Albany: J. B. Lyon, 1902. 3 vols.

———. *In Memoriam: James Samuel Wadsworth 1807–1864*. Albany: J. B. Lyon, 1916.

Nicholson, John P., comp. *Pennsylvania at Gettysburg*. Harrisburg: E. K. Meyers, 1893. 2 vols.

Nolan, Alan T. *The Iron Brigade*. New York: Macmillan, 1961.

Noyes, George F. *The Bivouac and the Battlefield*. New York: Harper and Bros., 1863.

Otis, George H. *The Second Wisconsin Infantry*. Edited by Alan D. Gaff. Dayton: Morningside, 1984.

Owen County Historical Society. *History of Owen County, Indiana*. Spencer, Indiana: Owen County Historical Society, 1977. 2 vols.

Peck, Theodore S., comp. *Revised Roster of Vermont Volunteers*. Montpelier: Watchman Publishing, 1892.

Phisterer, Frederick. *Statistical Record of the Armies of the United States*. New York: Charles Scribner's Sons, 1886.

Pierce, Frederick C. *Fiske and Fisk Family*. Chicago: W. B. Conkey, 1896.

Portrait and Biographical Record of Delaware County, Indiana. Chicago: A. W. Bowen, 1894.

Powell, William H. *The Fifth Army Corps, Army of the Potomac*. New York: G. P. Putnam's Sons, 1896.

Power, J. C. *Directory and Soldiers' Register of Wayne County, Indiana*. Richmond, Indiana: privately printed, 1865.

Prutsman, C. M. *A Soldier's Experience in Southern Prisons*. New York: Andrew H. Kellogg, 1901.

Quint, Alonzo. *The Potomac and the Rapidan*. Boston: Crosby and Nichols, 1864.

Ransom, John L. *Andersonville Diary*. Auburn, New York: By the author, 1881.

Record of Delaware and Randolph Counties, Indiana. Chicago: A. W. Bowen, 1894.

Record of the Movements, Camps, Campaigns, Skirmishes and Battles of the Seventh Indiana Regiment. Fort Wayne, Indiana: Fort Wayne Public Library, 1971. Photo offset copy of 1863 book by men in the regiment.

Report of the Unveiling and Dedication of the Indiana Monument at Andersonville, Georgia. Indianapolis: Wm. B. Burford, 1909.

Roll, Charles. *Indiana: One Hundred and Fifty Years of American Development*. Chicago: Lewis Publishing, 1931. 5 vols.

Ropes, John C. *The Army under Pope*. New York: Charles Scribner's Sons, 1882.

Roster of Wisconsin Volunteers, War of the Rebellion, 1861–1865. Madison: Democrat Printing, 1886. 2 vols.

Sandburg, Carl, *Abraham Lincoln: The War Years.* New York: Harcourt, Brace, 1939. 4 vols.

Schaff, Morris. *The Battle of the Wilderness.* Boston: Houghton, Mifflin, 1910.

Scott, Colonel H. L. *Military Dictionary.* New York: D. Van Nostrand, 1864. Reprint, Yuma, Arizona: Fort Yuma Press, 1984.

Scribner, Theodore T. *Indiana's Roll of Honor,* vol. II. Indianapolis: A. D. Streight, 1866.

Seeds, Russell M. *History of the Republican Party of Indiana.* Indianapolis: The Indiana History Company, 1899. 2 vols.

Shannon, Fred Albert. *The Organization and Administration of the Union Army 1861–1865.* Cleveland: Arthur H. Clark, 1928. 2 vols. Reprint, Gloucester, Massachusetts: Peter Smith, 1965.

Shaw, Albert D. *A Full Report of the First Reunion and Banquet of the Thirty-fifth New York Volunteers.* Watertown, New York: Times Printing and Publishing House, 1888.

Shaw, Horace H. *The First Maine Heavy Artillery 1862–1865.* Portland: n.p., 1903.

Smith, Abram P. *History of the Seventy-sixth New York Volunteers.* Cortland, New York: Truain, Smith and Miles, 1867.

Smith, Donald L. *The Twenty-fourth Michigan of the Iron Brigade.* Harrisburg, Pennsylvania: Stackpole, 1962.

Soldiers and Citizens Album of Biographical Record. Chicago: Grand Army Publishing, 1888. 2 vols.

Sparks, David, ed. *Inside Lincoln's Army.* New York: Thomas Yoseloff, 1964.

Stevens, C. A. *Berdan's United States Sharpshooters in the Army of the Potomac.* Dayton: Morningside, 1984.

Stevenson, David. *Indiana's Roll of Honor,* vol. I. Indianapolis: A. D. Streight, 1864.

Stine, James H. *History of the Army of the Potomac.* Washington: Gibson, 1893.

Survivors' Association. *History of the 121st Regiment Pennsylvania Volunteers: An Account from the Ranks.* Philadelphia: Burk & McFetridge, 1893.

Sutherland & McEvoy's Richmond and Cambridge City Directories. Richmond, Indiana: Sutherland & McEvoy, 1860.

Swinton, William. *Campaigns of the Army of the Potomac.* New York: Charles Scribner's Sons, 1882.

Taylor, Charles W. *Biographical Sketches and Review of the Bench and Bar of Indiana.* Indianapolis: Bench and Bar Publishing, 1895.

Tevis, C. *History of the Fighting Fourteenth.* New York: privately printed, 1911.

Thompson, Donald E., comp. *Indiana Authors and Their Books 1917–1966.* Crawfordsville, Indiana: Wabash College, 1974.

Thomson, Orville. *Narrative of the Service of the Seventh Indiana Infantry.* Published by the author, undated.

Thornbrough, Emma Lou. *Indiana in the Civil War Era 1850–1880.* Indianapolis: Indiana Historical Bureau and Indiana Historical Society, 1965.

Thornburg, Opal. *Earlham: The Story of the College 1847–1962.* Richmond, Indiana: Earlham College Press, 1963.

Todd, William. *The Seventy-ninth Highlanders, New York Volunteers in the War of the Rebellion 1861–1865.* Albany: Brandow, Barton, 1886.

Tomkins, Daniel A. *Company K, Fourteenth South Carolina Volunteers.* Charlotte: Observer Printing and Publishing House, 1897.

Truett, Randall Bond. *Washington D.C.: A Guide to the Nation's Capital.* American Guide Series. New York: Hastings House, 1968.

Tucker, Ebenezer. *History of Randolph County, Indiana.* Chicago: A. L. Kingman, 1882.

Tucker, Glenn. *Hancock The Superb.* Indianapolis: Bobbs-Merrill, 1960.

Vautier, John D. *History of the Eighty-eighth Pennsylvania Volunteers in the War for the Union.* Philadelphia: J. B. Lippincott, 1894.

Waite, Otis. *Vermont in the Great Rebellion.* Claremont, New Hampshire: Privately printed, 1869.

Walker, Charles M. *Sketch of the Life, Character, and Public Services of Oliver P. Morton.* Indianapolis: Indianapolis Journal, 1878.

Walker, Francis A. *History of the Second Army Corps.* New York: Charles Scribner's Sons, 1886.

Warner, Ezra J. *Generals in Blue: Lives of the Union Commanders.* Baton Rouge: Louisiana State University Press, 1964.

Warren, Horatio. *Two Reunions of the 142nd Regiment, Pennsylvania Volunteers.* Buffalo: Courier, 1890.

[Wasson, John Macamy.] *Annals of Pioneer Settlers on the Whitewater and Its Tributaries from 1804 to 1830.* Richmond, Indiana: Telegram Printing, 1875.

Wayne County Gazetteer. Chicago: John C. W. Bailey, 1868.

Weygant, Charles H. *History of the One Hundred and Twenty-fourth Regiment, NYSV.* Newburgh: Journal Printing House, 1877.

Wilmer, L. Allison, J. H. Jarrett, and George W. F. Vernon. *History and Roster of Maryland Volunteers, War of 1861–5.* Baltimore: Guggenheimer, Weil, 1898. 2 vols.

Winslow, Hattie Lou, and Joseph R. H. Moore, *Camp Morton, 1861–1865.* Indianapolis: Indiana Historical Society, 1940.

Young, Andrew W. *History of Wayne County, Indiana, From its First Settlement to the Present Time; with Numerous Biographical and Family Sketches.* Cincinnati: Robert Clarke, 1872.

Yount, Beverly. *Early Marriages of Wayne County, Indiana.* Fort Wayne, Indiana: Library of Fort Wayne and Allen County, 1979. Photocopy of 1967 typescript.

ARTICLES AND PAMPHLETS

Beck, E. W. H. "Letters of a Civil War Surgeon." *Indiana Magazine of History.* 27 (June 1931): 132–63.

Berwanger, Eugene H. "'absent So long from those I love': The Civil War Letters of Joshua Jones." *Indiana Magazine of History.* 88 (September 1992): 205–39.

Bonham, Milledge L. "A Little More Light on Gettysburg." *Mississippi Valley Historical Review.* 24 (1937–38): 519–25.

Brand, Carl. "The Knownothing Party in Indiana." *Indiana Magazine of History.* 18 (March 1922): 47–81.

Bushnell, A. R. "How the Iron Brigade Won Its Name." Unidentified article. State Historical Society of Wisconsin, Madison.

Byrnes, John P. "Recollections of a Private in Blue." *Confederate Veteran*. 12 (1914), 426.

"Civil War Letters of Amory K. Allen." *Indiana Magazine of History*. 31 (1935): 338–86.

Cook, J. D. S. "Reminiscences of Gettysburg." *War Talks in Kansas, Kansas Commandery, Military Order of the Loyal Legion of the United States*. Kansas City, Missouri: Franklin Hudson Publishing, 1906. 321–41.

Dennis, Mary. "West River Friends Cemetery." *Hoosier Genealogist*. 32 (December 1992): 209–20.

Drum, William F. "Work of the Fifth Corps Ambulance Train, Spring and Summer of 1864." *Glimpses of the Nation's Struggle, Minnesota Commandery, Military Order of the Loyal Legion of the United States,* series 3. New York: Merrill, 1893. 77–86.

Dudley, William W. *The Iron Brigade at Gettysburg: Official Report of the Part Borne by the 1st Brigade, 1st division, 1st Army Corps*. Cincinnati, 1879.

Ebersole, Jacob. "Incidents of Field Hospital Life with the Army of the Potomac." *Sketches of War History 1861–1865, Ohio Commandery, Military Order of the Loyal Legion of the United States*. Cincinnati: Robert Clarke, IV (1896): 327–33.

Fulton, W. F. "The Fifth Alabama Battalion at Gettysburg." *Confederate Veteran*. 31 (January 1923): 379.

Gaff, Alan D. "'Here Was Made Out Our Last and Hopeless Stand': The 'Lost' Gettysburg Reports of the Nineteenth Indiana." *Gettysburg Magazine*. 1 (Winter 1990): 25–31.

"Governor Morton's Report on Disbursements from Military Contingent Fund." *Documentary Journal of Indiana*. I (1863): 37.

Hadley, John V. "A Day with Escaping Prisoners." *War Papers Read Before the Indiana Commandery, Military Order of the Loyal Legion of the United States*. Indianapolis, 1898. 278–94.

Haight, Theron. "Among the Pontoons at Fitzhugh Crossing." *War Papers, Wisconsin Commandery, Military Order of the Loyal Legion of the United States*. Milwaukee: Burdick, Armitage and Allen, 1891. I. 416–23.

Haight, Theron W. "Gainesville, Groveton and Bull Run." *War Papers, Wisconsin Commandery, Military Order of the Loyal Legion of the United States*. Milwaukee: Burdick, Armitage and Allen, 1896. II, 357–72.

Haight, Theron W. "King's Division: Fredericksburg to Manassas." *War Papers, Wisconsin Commandery, Military Order of the Loyal Legion of the United States*. Milwaukee: Burdick, Armitage and Allen, 1896. II, 345–56.

Harries, William H. "Gainesville, Virginia, Aug. 28, 1862." *Glimpses of the Nation's Struggle*. Minneapolis: Aug. Davis Publishers, 1909. IV, 157–68.

Hawkins, Norma Fuller. "Sergeant-Major Blanchard at Gettysburg." *Indiana Magazine of History*. 34 (June 1938): 212–16.

Hogarty, William P. "A Medal of Honor." *War Talks in Kansas, Kansas Commandery, Military Order of the Loyal Legion of the United States*. Kansas City, Missouri: Franklin Hudson Publishing, 1906. 351–60.

Hudson, Helen. *Civil War Hawks: Story and Letters of Hawk Family in Civil War*. Hagerstown, Indiana: Historic Hagerstown, 1974. photocopy.

Kallina, Paul. "Lincoln's Quaker General." *The Lincolnian.* 6 (November–December 1987): 3–4.

Kelley, Margaret R. "A Soldier of the Iron Brigade." *Wisconsin Magazine of History.* 22 (March 1939): 286–311.

King, Charles. "Gainesville, 1862." *War Papers, Wisconsin Commandery, Military Order of the Loyal Legion of the United States.* Milwaukee: Burdick and Allen, 1903. III, 259–83.

King, Charles. "Memories of a Busy Life." *Wisconsin Magazine of History.* 6 (1922–23): 165–88.

King, Charles. "Rufus King: Soldier, Editor, and Statesman." *Wisconsin Magazine of History.* 4 (1920–21): 371–81.

"Letter from Major Thomas Scott Allen." *Civil War Times Illustrated.* 1 (November 1962): 32–33.

Madaus, Howard Michael, and Richard Zeitlin. "The Flags of the Iron Brigade." *Wisconsin Magazine of History.* 69 (Autumn 1985): 3–66.

McCall, W. M. "Letter to the Editor." *Confederate Veteran* 3 (January 1895): 19.

Meredith, Jaquelin M. "The First Day of Gettysburg: General Heth at Gettysburg." *Southern Historical Society Papers.* 24: 182–87.

Meredith, Solomon. "Truth Is Mighty and Will Prevail." Indianapolis: Douglass & Conner, 1866. Pamphlet.

Monroe, J. Albert. "Reminiscences of the War of the Rebellion of 1861–1865." *Personal Narratives of the Battles of the Rebellion, Being Papers Read Before the Rhode Island Soldiers and Sailors Historical Society.* Series 2, no. 11. Providence: N. Bangs, Williams, 1881. 1–78.

Monteith, Robert. "Battle of the Wilderness." *War Papers, Wisconsin Commandery, Military Order of the Loyal Legion of the United States.* Milwaukee: Burdick, Amitage and Allen, I (1896): 410–15.

Morrow, Henry A. "To Chancellorsville With the Iron Brigade." *Civil War Times Illustrated.* 14 (January 1976): 12–22.

Nineteenth Indiana Infantry Reunion Roster, 1913.

Official Program and Souvenir, 32nd Annual Encampment. Richmond, Indiana: Indiana Department, G.A.R., 1911.

Robertson, James I., Jr. "An Indiana Soldier in Love and War: The Civil War Letters of John V. Hadley." *Indiana Magazine of History.* 59 (September 1963): 189–288.

"Spirit of the Fair." Souvenir Program. New York City Sanitary Fair, April 7–18, 1864.

Stewart, James. "Battery B. Fourth United States Artillery at Gettysburg." *Sketches of War History 1861–1865, Ohio Commandery, Military Order of the Loyal Legion of the United States.* Cincinnati: Robert Clarke, IV (1896): 180–93.

"The Texans at Sharpsburg." *Confederate Veteran.* 12 (December 1914): 555.

Woodruff, C. A. "In Memory of Major General John Gibbon, U.S.A." *Personal Recollections of the War of the Rebellion.* 2 ser., New York: G. P. Putnam's Sons, 1897. 290–301.

Yaryan, John Lee. "Stone River." *War Papers Read Before Indiana Commandery, Military Order of the Loyal Legion of the United States.* Indianapolis: Indiana Commandery, II (1878): 157–77.

Zimmerman, Charles. "The Origin and Rise of the Republican Party in Indiana from 1854 to 1860." *Indiana Magazine of History.* 13 (December 1917): 359–412.

GOVERNMENT DOCUMENTS

The Medical and Surgical History of the War of the Rebellion. Ed. Joseph K. Barnes, Wilmington, NC: Broadfoot Publishing, 1990–91. 15 vols.

The Official Atlas of the Civil War. New York: Thomas Yoseloff, 1958.

National Archives, Quartermaster General Department, *Register of Burials in National Cemeteries,* Record Group 92.

National Archives, Record and Pension Office, Civil War Pension Files, Record Group 15.

National Archives, Record and Pension Office, Compiled Military Service Records of Volunteers, Record Group 94.

National Archives, Records of the Adjutant General, Regimental Record Books, Record Group 94.

National Archives, Records of the Bureau of Military Justice, Court-Martials, Record Group 153.

National Archives, Records of the Office of the Quartermaster General, Regimental Burial Lists, Nineteenth Indiana Infantry, Records Group 92.

National Archives, Records of the Ordnance Department, Ordnance Returns, Record Group 156.

Report of the Adjutant General of the State of Indiana. Prepared by W. W. H. Terrell. Indianapolis: State Printing Office, 1869. 8 vols.

Report of the Indiana Arsenal. Indianapolis: Joseph J. Bingham, State Printer, 1864.

Report of the Indiana Military Agencies to the Governor. Indianapolis: W. R. Holloway, 1865.

Report of John H. Vajen, Quartermaster General of the State of Indiana. Indianapolis: Joseph J. Bingham, State Printer, 1863.

Revised Report of the Select Committee Relative to the Soldier's National Cemetery, Together with the Accompanying Documents as Reported to the House of Representatives of the Commonwealth of Pennsylvania. Harrisburg: Singersly & Myers, State Printer, 1865.

Revised United States Army Regulations of 1861. Washington: Government Printing Office, 1863.

U.S. Bureau of the Census. Census of Population, Wayne County, Indiana. 1840, 1850, 1860.

U.S. Congress. House. *A Biographical Congressional Directory 1774 To 1903.* Compiled by O. M. Enyart, Washington: Government Printing Office, 1903. 57th Cong., 2d sess., H. Doc. 458.

U.S. Congress. House. Joint Committee on the Conduct of the War. *Report of the Joint Committee on the Conduct of the War 1863–1866.* 37th Cong., 3d sess., H. Rept. 108.

U.S. Congress. Senate. Committee on Veteran's Affairs. *Medal of Honor Recipients 1863–1973.* 93d Cong., 1st sess., October 22, 1973. Committee Print 15.

U.S. Congress. Senate. *Proceedings and Report of the Board of Army Officers Convened by Special Order No. 78, Headquarters of the Army, Adjutant General's Office, Washington, April 12, 1878, in the Case of Fitz John Porter, Together with Proceedings in the Original Trial and Papers Relating Thereto.* 46th Cong., 1st sess., 1879. S. Exec. Doc. 37.

U.S. Department of the Interior. *Report of the Secretary of the Interior for 1862.* Washington: Government Printing Office, 1862.

U.S. War Department. *A Report to the Secretary of War of the Operations of the Sanitary Commission and Upon the Sanitary Condition of the Volunteer Army, Its Medical Staff, Hospitals and Hospital Supplies.* Washington: McGill & Witherow, 1861.

U.S. War Department. *The War of the Rebellion: A Compilation of the Official Records of the Union and Confederate Armies.* Washington: Government Printing Office, 1880–1901. 128 vols.

Work Projects Administration. *Index to Marriage Records of Wayne County, Indiana.* Work Projects Administration, 1941. 3 vols.

MANUSCRIPTS

"The Army History of Captain Wilson." Privately owned by Daniel Tepfer, Beavercreek, Ohio.

Bachelder, John B. Papers. New Hampshire Historical Society, Concord, New Hampshire.

Benton, Thomas H. Letters. Indiana Historical Society, Indianapolis.

Bragg, Edward S. Papers. State Historical Society of Wisconsin, Madison.

Burnham, Uberto. Papers. New York State Archives, Albany, New York.

Byson, John. "A History of the Thirtieth New York Volunteers." Archives, Manassas Battlefield Park, Manassas, Virginia. Typescript.

Campbell Family. Papers. Privately owned by James Biltz, Pierceton, Indiana.

Carmen, E. A. Papers. National Archives, Washington, D.C.

Church, William H. Papers. State Historical Society of Wisconsin, Madison.

Conley, Robert G. Letters. Indiana Historical Society, Indianapolis.

Crull, Thomas. Letters. Privately owned by Thomas R. Pratt, Santa Barbara, California.

Dawes, Rufus R. Manuscript Report. T. C. H. Smith Papers. Ohio Historical Society, Columbus.

Earlham Cemetery. Interment Records. Earlham Cemetery, Richmond, Indiana.

Eaton, Samuel. Papers. State Historical Society of Wisconsin, Madison.

Fairfield, George. Papers. State Historical Society of Wisconsin, Madison.

Finney, George Edward. Diary. Indiana Division, Indiana State Library, Indianapolis. Typescript transcription by Joan Dearmin Finney.

Green, Sullivan. Papers. State Historical Society of Wisconsin, Madison.

Hamilton, Robert. Papers. Indiana Historical Society, Indianapolis.

Haskell, Frank A. Papers. State Historical Society of Wisconsin, Madison.

Hughes, Robert. Papers. State Historical Society of Wisconsin, Madison.

Jackson, William N. Diary. Indiana Historical Society, Indianapolis.

Johnson, John. Civil War Papers. Indiana Historical Society, Indianapolis.

King, Charles. Scrapbook. State Historical Society of Wisconsin, Madison.

Lincoln, Robert Todd. Papers. Lincoln Museum, Archives, Lincoln National Life Insurance Company, Fort Wayne, Indiana.

Marquis, George. Papers. Indiana Division, Indiana State Library, Indianapolis.

Marsh, Henry C. Papers. Indiana Division, Indiana State Library, Indianapolis.

Mead, Sydney. Diary. State Historical Society of Wisconsin, Madison.

Meredith, Solomon. Papers. Indiana Historical Society, Indianapolis.

Monteith, Samuel. Papers. State Historical Society of Wisconsin, Madison.

Moore, William Roby. Papers. Indiana Historical Society, Indianapolis.

Morton, Oliver P. Papers and Correspondence. Archives Division, Indiana State Library, Indianapolis.

Murray, Julius. Papers. State Historical Society of Wisconsin, Madison.

Murray, William E. Diary. Privately owned by John W. Green, Livermore, California.

Noble, William. Papers. State Historical Society of Wisconsin, Madison.

Odle, Elisha B. Letters. Archives, Fredericksburg National Battlefield Park, Fredericksburg, Virginia.

Orr Family. Papers. Manuscripts Department, Lilly Library, Indiana University, Bloomington.

Pattison, Alexander B. Diary. Indiana Historical Society, Indianapolis.

Perry, James M. Papers. State Historical Society of Wisconsin, Madison.

Quiner, Edwin. *Correspondence of Wisconsin Volunteers 1861–1865*. State Historical Society of Wisconsin, Madison. Ten volumes of newspaper clippings.

Rollins, Nathaniel. Papers. State Historical Society of Wisconsin, Madison.

St. Clair, John. Papers. State Historical Society of Wisconsin, Madison.

Scrapbook. Newspaper clippings and miscellaneous items. Archives, Wayne County Historical Museum, Richmond, Indiana.

Smith, T. C. H. Papers. Ohio Historical Society, Columbus.

Starbuck, Julietta. Civil War Papers. Indiana Historical Society, Indianapolis.

Wheeler, Cornelius. Papers. State Historical Society of Wisconsin, Madison.

Williams, Grear N. Diary. Privately owned by Mick Kissick, Albany, Indiana.

Winscott, Elliott. Letter. Privately owned by Rick Saunders, Martinez, Georgia.

Young, Henry F. Letters in Warner Papers. State Historical Society of Wisconsin, Madison.

NEWSPAPERS

Broad Axe of Freedom, Richmond, Indiana.

Cambridge City Tribune, Cambridge City, Indiana.

Charleston Daily Courier, Charleston, South Carolina.

The Christian Banner, Fredericksburg, Virginia.

Cincinnati Daily Commercial, Cincinnati, Ohio.

Daily Gazette, Janesville, Wisconsin.

Daily State Sentinel, Indianapolis, Indiana.

Daily Wisconsin, Milwaukee, Wisconsin.

Delaware County Free Press, Muncie, Indiana.

Delaware County Times, Muncie, Indiana.

Elkhart Weekly Review, Elkhart, Indiana.

Evening Star, Washington, D.C.

Grant County Herald, Lancaster, Wisconsin.

Grant County Witness, Platteville, Wisconsin.

Indiana True Republican, Centerville, Indiana.
Indianapolis Daily Journal, Indianapolis, Indiana.
Indianapolis Star, Indianapolis, Indiana.
Milwaukee Sentinel, Milwaukee, Wisconsin.
Milwaukee Sunday Telegraph, Milwaukee, Wisconsin.
Mineral Point Tribune, Mineral Point, Wisconsin.
Missouri Republican, St. Louis, Missouri.
Muncie Daily Herald, Muncie, Indiana.
The National Tribune, Washington, D.C.
New Castle Weekly Courier, New Castle, Indiana.
New York Daily Tribune, New York, New York.
New York Herald, New York, New York.
New York Times, New York, New York.
Prairie Du Chien Courier, Prairie Du Chien, Wisconsin.
Quaker City Telegram, Richmond, Indiana.
Randolph County Journal, Winchester, Indiana.
Richmond Daily Free Press, Richmond, Indiana.
Richmond Evening Item, Richmond, Indiana.
Richmond Palladium, Richmond, Indiana.
Rochester Daily Union and Advertiser, Rochester, New York.
Sun Telegram, Richmond, Indiana.
Weekly Racine Advocate, Racine, Wisconsin.
Winchester Journal, Winchester, Indiana.
Wisconsin Daily Patriot, Madison, Wisconsin.
Wisconsin State Journal, Madison, Wisconsin.
Wisconsin State Register, Portage, Wisconsin.

INDEX

ALAN D. GAFF is the author of *Brave Men's Tears: The Iron Brigade at the Battle of Brawner Farm* and *If This Is War: A History of the Campaign of Bull's Run by the Wisconsin Regiment Thereafter Known as the Ragged Ass Second*, and the editor (with Maureen Gaff) of *Adventures on the Western Frontier* by Major General John Gibbon.